IMPLEMENTING THE ENDANGERED SPECIES ACT ON THE PLATTE BASIN WATER COMMONS

T0350780

IMPLEMENTING THE ENDANGERED SPECIES ACT ON THE PLATTE BASIN WATER COMMONS

David M. Freeman

UNIVERSITY PRESS OF COLORADO

TO SANDRA

She has created a wonderful world
and kept the sparkle of dew in it.
With time
she has added the light
such that I see it better.

TO THE GRANDCHILDREN

Keep the sparkles; pass them on.

Navarre
Ren
Kira
Alexander
Kiana
Hannah   Shifa
Ishara
Nai'a
Noah
Remington
Lexington

Published by the University Press of Colorado
5589 Arapahoe Avenue, Suite 206C
Boulder, Colorado 80303

7͞5

AAUP 1937 2012

The University Press of Colorado is a proud member of
the Association of American University Presses.

The University Press of Colorado is a cooperative publishing enterprise supported, in part, by
Adams State College, Colorado State University, Fort Lewis College, Metropolitan State College
of Denver, Regis University, University of Colorado, University of Northern Colorado, Utah State
University, and Western State College of Colorado.

∞ This paper meets the requirements of the ANSI / NISO Z39.48-1992 (Permanence of Paper).

Library of Congress Cataloging-in-Publication Data

Freeman, David M.
 Implementing the Endangered Species Act on the Platte Basin water commons / David M.
Freeman.
    p. cm.
 Includes bibliographical references and index.
 ISBN 978-1-60732-054-8 (cloth : alk. paper) — ISBN 978-1-60732-055-5 (ebook) — ISBN 978-1-
60732-183-5 (pbk. : alk. paper) 1. Endangered species—Law and legislation—South Platte River
Watershed (Colo. and Neb.) 2. United States. Endangered Species Act of 1973. 3. Fisheries law
and legislation—South Platte River Watershed (Colo. and Neb.) 4. Wildlife conservaiton—Law
and legislation—South Platte River Watershed (Colo. and Neb.) I. Title.
 KF5640.F738 2010
 346.7304'69522—dc22
                            2010034837

Design by Daniel Pratt

21 20 19 18 17 16 15 14 13 12   10 9 8 7 6 5 4 3 2 1

FIGURES

MAPS

AEAM	adaptive environmental assessment and management
af	acre foot / feet
AMWG	Adaptive Management Working Group
BLM	Bureau of Land Management
bo	biological opinion
CA	Cooperative Agreement
C-BT	Colorado–Big Thompson Project
CDOW	Colorado Division of Wildlife
cfs	cubic foot / feet per second
CNPPID	Central Nebraska Public Power and Irrigation District
COHYST	Cooperative Hydrological Study (Nebraska)
CWCB	Colorado Water Conservation Board
DBO	draft biological opinion
DEIS	Draft Environmental Impact Statement
DNR	Department of Natural Resources
DOI	Department of the Interior (U.S.)
EA	Environmental Water Account
ED	Environmental Defense
EIS	Environmental Impact Statement
ESA	Endangered Species Act

FBO	Final Biological Opinion
FEIS	Final Environmental Impact Statement
FERC	Federal Energy Regulatory Commission
GASP	Groundwater Appropriators of the South Platte (Colorado)
GC-1	Governance Committee Program Alternative 1 in draft EIS
GC-2	Governance Committee Program Alternative 2 in draft EIS
GIS	geographical information system(s)
gpm	gallons per minute
IMRP	integrated monitoring and research plan
ISAC	Independent Science Advisory Committee
J-2	Johnson Lake power plant (unit 2 on CNPPID system)
LB-962	Legislative Bill 962 (integrating Nebraska surface and ground-water diversion law)
LSPWCD	Lower South Platte Water Conservancy District (Colorado)
M&I	municipal and industrial
MOA	Memorandum of Agreement
NAS	National Academies of Science
NCWCD	Northern Colorado Water Conservancy District
NDNR	Nebraska Department of Natural Resources
NEPA	National Environmental Policy Act
NPPD	Nebraska Public Power District
NRC	National Research Council of the National Academies
NRD	Natural Resource District (Nebraska)
NWF	National Wildlife Federation
NWS	National Weather Service
PRP	Platte River Project (organization of Colorado Front Range water users)
ROD	record of decision
RPA	reasonable and prudent alternative
SDF	stream depletion factor
SPLRG	South Platte Lower River Group (Colorado)
SPWRAP	South Platte Water Related Activities Program
USACE	U.S. Army Corps of Engineers
USBR	U.S. Bureau of Reclamation
USDA	U.S. Department of Agriculture
USFS	U.S. Forest Service
USFWS	U.S. Fish and Wildlife Service
USGS	U.S. Geological Survey

How does an environmental agenda, at the river basin scale, become incorporated into a typical western utilitarian water allocation system? Here is the detailed story of complex negotiations regarding habitat restoration on behalf of four species listed under the federal Endangered Species Act—the whooping crane, piping plover, least tern, and pallid sturgeon. The tale is documented by a sociologist who attended the bulk of the negotiating sessions across the final ten years, a person without attachment to any particular position, a person who wanted to closely observe and faithfully record the unfolding of contending positions and issues. All of this is couched within an analytical framework that highlights critical features of the problem and sustains an incisive examination of the central question: what are the fundamental requirements of a successful mobilization of self-interested water provider organizations to cooperatively undertake the burden of constructing a major multi-state, multilevel, state-federal habitat restoration program?

The negotiations evolved from scattered beginnings across the basin landscape starting in the mid-1970s and finally came to a conclusion in late 2006. The author provides a feel for their cadence, tenor, uncertainties, and participants' struggles. By portraying the evolving positions of the major participants—the United States Department of the Interior, the environmental community, and the states of Wyoming, Colorado, and Nebraska—the text captures aspects of western water negotiations not found elsewhere. The book reveals in striking detail at least two transcendent themes: (1) the ways people are learning to better govern themselves more along the river basin lines recommended by John

Wesley Powell and (2) the long elusive application of basin-wide integrated water resources management now birthed in the Platte River Basin.

By the book's conclusion, the reader will walk away with great admiration for those involved in the process that produced the agreement to undertake the collective effort. Water allocation rules and tools in the western United States have a long history of adaptation to changing requirements, and now the story is told about how the Platte Basin relationships have been reconfigured in the name of implementing the Endangered Species Act. There is a necessary messiness in this process that begs for understanding. This book provides insight in a most revealing and educational manner. It is a must-read for those who are, or who seek to become, involved in contemporary water management.

I have wondered how the author could continue to follow the negotiation process. As the years passed, I contemplated whether he could write an account of what eventually turned out to be a successful basin-wide water negotiation. It took a major twelve-year commitment. That is why we have not read books like this before. It is one-of-a-kind.

Robert Ward, PhD
PROFESSOR EMERITUS
FORMER DIRECTOR, COLORADO WATER RESOURCES RESEARCH INSTITUTE
COLORADO STATE UNIVERSITY, FORT COLLINS

Water is a social organizational phenomenon, and thereby invites sociological analysis, because people need to control water in ways that simply cannot be produced by individual action. When water diverted from a river to a canal hits a crop root zone at the right time, place, amount, and quality to grow our food and fiber, it is because people have organized to make it so. They mobilized themselves to construct river and ditch organizations essential to growing corn, dry beans, and the many other products we enjoy at the dinner table. Likewise, when river flows have shifted away from the natural cycles of spring flood peaks and summer rain pulses that inundate wetlands and nourish a great diversity of life forms in uncounted ecological niches, it was because people organized to make that so.

Around the world, water users go into marketplaces and are promptly provided—given sufficient capacity to pay—with desired agricultural implements, seeds, fertilizers, pesticides, herbicides, and all the other necessary items that directly benefit both buyer and seller. However, in no water culture have people been able to order up in those same private transactions a unit of ditchwater control, a "fair share" allocation of stream flow, a solution to the problem of the conjunctive use of well water with surface supplies by neighbors and others more remote, or an increment of improved ecosystem diversity. Such challenges require coordinated action by social organizations beyond the capacity of marketplaces alone to provide. The account of a river's degradation and restoration must therefore in critical respects be a social organizational story.

In their historical struggles with each other and with the arid high plains environment, people of the Platte River Basin have evolved a rich organizational capacity to do things collectively that could not be accomplished through private exchange in marketplaces. They organized to divert water into ditches, to share the "shrink" among parties on those leaky canals, and they employed their collectively owned and managed water systems as a foundation upon which to construct their communities. Then, to protect those communities from the depredations of newcomers upstream, they organized to allocate scarce water among ditch headgates along extensive stream systems. When surface water sources no longer sufficed, many people sought relief in the use of groundwater; this, in turn—at least in many places in the basin—has compelled additional organization to integrate generally newer groundwater exploitation with older surface water uses.

Now, this organizational tradition has been put to a more recent test in the Platte River Basin. Could the tradition that grew up on a heavy dose of utilitarian water use—largely blind to environmental consequence and forged around boundaries that divided the federal government from the states, the three basin states from each other, user from user, and environmentalist from environmentalist—foster a successful basin-wide program of collective cooperative action for integrating habitat needs of three birds and a fish within the water management agenda?

The purposes of this book are to (1) document the way organizational interests representing three states—Colorado, Nebraska, and Wyoming—and the federal Department of the Interior came to collaboratively seek remedies for degraded habitats under the terms and conditions established by the Endangered Species Act of 1973; (2) describe how these entities have mobilized to address the problems of habitat restoration; and (3) advance sociological propositions regarding conditions under which organizations of water providers were mobilized to transcend their narrower self-interests and produce a collective environmental good from which they can capture no greater benefit than any entity that was not involved in the negotiations or in developing the resulting habitat recovery program.

The method has centered on capturing the essential shape of multiple sets of negotiations that were ongoing from the mid-1970s to late 2006 in the Platte River Basin. Negotiations entailed an ambitious set of talks between water users and environmentalists, between rival water users within and among states, between water users and state authorities, and between states and the federal Department of the Interior. The research intent has been to be attentive to positions and processes, to the exertions of leaders and their organizations as they have collectively approached the creation of something new under the high plains sun—a set of agreements that will re-time Platte River Basin water flows to provide improved river and terrestrial habitat for threatened and endangered species.

Details of the evolution of the Platte River Habitat Recovery Program have been situated within a theoretical framework informed by an interdisciplinary tradition of analysis regarding humans' organization of their common property—in this case, the timeless flows of the Platte River Basin. The intent has been to extract empirically researchable propositions that will inform existing theoretical approaches to the analysis of organizational governance of common pool resources. The story of the Platte River Habitat Recovery Program may yet play out over lifetimes still to be lived. However, the more limited tale of putting a program in place can now be penned and analytically dissected for its lessons.

ACKNOWLEDGMENTS

The many facets of water humble me. I am frequently astounded by how much I have to learn in order to grasp how little I know. This project has been made possible by the assistance and goodwill of many people who have lived and breathed Platte Basin water and environmental issues. These citizens have helped me understand issues, problems, and perspectives in public forums, small groups, private homes, public offices, committee meetings, lunches, dinners, on the banks of ditches and rivers, in farmyards, and in parking lots. They have given me tours, fed me, and patiently educated me. They have represented federal and state policy and management positions, irrigation districts, mutual companies, natural resource districts, conservancy districts, power districts, municipalities, environmental organizations, and private agricultural enterprises. Their assistance has made this project possible, and many are recognized in Appendix A. I deeply appreciate their efforts.

I express gratitude most specifically to members of the Platte River Cooperative Agreement Governance Committee, established in 1997, who have constituted the epicenter of the negotiations. My research effort, among other things, has involved observing the fellowship at their table during regular meetings, as well as in negotiating team sessions, subcommittees, and special workshops. By the time the Platte River Habitat Recovery Program began in 2007, I had the benefit of a full decade of witnessing their negotiations within the formal structure of their meetings as well as the insight gained from documents and—beyond the negotiating arenas—in private and repeated individual interviews with both members and many interested parties outside the negotiating arena.

I can only hope that those who have contributed so much to my understanding will find this study of interest and fair to the contending perspectives. I hope that, with their help, I have the story straight and that they will find their efforts on my behalf to have been rewarded.

To minimize errors, I have assiduously applied the comments and insights of reader-reviewers representing the several negotiating communities. Yet the contents of this study do not provide any official record of the negotiations. The text has been written from my interpretation of interview responses, meeting observations and notes, and reviews of documents. The basis of any future negotiation or litigation must rest on the contents of the Final Program Agreement signed by the governors of three states—Colorado, Nebraska, Wyoming—and the secretary of the U.S. Department of the Interior. I have advanced my best formulations; any errors of fact or interpretation are solely my own.

IMPLEMENTING THE ENDANGERED SPECIES ACT ON THE PLATTE BASIN WATER COMMONS

PART I

Introduction

Problem and Significance

In a moment utterly without drama, on October 24, 2006, negotiators representing Colorado, Nebraska, Wyoming, the environmental community, and the United States Department of the Interior—each of whom had struggled for years in Platte River habitat recovery talks—assembled in a Denver hotel conference room. The mood was quietly positive as they sat in a horseshoe arrangement at tables covered with white tablecloths studded with notebooks, laptop computers, water pitchers, glassware, and soft-drink cans. For nearly an hour they had been reviewing for one last time electronically projected editorial changes to the bulky program document. Among some good cheer and subdued laughter, the negotiators then unanimously approved sending that record of their agreement to the printer. The first audience would consist of the governors and congressional delegations of the three Platte Basin states and the secretary of the United States Department of the Interior. Something new was being birthed under the Platte River Basin sun. These representatives had agreed to govern their water commons in important new ways.

They had been brought to the negotiating table by the requirements of the Endangered Species Act (ESA) of 1973. Since 1994—for twelve long years—negotiators had been slowly, haltingly, defensively shaping the terms and conditions under which they would voluntarily and collaboratively organize to re-time about 11 percent of the average annual surface flow of the Platte River (as measured near Grand Island, Nebraska) in conjunction with restoring 10,000 acres of critical habitat for whooping cranes, piping plovers, and least terns during the first thirteen-year program increment. In addition, they agreed to test the hypothesis that the basin-wide recovery program would demonstrably serve the needs of pallid sturgeon further downstream, near the river's mouth on the Missouri. The parties had constructed a habitat recovery program document, well over 500 pages long, that reflected more than thirty years of struggle among contending organizational interests as they sought ways to remedy the jeopardy in which historical water-use patterns in the basin had been found to place the ESA listed species. The program would be launched January 1, 2007.

On that sunny October day, there was no ceremonial public commemoration of the moment; not even a photo was taken to be buried deep in the pages of the region's newspapers. Within each coalition of interest—water user, state government, federal government, environmental—were constituencies opposed to the deal. On the one hand, it had been clear for years that each set of negotiators wanted—even desperately needed—the Platte River Habitat Recovery Program. On the other hand, each community of interest had points it disliked about the new basin-wide habitat recovery program, and each faced the prospect of defending the program to antagonists in their divided constituencies. While proud of their work, and knowing that what they had hammered into existence could make each of their constituencies much better off than they would have been if the project had been abandoned, there was no general enthusiasm for publicly trumpeting their accomplishment. Public displays of affection over what they had wrought risked the needless taunting of those opposed.

In recent years, negotiators had worked during the deepest and most extended drought in the basin's history and had persevered despite political leadership in the three states and Washington, D.C., openly hostile to the Endangered Species Act as written. Yet the deal makers had found a way to implement the ESA on a large multi-species, multi-state, multi-government landscape-scale river basin. It was a signal accomplishment. The principals had birthed a program baby, and they would be glad to quietly claim paternity. But each preferred not to make a big show of kissing that baby in public.

QUESTIONS

Two sets of questions are paramount. First, descriptive questions need to be addressed. What were the ecosystem issues? How have water users, environmentalists, and state and federal authorities found themselves locked in a prolonged discussion on how to mitigate the problem? What were the participants' agendas? What were their options, and how did they exert themselves in problem solving? What roles did the federal regulatory process, science, and politics play?

The second question set is analytical; it will be examined at the beginning and the end of this book. The social construction of the Platte River Habitat Recovery Program is of interest not only because it constitutes an instructive story but also because it provides analysts with grist for addressing crucial theoretical matters having to do with the way human beings transcend their individual self-interested rationality and cooperate to produce collective/public good—in this instance, a river basin–wide environmental good. Why do rational self-seeking resource appropriators neglect environmental matters in the first place? What does it take to mobilize them to undertake concerted and collaborative action to preserve available remnants of high-quality habitat and restore degraded segments? Case studies cannot provide adequate testing of hypotheses, but they can generate propositions worthy of further consideration in sociological theory building. (See Appendix B for discussion of research methods and theory.)

Descriptive questions will be addressed part by part, chapter by chapter. Analytical questions require a brief explanation.

ANALYTICAL PERSPECTIVE

Why do individually rational resource users degrade environments? What can be done to mobilize these same users to first stop and then reverse environmental degradation? A tradition of inquiry in the social sciences has emerged, contributors to which have closely examined problems of natural resource degradation, requisites of effective mobilization to reverse matters, and attributes of the most effective long-enduring resource management organizations (Baden and Noonan 1998; Bromley 1992; Burger et al. 2001; Dolsak and Ostrom 2003; Freeman 1989, 2000; Hanna, Folke, and Maler 1996; Keohane and Ostrom 1995; McCay and Acheson 1987; Ostrom 1990, 1998; Ostrom and Ostrom 2004; Young 1982, 1997, 1999).

The essence of the matter is that rationality is multiple. What is rational for the individual may not be rational for an assembly of individuals. The reverse is also true. What is rational for society may not be in the rational self-interest of any particular individual actor. Rationality also turns out to have different implications depending upon the kind of property resource addressed.

To clarify the problem, it is helpful to distinguish three kinds of property and reflect briefly on how rationality is affected by each (Figure 1.1). Each property type produces streams of benefits, but the nature of the benefit streams varies importantly on two conceptual dimensions—rivalness and excludability:

1. Rivalness is determined by whether use of the benefit by one user denies that benefit to other potential users. If one investor pays for production of the benefit and consumes what he or she can, will that same benefit be available for others who did not invest in providing it? If not, the property is said to be highly rival. Such is the case with investing in a slice of pizza. If one person eats the piece, it is not available to another. However, some kinds of property—for example, high-quality whooping crane habitat—are non-rival. One person's knowledge that whoopers have a good place on the central

Platte for their spring and fall stopovers does not interfere with another's awareness. Here, rivalness is zero.

2. Excludability is determined by whether it is easy to exclude the non-investor (free rider) from benefiting from the investment. If one invests in a type of property, can non-investors easily be excluded from sharing in the benefits produced? If so, excludability is said to be high, as would be the case with a slice of pizza. If, on the other hand, an investor invests in improved piping plover habitat in central Nebraska, the non-investor cannot be excluded from the benefits of enhanced ecosystem biodiversity. Non-investors reap as much of the benefit as those who have sacrificed to provide the improved habitat. Excludability, in such an instance, is zero.

Employing these two analytical dimensions, it is now possible to define three kinds of property and highlight implications of each for rational action and willingness to sacrifice for provision of high-quality wildlife habitat on the central Platte or anywhere else:

1. Private property (Figure 1.1a) is characterized by both high rivalness and high excludability. In matters involving private goods, investors can fully capture whatever benefit stream the property produces; they can deny non-investors the opportunity to take a "free ride" on their investment. Farmers who buy improved seed varieties capture the benefit of higher yields. Purchasers of automobiles capture the benefit of personal transport and, by controlling locks and ignition keys, exclude potential free riders. Pizza buyers literally internalize the benefit of their investments. In irrigated agriculture, a given quantity of water actually put to consumptive use on a farmer's field crop represents a private good; that would be the consumptive use fraction of the applied water that grows corn only on that field. Individual rationality works well in free markets to produce and distribute private goods. People employ their individual rationality to trade away the things they do not want in order to obtain the things they do. There is no need to organize an entire community to buy and use a pocket comb or a quantity of seeds.

2. Collective (public) property (Figure 1.1c) has the opposite attributes from private property. It is characterized by zero rivalness and excludability. A given quantity of patterned water flow contributing to quality plover habitat produces a public good. Markets do not emerge to provide collective (public) goods because the benefits that can be captured by an individual investor cannot be greater than those available to non-investors (free riders). Healthy ecosystems capable of sustaining species listed under the Endangered Species Act, in the absence of public policy and effective organizations to prevent private rationality from dominating the situation, will be degraded by people who—in the course of pursuing private rationality in market-places—exploit open access to the public and common heritage for private gain. In an open access situation, one has to be a fool or a major altruist to invest in things whose benefits will escape away and cannot be denied

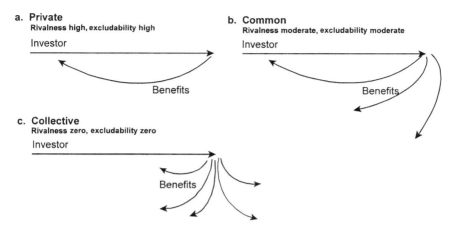

a. Private
Rivalness high, excludability high

Investor

Benefits

b. Common
Rivalness moderate, excludability moderate

Investor

Benefits

c. Collective
Rivalness zero, excludability zero

Investor

Benefits

FIGURE 1.1. *Types of property.*

to non-investors. Examples of collective or public goods include national defense, flood control, police and fire protection, forest and watershed protection, and, of course, provision of high-quality habitat for birds and fish on the central Platte River.

3. Common property (Figure 1.1b) is characterized by moderate rivalness and excludability. For example, a given quantity of water flowing though an irrigation canal to a farmer's field represents a resource that is moderately rival and excludable. It is rival in the sense that a delivery to one farmer cannot be simultaneously delivered to another. However, an important fraction of the water delivered to the first user will run off as tailwater or percolate deep into soils and move downslope to provide "return flows" to other users who thereby also share benefits. Given leaky earthen ditches and modest field application efficiencies, a substantial fraction of one user's water will flow to others in the irrigation community, and the others cannot be totally excluded from the benefits at reasonable cost. Since many benefit from the investments of others in highly interdependent flow networks, there is no particular interest in attempting to exclude the non-payers.

It is now possible to see the genesis of environmental degradation and, in principle, a path to a solution. Rationality in pursuit of private goods, undisciplined by higher-order organizational rationality, will generate a perverse logic that results in the destruction of collective property (such as environmental quality/biodiversity). Open access situations (defined as the absence of an organizationally viable discipline of property users' appetites) regarding collective property will produce destructive outcomes that have come to be called the "tragedy of the commons" (Hardin 1968; Ostrom 1990: 2–3). The dynamic that produces the "tragedy" has long been studied and is known as the prisoners' dilemma (Ostrom 1990: 3–5; Poundstone 1992).

The essence of the prisoners' dilemma dynamic is simple. The tragedy of the commons is a product of individual rationality that seeks to maximize individual gain in an open access resource situation. In the absence of effective social organization that empowers individual actors to discipline each other, monitor each other for compliance with rules, and share asset management costs in ways mutually accepted as legitimate, self-seeking actors will individually exploit the resource as best they can and thereby impose degradation to the detriment of all. Garrett Hardin's (1968) classic example centered on competitive grazers of cattle who put too many animals on an open access pasture, thereby so degrading the grazing commons in the name of private rationality that all were brought to ruin.

Self-seeking actors, in an unorganized open access situation, feel pressure to enter the resource extraction race so they can grab as much as possible from the commons before other, equally unconstrained, individually rational competitors do (Table 1.1). Any individual resource appropriator who exercises constraint in the name of long-run resource sustainability is thereby punished. Any actor who holds back from the race loses immediate gain while his or her competitors snatch it. In a finite world, resource exploitation races fueled by individual self-seeking rationality must inevitably bring ruin to all—the tragedy of the commons.

If the consequences of private actions place a burden on the environment external to the private goods exchange—such as toxic flows of waste products, channelization of rivers, and destruction of wetlands—no automatic constructive joint action by the players will occur to rectify matters. If player X invests in altruistic environmental rehabilitation practices on a small fraction of damaged streamside where no one else can be expected to join in, player X alone can do little to reverse the river degradation caused by numerous players. Player X finds the individual investment in restoration to be futile, and his or her investment is wasted. It is individually rational for X to defect from any proposed collaboration. If, on the other hand, all other players somehow altruistically collaborate in reversing the degradation without organizational inducement to do so, the collective task of restoration would proceed without player X's contribution. Therefore, either way the rational actor (individual or organizational)—with open access to the resource and no certainty of regulated cooperation by others by virtue of membership in an effective encompassing governance organization—will refrain from investing in a collective remedy and choose to be either a free rider on the contributions of others or a fellow competitor in the race to collective ruin. Because everybody is a self-interested, individually rational preference maximizer, everyone calculates in a similar manner, and the public/collective property is allowed to deteriorate. The open access commons is plundered. This will hold even if there is perfect knowledge of both the problem and the solutions. What is rational for the individual in such situations is not rational for the encompassing community over time.

Table 1.1. Logic of the Prisoners' Dilemma and the Tragedy of the Commons

Actor X	X Invests, Y Invests	X Invests, Y Defects
Decisions Regarding Collective Good	Best outcome Collective good produced by joint action Tragedy of the commons avoided	Worst outcome X's investment wasted Tragedy of the commons sustained
Actor Y	X Defects, Y Invests	X Defects, Y Defects
Decisions Regarding Collective Good	Worst outcome Y's investment wasted Tragedy of the commons sustained	No collective solution Both players suffer Tragedy of the commons sustained

Obviously, human beings in many societies have known a solution for thousands of years. People organize themselves such that any one investor can be assured that others will make coordinated and proportionate sacrifices to ensure that the collective good—in this case, the water commons—will be protected and enhanced (Bromley 1992; Freeman 1989; Ostrom 1990; Ostrom, Schroeder, and Wynne 1993). The organized work of all resource appropriators can produce and sustain collective property—the commonwealth. If actor X is a member of an organized community in which it is clear that all members will refrain from uncontrolled exploitation of the commons, will sacrifice proportionately so that one does not gain undue advantages over another, and will contribute to sharing costs of maintaining the commons, actor X can invest in collective property knowing that an organization is in place that will prevent free riders from eroding what organized restraint in resource use has gained.

The solution to the common pool resource problem, especially the pure collective property problem, raises two strategic questions: (1) under what conditions will individual self-seeking actors mobilize themselves to organize, and (2) what are the attributes of successful long-enduring social organization that empower people to transcend their individual rationalities and produce common and collective property? This study centers on the first question. The second question has been, and continues to be, addressed elsewhere (Dolsak and Ostrom 2003; Freeman 1989, 2000; Ostrom 1990). Inquiry into the design of such organizations, and the mobilization of actors to create them, should be a centerpiece of environmental and natural resources sociology.

The central message is that individual, private, self-seeking, mutually beneficial exchanges in marketplaces—as important as they are to a good society—necessarily take place within an organizational common property and collective goods context. Furthermore, while it may be perfectly rational for any particular actor to take out un-priced mortgages against the river water commons, never intended to be repaid, a historical accumulation of such unpaid mortgages in pursuit of individual private agendas can threaten important components of the commonwealth—in this case, represented by an ecologically degrading river system. Important components of a viable society cannot be captured in marketplace exchange and by their summation in gross national product accounts. At some point, in recognition of this truth, people must mobilize themselves through their representative governments and local common property management organizations to address matters by investing in the commons. In doing so, we add to our collective capacity to govern ourselves on our landscapes.

The Platte River Habitat Recovery Program negotiations are of interest precisely because they promise to build an organized set of collective governance arrangements that will permit water users and environmentalists in three states and the federal government to transcend their more limited traditional organizational agendas and cooperatively and voluntarily mobilize at the river basin level to produce a new form of collective/public property: quality habitat for threatened and endangered species.

To produce this new governance system for the environmental restoration and sustenance of this collective property, the players have had to agree to transcend and adapt their particular private and historical agendas. After years of wrangling, they have proposed to invest in creative solutions of their own making to produce a product from which they will capture no more benefit than anybody else in the basin, the nation, or the world. Like others, they did not know the value of a plover, a tern, a whooping crane, or a pallid sturgeon. Whatever that value, it is not to be measured in market exchange of private goods. They knew there was no private profit in sustaining these umbrella species and the life forms that flourish with them. They knew that to enhance the environment, their customers and members must pay a little more for an acre foot of water and a kilowatt hour of electricity and must accept a little less drought protection afforded by some basin reservoirs. They knew they would not have undertaken to produce this collective good if left alone. They now know they were capable of negotiating a new social organizational regime that will reflect somewhat more accurately the costs production and consumption of private goods have placed on the river and on other living things that depend on it. They had to adjust their former organizational rationalities to make room on the basin's rivers for a new collective agenda to enhance the Platte ecological commonwealth. All in all, the attempt to establish a basin-wide, multi-state, state-federal cooperative species habitat recovery program is an astounding development—undertaken by virtually no other society—that is well worth investigating.

Change on the River

> While I know the standard claim is the Yosemite, Niagara Falls, the Upper Yellowstone and the like offered the greatest natural shows, I am not so sure but the prairies and plains, while less stunning at first light, last longer, fill the esthetic sense fuller, precede all the rest, and make North America's characteristic landscape.
> —WALT WHITMAN (1998: 864)

The waters of the Platte River Basin are among the most intensively exploited on the planet. By the time the South Platte River meets the North Platte to form the main stem, both tributaries have been harnessed repeatedly for the utilitarian needs of industrial agriculture, urban life, and flat-water recreation—a pattern sustained on the river downstream across Nebraska (see Map 2.1). Hydrologists estimate that in some stretches the waters are used an average of eight times as diverted water returns to the river for reuse by agriculture, urban treatment plants, groundwater use, and recharge (Ring 1999). People and other living things are fundamentally dependent upon multiple reuses of uncounted return flows. Agriculturally, these streams supply surface water and groundwater irrigation to over 2 million acres of land in the three states. Human engineering of Platte Basin waters for these multiple uses has exacted a high toll on the ecological health of the river and associated riparian ecosystems.

THE TRADITIONAL PRE-SETTLEMENT RIVER

Platte

"Platte" is the French word for flat—an honest translation by French explorers of "Nebraska," the Omaha Indian name for the broad, shallow, braided river (Mattes 1969: 6). The North Fork of the Platte is 618 miles long, while the South Fork extends 424 miles before the two combine just east of North Platte, Nebraska, to form the 310-mile main stem. Measured by annual average volume at the mouth, the Platte River delivers an average of 6,926 cubic feet per second cfs) to the Missouri, a pittance compared with rivers such as the Ohio (281,000 cfs) or the Missouri (76,200 cfs) (U.S. Geological Survey 1990). Approximately 90,000 square miles in Colorado, Wyoming, and Nebraska contribute surface runoff and groundwater to the Platte River, yielding an average annual flow of 5,056,000 acre feet to the Missouri (Platte River EIS Team 2000). The Platte, like other western rivers that drain arid and semiarid lands, is long but not impressive when measured by volume.

Near the Continental Divide that runs along the eastern front of the Rocky Mountains, Colorado and Wyoming mountain snowpack thaws into rivulets that gather into plunging streams that flow through rough canyons and then abruptly run out onto flat prairie where the water settles into wide beds, which, well before the Nebraska borders, drop at an average rate of only 7 feet per mile (Ring 1999:13). Plains channels are typically broad, braided, and sandy, with low banks, sparse woody vegetation, and high sediment loads (Eschner, Hadley, and Cromley 1981; Wohl et al. 1998). Average annual rainfall slowly increases as one travels from west to east, from about 12 inches near the mountain canyon outlets to 20 inches at the 98th meridian two-thirds of the way across Nebraska. Aridity dictated a river bounded by a short-grass plains landscape of buffalo and blue grama grasses.

Prior to European settlement, the natural flow pattern consisted of a spring rise beginning in March, extending to a peak in late May or June, and then a sharp decline in late June into summer, fall, and winter. Spring and early summer floods cleared vegetation from sandbars, islands, and riverbanks and distributed sediment across a wide path. In the view of most analysts, channels had only small, infrequently distributed clumps of green ash, plains cottonwood, box elder, and willows growing along the banks. A mile wide in some places, the river was described as a burlesque of rivers, braided with islands and studded with sandbars. Early travelers complained that the Platte could not be ferried for lack of water and could not be bridged for lack of timber (Mattes 1969: 239). When John C. Fremont descended the North Platte in early September 1845, he attempted to float a bull boat with a draft of four inches; after dragging it on the sands for three or four miles, he abandoned the boat entirely (Simons and Associates Inc. 2000).

Analysts have vigorously debated the extent of the riparian forest in the pre–European settlement Platte River. The dominant view has been that the pre-settlement Platte was mostly an open, non-wooded prairie river dominated by sandbars and non-arboreal vegetation (Currier and Davis 2000; Currier, Lingle, and Van Der Walker 1985). However, historical accounts of the river and in-

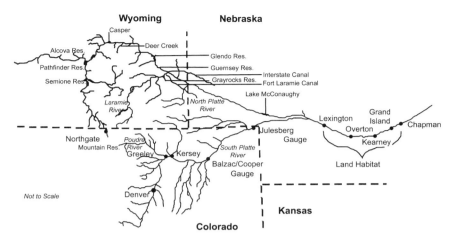

MAP 2.1. *Platte River Basin. Modified from map from U.S. Department of the Interior, Bureau of Reclamation, and U.S. Fish and Wildlife Service; Platte River Recovery and Implementation Program: Final Environmental Impact Statement, April 2006.*

formation from early settlers and the early General Land Office Survey have challenged that mostly treeless view of the Platte (Johnson 1994; Johnson and Boettcher 2000). The view developed from those accounts pictures the traditional Platte as a river with an abundance of trees and riverine forest that was cleared during exploration and early settlement. The "openness" reported by observers in the late nineteenth and early twentieth centuries was, in this view, an artifact of human deforestation, not of natural processes. The debate has important implications for envisioning river restoration targets, but definitive conclusions have been impossible to draw because the debate has not been about whether there were trees—everyone agrees that there were at least some—but instead about the extent and patterning of the riparian woodlands. The explorer-settler observations available in the record are not sufficiently quantitative to settle the argument. There is no disagreement, however, that the traditional plains Platte was a shallow, wide, slow-moving stream braided with sandbars.

Ecosystem Characteristics

Rivers in open, flat country typically support more complex ecological communities than do smaller woodland streams. More sunlight, algae, and zooplankton provide a broader base for the food chain. In addition, rivers with small gradients meander, demonstrating a dynamic equilibrium between erosion and deposition of sediment. Faster-moving water scours out earth from the outside curves of channels and deposits that load when the velocity slows at inside curves. Stretches of maximum velocity and the deepest part of a channel lie close to the outer side of each bend and then cross over near the inflection between the banks, resulting in zones of erosion and deposition (Outwater 1996: 57–58). River backwaters, oxbows, and chutes in a meandering pattern have been important to breeding, feeding, and resting habitat for resident and migrating waterfowl—such as sandhill and whooping cranes, ducks, geese, and a variety of shore birds, including the least tern and piping plover. Flood pulses reworked stream channels by clearing out woody vegetation and flushing out silt.

Most aquatic productivity has occurred in floodplains rather than in the main channel (Outwater 1996; Wohl 2001). The transitional zone between river channel and prairie grasslands acted as a buffer from the extremes of flowing water and arid uplands. Successive plant/animal communities occupied meander loops as they were slowly transformed from aquatic channels to isolated oxbows and finally to wet floodplain depressions. As long as the river system kept creating new loops and cutoffs, a succession of habitats suited to each type of ecological community was maintained. The larger river and floodplain sustained all stages of the process and thereby supported a rich diversity of life.

Habitat Change

Platte River Basin flows have been altered by 15 major dams and reservoirs supplemented by many smaller water diversion and storage projects. On the South Platte alone, 106 storage facilities hold an average of 2.8 million acre feet of water (Eisel and Aiken 1997). Upstream from Lake McConaughy on the North Platte River, there are 84 storage works with a combined capacity of 4.3 million acre feet. The total basin storage capacity is about six times the average annual flow of the Platte at Grand Island. Dams and reservoirs in the Platte River Basin provide a total storage capacity of over 7.1 million acre feet, with Bureau of Reclamation projects accounting for 2.8 million acre feet (Keyes 2002). Traditionally, river diversions were made primarily for agricultural use, but higher value-added uses in the urban, industrial, and postindustrial high-technology and recreational sectors have pulled water out of agriculture at a rapid rate, especially on Colorado's South Platte.

All of the hardware that social organizations have put in place in the Platte Basin has produced the economic wealth that accompanies extensive irrigated agriculture, hydroelectric power, urban and industrial development, and the kinds of wildlife that benefit from dense riparian vegetation, channelized streams, and added reservoirs (for example, neo-tropical songbirds, ducks, geese). Furthermore, there have been benefits in the form of recreational boating and other slack-water sports that are served by reservoirs and outstanding coldwater fishing of non-native species (for example, rainbow trout) below dams.

On the cost side of the ledger, however, the Platte in most places has become a stream of narrowed channels intersected by densely vegetated islands and floodplains. Many oxbows and meanders and associated natural wetlands have been destroyed. Native fish migrations have been blocked by dams and diversions, while growth of woody vegetation is no longer swept away at the seedling stage by naturally occurring ice scouring and flood pulses. Highly variable temperature fluctuations are produced as cold lake-bottom waters are periodically released through gates of dams. Over the course of the twentieth century, wetlands and meadows were significantly reduced as a result of the installation of drainage schemes to open lands for row-crop agriculture. It is estimated that native grassland and wet meadow habitat has declined by 73 percent since European settlement (U.S. Department of the Interior 2006: 31).

Two major factors that affect river channel width are average annual flows and peak flows that rise with spring snowmelt and sporadic intense summer precipitation events. Average annual flows, as measured near Overton, Nebraska, at the top of the designated critical habitat, dropped from about 2.65 million acre feet/year between 1895 and 1909 to about 1.4 million acre feet/year during the period 1970–1998 (U.S. Department of the Interior 2006: 26). Peak flows in the years 1895 to 1909 exceeded 17,000 cubic feet/second at Overton in two of every three years. Decades later, from 1970 to 1999, annual peak flows only exceeded 6,000 cubic feet/second on an average of two out of every three years (U.S. Department of the Interior 2006: 26).

Where did the water go? Much was diverted to human consumptive uses that accompanied expanding Platte Basin settlement. Why were flow peaks reduced so remarkably? Because they were largely impounded behind dams. Why are the declines in peak flows and annual flows a concern? Because high peaks traditionally ripped out young vegetation, shifted and reconstructed sandbars, and created open views for cranes, piping plovers, and least terns. Summer instream flows sustain connected biotic webs essential to the well-being of many life forms important in the food chain of plovers and terns, not to mention myriad other species.

The fundamental strategy human beings have pursued to build their agricultural, industrial, and postindustrial civilization on the Platte has been to divert water from streams during the few weeks of spring runoff, store it in reservoirs for later use, extract a fraction in consumptive uses over the annual calendar and pick up and store return flows where possible, extract additional consumptive uses, and continue this pattern again and again as the shrinking supply moves increasingly downslope. Continued cycles of diversion, storage, consumptive use, return flow, storage, consumptive use, and return flow reduce both annual flow and flow peaks.

Given that reservoirs in the river basin trap high proportions of the sediment (especially on the North Platte) and given that fast-moving clear water released through dams energetically picks up sediment—especially during an era of attenuated peak flows—the central Platte transports 410,000 more tons of sediment per year at Overton than upstream at Cozad, Nebraska (U.S. Department of the Interior 2006: 29). This interplay of dams, clear water, and flow peak remnants is the major source of erosion of the riverbed in the upper portion of the critical habitat that destroys the wide, shallow, braided channel characteristics by chewing out deeper and narrower channels than did the traditional river.

In general, therefore, the traditional flow regime has been changed to one characterized by lower and less frequent spring flood pulses, clearer water flows as sediment is trapped behind dams, more incised and straighter channels, and higher fall and winter flows because cities in the basin divert and store water year-round in a way the traditional natural regime did not.

HABITAT REQUIREMENTS

We are not trying to turn the river back to its pre-European historical condition. That is impossible. We are trying to maintain pockets of serviceable habitat.

—RALPH MORGENWECK,
former regional director, U.S. Fish and Wildlife Service (used by permission)

Birds and fish require substances from their habitats that are generally limited in supply—items such as food, shelter, and nesting or spawning sites. Birds and fish of the same or similar species make similar demands on the habitat—the more individuals in a given territory, the less supply for any given individual. Therefore, members of species compete among each other and with other species using their ecological niches. What is needed for the preservation and protection of species are larger quantities of habitat to support the numbers competing for available resources. As human impact has destroyed the wide, shallow, braided Platte in most reaches, the story of the whooping cranes, least terns, and piping plovers is one of being crowded into ever smaller reaches of viable habitat along with millions of other migrating birds that press into the same area. The story of the pallid sturgeon is less well-known, but there has clearly been massive destruction of its habitat on the Mississippi and Missouri rivers, and at least some of these fish make at least some use of the Lower Platte River near its mouth.

Whooping Cranes

The whooping crane, *Grus americana*, is the largest bird in North America. "Whoopers" stand about five feet tall and possess a wingspan of about 7.5 feet. Males weigh an average of 16 pounds and females about 2 pounds less. They frequently fly 200 to 500 miles per day during migration. They lay two eggs a year in the Far North and live as long as 24 years in the wild. They are brilliant white birds, with black wingtips and bare redheaded tops. Whooping cranes share the central Platte River habitat of the sandhill crane, a smaller, gray, much more numerous cousin. One of the most celebrated of the endangered species, the whooping crane is a loner—much less gregarious than its prolific relative, the sandhill. Whooping cranes have a convoluted windpipe as much as five feet long that can produce loud, resonant calls while flying. Audubon asserted that he could hear whoopers at a distance of three miles (Forbush and May 1955).

Flocks of sandhills, sometimes joined by a few whoopers, visit the Platte River in February–April and October each year as they first move from wintering grounds on the Texas gulf to breeding areas in northern Canada and then make their autumn return. The fossil record places sandhill cranes in Nebraska more than 9 million years ago, long before there was a Platte River—which, by comparison, is only about 10,000 years old. Well-drawn descriptions of whooping and sandhill cranes are readily available (Allen 1952, 1969; Matthiessen 2001; Pratt 1996; Walkinshaw 1973). Whooping cranes have come to symbolize a variety of things: conservation, royal beauty, and wilderness. They have now become the major symbol of a proposed reorganization of water in the three states of the Platte River Basin.

The population of whooping cranes prior to European settlement of North America has been estimated to have been about 15,000 (Matthiessen 2001: 274). They once ranged along the Atlantic seaboard, as did the sandhill. However, as European settlement increased, their numbers decreased. Very edible and of great size, whooping cranes were decimated by the settler-hunters' rifles and shotguns. In 1860, some estimated that the whooping crane population was in the range of 1,300 to 1,400 birds, while others estimated as few as 500–700 individuals (Allen 1952). During the nineteenth century the whooper retreated to west of the Mississippi, and by 1880 it was rare everywhere. A non-migratory population in southwestern Louisiana fell to disease in 1940 and soon became extinct. By 1941 the number of individuals in the recorded migrating wild population had declined to 16, with only 6 to 8 breeding birds (U.S. Fish and Wildlife Service 1997b).

The whooping crane population has rebounded somewhat because of habitat acquisition, federal protection, and intense management of breeding and wintering areas. In December 1937 the U.S. Fish and Wildlife Service established the 47,000-acre Aransas Wildlife Refuge on the Gulf Coast of Texas, with the hope that the tiny wild flock could be preserved and enhanced (Cottam 1996: 125). This refuge has provided winter habitat while the birds use the central Platte as a migration route to and from Wood Buffalo National Park in Canada's Northwest Territories. The Aransas–Wood Buffalo flock is the only naturally occurring wild migratory population of whooping cranes in the world. By 1987,

136 birds were in the wild, and populations fluctuated around that number until 1995 when what was then a peak wintering population of 158 birds was recorded (U.S. Fish and Wildlife Service 1997b).

By late 2006 the North American mid-continent flock hit a modern population peak—237 birds were counted in the mid-December census at the Aransas Wildlife Refuge (Whooping Crane Conservation Association 2006). That number, combined with a number of birds in captivity and those from East Coast flocks raised for introduction into the wild, brought the total whooper population to 518—a milestone in that it represented the first time since the initiation of national and international efforts on behalf of the birds that the total population had exceeded 500. Whooping cranes remain the rarest of the world's fifteen crane species. The U.S. Fish and Wildlife Service has a long-standing goal to recover the species to the point that it can be down-listed to the status of "threatened" under the terms of the Endangered Species Act. This would likely entail seeing the Aransas–Wood Buffalo population increase to about 1,000 individuals, including around 250 breeding pairs (Lutey 2002).

The big bend stretch of the Platte River in central Nebraska—the migratory bird mid-continental "waistline" (Figure 2.1)—has presented an extremely favorable combination of bird habitat types. This reach is made up of alluvial bottomlands, river terraces, and gently rolling bluffs along the river escarpment. Bottomlands are flat and extend for up to 15 miles on both sides of the river channel. Rich prairie soils support productive agriculture. Each year, this area provides for the needs of millions of migratory birds representing over 300 species (Grooms 1991: 20). To name a few, it hosts bald eagles, peregrine falcons, over 10 million ducks and geese, Eskimo curlew, and for a brief period each spring over a half million sandhill cranes along with their rare cousins, the whooping cranes. The area between Lexington and Chapman is witness to over 80 percent of the world's sandhill cranes, who spend 4 to 6 weeks there each spring resting, dancing, and feeding before continuing the migration north. As they rise from their shallow river channel habitat at daybreak and return at sunset, the approximately half million sandhill cranes put on one of the great natural wildlife shows on the planet.

Many, if not all, of the entire natural flock of whooping cranes are believed to migrate through this central Nebraska area between their wintering grounds at Aransas Wildlife Refuge and their summer nesting grounds in Wood Buffalo National Park (Currier, Lingle, and Van Der Walker 1985: 22). Whoopers fly in pairs and singly in daylight, relying on thermal updrafts to improve efficiency and minimize energy expenditures. Riding an updraft and then gliding northward, they steadily lose altitude until the next thermal lifts them and they repeat the process. Often flying a mile above the earth, they can soar to 20,000 feet above sea level. When they arrive in the central Platte, they descend from spring and autumn skies into Nebraska agricultural country with rolling hills and marshes,

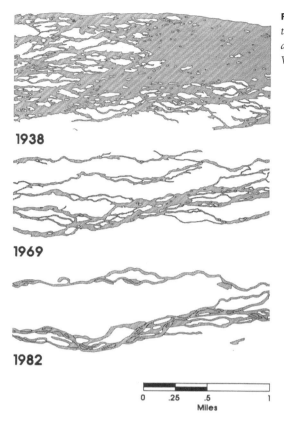

FIGURE 2.2. *Increased channelization of the Platte (channel is shaded area). From Currier, Lingle, and Van Der Walker 1985: 102.*

1938

1969

1982

in overall river flows than there was historically. The Pathfinder Reservoir, completed in 1909, was the first major impoundment on the North Platte, followed by Guernsey (completed in 1927), Alcova (1938), Seminoe (1939), McConaughy (1941), and Glendo (1957). These reservoirs dropped annual average peak flows on the North Platte by 86 percent (Currier, Lingle, and Van Der Walker 1985: 96). This change has resulted in a net loss of water-filled channel and an associated increase in vegetated riverbanks. This development, in turn, has meant the loss of roosting, nesting, and feeding habitat that comes with the loss of meanders and grasslands-wetlands near the main river channel.

Reduction of available habitat for all species of birds that have traditionally made use of the Platte Basin creates two forms of hardship: (1) competition for the limited food supply and (2) crowded conditions, which exacerbate disease transmission. Avian cholera and tuberculosis brought in by snow geese threaten the health of many birds, particularly cranes. As wetlands have been drained and woodlands have grown up along the banks, quality crane habitat has shrunk to less than 70 river miles in the Kearney–Grand Island area and downstream. Here, cranes and other birds crowd together dangerously close in the few good habitat reaches that remain (Currier, Lingle, and Van Der Walker 1985: 18; Grooms 1991: 116).

Interior Least Terns

The interior least tern (*Sterra antillarum*) is the smallest of the tern species, with a body approximately nine inches long and a twenty-inch wingspan. Adults are recognized by a white patch on the forehead that contrasts sharply with a black crown, a bright yellow bill with a black tip, a gray back, a white underbody, and orange-yellow feet (Forbush and May 1955: 235–236). In recent decades this species has been found on only a fraction of its former habitat, which in the early twentieth century had stretched from Texas to Montana and from the Front Range of Colorado and New Mexico to Indiana. The species was listed as endangered in 1985. Recent estimates place its population at about 4,800 (U.S. Fish and Wildlife Service 1997b), but fewer than 500 are estimated to remain on the central Platte (National Research Council 2005).

Interior least terns nest in colonies among sparse beach vegetation, in shallow, inconspicuous depressions in open sandy areas in the blinding glare of the sun. Their protection is their camouflage of eggs and young birds that so closely resemble the color tones of sandy beaches and scattered pebbles that the eggs can escape even the eye of the hawk. The tiny young squat so low that they barely cast a shadow. Two or three eggs are laid in May–July, incubation lasts 22–23 days, and the hatched chicks remain near the nest as a brood for a week or so. They are able to fly within about three weeks. Unlike the piping plover, interior least terns forage heavily on schools of small fish, which adults hunt from the air by diving for minnows near the water's surface. In Nebraska they are found on sandbars of the Missouri, Loup, Niobrara, and Platte rivers; on the beaches of Lake McConaughy; and on the shores of sandpits created by human extraction of gravel.

Least tern habitat on the Platte has been reduced and fragmented by encroaching trees and other woody vegetation. Traditionally, least terns would await the decline of spring peak flows and then scrape out their nests. With the advent of human manipulation of river flows all summer long for purposes of irrigation, power production, and municipal use, Platte River flows have tended to increase in mid- to late summer; therefore, high-flow periods are common long into the nesting season. The birds are vulnerable to being flooded out by high water that continues long past the time they can wait to nest. One obvious adaptation to sustained higher flows is to nest on higher, more exposed sandbars, where available, but today most of the main channel areas are clogged with trees and shrubs. The birds do retreat to gravel pits dug by construction crews and filled by high water tables near rivers, but the mortality of the young is high because of predators whose ability to find their prey is greatly increased in such small places. The pits also provide inferior food sources (Currier, Lingle, and Van Der Walker 1985: 38–39).

Piping Plovers

Piping plovers (Charadrius *melodus*) earned their name by virtue of their flute-like calls. They are similar to least terns in that they utilize much of the same habitat and compete for the same nesting sites. They differ slightly from least terns in that they are somewhat more tolerant of woody vegetation encroachment. This species was listed as threatened under the Endangered Species Act in 1985. A 2001 census estimated its population in both Canada and the United States to be about 6,000, but as a result of habitat degradation, the central Platte population was estimated at only about 85 nesting pairs. Trend data indicate that the northern Great Plains population declined by about 15 percent from 1991 to 2001 (National Research Council 2005). The population is distributed from southeastern Alberta to northwestern Minnesota and along prairie rivers and reservoirs to southeastern Colorado. About 10 percent of the birds are estimated to breed primarily along rivers, and 90 percent nest around lakes and ponds (U.S. Fish and Wildlife Service 1997b).

Piping plovers are a stocky, robin-sized shore bird about 6–7 inches long with a wingspan of about 14–15 inches (Forbush and May 1955). The head, back, and wings are pale brown to gray, with black-and-white highlights. They are most easily identified by a black strip across the forehead that runs from eye to eye, a single black neckband, and white eye stripes. Like terns, plovers are birds of the sandy shore, where they are capable of racing at such speed that it is easy to confuse their running with swift gliding. Beginning in May, females usually lay four eggs, one every other day. Incubation lasts 25 to 31 days, after which well-camouflaged downy chicks survive by flattening themselves into the sand while their parents feign crippling injury to draw away predators such as skunks, raccoons, coyotes, bull snakes, owls, and hawks. Young birds can fly about 21 days after hatching. Piping plovers walk or run from spot to spot, seeking to feed primarily on insects, larvae, and snails.

Much of their required habitat has gone the way of the habitat also needed by least terns and whooping cranes, and for the same reasons. The activities of both humans and domesticated livestock have been hard on shorelines in the region. Faster fluctuating summer flows moving through incised channels that lie between banks and islands supporting dense woody vegetation have increasingly confined least terns and piping plovers to ever more limited, fragmented, and scattered habitat.

Pallid Sturgeons

Sturgeons are a remnant from the Cretaceous period, the age of dinosaurs. Whatever killed the dinosaurs did not kill them. Yet within the last 75 years, this family of species appears to have rapidly declined virtually everywhere. From the Caspian Sea in Central Asia to the Chesapeake Bay, the Great Lakes, and in the Mississippi and Missouri river systems, sturgeon are threatened by pollution, the fragmentation of habitats by dams and their associated reservoirs, channelization of rivers, and the human appetite for caviar.

Pallid sturgeons (*Scaphirlynchus albus*) are of special interest to the Platte River habitat recovery effort because they are among the rarest fish in North America, and they may be significantly reliant on the Lower Platte near its mouth at the Missouri. Pallid sturgeons were not recognized as a species until 1905, and little is known about their historical population numbers. Catch records are incomplete and rare. Analysts at the U.S. Fish and Wildlife Service (USFWS) fear the species may be precariously close to immanent extinction (USFWS 2000c: 26–28). In the 1960s, records documented about 500 observations of the pallid per year across its historical range; that number had declined to 7 in the 1980s (National Research Council 2005). In 1990 the species was listed as endangered under the terms of the federal Endangered Species Act.

Pallids are a large fish, generally ranging from 30 to 60 inches in length and weighing up to about 85 pounds. They are bottom feeders that use their toothless mouths—located under a protruding flat snout—to suck up small fish, plankton, insects, larvae, and crustaceans. Equipped with highly sensitive, fleshy chin barbels that dangle in front of their mouths, they are highly efficient foragers in turbid waters. When water is too clear, the vision hunters gain a competitive advantage. Evidence indicates that pallid sturgeon prefer warmer, annually variable flows in wide braided rivers with firm sandy channel bottoms. They tend to reside in the deeper water areas of main river channels, especially the quieter places just below the downstream tips of sandbars and islands where energy expenditures are lower compared with areas of faster flow.

The Missouri River, which begins near Three Forks, Montana, drains about one-sixth of the land area of the United States below the Canadian border as it descends 2,466 miles to its confluence with the Mississippi about 20 miles north of St. Louis (Schneiders 1999: 12). The Missouri, like its Great Plains tributaries, historically provided extensive and diverse aquatic habitats produced by high spring flood flows, low summer volumes, and many divided channels, sloughs, sandbars, islands, oxbows, and meanders. The seasonal river changes prevented any one component in the complex habitat mix from becoming so dominant as to preclude others. As the river destroyed one habitat, it created another—permitting plant, fish, bird, and animal species to colonize and re-colonize. Through the process of endless formation and destruction, the Missouri River system nurtured the dispersal of life forms and rich biodiversity. It was an eco-system that sustained the pallid sturgeon.

During early European settlement in the Missouri Basin, people had to live, farm, and conduct their commerce primarily on and behind the bluff lines above the channel meander belts or risk losing everything to a river that too frequently threatened to sweep them away. Free-flowing, unruly water hindered what people in search of greater economic prosperity wanted to do—extend agriculture, commerce, and residences onto the floodplains and make economic use of all the good land between the bluffs on either side.

Although the U.S. Army Corps of Engineers had been channelizing segments of the Missouri since the 1890s, the big push for altering the river started with construction of northern Montana's Fort Peck Dam in 1933 and intensified after World War II (Ferrell 1993; Ridgeway 1955; Schneiders 1999). The Missouri River engineering story is too vast to be summarized here, but to name a few large projects, people near the river witnessed the Garrison Dam construction 75 miles upstream from Bismarck, North Dakota, beginning in 1947 and closing its gates in 1953; Oahe Dam near Pierre, South Dakota; Fort Randall Dam, 12 miles west of Wagner, South Dakota; and Gavins Point Dam, 4 miles south of Yankton, South Dakota. In the aftermath, the richest continuous stretch of sturgeon habitat in the Midwest has been replaced by a highly channelized, faster-flowing river made at least temporarily safer for an extensive urban-industrial-agricultural complex established behind rock-lined pile dikes, wing dams, revetments, and other water control works. Beneficiaries have been residents who have enjoyed the advantages of floodplain living, extensive highway networks, urban and suburban economic prosperity, the opening of new land for agriculture and industry, and the dredging of barge channels to improve the competitiveness of enterprises that deal in bulk goods.

In place of the wide range of ecological niches afforded by the natural flows of pre-dam construction and the dike-building era, there is now a much swifter-flowing channelized river bereft of the attributes essential to many forms of wildlife in general and to the pallid sturgeon in particular. Essential facts were documented in a USFWS biological opinion (USFWS 2000a). Today, as compared to the pre-dam era, between Sioux City, Iowa, and St. Louis, Missouri, less than 10 percent of the river's floodplain is inundated when floodwaters rise. In the same stretch of river channel, stream width has narrowed from an average of 2,363 feet to 739 feet, removal of oxbows and meanders has shortened the river by 70 miles, and flow velocity has increased from 1–2 miles per hour to roughly 6 miles per hour (American Rivers 2004; Schneiders 1999: 228). The "Big Muddy" now tends to run with much clearer water because its necklace of dams creates the slack water that drops its sediment to reservoir bottoms. As the riverbed is "down-cut" by faster-moving clear water, many side channels that have survived become inaccessible to fish.

The devastation of much pallid sturgeon habitat on the Missouri has placed its recovery agenda on the docket of Nebraska's Lower Platte. In the Upper Missouri (above Gavins Point Dam), no documented reproduction has occurred in recent years—all the fish seem to be large and mature. The reason, analysts hypothesize, is that little to no free-flowing river is found between reservoirs in the Dakotas, and pallids are thought to need a spring flood pulse to trigger spawning. Also, any pallid larvae are likely to end up in the next downstream reservoir, where conditions are hostile to their survival and growth. In the mid-basin—including the area around the mouth of the Platte River—is a place with the most natural geomorphology and greatest flow variability in the entire Missouri system (National Research Council 2005). The Lower Platte River, between the mouth of the Elkhorn River and the Platte's confluence with the Missouri, may be important for the pallid sturgeon's recovery.

SUMMARY

In summary, the three bird species on the central Platte and the one fish species that appears to make use of the Lower Platte confront the same general challenge—massively altered ecosystems that have diminished and fragmented their habitats. Opportunities for birds and fish to make a living have been curtailed by people organized to take the peaks off of high spring flows; to stabilize summer flows at higher than traditional levels; to drop sediment in slack water behind dams and diversions; to send clear, sediment-hungry water downstream at higher than traditional velocities; and to scour out, incise, and narrow channels. People have advanced their economic prosperity in many ways, but they have done so in part by taking out unpaid, un-priced mortgages against the river and its associated ecosystems to which all are tethered.

In analytical terms, people traded away the features of an open access collective good in the form of a traditional river to expand the production and consumption of private goods. But, in their wisdom, representatives of the people of the United States also put in place the Endangered Species Act of 1973. With its passage, citizens of the republic committed themselves to pay off a small portion of the mortgage extracted from Mother Nature, insufficient to restore native flow patterns but enough to preserve some bits of serviceable habitat in the cause of preventing knowing and deliberate extinction. How could this be done in the context of the Platte River Basin?

PART II

Social Construction of the Crisis

Into a Federal Nexus

> All great values of this territory have ultimately to be measured to you in
> acre feet.
>
> —JOHN WESLEY POWELL,
> speaking at the Montana Constitutional Convention
> in 1889 (quoted in Peirce 1972: 16)

The ecological problem became a social organizational and political problem
by virtue of the legal mandate encoded in the Endangered Species Act (ESA) of
1973. Degraded habitats for whooping cranes, piping plovers, least terns, and
the pallid sturgeon were intimately linked, at least in the view of the U.S. Fish
and Wildlife Service (USFWS) and the larger environmental community, to the
construction of Platte and Missouri basin water facilities, especially dams, reservoirs, and diversions. The ESA would force a confrontation between the activities of water users in the basin and the needs of four species listed under that
law. The ESA compelled a thirty-three-year conversation about how to negotiate reconciliation between human water demands and the needs of four listed
species—three birds and one fish.

TWO TRADITIONS

The American West has always been a major federal project. The federal government has been the purveyor of cheap homesteads, subsidizer of railroads and high-
ways, investor in military facilities, promoter of irrigation, builder of the Panama
Canal, fighter of Native Americans, provider of reservations for Native Americans,

organizer of grazing resources, steward and restorer of soils beginning with the "great blowout" of the 1930s, and owner-manager of parks and forests. In the eleven westernmost states (of the lower forty-eight), the federal government is by far the largest landowner. Federal agencies own almost half of the seventeen western states, as compared with eastern states whose landholdings have been overwhelmingly privatized. Nevada has the highest proportion of land under federal ownership (82.9%), Wyoming is 48.9 percent federally owned, and 36.3 percent of Colorado's land is federally owned, but federal holdings in Nebraska amount to only 1.4 percent of the state's total area (Riebsame and Robb 1997: 58).

The significant federal presence in the West has always meant that close relationships have existed among federal, state, and local natural resource interests. But in the 1960s and 1970s, the rules that governed that relationship drastically changed. For decades its powerful constituencies had promoted the U.S. Bureau of Reclamation (USBR) as a force for progress by advancing the story of the small, struggling community starved for essential services—educational, religious, health, commercial, and financial—transformed into a thriving population center by a USBR dam. In the early twentieth century, the USFWS served that same vision by attempting to remove predators that threatened to make the West unsafe for cows. When the USBR constructed the large dams and reservoirs on Wyoming's North Platte and built the system of Colorado Western and Eastern slope storage reservoirs and a series of pumps and tunnels that brought Colorado River water to the burgeoning population on the east side of the state, the federal-local vision was one of utilitarian commodity production (Pisani 2002). There were no ESA or other environmental mandates to fulfill. But a spate of environmental legislation began to change all that. In particular, the passage of the Endangered Species Act in 1973 transformed the USFWS into an agency that would define itself by the number of dam projects modified or blocked in the name of an alternative vision of social progress centered on free-flowing streams. In the 1970s and 1980s the USBR would partially and haltingly reorient itself toward a revised mission: that of water service at least somewhat constrained by environmental stewardship. Old constituencies in both agencies felt that their nineteenth- and early–twentieth-century compacts with the federal government had been betrayed. New urban, rural ranchette, and environmental resource constituencies pushed hard in the U.S. Congress and the courts for new visions.

THE ENDANGERED SPECIES ACT

I think the ESA is a remarkable piece of legislation. . . . It's the one federal environmental statute that deals with scientific uncertainty and makes it clear that the species will not bear the burden of scientific uncertainty.

—DANIEL F. LUECKE,
Environmental Defense (2002: 409)

North America's freshwater habitats continue to support an extraordinary diversity of biotic communities, particularly compared with those found in similar habitats around the globe. But U.S. freshwater habitats are also among the most threatened by flow alterations, habitat degradation and fragmentation, and introduction of non-native species. All this has taken a heavy toll. In the United States, only 2 percent of natural rivers and streams are free-flowing. The consequences of human disturbance have been staggering: 67 percent of freshwater mussels and 65 percent of crayfish species are rare or imperiled, 37 percent of freshwater species are at risk of extinction, and 35 percent of amphibians that depend on aquatic habitats are rare or imperiled (Abell et al. 2000). In the late 1960s the whooping crane, bald eagle, peregrine falcon, and Eskimo curlew were all considered endangered (U.S. Fish and Wildlife Service 1997c). Early concerns about this habitat loss and consequent threats to plant and animal species led to calls for protective legislation, and those efforts resulted in the eventual passage of the Endangered Species Act (1973).

Under the ESA, existing federal water projects may be subject to federal discretionary authority and control if they appear to affect habitat of listed species (Echeverria 2001). Under Section 7 of the ESA, any federal agency must ensure that activities it authorizes, funds, or implements are not likely to jeopardize the continued existence of any listed species. Further, no federal actions can adversely modify or destroy "critical habitat" of any species (Bean 1999; Rohlf 2001). Federal agencies are mandated to coordinate their efforts with the Fish and Wildlife Service to try to ensure that no species are jeopardized by any federal agency action. Section 4 of the ESA provides for the designation of critical habitat, which consists of land, water, and airspace sufficient to provide the primary elements required for the survival of designated species (Anderson 1998).

The ESA has therefore changed water policy in the West by changing the mandates of the USFWS, the Army Corps of Engineers, and the USBR. When dependent upon federal government projects or when non-federal water facilities need federal approval, water users planning to undertake actions that can reasonably be expected to jeopardize a listed species must find ways to achieve ESA compliance in order to gain essential permits. For over three decades, the ESA has been an unwelcome guest at virtually every western water user dinner party.

The concept of jeopardy, and the manner in which jeopardy is defined and implemented by the USFWS, resides at the center of ESA's operational meaning. The definition of *jeopardy* establishes a bar against which the USFWS evaluates all federal actions that affect listed species. Not surprisingly, the issues surrounding the jeopardy standard(s) are complex, subtle, and draw fire from virtually all resource constituencies. The essence of the concept is simple enough. Jeopardy for a listed species is created when an action is undertaken that can reasonably be expected to reduce the likelihood of survival and recovery of that species

(Rohlf 2001: 118). However, it is not a simple matter to draw a biological line in the policy sand and then halt threatening actions of other federal agencies, their state and local constituencies, and non-federal authorities. Environmentalists have pushed hard for strong interpretation of the ESA, while resource appropriators seek to gain permits with regulatory certainty at the least possible cost. The USFWS's struggle to define the jeopardy standard is grist for other studies (Rohlf 2001).

In 1978, in an effort to protect the whooping crane, the USFWS designated a 56-mile-long by 3-mile-wide stretch of the Platte River between Lexington and Chapman, Nebraska, as critical habitat. Five additional species in the central Platte area were also listed as threatened or endangered: the least tern and piping plover (1985), western prairie fringed orchid and American burying beetle (1989), and pallid sturgeon (1990) (Echeverria 2001; U.S. Fish and Wildlife Service 1997c). The USFWS, in an effort to implement its ESA mandate, would take a seat at the Platte Basin water users' repast.

THE NATIONAL ENVIRONMENTAL POLICY ACT

By the 1960s it was clear that in conjunction with state and local constituencies, federal programs had created significant environmental problems. It had become clear that if federal action was an important part of the nation's environmental problems, the federal government must also be the source of potential solutions (Andrews 1999).

In 1969, Congress enacted a critical piece of legislation—the National Environmental Policy Act (NEPA)—which declared that it would now be national policy to maintain "productive harmony" between humans and nature while fulfilling the economic and social requirements of present and future generations. NEPA stipulated procedural requirements that mandated preparation of an environmental impact statement (EIS) for each major federal action that would significantly alter the natural environment. Each EIS would assess the environmental impacts of proposed actions and would also advance suggested options to address the environmental impacts that would be caused by the proposed actions (Andrews 1999). NEPA analyses would be available to all citizens.

When some USBR water facilities in the Platte Basin, along with certain other non-federal projects, were found to have jeopardized listed species associated with the central Nebraska critical habitat, project sponsors had to begin to search for options to redress matters. Any solutions developed would be advanced for scrutiny under two lenses. One would be under the auspices of NEPA and would lead to the production of an EIS. The other would be directed by the USFWS as it worked to implement the ESA by formulating a biological opinion regarding the proposed action and, if jeopardy was found, working to offset projected harm to species by ensuring construction of a viable remedy—a reasonable and prudent alternative.

REASONABLE AND PRUDENT ALTERNATIVES

To obtain ESA compliance, any federal action agency proposing to undertake a project that may negatively affect one or more listed species is required under Section 7 to consult with the USFWS to determine whether that agency believes the proposed action will likely jeopardize the continued existence of endangered or threatened species (Freedman 1987). Any action agency that receives a USFWS "jeopardy opinion" is technically free to make its own decision about its proposed action's consistency with Section 7. However, since the biological opinion will be given weight in any citizen's legal challenge to the proposed action, other agencies are seldom willing to proceed with their challenge in the face of a biological opinion that specifies jeopardy. Furthermore, the USFWS will be unwilling to endorse any action agency's proposal that is inconsistent with its own biological opinion stating a jeopardy rationale. That agency would predictably find itself subject to civil lawsuits from citizens who closely follow the disposition of jeopardy opinions. The ESA has specifically empowered citizens to file suit against the Fish and Wildlife Service and other resource agencies and users for violations of the act.

Remedy for having been established to be a cause of "jeopardy" is found in a decision to shut down and thereby eliminate that cause of jeopardy or, more likely, to revise the project to eliminate jeopardy by installing a "reasonable and prudent alternative" (RPA) that permits the project to continue while providing relief for the listed species. The holy grail of the ESA Section 7 consultation process for a resource user, singly or in collaboration with others, is to construct an RPA that, in most instances, will be reviewed under the NEPA/EIS process. This, in turn, opens up a public discussion of the proposal and options and the opportunity to have it judged as satisfactory by the USFWS in the form of an agency biological opinion. Non-jeopardy biological opinions are issued if and when the RPA is determined to sufficiently offset or prevent original project-induced harm to the species. All this will produce the prize: a sanction to continue the operation with the promise of regulatory certainty. For project promoters, regulatory certainty is critical because it promises that deal-abiding players may count on future project permit approvals in streamlined review processes.

THE FUTURE WITHOUT A
COLLABORATIVE RECOVERY PROGRAM

Since the late 1970s, the Fish and Wildlife Service has issued "jeopardy biological opinions" for virtually all water projects that deplete flows in the Platte River

Basin. In principle, the barrage of jeopardy opinions could have caused major disruptions of water supplies for agriculture, cities, and power production. However, the relevant federal action agencies (following the lead provided by the USFWS's jeopardy opinions) granted temporary approval for continued operation of permitted facilities on the condition that serious negotiations would be undertaken by Platte Basin interests and that specific actions involving land, water, and money would be undertaken during the negotiation period to mitigate jeopardy. The purpose would be to create a basin-wide solution. There was a clear understanding that if negotiations failed, ESA Section 7 consultations would be reopened. Water users in the Platte River Basin were thereby provided an opportunity to voluntarily come into compliance with the ESA by constructing a reasonable and prudent alternative. The temptation to walk away from negotiations would be more than counterbalanced by the knowledge that serious negative consequences would result.

Any water provider intent on pursuing a "no-action option" would be confronted squarely with a fearsome action option—specifically, the provider would have to go into an ESA consultation individually and alone. Failure to accomplish a satisfactory collective solution on a basin-wide basis would result in individual consultations during which the USFWS would evaluate each individual water project against what the agency judged to be an average annual target flow shortage of 417,000 acre feet per year at Grand Island, Nebraska. Furthermore, individual water users would face a USFWS demand that they replace their project depletions on a one-acre-foot for one-acre-foot basis at their state lines (for Nebraska, at the top of the critical habitat) in both amount and timing. This demand threatened to derail critical existing and future water-use activities in the states. Even though users never agreed to the shortage numbers the USFWS presented, they were bound to them. If individual water users failed to build collective, reasonable, and prudent alternatives in an acceptable manner, the Fish and Wildlife Service would devise its own solution on an individual case-by-case basis as federal permit renewals came up. The agency would do so within a framework centered on what to water users was a shockingly high agency water shortage calculation, as well as its determination that there needed to be 29,000 acres of high-quality listed species land habitat on and around the central Platte.

The Platte Basin permit crisis led directly to the governors of three states and the secretary of the Department of the Interior signing a Memorandum of Agreement in June 1994 pledging that a good-faith effort would be made to construct a cooperative program to restore and protect critical habitat in Nebraska for the whooping crane and other listed species. If this cooperative effort failed, the USFWS would return to individual ESA Section 7 consultations that would lack the advantages potentially available under a basin-wide collaborative program. That threat constituted a strong incentive for basin water users to collectively seek relief from the jeopardy opinions to which they were subject.

To gain a modicum of control over their operating environment—to obtain "regulatory certainty"—water users had little option but to join in a collaboration with each other, environmentalists, and the Department of the Interior to create a basin-wide solution. They would have to cooperate to achieve what no water provider could possibly achieve individually and independently. Yet they were divided among themselves by a history of contention, state lines dividing their geographic areas, collisions of interests within and among their units and levels of government, incompatible water interests, and conflicting visions. How could they transcend their self-interests and cooperate to restore habitats?

CHAPTER 4

Colorado in a Federal Nexus

Defending the Water Tower

Citizens of this headwaters state, the most urbanized in the Missouri Basin, have constructed a hydraulic society that lives off a fraction of snowpack runoff for a brief period each spring and a small amount of warm-season precipitation. They know they must fulfill obligations to other states as required by compacts on virtually all of their drainages. The future for Colorado's economic growth, society, and environment depends on keeping the widest gap possible between what mountain watersheds produce in a given year and what is required at the state lines. The Colorado perspective is driven fundamentally by a need to defend as much flow as humanly possible while making maximum use of the water before releasing it for compact requirements and downstream uses across its borders.

LIVING ON THE GAP

About 80 percent of Colorado's surface water supply enters the local hydrological cycle in the form of snowflakes that begin cascading from the skies in the fall and continue sporadically through the spring. They lay down a narrow strip of snow—the pack is generally deepest between 8,000 and 11,000 feet elevation—along mountain slopes on both sides of the Continental Divide but preponderantly on the Western slope. As much runoff as possible is trapped temporarily in a network of reservoirs laced to streams that are not self-contained within state borders. Given that Colorado water supplies originate in a condition of highly variable precipitation, great uncertainty always exists about annual water supply.

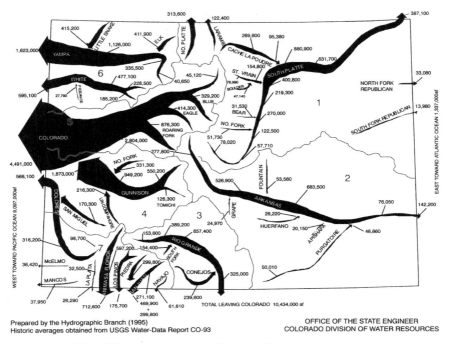

FIGURE 4.1. *Colorado historic average annual water outflows.*

Geography ensures that Colorado users will be defendants in virtually any western interstate water litigation (Figure 4.1).

The great nightmare of Colorado water policy makers—liberal and conservative, Republican and Democrat, Western slope and Eastern slope, rural and urban—is that Colorado will become a "pass-through" water collector, too subservient to the demands of other states without sufficient capacity to employ the resource in Colorado. No politician or water manager can make a career out of a vision of Colorado as too willing to share control over its own spouts. Generations of water people have passed along a deep paranoia as they have viewed themselves continually fighting rearguard actions on their drainages. To be "soft" on water on any one stream (for example, the South Platte) has always run the risk of setting a precedent for every other river in the state. Downstream of the Colorado segments of the Rio Grande and the Colorado River, to take two examples, are "high-dollar" entrepreneurs eagerly contemplating the possibilities inherent in any change in Colorado's rules of the game for Santa Fe, Albuquerque, Las Vegas, Phoenix, Tucson, or Los Angeles. When a Colorado representative enters any negotiation that has interstate reallocation implications, he or she does so with extreme caution and absolute determination to preserve that precious gap between the expected upstream water and water obligated downstream at state lines.

COLORADO USERS IN A FEDERAL NEXUS

Denver Water

The Denver Board of Water Commissioners (Denver Water) operates the largest public utility between Chicago and Los Angeles, with about 1,000 employees and a $180 million annual budget. Behind only the federal government, Denver Water is the second-largest landowner in Colorado (Bunch 2003: 4B). By the 1960s, Denver was the premier water provider in the greater Denver metropolitan area (Cox 1967; Lochhead 2000). By the 1970s it was operating 31 pumping stations, 32 storage reservoirs, and several water treatment plants and had launched a billion-dollar capital expenditure program (Gottlieb and Wiley 1982). By the turn of the twenty-first century, the agency was serving about 1.2 million people, approximately half the population of the metropolitan region. About half of its water supply comes from the Platte, with the remainder diverted from the Upper Colorado and transmitted by way of an elaborate trans-mountain plumbing system.

Historically, Denver Water did not rely on federal funding to capture and deliver its water supply. As a young city, Denver used its resources to purchase land, litigate rights, and develop the Moffat and Roberts Tunnel collection systems that brought to the city and its suburbs Western slope water captured in several reservoirs—including its crown jewel, the Dillon Reservoir. But by the early 1970s, Denver was no longer untouched by federal environmental laws. For example, Gross Reservoir (capacity 43,065 acre feet and part of the Western slope collection systems) had a 50-year Federal Energy Regulatory Commission (FERC) hydropower permit that was due for renewal in 2002; likewise, Denver Water's Williams Fork facility impounded the flows of a small stream tributary to the Colorado River, which included a small electrical power plant that put it squarely in FERC's clutches. The facility was scheduled for a re-licensing procedure just after the Gross review.

On the eastern side of the Continental Divide, by the time the Foothills Water Treatment Plant was proposed, many environmental laws were in place, and strong opposition to the project emerged from the Environmental Protection Agency and environmentalists. As Denver Water proceeded with its plans for Foothills and the Strontia Springs Dam, it had to confront the uncomfortable realities presented by the federal Clean Water Act, the National Environmental Policy Act, the Federal Land Policy Management Act, and the Endangered Species Act (ESA). The Foothills facility posed no ESA problems, but it took a long process of negotiations involving other federal environmental legislation before a 1979 settlement was reached and Denver received permission to proceed with the Foothills system, which was finally completed in 1983. In the face of much public controversy the Foothills Water Treatment Plant came on-line, but only under the agreement that Denver Water would conduct a system-wide environmental impact statement for its water projects, implement a water conservation program, and appoint a citizens' advisory committee to the Denver Water Board (Lochhead 2000). By that point, Denver Water was firmly immersed in a relationship with the federal environmental agenda.

Colorado–Big Thompson Project

By the 1930s, irrigators who were planting more than 3 million acres along the Front Range and the eastward fringes of the South Platte were annually running short of water as a result of new lands being brought into production and a shift from grain to more water-intensive crops. From 1925 to 1933, farms had less than half of the water they needed. Further motivated by a severe drought that started in 1931, by 1934 farmers had formed a coalition with the Great Western Sugar Company, Platte Valley ranchers, Colorado Agricultural College (now Colorado State University), and local newspapers and chambers of commerce and had organized the first Northern Colorado Water Users Association. Together, they lobbied hard for the diversion of water across the Continental Divide. The story has been well told (Abbott 1976; Tyler 1992), and in 1938 the U.S. Bureau of Reclamation (USBR) started construction on the Colorado–Big Thompson Project (C-BT). Most of the construction was finished by 1953, when some water began to flow. The C-BT diverts water from the Colorado River to the Big Thompson by way of the 13.1-mile Alva B. Adams Tunnel. Compensatory storage for Western slope users was provided by Green Mountain Reservoir, located on the Blue River.

The C-BT was one of the most complex projects undertaken by the USBR. It consists of over 100 structures integrated into a trans-mountain diversion system that provides supplemental water for agricultural and municipal users on over 720,000 acres of Colorado's northern Front Range and a stretch of the eastern plains along the South Platte. The project has annually diverted volumes ranging mostly between 220,000 and 260,000 acre feet (310,000 acre feet has been the maximum) from the Colorado River headwaters on the western side of the Continental Divide to the Big Thompson drainage, a tributary of the South Platte. By comparison, Denver Water's annual diversions from the Western slope have been in the range of 110,000 acre feet. The project is sponsored and operated by the Northern Colorado Water Conservancy District (NCWCD), which apportions the water to more than 120 mutual ditch company associations, 60 mutual ditch company reservoirs, and 11 towns and cities. Electric power revenues produced by six power plants through which water drops on its way down

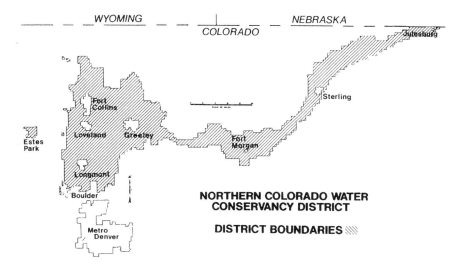

FIGURE 4.2. *NCWCD service area. From Northern Colorado Water Conservancy District, State of Colorado, Berthoud.*

the east side of the Divide have done much to subsidize the repayment of initial federal capitalization.

The C-BT's original mission was primarily to supply supplemental water to agriculture and municipalities within the NCWCD's boundaries (Figure 4.2). In 1957, the first full year of water deliveries, 720,000 acres of land were in production in the district; by 1990 urbanization had reduced the acreage to about 630,000 (Tyler 1992), and more than 50 percent of the diversions had shifted to municipal and industrial uses. NCWCD's interest is best served if water released by agricultural dry ups is put to beneficial use within district boundaries. Denver's suburbs particularly covet NCWCD water, and the district has set itself against water raiders from outside entities.

The NCWCD was created to sponsor and manage the operation and repayment of the C-BT within the terms and conditions established by contracts with the USBR and continually overseen by that agency as it exercised its ongoing discretionary authority. That, in turn, would entail consultation among the NCWCD, the USBR as the federal action agency, and the U.S. Fish and Wildlife Service (USFWS). Colorado's first and largest conservancy district was firmly entrenched in a relationship with federal environmental law, especially the Endangered Species Act. Congressional policy expressly stated in the ESA (Section 2 [c][2]) mandates that federal agencies (specifically the USBR) work with state and local agencies (for example, the NCWCD) to resolve water resource issues in ways that fulfill the needs of listed endangered species. The NCWCD had no room to wiggle away from the ESA agenda of the USFWS.

Poudre River Mountain Reservoirs

Mountain storage reservoirs at higher elevations are highly valued because they afford maximum delivery options as a result of gravity flow. In addition, deeper narrow canyons permit smaller dams and less water surface exposure per unit volume, and cooler temperatures reduce evaporation losses compared with plains reservoirs. These advantages have made mountain sites prime candidates for reservoir construction, and most such sites in the West were initially located on federal land, especially federal forestland. Many dams, reservoirs, canals, and pipelines have been constructed on U.S. Forest Service land—some well before the creation of the U.S. Forest Service (USFS)—and operate under permits granted by the USFS (Blumm 1994).

In 1991 six special use permits expired for reservoirs on the Upper Poudre River, the largest tributary of the South Platte. These facilities were owned by four Front Range cities, one irrigation mutual company, and the Public Service Company of Colorado (now known as Xcel Energy) and were located on the Arapaho-Roosevelt National Forest. It quickly became apparent to the reservoir operators that the USFS would consult with the USFWS as required under the terms of the ESA. During the permit renewal process, the USFS sought to impose "bypass flow" regulations on reservoir operators to advance its environmental forest habitat agenda. All of this threatened to reduce the yields of the water storage projects. Colorado water constituencies created a firestorm of protest in Colorado and eventually in Washington, D.C. (Lochhead 2000). Then, on June 2 and July 1, 1994, the USFWS issued two biological opinions that concluded that any USFS renewal of the six permits would jeopardize the existence of the whooping crane, least tern, and piping plover critical habitat in Nebraska and also that of the pallid sturgeon further downstream on the Lower Platte (Record of Decision 2006: 25; U.S. Department of the Interior, Bureau of Reclamation, and U.S. Fish and Wildlife Service 2006, vol. 2:2).

A prolonged period of legal wrangling ensued over federal authority to require bypass flows for federal forest purposes. Important portions of the story have been documented elsewhere (Gillian and Brown 1997; Gordon 1995; Neuman and Blumm 1999). During the bitter struggle, it became clear to all parties that issues involving species habitat for three birds and one fish on the main stem of the Platte River in Nebraska would compel negotiations, the purpose of which would be to address a federal ESA environmental habitat agenda. Neither the federal agencies nor state water users could obtain what they wanted without the cooperation of the other. At that point, the USFS only had seven permits under consideration for renewal on the Front Range, but the agency—along with the USFWS—contemplated that over a hundred would be coming up for review within a few years after the turn of the new century. The situation was quickly becoming impossible for all parties concerned. With deep reluctance, Colorado representatives agreed to voluntarily sit at the table with representatives from Wyoming and Nebraska and federal negotiators.

NEW COLLISIONS

Denver Water, the NCWCD, and operators of high mountain reservoirs on the Poudre River were firmly in the grip of the federal ESA by virtue of facilities they had long possessed. But that law had also reached into water user aspirations for new projects yet to be constructed. Those dreams collided with ESA realities.

Wildcat Creek Project

In the late 1970s, Riverside Irrigation Company and the Public Service Company of Colorado obtained from Colorado's Division 1 Water Court a right to store and use 60,000 acre feet of water on Wildcat Creek, a small tributary of the South Platte with an annual average flow of only about 1.1 cubic feet per second (cfs) at its confluence with the South Platte near Brush, Colorado (MacDonnell 1985; Tyler 1992).

By that time, construction of a dam virtually anywhere in the United States required a permit from the U.S. Army Corps of Engineers (USACE) under Section 404 of the Clean Water Act. For the purposes of the ESA, the federal action was a dredge-and-fill permit for construction of a dam on an intermittent stream at a site 250 miles upstream from the designated critical habitat of the whooping crane in Nebraska. Once the application was filed with the USACE, an ESA review by the USFWS was in order. The Wildcat project was then stymied by a USFWS jeopardy opinion that left the USACE with no choice but to stop the Riverside Irrigation Company from proceeding, given the dam's potential harm to whooping crane habitat far downstream in another state. The USFWS had determined that peak water flows were necessary downstream in Nebraska to clear out woody vegetation in a 70-mile riparian habitat that supported the whooping crane and other listed species. River diversions into Wildcat Creek would further diminish the South Platte's flood surges.

The Riverside Irrigation Company and the Public Service Company of Colorado, with the help of the Northern Colorado Water Conservancy District, filed suit in Federal District Court challenging the ruling. During the legal conflict, it became clear that Wildcat proponents would have to go through the expensive and time-consuming process of individual permitting with the USACE as it consulted with the USFWS (Tyler 1992). For all practical purposes, hopes for a Wildcat Reservoir were dashed.

Narrows Dam Project

The Narrows Dam Project on the South Platte River near Fort Morgan was first proposed in 1908 and in 1944 was introduced as one of many projects authorized by the Pick-Sloan Act (Reisner 1986). The Narrows facility was originally proposed as a multipurpose project to provide irrigation water, flood control, and recreational water use for northeastern Colorado. In 1931 the USACE sponsored the Narrows Project for the purpose of flood control (Tyler 1992). After World War II, the Bureau of Reclamation took over responsibility for pushing the project and drafted plans that would create a dam approximately 147 feet high and 4 miles long, with the capacity to store 973,000 acre feet of water (Reisner 1986; Woodward 1981).

Protection of the whooping crane under the ESA soon became one of many issues and would ultimately play a major role in the termination of plans for the project. Years of haggling over the Narrows Dam led the USFWS to construct the benchmark figure of at least 10,000 acres of habitat to be restored in central Nebraska and prompted the general concept of re-timing Platte Basin water flows to achieve target flow volumes for preserving and restoring the central Platte habitat. The discussion was critical to the emergence of the concept of a basin-wide federal-state collaborative plan—something the Department of the Interior and governors of the three basin states eventually agreed to begin to negotiate in 1994.

In the end, the Narrows Project failed for many reasons. The proposed location of the dam site was questionable on geological grounds. There was sharp conflict between upstream and downstream users—a serious political liability when supposed beneficiaries could not agree on the project's merits. Shrinking access to federal treasury dollars under Presidents Jimmy Carter and Ronald Reagan signaled changing federal priorities. Opposition to USBR river storage projects in general, and to the Narrows in particular, had increased to the point that the proposal had become politically contentious in both state and federal arenas.

Finally, on January 20, 1983, the Fish and Wildlife Service issued its jeopardy opinion, which had emerged from its evaluation of the Narrows proposal (Record of Decision 2006: 25). The USFWS found that the net annual depletion of flows to habitat would be 91,000 acre feet. Such a massive impact on South Platte flow volumes and pulses could only damage the whooping crane habitat (MacDonnell 1985). The doomed project was not yet dead, however. It lingered for years in the vain hope that it could be revived. By the late 1990s its organizational sponsor, the Lower South Platte Water Conservancy District, quietly dropped any effort to prove diligence on behalf of project water rights—a decision that effectively killed any future for the Narrows Dam.

Two Forks Dam and Reservoir Project

The story of Two Forks is a tale of how Denver Water invested heavily in its proposed project on the South Platte, hit a wall made up of environmental considerations, picked up the pieces, and re-made itself. When the history of Denver Water is written, it will be told in two parts—before and after Two Forks. The defeat of the Two Forks Dam and Reservoir Project changed everything about the way the city of Denver has managed its water assets. Before the Two Forks Project proposal failed, Denver Water's mission was to provide water for the greater metropolitan area and promote economic growth among its constituencies—and to do all that as cheaply as possible. With a budget and staff much larger than those of any other metropolitan supplier between Los Angeles and Chicago, Denver Water was a major battler for water—especially for trans-mountain diversions from Colorado's Western slope—and thereby became a nemesis of those who stood in its way. After the Two Forks Project failed, Denver Water would trim and reconfigure its mission in ways that were more accepting of federal environmental legislation, that showed a greater willingness to invest the funds necessary to incorporate environmental considerations into its project planning, and that opened up to more public involvement, especially with regard to Western slope water interests (Barry 1997: 22–23).

For nearly 100 years, Denver Water had entertained a proposal to build a massive dam on the Eastern slope to store South Platte River water and flows it had been diverting through Roberts Tunnel from the Upper Colorado River. By the early 1980s Two Forks Project plans had been drafted in detail and were seen as an answer to future water needs in the Denver metropolitan area. Sustainable flows could be tapped in the South Platte River above Denver and in the Blue River (tributary to the Colorado River) above Dillon. Capturing such flows would require the largest water project in Colorado's history, one that would create a 31-mile-long reservoir covering a surface area of 7,300 acres in Cheesman Canyon on the main stem of the South Platte River (MacDonnell 1985). In the end, Two Forks would promise to deliver 98,000 acre feet per year to 41 cities and utilities in the Denver metropolitan area.

There were problems, however. In addition to the obvious negative environmental impacts associated with high dams and slack waters, there would be the loss of prime recreation area in a beautiful canyon and a pristine free-flowing stretch of the South Platte. The large storage reservoir (more than a million acre feet) was projected to yield less than 100,000 acre feet annually. In addition, the state of Nebraska joined environmentalists in opposing construction of the Two Forks Dam on the grounds that the huge storage project would undercut the historical regime of the river and that there would be loss of flows in excess of Nebraska-Colorado compact minimums and a loss of flood pulses, which would be damaging to listed species habitat in central Nebraska.

The politics quickly became ferocious. Eastern/Western slope water interests became deeply mired in a polarized conflict, and sharp divisions emerged within these two major blocs. The Two Forks Project review eventually took 10 years and cost nearly $40 million (Lochhead 2000). Much to the dismay of environmentalists and Nebraska water interests, on October 14, 1987, the USFWS issued a non-jeopardy biological opinion (Record of Decision 2006: 25). Proponents pushed on. In 1989, after years of working amid intense wrangling by conflicting parties, the Army Corps of Engineers completed its environmental impact statement and was ready to issue the key permit. The only necessary signature left to obtain was that of President George H.W. Bush's newly appointed administrator of the Environmental Protection Agency, William K. Reilly. Over the objections of water interests in Colorado and his own agency's senior staff, Reilly had initiated a final review process that had taken 19 months. In a shocking move for a Republican administration that had been solicitous of western water user perspectives, in March 1989 Reilly vetoed Two Forks on the grounds that the project would violate Section 404 of the Clean Water Act.

Shock reverberated among water users throughout the West. Wherever they stood on the Wildcat, Narrows, and Two Forks projects, all parties involved could see that virtually any water project proposal would raise basin-wide issues that would compel action across state lines. Federal laws and agencies were scratching new environmental handwriting on state water user walls.

CHAPTER 5

Nebraska in a Federal Nexus

Threat to the Big House

Nebraska is the place where the arid West begins. Two-thirds of its length falls on the western side of the 98th meridian, the fixed marker of a variable point—shifting from wet to dry years—that defines precipitation of twenty inches a year or less. Nebraska farmers are world leaders in the production of grain, and the state's economy is dominated by high-input, high-output–production agriculture and its support services. This is all made possible by extensive reliance on irrigation water, most of which is pumped to the surface by wells tapped into aquifers tributary to the Platte River and to other surface streams that, in turn, are Platte tributaries.

Nebraska's Platte River water sources change character from west to east. Snowmelt from Wyoming (the North Platte) and Colorado (mostly the South Platte) is critical to the entire river but especially so in western and central Nebraska, where there is high dependence on return flows from diversions in the upstream states. To the east, the river is greatly supplemented by flows from two major tributaries; near Columbus, the Loup River drains into the Lower Platte, and further downstream the Elkhorn contributes its flow at a point north of Ashland. Each of these tributaries, along with other streams, is importantly fed by waters stored in a portion of the Ogallala aquifer underlying the grassy sandhill region north of the central Platte.

Nebraska is second only to California in irrigated area within the United States (Table 5.1). The story of Nebraska irrigation has been well told by others (Ashworth 2006; Dornbusch, Vining, and Kearney 1995; Dreeszen 1993; Opie 1993; Smith 1989), and I will not attempt to repeat it here. By the time the Platte empties into the Missouri, it has drained about two-thirds of the state.

Table 5.1. Irrigated Acreage, Selected States, 1997 and 2002

State	1997 Acres	2002 Acres
California	8,886,693	8,709,353
Nebraska	7,065,556	7,625,170
Texas	5,764,295	5,074,638
Kansas	2,695,816	2,678,277
Colorado	3,374,233	2,590,654
Wyoming	1,749,908	1,541,688

Source: USDA, National Agricultural Statistics Service, 2002 Census of Agriculture, State Data. At http://www.nass.usda.gov/census/census02/volume1/us/st99, table 10, accessed December 8, 2006.

Whereas irrigated acreage in every other state listed in Table 5.1 declined over the reported six-year span, it is notable that irrigated land expanded in Nebraska; the increase was almost entirely the result of additional agricultural irrigation wells. In the interior West, Nebraska is truly the "big house" of irrigated agriculture.

NEBRASKA WATER USERS IN A FEDERAL NEXUS

Kingsley Dam, the heart of a non-federal project, closed its gates in 1941 to begin filling Lake McConaughy on the North Platte near Ogallala, Nebraska. The hydraulic earth-fill dam is a 3-mile-long mound that has created the largest reservoir in the Platte Basin and, for that matter, is by far the largest pool of surface water in Nebraska. Knowledgeable Nebraskans are fond of pointing out that the volumes of all the other lakes in the state could—conceptually at least—be poured into Lake McConaughy twice and still leave remaining capacity. When full, the surface area is about 30,500 acres and consists of a maximum allowable storage capacity of 1.79 million acre feet (USFWS 1997a: 15). When filled to capacity Lake McConaughy measures 3 miles wide and more than 20 miles long. In addition to providing a historical average of 285,200 acre feet of irrigation water each year, the lake's water serves hydropower needs, flat-water recreation, and groundwater recharge for irrigation wells. In its early years, the Central Nebraska Public Power and Irrigation District (CNPPID, or Central) managed its own marketing of electrical power, but in 1970 a specialized organization was established for this purpose—the Nebraska Public Power District (NPPD).

Two Districts

The CNPPID delivers irrigation water to farmers who work 215,000 acres of high-quality farmland in central Nebraska. Central's network of canals and hydroelectric production facilities stretches over 170 miles along the North Platte and the main stem (Figure 5.1). CNPPID operates a 75-mile-long supply ditch, the Tri-County Canal, which delivers water to three major canals that together serve 105,000 acres in three counties (Gosper, Phelps, and Kearney) and another 5,600 acres in Lincoln and Dawson counties. On the Tri-County Canal, Johnson Lake serves as a re-regulating pool to ensure stable controllable flows into the three lower distributaries.

Lake McConaughy is filled by North Platte River flows that are highly dependent upon return flows from irrigation diversions out of Wyoming's string of North Platte reservoirs (Figure 5.1) and from diversions to irrigation district lands in the panhandle region of western Nebraska. Roughly 80 percent of the water stored in Wyoming's six major reservoirs is designated for irrigators in the western Nebraska panhandle. Substantial fractions of flows diverted onto Wyoming projects for initial uses find their way downslope to McConaughy. As has been the case in many places in the arid and semiarid West, so-called waste from a user above becomes an essential supply treasure for the diverter below. McConaughy Reservoir is therefore primarily filled by water that has been repeatedly diverted upstream. Basic CNPPID-NPPD management strategy is to release these re-captured flows from Lake McConaughy to coordinate with and supplement South Platte flows from Colorado.

The CNPPID releases Lake McConaughy water through turbines at Kingsley (50,000 kilowatts) and then spills the flow into Lake Ogallala, created by the excavation of earthen material used in constructing the dam. Water then travels downriver and into the canal system through hydroelectric plants (see Figure 5.1). Central's hydro plants—Jeffrey, Johnson No. 1, and Johnson No. 2—each with a capacity of 18,000 kw, are remotely operated from Central's control facility in Gothenburg, in combination with the Kingsley Dam unit. These power plants generate up to 104,000 kw of electricity.

Power revenues produced at Kingsley Dam subsidize operational costs of the CNPPID irrigation project and make possible substantially lower irrigation water rates for agricultural users. Central coordinates its water releases under the terms of several contracts with the NPPD. The CNPPID-NPPD relationship is anything but simple, but its essence revolves around the fact that CNPPID wholesales its electrical power production to NPPD, which then retails it to end users. Complexity arises from the necessity of melding CNPPID's farm irrigation mission during the summer with NPPD's demand for electricity to serve baseload and peak demands year-round; meshing the two organizational agendas has never been easy. Furthermore, during the summer months the NPPD moves beyond its role as electricity producer and distributor when it uses McConaughy storage rights, which it administers on behalf of seven older, smaller irrigation systems that hold river diversion priorities senior to those of the Kingsley Dam Project and are operated by mutual companies located between Brady and Kearney—altogether providing surface irrigation water to about 75,000 acres of farmland.

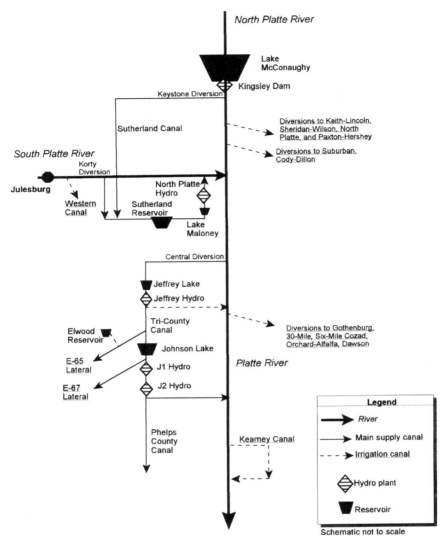

FIGURE 5.1. *Nebraska diversions and facilities. Modified from map from Mark Butler, U.S. Fish and Wildlife Service EIS Office; U.S. Department of the Interior, Bureau of Reclamation, and U.S. Fish and Wildlife Service; Platte River Recovery and Implementation Program: Final Environmental Impact Statement, April 2006.*

Federal Energy Regulatory Commission

The Federal Energy Regulatory Commission (FERC), created in 1977 as the successor to the Federal Power Commission, reviews permit renewals for about 2,600 hydropower dams in the United States. Established by the U.S. Congress in

1920 to promote and regulate private development of hydropower facilities, the original Federal Power Act was a signal achievement of progressive American politics. It provided for a detailed regulatory review process to ensure that future citizens could have discretion in deciding the terms and conditions for granting new licenses—or whether to grant them at all. The Federal Power Act, through the Federal Power Commission, authorized private enterprises to own and operate power projects on public waterways subject to conditions specified in project licenses that had maximum terms of fifty years. Re-licensing proceedings are best understood as a careful reevaluation of the use of water and of public needs (Pitzer 2005). Rivers are a public resource, and U.S. citizens, through their government, allow an enterprise to use that public asset to serve society and generate financial returns. Knowing that societal needs are ever changing, Congress was careful to create no vested right to re-licensing. Located in the U.S. Department of Energy, FERC now regulates the operation of most non-federal hydropower capacity—about 20,000 megawatts (Western Water Policy Review Advisory Commission 1997).

In 1986, amendments to the Federal Power Act directed FERC to give equal consideration to fish, wildlife, recreation, and other uses—along with power production—during its licensing decisions. Among those same amendments, Congress directed FERC to include conditions—in addition to those imposed by the Endangered Species Act (ESA)—that protect, mitigate, and enhance fish and wildlife based on USFWS recommendations. FERC is required to consult with federal, state, and local resource agencies in its licensing decisions and under the National Environmental Policy Act (1969) is obliged to prepare environmental impact statements. About two-thirds of licenses for non-federal hydropower capacity in the West expired between 1997 and 2010.

Original licenses were issued for CNPPID and NPPD operations in 1937. They expired in 1987. Environmental interests had fervently pointed out that the Platte riverine habitat had been dramatically and, in their view, negatively impacted by the complex of the CNPPID-NPPD river works (Echeverria 2001). Given the requirements of the ESA, there was little alternative but to begin consideration of listed species habitat requirements. The re-licensing discourse that had begun years prior to 1987 was an obvious place to insert the new environmental agendas that had come with passage of the Endangered Species Act in 1973. The two districts were squarely in the grip of federal regulatory agencies and the ESA.

RE-LICENSING

In 1984, CNPPID and NPPD began formal work on re-licensing their projects with FERC (Gaul 1993: 224). In May 1987, just prior to the expiration of the original licenses, the ESA required FERC to fully consult under Section 7

(U.S. Fish and Wildlife Service 1997c: 6). The licensing procedure was of interest to the Department of the Interior, Wyoming, Colorado, the Environmental Protection Agency, environmental organizations, and more than fifty other parties. Discussions among the USFWS, FERC, NPPD, and CNPPID were extended, detailed, energy-consuming, costly, and torturous. In the early negotiating years, the districts did their utmost to fight the notion that they should seriously contemplate yielding to the ESA agenda.

In February 1996, given that the districts had been less than enthusiastic partners in the new environmental discussion, FERC requested a formal consultation with the USFWS on the proposed re-licensing of the districts' facilities, prompting issuance of a USFWS biological opinion. That opinion concluded that re-licensing the Kingsley Dam facilities would jeopardize the continued existence of the endangered whooping crane, least tern, and pallid sturgeon and the threatened piping plover. Also, it would result in adverse modifications of federally designated whooping crane critical habitat on the central Platte (U.S. Fish and Wildlife Service 1997b). In its biological opinion of July 1997, the USFWS presented two options to the districts: (1) a stand-alone option, in which the districts would be individually responsible for their portion—as calculated by the USFWS—of preservation of the critical habitat along the Platte; and (2) making the proposed re-licensing action an integral part of the Memorandum of Agreement initiating the Platte River Habitat Recovery Program. The CNPPID and the NPPD chose to integrate their re-licensing efforts with the basin-wide collaborative effort that had been launched in June 1994, which had produced an outline of a basin-wide solution by June 1997. In July 1998, after thirteen years and an expenditure of over $30 million, the districts received their renewed forty-year licenses from FERC.

FERC–KINGSLEY DAM OPERATING REQUIREMENTS

While FERC has the authority to deny a license, its focus is primarily on the terms and conditions to be included in a new license. FERC insisted that the districts' facilities be managed in a way that would trade away some drought protection and power production to improve the health of aquatic ecosystems. The changes would be modest, but they required the acknowledgment of a very different operating philosophy than the one that had informed the original licenses (Gaul 1993: 224). The licenses issued to the districts incorporated a mix of conditions to be followed in the operation of facilities and included a general mandate to cooperate in the implementation of the 1997 Cooperative Agreement. It was made clear that more demanding requirements would go into effect if the Cooperative Agreement effort were to fail, and paramount among the re-licensing conditions imposed was a "reopener" clause that reserved FERC's authority to modify licenses in the future based on changed conditions or compelling new information (Echeverria 2001: 576). In principle, therefore, the re-licensing arrangement was made dependent upon the successful development and implementation of the Cooperative Agreement.

Prior to issuing the USFWS's final biological opinion, the districts and the U.S. Department of the Interior—along with the other parties to the proceedings— reached an agreement in principle for fulfilling license conditions for the Kingsley Dam. The districts accepted an obligation to take special actions for the benefit of endangered or threatened species and other non-listed species. Actions essential to fulfill FERC licensing requirements were constructed as components of the proposed Cooperative Agreement. Among other things, the USFWS called for an environmental water account at Lake McConaughy, specifically allotting a fixed percentage of inflows to that account. This water would then be managed by the USFWS on behalf of habitat for the listed species. During the three-year period (1997–2000) then planned for negotiating a viable Cooperative Agreement as required by the FERC re-licensing, the districts agreed to begin re-operation of their facilities and to undertake land acquisition for species habitats, habitat restoration, and water conservation and supply measures. The two Nebraska districts were not only caught up in a federal nexus, as they had been since the beginning of their operations, but they had now become a centerpiece in the development of a basin-wide collaborative solution with water users and environmentalists in two other states.

Wyoming in a Federal Nexus

Defending the Mountaintop

Wyoming's North Platte water users have been in a relationship with the federal government and the mandates of the Endangered Species Act (ESA) because they have been beneficiaries of federal dams, reservoirs, river diversions, and canals that capture over 2.8 million acre feet of North Platte River water for irrigation and hydroelectric power. The U.S. Bureau of Reclamation (USBR) owns and manages—on behalf of four Wyoming irrigation districts and nine Nebraska districts—the infrastructure that has significantly altered stream flows, sediment loads, and consumptive uses across a wide stretch of high semi-desert. All of this federally constructed North Platte River plumbing meant that Wyoming water users, along with their Nebraska compatriots downstream across the state line and along the Upper North Platte above Lake McConaughy, would be in the grasp of federal environmental laws and regulations.

North Platte River water users on federally funded and managed USBR irrigation projects must face the prospect of consultations with the U.S. Fish and Wildlife Service (USFWS) under Section 7 of the ESA and Section 404 of the Clean Water Act. Wyoming's facilities are large and impose major impacts. Section (2c)(2) of the ESA declares that federal agencies shall cooperate with state and local agencies to resolve water resource issues in concert with the conservation of endangered species (Record of Decision 2006: 2–3).

BACKGROUND

Wyoming's boundaries encompass an ancient and gigantic mountain mesa, the geologic nucleus of North America. Mountain peaks that hover over water-sheds such as those of the Medicine Bow Range are merely pimples on the massive up-thrust that in many places consists of pre-Cambrian rock 4.1 billion years old, an impressive figure on a planet only about 4.6 billion years old (Knight 1990; Ostresh, Marston, and Hudson 1990). Colorado and Nebraska, by comparison, are geologic afterthoughts. The broad mountaintop that is Wyoming tends to level out in the southern part of the state and thereby afforded a path that provided the best route west for nineteenth-century folks of European stock who followed the Missouri, then the Platte main stem to North Platte, Nebraska, then the North Platte to Wyoming's Sweetwater River, then over the Continental Divide to Utah, Oregon, or California. Today, Interstate 80—paralleled by the Union Pacific Railroad—roughly follows that same trail. The state's history has been well told elsewhere (Larson 1965).

Only about 15 percent of the state has an average annual positive water balance, meaning areas where more water is received from precipitation than is lost through evaporation and transpiration by way of vegetation. These areas are generally found in the mountains (Ostresh, Marston, and Hudson 1990: 24). At lower elevations, where cropping seasons are the longest, water balances tend to be negative—a fact that harshly constrains dry-land farming. Aridity, combined with high elevations and short crop seasons, has meant that the Wyoming post-settlement agricultural landscape has always been dominated by grass range for sheep and cattle. The agricultural and urban-industrial frontiers have been held in check. The state has the smallest population of the lower forty-eight U.S. states. Its urban centers, by the standards of most states, are little more than small towns. Old-timers are fond of saying that "the whole state is a small town, just with very long streets."

NORTH PLATTE WATER PROJECTS

The North Platte River originates in north-central Colorado near the Continental Divide and plunges through Northgate Canyon into Wyoming. Major Wyoming tributaries, capturing and channeling high-country snowmelt, feed the stream; the most prominent are the Encampment, Sweetwater, Medicine Bow, and Laramie rivers. After leaving Colorado, the stream flows in a northerly direction until it hits the slack waters of a string of federally constructed reservoirs. When released through gates at Seminoe and Pathfinder, some flow is diverted toward Kendrick Project lands at Alcova Dam. A larger annual fraction moves northeast to Casper, after which the river bends southeast to fill Glendo Reservoir, on to Guernsey Reservoir, then across the state line to western Nebraska panhandle country where—after multiple uses and return flows—it fills Lake McConaughy (Map 6.1). About 80 percent of the North Platte storage water pooled in Wyoming reservoirs is destined for Nebraska panhandle water users above Lake

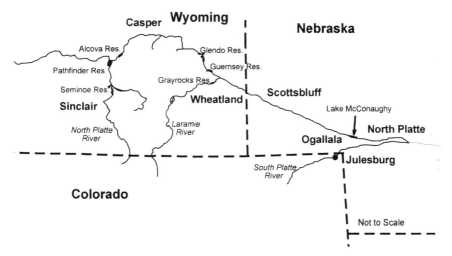

MAP 6.1. *North Platte River Basin. Modified from map from U.S. Department of the Interior, Bureau of Reclamation, and U.S. Fish and Wildlife Service; Platte River Recovery and Implementation Program: Final Environmental Impact Statement, April 2006.*

McConaughy. From that point it will again be released to downstream water providers in central Nebraska. Obviously, the greatest proportion of irrigated land in the North Platte Project is downstream of the Nebraska boundary. The smaller Wyoming irrigated command areas are primarily on the south side of the river along the Fort Laramie Canal below the diversions at Whalen and are commercially served by Torrington, an agricultural trade center made possible by the North Platte Project.

As Table 6.1 reveals, the three major Wyoming USBR projects on the river are the North Platte, Kendrick, and Glendo (Water and Power Resources Service 1981). The North Platte Project extends 111 river miles from near Guernsey, Wyoming, to Bridgeport, Nebraska. The city of Scottsbluff, Nebraska, is located near the center of the irrigated area. About 8 miles below Guernsey Dam, the Whalen diversion in Wyoming directs flows into two large canals: (1) water heads from the south bank for 130 miles in the Fort Laramie Canal along bench land commanding Wyoming fields below, and (2) the Interstate Canal similarly serves irrigated land on the north bank along its 95-mile length and tails off into two Nebraska reservoirs, Lakes Alice and Minatare. The North Platte Project features two major storage reservoirs: Pathfinder (completed in 1909), 47 miles upstream of Casper, and Guernsey (1928), located well downstream. Together they hold water for more than 2,000 miles of supply canals and drains. Pathfinder Reservoir, which originally provided 1.07 million acre feet of capacity, stores river flows under a 1904 priority. Waters released from Pathfinder and other upstream reservoirs, supplemented by return flows, travel the river channel to Guernsey Dam, where managers fine-tune flows for releases at Whalen. Guernsey Reservoir originally had a capacity of almost 74,000 acre feet, but siltation has much reduced its volume.

Table 6.1. Select Wyoming North Platte Basin Water Facilities

Name	Project	Priority	Storage Capacity (acre feet)
Seminoe	Kendrick	December 1, 1931	Permitted: 1,026,360 Current: 1,017,273
Kortes	Pick-Sloan Missouri Basin	September 11, 1933	Permitted: 4,640 Current: 4,739
Pathfinder	North Platte	June 21, 1904	Permitted: 1,070,000 Current: 1,016,507
Alcova	Kendrick	April 25, 1936	Permitted: 184,295 Current: 184,405
Glendo	Pick-Sloan Missouri Basin	August 30, 1951	Permitted: 800,000 Current: 789,402
Guernsey	North Platte	April 20, 1923	Permitted: 71,040 Current: 45,612

Source: USBR, North Platte Basin Reference Map, March 31, 1987, Mills, Wyoming. No. 20-703-5199.

The Kendrick Project consists of Seminoe Dam (its gates closed in 1939), just above Pathfinder, and Alcova Dam (1938), located below Pathfinder, to divert Seminoe water into the 59-mile Casper Canal along which water flows to an irregular patchwork of irrigated land between Alcova and Casper—about 24,000 acres in all. Seminoe Dam backs up water available under a relatively junior 1935 water storage right. Constrained by this late right to divert and hold water, Seminoe Reservoir can be filled only in wet years. Today, about 70,000 acre feet of average annual water demand is placed on the tub. Yet Seminoe rivals Pathfinder in capacity: 1,017,273 acre feet. Seminoe's designed duty has therefore been to carry water over long periods. Given limits as a result of areas of dead storage and sedimentation that inevitably compromise capacity, the reservoir can be relied upon to serve its demand for ten or more years between high spikes in North Platte water availability.

Glendo Dam (completed in 1958) and Reservoir are components of the Missouri Basin's Pick-Sloan plan, along with the upstream Gray Reef Dam, the Fremont hydroelectric power plant, and its re-regulating reservoir. The Gray Reef unit is located just 2 miles below Alcova Dam and was designed to hold and modulate the wildly fluctuating releases from Alcova. The Glendo and Gray Reef facilities (finished in 1961) have been managed in conjunction with the North Platte and Kendrick projects. The Glendo unit was designed primarily as a power production facility and secondarily as a flood control facility. When at capacity, the reservoir extends 14 miles above Glendo Dam. Space was provided for eventually storing 115,000 acre feet of sediment—an estimated 100-year buffer for irrigators below. Although a large tub and a critically important workhorse for the USBR's management of the North Platte, Glendo provides only 40,000 acre feet each year for irrigation and other uses in Wyoming and Nebraska, especially along the Fort Laramie and Interstate canals. Of this sum, 15,000 acre feet are designated for Wyoming users, and 25,000 acre feet are to serve Nebraskans.

In the Wyoming-Nebraska negotiations that cleared the way for the Glendo Project construction, Nebraskans were intensely interested in ensuring that consumptive uses in Wyoming and western Nebraska be capped with an eye to preserving the pre-Glendo regime of the river, with the intent to keep Lake McConaughy as full as possible. Therefore, the Glendo unit is the only facility on the North Platte expressly designed with such a large flood control feature, one that included a commitment that its impounded floodwaters would not be dedicated to any large Wyoming beneficial use. An amendment to the Wyoming-Nebraska North Platte River U.S. Supreme Court decree of 1945 protected Nebraska's interest in filling Lake McConaughy by providing that not more than 40,000 acre feet (plus space needed to compensate for evaporation losses) of water could be stored at Glendo for irrigation purposes in any given year. The 2001 U.S. Supreme Court–endorsed settlement in *Nebraska v. Wyoming* (Olpin 2001: 43–45) abandoned historical water-use restrictions and freed both Nebraska and Wyoming users to use their Glendo allocations anywhere within the Platte River Basin for legitimate beneficial uses.

NEW COLLISIONS: BIRDS GET A VOICE

Given its federal ownership, each Wyoming North Platte Project facility would be required to comply with federal law and regulatory policy, as the U.S. Bureau of Reclamation—the action agency—would be required to consult with the USFWS about incorporating a new ESA agenda into traditional water management. When the ESA was passed into law during Richard Nixon's Republican administration in 1973, it would not take long for this new conversation to begin. However, it was Wyoming's ambitions to expand water storage at two locations that sparked the arguments.

Grayrocks Dam and Reservoir

The Grayrocks Project began in the early 1970s, when a coal-fired electrical generating plant was proposed for construction on the outskirts of Wheatland, Wyoming. Grayrocks Dam and Reservoir—to be built on the Laramie River in southeastern Wyoming, a tributary of the North Platte—was needed to provide 104,110 acre feet of cooling water (Simons and Associates Inc. 2000). The

Rural Electrification Administration granted a loan guarantee, and the Army Corps of Engineers issued a construction permit to the Basin Electric Power Cooperative.

The state of Nebraska and the National Wildlife Federation countered with a lawsuit alleging that the two federal agencies had failed to comply with the ESA and National Environmental Policy Act (NEPA) and also claimed that the diversion of Laramie River water would jeopardize irrigation and wildlife habitat in Nebraska (Gaul 1993). Neither Nebraska nor the environmentalists wanted more than 20,000 acre feet of water each year to be evaporated through cooling towers—water that had been flowing to Nebraska even though Wyoming asserted a prior right of appropriation to use it (Kappas 1997: 17). As a downstream state, Nebraska had found a silver lining in the ESA cloud, a means to prevent upstream states from fully exploiting water rights under existing state water law and court settlements.

Grayrocks also threatened some local Wyoming water users, as well as Nebraska irrigators, hydropower producers, and environmentalists who rose to the defense of critical whooping crane habitat. It also brought the new federal environmental agenda into the North Platte Basin for the first time. When the power plant was in the early planning and permit stage, members of several local Wyoming interests and Nebraska water organizations, along with environmentalists, gathered; for the first time in history, instead of fighting each other, they found themselves on the same side in opposition to Basin Electric (Bethell 1986). Opponents argued that Basin Electric Power Cooperative had failed to consider the project's downstream effects and had ignored everything beyond the Wyoming-Nebraska state line, including the needs of whooping crane habitat. The intent of local Wyoming opponents was to limit the size of the power plant in an effort to hold down the draw on local water supplies and to constrain Basin Electric from letting any more water go downstream than necessary, as well as to limit the project's impact on local schools, streets, taxes, and the immediate environment (Bethell 1986).

With the filing of the lawsuit, for the first time the weight of the ESA was applied to North Platte River water management. Because the ESA was still new at the time of the Grayrocks discussion and what would be the 1978 amendments to the ESA had not yet clarified Section 7 procedures regarding the taking of listed species habitat, implementation of the ESA was still murky. The Army Corps of Engineers argued that it did not have to consult under Section 7 because Grayrocks Dam's potential effects on endangered species were too far downstream. Amid the procedural confusion, in December 1978 the U.S. Fish and Wildlife Service issued a jeopardy biological opinion to the Army Corps of Engineers (Record of Decision 2006: 24–25). It found that up to 23,250 acre feet of annual water depletions would create a negative impact on whooping crane habitat over 300 miles downstream.

The federal court ruled in favor of the plaintiffs and issued an injunction against construction of Grayrocks Reservoir. Further negotiations between the parties resulted in an out-of-court settlement that earned court approval. Basin Electric agreed to limit its water use, provide seasonal water releases from Grayrocks for downstream habitat, and establish a $7.5 million trust that would fund the enhancement of whooping crane habitat to offset consequences of the power plant project (Gaul 1993). These funds provided the core asset of a new entity to speak for the birds and riverine habitat in central Nebraska—the Platte River Whooping Crane Habitat Maintenance Trust.

The principal objective of the trust has been to protect and improve habitat for whooping cranes, sandhill cranes, and other migratory birds on the seventy-mile stretch of the "big bend" portion of the Platte River. Its funds can be spent for the purchase of rights to land, water, and water storage and for management of those assets. The trust board was established with three members representing the state of Nebraska, Wyoming's Basin Electric Power Cooperative, and the National Wildlife Federation. The trust has acquired over 9,000 acres of quality habitat through fee title purchase and easements. Cranes, eagles, plovers, terns, and pallid sturgeon do not partake in the market economy and political debates; they had therefore been ignored. Now they had an organized voice.

Deer Creek Project

Within a few years of the collision at Grayrocks, another unhappy episode occurred for Wyoming water providers. This time it was upstream on the Deer Creek drainage tributary to the North Platte at a point near Glenrock, southeast of Casper. Some water users had approached Wyoming authorities in the early 1980s with a proposal for a dam and a 66,000-acre-foot storage reservoir at a location on Deer Creek. The plan was to serve Casper's water needs through an exchange whereby the city would take upstream water out of priority and then pay back the senior appropriators with what would become Casper's Deer Creek supply.

There were two problems. First, promoters found themselves in an unwanted Section 7 consultation with the Fish and Wildlife Service. They learned that their proposal did not contain an adequate "reasonable and prudent" alternative to deliver water to designated habitat in central Nebraska. Not to be denied their Deer Creek dream, by 1985 promoters—after considerable wrangling—struck a deal with federal administrators of the ESA; among other things, it involved the state of Wyoming purchasing 470 acres of Nebraska whooping crane habitat near Kearney. The USFWS agreed to manage this land under an arrangement with the Wyoming Water Development Commission. Given that Wyoming had agreed to undertake mitigation measures, the USFWS then issued a non-jeopardy biological opinion to the Army Corps of Engineers and the Wyoming Water Development Commission in July 1987 (Record of Decision 2006: 25).

Then a second problem erupted: Wyoming's downstream neighbor was hostile to the entire concept. In Nebraska's eyes, the prospect of its neighboring state seeking to expand its upstream water uses by intruding into Nebraska's central Platte territory to retire agricultural and river bottomland was an anathema. To make matters worse, Wyoming was rubbing proverbial salt into the wound by bringing in a federal agency to manage habitat for an environmental agenda. Some even saw the proposed arrangement as an evil plot by which Wyoming was abetting the onset of federal control over Nebraska's river. By 1986 Nebraska had filed a lawsuit against Wyoming alleging that Wyoming was wrongly capturing flows from North Platte tributaries, in violation of the 1945 U.S. Supreme Court decree. Deer Creek Project promoters found their plans halted. The project remained in legal limbo until a 2001 U.S. Supreme Court settlement, in the form of a modified North Platte decree, put a stop to the Deer Creek plans.

As Deer Creek promoters licked their wounds, Wyoming and USBR authorities knew another source of water was available for municipal purposes: restoration of storage lost to sedimentation at Pathfinder Reservoir. But the Pathfinder option was a USBR project, and any arrangement that could be worked out would require compliance with federal law and regulatory policy, especially the requirements of the ESA.

The unhappy episodes at Grayrocks and Deer Creek had ensnared two basin states and the federal government in skirmishes that nobody won, that had bruised everyone, and that signaled that the ESA had to be served. Attempted arrangements, unhinged from an overall basin perspective, could easily inflame long-standing interstate conflicts. Thirsty Casper-area water users would have to find ways other than Deer Creek to augment their supplies.

The lessons of Grayrocks and the need to replace the stymied Deer Creek Project drew a highly reluctant Wyoming into basin-wide discussions by the late 1980s. At least three things had been established. First, Wyoming water users were in a historically troubled relationship not only with Nebraskans but also with the U.S. Fish and Wildlife Service as that agency began to implement the ESA. Second, the new environmental legislation of the late 1960s and early 1970s, especially the newly minted ESA, could be a tool Nebraska could employ to advance its interests by blocking new Wyoming upstream water uses. Third, the dynamic had established an important new participant in basin water planning—the Platte River Whooping Crane Habitat Maintenance Trust. The birds had a voice at the table. The Whooping Crane Trust would not be silenced, and it was backed by the ESA and a multi-million-dollar endowment.

PART III

Initiating Negotiations

Options

Individual Consultations, Litigation, or
Constructing a Cooperative Program

> If every speaker who has talked in the last twenty years or so about federal-
> state relationships in water law was to be laid end to end, it would be a good
> and merciful thing.
>
> —CHARLES E. CORKER, 1972 (quoted in Pisani 1989: 282)

The drafting of the U.S. Constitution was an occasion for struggling with the vexing question of how to balance power between states and the federal government. Federalism as a system of dual sovereignty was cobbled together on a fundamental principle: "The powers delegated by the proposed constitution to the federal government are few and defined. Those which are to remain in the state governments are numerous and indefinite" (U.S. Constitution, Amendment 10). Federal environmental legislation, particularly the Endangered Species Act (ESA), needed to be implemented within the locus of state water administration. Therein lay a problem.

FEDERAL WATER POLICY

Aridity in the West meant the federal government, which had paid little attention to the importance of water and systems of its appropriation in the late nineteenth century, would be paying detailed attention in the late twentieth century. Furthermore, federal policy has not been coherent. It has been developed in an ad hoc manner, with no agency of the executive branch and no congressional committee maintaining a unifying vision. The discourses have been unhinged from any defensible guiding principles. Federal water policy has been characterized by competing agendas, agency turf battles, protracted disputes, and an inability to provide policy views in any predictable manner (Rogers 1996). The fact that federal water policies had been a muddle for decades prompted Congress to pass the Western Water Policy Review Act (P.L. 102-575) in 1992. This legislation directed the president to undertake a comprehensive review of federal activities in nineteen western states that affected the allocation and use of water resources, both surface and subsurface. To that end, the Western Water Policy Review Advisory Commission was launched. The commission found fifteen federal bureaus and agencies with water-related programs in seventeen western states (of the lower forty-eight); they were responsible to six cabinet departments, thirteen congressional committees, and twenty-three subcommittees and were funded by five different appropriations committees (Western Water Policy Review Advisory Commission 1997).

Given that historically the "federal family" has not been particularly functional, Platte River Basin negotiations would have been challenging enough. But the basin initiatives were also tethered to regional social and political networks of influence that added their own impact—the "sagebrush rebellion" and the "wise-use" movement.

As state water user representatives were attempting to devise ways to work with new federal environmental mandates, at least some of their constituencies were organizing to challenge federal natural resource policy in general. Federal water policy became entangled with federal land and grazing policies, especially in light of the way the Bureau of Land Management (BLM) and the U.S. Forest Service (USFS) began to change the manner in which they regulated federal land uses. Traditionally, water users in the West gained more from keeping lands under federal control as long as the BLM was politically subservient to their needs. Traditional users of BLM land had no more guaranteed rights to these public assets than anyone else, but many ranchers and farmers depended on easy access to public BLM and USFS land for much of their revenue as an extension of their private operations. Bankers and other financial institutions had capitalized low-cost access to these public assets into the valuation of their businesses (Andrews 1999). Any threat to their cheap availability would be energetically resisted by farmers and ranchers, who were struggling to survive in an economy organized to extract the maximum from them while rewarding most of them minimally. In some circumstances, the threat would appear when any of the federal natural resource management agencies consulted with the U.S. Fish and Wildlife Service (USFWS) under the terms of a new and unwelcome reality—the Endangered Species Act (ESA).

As the BLM and the USFS undertook to implement their increased environmental mandate and used their authority to begin to seriously constrain access to public land and water, the agencies triggered a backlash among some western public land users who fought for continued access on the old terms. Those users organized a lobbying campaign—the sagebrush rebellion—in an attempt to intimidate the agencies and to reduce, if not stop, meaningful federal intervention in their traditional local control. A smoother, more sophisticated successor came to be known as the wise-use movement. It continued the fight for traditional uses of land and water free from significant constraint by federal agencies with environmental mandates. By the early 1990s the wise-use movement consisted of 600 property rights groups formed under an umbrella organization called the Alliance for America (Nestor 1997).

When Ronald Reagan took office in 1981, the president began to reverse many of the Carter administration's environmental advances. Reagan adopted much of the sagebrush rebellion's agenda and placed leaders of the movement in positions of federal authority. With this political shift, farmers, ranchers, and state water user interests were able to push back hard against biologists in the Fish and Wildlife Service who issued biological opinions that favored "varmints" over people. They attempted to build a coalition of forces that would try to "gut" the ESA and other environmental laws governing ranching, logging, and mining; but they soon found that more environmentally conscious members of Congress from other regions would prevent them from overturning the new U.S. environmental priorities. The subsequent George H.W. Bush administration (1989–1992) moderated the anti-environmental priorities of the early Reagan years, although it honored environmental priorities more by simple neglect than by active involvement.

During the 1992 election, the wise-use movement divided its energies between George H.W. Bush and Ross Perot and thereby lost impact. William Jefferson Clinton won the election and, after entering office, appointed strong environmental protection advocates to positions in the Department of the Interior (DOI). But in 1994, in the elections of the 104th Congress, voters—especially in the West—chose anti-Clinton politicians who had no love for environmental agendas. The anti-Clinton and, in part, anti-environmental backlash had given a Republican majority control of the House of Representatives for the first time in forty years. Control of important congressional committees shifted to a group of aggressively anti-environmental legislators. Over the next two years—1994–1996—conservative Republicans mounted an all-out assault on the center of environmental law that had been constructed in the 1960s and 1970s. This attack produced congressional logjams and repeated Clinton vetoes, which sometimes very narrowly derailed mounting efforts to overturn environmental legislation, including the ESA.

During the years leading to an eventual 1994 agreement to negotiate water issues in the Platte River Basin and the subsequent period of actual systematic negotiations between 1994 and 1997, the Clinton administration struggled to hold together a coalition that could preserve and protect the legacy of environmental legislation constructed prior to the "Reagan revolution." There would need to be an emphasis on negotiation with water interests, collaboration, and flexibility to adapt to local opportunities and constraints. It was important to demonstrate to environmental supporters and opponents alike that the ESA and other environmental laws could be administered with sensitivity and flexibility while still fulfilling their letter and spirit.

Somehow, a path would have to be created that would protect and even enhance support for the ESA, not erode it. Clinton's secretary of the interior, Bruce Babbitt, sought to accomplish that feat while also finding ecologically viable solutions to environmental problems. From DOI's perspective, Platte River issues presented an opportunity to implement an emerging strategy for addressing the political challenges created by natural resource users' opposition to the ESA.

LITIGATION RISKS

Department of the Interior authorities did not want to enter into litigation with the states over water rights for several reasons. First, the USFWS cannot directly intrude into state water rights systems; it can issue biological opinions that can only be enforced when environmentally aware citizens choose to file suit and succeed in having a judge rule in their favor. The system forces environmentalists, not the federal government, to engage in the litigation process. Federal action agencies (such as FERC, the USFS, BLM, and USBR) must operate with the power they have—that is, the power to issue permits and grant licenses for water facilities such as dams and river diversions. As they proceed through their decision-making processes, they keep in mind the positions and postures of the USFWS, especially as documented in its biological opinions.

Second, agency inflexibility and rigidity in a succession of nationwide attempts to enforce ESA mandates could erode political support and place the ESA and other environmental legislation in jeopardy. The ESA itself could be in peril if clumsy handling of the act drove away congressional allies. Third, legalistic rigidity would drive away the very interests—local people, their organizations, and their water knowledge—that must eventually be involved as partners in implementing any solution. Fourth, federal action agencies and the USFWS would be overwhelmed by the burdens of individual Section 7 consultations that would be required in administering the ESA in situations as complex as the Platte River Basin. Finally, time and money spent on litigation could be better spent on behalf of species. It would be better to embrace local interests, educate them as to their responsibilities under the law, convince them to subscribe to the collective cooperative habitat recovery agendas, and move forward with the process of actually improving habitats.

Across the years of discourse, local water users in the Platte River Basin were reluctant to litigate because they did not trust a court—especially a federal court—to responsively consider water interests involving multiple and conflicting uses. Court litigation was thought to be an expensive gamble. State water providers feared they would lose control over their future in the courts. The thought of legal minds reasoning based on obscure precedents with little knowledge of the implications for delicately balanced water arrangements was scary. In the view of many, judges inhabit a professional universe largely divorced from the complexities of life on rivers and aquifers; they may understand little of the context of the actions under review and might decide a case on a point of law far removed from what a given litigant thought the case entailed. Judicial interpretations could easily carve out water arrangements in technically, economically, and politically untenable ways. Also, states did not have the money for protracted struggles against federal agencies in long successions of cases. All in all, court-imposed solutions were to be feared more than anything the Fish and Wildlife Service could develop in cooperation with local water users.

THE NO-ACTION OPTION

Some water users seriously considered the no-action option—no cooperative action among the states and the DOI while taking their chances with individual ESA Section 7 consultations. As time went by, however, it became clear that refusal to collaborate with the Department of the Interior could lead to unacceptable outcomes. Doing nothing would not make the ESA go away. Water providers who were tied to federal programs would be individually responsible for offsetting adverse impacts on listed species habitats, and they would do so on USFWS terms that included an annual average water shortage calculation of 417,000 acre feet and 29,000 acres of quality land habitat. The USFWS dangled the prospect of settling for substantially less water and land during any first program increment if the essential players would sign on to a collaborative approach. How, though, could any single actor address species needs from far upriver in Colorado, Wyoming, or the Nebraska panhandle? Why would the Nebraska districts wish to proceed without the collaboration of water users in upstream states? Under the no-action prospect, project operators would not know in advance of the ESA Section 7 consultations the requirements that would be placed upon them.

Water providers that refused to undertake cooperative action would lose the extended time provided for joint planning by the proposed Cooperative Agreement (CA) concept. During such a period, under a DOI-approved CA they could obtain annual permit approvals for their water facilities and participate in constructing their own futures. Without a basin-wide cooperative program, it was clearly possible that lawsuits filed by water users or environmentalists might bring about court orders to cease or curtail operations until ESA Section 7 consultations were reinitiated; such scenarios were frightening. Therefore, many perceptive water users saw the no-action option as intolerable.

BABBITT'S COLLABORATIVE STRATEGY

Many within federal agencies have long noted the need to move away from simplistic "command and control" approaches to environmental regulation and toward more collaborative ecosystem management (Interagency Ecosystem Management Task Force 1996; Melious and Thornton 1999; Ruckelshaus 1997; Smith 2000). Given the sheer number of permit renewals to be processed, it was prohibitive even to contemplate an individual case-by-case approach in a complex river basin when no single user organization could provide the needed collective good but each could muster allies in the struggle against constructive engagement with the problem of providing improved habitat. In the politically charged context created by the divisive struggle in the Pacific Northwest over old-growth logging in the domain of the spotted owl and the broad regional wise-use movement, Bruce Babbitt developed an ambitious plan to abandon traditional command and control approaches to ESA implementation. Policy would consist of:

1. Bringing U.S., state, and local governments and resource users together to build comprehensive local negotiated solutions.

2. Making partnerships around large regional watershed strategies that would get ahead of the many crises that arose from isolated ESA consultations; federal authorities did not want to administer the ESA from an individual species perspective any more than local users wanted to renew their water rights permit by permit.

3. Providing incentives to water users by

    a. Conducting multi-species consultations that could anticipate subsequent individual species listings.

    b. Crafting a general road map so everyone would know what sort of action would be considered if reinitiation of consultations were required—to anticipate future reasonable and prudent alternatives.

    c. Giving participants some assurance that if they "signed on" to a recommended plan, they could obtain "regulatory certainty" over reasonable periods of time.

Playing the endangered species game on a project-by-project basis across the basin had been costly for all parties. Each had a need for accommodating the ESA; that was the lesson of Pathfinder, Deer Creek, Grayrocks, Wildcat, Narrows, the Poudre River reservoirs, Two Forks, and the need to fulfill FERC re-licensing requirements at Kingsley Dam. Collaboration and negotiation would do more for the species—and for preserving the ESA—than would litigation and confrontation. A strong impetus for the Platte River Habitat Recovery Program was to see how well Babbitt's plan to radically change the traditional approach to implementation of the ESA would work. The political objective was to fend off attacks on the ESA directed at gutting it, if not repealing it altogether

(Echeverria 2001). The Platte Basin negotiations have been all about whether the ESA can be implemented in a collaborative multi-species, multi-user, multi-state, multi-interest manner.

The collaborative concept was not originated by agents in Washington, D.C. Rather, it had emerged out of experience with developing the Upper Colorado River Endangered Fish Recovery Program launched in 1988 (Brower, Roedy, and Yelin-Kefers 2001; MacDonnell 1999; USFWS 2004–2005: 6). To a lesser extent, federal authorities also benefited from habitat restoration work in the 1980s as part of the San Francisco Bay–Sacramento–San Joaquin River Delta (CALFED Bay-Delta) Program (Aiken 1999: 143). The Upper Colorado Cooperative Agreement had been signed by authorities from Colorado, Utah, and Wyoming, as well as by the U.S. secretary of the interior and representatives of the Western Area Power Administration. The objective was to recover populations of the humpback chub, bonytail, Colorado pikeminnow, and razorback sucker. The concept of a basin-wide, multi-species, multi-federal-agency–state collaboration was hammered out during the course of developing a viable approach to species recovery. It was here that a format for proceeding with the Platte River Habitat Recovery Program was birthed, applied, and placed on the tool shelf for Secretary Babbitt to work with in the Platte River context.

Individually, rational water users had a choice; they could have litigated and refused to come to the table. Nevertheless, the workings of the ESA brought those parties into a federal nexus and kept them there. Yet, one major element of this story is missing—the sense of how a basin-wide cooperative effort could actually produce improved habitat.

ASSEMBLING A VISION:
THE PLATTE RIVER MANAGEMENT JOINT STUDY

In 1983, when the USFWS issued a biological opinion that found that the Narrows Project on Colorado's South Platte River would jeopardize listed species in central Nebraska, the repercussions were felt around the basin and beyond. Within the Department of the Interior, in recent history two agencies had not gotten along especially well. The USBR, dam builder extraordinaire, and the USFWS, enhancer of wildlife habitat and custodian of the ESA, were at loggerheads. Clearly, the status quo would not suffice.

In this context and in light of the post-Narrows wreckage on the administrative and political landscape, in 1983 the regional directors of the USFWS and the USBR initiated a Platte River Management Joint Study. The following year the secretary of the interior was petitioned by water interests in Colorado, Nebraska, and Wyoming who wanted to be included (Platte River Management Joint Study 1993). If federal authorities were going to be discussing the future of water use in their basin, state authorities and water interests wanted their voices heard. The result was the establishment of the Platte River Coordinating Committee, composed of the regional directors of the USFWS, the USBR, and water authorities from each of the three states. Soon, working groups were established to consider specific aspects of the basin-wide water-use and listed species habitat agenda—items ranging from species habitat needs to land and water management alternatives, research and habitat monitoring, public information and education, possible institutional arrangements, projected costs, and potential funding sources. The memberships of the working groups were much more inclusive than was that of the core coordinating committee. They drew upon the talents, experience, and perspectives of environmental organizations, the Army Corps of Engineers, the Environmental Protection Agency, and a diverse array of local water users.

During the remainder of the 1980s and the early 1990s, study participants cajoled, wrangled, and battled over how to design a solution that would serve the requirements of the ESA, state appropriation doctrines, apportionments among the states mandated by U.S. Supreme Court decrees, and the interstate South Platte water compact. They did their homework, consulted with their constituents, and struggled to frame a vision for addressing how the habitat needs of the listed species could be met while preserving water user interests. In particular, they found inspiration in the Upper Colorado River Basin Program for recovery of endangered fish species, which was under way by 1988 and was advancing under the watchful eye of the Department of the Interior. In May 1993 the Platte River Coordinating Committee issued its draft report (Platte River Management Joint Study 1993), which envisioned a basin-wide habitat recovery program. Its work constituted an essential component of what would become a 1994 agreement among the three basin states and the Department of the Interior to launch a cooperative habitat recovery program. The committee had set forth a preliminary vision, albeit one that was sketchy. But it succeeded in anticipating how necessary habitat lands could be acquired and how water assets could be made available, in addition to outlining a research and monitoring program along with a budget and identifying proposed sources of funding. The framers foresaw an organizational structure and a system of representative basin-wide governance.

AGREEING TO TALK

The Platte River Coordinating Committee's study effort had provided an initial vision for moving ahead. But how were the several actors actually going to initiate negotiations?

Following Clinton's 1992 election victory and Babbitt's installation as secretary of the interior, the new appointee wanted to find a collaborative way out of what seemed an impossible quagmire. He soon received a boost from a friend of the Clinton administration, Colorado governor Roy Romer. Romer was a leading figure in Democratic Party politics and later served as chair of the Democratic National Committee. He had not placed environmental issues on his campaign agenda in Colorado, but after working on the problems caused by the permitting logjam involving the Poudre River mountain reservoirs, he saw the impossibility of the emerging situation. He then decided to be open to environmental arguments. Furthermore, he wished the Clinton administration well in its efforts to reform policy and practice in the Department of the Interior.

Governor Romer had direct conversations with the DOI secretary and invited Babbitt to speak in Colorado, where he would propose a comprehensive, collaborative Platte River Basin–wide negotiated approach to the problem. The secretary felt a need to be in Colorado, among other things, to address BLM and USFS livestock-grazing disputes. While there, he had breakfast with water users at the Governor's Mansion. This led to a series of meetings involving senior officeholders and water users in all three basin states in 1993 and early 1994. Many were people who had experience with the Platte River Coordinating Committee, who knew well the bitter aftermath of the collapse of Two Forks in Colorado, the grindingly slow progress in the FERC discussions at Kingsley Dam, the scary possibilities contemplated on Poudre upstream reservoirs, and Wyoming's stymied efforts to capture water for its own purposes—especially to serve economic growth needs in and around its second-largest city, Casper.

On June 10, 1994, an early draft agreement to begin systematic talks was signed by the Department of the Interior and the governors of Wyoming, Nebraska, and Colorado. Signatures were put to paper just one week after the USFWS issued its biological opinion finding that species were jeopardized by the operation of the Arapaho-Roosevelt National Forest Poudre River reservoirs. This first three-state and DOI agreement was only five pages long including the signature sheet; it lacked much substance and took much of what little detail it contained from the coordinating committee's effort. But it made a critical point: basin-wide collaborative negotiations would be undertaken. The governors of Nebraska, Wyoming, and Colorado and the secretary of the interior had made a commitment to build a Platte River Endangered Species Partnership.

All parties agreed to work within the existing frameworks of federal and state law. If the effort to construct a viable reasonable and prudent alternative failed, it was agreed that all biological opinions would be reopened. Platte River Basin habitat recovery negotiations would now proceed.

Organization of Negotiations

We need to recognize that adversarial, winner-take-all, showdown political decision-making is a way we defeat ourselves. Our future starts when we begin
honoring the dreams of our enemies while staying true to our own.
                                         —WILLIAM KITTREDGE (1996: 142)

Following the signing of the 1994 Memorandum of Agreement (MOA), the Department of the Interior's (DOI) assistant secretary of water and science was appointed to lead the federal negotiation team. The governors of each of the three
states appointed staffs to represent their interests. Representatives of the water provider organizations were appointed by their respective authorities, including the
Central Nebraska Public Power and Irrigation District (CNPPID), the Nebraska
Public Power District (NPPD), Denver Water, the Northern Colorado Water Conservancy District (NCWCD), and the Pathfinder and Goshen irrigation districts.

How would environmentalists be incorporated into the negotiations? Unlike
representatives of federal and state agencies or water user representatives of
state political subdivisions such as irrigation, public power, and conservancy districts, environmentalist organizations function in civil society beyond any state
apparatus. What standing would they have amid state, state water provider, and
federal authorities?

ENVIRONMENTAL ORGANIZATIONS

The Platte River Whooping Crane Habitat Maintenance Trust (Whooping Crane
Trust) was formed in 1978 and funded with monies generated by the endowment

provided by the Wyoming Grayrocks settlement. By the time of the governors' sponsored talks, it had acquired almost 10,000 acres of wet meadows, river channels, woodlands, and cropland along the Platte River. By using litigious means and the threat of such means, the Whooping Crane Trust had been active in the struggle over Federal Energy Regulatory Commission (FERC) re-licensing requirements at Kingsley Dam and had also strongly advanced environmental interests in the conflict between Wyoming and Nebraska over the division of North Platte River flows. The trust would remain an important environmental player throughout the Platte River collaborative process.

The National Audubon Society was originally incorporated in 1905 to stop the slaughter of birds for millinery commerce. After that success, the Audubon Society continued to advocate for wild birds. By the mid-1990s it had 300 employees and 570,000 members. Audubon has a long history of lobbying for state and federal protection of habitat and has developed its own system of about 100 bird sanctuaries, one of which is located on high-quality Platte habitat at Gibbon, Nebraska. Audubon had become interested in the status of the whooping crane on the central Platte in the 1940s. In 1973 it purchased 782 acres of pristine crane habitat along the Platte east of Kearney, known as the Rowe Sanctuary, and became deeply involved in discussions regarding Platte Basin water diversion and storage proposals. Additional acreage has been purchased since, and cooperative agreements have extended protections beyond the sanctuary. The society was active in the re-licensing of Kingsley Dam and became an important force in Platte River recovery negotiations.

Environmental Defense (up to 1999, the Environmental Defense Fund) was originally incorporated in 1967 by a group of Long Island conservationists to ban the use of the pesticide DDT. Environmental Defense (ED) played an active and important role in negotiations until early 2002, when the organization announced a reallocation of its assets and a review of its priorities and withdrew its representative from the negotiations. In the aftermath, the National Wildlife Federation (NWF) stepped forward to occupy a lead role. The person who had served as Environmental Defense's representative in the negotiations resigned from his ED position to continue to work on the Platte River agenda as an NWF consultant.

The National Wildlife Federation is one of the largest, oldest, and most active environmental organizations. As one of the major actors in the North American environmental movement (Shabecoff 2000), the NWF has been a major force for environmental causes across the U.S. landscape. The NWF was involved with bird habitat—especially for whooping cranes—decades before the basin-wide negotiations were undertaken. It was party to the Wyoming Grayrocks settlement, and it has a member on the board of the Whooping Crane Trust. The NWF intensified its involvement in the Platte talks following Environmental Defense's departure.

After ED chose to put its resources into serving other priorities, another national nonprofit conservation organization—American Rivers—would move to play a supporting role in the negotiations. It was founded in 1973, with the initial objective of increasing the number of rivers protected by the National Wild and Scenic Rivers System. Over the years, American Rivers has collaborated with many river restoration entities in dismantling existing dams, blocking proposed dams, and restoring natural flows where possible. With its headquarters in Washington, D.C., and a field office in Nebraska, American Rivers chose to assist the environmental leaders at the Platte table.

From 1994 into the first years of the twenty-first century, the environmental "big three" in the negotiations were the Whooping Crane Trust, Environmental Defense, and Audubon. The National Wildlife Federation and American Rivers became active in the negotiations at a later date. Essentially, the story of environmentalist participation in the Platte Basin negotiations after 1994 was one of environmentalists bringing true substance to the basin-wide collaboration. They owned significant quantities of quality habitat, the Whooping Crane Trust and Audubon had much knowledge of local rivers and habitat, and the local representatives were backed by important national organizations.

In early 1994, in discussions with the three states and the DOI, environmentalists had no well-defined standing and no vote. But senior administrators in the Department of the Interior were friendly to environmental voices and did what they could to encourage representatives from the Whooping Crane Trust, Audubon, and the Environmental Defense Fund to participate. Furthermore, overtures made to the environmental community were motivated by a political reality: excluding environmentalists from the talks and denying them voting rights would almost certainly cause difficulties in eventually securing their endorsement of any eventual river restoration agreement Eventually, DOI was able to arrange for environmentalist representatives to be considered full members of the Governance Committee. They were then invited into the talks by the Mountain and Prairie Region of the U.S. Fish and Wildlife Service (USFWS), with the approval of upper echelons of the DOI. The various environmental organizations (plus American Rivers after 2002) would share two votes on the Governance Committee that was created in the July 1, 1997, Cooperative Agreement (CA). It was mutually agreed that the Whooping Crane Habitat Maintenance Trust and the Audubon Society, because of their extensive local presence as property owners, should have primacy in occupying the two voting seats. Other environmental organizations would serve in support roles.

NEGOTIATING DYNAMICS

As the participants found their way to the table, they recognized that while the process was to be based on advancing toward objectives by consensus, the discussion itself was forced by the Endangered Species Act (ESA), about which there was no consensus. However, the ESA provided the "bad cop" common enemy the states needed. The states could not trust one another to fulfill their commitments; however, they could depend on the ESA to act as a sufficient threat to ensure that each party stayed honest and fulfilled its promises (Zallen 1997). Each interested party came to the table with historical animosities, its own incompatible positions, as well as uncertainty about—and antagonism toward—the federal policy requirements they were there to somehow satisfy.

After July 1994, a series of meetings along the I-80 and I-25 corridors of the three states took place—meetings were held in Cheyenne, Wyoming; Kearney, Lincoln, Omaha, and Grand Island, Nebraska; and Denver, Colorado. These sessions originally included only representatives from the DOI and the three states. Federal representatives and three governors were in charge and imposed a rigid order to the proceedings. This structure included assigned seats for federal and state representatives, with water user representatives and environmentalists sitting as an audience, away from the table. This frustrated and discouraged those who were held apart. As time passed and rancor diminished, the talks expanded to include water users and environmentalists, and discussion formats became less formal.

The process dragged on for one year, then a second; the meetings were long, and many were tedious. The talk was tough, often confrontational, and frequently involved emotional venting and angry claims of injury. Representatives of host states demonstrated solidarity with their constituencies by "grandstanding" (Zallen 1997). Nearly every term or condition put forth was untenable to some important party. Federal agencies were not always the target of attacks. Some of the most difficult issues were those between states, and their representatives met repeatedly without the DOI present to address interstate problems. To many, the process seemed deadlocked, a futile waste. But no party was willing to be the first to step away from the table. No one wanted the dead body of a failed negotiation placed at its doorstep.

A fundamental common interest kept water user parties moving ahead with the talks. The U.S. Bureau of Reclamation (USBR) owned facilities critically important to water users in all three states, and the agency needed to secure ESA coverage for them. There was no option. That meant the USBR had common ground for working with the states and their water users that could not be abandoned in a cavalier manner. It also meant that two federal agencies that had frequently been adversaries over water issues elsewhere (the USBR and the USFWS) would, by sheer necessity, be compelled to cooperate with each other regarding Platte Basin matters.

Negotiations were open to the public. As the discussions slowly showed signs of progress, more people thought they were worth attending. At times, meetings were witness to large gatherings; 50 to 100 and more people crowded into rooms designed for considerably fewer participants (Ring 1999). It was then agreed to break into small work groups and reduce the meeting size to about 30 people. Overall, the negotiations were labor- and time-intensive; this was a problem because none of the parties had adequate staffing or funding to sustain their efforts. Federal and state budgets were limited and in some cases were being reduced. Individual ranchers and farmers were at the greatest disadvantage because they had no specialized assistance and no travel budgets, and they found it difficult to participate during the busy spring, summer, and fall seasons. Constrained resources created more than complaints; they were also the source of pressure to get serious and make a deal. Representatives of the various interests knew, however, that the price of acquiescing to a "bad deal" would be having their heads handed to them by their own constituencies.

CONSTITUENCIES DIVIDE

Bruce Babbitt's attempt to push a collaborative approach in an effort to demonstrate that the ESA could be wielded with sensitivity and openness to local creative solutions would split environmentalists and commodity producer constituencies alike.

Environmentalists Split

From the beginning of the organized talks, environmentalists feared they would have too little impact, that their presence would be little more than an implicit endorsement of a process that would deliver too few benefits for listed species (Ring 1999). They soon split along ideological lines.

Some in this camp wanted the ESA to be employed as an uncompromising legal hammer, not an invitation to negotiation with despoiling devils. Collaboration would allow developers, industrialists, agriculturalists, and extractive industries to construct a path around ESA requirements. Environmentalists had to confront their big strategic choice:

1. Working within Babbitt's framework of negotiations, which would mean compromising with coalition partners, accepting certain things as given, and working out solutions within the parameters established by the coalition; or

2. Working outside the framework of negotiations, staying "pure," and being prepared to challenge any negotiated outcome in court; this would mean sacrificing the local knowledge that comes with getting to know your opponents and allies and giving up on the idea of getting something positive done on the ground sooner rather than later, if at all.

The question became: when is it time for environmentalists to be divisive holdouts, and when is it time to enter the fray, cut deals, and help get something done on the ground, even if it is less than perfect?

Some environmentalists saw the USFWS as too willing to compromise, thereby weakening the intent of the ESA and unduly risking species survival. They noted what they considered an infrequency of jeopardy findings and declared that compromise in negotiated settlements was inadequate to ensure the survival of species (Wood 1998). Collaboration was seen as risking the surrender of national interests to local interests, and these environmentalists felt it would allow resource users to retain too much control. Such voices held that it would be better to stay remote and uncooperative and to force issues through the courts.

Environmentalists had participated in talks throughout 1994, 1995, and well into 1996. However, at one point in late 1996 the Whooping Crane Trust and the Audubon Society decided to abandon the Platte River negotiations because their representatives did not believe the water users were open to their concerns or took them seriously enough. One disaffected representative of Audubon who left the table and did not return later wrote that it should be a matter of no small concern that the Platte Basin negotiations could be proclaimed as a particularly deficient model for environmental planning—a "good horrible" example (Echeverria 2001).

The issues that drove the split and the walkout revolved around the controversial 417,000-acre-feet proposed target flow in the biological opinion on the whooping crane, the handling of land objectives, and the status of the Platte River discussions relative to talks ongoing with FERC at Lake McConaughy. The highly contentious target flow figure was at the center of negotiations and had to be addressed. The states were adamant that the proposed target flow was wrong and totally unjustified. The USFWS saw fit to divide that amount of water into more manageable chunks, with the first 10- to 13-year program incremental proposed quantity to be in the range of 130,000 to 150,000 acre feet per year. Its willingness to step back from its 417,000-acre-feet target flow figure kept water users in the negotiations, but environmentalists' reactions were divided. Some wanted to stay at the table, debate the amount of water, and remain positive about the direction of the discussions. A "rejectionist camp" was concerned that the biological opinion should not be compromised up front (Echeverria 2001; Ring 1999). In addition, divisions existed regarding the wisdom of the USFWS decision to compromise on the matter of land habitat acreage. The original biological opinion specified a target of 29,000 acres. Yet the agency was prepared to break that figure down into thirds, setting 10,000 acres as the target for the first program increment. That concession was not well received by the rejectionists. Furthermore, the Audubon representative who left the discussions had been deeply invested in the FERC re-licensing negotiations and felt that process was bearing fruit. When Secretary Babbitt and Governor Roy Romer initiated the Platte MOA process, it seemed to the representative that energy and focus were being diverted from possible success within the FERC framework (Echeverria 2001). Superseding the FERC process for wider Platte Basin efforts was not welcome. For the Whooping Crane Trust and Audubon, it was time to walk away.

However, some environmentalists felt strongly enough about the merits of the process that they never left or soon returned to the table, including the representative of the Environmental Defense Fund. These environmentalists knew they would be mainly on the sidelines even as they sat at the table as voting representatives because the states and their water users controlled the Platte waters, while the USFWS would have no other option than to figure out ways to collaboratively rework state water resources on behalf of ESA objectives. It was frustrating, but environmentalists would have to defer to the federal negotiators and try to help the talks when possible. Furthermore, these environmentalists saw potential in the negotiating process that could reward their patience. One attractive element was that the CA being forged at the table for signing in 1997 clearly laid down an environmentally desirable policy—no new depletions on the Platte could be made post-1997 without full replacement. That alone was viewed as a compelling reason to continue the negotiations. Another reason to remain engaged was the larger political and ecological issue of big multi-state landscape-level planning, something the FERC discussions could not deliver. Nebraska alone could not be expected to satisfy the needs of cranes without the contributions of the upstream states—Colorado and Wyoming—that had the basin watersheds. No individual state could politically and technically achieve the essential habitat improvement goals. Scientifically and politically, a basin-wide program was critical to habitat restoration. The basin encompassed the important actors, as well as the options of a large area and many different access points for change. The Platte River negotiations gave environmentalists what they needed and were not likely to get any other way—a basin-wide effort.

When the Whooping Crane Trust and Audubon representatives stepped away from the table in the summer and fall of 1996, the Environmental Defense Fund representative was left without coalition partners. The representative became concerned that the walkout risked unnecessarily alienating DOI, particularly in light of that agency's relatively recent efforts to ensure full membership status for environmental representatives. Furthermore, the walkout threatened to throw away a golden opportunity for basin-wide water re-timing. Meanwhile, DOI authorities maintained linkages to the walkouts. Later, in the spring of 1997, representatives of the Whooping Crane Trust and other delegates from Audubon returned to the discussions. They knew a CA was being forged and would likely be signed by mid-1997. It was better, they calculated, to be party to the deal and help the program work. After all, they had already won a significant victory. The nature of the debate had changed in the Platte Basin. It was no longer about defending the old status quo. Discussion was now about how to reorganize water flows, replace any new depletions, acquire terrestrial habitat, and work out program monitoring plans. It was all about species recovery. In the final analysis, environmentalists who stayed at the table would have a hand in developing an exciting new agenda, and they still had the ESA as a backstop. If the DOI and the states were to trade away too much of the environmental agenda, sharp-eyed environmentalists involved in the process still had the litigation option.

Agricultural Water Users in Opposition

Many agricultural water users also questioned the wisdom of entering into basin-wide discussions. Their discontent emerged soon after the 1994 pact was signed, but it erupted most strongly soon after the 1997 CA was launched. The agriculturalists' opposition was different from that of the environmentalists in that whereas the environmentalists were divided over whether to be present at the negotiating table, agriculture had representatives at the table. Rejectionists within agricultural water user communities stood in opposition to what they feared their representatives would agree to do. Opposition mounted especially in Nebraska among agricultural well owners, who saw that the two districts—the CNPPID and the NPPD—in seeking their renewed licenses, were bringing the federal government into Nebraska water supply issues. Those issues, in turn, could impinge upon historical Nebraska tensions between ground and surface water interests. The intrusion of federal environmental agendas, they believed, needed to be energetically resisted.

Nebraska opponents received support from some irrigators on the Upper North Platte in Wyoming and a few in Colorado, especially those in the Central Colorado Water Conservancy District with headquarters in Greeley. This minority had been at least partially radicalized by the botched Wyoming-federal deal at Deer Creek, which some saw as indicative of the federal intent to exert control over state water resources in unacceptable ways. They became particularly vocal and disruptive in 1997–1999, after the MOA was signed and a Governance Committee and its advisory committees had been established, at least on paper. Their story will be addressed in part in Chapters 14 and 15 (science and junk science) and 16 (land habitat).

Despite the presence of rejectionists in each of the camps—water user and environmental—the collaborative process was beginning to work. The Babbitt and Romer initiative that had led to the 1994 agreement to talk about habitat recovery on the Platte was beginning to create a de facto coalition that could hope to provide and manage resources in critical habitat over the long run.

SIDEBOARDS, MILESTONES, AND RELIEF FROM JEOPARDY

The essence of the federal approach was to offer the promise of long-term regulatory certainty for water users in return for state and water user willingness to fulfill species habitat needs, blend in the milestones to be negotiated—fulfillment of which would provide temporary relief during and after the negotiations—and demonstrate federal willingness to collaborate in a mutual learning process called adaptive management.

By March 1995 the negotiations had produced a preliminary vision built on the earlier Platte River Coordinating Committee, a rough outline of what a negotiated solution might look like (U.S. Fish and Wildlife Service 1995). Referred to as the "Sideboards Document," the study envisioned ESA implementation in a fair and scientifically sound manner, emphasized collaboration in adaptive management, and encouraged a comprehensive, multi-species approach. It kept the negotiators together, established a history and a justification for talks, and advanced a sketchy vision of a direction negotiators could follow and share with their constituents. The sideboards statement provided an essential vocabulary of concepts that would serve negotiators in the years to follow, principles for the expenditure of federal funds, financial protocols, adaptive management, a route to develop a reasonable and prudent alternative that would provide quantities of land and water, essential milestones to be fulfilled, and a list of issues yet to be negotiated.

The milestones embodied the concept of "sufficient progress," as defined and required by the USFWS. Milestones represented systematic goals, the achievement of which would become measures of progress. They allowed for adjustment in the face of unforeseen circumstances and created incremental targets on the road to constructing a viable, reasonable, and prudent alternative. Milestones would be assessed year by year, state by state, and organization by organization. If progress was deemed insufficient, the USFWS could threaten to withdraw relief from jeopardy and reopen any biological opinions that had been issued. Milestones would be negotiated and employed in the domains of water, land, research and monitoring, and program governance and administration. Milestones were the most predictable performance standard the states would have—standards that would provide measurable benchmarks against which the efforts to build a program could be assessed.

In exchange for the temporary grant of ESA compliance during the proposed CA period following mid-1997, states and water providers would deliver specific items regarding the provision of land, water, integrated research and monitoring, governance, and money. States and their water users were extremely concerned about not fulfilling a milestone as a result of circumstances beyond their control and the resulting consequences of that failure. For example, if budgets and market conditions would allow acquisition of only a portion of required land for habitat, how quick would the USFWS be to withdraw the promise of regulatory certainty? Essentially, the USFWS walked a fine line between reasonable flexibility in an uncertain world and toughness in holding to expectations that would induce good-faith efforts to push ahead. The USFWS mantra was "let's talk, make milestone commitments, evaluate, discuss options, and adjust milestones as compelling lessons are learned." USFWS personnel pointed to examples of agency reasonableness in other collaborative efforts, such as the Upper Colorado where milestones had been adjusted and new ones created in an effort to deal flexibly with unanticipated problems (Morgenweck 2001). Adaptive management and fulfillment of milestones were two concepts that became closely allied as negotiations progressed.

Eventually, the USFWS promoted constructive discussion by calling for and collaboratively arranging workshops every few months. Small groups representing the various interests met to define problems, do homework, and envision solutions and then feed proposals into the workshops. A basic dynamic was repeated across the years:

1. Members within each network (each of the three states, the federal interests, and environmental communities) would consult and sort out issues among themselves. Within networks, home coalitions had to be constructed.

2. After building a coalition and a strategy, states could then talk with the other states, and environmental groups could share ideas with other environmental groups.

3. Representatives of each network could then work with other parties at the committee level. As issues and positions emerged, members of each network would retreat to reconfigure their positions as new information and opportunities arose.

Because negotiations grew out of many conversations within and among the sub-networks, leaders could not simply sign documents and expect successful outcomes. Collaborative efforts, by their very nature, are slow to develop because leaders must build coalitions in an effort to retain the support of players who are there voluntarily.

Target Flow Challenge

Over the course of several confrontational episodes in the Platte Basin (including Grayrocks, Deer Creek, Wildcat, Narrows, Two Forks, the Poudre River mountain reservoirs, and FERC re-licensing at Kingsley Dam), the USFWS had developed its capacity to model Platte flows and contemplate the habitat needs of listed species. A team of people representing the USFWS and the National Biological Survey then created a table of target flows that, on the assumption that inadequate river flow volumes were the most important limiting factor in restoring and sustaining the central Platte riparian ecosystem, led to an agency conclusion regarding the average annual amount of water needed at the critical habitat during certain times.

Between 1994 and 1997, the primary substantive challenge for negotiators was to find a way to deal with the USFWS's judgment, as expressed in its biological opinions, that the history of water diversions in the Platte River Basin had shorted the critical habitat of an annual average of 417,000 acre feet at key times of need. Using historical river flow data (1943–1994), the USFWS had defined times—counted in specific days during spring and summer—when additional desired flow volumes were, at least in the agency's view, needed to sustain agency-stipulated habitat characteristics. Observed flows were then compared with USFWS definitions of desired flows, differences between the observed and the desirable were averaged across years, and analysts cumulated daily deficits into the overall shortage-to-target-flow value. Target volumes were categorized by dry years, normal years, and wet years. Decisions regarding what kind of year managers would face were based on estimated gross water supply, estimates of groundwater and precipitation, and snowpack in the entire basin (Bowman 1994).

Negotiations threatened to flounder on the question of whether the annual 417,000-acre-foot shortage conclusion was justifiable. For its part, the USFWS could not play fast and loose with its biological opinions, which constituted the basis of the entire basin discussion, and water users were not about to accept that number or the analysis that had generated it. The USFWS insisted that the target quantity of water be re-timed on behalf of the ESA agenda. Water users insisted on obtaining regulatory certainty without promising anything close to the USFWS target flow.

Reorganized water quantities (water shifted from times of excess flow to times of shortage) would be required to recover critical habitat components, including channel roosting, wet meadows, sandbar nesting, fishery, and foraging habitats. This part of the envisioned program would address historical depletions to the river prior to July 1, 1997. Another portion of any plan would be for states and their water users to offset their "future" depletions, defined as those caused by water uses begun on and after July 1, 1997. All of these components were seen as essential for recovery of federally listed species. Re-timed flows would recover damaged habitat, prevent the need for listing additional species, and provide for conservation of natural biotic ecosystem components.

In addition to enhancing the general aggregate volume of shortages to target flows, the USFWS identified pulse flows as the highest priority. They were viewed as essential to maintain and enhance the physical structure of wide, open, un-vegetated, and braided channels; to supply soil moisture and pooled water during the growing season for plants and animals lower in the food chain in meadow grasslands; to rehabilitate and sustain biologic webs in main and side channels as nursery habitats for fish, shellfish, and other aquatic organisms; and to facilitate nutrient cycling in floodplains. Pulse flows also raise groundwater levels in wetlands adjacent to rivers and bring organisms close to the soil surface for predation by migratory birds and other species. Pulse flows contribute to the breakup of winter ice and thereby induce the scouring of vegetation off of sandbars, which is especially important in years of low flow. Except in the driest years, at least 50 percent of the pulse flows should occur during the period May 20–June 20 and should emulate traditional flow patterns of 10 days ascending, 5 days cresting, and 12 days descending (U.S. Fish and Wildlife Service 1997b).

Water users ferociously attacked the Fish and Wildlife Service numbers. They believed the figure of 417,000 acre feet of water for habitat recovery was not based on river flow history or defensible logic. In the often heated discussion of target flows, even basic facts about the river's physical structure could not be agreed upon—especially the most crucial element, which was how much water would actually be required to restore and sustain habitat. The USFWS was fixed on its biological opinion and its target flow analysis; there was no way the agency would negotiate away the analysis that had been the basis of its jeopardy biological opinions. Target flows had become nonnegotiable. Yet water users vehemently rejected the analysis. The collision threatened prospects for a negotiated river basin solution.

Some path had to be found to keep the talks from floundering. A way to keep them alive was secured by two agreements. First, the parties accepted the concept of adaptive management, a term that would be the subject of much pulling and hauling in future negotiations. The idea of adaptive management allowed water users and states to reject the federal target flows analysis while the federal government held to it and thereby protected its biological opinions. Adaptive management allowed all parties to make peace, not around any agreed target flow number but around the idea that collaborative work, research, and monitoring over the duration of the first 10- to 13-year program increment would allow all parties to determine actual species needs. This mutual commitment to adaptive management allowed all parties to move past the impossible target flow discussions by agreeing to disagree about target flows. Second, it was agreed that the USFWS would accept a 1997 CA stipulation that would call for the first 13-year program increment to include an average annual reduction of shortage to target flows of 130,000–150,000 acre feet. The agency would thereby obtain a meaningful promise to address Platte flow issues and fully retain its biological opinion as an uncompromised policy document. If the first increment's water objectives were fulfilled and the volumes were found to be inadequate, DOI could always ask for more under the terms of the original biological opinion that had launched the search for a workable recovery program. Meanwhile, the talks were back on track.

1997 Cooperative Agreement: Essential Elements

On July 1, 1997, the secretary of the interior and the governors of Colorado, Wyoming, and Nebraska entered into an arrangement called the Cooperative Agreement. The parties agreed to negotiate a program to conserve and protect the habitat of four species listed as endangered and threatened under the ESA. The CA was almost 150 pages long and included several documents:

1. A milestone document describing the parties' obligations during the three-year Cooperative Agreement period (1997–2000)

2. A water conservation/water supply document describing studies needed to develop water for program purposes

3. The proposed program, describing water supply and re-timing projects to provide water to the habitat and land, money, and other contributions by the states and DOI, and

4. A governance document that, among other things, established an oversight committee (the secretary of DOI and the governors of each of the three states) and a governance committee to conduct the negotiations (see Appendix C)

The anticipated 3-year CA period would be employed to (1) complete negotiations of unresolved issues pertaining to land, water, research, and monitoring; (2) provide time for a USBR–environmental impact statement (EIS) team to assess the proposed program, as required by the National Environmental Policy Act (NEPA); and (3) provide opportunity for the USFWS to evaluate the emergent program for sufficiency as a reasonable and prudent alternative. Assuming that all this was accomplished by June 30, 2000 (a provision had been made for possible extension to December 31 of that year, and that provision would be exercised), a viable program would be launched in its first increment of 13 years. The USFWS had advocated a 10-year first increment, while the states held out for 15 or 20 years to fulfill the program goals. The compromise was a 13-year first program increment. The federal community was willing to extend the time because members estimated it would probably take that long to detect the results of program manipulations and determine possible courses of action for a subsequent program increment. Water users would enjoy regulatory certainty by fulfilling milestones to the USFWS's satisfaction.

A successful program will extend indefinitely but be implemented in increments. After successful completion of increment one, the parties will negotiate the terms and conditions of the second and subsequent increments. The USFWS's mandate is to review matters as the program moves to the conclusion of the first increment, negotiate amended terms and conditions for the future increments, if necessary, and reopen consultations if the program has seriously broken down.

The Cooperative Agreement pledged that in the first 13-year program increment the states and their water users would acquire, protect, and restore at least 10,000 acres of terrestrial habitat and would re-time basin waters to reduce shortages to USFWS target flows by 130,000 to 150,000 acre feet, as measured at Grand Island, Nebraska.

By 1997, water users in the three states had sketched out three sources of program water that the USFWS estimated, in combination, would provide an average total of about 80,000 acre feet/year (see Table 12.1). Nebraska's contribution would come from an environmental account established at Lake McConaughy. In Nebraska the two districts (CNPPID and NPPD) were nearing the conclusion of their re-licensing process with FERC. As part of this bureaucratically torturous process, each district had agreed to join in the Platte River Habitat Recovery Program negotiations, with the understanding that the FERC re-licensing deal would be reopened if the Platte River talks failed. The districts therefore had incentive to ensure successful Platte habitat recovery outcomes through the larger Platte Cooperative Agreement negotiating process. One part of that FERC deal established an environmental water account (EA) at Kingsley Dam and Lake McConaughy. A USFWS employee who worked at the Grand Island field office would request releases by the Central Nebraska Public Power and Irrigation District just like any other customer and would manage the account waters on behalf of the listed species in accordance with license requirements.

The McConaughy EA would be filled by water inflows equal to 10 percent of the storable natural inflows to the lake in the months October through April, up to a maximum annual addition of 100,000 acre feet (Cooperative Agreement 1997). Yield at Grand Island would average about 36,000 acre feet per year. Water remaining in the EA after September 30 could be carried over and added to the following year's contributions. Total EA water in the McConaughy tub can fluctuate across time but can never exceed 200,000 acre feet at any time during the water year (Cooperative Agreement 1997). Wyoming's proposed Pathfinder Dam and Reservoir modification project promised to increase storage by 54,000 acre feet. About 34,000 acre feet of that restored storage capacity would also serve as an environmental account, like that of Lake McConaughy. The remaining 20,000 acre feet would be held for Wyoming municipal uses; for example, Casper-area municipal needs that were not addressed by the failed Deer Creek enterprise. Colorado pledged to construct what came to be known as the Tamarack Plan (after an old ranch by that name), designed to produce an annual average yield at the Colorado-Nebraska state line of 10,000 acre feet through groundwater recharge that would generate return flows to the South Platte at times needed for recovery of species habitat. The difference between what these sources could produce as an annual average shortage reduction (about 80,000 acre feet) and what was necessary to reach the first increment goal of 130,000–150,000 acre feet would be addressed during the CA three-year period by a $900,000 state-funded water conservation and supply study.

In addition, each state pledged to construct a future depletions plan by the end of the CA period (then expected to be either June 30 or December 31, 2000). Any new depletions water users placed on the river would have to somehow be replaced if they increased shortages to target flows, regardless of whether the depleter was in a federal nexus. Each state would develop important portions of its own water contribution in a manner that would reflect its unique opportunities and constraints. For existing water projects, in place prior to July 1, 1997, as long as the milestones of the CA period and of the program's first increment were met, the evolving program would serve as a reasonable and prudent alternative. That, plus known rules for replacing future depletions (post–June 30, 1997), would provide justification for providing regulatory certainty to water suppliers.

In the end, everyone could see the advantages of pursuing a collaborative recovery program within the framework of the Cooperative Agreement. The federal government obtained a path to improved flows, restored habitat, and effective working relationships with water interests in the three states. The ESA would be served. The water users and the states stood to gain regulatory certainty and secured means by which land and water acquisitions would be made on a willing seller-buyer basis. Nebraska obtained re-licensing of Kingsley Dam and associated CNPPID and NPPD facilities. Wyoming would get a 40 percent portion of restored storage, to be made available at Pathfinder. Colorado gained a path to needed permits for its headwaters projects and city water facilities.

THE ROAD AHEAD

The July 1997 Cooperative Agreement was far from perfect in the view of negotiators, but it framed a potentially livable future. Alternatives were more frightening. Over the next three-and-a-half years (July 1, 1997–December 31, 2000), a plan was developed to supplement the 80,000 acre feet/year already identified at Wyoming's Pathfinder Reservoir, Nebraska's Lake McConaughy, and Colorado's Tamarack with another 50,000–70,000 acre feet. People involved in the process would see issues hammered out for the acquisition and management of habitat, and negotiators would grapple seriously with the fundamentals of measuring progress toward defined program goals.

Negotiations up to mid-1997 had established precedents that took water users and state authorities well beyond their comfort zones. Every perspective constituted a platform from which complaints were launched. Wyoming and Colorado users especially lamented that the Bureau of Reclamation had betrayed its original mission and changed their universe; Nebraska irrigation and power districts disliked the establishment of an EA at Lake McConaughy. Nebraska groundwater users complained that the two districts operating at Kingsley Dam were securing their permits at the cost of dragging them into a discussion with water policy makers in Lincoln and with federal authorities, of which they wanted no part. Colorado users expressed fears that an implicit federal junior water right was taking form to serve the recovery program and that it would reorganize at least some Lower South Platte River flows in a manner that would place state water rights at a disadvantage. In the federal view, agency representatives had displayed flexibility in dealing with target flows, had scaled back their demand for the desired 29,000 acres of land habitat to 10,000 acres for the first program increment, and had proffered a philosophy of adaptive management for working things out. Yet they had received little appreciation from the states' representatives, who appeared to be dragging out discussions in what federal negotiators took to be a stalling game. Environmentalists fretted about the danger that the federal negotiators would cut environmentally unprincipled deals to create coalitions with users that, in saving the Endangered Species Act in Washington, D.C.'s congressionally hostile political environment, would gut it on the high plains.

Meanwhile, the USFWS sat in the middle of the contending forces as its leadership attempted to steer a path that would serve the listed species and keep opposition from getting out of hand—all this with insufficient personnel, time, and money. The U.S. Congress, divided over the wisdom of the ESA as presently constructed, had not devised legislative solutions. Congress had clearly determined one thing, however: it would hold the USFWS on a short leash by seriously constraining its budget. Whatever the USFWS did by way of implementing the ESA through large-scale basin-wide collaborative programs, it would do with seriously overworked staff and tight funds. But for all its constraints, the USFWS controlled the road to the Eldorado of regulatory certainty for water users.

PART IV

Negotiating Interests

Colorado's Interests

In defense of their water tower and to assemble their contribution to a habitat recovery program, Colorado's South Platte water providers configured their designs to fit the fundamental realities of their situation. They needed to preserve the integrity of the Nebraska-Colorado Compact, develop alliances with water interests on the lower river near the Nebraska border, prevent opportunistic destructive water raids in the name of legal compliance, and secure water flows for listed species in a heavily appropriated basin.

NEBRASKA-COLORADO COMPACT

Interstate water compacts allocate rights to consumptive use (Corbridge and Rice 1999: 534–540; Dunbar 1983). They are treaties made among states, ratified by the respective state legislatures, signed by governors, and adopted by the U.S. Congress. Colorado pioneered the use of compacts to resolve interstate disputes, and its waters are the most compacted of any state (Tyler 2003).

On the South Platte River, Colorado's water consumption is limited by a compact agreement with Nebraska mandating that if flows fail to equal or exceed 120 cubic feet per second (cfs) of natural flow to Nebraska from April 1 to October 15 each year, Colorado is obligated to curtail the diversions of a specific set of Colorado users with priorities junior to June 14, 1897. Users subject to curtailment are those located downstream of the Washington County line where the South Platte flows through the Balzac/Cooper gauge and is measured into what becomes the "lower river," about 100 miles long as it winds its

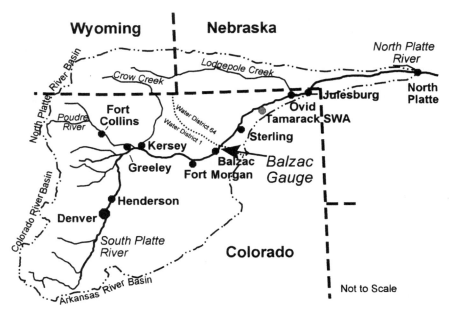

MAP 9.1. *South Platte River Basin. Modified from map from U.S. Department of the Interior, Bureau of Reclamation, and U.S. Fish and Wildlife Service; Platte River Recovery and Implementation Program: Final Environmental Impact Statement, April 2006.*

way northeast to the Julesburg gauge at the Colorado-Nebraska border (Map 9.1).*

When flows exceed 120 cfs at the border, all Colorado diverters can be "in" the lower river, subject to the constraints imposed on their priorities by Colorado's appropriation doctrine. When flows fall below that amount, Colorado users below the Balzac/Cooper gauge with priorities junior to June 14, 1897, must curtail their diversions to the extent that they diminish flows at the state line (South Platte River Compact 1923). All this has been a bequest of an earlier generation of water negotiators who hammered out the compact in the years leading up to April 27, 1923, when it was signed in Lincoln, Nebraska (Tyler 2003: 108–109).

The compact divided the South Platte River at the Balzac gauge because above the gauge the entire river's ordinary flow was established long before canal construction commenced on the Lower South Platte River in Colorado or in western Nebraska. Prior to the growth of irrigated agriculture along the upper reaches of tributaries, there was little, if any, surface flow at the Colorado-

---

*Note: The Balzac gauge has been decommissioned. Water is now measured about four miles upstream at the Cooper gauge.

Nebraska state line after spring runoff subsided. Settlers had moved up past the Nebraska South Platte and what is now known as the lower river in Colorado for the simple reason that almost nothing flowed there during the summer months. They sought the more bountiful supplies on the tributaries (such as the Cache la Poudre, Big Thompson, St. Vrain, and Boulder Creek), which were also easier to divert because they were not a "mile wide and an inch deep," as was much of the lower river. The lower river grew in summer flow volume as European tributary settlement trapped spring flood flows in small reservoirs and as farmers diverted water onto their fields and let ample fractions escape back to the river through surface runoff and deep percolation. All this, combined with late–nineteenth-century and early–twentieth-century trans-mountain diversions of water from the Colorado and Laramie rivers to Colorado's eastern streams, meant increasing flows on the South Platte that would permit later construction of irrigation works on Colorado's lower river and along Nebraska's South Platte and the main stem. These water return and flow facts and the slow but steady pattern of irrigation canal construction from the upper to lower river segments justified the exclusion of the Upper South Platte and its tributaries from the provisions of the Nebraska-Colorado Compact. Above Balzac/Cooper, Colorado could enjoy expanded water use unhindered by Nebraskan appetites.

On the whole, Colorado water users have viewed the Nebraska-Colorado Compact as a "good deal" because it placed a firewall at the Washington County line (the Balzac/Cooper gauge), and Colorado diversion priorities junior to June 1897 are vulnerable to shutdown only below that point. Most Colorado consumptive use on the South Platte occurs above that gauge. Over the years, Nebraska has come to see the disadvantage of its position. It is compelled to focus only on juniors on the lower river when it would prefer to look upstream into Colorado usage. For decades, many in Colorado have held to the view that Nebraska has sought an opportunity to renegotiate the matter. They feared the Platte River Habitat Recovery Program presented such a chance.

Colorado's interest was to ensure that the compact not be renegotiated. A practical implication was that no Colorado water facility upstream of the firewall could serve the basin endangered species recovery program. Any Colorado water contribution would have to occur in the lower river to preserve the firewall, and it would be preferable to locate it as close to the border as possible to avoid having to work any program water through or past Colorado diverters.

COLORADO SIDE PAYMENT

Colorado users who needed federal permits to continue their operations were not located on the lower river. Rather, they were operating facilities much farther upstream in the Denver, Boulder, Longmont, Greeley, Loveland, and Fort Collins areas and in the mountain watersheds on both sides of the Continental

Divide to the west. Given compact considerations, the Colorado contribution to the Platte River Habitat Recovery Program would have to come from far downstream in the lower river segment. Yet no water appropriators that far downriver were troubled by the consideration of a federal nexus. What could water providers in the federal Endangered Species Act (ESA) nexus do for them that could make lower river users willing partners in a central Nebraska habitat recovery effort?

The South Platte River, downstream from Denver and continuing all the way to Nebraska, is underlain by valley-fill sediment saturated with water. This alluvial aquifer varies from about a 20-foot thickness near Denver to as much as 200 feet thick at the state line. This underground sponge, hydraulically connected to the surface river, has been estimated to hold as much as 8.3 million acre feet in storage (Colorado Water Conservation Board 2004: 3–65). In the Lower South Platte alluvium are about 10,800 permitted wells, with yields ranging from 1 gallon per minute (gpm) to 3,000 gpm. The average yield has been estimated to be about 430 gpm, but around half of the total wells are domestic wells averaging less than 30 gpm. The major threat to surface flows in the lower river is posed by the large agricultural irrigation wells that pull volumes way above the average (Colorado Water Conservation Board 2004: 3–65).

Most surface water canal diversions on the lower river in Colorado are senior to the Nebraska-Colorado Compact date of mid-June 1897. Those junior to that date have long since gone out of business. The real problem for irrigators in Colorado downstream of the Washington County line is the fact that virtually all groundwater wells are junior to the compacted date; unless their depletions to the river are fully augmented, they are subject to being curtailed whenever flows drop below 120 cfs at the Julesburg gauge. It was long after 1897 and primarily after World War II before high plains agriculture was served by the technologies of high-capacity turbine pumps, rural electrification, and highly mobile drilling rigs that could quickly and cheaply punch deep holes into underground aquifers.

The typical Colorado irrigator in the area is a surface water canal user who supplements ditch supplies that are likely to be senior to the compact date with well water that is certain to be junior to the date. Typically, when river flows drop below the compact requirement, it is a sign that the countryside is dry. Dry times are exactly when farmers want their irrigation pumps to be on to bring their crops through the arid period. But wells below the Balzac-Cooper gauge are subject to shut down under the compact just when irrigators need them most.

Colorado and Nebraska negotiators of the 1923 compact counted on a continuing increase in South Platte River flow during summer months, given the rescheduling of spring surges in the form of delayed return flows by cities, towns, and especially upstream irrigated agriculture. In April 1923 their vision was one of a continuously "growing regime of the river," less and less likely with the passage of time to fall below the 120 cfs compact requirement. This was a happy vision for everybody on both sides of the border.

By the 1950s and early 1960s, however, increased groundwater pumping along Colorado's South Platte was causing problems, at first primarily for Colorado surface water canal appropriators. When a pump switch was flipped on and water gushed from a tributary aquifer beneath the ground, those molecules were emerging at an alternate point of diversion as compared to a surface flow through a canal headgate, and those molecules consumptively used were denied to a senior canal right somewhere on the river. The idea that a junior well owner would divert water out of priority as compared to a senior surface water user was unacceptable. It violated the state appropriation priority doctrine by permitting junior investors to plunder water owed to seniors.

Something had to be done, and it was politically possible to do it because most irrigators were using both water sources. No one liked being accused of depriving another irrigator of justly owed water, and in particular no one liked being thus deprived by others. By the 1960s Colorado irrigators were launched upon a voyage of discovery that would lead to river flow augmentation. Owners of junior wells joined a variety of social organizations that collectively repaid the river in ways that protected senior canal priorities from the depredations of junior well pumping (MacDonnell 1988).

A variety of river augmentation organizations were in existence by the mid-1970s, and there were important differences among them. What they had in common was that junior priority well beneficiaries had organized to protect senior canal diverters from injury. One method was for junior well owners to organize to collectively purchase wells at or near the headgates of senior canals and pay the costs of ensuring that each headgate would obtain its priority-declared ration (MacDonnell 1988). This freed wells to be pumped out of priority without injuring surface water seniors. Another method diverted water from the river at times of excess flows (fall, winter, and spring months) and placed it into recharge pits calculated to produce return flow volumes at times and places necessary to prevent injury to senior right holders the following summer. All of this was made possible by the Colorado Water Right Determination and Administration Act of 1969 (MacDonnell 1988) and a set of technical practices (Warner, Altenhofen, and Odor 1994). By the early 1990s, Colorado water culture had produced one major headgate management organization (Groundwater Appropriators of the South Platte) that worked on behalf of well owners from the headwaters of the Platte all the way down to the lower river and about sixty artificial recharge projects, most of them on the South Platte (Warner, Altenhofen, and Odor 1994).

However, a compact problem with Nebraska loomed. In looking at the overall annual flows of the South Platte across the state line, the happy vision of a continuously growing "regime of the river" came to pass when measured across an entire water year, but it was not sustained during high-demand summer irrigation periods. Colorado surface water users and Nebraska could not deny that the river was larger in summer than had traditionally been the case under pre-settlement conditions, but it was not the summer river the Colorado or Nebraska compact negotiators had envisioned. High-capacity Colorado agricultural wells had intervened between dreams and reality above and below the Julesburg gauge at the Colorado-Nebraska state line.

Colorado's administration of the South Platte Compact was never an issue. Obligations would be fulfilled. Yet there was a problem. In average to wet years, the lower river had been fully augmented for many years, but western snowmelt rivers are notoriously variable from season to season. Even in a good year, during the month of August, South Platte flows into Nebraska have averaged only 153 cfs (Ugland et al. 1993), thereby exceeding the compact standard by an average of only 33 cfs—a narrow margin on which to hang the lower river's agricultural economy.

In 1999 the river dropped below 120 cfs at the Julesburg gauge only twice. However, the following summer, by mid-August flows had failed to rise to that desired level for over 100 days. Two adjacent years, two extremes. Following a short drought in 1976–1977, until 2000 the South Platte had enjoyed above-average flows in all but 6 years. In fact, the period 1977–2000 was the wettest in recorded South Platte history following the 25-year wet spell that occurred from 1905 to 1929. This happy circumstance provided effective cover for Colorado appropriators to construct their augmentation projects and buy insurance against the inevitable summer season that would fall far enough below average to force a terrible choice: face down and curtail the wells of angry, struggling farmers who had wet-year assumptions capitalized by bankers into their farms or mobilize Nebraskans into a dreaded lawsuit.

There was a way out, however, a third path that became clear in the years leading up to the 1994 governors' agreement to negotiate a solution for endangered species. Some groundwater well users saw an opportunity to further augment their wells in a manner that would replace depletions at times of high demand during summer irrigation months. Totally sufficient river augmentation—which would keep wells pumping under the deepest and most extended drought conditions—would not likely be practical, but a program of systematic expansion of augmentation capacity would keep the large tributary aquifer in much greater play when needed for conjunctive use with surface water.

This was an agenda that could gain enthusiastic participation by lower river water users. Assistance with augmentation to replace depletions of lower river agricultural wells, as part and parcel of the proposed ESA habitat recovery program, would win lower river allies for Front Range users in their quest for federal relief from jeopardy. Many irrigation farmers who had any meaningful level of well water dependency could easily see that their farms would be worth little if they were required to curtail their well usage during the irrigation season. Without timely access to adequate supplementary groundwater, many of their enterprises would fail. Spurred by signs of drought in 2000, within a few months that fall and early spring of 2001, private entrepreneurs started twenty-one augmentation projects on private lands. By the summer of 2002, private landowners had installed twenty additional river augmentation wells that re-timed water from off-season surplus periods to high-demand summer flows. The exceedingly dry summer of 2002 also witnessed a frenzy of installations of river augmentation wells and recharge pits, plus augmentation from off-season use of surface flow canal seepage.

In this context, from the early 1990s onward, with the knowledge that they were living on borrowed time provided by an inordinately wet period that had started in the late 1970s, Front Range water users who required federal permits made an alliance with lower river users. The Colorado Tamarack Plan would emerge. It was initiated on public lands to demonstrate the concept of recharge for re-timing flows from winter to summer, which then produced a burst of private land recharge projects for the same purposes. Lower river interests would advance toward their dream of a "bulletproof" river vis-à-vis Nebraska. Front Range water users would obtain re-timed water to contribute to listed species habitat restoration and thereby obtain essential federal permits. The problem would be to sell all this to Nebraska and to the U.S. Fish and Wildlife Service (USFWS).

AVOIDING A SACRIFICE ZONE

An alternative way to secure water for the collaborative Platte River Habitat Recovery Program would be to dry up some fraction of Lower South Platte Colorado agriculture and send the consumptive use fraction of that "saved" water across the border. It would be easy for Front Range water users in need of federal permits to place lower river communities on the auction block and sacrifice them on the altar of the ESA. It would be uncomplicated for any Front Range entity with sufficiently deep pockets to send agents to quietly explore lower river land and water markets and cut mutually beneficial deals on a willing seller-buyer basis. The poor agricultural economy in the 1980s and 1990s and the early years of the twenty-first century set up many farmers for a water sellout. The farm would return to dry-land agriculture, and the water would be put to use when needed for federal permitting purposes. It was a perfectly reasonable capitalist market-based solution to the problem.

The social and economic forces at play had clearly placed Lower South Platte communities in a vise. One jaw was the poor agricultural economy, which placed many irrigators in an economic squeeze—years of rising farm input costs, especially energy, combined with low prices for farm products, had resulted in poor financial returns. The irrigator's most valuable asset was often water, the consumptive use portion of which could be moved to other uses by urban and industrial buyers. For many irrigators, the sale of water assets promised salvation. The other jaw was composed of Front Range water providers that needed to expand their water supply portfolios.

In a region where land-use planning has been largely disconnected from water planning, the assumption has always been that economic growth would supply revenue for acquiring additional water supplies. The problem, of course, was that by the 1990s and thereafter, the available water supply was rapidly diminishing. Managers of the newly acquired tax revenues, produced by combinations of new homes and big-box stores, searched aggressively for available water wherever it could be found.

The prime group to look at for new supplies was the financially squeezed lower river irrigators. It was possible to dry up economically hard-pressed irrigators by giving stressed farmers a "fair market" price and committing the consumptive use portion of the purchased supply to uses endorsed by entities above the Balzac/Cooper gauge. The new users would then offset their new consumptive uses by replacing depletions somewhere along the river as required to protect other water rights under the Colorado appropriation doctrine and to fulfill any federal ESA requirements.

The reality that lower river ditch communities could be turned into sacrifice zones for the purposes of wealthier upscale Front Range cities was always a given. The only real question was, why did most Front Range organizations that needed federal permits wait for years while negotiations for a proposed habitat recovery program dragged on? What was the source of their patience?

A buy-up and dry-up scenario entails nontrivial problems. The conscious and deliberate creation of a "sacrifice zone" would be divisive for the Northern Colorado Water Conservancy District (NCWCD), sponsor of the U.S. Bureau of Reclamation (USBR)–constructed Colorado–Big Thompson Project. The district's boundaries include the upper river tributaries of the South Platte (including Boulder Creek and the St. Vrain, Big Thompson, and Poudre rivers), where the large urban-industrial-financial-educational cities are centered, and the lower river small agricultural towns. The district's board includes members from both the upper and lower river segments. The NCWCD's fundamental mission is to serve the people and communities of the lower river, not to sacrifice them. A willing seller of water, by definition, sees his or her interest as well served by the sale. But others who share the ditch system can be expected to suffer as they struggle to maintain their collectively owned and managed canal property with fewer producers. Taking land out of irrigated production also reduces the county tax base and the flow of dollars among agricultural product and service providers in local communities. The idea that other water users that needed permits upstream were attempting to fill the recovery program "bucket" by drying up lower river communities could be expected to create immediate opposition.

The balance of economic and political power within the district had shifted in favor of the much more urbanized upper system users who needed permits, but any crude attempt to bail out their permit needs by sacrificing lower river communities would encounter feelings of betrayal, resistance by those left behind, and anger that could make life in the NCWCD boardroom an unpleasant trial. If all other options were exhausted, it might be speculated that the NCWCD could sacrifice the lower river interests to serve its larger, more prosperous, upstream urban-industrial-research institution and high-technology clients, but that option has not been willingly contemplated. The NCWCD would ask Denver Water and any other user in an Endangered Species Act Section 7 consultation to support a collective effort on the lower river that could deliver water to the recovery program and avoid a rush to buy out and sacrifice lower river communities and economies, which would be an individually rational move but would lead to collective problems. For its part, prior to the Two Forks episode, Denver Water had notoriously played the role of villain in its relationships with other water providers on both sides of the Continental Divide; in its reconstructed, post–Two Forks incarnation the agency clearly preferred not to play that role again if it could avoid doing so.

A permit-hungry water user rush to the lower river land and water market posed other problems. A dry up of irrigated agriculture would create a supply of water for the recovery program, but that released supply would then have to be ushered downriver past headgates that, under Colorado's appropriation doctrine, had every right to take the newly added increments into their systems. Only a tiny fraction of the newly released flow would survive repeated diversions, deliveries, and field applications. Any attempt to run "bought-out" water past headgates to the recovery program would create massive legal and technical problems. Also, it would be technically impossible to measure small volumes of water produced by scattered farm dry ups. How would one solve the problem of high shrinkage of small flows as a result of seepage and evaporation in low-flow river bottoms? The dry up that comes with willing buyers and sellers is difficult to organize in a concentrated viable pattern that would consolidate flows. There was little probability that water released as a result of helter-skelter dry-up initiatives by agents for different and competitive permit-needy buyers without any overall plan would lead to a coherent solution. Finally, a dry up of irrigated farm fields that have been the source of runoff and return flows for a century or more can disrupt wetland wildlife habitat that has developed around leaky canals and reservoirs. How much neo-tropical songbird habitat might be destroyed in northeastern Colorado by a dry up that would put sufficient water into the summer river for the recovery program? The welfare transfers among listed and non-listed species that accompany a dry up of irrigated agriculture are not easily analyzed and scored. All in all, there was every incentive to avoid confronting the legal, technical, administrative, and ecosystem welfare transfer problems associated with drying up irrigated agriculture in the Lower South Platte River.

In addition, there was a major interstate policy concern. The 1923 compact gave Colorado citizens the right to consumptive use of South Platte water under stipulated conditions. As long as Colorado is fulfilling those conditions, why should the state, as a matter of policy, promote mechanisms whereby the consumptive uses of its own lower river communities are undermined so Nebraska can be the beneficiary of the expanded consumptive use that accompanies enhanced river flows? In the view of many Colorado residents, the Nebraska camel had long been trying to get its nose under Colorado's tent flap, and a Colorado policy of relying on a dry up would push at least some Colorado users and communities out of the shelter. Such an action would throw away the bequest the compact negotiators had left to Colorado citizens.

If Colorado water—released at the expense of Lower South Platte communities—were to be generated for the endangered species program, it would flow immediately and directly into Nebraska's Western Canal ditch, and the compact would have been effectively renegotiated by Front Range permit-hungry users seeking federal permits to advance their higher levels of production and consumption. This would have occurred at the expense of small, agriculturally based trade centers on the lower river. What would have been rational for an individual Front Range permit seeker in the hunt to find water arguably would not have been rational for the larger community and Colorado policy. A better option had to be found.

COLORADO SOLUTION: TAMARACK PLAN RECHARGE

Given the 1923 compact and a desire not to renegotiate it, a river with an increasing annual aggregate flow volume, a need for Front Range water users with federal permit requirements to develop an alliance with lower river users who had dry-year well augmentation needs, and a need to forestall a free-for-all market solution that would sacrifice lower river irrigation communities and place water administrators in impossible legal and technical situations, local water managers in the Upper and Lower South Platte Basin began to search for a viable option to serve the basin-wide recovery program.

To conduct that discourse, it would be necessary to construct two organizations:

1. The Platte River Project (PRP) assembled a coalition of about twenty-five water users with a stake in the basin-wide endangered species program. Together they represented over 2 million people dependent on the South

Platte. Organized as a special quasi-autonomous unit within the Colorado Water Congress and promoted by Denver Water and the NCWCD, this organization was designed to seek ways to support the creation of a Platte Basin endangered species recovery program and to collaborate with Colorado state authorities in developing an option consistent with Colorado law and the Nebraska-Colorado Compact. The PRP secured contributions from each participant to cover costs (primarily for legal services) and created an executive committee to organize discussions, develop policy direction, and ensure that business was completed. Each contributing entity secured one vote. The Platte River Project held regular meetings and created the socio-political space within which the diverse interests of South Platte water users could be heard, considered, and incorporated into Colorado's lower river option.

As years went by and implementation of the Platte River Habitat Recovery Program loomed ever closer on the horizon, in 2005–2006, members of the PRP established a follow-up organization to implement what would eventually become Colorado's contribution to the three-state recovery program. The organization, called the South Platte Water Related Activities Program (SPWRAP), would be designed to mobilize financial resources from Colorado's Front Range water providers that had a present or future need to participate in the proposed habitat mitigation program and thereby be in a position to secure non-jeopardy biological opinions for projects under way or yet to be initiated. SPWRAP membership represented the best path to regulatory certainty under the ESA. When SPWRAP was fully activated in 2006, the PRP ceased to function. (See Chapter 29 for more about SPWRAP.)

2. The South Platte Lower River Group (SPLRG) was incorporated as a Colorado nonprofit entity in the spring of 1996. SPLRG included members in the lower river (below the Balzac-Cooper gauge) as well as some upstream water user organizations that were also members of the PRP, including Denver Water and the NCWCD. Members undertook technical analyses of possible options for generating Colorado water for the Platte Basin recovery program; the focus was on hydrological analysis and database construction, project identification, and demonstration of water re-timing facilities at the Tamarack Ranch site. When the Tamarack Plan was created and money was required to build river recharge and augmentation works, SPLRG secured grants and in-kind services from several sources, including the Colorado Water Conservation Board, Colorado Division of Wildlife, Ducks Unlimited, the USBR, and proceeds from the Colorado state lottery. Officially, the articles of incorporation named four organizations as voting members:

   a. The Lower South Platte Water Conservancy District (LSPWCD), headquartered in Sterling, Colorado, was originally established to sponsor the ill-fated Narrows Dam and Reservoir Project. It shifted its mission to the construction and operation of well augmentation projects on private lands surrounding the lower river.

b. Groundwater Appropriators of the South Platte (GASP) was created in the wake of the 1969 Colorado Water Right Determination and Administration Act, which required junior priority well owners to repay the river for depletions imposed on surface flows. By organizing collectively, well owners could find the means to ensure that senior surface priorities would not sustain injury from their pumping. GASP's major strategy was to pay the costs of installing wells at or near the headgates of senior surface water priorities in a pattern that would prevent senior surface users from being harmed by groundwater pumping and to serve as a stable buyer of augmentation water credits produced by the many private owners of wells and sanctioned recharge pits. GASP was headquartered in Fort Morgan. It was unable to adequately provide offset water to replace specific depletions during years of extreme drought (2000–2004) and stopped functioning in 2005. The work of providing water to the South Platte to offset well depletions shifted to an array of smaller augmentation organizations better suited to the task of providing specific senior canal water users insufficiently supplied by the GASP model.

c. The Platte River Project was the coalition of water suppliers (urban and agricultural) on the South Platte discussed earlier. Denver Water led PRP participation in SPLRG (see p. 102).

d. The Northern Colorado Water Conservancy District (NCWCD) was established to sponsor the Colorado–Big Thompson trans-mountain diversion project that captures water on the Western slope of the Continental Divide and delivers it through the thirteen-mile-long Adams Tunnel to users on the east in the South Platte Basin. The NCWCD provided essential leadership and technical support for SPLRG.

The four voting member organizations assessed themselves about $5,000 a year apiece to cover the costs of discussion—primarily costs of legal counsel— as well as some equipment and demonstration project construction charges. SPLRG, as an incorporated entity, received and managed grants from interested public and private entities to advance the work of demonstrating water re-regulation for local, state, and national agendas. Its meetings were valuable, not so much for bringing issues to a vote but for providing a forum within which the South Platte Basin players could meet, discuss, evaluate, modify, and come to a consensus about courses of collective action. On a given meeting day, the parking lot typically contained vehicles representing the four voting organizations and also ditch riders, local community leaders and town managers, area politicians, state of Colorado Department of Natural Resources personnel, Colorado Water Conservation Board members, representatives of the Colorado Division of Wildlife and Ducks Unlimited, local farmers, and citizens at large.

Compared to the Platte River Project, SPLRG was more essential to the creation of alliances between upper and lower basin water interests and the design of the Tamarack Plan. The PRP was more focused on keeping upper basin city and town managers informed of progress and ready to push the Tamarack Plan to state authorities. The fact that Denver Water, the Northern Colorado Water Conservancy District, and the Lower South Platte Conservancy District were members of both organizations kept a rich set of cross-linkages active in the dissemination of information and perspectives within the two overlapping networks. Each organization sustained a high quality of civic discourse about the challenges presented by the Endangered Species Act and the options and implementation of the proposed Colorado program: the Tamarack Plan.

COLORADO'S TAMARACK PLAN

Continued construction of water facilities has occurred along Colorado's Front Range, fed by trans-mountain diversions and agricultural-to-urban transfers. Depending on exterior landscaping and lot size, it often takes less water to grow houses than it does to grow corn. This water gain can feed growing stream flows. Furthermore, non-tributary groundwater development in the Denver basin has also ensured that South Platte flows have been increasing over time, and the trend is expected to continue (Hydrosphere Resource Consultants 1999). New flow creation was not necessary to serve the species recovery program, but a change in the timing of flows has been required. Analyses of the history of South Platte flows established that in any given year, there had been more months of flows in excess of the USFWS target at the Grand Island gauge than there were months of deficit (Hydrosphere Resource Consultants 1999). Therefore, the trick was to re-time flows from periods of excess to USFWS target flows to those of periods of shortage.

How would Colorado's habitat recovery contribution be constructed? Recharge projects for reorganizing Lower South Platte flows had to be at places with suitable soils and geologic features that permitted the required fraction of water to return to the river channel within the intervals required, 60–300 days. The U.S. Geological Survey (USGS) had constructed a logic of stream depletion factors (SDFs) that denoted the number of days a given recharge site would require to return to the river 28 percent of a given quantity of water placed in a recharge pit (Warner, Altenhofen, and Odor 1994).

Initially, no one could expect a small number of private landowners to be willing to compromise their private for-profit operations to serve the needs of a South Platte environmental agenda. Therefore, public lands were needed in addition to continued private river augmentation efforts necessary to protect Colorado senior surface water priorities. Several state wildlife areas on the lower river had good groundwater recharge potential. SPLRG discussions would lead to the selection of the Tamarack Ranch State Wildlife Area on the south side of the river near Crook, Colorado, about forty miles upstream of the Nebraska

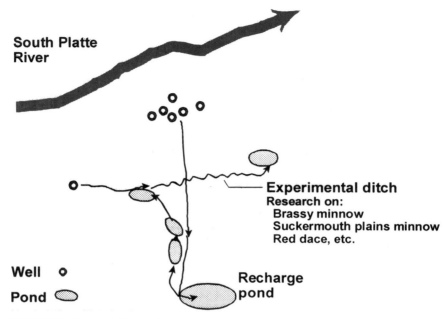

FIGURE 9.1. *Tamarack Project elements.*

border. As the name implies, the site is owned and managed by the Colorado Division of Wildlife (CDOW). With the eventual organization of the South Platte Water Related Activities Program, by 2006 SPWRAP was in a position to provide funding for Tamarack Plan facilities, including those of CDOW's Tamarack Ranch State Wildlife Area.

The Tamarack Plan (Boyle Engineering Corporation 2000), as it evolved over years of SPLRG discussions, would produce Colorado's re-timed water in two parts: (1) a set of public facilities located on public lands such as Tamarack but not limited to that site, and (2) recharge pumps, pipelines, and pits installed on private properties that, in return for augmentation credit and revenue in the range of twenty-five dollars per acre foot or more, would be sold or leased to the public agenda. CDOW's cooperation was secured by virtue of water provider willingness to pay for the installation of facilities necessary to conduct research on several Colorado native fish species of concern (Figure 9.1). The objective was to address the needs of such species before they became listed under the federal ESA.

At the Tamarack Ranch State Wildlife Area and other public and private lands closer to the border, the plan has been to divert water at times of excess flows at Grand Island through canals or wells adjacent to the river. The diverted flows are then conveyed to recharge sites at various distances from the river, where they are quickly absorbed by sandy soils. They then move into the aquifer and eventually back to the river (Figure 9.1). Return flows accrue to the river for a period of time after entry into the recharge pit, depending on known hydro-geological conditions and distance to the river channel. Tamarack Plan river aug-mentation was planned to unfold in three phases:

Phase I. During the first recovery program increment (thirteen years), Tamarack Plan facilities for recharge were committed to have the capacity to produce a minimum average of 10,000 acre feet/year of augmentation water during times of shortage to target flows measured at the Grand Island gauge.

Phase II of the Tamarack public land recharge included planned facilities to repay the river for "new depletions" placed on it as Colorado economic growth projects (post–June 30, 1997) imposed diversions and their associ-ated consumptive uses on the stream. Careful analysis suggested that based on historical experience in the basin, every 100,000 additional people would result in a net seasonal depletive effect on the river of a little less than 1,800 acre feet/year. Therefore, the output of Phase II facilities will be driven by the rate of population growth in the Colorado South Platte Basin. Tamarack II will consist of river augmentation facilities identical to those serving other phases, but unlike Phase I or III operations, Tamarack II addresses Colorado's "future depletions" requirement strictly within a Colorado legal framework that does not include river flow conditions at Grand Island. Recharge pumps will be switched on and off according to the dictates of the Colorado appropriation doctrine and those of the Nebraska-Colorado Compact. Environmentalists have been generally pleased with the Phase II concept because groundwater recharge costs send a price signal back to wa-ter suppliers that reflects something of the cost of the depletions they place on the river in their quest to serve economic growth.

Phase III. The 10,000-acre-foot/year average for Phase I was agreed to as part of the negotiations that took place between 1994 and 1997, and that commitment was built into the 1997 Cooperative Agreement. But that agreement had only worked out the means to produce a total of 80,000 acre feet/year; it had been agreed that something in the range of 130,000–150,000 acre feet of target flow shortage reduction would be required to build a reasonable and prudent alternative acceptable to the USFWS. Phase III of Tamarack was conceived as the method to produce Colorado's proposed share of the 50,000- to 70,000-acre-foot/year difference—specifi-cally, a commitment to re-time an average of 17,000 acre feet/year during the first program increment. Phase III would consist of additional recharge at Tamarack, other public land sites (for example, Pony Express), and other private land–state program partnerships along the Lower South Platte River.

All of this was about finding a path to a solution for Colorado South Platte water user communities that would keep the 1923 compact intact, preserve the firewall, avoid the rush of permit-hungry Front Range water users to dry up lower river agriculture and town trade centers, and keep the effort close to the border to minimize the technical and legal problems associated with ensuring that gravity would pull obligated flows to Nebraska.

Nebraska's Interests

The buildup of return flows that sustained successively lower-elevation irrigation canals on Colorado's South Platte and Wyoming's North Platte were longer in coming to western Nebraska, and they were more modest in quantity.
Many Nebraska farmers therefore moved away from their dry-land beginnings
to irrigation by groundwater as soon as possible. By the mid-twentieth century,
Nebraska agriculture relied far more on groundwater pumping than on surface
diversions of river flows into canals.

The big house of Nebraska irrigation therefore raised two offspring—a minority of canal water users and a large majority of well owners who historically felt no responsibility for any negative impacts to surface water supplies.
Surface water users, virtually all of whom would be senior to groundwater users
in a unified priority system, had an inherent interest in the hydraulic connection
between surface water availability and groundwater withdrawals not shared by
well owners with no dependence on canal deliveries. This difference in interest,
and its implications for the proposed Platte River Habitat Recovery Program,
accounted for much of the Nebraska story.

THE BIG HOUSE DIVIDED AGAINST ITSELF

Given that irrigation is concentrated in the more arid two-thirds of the state
west of the 98th meridian and given the fact that the Platte drains the greatest area in the state, it is not surprising that the largest number of agricultural
groundwater wells is found on land overlying aquifers tributary to the Platte.

As of 1997, there were 78,373 registered groundwater wells in the state, with the greatest concentration situated along the Platte in western and central Nebraska. By 2005 that number had grown by almost 13,000, to 91,328 (Official Nebraska Government Website 2006: 1). By 1990 the ratio of acres irrigated by agricultural wells to area irrigated by surface water canals was about seven to one (Dreeszen 1993). Irrigated agriculture accounted for about 94 percent of groundwater withdrawal, with towns, cities, livestock watering, and industry accounting for the remainder. Eighty-two percent of Nebraska's population has been estimated to be dependent on groundwater wells, in varying degrees (Dreeszen 1993).

In many places in western Kansas, Oklahoma, and Texas, the individually rational race to pump the insufficiently organized groundwater commons (which thereby became collectively irrational) has meant that the Ogallala aquifer has been drawn down to levels such that irrigators in many places can no longer economically pump it (*Platte River Odyssey* 2006: 12). But Nebraska sits on about two-thirds of the massive Ogallala underground reservoir, perhaps the world's largest confined aquifer. Nebraskans are fond of pointing out that it has been estimated that if all the groundwater were elevated to the surface, they would be swimming in roughly thirty-three feet of water from border to border. No state west of the Mississippi has as much water. An estimated 2 billion acre feet of usable water stored in Nebraska's groundwater mounds has built up through a combination of rainfall, river seepage, losses from leaky irrigation supply canals and reservoirs, and field runoff. This quantity amounts to 700 times as much as that stored in all surface reservoirs in the state (Bleed 1993). Compared to other states in the arid West, Nebraska is the Saudi Arabia of groundwater.

Given a history of easy and open access to the groundwater resource, Nebraska groundwater law has been notoriously underdeveloped because resource abundance postponed user conflicts that spur legislative and judicial action (Aiken 1980: 919). For most of the state's history, Nebraska water leaders in groundwater-dominated irrigated areas had little incentive to address any depletions to surface flows or to each other because (1) there was so much groundwater in so many places, (2) groundwater users were so politically dominant that surface water user challenges appeared futile, and (3) leaders in Kansas were thinking about bringing a lawsuit against Nebraska regarding the Republican River, asserting that Nebraska well users were depleting water promised to Kansas under an interstate compact. If Nebraska formally declared a connection between groundwater and surface water, the explicit admission could give Kansas an advantage in any legal proceeding. For years Nebraska just wanted the groundwater–surface water issue to stay out of sight.

The split in interests between groundwater and surface water users has historically been so deep that it has been reflected in two distinctly different systems of water administration.

1. The Nebraska Department of Natural Resources, headquartered in Lincoln, administers all surface flows in accordance with Nebraska's doctrine of prior appropriation. Surface water exploitation, beginning in the 1860s, produced that doctrine for Nebraska, for the same reasons it was adopted in other arid states in the West. Those who had sacrificed much to divert water and build their communities did not want to be placed in jeopardy by latecomers who opportunistically took water upstream and thereby destroyed the investment made by those first in time. For several decades during the late nineteenth and early twentieth centuries, surface water users were the only significant players in Nebraska water. The Central Nebraska Public Power and Irrigation District (CNPPID, or Central), to take one example, designed its facilities in the 1930s prior to the innovation and diffusion of the high-capacity turbine pump and center-pivot irrigation technology, which could irrigate rougher land surfaces than more traditional furrow irrigation and thereby spread water over areas never contemplated for irrigation with the older technology. Central's design engineers computed water availability in Platte surface flows without taking into account a future with thousands of high-capacity wells sucking from aquifers hydraulically connected to the Platte.

2. With the emergence of new groundwater technologies in the 1930s that dispersed rapidly across the countryside after World War II, groundwater irrigation went through a phenomenal period of growth that soon dwarfed the acreage served by surface methods. Well users were latecomers on the scene; in any system of integrated priorities between the two sources of supply, well users would thus be clearly junior. In their view, therefore, it was critical that they succeed in operating independent of the prior appropriation doctrine. Given the abundance of Nebraska groundwater and the fact that they held a large majority status among irrigators, well users were able to do just that.

In 1969 the Nebraska unicameral legislature passed a bill reorganizing 150 single-purpose water districts into 24 multipurpose Natural Resource Districts (NRDs). NRDs were designed to address a wide range of issues—for example, soil and water conservation, flood and erosion control, drainage, pollution control, wildlife habitat management, recreation, forest and range management, and water supply (Gaul 1993; Longo and Miewald 1989; Stephenson 1994). NRDs are local units of government generally organized along river basin lines, financed by district property taxes, and governed by locally elected boards that employ a full-time manager and staff to do the daily work. In 1975 the Groundwater Management Act authorized NRDs to form groundwater control areas. In 1982 NRDs received legislative sanction to develop groundwater management plans if local interests saw the need for them.

By 1991 three groundwater control areas had been created in areas with declining water tables. The major problem in all this is that NRDs may have had the potential to limit well drilling. There was no incentive to constrain private appetites for withdrawing groundwater. In addition, NRDs have historically operated independent of state appropriation doctrine. Groundwater interests ensured that NRD boards of directors would be dominated by their representatives, who were careful to protect the dual system of water management—prior appropriation for surface waters and the correlative rights doctrine (share and share alike) for groundwater. In groundwater matters the state was largely confined to well registration and data collection. Until the passage of legislation in April 2004 (Legislative Bill 962) that preserved the dual management system but imposed constraints on groundwater uses, NRDs were not required to follow any state-imposed decision rule(s) that would lead to integration of groundwater and surface water management. The passage of new state legislation in 2004 was viewed as a landmark in Nebraska's struggle to integrate groundwater administration within a legal framework that over time, it is hoped, will protect well owner from well owner, the supplies of surface water diverters from exploitation by well owners, and Nebraska's Platte River system itself.

THE GROUNDWATER DEPLETIONS ISSUE GAINS FOCUS

Central was critical to getting discourse started in Nebraska regarding the connections between groundwater and surface water. The CNPPID was in the federal nexus and needed Federal Energy Regulatory Commission (FERC) licenses. To this end, Central could only satisfy FERC and the U.S. Fish and Wildlife Service (USFWS) by addressing the issue of groundwater depletions to Platte in-stream flows. Central was a major surface water supplier to agricultural users and needed to be concerned about depletions to those senior rights by junior wells, especially wells imposing depletions above Lake McConaughy. Central also had allies in the cities, the water managers of which knew they were dependent on protecting appropriate levels in the groundwater mound and were generally in favor of limiting wells—especially upstream of their areas.

A complex interaction exists between the Platte's surface flows and its numerous groundwater mounds. What is clear to all observers is that the CNPPID surface delivery systems operate in a manner highly interdependent with groundwater. Central's operations are testimony to Nebraskans' deep understanding of the interrelationship between surface and groundwater (Bleed 1993; Diffendal 1993). Yet that which was clearly understood as established fact for decades was not to be accepted as a matter of law, social organization, or management of the two types of water assets—at least up to 2004.

The large water mound created by the complex of Nebraska Public Power District (NPPD) and CNPPID canal and storage facilities produced an unplanned surface-groundwater conjunctive use system that nobody foresaw when Central facilities were still on the drawing board (*Platte River Odyssey* 2006: 19). The Central Nebraska Public Power and Irrigation District service area and downstream from that area were places in Nebraska where many water users employed both water sources, where surface water users had organizational control and wanted to ensure that junior well pumping did not injure senior surface rights. Here was a place that would support reform of Nebraska water law in a manner that would incorporate groundwater rights into Nebraska's doctrine of prior appropriation. Here was support for carrying on the difficult discussion the state had postponed: how to integrate groundwater into the surface water agenda to protect senior surface rights.

One of CNPPID's strategic goals was to protect senior surface flows from the depredations of what should have been junior well owners. The surface-groundwater fight had been brewing for years. Nebraska had a major problem to confront within its legal and administrative house, and that problem was looming larger even if the federal Endangered Species Act (ESA) habitat recovery agenda went away.

ENTER FEDERAL AGENDAS

Central and the NPPD spent over $30 million between 1984 and 1998 dealing with FERC re-licensing issues under the Endangered Species Act. By 1994, after the governors of the three basin states had signed the agreement to work with the Department of the Interior, the FERC discussions at Kingsley Dam and Lake McConaughy became clearly tied to the Platte River Habitat Recovery Program. After an additional three years of talks within the three-state framework, the USFWS issued a jeopardy biological opinion on July 25, 1997, regarding the negative impacts of the two Nebraska districts' facilities and operations on the listed species. The agency put forth in that same document a route to obtain a satisfactory "reasonable and prudent alternative." Re-licensing would rely on implementation of the Cooperative Agreement signed by the three state governors and the secretary of the interior just weeks earlier, on July 1.

If negotiations for a basin-wide solution failed, the two districts were put on notice that they would have to return to individual consultations under Section 7 of the ESA and reinitiate the re-licensing process. This was a powerful incentive to make the recovery program negotiations succeed.

When it came to defending surface water priorities, Central found allies in the western Nebraska panhandle North Platte irrigation districts, including Pathfinder, Gering–Fort Laramie, Mitchell, and Enterprise. Those irrigators had good reasons to fear what might happen to their Wyoming sources of supply in a formal ESA Section 7 consultation. The districts operated under the terms of contracts with the U.S. Bureau of Reclamation (USBR). Across the West, the USBR was careful never to guarantee a specific quantity of water delivery. Quantities could be adjusted according to the dictates of weather, levels of impounded supply, or for any other compelling reason—including changes in the administration of federal law that could potentially be imposed as outcomes of

ESA Section 7 consultations. It would be much better to voluntarily negotiate a cooperative habitat recovery program as a route to regulatory certainty. The districts were also vulnerable to unconstrained groundwater depletions of their canal supplies.

The 1994 governors' Memorandum of Agreement, which cast a vision of the new world to be negotiated by 1997, had two appealing features. First, the concept of "adaptive management" promised a partnership arrangement among local users, state authorities, and federal agencies within which new information and options could be incorporated in ways that would reward local knowledge, initiative, and creativity. Second, the agreement made it clear that there would be allowance for future growth in water use as long as any new depletions to flows protected by the program were offset. This was exactly what Central and other surface users had been angling for over the years with regard to the state's internal surface water–groundwater problem. No local water leader wanted to be caught saying anything "too nice" about federal environmental agendas, but this requirement of an environmental agenda suited Central and other surface water users.

A Central annual report (CNPPID 1995: 5) noted that, under pressure from the ESA, Nebraska was moving toward some form of integrated management of surface and groundwater, at least in terms of general policy. ESA considerations were driving Nebraska to undertake extensive groundwater investigations and modeling activities (Cooperative Hydrological Study, or COHYST). Municipalities with multi-million-dollar investments were heavily dependent for their supplies on recharge from surface water, which was in danger of being intercepted by new well installations and increased pumping. Central was a major player on the Nebraska stage, it had allies in the panhandle districts and cities, and it wanted federal permits.

The convergence of Central's long-standing concern with having well owners offset their depletions along with the federal need to address the same issue ensured that two difficult discussions would occur simultaneously:

1. In a state with two separate water administrations, how could groundwater administration be integrated into the surface water agenda to protect surface senior rights?

2. How could the state of Nebraska confront the federal ESA agenda, which meant finding water to offset a history of depletions (before and after the 1997 Cooperative Agreement) to the critical stretch of the central Platte to which the listed species were linked?

THE LOOMING DECISION

The vast majority of well owners did not appreciate falling into the embrace of any discussion that was going to "pick their pockets" so that the two districts—

the CNPPID and the NPPD—could secure federal permits. Two Nebraska governors—Mike Johanns and Dave Heineman—saw the mounting political problem. To gird himself, Johanns (who left the governorship in January 2005 to serve as secretary of agriculture in George W. Bush's administration) appointed a twenty-three-member Citizen Advisory Committee representing a variety of agricultural water interests. They included representatives of irrigation districts and NRDs, center-pivot sprinkler irrigation equipment manufacturers, agricultural businesspeople, groundwater users, and surface right appropriators. Some were involved in the Platte Basin habitat recovery negotiations; others were not. Generally meeting about every other month to review the Platte habitat recovery negotiation effort, they were charged with making a recommendation to the governor in a "yes/no" format as to whether he should endorse the Platte River Habitat Recovery Program. After assuming office, Dave Heineman, formerly the lieutenant governor, kept the advisory committee intact. In the years leading up to the actual decision in November 2006, no one close to the negotiations in Nebraska could predict what the council's recommendation would be or what the governor would do with it. That would be the case right up to the eve of the decision. Amid this political murkiness, it is safe to say that Nebraska Platte River Habitat Recovery Program negotiators kept in mind the advisory committee, the constituencies represented within it, and the governor's political problem as they confronted a deeply divided Nebraska house of water.

NEGOTIATING THEMES: CHALLENGE COLORADO ON THE SOUTH PLATTE

In each of the three Platte Basin states, the problems of reorganizing water for the endangered species recovery program were much more political than technical. Water could be re-timed by various means; the greater problem was how to formulate a negotiating strategy that would build a coalition of support. In Colorado, in putting together the Tamarack Plan, local users had to weave together Upper and Lower South Platte interests. In Wyoming, state authorities built a coalition around the restoration of reservoir capacity at Pathfinder, dam safety, and how to address selenium in the Kendrick Project. In Nebraska, given the divided house of irrigation, what plan would win support across the countryside, within the state's unicameral legislative assembly, and among members of the governor's Citizen Advisory Committee?

As residents of a downstream state, Nebraskans have always looked upriver with anxiety about future flows. Nebraska interests had vigorously opposed the Grayrocks and Deer Creek projects in Wyoming. The lawsuit the state filed against Wyoming in 1986 attacking expanded use of North Platte waters had, in the 2001 settlement, turned out about as well as could have been hoped by effectively preventing any future net increases in Wyoming consumptive uses (see Chapter 11). Although Nebraska negotiators could not then foresee how *Nebraska v. Wyoming* would be resolved, they knew they were making an all-out effort against Wyoming on the North Platte and that they would have to go after Colorado on the South Platte where, over the years, Nebraska had clearly opposed Colorado's Narrows and Two Forks proposals.

To the extent that their depletions reduce flows to a volume of less than 120 cubic feet per second (cfs) at the Nebraska state line from April 1 to October 15 in any given year, Colorado water users below the Balzac/Cooper gauge with priorities junior to June 14, 1997, must curtail their diversions. But water in excess of compact minimums is always welcome, and it had even been expected, given that the river has been historically "gaining." Neither Nebraskan nor Colorado framers of the 1923 compact could foresee the future extensive well depletions that would send summer flows at the Julesburg gauge too close to and even below the 120 cfs minimum. Nor did their crystal balls permit them to foresee the incredible growth of Colorado Front Range cities' water demands, which would threaten to diminish the gain in summer flows. Nor did they anticipate that urban water suppliers—especially Denver Water and Aurora in the wake of the Two Forks Dam debacle—would launch plans for water reuse projects that would recycle effluent back into the cities, thereby adding another consumptive use, and further diminish return flows. As the years passed after the compact signing, Nebraska began to see the disadvantages of its position and would seek ways to renegotiate arrangements on the river without explicitly bringing up compact matters.

Two languages would emerge in negotiations before and after 1997. Colorado used a language that emphasized fulfilling compact obligations, thereby reminding everyone that it could consumptively use all waters on its side of the border as long as compact conditions were fulfilled. For its part, Nebraska adopted the language of a "regime of the river" and thereby advanced the view that waters traditionally available in "excess" of compact minimums were open to discussion and could be divided up in the context of recovery program needs. If Colorado resisted such regime-of-the-river considerations, the state would simply have to realize that they were essential to Nebraska's participation in a recovery program. Discussions would center on the sword thrust of Nebraska's insistence that the South Platte regime of the river needed to be preserved and enhanced. Colorado would parry with its compact shield.

The essence of Nebraska's negotiating effort was to get Colorado in an embrace and then push discussions about the regime of the river and "fair share" contributions to reduce shortages to target flows in the required amount. Colorado would be determined to back away. Nebraska's gambits to preserve and enhance the regime of the river presumably played well at home, but a mostly silent Colorado water priesthood would only utter its incantation: compact, compact, compact; Tamarack, Tamarack, Tamarack.

Nebraska sword thrust: Tamarack is not "new" water; it is simply what Nebraska is going to receive anyway from Colorado and is just re-timed from fall and winter to spring and summer. Colorado should dry up some existing consumptive uses—irrigated agriculture would be a prime target—and allow the water saved to flow by gravity downstream to Nebraska. Doing so would establish that Colorado was serious about the proposed recovery program, that Colorado users were prepared to make sacrifices as Nebraska's citizens were being asked to do. In addition, it would preserve the regime of the river (sustaining or increasing the level of flow excess to the compact) to serve the habitat recovery program.

Colorado parry: the compact preserved Colorado's right to its consumptive use, and there was no need to dry up anything. Forced dry up on behalf of the recovery program would simply amount to a betrayal of the compact. The South Platte is a gaining stream, and Tamarack re-timing simply shifts a small fraction of that historical gain so it reappears at the right time—during the spring, summer, and fall months—for recovery of the critical habitat. All water is "old" water in the sense that it has been used and reused several times before it hits the border, but Tamarack water is "new" in a meaningful sense because it appears as added flow when needed for listed species habitat.

Nebraska sword thrust: let us see some real diversity in Colorado's project options. Let there be a systematic comparative analysis of several possibilities for producing program water. Let us show Nebraskans who are asked to endure pain to make the recovery program work that Colorado users are also willing to consider making a real sacrifice by creating a wide scan of water supply options. If careful analysis of all other options establishes them as inferior to Tamarack and if Nebraska can be party to evaluating those options, then Nebraska will feel comfortable explaining that fact to its water constituencies, particularly the governor's Citizen Advisory Committee. For example, Colorado has an opportunity to produce significant water at Beebe Draw, a shallow alluvial aquifer located between Barr Lake and Milton Reservoir east of Fort Lupton and Brighton. It could be a groundwater recharge project similar in principle to the one at Tamarack, with high-capacity wells pumped to deliver water back to the South Platte when shortages to target flows exist at Grand Island. Beebe Draw is a possibility that should be the subject of inspection and in-depth analysis.

Colorado parry: putting Beebe Draw on the negotiating table is tantamount to flirting with the possibility that Nebraska (and federal agencies) would have an interest in a recovery program project activity upstream of the compacted firewall at the Balzac gauge. Colorado will not engage in a serious discussion of Beebe Draw (subtext: or any other option upstream of the compact firewall). Colorado will do nothing that will permit Nebraska to trespass beyond that line, mutually agreed to in 1923.

Nebraska sword thrust: if Colorado really wants a partnership with Nebraska in an effort to make a basin-wide recovery program successful, Colorado must be responsive to Nebraska's need to preserve the historical regime of the river. The compact was not written to address ESA recovery program issues that are entirely independent of the compact. The price of Nebraska's participation in a collaborative recovery program is protecting the regime of the river. Colorado should not stand rigidly and mutely behind the compact but instead should reach out and work creatively and collaboratively with Nebraska.

Colorado parry: while Colorado agriculture is declining along the South Platte as a result of rapid industrialization and urbanization along the Front Range, a groundwater-fed irrigated agriculture continues to expand in Nebraska. Nebraska is less concerned with recovery of species habitat and more intent upon enlarging flows of South Platte water so the state can continue its history of not replacing its well depletions. Colorado will not renegotiate the compact as the price of having a habitat recovery program, and it is not interested in bailing out Nebraska well owners who must confront the costs they have imposed on each other, surface users, and the river.

Nebraska sword thrust: Colorado should apply for a Nebraska water right to convey Tamarack water downstream to critical habitat. Colorado's Tamarack contribution cannot flow "unprotected" and must be registered by the proper authorities in the Nebraska Department of Natural Resources. Technically, Nebraska could assign that right to the U.S. Department of the Interior (DOI) if the federal agency were to apply. However, such a move would be a public relations nightmare, as Nebraskans of all stripes would protest vehemently if any water right fell into the hands of a federal agency. One of the two districts (CNPPID and NPPD) could hold the right to Tamarack flows, but from a Nebraska perspective it would be much cleaner if Colorado held a Nebraska right to conduct its contribution to the program.

Colorado parry: Colorado will not apply for any water right in Nebraska. It is Nebraska's responsibility, by whatever means, to usher Tamarack flows to critical habitat. Nebraska's invitation to Colorado is little more than a thinly disguised subterfuge to get Colorado in its grasp on Nebraska turf and force a review of virtually every aspect of Colorado's water contribution. Colorado has nothing to gain from mounting a defense of its water contribution in unfriendly territory.

Nebraska sword thrust: a "fair share" solution is needed that reflects, at least roughly, state user depletions in the basin. In the domain of money for constructing the first phase of the program's water supply projects (producing an annual average of 80,000 acre feet) agreed to at McConaughy, Pathfinder, and Tamarack in 1997, it was stipulated that the states' share of the cost should be divided on a 40/40/20 basis. Nebraska and Colorado agreed to pay 40 percent each, while Wyoming will contribute 20 percent. Now that we are discussing how to get the balance of required water needed to achieve the full 130,000- to 150,000-acre-foot annual average reduction to target flows, something approximating that same split should be employed. To reach a 40 percent contribution, Colorado must produce much more water than it has offered at Tamarack. Nebraska understands that the closer the water source is to the critical habitat, the easier it is to arrange to deliver program water. There will be less conveyance loss, fewer negative third-party impacts, easier measurement of flows, and smoother administration of water rights. Even though all of this holds true, Nebraska citizens will not allow the state to give away their consumptive use rights too disproportionately. Wyoming's efforts are much more proportionate to the entirety of the program than are those of Colorado. Colorado must supply more water.

Colorado parry: Colorado users will divert from the South Platte according to their appropriation doctrine and compact entitlement. Tamarack water that is "new" will be available at the border; Nebraska can deal with it on its way to the critical habitat. Nebraska's call for a 40 percent water share from Colorado is nothing less than a call for a major renegotiation of the 1923 compact—a division of the waters accepted by both state legislatures, signed by the respective state governors, and endorsed by the U.S. Congress. Nebraska is treading on dangerous territory if it continues to insist that Colorado abandon that agreement and revise its obligation upward. Furthermore, compact issues aside, Colorado has not done the damage to basin flows—especially to pulse flows and sediment movement—that the dams and diversions of Wyoming's and Nebraska's North Platte have imposed. The South Platte is a gaining river that produces greater supplies than were available historically (although Nebraska has seriously questioned this assertion); most of all, the absence of on-stream storage below Denver has meant that the South Platte contributes virtually all of the natural flood pulses and sediment for sandbar building. Any fair share calculations in terms of costs imposed on critical habitat must reflect that Colorado's imposed damages are far lower than those of the other two states, which together "broke their river." Colorado did not "break" its river.

Nebraska sword thrust: in negotiating the conditions of FERC re-licensing of the Kingsley Dam and associated facilities, federal regulators developed an analysis of how the environmental account at Lake McConaughy would work. As they did so, the federal analysts did not take into account Nebraska-Colorado Compact considerations or constraints; nor did they incorporate the Supreme Court–endorsed settlement with Wyoming (see Chapter 11), something that became final after the Kingsley Dam re-licensing. They simply built the historical flow regimes on the South and North Platte into their calculations and employed their estimates of flow volumes in specifying CNPPID and NPPD re-operation obligations. Nebraska had little choice but to accept these USFWS-FERC–imposed conditions as a condition of re-licensing. Therefore, Nebraska has little choice but to release flows downstream in a regime mandated by the USFWS and FERC, but it must do so without full control of what is happening upstream on either the North or South Platte. About 80 percent of flows into Lake McConaughy have been return flows. The recent Nebraska-Wyoming

Supreme Court settlement did not address the issue of whether Wyoming could add winter-season consumptive uses below Guernsey Reservoir. Insofar as Wyoming places new consumptive uses on the North Platte, there will be less return to Nebraska. New consumptive uses in Colorado will also impose costs on Nebraska that must be made up by North Platte waters. Management of the North and South Platte is highly interdependent; Nebraska has been placed at risk as a result of factors under the control of Wyoming and Colorado. Loss of water on either the North or South Platte will place pressure on the other to produce compensating flows for the critical habitat, or Nebraska will have to unfairly "eat" the loss. Colorado and Wyoming must accept their share of the burden imposed by the program by not eroding the historical regime of the river with new consumptive uses.

Wyoming parry (with Colorado's endorsement): there is actually little real problem to be solved. The USFWS, in ensuring that the mandated program flow volumes reach critical habitat and in exercising its powers of review, will protect Nebraska interests. If a water user applies for a permit to place a new consumptive use in either Wyoming or Colorado, it will either be in a federal nexus or it will not. If it is in a federal relationship, it will have to seek approval for its enterprise in an ESA Section 7 consultation. The USFWS can be expected to deny any new water use that would place critical habitat in jeopardy; that would mean protecting inflows to Lake McConaughy and outflows from Colorado's South Platte. If the new user is not in a federal nexus, that user must still acquire state approval for the use under the state's future depletions plan. One way or another, that plan will provide compensating water. Such offsetting supplies will protect Nebraska. If the new consumptive use is not acceptable within the framework of that state's depletion plan, the new user will have to surmount a series of tests: (1) it would have to establish that it was not in any federal nexus and would in no way compromise flows into any of the big three recovery program re-regulation projects—specifically, the environmental accounts at Pathfinder and McConaughy and Colorado's Tamarack Plan; (2) it would have to establish that it would not injure any existing priority under the state's appropriation doctrine; and (3) it would have to establish that it would not damage any state's new depletions plan. To get by any or all of the tests, the promoter of any new consumptive use will likely have to provide offsetting water. Nebraska is in little danger of any nontrivial loss. Any minor losses will pale in comparison to what undisciplined Nebraska groundwater use imposes on the river.

WATER ACTION PLAN: PROTECTION AMID UNCERTAINTY

Nebraska's plan for contributing program water was centered on protecting all Nebraska surface and groundwater for the state's purposes to the fullest extent possible. That would be critical to any hope of securing the support of the governor's Citizen Advisory Committee and the unicameral legislature. Like other states, Nebraska has always feared losing the benefits of its waters to outsiders. Now the state was confronting a federal environmental agenda in the context of a deep intrastate conflict of interest between surface and groundwater users. Any path forward was going to require access to water. Nebraska is not likely to become a major tourist destination, as Wyoming and Colorado are; nor do Nebraskans see themselves as likely to host major high-technology or large industrial centers. Nebraska's future is heavily dependent on sustaining a viable agriculture supported by the essential service and smaller-scale industries. All this will require preserving and enhancing Nebraska water sources in general and, in particular, the great central groundwater mound.

Nebraska authorities, at least in Lincoln, were determined not to permit the "mining" of the state's groundwater—especially for federal program purposes—because that water was viewed as essential to long-term economic and ecological sustainability. Sustainable groundwater use was absolutely necessary for protecting senior surface water user rights because under the program, Nebraskans would have to offset a history of depletions caused by unconstrained groundwater exploitation. If Nebraska was to join the cooperative basin habitat recovery program, it would have to engage in well regulation and, even more important, organize means by which at least some well owners (see discussion of the depletions plan later in the chapter) could pay back—with or without assistance from the state—depletion debts to the river. Finding supplies of water to offset historical well depletions will take an as yet unknown fraction from the water mound. There were two beneficiaries to protect: (1) Nebraska surface irrigators, whose canal service has been undercut by undisciplined well depletions; and (2) the federally mandated endangered species habitat recovery program. Nebraska was willing to use water from the mound to protect the first group—Nebraskans, who have every right to expect redress under the state appropriation doctrine—but state authorities were not prepared to place any meaningful fraction of the water mound on the negotiating table for the federal endangered species agenda. But how much water would be required to offset Nebraska well depletions? Where would it be extracted? No one knew. In a highly uncertain world, it was in Nebraska's interest to proceed by protecting water everywhere, particularly in the central Platte Valley groundwater mound.

Early on, Colorado and Wyoming did what they could to have water in the central mound placed on the negotiating table. They argued for a "least-cost" approach to finding program water. Let program participants go out and find the least expensive supplies (those would be Nebraska supplies available in the central mound closest to critical habitat), then other partners could simply contribute two-thirds of the necessary cash to pay the costs of getting that least-cost water to the critical habitat. The logic was simple and compelling to anyone who thought least-cost economics should rule the world.

Negotiators in Lincoln, not about to allow federal agencies to get their hands on the mound, were in no mood to countenance such talk. Money from Wyoming and Colorado would never be equivalent to retaining full control of the mound. It would be politically disastrous for Nebraska to take on such a disproportionate share of the water burden while being bought off by Colorado and Wyoming money. Citizens representing many interests would be infuriated. Money reflects a claim on wealth; it takes wet water to produce wealth. The powers-that-be in Lincoln insisted that discussions focus on issues of fair share and the regime of the river at the borders.

Offsetting Depletions after June 30, 1997

It was one thing to agree in principle to make post-1997 well installations and new surface water projects accountable to the river for their depletions, but it was quite another to implement that plan within the context of Nebraska water politics. Nebraskans needed time to think, to plan, to build a coalition of support for a changed water regime. Authorities pursued a two-pronged approach:

1. In 1998 they initiated what was originally intended to be a three-year study of central Platte aquifers and their connections to surface water (Ring 1999). A Cooperative Hydrological Study (COHYST) was launched to provide a database for the design of Nebraska's recovery program projects, to provide policy makers with essential information, and to promote considered discussion among Nebraska's many water voices—agricultural, municipal, environmental, and industrial (see www.cohyst.nrc.state.ne.us). The objectives were to identify gaps in existing data, gather data to fill those gaps, and build a model of the Platte River and its interaction with groundwater. Many Nebraska water people knew such an effort should have been made years earlier, but there was no support for such a project until the federally mandated habitat recovery program loomed on the horizon and made it essential. It took the "crisis" of signing the 1997 agreement to get the study started.

2. Also in 1998 they announced that depletions created by well installations after July 1, 1997, up to the end of 2001 would be covered at state expense. Exactly how Nebraska would create mechanisms to offset the depletions was never clarified. After all, the NRDs had statutory responsibility for groundwater management, and it was not clear that leaders and memberships at that level were going to support any depletions program that had, at that point, not been thoroughly discussed and that many opposed ideologically. It soon became apparent that groundwater users' determination to expand their usage with added wells was creating a runaway train that could not be politically controlled by the end of 2001. Stepping back in the face of energetic well user opposition to control, at the January 2001 Governance Committee meeting, state authorities announced that they had extended the

time period for state coverage of new well depletions to December 31, 2003 (later extended to December 31, 2005). If an existing or new groundwater user could not, after years of notice, get the necessary additional straws in the ground before January 1, 2004 (later, January 1, 2006), they would be responsible for their own depletions.

The state of Nebraska's willingness to promise use of the public purse to supply offsetting water for depletions of wells installed after the 1997 Cooperative Agreement represented a considerable gift (side payment) to groundwater users. The repeated extension of deadlines was testimony to the political power of the groundwater lobby.

Offsetting Historical Depletions Prior to July 1, 1997

With an eye to protecting its central groundwater mound as much as possible, Nebraska pieced together its contribution to the three-state effort to secure an additional 50,000- to 70,000-acre-feet annual average reduction in the shortage to USFWS target flows required to supplement the original 80,000 acre feet identified by June 1997 (see Table 12.1).

The CNPPID operates several reservoirs that would function as surface equivalents of Colorado's Tamarack. They would capture water at times of excess flows in the river and hold it until needed for release back to the river for program purposes. (For a discussion of all Nebraska water projects, see Boyle Engineering Corporation 2000.)

Another water re-timing effort was planned for the Dawson and Gothenburg canals, located on the north side of the Platte River. The idea was to divert surface water directly from the Platte River into these canals during the non–irrigation seasons and then allow it to seep into the aquifer storage. During the irrigation season an equivalent amount would be available for irrigation pumping. That would mean saving water not released from Lake McConaughy, which, in turn, could be directed to habitat recovery program objectives.

Additional program water could be found through water leasing. The plan would rely on economic incentives to farmers who would annually lease to the Platte River Habitat Recovery Program their reservoir water allotments that would otherwise be used for irrigation. The consumptive use portion of the saved water would be stored in Lake McConaughy for release in ways that would serve program needs, especially at times of shortage in the critical habitat.

Nebraska also planned to employ program funds to create incentives that would encourage farmers to adopt practices of conservation cropping, deficit irrigation, leaving land fallow, and improving on-farm water delivery and field application efficiency. The general idea was that farmers with irrigation water stored in Lake McConaughy would be paid to reduce their water demand. These reductions in consumptive use would be saved in the lake and released when required. Conservation cropping also meant a shift from more to fewer water-intensive crops. Deficit irrigation would mean that a given farmer, in exchange for a payment from the program, would cut back a fraction of the water he or she used. A reduction of, say, six inches/acre/year could cumulate to significant amounts of water remaining in McConaughy storage for the program. Some farmers may decide to leave their land fallow in exchange for a payment. Finally, there are areas where irrigation water applications generate return flows in patterns that do not return to the river at all, that produce returns to areas of already troublesomely high water tables, or that generate return flows below critical habitat. In these cases and where the irrigation is occurring near the critical habitat, Nebraska authorities will initiate voluntary programs to increase canal delivery and field application efficiency. The water saved will be made available to the habitat recovery program.

The state of Nebraska has selected areas of high groundwater tables that it wishes to explore for their potential to supply water to future depletions plans. Authorities want to ensure that no "mining" of the groundwater (no net loss) will occur, and they wish to study matters carefully. Nebraska will reserve the yields of these exploratory groundwater management areas (under the Phelps County Canal system, the Reynold's and Robb Wetland, and other areas in Phelps and Kearney counties) for its own depletions offset program.

Finally, Nebraska plans to have a fraction of water it makes available to the program come from power interference arrangements at Kingsley Dam and several smaller hydroelectric plants located downstream on Central's canals. This will entail making a cash payment to the electricity producer sufficient to change the pattern of water releases through turbines. There are at least two possibilities: (1) bypass water around the turbines to get it started on a path to critical habitat when generators have no need for it (2) change the timing of the generation such that electric current is produced at a time when it has less value on the grid. In general, at times of excess flow at the critical habitat, Central and NPPD would be compensated for holding back electricity production.

SUMMARY

In sum, Nebraska's Platte River Habitat Recovery Program negotiation team did its work within a deeply troubled Nebraska house of water administration. To implement the ESA, federal authorities were pushing for re-timed Platte flows, discussion of which necessarily became entangled in Nebraska's long-brewing in-house surface water–groundwater struggle. Either issue in itself was challenging. In the midst of these interrelated discourses, Nebraska authorities were able to put together an outline of proposed water re-regulation actions designed to offset historical and "new" depletions. Their efforts were sufficient to maintain the basin-wide talks with federal authorities and Nebraska's upstream state neighbors. The state thereby secured annual relief from the jeopardy biological opinions. But either the externally imposed Platte habitat recovery issues or the ongoing internal discourse regarding integration of surface and well water could potentially blow up and take Nebraska out of the basin-wide Cooperative Agreement talks. Nebraska's capacity to deliver solutions was in question until the last moments of the 1997–2006 negotiations.

Wyoming's Interests

LOW-HANGING MOUNTAIN FRUIT

A federal agency, the U.S. Fish and Wildlife Service (USFWS), was on the prowl for 417,000 acre feet per year with which to fulfill its central Platte River target flow aspirations in Nebraska. Another federal agency, the U.S. Bureau of Reclamation (USBR), held potentially available water in its string of Wyoming North Platte River reservoirs—Seminoe, Kortes, Pathfinder, Alcova, Glendo, and Guernsey. The obvious juxtaposition of water demand for a new federal environmental agenda and a potential federal supply for that agenda deeply worried state water providers.

Furthermore, Wyoming water interests wished to pursue a modification of Pathfinder Dam that would restore storage capacity lost to years of sedimentation. The plan to raise the elevation at Pathfinder Dam promised to reclaim 54,000 acre feet of capacity, an amount permitted under the facility's 1904 water right. Given that the Deer Creek option had been stifled, the Pathfinder modification was the most realistic and cost-effective course of action that could be devised to serve economic growth agendas in several North Platte River communities, especially in the Casper area.

CONSULTATION CONTEXT

The USBR began informal consultations with the USFWS regarding the Wyoming and Nebraska North Platte projects in 1989 (Record of Decision 2006).

Beginning in 1994, when the three state governors and the Department of the Interior agreed to negotiate a comprehensive basin-wide habitat recovery plan, the focus of the informal USFWS-USBR consultations was on negotiating the terms and conditions of the voluntary Cooperative Agreement, the deal everyone was counting on to eventually produce the Platte River Habitat Recovery Program. However, if the negotiations collapsed or if any subsequent program increment fell apart, Wyoming's North Platte federally funded water facilities would be reexamined in light of the Endangered Species Act (ESA). The water users proceeded to appropriate their water from federal facilities under Wyoming's appropriation law, but they operated from year to year within the shadow of the ESA hammer.

In Wyoming, agricultural users put water to highly consumptive uses in a system with high elevations, comparatively short growing seasons, a small agricultural economy in the regional perspective, and large water storage projects. In the words of one well-informed observer, "We are indeed low-hanging fruit." The implication was clear: Wyoming and western Nebraska irrigators who worked under USBR contracts had better get together and push for a cooperative basin-wide ESA listed species habitat recovery program. To do anything less was to invite much greater loss of yields from their precious federally constructed and managed water storage projects than the amount they could expect to lose under individual ESA Section 7 consultations.

Some strategists in the environmental community, noting Wyoming's potential squeeze, contemplated staying away from program negotiations with the thought that without a viable program, Wyoming's reservoirs could be a source of much more water for environmental purposes than the amount any foreseeable voluntary recovery program would extract. However, any such prospects for major shifts in water use would be intensely and expensively conflictive and, in all probability, could not materialize for more than a lifetime, perhaps several lifetimes. Therefore, more pragmatic environmental leaders advocated working with Wyoming at the negotiating table.

Wyoming's situation under a viable proposed voluntary habitat recovery program could be expected to be a "good deal" compared with virtually anything that could be expected if no such program existed. Given these realities, Wyoming representatives proved to be the most steadfast among the state delegations in finding ways to solve problems that came up during years of difficult negotiations. A small group of senior leaders had put together a vision of what Wyoming could do; they knew well before 1997 the direction they needed to take with any cooperative basin-wide program; they worked with their constituencies in consistent ways, and they were relentless in their attempts to keep the negotiations moving forward at moments when the future of the talks was most in doubt. But they would have to surmount tribulations, especially a legal challenge from Nebraska.

NEBRASKA V. WYOMING

In 1986, in the context of the Deer Creek struggle, Nebraska authorities filed a lawsuit against Wyoming in the U.S. Supreme Court, alleging that Wyoming was wrongly capturing flows from tributaries to the North Platte in violation of an original 1945 decree (*Nebraska v. Wyoming,* 483 U.S. 1002 [1987]) (Olpin 2001). In that litigation, Wyoming's ambition to secure more storage at Deer Creek was merely one of several points of contention. Challenged by both the USFWS and Nebraska, Wyoming agreed to trade away its prospects for Deer Creek permits in return for Nebraska and USFWS acceptance of a modification of Pathfinder Dam accompanied by the installation of an environmental water account at Pathfinder Reservoir.

Nebraska v. Wyoming dragged on until early 2001 and posed problems for Platte River recovery negotiations. Open discourse was difficult; sharing data was a risky proposition for both adversaries. Negotiators working on behalf of each state found themselves in a difficult position with their respective state legislators. On the one hand, they had to go hat in hand seeking financing to prepare their legal cases. On the other hand, they had to simultaneously ask those same legislators for money to fund a Cooperative Agreement that would require holding hands not only with the federal agencies and their environmental agenda but also with their adversary—all without knowing the eventual Cooperative Agreement's impact on the lawsuit or the lawsuit's meaning regarding the eventual 1997 collaborative understanding. It was all extremely awkward. How could either party make commitments to the recovery program without understanding the final outcome of the interstate legal battle?

In 1934, in the context of the Great Depression and severe drought on the high plains, Wyoming water users held back as much water as possible in the state's reservoirs and thereby earned the enmity of downstream Nebraska irrigators. Wyoming was also at work on its Kendrick Project, which would create new storage for North Platte water behind Seminoe Dam. The very concept of such a project worried Nebraska authorities. The case went to the U.S. Supreme Court in 1934 but was not decided until 1945 (*Nebraska v. Wyoming,* 325 U.S. 589, 671 [1945]; modified 345 U.S. 981 [1953]) (Rundquist 1993; Weiss and Montgomery 1999). The court ruled that Wyoming should allow 75 percent of the natural flow on the lower section of the river to go to Nebraska during the irrigation season but did not address usage along the tributaries in Wyoming; nor did it satisfactorily address issues pertaining to what became an increase in groundwater exploitation. In the decades that followed, Wyoming water users installed water facilities on tributaries to the main stem, proposed building water catchments at Deer Creek and Grayrocks, and spurred the growth of hundreds of wells upstream of the Nebraska border. All of this, in Nebraska's view, either interfered or threatened to interfere with the 1945 adjudicated split. For Nebraska water providers, the 1945 Supreme Court decision could not stand; it would have to be reopened.

129

At the extremes, Nebraska contended that its 1945 apportionment froze Wyoming's depletions at their 1945 levels. Wyoming countered that its users could add new depletions at will as long as the express injunctions in the 1945 decree were not transgressed. But neither adversary could long contend for the extremes, and they began to find a middle ground. The case was argued in subtle and multifaceted ways that will not be traced here. A glimmer of insight into the challenges for each side can be gained by noting that after years of expensive pre-trial maneuvering, when Nebraska's team made a discovery trip to Wyoming in April 1999, Wyoming produced and sent its adversary over 1 million pieces of material. Then, after fifteen years of litigation that cost each of the two states more than $20 million, in March 2001 the parties agreed to an out-of-court settlement. Peace was made literally on the courthouse steps in Pasadena, California, on the day the case was to go to trial. The following November, the U.S. Supreme Court approved the deal, which reflected the recommendations of the Court-appointed special master (Olpin 2001).

Fundamentally, the agreement specified that Wyoming must administer its water rights in accordance with the basic 1945 decree but with modifications that included additional enforcement provisions. Nebraska had asked Wyoming to cut back its North Platte River water users to 1930 levels and to pay Nebraska $100 million in damages. Under terms of the 300-plus-page settlement, however, no Wyoming users were cut off (although some uses were curtailed), and the state was not obligated to pay anything. However, the states agreed to form a North Platte Decree Committee made up of water officials from the USBR, Nebraska, Wyoming, and Colorado (the latter two were Platte River headwater states). This unit has served as a conflict management forum. Nebraska obtained greater certainty that Wyoming would administer North Platte rights in accordance with the 1945 decree. Nebraska accepted the reality that Grayrocks Dam and Reservoir had been completed on the Laramie River and endorsed the proposed restoration of storage capacity at Pathfinder to serve endangered species in Nebraska, the city of Casper, and other Wyoming North Platte communities. Wyoming accepted the fact that its plans for Deer Creek had been stopped. Since Wyoming had protected its existing users and Nebraska had received clarification of its rights to North Platte water in a way that effectively capped any new Wyoming summer-season water uses, each side claimed victory.

DEFENSE THROUGH PATHFINDER RESTORATION

Pathfinder Dam and Reservoir stands at the center of Wyoming's contribution to the Platte River Habitat Recovery Program (Boyle Engineering Corporation 2000). Completed in 1909 and served by a 1904 water right, it is located about 47 miles southwest of Casper on the North Platte, just below the mouth of the Sweetwater River. In the years leading up to the signing of the 1997 Cooperative

Agreement and incorporated in that deal, Wyoming proposed restoring 54,000 acre feet of storage capacity lost to years of sedimentation. Of that amount, 34,000 acre feet of the restored storage capacity would be dedicated to an environmental account serving the needs of the habitat recovery program. The program environmental account manager, operating at Nebraska's Lake McConaughy, would be provided with a known quantity of water upon which to call in upstream Wyoming (see Table 12.1). The anticipated yield from the Pathfinder environmental account at the critical habitat in Nebraska was estimated to be about 26,000 acre feet. Pathfinder's water, with its 1904 priority, can be handily moved by USBR managers—directly or by exchange—to any of the major North Platte River reservoirs (such as Seminoe, Glendo, and Guernsey in Wyoming and Lakes Minatare and Alice in Nebraska). Much intra–North Platte water basin trading has always taken place on behalf of agriculture; now that the basin habitat recovery program has been created, it will be possible to employ traditional flow and trading mechanisms on behalf of Nebraska species habitat under the direction of the USFWS environmental account manager operating at Nebraska's Kingsley Dam and Lake McConaughy.

For years after its construction, Pathfinder was the most upstream dam on the river, so it necessarily trapped sediment. The high mountain streams that filled it did not have particularly erodible streambeds. Yet with each spring run-off after the gates were closed at Pathfinder Dam in 1909, storage capacity was incrementally lost to particulates captured by once-fast-flowing water that fell out of stilled water. Although the rate of sedimentation was greatly reduced after Seminoe Reservoir was built upstream in the years 1936 to 1939, by the early 1990s calculations revealed a 54,000-acre-foot loss of storage capacity at Pathfinder. Restored capacity there was filled under a 1904 priority, the oldest among the large North Platte storage projects.

The remaining 20,000 acre feet of re-captured Pathfinder storage is destined to serve municipal uses of several North Platte communities, especially Casper. Loss of the ill-fated Deer Creek plan will be compensated thereby. The total municipal storage account has been estimated to sustain a firm annual yield (as distinguished from average yield) of 9,600 acre feet per year for urban use, after which most of the water will flow back into the river for other users in Wyoming and Nebraska. A second priority is served by such return flows—augmentation to replace depletions placed on the river by groundwater wells situated below Guernsey. Finally, in years of relative abundance, the Pathfinder municipal account can serve a third priority. During years in which urban demand is less than 9,600 acre feet, Wyoming at its discretion will be able to release the remainder in ways that will maximize benefits to program critical habitat recovery.

Glendo Dam and Reservoir is located on the North Platte River about 75 miles downstream of Casper and about 60 river miles above the Nebraska border. Glendo is a large reservoir dedicated mostly to flood control, but 40,000 acre feet were traditionally designated during any water year for irrigation of Wyoming lands below Guernsey Reservoir (15,000 acre feet) and lands in the western Nebraska panhandle (25,000 acre feet) (Water and Power Resources Service 1981). However, in the 2001 U.S. Supreme Court settlement stipulations, it was agreed that each state could use its Glendo allocation anywhere in the Platte River Basin for any beneficial purposes (Olpin 2001: 44). New flexibility in water use was at hand. Of Wyoming's 15,000 acre feet, 4,400 are permanently contracted to users, leaving 10,600 acre feet of temporarily contracted storage available in Glendo for a Wyoming contribution to the basin habitat recovery program.

Another 5,000 acre feet of water is available for a Wyoming donation from LaPrele Reservoir, located on a tributary to the North Platte by the same name where the water enters the main stem about 125 miles downstream of Pathfinder. A complicated set of considerations makes yield estimates problematic, but releases can be timed to meet the program environmental account manager's requirements.

In addition, Wyoming's water contribution will be enlarged by a program of voluntary water leasing. It was anticipated that the eventual recovery program would provide financial incentives to farmers to annually lease water supplies that would otherwise have been dedicated to irrigated agriculture. The recovery program would receive the component of the leased water that represents the actual reduction in crop consumptive use (thereby preserving the return flow fraction for traditional uses under the Wyoming appropriation doctrine and preventing injury to appropriators who have become dependent on such flows from neighboring irrigators). The leased water will be conveniently held in one or more storage reservoirs until the USFWS environmental account manager at McConaughy calls for them to be sent downstream to meet critical habitat needs. It is estimated that leasing about 22,700 acre feet annually will correspond to about 16,400 acre feet delivered to farms and, in turn, amount to about 8,200 acre feet of historical consumptive use reduction that can be made available to the recovery program.

WYOMING SIDE PAYMENTS

First and foremost, Wyoming's proposed contribution of approximately 34,000 acre feet in the environmental account, to be extracted from 54,000 acre feet of restored Pathfinder storage capacity, was accompanied by something Wyoming water interests had long and dearly wanted—additional water for North Platte River municipal demands. Obtaining federal approval for the Pathfinder modification (raising the height of the dam), which also included 20,000 additional acre feet of water for Wyoming agendas, was a significant step ahead for Wyoming authorities. What Deer Creek could not deliver, the Pathfinder modification replaced. By doing something for listed species in Nebraska, Wyoming found a way to improve its municipal water supply situation.

Also, state authorities have worked with local irrigators and federal agencies on two local problems in ways that have helped farmers in irrigation communities make peace with the proposed habitat recovery program. Within the canal command area of the Kendrick Project, there had long been a serious problem created by the fact that some project water, after irrigating certain areas, had moved into naturally occurring selenium deposits that then became a highly toxic wetland soup that threatened numerous life forms but especially migratory waterfowl (Ostresh, Marston, and Hudson 1990: 88; Pitzer 2006). Some Kendrick Project land had thereby become a selenium hotspot. In most instances the wetlands were created by artificial barriers built by irrigators decades ago to capture runoff. Breaking down the barriers and drying up the artificial wetlands would pose little technical challenge, but it did create some difficult legal problems in the context of federal environmental legislation—especially the Migratory Bird Treaty Act (1918). The state of Wyoming has committed itself to work with irrigators and federal authorities to address the problem. Farmers, hard-pressed by a history of receiving low prices at the farm gate in the context of the escalating costs of virtually all farm inputs, have welcomed the state of Wyoming's willingness to assist them with the unwanted selenium seeps.

Furthermore, farmers up and down Wyoming's North Platte have been kept onboard the recovery program because Wyoming authorities are working closely with irrigation districts confronted by varying but significant dam safety problems. In the first half of the twentieth century, when Wyoming interests eagerly invited the USBR to build dams on the North Platte drainage, a fundamental contractual stipulation applied to bureau projects across the West. Each project had to be sponsored by a locally controlled incorporated entity chartered under state law—typically an irrigation district. This has also been the case in Wyoming's North Platte Basin. These districts have been held accountable for managing their respective projects under USBR supervision, paying for annual operations and maintenance, and repaying project capital costs (Pisani 1989, 2002).

In this context, there has been a problem—a dam safety problem. Wyoming's large, expensive federal dams are sponsored by irrigation districts, farmer-members of which work lands that tend to be economically marginal at best. District budgets have been severely constrained. Yet as the years have gone by, facilities have aged, new design considerations have applied as populations of non-irrigators fill in the valleys below, and new federal safety regulations have come into effect. The problems vary in type and severity from site to site and district to district, but virtually all four Wyoming North Platte irrigation districts are operating USBR dams that in one way or another cannot entirely fulfill the federal Safety of Dams Act (1978), which among other things establishes high standards for a qualifying dam to be able to contain maximum probable flows. A world of low agricultural commodity prices, combined with escalating costs of farm inputs, is not conducive to the aggregation of large amounts of capital in irrigation district budgets.

Considerable portions of the large sums required to rehabilitate dams to fulfill federal standards will have to come from sources other than the district water allotment holders. Such money is potentially available from the Wyoming Water Development Commission (funded by state mineral severance taxes), but work on dams built by the USBR must fulfill review standards by federal authorities in the bureau. That, in turn, means consultation with the Fish and Wildlife Service, which, of course, means doing things in a manner consistent with the objectives of the basin-wide endangered species recovery program. The quid pro quo is clear: farmer support for recovery of habitat for three birds and one fish will, in turn, provide access to additional state resources needed to address important dam safety problems. Side payments in the form of selenium mitigation and dam safety subsidies have lowered farmer–water user resistance. Furthermore, urban users are beneficiaries of a state of Wyoming investment in restoring long-lost Pathfinder capacity to increase the municipal account. All users know that urban return flows will enlarge downstream flows. Also, some fraction of environmental program flows will be caught and delayed for Wyoming's benefit in riverbank storage, a momentary loss to the program that would be a gain for local users in the right locations.

All in all, when many looked at the details of what had been an unwanted federally mandated basin recovery program, they found it not so objectionable after all. Actually, for some—especially those lower on Wyoming's North Platte—it represented a real improvement in their prospects.

HIGH OBJECTIONS

Some irrigators working in Wyoming's Upper North Platte Valley—above Seminoe and Pathfinder—have been displeased with the proposed arrangement at Pathfinder. Some joined opponents of the recovery program in Nebraska, especially supporters of Nebraskans First (see Chapter 15). Some were participants in overt protests that occurred in the months following the mid-1997 establishment of the Governance Committee and its land and water advisory committees. Objections arose from farmers who operated in a wide range of circumstances. Many came from those with at least some surface stream priorities junior to Pathfinder (1904)—about half of the diverters above the reservoir. For decades, these users had diverted from the North Platte and its tributary creeks on a run-of-the-river basis. They organized two associations to push their case against Wyoming state authorities and the USFWS: the North Platte Valley Water Users' Association and the North Platte Valley Water Conservation Association (Wyoming Board of Control 2008).

Historically, after construction of the North Platte reservoirs, Wyoming irrigators had frequently operated in a water-abundant context. Given modest irrigation water demands on large tubs, during many years the diversion priorities could be filled without placing the North Platte stream under strict state administration. This situation occurred when Pathfinder's 1904 storage right (currently 1,016,507 acre feet but to be restored to 1,070,507 acre feet) could be completely filled and still leave sufficient flows for junior rights and fulfillment of the Supreme Court decree stipulations binding on Wyoming for Nebraska. However, during years when water supplies were forecast to be insufficient to fill Pathfinder (and Guernsey Reservoir also, as another part of the North Platte Project), USBR managers would place a call on the North Platte River system—a request to store water prior to the start of the irrigation season from February 1 to April 30. This, in turn, meant that the Wyoming state engineer would be asked to impose a regulation on river diversions. The Office of the Wyoming State Engineer would then evaluate the federal call. If it found the call to be valid, the office would comply with the request. In such a year, water diverters with priorities junior to Pathfinder would not be allowed to divert during the February–April period unless and until Pathfinder filled. Under some extreme drought scenarios, the winter-spring diversions of Upper North Platte juniors could in principle be curtailed.

Given the imposition of river regulation during dry times, water rights upstream of, and senior to, Pathfinder are limited to one cubic foot per second per seventy acres (Olpin 2001: 191–192). Therefore, a possible small disadvantage would be imposed on diverters with water rights senior as well as junior to Pathfinder's. Therein lay the rub: irrigators with rights far senior to any new environmental or municipal water uses could, under some possible scenarios, suffer a loss—however small—in deference to newly installed uses at Pathfinder and Guernsey.

There was another potential problem. Seminoe Reservoir, located just upstream of Pathfinder, has a late 1931 priority on the river, and that junior date means it cannot store water in average to dry years—in effect, most years. Therefore, state and federal officials have not wanted to store endangered species habitat program water there. They wanted storage under the 1904 priority that applies to the Pathfinder facility. Many upper valley water users have opposed the insertion of a federal environmental water claim that was hammered out in the 1990s and affects the two reservoirs of fixed capacity with the knowledge that the environmental account of up to 34,000 acre feet will be fully exercised each year. By annually draining that water required to serve this new federal environmental need (which would ride on the original 1904 Pathfinder priority), the demands of the recovery program's environmental account manager would at least potentially represent a threat to much more senior Wyoming rights. The more junior the Wyoming user right, the greater the jeopardy; there would be a greater likelihood that after the federal recovery program is served, less water will remain to fulfill traditional Wyoming priorities even though they are many years senior to the late–twentieth-century / early–twenty-first-century arrangement for federal habitat recovery program water.

In average to wet years—even sporadic dry years—all this will be irrelevant; there will be enough water to go around. However, Seminoe and Pathfinder reservoirs may be squeezed in an extended series of dry years. Prior to the habitat recovery program, a major fraction of the 54,000 acre feet for municipal and environmental accounts in the restored Pathfinder would have filled Seminoe accounts and contributed to serving more junior priorities there. It is easy for at least some of the upper valley right holders (who used the storage water for exchange) to imagine a drought scenario in which depleted Seminoe and Pathfinder reservoirs will have too little water in storage to serve everyone. At that unhappy moment it will not be the junior-most federal environmental storage claim (or a municipal right) that will be cut off under terms of the proposed program. In a sufficiently dry context, the constant drawing down of the full environmental account at Pathfinder will inevitably push state juniors, in order of priority, out of storage at the two reservoirs, successively nudging aside higher and higher Wyoming user priorities in shrinking tubs—all this while a recently installed state-federal habitat recovery arrangement and state municipal accounts release water downstream for new agendas. If this were to occur, a welfare transfer will have taken place from the Upper North Platte Valley to lower valley interests not sanctioned by Wyoming's water appropriation doctrine.

State and federal representatives have replied that the "resisters" were seeing a problem that did not really exist. They argued that restoration of Pathfinder's capacity could not hurt upper valley irrigators. They contended that the state would never make a call on the upper valley to furnish any portion of the 54,000 acre feet of expanded Pathfinder volume by shutting down upper valley users with priorities junior or senior to Pathfinder. Instead, they would simply regulate the upper valley users to their traditional diversions. Rights junior to Pathfinder's could be shut down, while rights senior to Pathfinder's would be limited to their original legal ceilings—one cubic foot per second per seventy acres.

Wyoming authorities would not permit administrators of the river to actually cut off the juniors. The 1997 Cooperative Agreement stipulated that the USBR would not make a call on rights upstream of Pathfinder to fill the 54,000 acre feet of storage to be restored through Pathfinder modification (Cooperative Agreement 1997: tab 2A, IA). This was a roundabout way of saying that the state and the Habitat Recovery Program Governance Committee promised to respect the traditional and legally sanctioned consumptive uses of upper valley users.

State and USBR authorities pointed out that practical steps could be taken to hedge against such worst-case scenarios. The state can never keep irrigators anywhere from harm in the face of Mother Nature's droughts, but potential program injury to upper basin users can be eliminated for all practical purposes. Water conservation practices up and down the river, especially at Seminoe, can do much to reduce water demand on that tub. Lining Kendrick Project canals (to reduce selenium seepage problems) and creating better water control facilities on distributaries can lower the demand on Seminoe Reservoir by thousands of acre feet per year, creating more of a cushion for Upper Platte diverters. Also, state water authorities have pointed out that Upper North Platte irrigation farmers will eventually face federal permitting issues on their water catchments and supply lakes high in the Medicine Bow National Forest and on Bureau of Land Management (BLM) lands. At such moments they, too, will be in a federal nexus and will then appreciate the coverage provided by a viable basin-wide habitat recovery program.

In addition, proponents of the environmental and municipal accounts at Pathfinder have contended that farmers above Seminoe benefit from the operations of the North Platte plumbing system much more than the "resisters" have acknowledged. For example, in average to wet years, USBR managers can make good use of Glendo storage to serve water demands on the lower Wyoming Platte in the vicinity of Torrington. This, in turn, keeps water levels in Pathfinder higher than would be the case if Pathfinder had to release its supply downriver all the way to project users close to the Nebraska border. Keeping water in Pathfinder is greatly to the advantage of Upper North Platte water users, who benefit from thicker cushions there. If the cooperative habitat recovery program were canceled, the USFWS would have no other option than to pick some of Wyoming's lower-hanging fruit in the form of water yields in reservoirs such as Pathfinder, Seminoe, Glendo, and Guernsey. Any failure of the proposed cooperative program will place the federally constructed storage facilities in the crosshairs of the USFWS and environmentalists. A loss of yields anywhere would diminish federal USBR project yields for all Wyoming users at all points on the river. Any such specter would be far worse for Upper North Platte water users than any low-probability scenario about which they had tormented state and federal USBR authorities. They were therefore advised to embrace the proposed Pathfinder modification project.

Upper valley opponents replied that unless the state and proposed program authorities could ensure that there will never again be a prolonged drought, there will be no place to obtain the water for the 1997 federal environmental account priority except by subordinating and extracting the water from state priorities senior to that of the habitat recovery program. They did not trust the state of Wyoming and habitat recovery program leaders to keep their word never to compromise a state priority given the intense pressures that would be expected to fall on federal and state authorities during a prolonged drought.

There were no effective side payments with which to draw Upper North Platte water users into the Wyoming coalition. They would remain intransigent;

the fight would go on until the last days of negotiations—even into the federal dollar authorization politics in the years 2006–2008. The Wyoming negotiating posture, therefore, was one of working hard to solve problems that stood in the way of obtaining a viable cooperative habitat recovery program to protect the state's water project yields, working within the terms of the 2001 *Nebraska v. Wyoming* settlement, and all the while swatting away challenges from Upper North Platte Valley water users who had water yield concerns of their own.

CHAPTER 12

States, Federal Agencies, and the Water Plan

Representatives of the U.S. Fish and Wildlife Service (USFWS) and the U.S. Bureau of Reclamation (USBR)–environmental impact statement (EIS) team were engaged in continual discussions with each other, the states, environmentalists, and basin water users. Federal authorities played a critical role in support of negotiations that had brought them to the point in the fall of 2000 when a water action plan had been pieced together. There were hopes that an agreement could be reached in time for last-minute signatures by Clinton administration authorities.

The USFWS kept up an intermittent and clear drumbeat heralding that the Endangered Species Act (ESA) had to be implemented. If efforts failed, individual Section 7 consultations would be reinitiated. There is no question that without a strong federal presence working on behalf of a tough ESA, the water user community would not have sustained a minimal interest in negotiations. The quest for regulatory certainty by Platte River Basin water appropriators was what kept them at the table—seats they would have gladly abandoned if they had viable options other than to act in concert.

The question that arose was how to best employ the ESA hammer. When, how much, and under what circumstances should the threat of returning to individual consultations be employed? When does a responsible federal administrator threaten, cajole, or back away? How is one to distinguish stalling from spadework?

The most dramatic instance of threatening to use the ESA hammer, one that went beyond the negotiating rooms, occurred in April 2000 in anticipation of a possible December signing of the recovery program agreement. Farmers, especially in Nebraska, were restless and sending signals of opposition. They were listening to a daily barrage of conservative talk radio lambasting the Clinton administration and a litany of unwanted federal intrusions without mention of the federal dollars that were sustaining agriculture. Politicians, again especially in Nebraska, were nervous. Things looked much more positive for the recovery program in Colorado and Wyoming, but with the clock ticking its way toward a December deadline, a question emerged: would Nebraska bolt from all that had been accomplished?

In this context, Ralph Morgenweck, regional director of the USFWS in Lakewood, Colorado, conducted an interview on April 25 with a reporter from the *Omaha World-Herald*. The message was published the next day, neatly coinciding with a scheduled Governance Committee meeting where the statement was read to a roomful of silent negotiators and their staffs. Morgenweck spelled out for readers across the state the "nightmare" of the no-action alternative. Everyone involved in federal programs—ranging from flood control to commodity price supports, municipal water supply systems, rural electrification cooperatives, and soil and water conservation programs—could be accountable for compliance with the ESA. Individually, they would be required to make appropriate contributions to improved habitat for the listed species. All entities receiving federal permits or payments would be judged individually as to whether they were in compliance with the ESA. However, if the proposed recovery program could serve as a "reasonable and prudent alternative" to either forcing thousands of entities into compliance or shutting them down, such difficulties would disappear. The specter of federal authorities establishing "standards" for beneficiaries of federal dollars and attempting to enforce the law enterprise by enterprise across three states in the basin was a terrible thing to contemplate for all parties. The only way out, Morgenweck made clear, was to support the cooperative recovery program building process. Failure carried a high price. Readers got the message that people could no longer simply write off the proposed program as important to two Nebraska districts or other remote water users. Program failure would hit home where people lived, worked, and played all across the basin.

No one can know the impact the published interview had as it was picked up at breakfast tables and office desks by political elites and organizational managements across the state and around the basin. Political elites and their attentive audiences had the debate framed for them in a manner that could not be blithely dismissed. On the one hand, pressures mounted from important water constituencies to "pull out" of the talks rather than tolerate the USFWS's "blackmail." On the other hand, the message gave important political cover to any leader—especially the governor—looking for reasons to stay in the conversation, at least for a while. In the event, neither Nebraska nor any other state delegation left the negotiations. There would be no signed agreement in December 2000 as originally scheduled, but the reason would have to do with a problem the Department of the Interior (DOI) itself would advance: sedimentation and vegetation in the central Platte channels (see Chapter 16).

The USFWS and USBR-EIS team also played a critical role in advancing negotiations. Many state organizational water staff members are inveterate data analysts and model builders. But federal agency staff members are these things as well. State and local models of specific segments of the basin critical to water administration were important to recovery program discussions, but only the USBR-EIS team had constructed an overall basin model that could be used to evaluate the proposed recovery program and alternatives to it. The model was employed to estimate how much the combined state water projects, as they interacted with one another in the action plan, would reduce shortages to the controversial target flows. EIS team basin modeling and water volume scoring methods were of intense interest to everyone; they bridged state lines and gaps between locals and federal analysts.

The USBR-EIS team's model had been developed in the 1970s as a generic river model. It had been modified and developed for the Federal Energy Regulatory Commission (FERC) re-licensing process at Kingsley Dam and Lake McConaughy in the 1980s and 1990s. Given the fact that it had been closely scrutinized by a combination of federal, state, and local groups, including environmentalists, and that it had been cleaned up and made more user-friendly over the years, it was the tool of choice for evaluating the proposed recovery program (U.S. Department of Interior 2006: vol. 3). It was basically an accounting model that tracked inflows and outflows along the river from the Julesburg gauge in Colorado at the Nebraska state line downstream to the main stem and from Kingsley Dam through the critical habitat. The model employed time-series data that reflected current conditions on the river. Then analytical "runs" were made, each with a selected proposed program change to see how it would affect river attributes. Validity was checked by comparing observed results of model runs to known historical flow conditions.

When policy talks became animated, confrontational, and potentially explosive, sending matters back to the technical level often provided at least a temporary escape. Policy people, heading home after difficult sessions, heard from their technical people that possible ways of coping had emerged in technical-level discussions driven by the river model. This also sometimes worked in reverse; when technical discourse bogged down, staffs could seek direction from policy people in a data-rich context. Data analyses and modeling activities by state and federal teams were central to shifting the discourse back and forth, and the federal team's modeling efforts were critical to the dynamic.

A crucially important example of interaction between technical and political-policy discourse was seen in the difficult negotiations leading up to the

Table 12.1. Program Water Sources

Sources Negotiated, 1994–1997	State	Estimated Average Annual Reduction to USFWS Flow Targets (acre feet)	
McConaughy EA	Nebraska	44,000	
Pathfinder EA	Wyoming	26,000	
Tamarack Recharge Plan	Colorado	10,000	
Three-state subtotal		80,000	
Sources Negotiated, 1997–2000			
Re-regulating reservoirs Water leasing Water conservation Groundwater pumping Canal recharge, such as on Gothenburg and Dawson canals Payment for project interference	Nebraska (see Chapter 10)	Because individual projects were assessed in interaction within Nebraska and with Wyoming's, no individual project values are reported.	
Pathfinder municipal account Glendo storage Water leasing LaPrele Reservoir	Wyoming (see Chapter 11)	Because individual projects were assessed in interaction within Wyoming and with Nebraska's, no individual project values are reported.	
	Neb./Wyo. subtotals	*Minimum* 33,000	*Maximum* 43,000
Tamarack Phase III	Colorado (see Chapter 9)	*Minimum* 17,000	*Maximum* 17,000
Total average, 1994–2000		130,000	140,000

Source: Author, with the assistance of the USFWS-USBR Operational Study Team.

completion of the water action plan. Taken together, the three states had come up with an assembly of river re-regulation projects roughly estimated to yield an annual average of 130,000–140,000 acre feet deliverable to the critical habitat, as measured at the Grand Island gauge (see Table 12.1).

After discussion, all parties agreed that the quantity of water to be produced would be more than sufficient to fulfill the 1997 understanding that there would be reductions in shortages to target flows averaging 130,000–150,000 acre feet/year. Table 12.1 summarizes state contributions to the proposed program's water action plan. Individual water supply project yields are not produced in isolation. Rather, they interact in ways that may either add to or subtract from total program yields. There can be no simple linear cumulation and addition of individual project supplies. Therefore, Table 12.1 reports only general values and the estimated overall total program yield.

Federal representatives were therefore much more than taskmasters threatening to bring the ESA down on the heads of recalcitrant state water users. They were, among other things, becoming partners in data analysis and the modeling of complex aspects of basin water flow. People who had approached problems of water re-regulation from different perspectives shared the same concepts involved in data analysis and interpretation; they worked with models constructed out of common educational backgrounds and had the same respect for shared logics. An analytical coalition of states and federal agencies that had been gestating for five to six years had been birthed in the form of a water supply action plan that earned a passing grade in the federal assessment.

Unknown to negotiators at the table in late 2000, there would be six more years of serious and at times deeply troubled negotiations before a deal was made. However, during the conflict and tumult yet to come, the water program pieced together in the 1997–2000 conversations continued to earn the support of all parties. The water supply plan, summarized in Table 12.1, would take its place at the core of the ultimate Platte River Habitat Recovery Implementation Program Document (2006).

Politics and the Roles of Science

Defining Success

Science as a Referee in a Game Where No One Knows the Score

The three basin states and the Department of the Interior signed on to the 1997 Cooperative Agreement on the premise that they would find ways to negotiate a program rooted in solid, peer-reviewed science. That vision has been noble but deeply problematic. How do program participants balance today's need for immediate action on behalf of listed species with the need for further study to understand habitat requirements? What observable indicators can establish that the program is or is not working? Who gets to define those indicators and the criteria for assessing progress? The promise of "regulatory certainty" had been the bait the U.S. Fish and Wildlife Service (USFWS) used to keep water users at the table, but how could that concept be meshed with inevitable scientific uncertainty amid dynamic ecosystems?

The USFWS is statutorily responsible for determining whether the program has served as a reasonable and prudent alternative, but what is the status of state critiques? Who will pay the considerable costs of doing "good" science in a complex world that is always richer than the simplifications captured by theoretical and methodological models? When important issues remain unclear after time and money have been expended in the quest for understanding, who will bear the burdens of uncertainty—species habitat or water users? The Endangered Species Act (ESA) clearly places the burdens of uncertainty on human society, not the species. That is the glory of what has come to be known as the most important and powerful environmental legislation the world has ever seen. Yet everybody knows that the USFWS has limited means to protect species, and if it pushed too hard, the ESA itself would become politically endangered.

The USFWS unquestionably has the authority under the ESA to function as the referee who blows the whistle when state actions are found to be deficient, but when is that federal call based on sound scientific understanding and when is it little more than arbitrary and capricious dictates reflecting the agency's political, legal, and other non-scientifically grounded requirements that come and go with the passing of administrations, middle-level managers, fad, and fashion? These issues, along with more technical matters, were primarily addressed by members of the recovery program's Technical Committee, an advisory group organized to make recommendations to the Governance Committee in the areas of program research and monitoring.

PROGRAM OBJECTIVE

At a basic level, the program's objective seemed simple enough. Benefits for species in the form of improved habitat must be sufficient to ensure that the designated area of the Platte River does not impede recovery of the listed species. If the program succeeds in accomplishing that goal and if that success is underpinned by solid, scientifically based efforts at research and monitoring, it should be passed as a reasonable and prudent alternative to shutting down or modifying water projects in the basin that have "taken" the habitat of listed species. Life is simple.

Unfortunately, analysts do not know precisely how to justifiably define required baseline conditions on the river. Although biologists have a solid grasp of many fundamental considerations in defining habitat requirements of the three listed birds, no one has a complete picture of how the birds used the traditional habitat and which aspects are critical and which are not. What kind of habitat does the program want to produce over the next 13 to 50 to 100 years? The problem of defining "best habitat" is complex in many ways not addressed here. One thing that is clear, however, is that during recent decades, mainstream ecologists have largely abandoned any assumption that nature, in the absence of modern humankind, would somehow be self-regulating in the direction of some "natural" standard of stability or equilibrium (Krech 1999; Wood 1998). The concept of a "pristine environment" is deeply problematic and has no justifiable meaning for guiding the construction of program criteria for success.

The central and Lower Platte is only one link in a large continental complex of ecosystems that sustain the whooping crane, least tern, piping plover, and pallid sturgeon. For example, the future of whooping cranes will depend heavily on what happens in the Texas Gulf Coast, in the prairie pothole country of the Dakotas, and in the Northwest Territories of Canada. Even if habitat on the Platte were restored to conditions ideal for the species, forces at work in many other places could easily account for their extinction. It is possible to have a raging success, however defined, on the Nebraska designated critical habitat and still suffer the loss of the targeted birds. Can the recovery program be given good marks when, over time, the population of listed cranes continues to decline?

What will be the definition of program success? Many variables that affect the rise or decline of any given listed species are beyond the control of the recovery program. Should the program limit itself to establishing that the habitat is not a factor responsible for species decline, or should the integrated monitoring and research plan (IMRP) be much more ambitious? Should it attempt to establish that the listed species are actually recovering? There are deep epistemological problems here (Gerber, DeMaster, and Roberts 2000). How can science determine when a population has recovered with any certainty? The mere fact that a population increases over a given time period does not necessarily indicate that the species is on the road to sustained recovery. If the numbers fall over a twenty-year period, it does not necessarily mean—given our limited knowledge of particular species biology and habitat requirements—that program manipulations are causing the problem.

Uncertainty about the linkage of action and species response is inevitable; the domain for legitimate disagreement among thoughtful and knowledgeable scientists is large. Real-world action programs implemented as quasi-experiments take decades, arguably centuries, to have the desired impact. Given the number of uncontrolled variables, science may not even then be in a position to establish clear-cut connections between policy action and biological response.

If the program cannot simply count up numbers of birds and fish, what can it do? The USFWS begins by acknowledging that the Platte River Habitat Recovery Program is designed to assist in species recovery (Lutey 2002). The Platte River program cannot logically be held accountable for recovering the listed species per se. The awkward reality is that the ESA places people and ecosystems in its grasp not because they add up to viable ecological management domains that can be manipulated in concert; rather, the ESA works on those places and organizations it can touch because they are in a political-bureaucratic-dollar relationship with a federal action agency. Restoration ecologists would prefer to work in a coordinated fashion across the whooping cranes' great North American flyways, but not all parts of those ecosystems are under the ESA's thumb. Therefore, the USFWS cannot hold any particular recovery program responsible for the recovery of the listed species. This means science will be employed to do two things simultaneously that do not necessarily work together smoothly:

1. The objective of the recovery program will be to use the best available science to produce the best possible habitats for the listed species without regard to particular population fluctuations. Habitat systems will be restored. The best possible "species hotels" will be constructed regardless of whether occupancy rates rise or fall in any given time period. The adequacy of the recovery program will be evaluated according to its success or failure

in producing these best possible habitats as limited science can help define them. This requires program compliance science and monitoring and has to do with meeting milestones by acquiring and protecting land, acquiring and delivering water, and undertaking efforts to monitor and conduct scientifically grounded evaluation.

2. The USFWS, working independent of particular Platte River recovery program results in any given time period, cares greatly about the particular population dynamics of the listed species. It is critically important to the agency whether whooping cranes (and other listed species) appear to be gaining or losing numbers. The agency therefore has an internal objective to monitor and evaluate biological responses of particular species at particular sites under specific conditions.

How can these two different science and monitoring concerns be reconciled? Adaptive management is the answer.

ADAPTIVE MANAGEMENT

Over recent decades, adaptive management strategies for restoring and sustaining ecosystems have become popular because they provide a path for dealing with scientific uncertainty. There have been a growing number of applications of the concept, especially in riparian and coastal marine ecosystem management (Walters 1997). Adaptive management strategies have become the centerpiece of policy initiatives in the Colorado River Basin (Collier, Webb, and Andrews 1997) and the Columbia River Basin (Lee 1993). Under the label of the adaptive environmental assessment and management (AEAM) process (Holling 1978; Walters 1986), the concepts have been used in restoring the Upper Mississippi River Basin, the Florida Everglades (Ogden and Davis 1994; Walters, Gunderson, and Holling 1992), and the Great Barrier Reef in Australia (Mapstone, Campbell, and Smith 1996).

Adaptive management strategies have been variously defined. According to C. L. Halbert, "Adaptive management is an innovative technique that uses scientific information to help formulate management strategies in order to 'learn' from programs so that subsequent improvements can be made in formulating both successful policy and improved management programs" (Halbert 1993: 261–262). K. N. Lee and J. Lawrence (1986: 431–432) defined adaptive management as "a policy framework that recognizes biological uncertainty, while accepting the congressional mandate to proceed on the basis of the 'best available scientific knowledge.' An adaptive management policy treats the program as a set of experiments designed to test and extend the scientific basis of fish and wildlife management."

Adaptive management, as adopted by participants in the Platte River Habitat Recovery Program, is about using a recovery program–funded IMRP to test assumptions and predictions built into program manipulations of riverine and terrestrial habitat and then incorporating that information to improve program efforts (Marmarek and Peters 2001). Peer-reviewed science is used to construct conceptual models, to guide the formulation of restoration options, to monitor and evaluate outcomes, and ultimately to move toward improved understanding of what the problems are (Luecke 2000).

What can adaptive management change under the terms of the 1997 Cooperative Agreement? Anything, in principle, can be open to renegotiation and change with the approval of the Governance Committee and the endorsement of the USFWS. Given such open-ended possibilities, the states pressed for clarification and assurance that they would not immediately be confronted with peer-reviewed science that calls for significant increases in terrestrial habitat (above 29,000 acres) or greater water contributions. The USFWS gave assurance that during the first thirteen-year program increment, it would refrain from pushing such proposals in the Governance Committee.

Adaptive management means fundamentally that the various state and federal partners are willing to play together respectfully on the Platte Basin field. It will be a game with no end in sight and much room for disagreement about how points are scored. Play-making discourse can be expected to be as wide-ranging as a diverse constituency can make it; water users, state authorities, federal agencies, academic researchers, and environmentalists will all enter the arena and pound out their points of view and courses of action under the scrutiny of friendly critique and hostile opposition. There will be nothing neat and tidy about the process. But, in the final analysis, good science will mean civic science, the kind of science that stands up to the best tests friend and foe can bring to bear, the kind of science that understands that today's best hypotheses will be re-thought tomorrow, the kind of science that understands retreating to re-think in the face of compelling evidence, better methods, and improved theoretical insight.

Adaptive management, rooted in the best civic science, is a scary proposition for political leaders and administrators who want to know in advance exactly what to expect, what financial commitments need to be made to produce predetermined results and predictably obtain permits for their agencies and enterprises. It is frightening to politicians and administrators who want to keep control of the agenda and who see the danger of an unwanted finding dividing a winning coalition. Who in either the public or the private sector wishes to go to their superiors repeatedly to request more money to address unforeseen issues?

Environmentalists worry that state water users will employ adaptive management to tie up otherwise viable action proposals in endless peer reviews. What happens when program projects do not achieve their projected results? How long will water users and the states be allowed to do their analyses and re-analyses: 1 year, 10 years, 25 years? The states and water users worry that adaptive management is little more than a code word for tapping into their treasuries to pay for half-baked environmental schemes put together by "loopy biologists" who do not understand how rivers work physically, legally, socially, or politically. Adaptive management—and this may be the most frightening point of all—means continual river basin–level planning and concerted action by feuding water users and environmentalists, three bickering states, and at least three federal agencies (USFWS, USBR, and USFS) infamous for their inability to coordinate with each other or with the states. A new river basin arena of public policy discourse is slowly, haltingly, grudgingly being birthed, and it has not been particularly comfortable for anyone involved.

TERMS AND CONDITIONS

The Technical Committee became a forum for addressing crucial issues. Much work was accomplished on matters such as writing monitoring protocols for the listed species and proposing budgets for IMRP activities during the first program increment. But the big question was always, if the states and the Department of the Interior (DOI) were going to play cooperatively in Platte Basin ecosystems, about which little is known, what would be the terms and conditions of that game? In particular, how flexible will the program referee—the USFWS—be in dealing with state perspectives? Alternatively, what status would state and water user critiques have?

On the one hand, the USFWS cannot simply yield to state definitions of what constitutes best habitat or what water flow regimes are "good enough." To do so would be to abandon its mandate to be the effective steward of the ESA and would invite a blizzard of lawsuits from environmental groups seeking to ensure that the USFWS preserves the ESA's integrity. On the other hand, states have had to obtain reasonable standing during the process. Their voices must be heard and their messages given judicious consideration. Only water user communities within the states can actually implement the changed water regime. They must not be driven away by uncompromisingly rigid insistence that unobtainable standards be upheld.

How much could the USFWS give away in flexible language to obtain state buy-ins? How much could states afford to resist federal definitions of program success when after the first thirteen-year program increment, if not sooner, it will be the USFWS that declares whether the program is sufficient to provide states with regulatory certainty? Failure to accommodate USFWS needs would simply place a too compliant USFWS in a position to be sued by environmentalists. That would bring into the discourse outside lawyers, consultants, judges, and other environmentalists not party to years of delicate negotiations. A few court rulings that make sense in terms of legal precedent but not for the players in the recovery program could quickly turn the process into one of maladaptive management. Each side has needed and continues to need the other. For the states, the problem is that only one side—the federal agencies—has had a player who controlled the referee's whistle.

As 2000 progressed and it became clear that no agreement would be signed by the end of the year, discussions in the Technical Committee actually showed signs of greater effectiveness. The regional director's office reined in some of the more relentless biologists, and the USFWS showed greater willingness to be collaborative. Each state wanted to avoid having the dead body of a failed program on its doorstep. If any state delegation raised objections too strongly, it would create an opportunity for another state(s) to jump on the issue, use it as pretext for abandoning the program, and point the finger at the vociferous one. Each party pushed, but not too hard; it was important to control confrontations and keep the game going. They simply moved ahead with talks that were better than any imaginable alternative while hoping that the USFWS referee would be reasonable. If the game got too far out of hand, environmentalists could go to the courts, and water users had recourse in their congressional delegations.

CHAPTER 14

Science as Justification for Sacrifice

The Junk Science Controversy

In science, truth is procedural. Truth is dependent on the logical procedures used to arrive at it. A fact is judged according to the quality of procedures that produced it. The person who has only one watch knows what time it is, but a group with multiple watches may never be certain. But there are better and worse watches, better and worse methods for employing them, and better and worse logics by which to draw conclusions from the readings. Open, reasoned discussion of the use and maintenance of watches will tend to ensure that potential abuses of time keeping are minimized. People in a time-sensitive contest where the stakes are high will want to be sure to organize the keeping of time in a manner that is open to inspection by all and will attempt to ensure that all parties have confidence that the watch is read in an unbiased manner. "Junk" time keeping (and science) is therefore self-interested and advances the agenda of one player over another in ways not openly disclosed. "Good" time keeping (science) is that which is open to continual civic inspection and responds to reasoned critique with carefully argued, logical justifications for its practices.

The Endangered Species Act (ESA) is fundamentally science-driven. It is science in some form that establishes the listing of species; it is science that justifies the selection of critical habitats; it is science that must grapple with the perplexing issues that surround defining "habitat recovery"; it is science that is somehow to be an important guide to adaptive management in implementing habitat recovery options. The U.S. Fish and Wildlife Service (USFWS) must be in a position to say that the best science available underpins the logic of recovery program actions. Sacrifices entailed in implementing the recovery program must be justified by science. If the science utilized is seriously questionable, the entire edifice of recovery program justification loses its legitimacy. Good science potentially justifies sacrifice. Program opponents waved the flag of alleged junk science to attempt to discredit those who would have advanced the recovery program and its objectives.

Allegations that the USFWS had employed junk science to justify actions on behalf of endangered and threatened species circulated widely. Two examples in particular received widespread hearings among opponents of the Platte River Habitat Recovery Program negotiations. The first was a story about a so-called lynx hoax. The second involved a series of confrontations over USFWS–U.S. Bureau of Reclamation (USBR) actions in the Klamath River Valley of southern Oregon and northern California.

LYNX HOAX

On January 24, 2002, the *Wall Street Journal* ran a front-page story reporting a scandal regarding a high-profile Canadian lynx survey conducted by the state of Washington in cooperation with the USFWS during the preceding months. This followed a similar story in *The Washington Times* the preceding December 17. Seven employees of the USFWS and the U.S. Forest Service (USFS) were alleged to have submitted hair samples from captive lynx—a threatened species—and tried to pass them off as wild to establish lynx use of certain national forest areas. Their alleged goal was to eventually block those areas to human uses, such as logging, ranching, and mining. This story flashed across the country and was particularly welcomed into the arsenal of stories offered by ESA and proposed Platte program irreconcilables. To this vocal minority at least, the episode showed the USFWS for what it was—an agency "out of control" that had been willing to use junk science to expand its power to elevate the needs of wildlife over the needs of economically hard-pressed working folks. Some media implicated field biologists from the USFS, the USFWS, and the Washington state Department of Fish and Wildlife. The story became a rallying point for property rights activists and their representatives at the state and federal levels. There were calls for investigations into unethical practices by scientists, disciplinary actions, and—most important—a complete revision of the Endangered Species Act (Williams 2002).

A more careful examination of the events revealed that nothing of the sort had actually occurred (Williams 2002). There had been no unethical activity. Rather, scientists had submitted blind samples of a variety of furs to laboratories because of concerns about the accuracy of analyses from previous data collection efforts. It was common practice to check the validity of laboratory analyses so field samples could be correctly distinguished and identified. However, an informant within the USFS "leaked" information about the submission of blind samples to the lab as if the practice were suspect and newsworthy. Some media repeatedly ignored the realities of the case, including the fact that no illegal or unethical activity had occurred, no data had been falsified, and no confessions or refusals to cooperate with investigations had taken place. Internal and externally contracted investigations resulted in the alleged perpetrators being cleared of wrongdoing. However, the corrections to the story never received the widespread dissemination—especially among water users—the original allegations had enjoyed. The scientific reputations of the USFWS, the USFS, and the state of Washington Fish and Wildlife Department had been harmed.

CALAMITY ON THE KLAMATH

Based on a USFWS biological opinion that assessed the needs of endangered suckers and threatened coho salmon, in April 2001 the USBR shut off irrigation water to about 90 percent of the 220,000 acres watered by the Klamath Project in southern Oregon, where the fields had been irrigated since 1907. A coalition of downstream commercial fishing and environmental groups had sued the USBR under the terms of the ESA to force the shutting down of supplies to agriculture and to bypass flows into the Klamath River for salmon and other fish (Clarren 2001, 2008; Jenkins 2008). Farmers rebelled, and the long-ignored Klamath River Basin became an ESA flashpoint.

From its headwaters in southern Oregon, the Klamath River flows southwest to the seacoast in northern California (Ryman 2008: 134–155). It was once one of the most productive rivers in North America for salmon, but in recent decades the salmon population has declined to a small fraction of historical numbers (National Research Council 2004a: 71). Commercial fishermen, whose main money fish had traditionally been salmon, were experiencing lean times. They therefore allied with environmentalists and Native Americans on the Lower Klamath to seek redress in the courts (Blake, Blake, and Kittredge 2000; Levy 2003).

By July 2001, angry farmers had formed a local social movement aimed at the USFWS and the USBR; hundreds, along with their supporters, used torches and crowbars to open the headgates of an irrigation canal four times in a single month while clearly sympathetic local law enforcement stood by passively. The ESA was being attacked, directly and violently. Federal officers eventually stood inside locked gates guarding water valves against hostile locals. It was a bitter scene and testimony to what could go wrong in administering the ESA.

The Bush administration's secretary of the interior, Gale Norton, later announced that the farmers would receive about 15 percent of their usual annual water allotment in late summer, but this light and late sprinkling did not extinguish the rancorous conflict. By August, the Bush administration had asked the National Academies of Science (NAS) to review the USFWS biological opinion that had justified cutting off the irrigation flows. On February 5, 2002, NAS issued an interim report that, among many other points regarding the need for wetland and habitat restoration, stated that available scientific evidence did not support the need to require water levels as high as federal agencies had originally proposed in Oregon's Upper Klamath Lake or on the Klamath River (Gellman 2008: 195–213; National Research Council 2002). This news was received by water users around the West—who preferred to overlook the NAS call for wider habitat restoration—as confirmation that the USFWS's science was agenda-biased and self-interested and that it could not be trusted to stand up to independent review. Unreconciled opponents of the recovery program negotiations were always seeking ammunition; now they felt they had some (Levy 2003). They clung to the stories of junk science associated with the lynx and Klamath cases.

Later, in its final 2004 report, the National Research Council (NRC) endorsed the quality of the science and professional judgment incorporated in the USFWS biological opinion that had been the basis for the USBR's flow shutdown in spring 2001 (National Research Council 2004a: 37, 44–45). The report called for geographic expansion of restoration efforts beyond the lakes and main stem of the Klamath as essential to the recovery of listed species. The authors concluded with a scathing assessment of federal, state, and local organizational management of the Klamath restoration effort: "Ecosystem management in the Klamath basin today is disjointed, occasionally disfunctional, and commonly adversarial. Thus, it is often inefficient and ineffective" (National Research Council 2004a: 331). The fact that the USFWS's science was eventually endorsed by the National Research Council did not assuage the anger of hostile onlookers in the years 2001–2003 and sometimes thereafter. However, as the years went by and the adversaries exhausted each other fruitlessly, they arrived at the main features of a settlement accommodating fish, fishing interests, and farmers in 2006–2007 (Jenkins 2008: 12–19, 28).

NEGOTIATING AWAY SCIENCE AS AN ISSUE

For years, at least some representatives of each of the three Platte Basin states had asserted that the USFWS science regarding Platte River Basin realities was "flat-out bogus." The charge was directed especially at recommended target flows. To them, the science undergirding the USFWS definition of target flows for critical habitat (417,000 acre feet/year) did not stand up to reasoned inspection. These representatives had questioned much of the science that informed the biological opinions at the proposed Narrows Dam Project in Colorado, on the Poudre River mountain reservoirs, and at Nebraska's Kingsley Dam—which, in turn, had provided the foundation for the federal case that Platte Basin water uses had imposed jeopardy on the listed species.

State delegations had been divided about how to handle the issue of the so-called bad federal science. From the very beginning, some had advocated a confrontational approach: question the science; do not cooperate in building a recovery program. For the most part, these stridently negative voices were weeded out or tempered as it became clear that a Cooperative Agreement would be launched on July 1, 1997. Those who remained at the table could see that if they were too negative about what they regarded as serious deficiencies in the federal science, the negotiations would never proceed. If negotiations were halted, they would immediately fall into the grip of individual Section 7 consultations. Compromise seemed highly desirable. The USFWS had backed off its insistence on the 417,000 acre foot/year target flow number and had accepted a first program increment average annual value in the range of 130,000–150,000 acre feet; in addition, it had split up its demand for 29,000 acres of habitat and requested that only 10,000 acres be in place by the end of the first thirteen years of the program. For the pragmatists left at the table, the issue was resolved not by obtaining definitive science but instead by working to deliver some of what the USFWS wanted, avoiding the "nightmare" of individual Section 7 consultations, and obtaining regulatory certainty for their operations. A political compromise had substituted for a debate about the nature of quality science.

MR. OSBORNE'S HEARING

Meanwhile, as the crisis on the Klamath was unfolding and stories of the lynx hoax were circulating, Nebraska political elites were coming under pressure from constituents unhappy with the prospects of an endangered species recovery program. Among them was freshman congressman Tom Osborne (Republican–Nebraska). He was well aware that voters in his district were watching the events on the Klamath. He further knew that Nebraska farmers upstream of Lake McConaughy were contracted to the USBR in ways very similar to the contracts on the Klamath.

As political pressure mounted, he would have to take the lead one way or another. Toward this end, he arranged to conduct a Congressional Field Hearing on Saturday, February 16, 2002, in Grand Island. The assembly gathered in the largest auditorium on the College Park campus. The room was packed with a variety of intensely interested citizens, over 300; notable in the crowd, wearing red jackets and caps, were several dozen Nebraskans First lobbying group members who had sent out flyers to mobilize groundwater users. Under the banner "Protecting Nebraska's Groundwater for Agriculture" was the statement: "Once again, the USFWS has been exposed as being a rogue, out of control, and a dishonest federal agency." The text cited the conflict on the Klamath and the "lynx hoax" (NebraskansFirst.com/2262002.jpg). It alleged that the USFWS had not used sound science to support its decisions, which imposed harm on people.

Citizens were called to put an end to unspecified USFWS abuses in Nebraska. Nebraska elected officials were requested to order the USFWS to "close all species and habitat activities in our state" until an "independent scientific analysis" could be undertaken. The group proclaimed, "We are not asleep at the switch" (NebraskansFirst.com/2262002.jpg).

Representative Osborne opened the session by noting that no disturbance of any kind would be tolerated, a reference to threats of violence that had occurred in Nebraska land committee sessions. He lamented the calamity that had occurred the preceding summer in the Klamath River Basin. USFWS and USBR activities there had hurt people without helping target species. It was time, he said, to be proactive in Nebraska.

The Nebraska Platte River Habitat Recovery Program negotiating team, several Nebraska state agricultural leaders who had not directly participated in the negotiations, a representative of Nebraska's Audubon Society, and representatives from the Lakewood, Colorado, USFWS Regional Director's Office were all in the dock. One by one they made their respective cases for the recovery program. Osborne's tactic was to hear their brief presentations and then question them. He began by saying, "They have some explaining to do." Testimony emphasized repeatedly that the program would not take water from any irrigator except on a "willing lessee/lessor" or "seller/buyer" basis. Two presenters, one from the state Department of Agriculture and another representing the Central Natural Resources District, expressed concern that economic growth might suffer and, furthermore, that the USFWS's science could not be fully trusted. Members of the Nebraska recovery program negotiating team and the USFWS provided overviews of the proposed program and explained why it was needed.

Sitting in the audience, one had the sense that most citizens were hearing for the very first time what the program would entail. They heard summaries of the major considerations that had driven the need for the program, that it would not place heavy burdens on anybody, that there were benefits to be had. Almost five years after the Cooperative Agreement had been signed, most were learning for the first time about what had brought their Nebraska leaders to the negotiating table and that there were compelling reasons for what they had been doing.

In his summation, Representative Osborne stressed that the ESA needed reform. It protected species, he said, without any regard for economic impact, and that was a problem. But, he noted, many people in urban areas of the country, especially on each coast, liked the ESA as it was; politically, Nebraskans could not easily change it. But everybody agreed that decisions must be based on the best peer-reviewed science. He allowed that the Cooperative Agreement was solid in principle; it offered a political solution to an important problem. The negotiations on behalf of the proposed recovery program had raised issues with Nebraska's water law and planning. Nebraska had an excellent water situation overall, Osborne emphasized, and Nebraskans needed a state water plan to be proactive and to protect themselves.

Many people close to the recovery program negotiations worried about the effect the Osborne hearing would have. In the weeks leading up to the hearing, there had been serious concern that groundwater users might hijack the session and that the turmoil would place Nebraska authorities in even greater political difficulty. The disciplined conduct of the session prevented that scenario and did succeed in getting reasoned arguments out to community leaders around the state. However, one repercussion raised deeply problematic issues: Mr. Osborne would write a letter.

BRINGING BACK SCIENCE AS AN ISSUE

Congressman Osborne sent a letter to Secretary Norton dated February 26, 2002, noting that his constituents were concerned that the USFWS was planning to designate critical habitat for the piping plover in riverine areas the birds used much less than they did off-channel habitat around sandpits and lakeshores. He asserted that the USFWS's science was suspect and should be reviewed by the NAS or a similar independent qualified scientific authority. The message was clear: the USFWS could not be trusted to do "good" science. This point had been groused about at the negotiating table for years, but it had been subordinated to state water users' political desire to build a reasonable and prudent alternative and obtain regulatory certainty. A popular politician had now entered the fray; he had picked up that old theme and elevated it to the highest levels of the state and federal governments.

One can surmise that the governor of Nebraska, facing a difficult choice as to whether to sign the completed recovery program agreement, would have found important political cover in endorsing Congressman Osborne's call for an NAS review of the USFWS's science. By mid-June 2002, it was clear that Nebraska authorities were promoting a broad NAS review of the proposed Platte River Habitat Recovery Program and the science on which it is based. Nothing would be held aside. Reviewers would be asked to examine the science related to establishing habitat requirements, how flow regimes had affected target species and their habitats, whether the proposed habitat restoration activities were grounded in solid science, and whether the proposed monitoring and research activities were scientifically justifiable. They proposed a timeline in which NAS funding for the review would have been available by October, work would begin no later than December 2002, and a final report would be issued by September 2004. Nebraska was leading the way to an additional delay in implementing the program.

Wyoming negotiators and Colorado representatives, who for years had pounded out the program details with federal authorities, strongly disagreed with Nebraska's tactic and lamented that the option to conduct an NAS review had been raised. Over the years, all parties to the negotiations had whittled the water and land components into a condition with which each could live. Who was to say that an NAS review of the science behind the program would not conclude that there was a need for more terrestrial habitat or for qualitatively different habitat than that negotiated? What if NAS concluded that more, not less, water was required? Everything that had been so laboriously assembled could come crashing down under the weight of an outside review. A fallen program would not serve anybody's interest—federal, state, or local. Furthermore, even if an NAS review undermined the overall justification for the basin-wide program and caused it to be abandoned as some groundwater users in Nebraska wanted, the ESA would not go away. The need for Section 7 consultations would not evaporate. All an NAS review would do was risk "blowing up" a carefully negotiated recovery program and force water users to undergo the nightmare of the individual permitting process. Nebraska had taken a tack that was extremely dangerous. As one longtime state negotiator said, "If the Osborne strategy blows up the recovery program and we lose our chance at regulatory certainty, we will be all over him like stink on cow manure."

Negotiators had successfully pushed the issue of federal science off the table years ago, and most had no desire to bring it back. In spite of their wishes, however, the issue of questionable federal science was gaining life in the political hands of the three state governors—Mike Johanns of Nebraska, Wyoming's Jim Geringer, and Bill Owens of Colorado.

In Wyoming, Geringer appeared to be moving, with some reluctance, toward giving qualified support to an NAS review. His thinking was, how do you ask your people to make sacrifices if the science that justifies the program is no good? In Colorado, the Owens administration eagerly grasped the opportunity the issue provided. The idea of requesting an NAS review served the administration's politics well. As one Owens appointee put it in a conversation with Colorado supporters of the Tamarack Plan:

> The politics of this is that you guys [Colorado South Platte water users] don't want NAS to take an independent look at the science on which the whole program is based. You want to promote and defend your negotiated solution. . . . How do you go to a Governor during the biggest drought in a hundred years and ask him to sign on this program without a NAS review that the Governors of Nebraska and Wyoming are calling for? Governor Owens is not prepared to sign on [to] the recovery program without a NAS review.

In Colorado, local people working within their local constraints and opportunities had spent years putting together their contribution to the basin-wide recovery program, but they faced rejection by their state's Republican administration, which chose to place its anti-ESA ideology above local Colorado water users' efforts. In Nebraska, a different scenario was playing out. State negotiators had built a Nebraska program that had aroused sufficient opposition among local groundwater users that the governor was feeling intense pressure not to back his own negotiating representatives.

So it had come to pass that by midsummer 2002 the issue of the integrity of federal science, deftly put away in time to build the 1997 Cooperative Agreement, had once again emerged as a hovering specter. Colorado's highest administration officials chose to hold hands with an enthusiastic Nebraska governor and a more reluctant Wyoming governor. The negotiating teams in each of the three states saw the dangers inherent in the choice. Wyoming and Colorado water user representatives in the negotiations were adamantly opposed to the NAS review. Nebraska's team was split. In the waning days of 2000, for reasons discussed in Chapter 15, the Cooperative Agreement had already been extended until June 30, 2003. But time had passed quickly, and with the latest deadline little more than a year away, the governors' call for an NAS review of the federal science was a massive headache for negotiators. The thought of another delay in the program signing—at least another 18–24 months—was unwelcome. Even more worrisome was the threat that an unknown review team—competent, to be sure, but insensitive to the myriad considerations that had gone into the proposed program—would carve up the world in new ways, undo years of handiwork wrought by the most thoughtful people the several parties could muster, and leave everybody facing nightmarish independent Section 7 consultations.

The decision to undertake the NAS review, pushed by state political forces loosely linked to the negotiating room, marked a stunning shift in the entire negotiating process. The justifications of science had brought negotiators to the table; now a new NAS-NRC twist in those justifications could potentially unravel everything.

CHAPTER 15

Science as Faith

Negotiating an Adaptive Management Deal for Terrestrial Habitat

One aspect of Endangered Species Act (ESA) implementation has been the designation of critical habitats—the geographic areas requiring special management on behalf of target species. On the Platte, no critical habitat has been designated for the least tern or pallid sturgeon. For the whooping crane, designated critical habitat begins at the upstream end at the junction of U.S. Highway 283 and I-80 near Lexington, Nebraska, and extends eastward along the river and downstream to a point near the community of Shelton. Piping plover critical habitat is contiguous with that of the whooping crane but extends farther downriver to its mouth. The June 1997 Cooperative Agreement established a Land Committee, advisory to the Governance Committee, to address the vexing issues pertaining to evaluating, acquiring, crediting, managing, restoring, and monitoring land habitat for the three listed birds within the larger critical habitat.

ESTABLISHING A FORUM FOR DISCOURSE: TUMULTUOUS TIMES FOR THE LAND COMMITTEE

Recovery program leaders had to confront the problem of initiating an orderly Land Committee process. They needed to establish a viable and stable membership, create a charter, establish procedures for discussion and voting, select leaders, and develop criteria for purchasing or leasing habitat. These matters would constitute a multi-year challenge.

In Colorado, the Tamarack Plan had been pieced together by local water users who represented irrigation districts, mutual ditch companies, Denver Water, and the Northern Colorado Water Conservancy District. However, in Nebraska the water action plan had been assembled primarily by state-level authorities and representatives of two districts—the Central Nebraska Public Power and Irrigation District (CNPPID) and the Nebraska Public Power District (NPPD)—which needed to re-license their facilities. Groundwater users, organized in Natural Resource Districts (NRDs), did not participate actively in the proposed Platte River Habitat Recovery Program negotiations because their leaders were hostile to the entire concept. NRDs were therefore not the most effective conduits for the full flow of information regarding Platte Basin negotiations.

Immediately following the signing of the July 1997 Cooperative Agreement, only a small group of those closely associated with the negotiations attended Land Committee meetings. However, that period of quiet did not last. The sessions soon became deeply troubled.

Groundwater User Protest

The signing of the Cooperative Agreement had not been well received by many irrigators in Nebraska, especially groundwater users who elected to join an association known as Nebraskans First (www.nebraskansfirst.com/). Nebraskans First was formed in June 1991 (*Omaha World-Herald* 2007). Its express purpose had been to mobilize against the interests of surface water irrigators who were pushing a legislative bill (LB 306) that would have shifted control over groundwater exploitation to state authorities and thereby substantially diminished the capacity of NRDs to determine the future of groundwater pumping. The NRDs were overwhelmingly in the grasp of groundwater pumpers, and the specter of state control promised surface water right holders greater leverage in water policy debates.

Now, after the signing of the Cooperative Agreement in 1997, a new threat existed across central and western Nebraska—a federally induced habitat recovery program that would again raise the unwelcome question, what is the relationship between groundwater extraction and surface flows in the Platte River? Members of Nebraskans First would mobilize to assert their opposition to any such program at the most accessible point available to them—the Land Committee—and they would be joined by some from Wyoming's Upper North Platte region and even a few from eastern Colorado.

In this context, worried groundwater users fed themselves on slim rations of program knowledge and large helpings of fear-laden rumor. Nebraskans First had been ideologically opposed to many federal government programs in many policy domains and was outright hostile to the very thought of reorganizing Platte River water for endangered or threatened species. Furthermore, to the group's members the idea was repugnant that outsiders from Wyoming, Colorado, and the Department of the Interior (DOI) would "move in" on Nebraska land and use it for purposes the group averred Nebraskans did not want.

In late 1997 and throughout 1998, Land Committee meetings were targeted by protestors—many galvanized by Nebraskans First—who chose to vent their anguish at the program forum most conveniently available to them because the committee met in various Nebraska towns. Meetings were besieged by protesters who arrived by car, truck, and loaded buses.

The committee became virtually paralyzed by the vehemence of repeated protests. Packed meeting rooms were stages for the venting of opposition by farmers who were clearly not interested in a smooth committee startup. At times, moderate voices went largely unheard by more radical attendees. Thoughtful voices attempting to articulate fundamental program concepts were repeatedly shouted down. Attempts to explain program principles drew scorn. Angry attendees were not prepared to hear things such as the fact that program land would be acquired on a willing seller-buyer basis, that there would be no condemnations, that designation of critical habitat would not affect private ownership rights within critical habitat boundaries, that government agents would not have access to private lands, and that the program would not deny access to private property.

Sessions in the summer and early fall of 1998 were especially difficult. At the Ramada Inn in Kearney, at the Central Platte Natural Resource District Building in Grand Island, and again in Lexington, people packed into overflowing rooms. Those who could not squeeze inside milled in the parking lots. Thoughtful observers and participants sensed that the process was on the edge of erupting into overt violence. Some Nebraskans First members especially displayed hostility. It was an intimidating atmosphere for those who came to work—especially representatives from Colorado and Wyoming—and who rose occasionally to at least attempt to speak on behalf of the need for orderly discussion; it was also intimidating for those who merely wanted to share information or make a case for the program. They were repeatedly shouted down by people convinced that the federal program would dispossess them of their land. A few even saw connections between the proposed program and black helicopters allegedly spotted in the countryside, supposedly carrying agents hostile to the "American way."

Background

Some of the opposition to the proposed habitat recovery program was rooted in a series of events that took place in the context of preliminary Federal Energy Regulatory Commission (FERC) re-licensing discussions in the late 1980s. Some leaders of the opposition remembered what for them was a very threatening episode and recalled it as an example of what had made them afraid of federal penetration into the Nebraska Platte region. In April 1987, with the original Kingsley Dam hydropower licenses about to expire following an FERC extension, the CNPPID and the NPPD were caught up in renewing their annual operating licenses. The Whooping Crane Trust saw this as an opportunity to request that environmental conditions in support of habitat restoration be established as part of annual license renewals (Aiken 1999: 138–139). The trust did nothing more than ask FERC to hold administrative hearings regarding what habitat mitigation conditions might be established. FERC refused the trust's request on the grounds that the commission was not authorized to establish new conditions in annual license proceedings. Such conditions were appropriate to discuss in forthcoming negotiations with the two districts regarding the renewal of their fifty-year licenses (Aiken 1999: 138–139).

In 1989, FERC (still in consultation with the U.S. Fish and Wildlife Service [USFWS]) considered whether to impose in-stream flow requirements on interim Central and NPPD hydropower operations licenses during the extended long-term re-licensing process. NPPD's license was written in such a manner that FERC had latitude to insert new conditions. However, CNPPID's license authorized FERC modifications only with the district's consent (Aiken 1999: 138–139). On February 14, 1990, FERC required NPPD to release water through Kingsley Dam to enhance in-stream flows at Grand Island and downstream in the name of improved bird habitat. FERC had asked for Central's cooperation in this endeavor but was refused. After about 70,000 acre feet of Lake McConaughy water had been sent downstream over Central's objections, NPPD received a temporary stay from FERC on May 10, and an indefinite stay was put in place on May 30, 1990. The Whooping Crane Trust did not appeal the stays and requested no further interim releases (Aiken 1999: 140).

Those flow releases ordered by FERC in consultation with the USFWS shocked and enraged managers in the CNPPID and the NPPD, as well as many other Nebraskans. The Whooping Crane Trust could see that whatever benefits were forthcoming from enhanced in-stream flows, the organization had insufficient political capital to try to sustain the practice. Environmental organizations need friends, especially friends in their locality, and the federally ordered water releases meant the trust was losing friends fast. An experiment on the river had been conducted, but it had been costly for everyone.

Those with environmental sympathies lamented Central's hard-line stance. Those in the water community expressed fear of an "out-of-control" federal government. The issue was politically hot at the state level. Governor Benjamin Nelson personally intervened. On the one hand, Nebraska water constituents had been roused in opposition to the new federal environmental agenda. On the other hand, it was a fact of life that the two districts needed to be re-licensed over the long term by a federal agency. After due deliberation, the governor proposed the concept of establishing an environmental water account at Lake McConaughy. Subsequently, over years of negotiations the state of Nebraska, the two districts, FERC, and the USFWS would accomplish exactly that as part of the FERC re-licensing process. The districts would make "water deposits," and a USFWS manager would allocate those waters to ESA listed species needs.

But water users' hearts especially had been hardened. The CNPPID and the NPPD would thenceforth fight hard not to give up anything more in what would become the Cooperative Agreement negotiations during the years 1997–2006. Other Nebraska water users, especially on the groundwater side, sustained their deep paranoia about federal intrusion into Nebraska water agendas. Repercussions of that 1990 event would be felt all the way to the Land Committee negotiations years later.

The Aftermath

Social interaction within and surrounding the Land Committee had become highly polarized; civil discourse was threatened. Something had to be done before things spiraled further out of control. Ways and means would have to be found to de-polarize the situation, to find crosscutting attachments that would create more common ground. Such a situation started to develop in the fall of 1998 and continued throughout 1999.

The atmosphere at Land Committee meetings improved as time passed, as emotional venting over repeated themes became predictable and tedious, and as a public information table was made available at all meetings. After discussions with Nebraskans First leaders, it was agreed that no more busloads of people would be rounded up and delivered by the organization; rather, Nebraskans First would send a small number of representatives to observe committee proceedings and, along with others, be permitted to speak at specified times.

Information began to flow. The Land Committee was inadvertently becoming the most effective channel available to Nebraska authorities for outreach and education. As difficult as many committee sessions had been, people who had come to protest learned essential program facts. While some in the audiences continued to reject the message of speakers on behalf of the proposed program, others found that the proposed program was not the threat they had been led to envisage. Many heard the program side of the story for the first time, concluded that the threat was not that serious, and returned to their farms, ranches, and places of business. Radicals had overplayed their hand, in the minds of many. Moments of rancorous conflict diminished, and periods of authentic exchange of information increased.

By November 1998 the Land Committee was moving rapidly toward being organized, with subcommittees and a clearly specified membership consisting of two representatives from the federal government, one from each of the three basin states, Nebraska landowners, a hydropower representative, and an environmentalist—a profile that reflected the composition of other advisory committees. Sessions began to settle into a general pattern with which people could live. Monthly meetings of the full Land Committee were held in the fall, winter, and spring months with time off during the busy summer growing season, when farmers needed to be in their fields from before dawn until after dusk. Sessions still drew those who persisted in venting opposition, but they were speaking out during times set on an agenda that made space for comments from the floor. Meanwhile, away from the main stage, subcommittees began their substantive work.

There was much to do. Criteria needed to be formulated for assessing suitable habitat. Procedures had to be constructed that would permit speedy and flexible acquisition of land, and strategies needed to evolve for entering local land markets without playing the part of city people with too much money, too little sense, and too much vulnerability to being taken for a pricey ride by colluding locals. How could a program put together by three states and the Department of the Interior function as a "good neighbor" capable of responding quickly and effectively to local problems (for example, weed control, fencing problems, wetlands soaking neighboring property)? Consideration had to be given to the nature of the organizational entity that should be engaged to manage program lands. A system had to be created for crediting each participant-donor to the land budget with a land equity stake so assets could be justly distributed in the event the program collapsed. How could Wyoming and Colorado hold equity stakes in Nebraska? What methods should be used to acquire land?

All these issues and more required the committee's attention. Here, however, only one issue will be addressed: the problem of employing faith in science as an informant to a continual adaptive management process. How was suitable habitat to be defined?

WHAT CONSTITUTES ADEQUATE HABITAT?

What acreage would count against the 10,000-acre first increment goal in any USFWS scoring system? Would only parcels count that fulfilled "idealized" criteria to the greatest extent? If so, the availability of suitable land would be sharply diminished, and prices would escalate. If the highest standards in land selection were compromised, how much compromise would be acceptable to the USFWS? In March 2001, after lengthy—at times even bitter—discussions, the Governance Committee provisionally agreed on a policy statement that incorporated a principle of flexibility in the selection of habitat lands. The language of the statement made it clear that certain lands could count as suitable habitat even if their characteristics were found to be less than ideal and that program funds could be used, within limits, to acquire some alternative habitats for the purpose of determining over time whether they provided demonstrable benefits to the listed species. Alternative habitats were understood to consist of sandpits and non-riverine wetlands that would exist beyond the boundaries of USFWS-defined "habitat complexes."

The land habitat discussion labored under constraints different from those of water acquisition and use. Whereas water is a common pool resource, land on the Central Platte was overwhelmingly a private good. In the world of water, the asset is publicly owned, and water records had been well kept for over a century by all parties. Everybody roughly knew the pattern of basin flows and exactly which parties managed specific flows in each stream segment. With the exception of the *Nebraska v. Wyoming* legal struggle, there was no constraint on publicly sharing data about the availability of water among all parties. Nobody could hide a significant fraction of flow from anybody else. In the domain of land, however, the situation was different.

The Politics of Data and Markets

The USFWS had utilized land information produced by the U.S. Geological Survey's (USGS) geographical information systems (GIS) technology. The U.S. Bureau of Reclamation (USBR)–environmental impact statement (EIS) team then added its own analytical system to map the critical habitat. The USFWS was thereby able to identify with a high degree of precision and certainty which land parcels had the best habitat potential. The problem was that although GIS mapping products are a matter of public record, the USFWS dared not release information regarding its acquisition priorities. Furthermore, if the information were to be employed in making policy decisions prior to the conclusion of the negotiations, it would likely be subject to dissemination under the open records law. One thing the state, federal, and environmental representatives could readily agree upon was that any "hypothetical" analysis of land parcels in an effort to show how the 10,000- or 29,000-acre objective could best be achieved should not get beyond the negotiating room. If it did, the analysis would be variously interpreted, alarm some landowners while delighting others, be the subject of attention among citizens worried about the potential negative impacts to their communities, and—most of all—initiate spasms of land speculation that could work to the disadvantage of all parties. If such analysis ever reached the streets, the program would not be able to afford those lands targeted as most desirable.

Therefore, the USFWS could not show its maps to the Governance Committee or to Technical Committee members. Talk about GIS analysis of habitat was so potentially dangerous that it was best postponed until after a program had been put together and endorsed by the signatories and the Governance Committee was actually prepared to initiate habitat acquisition. The USFWS could only put out a message to the effect that land with certain attributes was desired.

The negotiators did not work with the same level of specifics used in the water domain. A cost to the negotiations accompanied the lack of specific

Governance Committee discussions of land habitat particulars. The choice not to employ real maps to tentatively advance specific options for assembling the most desirable habitat complexes meant that state representatives could back away from involving themselves in a collaborative construction of solutions, much to the dismay of environmentalists and federal representatives at the table. At no time were state negotiators willing to authorize the detailed formulation of program options by members of their staffs; an evil world had given them a reason not to join in collaborative problem solving with federal authorities on issues involving terrestrial habitat.

Even after the program launched, adaptive management—informed by the best available science—had to proceed with sensitivity, patience, and care, all the while never fully revealing the larger pattern of desired habitat. It would require the education of scientists, the faces of preachers, the hearts of gamblers, the souls of realtors, and the patience of quilters who would somehow stitch river channels to wetlands and buffer zones, with sandpits on the fringes.

Moving toward Sufficiency

If basin water users, environmentalists, and two agencies of the DOI were to agree to play an adaptive management game together for many years, some agreement had to be reached as to what terrestrial habitat goals were going to look like. The 1997 Cooperative Agreement had set forth a vision that during the first thirteen-year increment, the program should move as rapidly as possible toward establishing three large habitat complexes, each of which would be at least around 2,500 acres in area—one upstream of Kearney, Nebraska, one near Kearney, and one downstream of Kearney. Habitat complexes for the three birds were understood to incorporate sufficiently wide and braided channel areas, adjacent wet meadows, and buffer lands to protect the species from human disturbance. The first program increment pledged to develop 10,000 acres of suitable habitat. After completion of the first increment, the program would continue to acquire suitable habitat up to a total of 29,000 acres.

The three proposed complexes would serve in connection with 2,650 acres of habitat, locally known as Cottonwood Ranch, already acquired by the NPPD as part of its FERC re-licensing agreement. It was understood that given restoration, the Cottonwood Ranch property would count toward the 10,000-acre goal. Together, these ecosystem assemblies would provide over 10,000 acres of

1. Continually shifting barren sand islands in wide, shallow river channels for cranes, least terns, and piping plovers.

2. Roosting habitat on and around sandbars that would provide shallow water depths for cranes at sites where fields of vision would have a radius as long as 650 feet; least terns and piping plovers need nesting sites on un-vegetated

sandbars with sufficient height above water flow levels (for nesting) so that summer storm precipitation does not inundate nests.

3. Adjacent wet meadows where cranes can obtain protein as they prepare for further migration and egg laying; many of the food organisms eaten by migrating birds in general, and cranes in particular, are dependent upon the moist and saturated soils of wetlands for all or part of their life cycles.

4. Buffer zones to protect the birds from human disturbance.

USFWS authorities knew they could not expect the program to immediately obtain everything the agency most preferred. It simply wanted to make every effort to approximate the model as much as possible in an imperfect world. The closer the program could come to this ideal of large, complete complexes, the stronger the case for evaluating the program as a sufficient reasonable and prudent alternative that could earn a non-jeopardy biological opinion. This kind of language, which was reasonable to the USFWS, made the states very anxious.

At its core, the struggle between the USFWS and state negotiators was simple. The agency had prepared a biological opinion (U.S. Fish and Wildlife Service 1997b) that found listed species to be in jeopardy by virtue of human-caused habitat destruction. Under the law, the USFWS could not negotiate away the import of that finding. Therefore, the agency had little option but to take a hard line to ensure that its jeopardy standard would not be easily assailable in the courts by disgruntled environmentalists who would inevitably scrutinize the program agreement. The USFWS had every incentive to operate with the idea that there was ample land that could fulfill the rather rigidly constructed high standards for virtually all program acreage. Agency representatives therefore strove to reduce to a minimum the latitude of water users in the states to define sufficient habitat in the adaptive management process. The USFWS pressed for high-quality habitat standards and for explicitly specifying those standards in any program documents.

The states, in turn, energetically pushed back against what they considered an unjustifiable USFWS "straightjacket." States pressed for the maximum possible latitude in defining serviceable habitat. They had every incentive to construct the vision of a scarcity of land that would fulfill the USFWS's high standards, they argued for looser language that would permit maximum flexibility, and they resisted too much written detail.

Voices for the USFWS replied by pointing out that state representatives needed to keep good faith with the 1997 Cooperative Agreement, which had been hammered out between 1994 and 1997. From the federal point of view, the states were way off base in their attacks on so-called agency rigidity. The 1997 document clearly articulated the habitat goals of the projected first program increment. The 1993 Platte River Coordinating Committee's study (see Chapter 7) had envisioned the future program as acquiring and managing "large contiguous parcels of terrestrial and aquatic habitat" that would cumulate to 29,000 acres.

Given all this, DOI representatives believed they had succeeded in obtaining a commitment from the states to accept the concept of acquiring large, high-quality habitat complexes as quid pro quo for their compromise in lowering the acreage target to 10,000 acres. They were dismayed in the extreme when representatives of the states began to try to renegotiate what federal representatives had felt was a commitment to seek the best possible contiguous habitat complexes. In federal eyes, state representatives were exhibiting bad faith in having spent five years (1998–2002) pecking at and trying to renegotiate the habitat language in the Cooperative Agreement.

For their part, many state representatives began to advance the view that the difficult discussions about the definition of adequate habitat revealed the collaborative process as a fraud, an illusion. There was, they said, no authentic collaboration, just questionable dictates from the USFWS Grand Island field office. The biggest issue centered on the question, should off-channel habitat used by the three bird species but disconnected from the large habitat complexes specified by the USFWS have a priority place in the proposed program? The states argued that when it was demonstrable that birds were using these alternative habitats—especially sandpits and non-riverine wetlands—the program should spend at least some of its budget on acquiring them, and such habitat should be counted. The USFWS resisted the move.

Sandpits had been artificially created along the Platte River corridor by various Nebraska construction projects that needed gravel. The major project that accounted for most of the sandpit digging was the construction of Interstate 80, which roughly parallels the Platte River across the greater portion of Nebraska. As depressions were created by the removal of gravel, water seeped and made ponds in the holes. All parties agreed that at least two of the three bird species—terns and plovers—had made use of them. But USFWS biologists intensely resisted the idea of permitting the states to construct a reasonable and prudent alternative with a significant fraction of habitat in scattered, disconnected 40- to 250-acre parcels incorporating one or more sandpits near an interstate highway. The states—especially Nebraska—wanted an explicit program sanction to explore the idea. Such sites are numerous, they can generally be purchased cheaply, and at least some of the listed birds demonstrably used them. Should states get credit under the program for providing a significant amount of "alternative habitat?" The states said yes; the USFWS said no.

There were two possible ways to proceed. First was the option preferred by the USFWS: let there be no explicit endorsement of sandpit habitat and wetlands divorced from the river. However, the agency was prepared to defer to the states by indicating that a program of research and monitoring could be developed to assess the value of the alternative habitats over time. As evidence mounted one way or another during the first 10- to 13-year program increment, the adaptive management process could incorporate the lessons learned. The agency pointed out that it was possible to study how sandpits and non-riverine wetlands served the listed birds without spending any money on acquiring them.

The second option, pushed by the states, was to specify that program monies would be used to acquire habitat units of both types—larger complete complexes, as desired by the USFWS, and alternative habitats—and then early in the first increment begin to compare one type to the other in experimental fashion. This would make the acquisition and protection of sandpits and disconnected wetlands an acknowledged program priority. The states wanted this option not only because it made some sense but because it would serve as a litmus test regarding the limits of federal flexibility. The struggle was over how to define the arena for discourse about options and about the terms of the state-federal partnership.

Under sustained attack from the states over a period of many months, the USFWS refused to shift away from its strong defense of positions taken in its biological opinion, particularly that both riverine and sandpit habitats should be managed for tern and plover production but that sandpits could not serve as a substitute for quality river channel habitat (Lutey 2002: iv). Agency analysts had good reason to believe, in their view, that the three bird species had been listed in the first place because their preferred habitats had been damaged and even destroyed. It was not logically defensible, the agency argued, simply to conclude that because a species does not use a given patch of degraded riverine habitat, it does not need that habitat and furthermore that inferior habitat now occupied (primarily sandpits) could somehow be defined as "good enough" simply because terns and plovers had been displaced to them.

The issue became hotly contentious. State representatives asked: would the USFWS count a parcel of land disconnected from one of its idealized habitat complexes as providing a demonstrable benefit if

1. Birds were confirmed to be using a sandpit? USFWS: no.
2. Birds were confirmed to be using a sandpit and fledging their young there? USFWS: no.
3. Birds were confirmed to be using a sandpit, fledging their young there, and surviving to adulthood? USFWS: not necessarily.

In the agency's eyes, just because a bird has been found nesting on an asphalt parking lot, that fact could not support a rationale for acquiring paved habitats at shopping centers. The USFWS also feared that giving credit to noncomplex habitat would reduce the states' willingness to push for land in quality complexes. For months the agency held to the position that to have a demonstrable benefit, habitat acquisitions would have to be located within, or be adjacent to, an agency-endorsed and properly buffered riverine/wetland complex—at least until years of data gathering and analysis could establish beyond any reasonable doubt that sandpits and non-riverine wetlands could work for the species. Only this position could stave off pressure from the states, who were seeking maximum latitude and least-cost solutions, and environmental critics, who feared the USFWS would trade away the best biology to keep its coalition together.

Compromise

By May 2002, negotiators had produced a draft habitat protection plan that explicitly reflected compromise, a gesture toward the states. It included the possibility of spending first program increment dollars on acquiring up to 800 acres of "noncomplex habitat lands," as part of the 10,000-acre goal. Several reasons emerged for this move. First, it was clear to everyone that at the end of the day, the USFWS held effective veto power over the proposed purchase of any piece of habitat. Every land acquisition would require virtual consensus by the Governance Committee, and all habitat purchased with program dollars would have to fulfill agency criteria. Knowing this, agency negotiators could soften the language a bit to assuage the states' concerns. It was a small price to pay for showing willingness to incorporate state water user perspectives.

There was a second consideration. The real world would not deliver neatly packaged units of uniformly high-quality habitat; instead, land would become available on the market as a bundle of mixed qualities. In a true willing seller–willing buyer situation, sellers would not generally carve up their properties into subunits categorized according to USFWS habitat criteria and sell only those units the rigid agency program language endorsed. The program would have little option but to purchase some lower-quality land in order to obtain the best. Fighting over program language around the negotiating table would not make that reality go away. Decisions would have to be made on a case-by-case basis. Criteria for selecting particular site-specific habitat would emerge during the actual experience of putting the habitat together. Some sandpit and disconnected wetland habitat was seen as at least somewhat likely to be bundled in messy real estate transactions. Why not diffuse the fight a little and accept that up to 8 percent of the acquisitions could be alternatives to the main thrust of large connected habitat complexes?

Third, land acquisition requires speedy and deft flexibility to grasp fleeting opportunities. Willing sellers will not patiently wait for clumsy program procedures to be circumvented and extended Governance Committee debates to occur; recovery program administrators need to have their general guidelines in hand and be ready to move with dispatch or risk losing out to competitive buyers who have no wildlife agenda in mind. The reality would be messy and dynamic, and no amount of fussy bureaucratic rigidity in the program document could make the world tidy. The Platte River Whooping Crane Habitat Maintenance Trust had been operating in local land markets since the mid-1970s and, along with the Audubon Society, had acquired a great deal of local experience. Representatives of these organizations would need to assist the recovery program in its habitat acquisition efforts. If USFWS rigidity became a problem that seriously constrained effective land acquisition, these experienced local environmentalists would be expected to join with states and their water users to pressure the agency into greater responsiveness.

The Land Committee was established amid rancorous conflict. After it surmounted that early threat, it soon became embroiled again in a sharp dispute about how to define acceptable habitat. Negotiators who had earlier agreed to disagree about target flows had now agreed to disagree about what constituted justifiable habitat. The only way out of the troubled discourse was for the states to recognize that the USFWS had a biological opinion to defend and that they would have to accept fully configured habitat complexes as the overwhelming component of any viable land program. In turn, the USFWS eventually explicitly recognized that the states' contention that alternative habitats might also serve species needs had at least some merit. All parties were staking their futures on faith in a concept most had never heard of prior to the negotiations—adaptive management. Adaptive management would be used to bind up the wounds left by the inability to resolve fundamental issues, but the process would lead to the salvation of ESA compliance and regulatory certainty. The ESA, a challenging piece of science-dependent legislation, was requiring enormous amounts of good faith. As the law forced big questions to be asked that were beyond the capacity of the best science to answer, faith in adaptive management, science, and civil discourse had to increasingly fill in the gap.

Science as Faith

Putting Adaptive Management to Its First Test with
the Sedimentation-Vegetation Problem

Sediments washed down from the Rocky Mountain Front Range have long provided much of the muddy glop on which Lower Mississippi River Valley ecosystems and civilizations have been built. Sedimentation had been crucial to the
construction of traditional tern, plover, and crane habitat along the Platte. The
capacity of basin water flows to move a range of sizes of earthen particles would
loom large in recovery program negotiations. The problem of moving sands and
gravels by Platte flows to the right places and in the right shapes would bring the
negotiations to their lowest point, to the very edge of a blowup. It would not be
science per se that would save the day because available science lacked sufficient
answers. It would be faith in science, within an adaptive management framework,
that would get negotiators through to a tenuous resolution—albeit one barely
adequate to allow the construction of a reasonable and prudent alternative.

UNEXPECTED BAD NEWS

Members of the Governance Committee, their assistants, and other observers
gathered in the U.S. Fish and Wildlife Service's (USFWS) third-floor conference
room in the agency's office suite in Lakewood, a western Denver suburb. It was
August 3, 2000, and there was reason to feel good about the direction of things.
The water, land, and research-monitoring agreements had been sketched, even
if they were not fully complete. The forthcoming November elections would
put a new administration in place the following January, but there was guarded
hope that the recovery program was far enough along to produce a reasonable

and prudent alternative that could be signed in the last days of the Clinton administration. If not, the signing could occur in the early months of the newly installed presidency. The major general concern had been Nebraska's problem in finding sufficient support for the proposed program.

Ralph Morgenweck, the USFWS regional director, opened the meeting with a three-minute statement. The environmental impact statement (EIS) team had completed a preliminary analysis of the proposed water action plan (along with other alternatives the team had constructed over the past months, with the knowledge and consent of the Governance Committee as required by the National Environmental Policy Act). The EIS team had found that none of the alternatives served as a reasonable and prudent alternative. Years of work lay in disarray.

Sediment issues had been mentioned only sporadically in discussions prior to the signing of the Cooperative Agreement in July 1997. In the discourses that followed, no attention had been paid to sedimentation. Negotiators had pieced together a proposed water action plan on the premise that an average of approximately 130,000–140,000 acre feet added to the spring and summer flows would do much to help produce the desired wide, shallow, braided river required by the listed birds. However, now the EIS team had found that the laboriously constructed action plan produced mostly clear water that had dropped its sediment in reservoirs behind North Platte dams. When released for program purposes, this clear water would scrub up sediment and thereby scour out and further incise channels.

The EIS team determined that following installation of the Kingsley Dam, which created Lake McConaughy, and construction of the Central Nebraska Public Power and Irrigation District (CNPPID) canal system, three factors pertaining to sediment were at the core of the problem. First, Lake McConaughy was itself a sediment trap that made for clear water releases out of Kingsley. Second, the CNPPID plumbing constituted another sediment trap, resulting in clear water releases from the Johnson Lake power plant return (J-2) (see Figure 5.1). Third, the proposed program made the situation worse by moving additional flows through the CNPPID system as a method of delivering program water to critical habitat. Roughly half of the water flowing to the critical habitat was projected to come out of the J-2 return as clear flows that gouged river channels. Just a few months before the December 31 deadline for producing a viable program, the proposed collaborative program option, as it stood, was estimated to contribute to the very problem it was supposed to help solve.

Morgenweck made it clear that the action plan as negotiated was necessary to any reasonable and prudent alternative, but it was not sufficient. Unless changes were made, the negotiated program would only aggravate conditions that had led to the original jeopardy opinion in the first place. Furthermore, the issue had to be faced squarely; it could not be deferred. Water users could not expect to obtain regulatory certainty on the basis of what had turned out to be a deeply flawed reasonable and prudent alternative. The USFWS was prepared to explore options for constructively dealing with the problem.

This announcement had the potential to unravel everything. The best available science had undercut a key program premise. Negotiators were looking at years of effort in serious danger of falling apart. Federal authorities, who had frequently expressed frustration with what they had viewed as delay tactics by the states and their water users, had brought forward an issue at the last moment that was potentially a showstopper and, at the very least, would necessarily cause significant delay. A major extension of the Cooperative Agreement would be necessary; in fact, by the end of 2000, arrangements had been put in place to extend the deliberations for thirty months, to June 30, 2003.

The states saw great danger in the announcement. Was this just one more instance of loosely constructed federal science—in the form of incomplete and insufficiently validated models—threatening to place new, unwarranted, and open-ended demands on state treasuries? Was it ever going to be possible to walk into unknown territory with federal agencies and not get "mugged"? Given the succession of dams on the North Platte, the major source of sediment would have to be Colorado's South Platte. Would that mean a major renegotiation of Colorado's contribution at Tamarack? Would the federal agencies push for releasing sediment-laden water out of a reservoir or two above the Balzac gauge—the compact firewall—and run it on the crest of spring flood pulses? Such possibilities became a Colorado nightmare.

Would the USFWS be prepared to actually require the insertion of sediment into the river at Nebraska Public Power District's (NPPD's) Keystone diversion, where that district had been struggling for decades to remove the buildup? What would major insertions of sediment do to people who lived along the river? The Nebraska negotiating team had too few constituents pushing for the recovery program as it was. The program could lose much of what little Nebraska support it enjoyed if locals started thinking about federal agency managers becoming involved in Nebraska Platte River management, with little regard for their well-being. Also, for years, farmers in all three states had worked with the U.S. Department of Agriculture's (USDA) Natural Resources Conservation Service (formerly the Soil Conservation Service) to learn how to minimize erosion of soils into the river. Now, a federal agency actually wanted to put sediment into the river to build sandbars. To many, this was another instance of the federal government's right hand not knowing what its left hand was doing.

The states were perplexed that the USFWS had seemingly acted capriciously by suddenly changing the rules of the game so late in the negotiations. Up to this point, the route to regulatory certainty had been paved with commitments to re-time water, to acquire and manage habitat, and to do research and monitoring. Now it appeared that the USFWS wanted the program, in an open-ended way, to somehow manipulate more than eighty miles of river above the critical habitat—a long segment that any conceivable program flows could impact only marginally. The states might be placed on the hook forever for ongoing undefined commitments. How could such a proposal be ushered through a state legislature, assuming it made sense even to try to do so? A revised program would have to be devised. What form should that revision take? Who knew? How much time was there to think about this? The answer: all too little.

Morgenweck's official August speech on the subject was not entirely a surprise to those who had been following the negotiations closely. In Sterling, Colorado, the preceding April 25, after a day of Water Advisory Committee meetings and prior to the meeting of the full Governance Committee two days later, the USFWS and the U.S. Bureau of Reclamation (USBR)–EIS team organized an evening presentation that signaled their concern about the sedimentation problem. The sediment transport model that had generated problematic results was unfinished and un-calibrated, and the data shared that night did not fully justify any particular conclusion. But the federal partners wanted to share their concerns and the evidence as it existed at that moment. After all, the finished version of the proposed water action plan was due on May 15, only three weeks hence. The sediment model, one nobody was yet willing to trust, produced many preliminary scenarios—one of which was that a segment of wide river, enhanced by program flows, might erode a trench on one side of the main channel as deep as twenty-five feet. This was not what anybody wanted to hear. Program flows might become canyon makers.

Nobody took the figures too seriously, but those in attendance were put on notice. Something was seriously wrong with the proposed water action plan, and it would have to be fixed. At the May Governance Committee meeting, the issue was again discussed; the USBR-EIS team's sediment transfer model was being improved. Prospects were not bright for the proposed program to pass muster. During the last two weeks in July, after the EIS team had completed its assessment, Morgenweck informed Governance Committee members in advance that there was no viable alternative in sight; at that point, nobody had a clear idea of what to do to fix the problem.

The sedimentation issue revealed something about the limits of available knowledge in how to deal with complex, theory-defying ecosystems. Various hydraulic models of at least portions of the river had been employed for years. Other models were available that examined interactions among soils, water, and vegetation. But there was no rich history of putting the hydraulics of water flow together with vegetation growth patterns.

THE FEDERAL CASE

The USFWS saw in this episode a prime example of the need for effective adaptive management. Science had instructed the players on a crucial overlooked point. The key to everything was to keep focused on the needs of the species. Basically, the problems for the species had been caused by federal dam and reservoir projects on the North Platte combined with the non-federal Lake McConaughy, which traps sediment and releases clear sediment-starved water. The South Platte has a slightly higher rate of fall across its plains section than the North Platte, which is good for picking up sediment. Furthermore, there are no on-stream plains reservoirs downstream of Denver to serve as sediment traps. Therefore, for most of the twentieth century the South Platte was the main source of sediment for the central Platte. But the South Platte is a smaller stream still compromised in its sediment production potential by some upstream dams and off-stream reservoirs. All this means that human and natural forces have not established a dynamic that digs enough holes in the South Platte to fill the sediment-needy holes of the central Platte.

Sedimentation-Vegetation

When the most downstream dam on the North Platte, Kingsley, shut its gates for the first time in 1941, the central Platte eventually stabilized around a new regime of clearer and more constant flows that eroded listed bird habitats upstream of Kearney, Nebraska, but that—in the view of the USFWS—still supported a residue of effective bird habitats further downstream. The USFWS contended that during periods of low flow, vegetation was established as it always had been; thanks to Kingsley and the other dams above Kearney, however, the river no longer provided sufficiently high pulses to move sediment and scour out seedlings, leading to the growth of densely vegetated islands and riverbanks. The river, in this view, tended to deepen because when higher flows did occur, they were seemingly less erosive of densely vegetated riverbanks and islands and more erosive of channel bottoms. The river thereby became more channelized.

By 2000, preliminary studies had revealed that proposed program-enhanced water flows would likely cut deeper, narrower channels that would further degrade the prized but limited residual bird habitat (Murphy and Randle 2001; Simons and Associates Inc. 2000). Given all this, the USFWS saw that increased channel degradation had been slowly progressing from western upstream areas to eastern downstream points (see Table 16.1). It found upper reaches of the big bend in the river to be much more wooded and narrow than areas further downstream, where the good habitats had survived in the lower part of the big bend stretch. The objective of any viable program would be to halt and then reverse the slow advancement of increased downstream channel incision and narrowing.

Table 16.1. Average Channel Widths (in feet), 1865–1998

Location	Year		
	1865	1957	1998
Upstream at Overton	4,900	1,000	800
Downstream at Grand Island	2,800	1,900	1,300

Source: Murphy and Randle 2001.

Envisioning a Solution

At the May 2000 Governance Committee meeting at the Herschler State Office Building in Cheyenne, Wyoming, the USFWS had promised users that the agency would put together a statement indicating in general terms what it would take to construct a winning program. By September that package of basic concepts had been drafted and circulated among negotiators. In essence, the proposal was to employ the philosophy of adaptive management to increase the active area of the river channel—within existing banks—by reducing flow velocities and preventing the encroachment of vegetation between banks. Tinkering with the riverbank properties of hundreds, if not thousands, of Nebraska property owners would be the kiss of death for any proposed program, so the idea was to obtain the necessary habitat characteristics within existing river channels. It was estimated that removing vegetation from islands and moving sand off of higher islands could result in as much as a 50 percent increase in quality bird habitat. This proposal would entail the implementation of several management practices:

1. There would be an increased emphasis on generating pulse flows from whatever sources were available; the largest of these would be the environmental account at Lake McConaughy, recharged by waters held upstream at Pathfinder and Glendo. Over time, an elaborate schedule of pulse flows would evolve, but the central thrust would be to organize annual pulse flows of 6,000–8,000 cubic feet/second (cfs) for an average of three days in two of every three years. Pulse flows, along with the scouring action of the late winter–early spring breakup of ice sheets, would rip out young vegetation and prevent it from flourishing.

2. To cope with the clear water erosion problem, the concept would entail bulldozing island sand into the stream—about 500 tons of material per day for varying numbers of days depending upon wet-, dry-, or normal-year conditions—to destroy the larger, higher islands that had dense vegetation and to create a constantly shifting pattern of barren sandbars, the kind of habitat suitable for migrating whooping and sandhill cranes, nesting piping plovers, and least terns. For example, sand added to the channel at the rate of 500 tons/day would amount to 100,000 cubic yards of material per year, or the equivalent of about 20 acres of island sand cut to a depth of 3 feet per

year. Over a 64-year period, this would cumulate to 2 square miles of island area. Island chopping and pushing would lead to river sandbar building and a net increase in braided river.

3. To serve policy needs, protocols would be devised to guide systematic gathering of data to determine the effectiveness of the manipulations. This would become a major research and monitoring activity.

The USFWS made it clear that the proposed "concept package" did not mean the agency was attempting to take the river back to its pre-dam 1865 condition. The agency did intend, however, to increase the usable habitat in braided channels cleared of vegetation and to reverse as much as possible the advancement of channel degradation toward Grand Island. The river would necessarily remain constricted at bridges, but the channels were expected to re-widen between those structures.

THE STATES' RESPONSE

The states were less interested in species needs; they were more focused on holding together the architecture of their negotiated agreement, a deal that up to that point had promised what they wanted most: regulatory certainty. Visions of such certainty were dissipating infuriatingly. The best available models of sedimentation-vegetation dynamics were new, crude, incomplete, and untested; their broad error terms could not distinguish between a degrading river and one that was improving. Yet these admittedly inadequate models of complex river phenomena were being used to reject the proposed program and to make policy. The states wanted to know how regulatory certainty would ever become a meaningful concept if the USFWS kept reserving the right to re-think program matters at the last minute and threatening to withdraw the prize of regulatory certainty every time a new issue emerged that was rooted in questionable interpretations of inadequate models and data.

Was regulatory certainty ever to be anything more than a wisp that appeared and disappeared for less than compelling reasons not carefully examined by all parties? States were not alleging that the Department of the Interior (DOI) was conducting bad science because many had high regard for the federal sediment-vegetation modelers. They were angry because the DOI—with its positions encapsulated in the stone of biological opinions and Endangered Species Act (ESA) sufficiency mandates—would not meet with them, admit that too little was known, sign off on the proposed program, grant relief from jeopardy, and then work collaboratively within an adaptive management mode to address the problems.

Negative emotions were running high within state delegations. Representatives in each state advocated a confrontational approach: scrap the entire water action plan and start over. Some members of the Colorado delegation said it was time to go to court and put the Nebraska-Colorado Compact up against the ESA in a way that would reduce federal authority and break the federal case once and for all. But prudence dictated that the states abandon thoughts of rash action. If Colorado, with Nebraska's consent, were to undertake a final once-and-for-all legal battle, it would be risky, expensive, and time-consuming. Destroying the program by pulling out would deprive water users of their temporary grants of relief from jeopardy. If Colorado and Nebraska lost the case, everything would be lost forever. Wyoming was not ready to push for such an extreme tactic, Nebraska merely wanted to play for time, and Colorado decided that discretion was the better part of valor.

The October 2000 discussions did not go well. The USFWS was attempting to advance its concept package, but the states were focused on the troubled state-federal partnership issues. Some state representatives kept verbally attacking the federal negotiators, and the USFWS felt it had little recourse but to state openly that while the agency wanted constructive input from the states, it reserved its right under the law to reject their positions. Negotiations had reached an all-time low. To the states, the USFWS—employing the USBR-EIS team's analysis—had pushed too far in its quest for a "designer river" and had badly overreached its flimsy scientific case. No matter what you gave it, according to a common state sentiment, the USFWS always wanted more.

To federal representatives, the states had failed to understand that the ESA was about the needs of species and that the USFWS had a mandate to serve their habitat requirements. States needed to stop being so paranoid, stop whining, and engage in constructive problem solving. Furthermore, state allegations that federal authorities wanted a "designer river" did not pass the laugh test. There was a designer river out there, to be sure, but it had been "designed" by the state water users and, in some instances, their USBR partners during years of dam building and canal construction. In addition, its design had been found to have created jeopardy for listed species.

Target Flow Implications

The states took cold comfort in pointing out that they had been proven right all along about the DOI's target flow analysis. Now, by the USBR-EIS team's own light, it was clear that quality species habitat was not a simple function of enlarged flow volumes—the central premise of the proposed water action plan. If average annual flows of less than 140,000 acre feet per year could do damage to the river, think of what 417,000 acre feet/year could do. There would be too few islands to churn up to put a meaningful sediment load into that kind of volume. Perhaps, the states suggested, habitat improvement would be found to require even less than the negotiated first increment target flow figure of an average of

130,000–150,000 acre feet per year. Such talk had little consequence at the moment, but the implication existed that subsequent target flow figures in future increments might be negotiated downward.

Struggle for Agenda Control

Over the years, the states had found ways to develop a quasi-collaborative agenda with the federal community. But the USFWS's handling of the sedimentation-vegetation issue had hijacked the collaboration and threatened to spin it into domains where no state wanted to go. Would the USFWS use its control of the sedimentation issue to place specific program requirements on the states up front as a condition of developing a reasonable and prudent alternative? That would mean re-thinking many parts of the program under the duress of limited time, a scary prospect. Colorado was particularly alarmed that discussions might turn toward possible sediment sources in the state's South Platte reservoirs, which could scramble the carefully formulated set of tradeoffs that had gone into the Tamarack Plan. Furthermore, the USFWS had no clear standard for how wide a channel needed to be or how sediment should move in it. The states could not simply let the federal authorities treat such an important program outcome so casually, allowing the DOI to simply "know" when the sediment-vegetation dynamics were right or wrong. The states needed to regain initiative and re-capture the agenda. The way to do so was to bring on more science and model building.

The USFWS had been saying that although its science was not perfect, it was good enough to justify rejection of the program as developed so far and to serve as the basis for devising a revised water action plan that could prevent further river degradation. These assertions were open for review. As a way to regain at least some initiative, the states would have to hire their own consultant and pay the costs of a thorough review of the federal sedimentation-vegetation logic. The effort would be well worth it if serious questions could be pursued and areas of uncertainty be legitimately opened up. Expectations were not so much that weaknesses in the federal case could be used to sustain an anti-federal lawsuit—at least some state representatives believed the federal science was probably too good to warrant such an action—but problems might be found that would require federal humility in the face of uncertainty, the kind of humility that acknowledges multiple interpretations and alternative possibilities. That might keep "sedimentation-vegetation hell" out of any program agreement, where it would be tied closely to USFWS acceptance of a reasonable and prudent alternative. The states could then put that "hell" into a post-agreement adaptive management mode.

By November and December 2000, the states were making progress in developing their consultant solicitation. At first, the USFWS did not warmly embrace the idea. Tension increased in January–February 2001 as word went out to the effect that the USFWS was not looking favorably on a review designed entirely by the states. The states, in turn, ventured the thought that the USFWS was arrogant.

STATE PEER REVIEW PRODUCES STATE-FEDERAL SCIENCE

At the January 2001 Governance Committee meeting in Cheyenne, the states announced that plans were well under way toward having a consulting firm employed by March and that their contract would stipulate that a report be available by August. A senior federal decision maker made a case for the full sharing of analysis between the states' contractor and the USBR-EIS team. Tension in the room was broken and laughter generated when a participant suggested, "Maybe we can do data exchange the way nations do prisoner exchange. When one side delivers, it gets the other side's stuff immediately."

Parsons Engineering Science of Denver, Colorado, was hired to do the peer review. It began work in late March 2001, presented the essence of its findings in a July workshop, delivered a draft report in August, and submitted its final report in January 2002. Parsons was guided in its work by a three-member team, one from each state. Parsons had been hired to address USFWS credibility on the issue of sedimentation-vegetation. There were two ways the states could lead Parsons: (1) reject the federal plea for collaboration and attempt to use Parsons's work to drive a wedge between the states and the USBR-EIS modeling team that would set up a confrontation with the USFWS, or (2) use Parson's review effort to collaborate and share perspectives.

The choice was to collaborate. In the spring and early summer of 2001, an agreement emerged that Parsons and the EIS team should work openly together. Using the mutually accepted premise that a complete understanding of the processes determining the shape of the river channel did not exist, they would work to improve the existing USBR-EIS model to the fullest extent possible and produce a plan for continued systematic investigation of the physical channel, sediment, and vegetation dynamics with an eye to finding the best channel restoration methods. All of this was eventually incorporated into the program's integrated monitoring and research plan (IMRP).

The Parsons team undertook the contract with the understanding that it would review a finished federal product and arrive at a formal set of findings to be presented on behalf of the states. That did not happen. The federal agencies' work had not yet been produced in a neat, tidy final package. Initially, the Parsons-USBR attempt at collaboration was troubled, but a state-federal decision was soon made to have the Parsons team join the unfinished analytical USBR-EIS team effort. In the end, the Parsons review led to several lines of collaborative inquiry. As the Parsons team examined the various aspects of the federal analysis, it built linkages with the federal USBR-EIS group and entered into a discussion as federal analysts advanced their model to a more finished state. As word got out that Parsons and the federal team were sharing modeling approaches and that the EIS team had refined its sedimentation-vegetation model, in part thanks to constructive exchanges with Parsons, negotiators representing the states became more comfortable with the direction the plan was taking.

In anticipation of releasing its draft report in mid-August, the Parsons team presented its findings to an assembly of negotiators and staff members on July 17, 2001. The workshop was chaired by a senior Colorado representative, who welcomed everyone and noted that the "objective was to share data, hypotheses, information, and to avoid litigation." Parsons analysts took the floor and noted that they had relied heavily on data from the USBR-EIS team and 350 other sources. They had not attempted to replicate the federal model; given the constraints of time and money, Parsons reviewed the EIS team's model, data, and interpretations. Furthermore, Parsons had identified data needs that would have to be addressed in the future.

What did all this mean? Were the USBR-EIS team's conclusions justified? Parsons identified twelve "building blocks" in the EIS argument. Each "block" was then examined systematically for its uses and limits. The discussions were at least somewhat collegial and geared toward problem solving. In addition, Parsons's investigations went beyond the twelve building blocks and asked questions not raised in the original federal effort. For example, Parsons examined the impact of regional climate variations not addressed by the federal team. It found that, given the considerable variation in the natural climate cycle, it was not justifiable to simply pick a spot in the larger cycle and think that such a point represented the "natural river," as federal analysts had done when selecting the 1860s as a baseline.

Parsons's analysts found that while pulse flows are important to sedimentation-vegetation dynamics, the federal argument had overstated their significance. Evidence suggested, according to Parsons, that the breakup and movement of ice sheets independent of flood pulses were a more important channel-scouring mechanism than pulse flows were. The USBR-EIS team assumptions that provided foundations for specific logics within a few of the twelve building blocks were found to be based on insufficient data. In sum, the Parsons team concluded that while there was much to recommend the federal sedimentation-vegetation analysis, the federal team had been found to have inadequately supported its conclusions. Important unresolved questions needed to be addressed before the federal model could be employed to adequately justify decisions about the sufficiency of any proposed program alternative. The way forward, then, would be for the entire issue to employ adaptive management during the first increment.

Collaboration between the USBR-EIS team and Parsons had reached such a level that together they placed on the table a plan to test alternative hypotheses regarding sedimentation-vegetation dynamics. The plan centered on performing pulse flow and "island-squishing" tests, beginning with small ones and incrementally increasing their scale. The tests would be preceded by detailed evaluations of channel capacity; initial flow pulses would be held well below those capacities. Tests would be run only in dry weather conditions and would be coordinated with highway and bridge maintenance crews. Numerous observers would be placed at strategic points along the channel with a checklist of items to guide systematic documentation of conditions prior to, during, and after each pulse flow. Tests would be implemented before or after the irrigation season so that diversions and water deliveries would not be negatively affected. The number and acreage of islands proposed for initial squishing would be small, only about 5 percent of the acres needed, according to USBR-EIS team estimates. All tests would be performed early in the first increment so there would be time to identify the most favorable treatments and begin to implement them on a wider scale before the end of the first ten to thirteen years. The Parsons-EIS team also provided a first program increment cost estimate for conducting the work. At the moment, negotiations were getting back on track.

RESOLUTION

Ultimately, this is a voluntary program. We cannot pit one interpretation against another and thereby create a stalemate. We need to find a way around that.

—SENIOR FEDERAL NEGOTIATOR

The Parsons study had paid off for the states; it had created enough new questions and grounds for doubt that the USFWS had to admit to the need for a longer-term learning process. It would have been extremely foolish to lock program participants forever into a particular path of action that was not based on even a minimally adequate understanding. But it was possible to contemplate writing an aggressive adaptive management agenda into proposed program documents.

"Sedimentation-vegetation hell" had been wrestled into a shape with which the states and the federal community could live. All parties had sidestepped an issue that could have caused the entire plan to collapse. They had been as deeply polarized as at any time since well before 1997. The meaning of a federal-state partnership had been at stake. Federal representatives from the Department of the Interior faced state representatives as opponents in at least three critical conflict cleavages: the acceptability of alternative habitats in the land discussion, the meaning of the sedimentation-vegetation problem, and the advisability of states undertaking their own independent review of federal sedimentation-vegetation science. They had become adversaries on all these issues, allies on none. The cleavages had stacked up in a polarized pattern (Freeman 1992: 132–136), the legitimacy parties attributed to each other was diminishing, and their sense of mutual interdependence was turning decidedly in the direction of a zero-sum game: whatever one side won, the other had to lose.

However, at least two significant crosscutting cleavages provided common ground and kept the negotiators at the table: (1) a tough ESA, which held out the prospect of individual accountability for the construction of reasonable and prudent alternatives as the price of failure—an outcome no party wanted; and (2) a mutual commitment to the value of open scientific inquiry for reasoned inference. An independent review that could have been used to heighten confrontation and division instead became a place where quiet technical talk could set aside partisan posturing, cool emotions, build linkages among adversaries, and eventually lead to a joint plan for adaptive management. This became the stuff around which a future relationship might be forged. The mutual commitment to science grew within a context in which a powerful ESA provided the strongest incentive to make a state-federal relationship work. Rigidity in the law was essential to keep negotiators together; in this instance at least, it did not prove to be an obstacle to flexible action.

Scent of Victory and Impasse

By the summer of 2002, the construction of a reasonable and prudent alternative was well under way. A water action plan had been outlined, a terrestrial habitat plan had been sketched, and protocols for research and monitoring efforts were being put in place. If the U.S. Fish and Wildlife Service (USFWS) would accept a general conceptual plan that left much to be negotiated in the first program increment and if Nebraska could resolve its internal problems, it was possible for water users to imagine that the prospect for a thirteen-year period of regulatory certainty was tantalizingly close.

VICTORY?

On July 17, 2002, in a motel conference room in Kearney, Nebraska, negotiators and other participants in a U.S. Bureau of Reclamation (USBR)–environmental impact statement (EIS) team workshop heard the results of an analysis performed using the team's enhanced sedimentation-vegetation model. The news was good. A way had been found to make the water action plan work by decreasing the frequency of low flows, increasing the frequency of pulse flows, increasing spring-summer base flows for species, and reducing winter flows. The upgraded model of the river showed that a revised set of program flows could pass muster if they were properly integrated with clearing and leveling 750 acres of wooded islands within the areas of five river bridge segments during the first program increment.

The model produced numbers that showed that island "squishing," along with other practices, would mitigate and reverse clear water channel incision.

Furthermore, the model showed pulse flows building low sandbars not yet inundated by summer peak flows, something important for plover and tern nesting. Bird sight distances had increased to acceptable values. Cross-sections of the river that would receive the proposed program treatments for thirteen years would be sustainable for over forty-eight years, with much less vegetation management in the second and subsequent program increments. The essential geomorphological results could pass muster for whooping crane habitat. More work would have to be done, however, to get program flows right for least terns and piping plovers. There was also a need to address the situation regarding the pallid sturgeon.

After at least five years of pulling and hauling, the negotiations had produced a proposed program, major components of which would serve as the greater part of what could eventually become a reasonable and prudent alternative. It could be the source of relief from jeopardy and for regulatory certainty. Yet the state delegations took the good news with no visible display of joy or any other emotion: no laughter, no handshakes, no relieved congratulations. Stoic silence governed the moment. Why?

THE FEDERAL QUESTION

The problem was that the EIS team had just presented a positive evaluation of an important proposed program component. But the proposed program itself and what it would require next were a source of serious divisions within Colorado, Nebraska, and Wyoming. Negotiators representing the three states faced the awkward prospect that their "preferred alternative" had significant opposition back home. Nobody in the room found it pleasant to contemplate putting an EIS on the street without full good-faith backing of the program in central Nebraska as well as in Lincoln, in Bill Owens's administration in Denver, and among all North Platte constituencies in Wyoming. A federal leader asked, "Does anybody really want an EIS on the street that has states disavowing it?" Silence. Federal voices then expressed a wish to know when the three states would be able to declare agreement with the proposed program and actively move ahead to finish addressing issues, the details of which would have to be put in place so the three governors could sign off on the plan in less than a year, by June 2003. Federal voice: "We are at our wits' end trying to figure out how to drive this process forward." Silence.

At that moment, there was no easy answer to the federal question. Victory of a sort was at hand. But even the scent of victory threatened to deny Nebraska time. Victory would force unwanted confrontations within Colorado and between Colorado and federal negotiators over the division of peak flows and between the three states and the USFWS regarding the organization of pulse flows. It would compel difficult talks about the regime of the river between the

three states and another federal agency, the U.S. Forest Service. It would ne-
cessitate clashes over incompatible visions of river restoration with which to
guide adaptive management. State representatives could only see dimly into the
near future, but they could clearly predict that these matters had to be resolved
in a manner that would be supportable by majorities in their state legislatures
and by their governors. The contemplation of victory on the near horizon and
its implications brought a roomful of people to silence. No state representative
could see a clear path through it all at that moment. The scent of victory meant
confronting an impasse.

PART VI

Reaching Sufficiency

Wrestling with Skunks

On Wednesday, February 19, 2003, soon after the Governance Committee gathered in a motel conference room near Denver International Airport, the leader of the U.S. Fish and Wildlife Service (USFWS) team stepped up to a flip chart. He listed in two or three words each item that had to be addressed if there were to be any hope of putting together a successful reasonable and prudent alternative. Each item had been lurking around the negotiating table in unresolved form for years. The long-postponed searches for solutions to critical problems had to be meaningfully addressed in ways that would give substance to an eventual environmental impact statement and a biological opinion.

The list included protection of peak flows on the Colorado South Platte, the necessity of building pulse flows on the central Platte for habitat restoration and maintenance, the challenge of addressing "choke point" restrictions on North Platte flows that threatened to compromise the delivery of environmental account water to the habitat as well as pulse building, the needs of the pallid sturgeon, and the importance of giving substance to an amorphous adaptive management plan. In addition, everyone knew that state and federal future depletions (post–June 30, 1997) offset plans needed to be completed and endorsed. Therein lay deeply troubling issues.

After some discussion, a state representative rose from the table and declared, "The skunks are on the table now." From 2003 to 2006, problems mounted seemingly faster than negotiators were able to cope with them. The federal regulatory process required that federal and state authorities find a way to embrace each other, but how? How would negotiators find ways to deflower a pack of skunks?

Prior to an examination of the particulars, however, it is important to establish the context within which negotiators were struggling. Through 2000, during the Clinton administration, the Department of the Interior was led by political appointees friendly to large-scale voluntary cooperative habitat restoration programs, as evidenced in the Florida Everglades, the Chesapeake Bay, Upper Colorado, the San Francisco Bay/Sacramento San Joaquin Delta (CALFED Bay Delta) Program, and the Platte River Basin effort (Doyle and Drew 2008). It was also a time of federal budget surpluses. Furthermore, the 1990s were characterized by above-average Platte River Basin flows. Then, the context of the negotiations shifted significantly, as traced in Chapter 18.

Negotiating Context, 2000–2006

DROUGHT

Periodic drought has long been part of life in the West, especially in the Platte Basin (McKee et al. 2000). Drought returned to all three basin states in 1999 and 2000, and it was severe, reaching record-breaking levels by 2002. It remained a factor for the duration of the negotiations, through 2006. Depending on the location, the last years that had experienced generally average or above-average precipitation were 1998 and 1999. By the summer of 2002, the lack of precipitation had placed Platte Basin water supply constraints in sharp relief (see Tables 18.1, 18.2, 18.3, and 18.4). In late 2004, analysts at the U.S. Geological Survey reported that the region was likely experiencing the worst drought in 500 years, as established by a combination of records and tree-ring studies (Martinez 2004: 3A).

By the end of the 2006 irrigation season, North Platte reservoirs were exceedingly low—Seminoe was at 26 percent of its normal amount, Pathfinder at 21 percent, and McConaughy (highly dependent on return flows from Wyoming's plumbing) at about 22 percent of its average (Hendee 2006). An indicator of the North Platte situation is seen in Nebraska's Lake McConaughy data in Table 18.3 and Wyoming's Pathfinder Reservoir data in Table 18.4.

In the area commanded by the Central Nebraska Public Power and Irrigation District's (CNPPID) canal system, normal irrigation season deliveries had historically taken place over a period of twelve weeks and consisted of 15 to 18 inches of water per acre. However, by the summer of 2005, irrigation deliveries had been cut back to eight weeks and were limited to 6.7 inches per acre. This reduction continued in 2006 and 2007 (*Kearney Hub* 2007). In Colorado (see Table

Table 18.1. Wyoming North Platte Snow-pack Accumulations, 2000–2006 (% of historical average)

Year	Percent of Average
2000	68
2001	56
2002	16
2003	68
2004	37
2005	89
2006	70

Sources: CNPPID 2005a: 1; Hendee 2006.

Table 18.2. Colorado South Platte Snowpack Accumulations, 2000–2006 (% of historical average)

Year	January (% of average)	February (% of average)	March (% of average)	April (% of average)	May (% of average)	June (% of average)
2000	64	85	84	98	85	25
2001	84	65	69	81	80	22
2002	54	49	52	54	23	02
2003	73	63	79	114	109	58
2004	67	65	69	51	65	13
2005	92	84	80	84	77	47
2006	130	112	101	103	74	16

Source: www.co.nrcs.usda.gov/snow/snow/watershed/current/monthly/data/snowpercentagestxt. Accessed March 3, 2008.

Table 18.3. Water Storage at Lake McConaughy, 2000–2006 (acre feet and % of total storage capacity [1.79 million acre feet] as of June 1)

Year	2000	2001	2002	2003	2004	2005	2006
Acre Feet	1,438,200	1,227,800	1,118,400	815,000	631,400	643,000	702,300
Percent	80	69	63	46	35	36	39

Source: Central Nebraska Public Power and Irrigation District, Holdrege, Nebraska, personal communication, September 5, 2007.

18.2), after two years in which no month attained average snowpack conditions, the drought reached record levels in 2002 and continued, somewhat less severely but still intensely, in subsequent years.

In any given year, June 1 represents reservoir levels prior to the main irrigation water release season. Levels over the course of an irrigation season fall markedly and typically begin recovery in the fall and winter months.

As water was lost to drainage, river flows diminished and remnants of peak channel flows shriveled. Subsoil moisture disappeared from farm fields as a

Table 18.4. Water Storage at Pathfinder Reservoir, 2000–2007 (acre feet and % of total capacity—1,016,507 acre feet)

Year	June 1	September 1
2000	994,653 (98%)	650,187 (64%)
2001	797,951 (79%)	476,697 (47%)
2002	549,621 (54%)	285,768 (28%)
2003	382,500 (38%)	272,773 (27%)
2004	295,172 (29%)	191,120 (19%)
2005	210,959 (21%)	236,279 (23%)
2006	301,514 (30%)	208,916 (21%)
2007	274,524 (27%)	182,954 (18%)

Source: www.usbr.gov/gp-bin/hydromet-archives.pl. Accessed March 3, 2008.

result of the lack of late winter and spring precipitation on the plains, leaving farmers to cut back planting acreage, begin irrigation earlier, or both. When earlier than normal first irrigations were required on farms, their suppliers—irrigation districts and mutual companies—placed their ditch priority calls on the river sooner. Then, water that would normally have gone into storage for late summer use had to be diverted directly onto fields in spring and early summer. Storage tubs therefore stopped filling much earlier than usual. As surface water supplies dwindled, farmers desperate to bring their crops through so they would stay in good standing with their credit suppliers switched on their groundwater wells earlier and ran them longer, thereby sucking down water tables. In places, wells that had served sufficiently for decades declined in productivity and sometimes went dry when the underground water commons was no longer sufficiently recharged.

Drought undercut historical recharge patterns by denying direct precipitation, depleting surface reservoirs, and reducing canal flows—the sources of aquifer replenishment. Depleted surface tanks meant hydroelectric power facilities cut back production, and lucrative slack-water recreation enterprises were hurt. The lack of peak, pulse, and continuous in-stream flows on important river segments also meant increased vegetation, which choked river channels.

Many Platte Basin ranchers who had irrigated feed crops for their cattle found that the drought so severely compromised their capacity to produce feed that they had little option but to sell substantial fractions of their herds to buyers in wetter places. In the aggregate, hundreds of thousands of cattle left the basin to follow water. As crops and cattle diminished, small-town economies across the basin suffered. Lower crop yields and reduced herds meant reduced or nonpayment of local debts to banks and suppliers of other agricultural inputs. Debt repayment problems quickly translated into smaller loan volumes for equipment, supplies, and living expenses. That, in turn, forced some agricultural supply businesses into retreat, if not extinction.

Water interests were being asked to hammer out a Platte Basin Habitat Recovery Program at a time when water scarcity issues were highly salient for their constituencies, and water for wildlife habitat did not seem to be much of a priority for many. Negotiators representing the states knew well that their economic growth constituencies would not be particularly willing to make sacrifices for habitat purposes.

NATIONAL POLITICAL CLIMATE

The Bush Administration has been hostile to the Endangered Species Act.
—JOHN KOSTYACK, DIRECTOR,
Wildlife Conservation, National Wildlife Federation
(quoted in Lipsher 2007: 7A)

There had been a long-standing backlash against the Endangered Species Act (ESA), especially in the interior West. In 1994, after one of the most anti–federal government campaigns in U.S. history, Georgia Republican Newt Gingrich led his party to a position of control in the U.S. Congress. Many Republicans had campaigned waving an anti-federal "Contract with America" that promised roll-backs of federal regulations and a shrinking federal government. The document did not specifically mention environmental policy, but much of the language had been inspired by right-wing think tanks that had a history of attempting to discredit environmentalist agendas (Kraft 2006: 134–136). Within a year, Republican leaders had slapped a one-year moratorium on new species listing and critical habitat designations. Many lawmakers went further, threatening wholesale roll-backs of environmental legislation, most notably the ESA.

If the policy goal of gutting the ESA through a direct attack was beyond the reach of opponents of the law, the Republican strategy—beginning in the Ronald Reagan years and picked up again in 1995 under Gingrich's leadership—would be pursued in an intensified manner by George W. Bush's administration after its inauguration in 2001. The party employed its control over appropriations to slash the budgets of agencies that did environmental work, with special attention paid to cutting the U.S. Fish and Wildlife Service (USFWS). One avid supporter of this tactic was Representative David McIntosh (R-Indiana, member of freshman class of 1995), who stated: "The laws would remain on the books but there would be no money to carry them out" (quoted in Kraft 2006: 136).

After Bush took office, the new president moved quickly to appoint pro-business officials to nearly all the environmental and natural resource agencies (Kraft 2006: 136). When newly appointed secretary Gale Norton took over the reins of the Department of the Interior (DOI), she moved the department's affairs in a sharply anti-environmental direction.

At the Platte River negotiation tables, water users could see that they were working within a friendlier political context than had been the case under President Clinton. But that fact presented a conundrum. On the one hand, they could expect Bush administration authorities to be easier on them, which meant holding out for the best possible deal. On the other hand, there was the reality of a regulatory process that required publicly open inspections of draft and final environmental impact statements (EISs) and also of any biological opinion that gave the program a passing grade. A grossly deficient program deal would invite a flurry of lawsuits from the environmental community. Courts of law were no place water users wanted to go because they would face extended, expensive deliberations with highly uncertain outcomes. Water users enjoyed greater latitude than they might have under another, more environmentally friendly federal administration. However, they knew they did not have carte blanche to impose their will, produce a document the environmentalists at the table could not legitimately defend, and end up in legal battles they did not want to fight.

In the wake of the 2004 elections, Richard Pombo (R-California) saw a long-awaited opportunity to decisively undercut the Endangered Species Act. With both houses of Congress firmly in Republican hands and a sympathetic president occupying the White House, Representative Pombo introduced another ESA "reform" bill for the twelfth time in eight years. The ESA was facing its most extreme shakeup since another California Republican—Richard Nixon—had signed it into law in 1973. On September 29, 2005, Pombo's U.S. House of Representatives version passed by a vote of 229 to 193; supporters included 36 Democrats representing mostly rural western districts (Farquhar 2005: 3). If passed by the U.S. Senate and endorsed by President Bush, the reform bill would impose far-reaching changes—all in favor of business over species habitats.

Among other things, the reform version produced by the House would have permitted the secretary of the interior to determine what science could be used to make decisions about listed species. Furthermore, federal agencies and industries would have been allowed to harm listed species and their habitats through actions such as road building without consulting the USFWS. Species recovery plans would have needed to be developed within two years of listing (no time limits were specified in the existing law), and if the federal government failed to meet the deadlines, project promoters could proceed with impunity. Furthermore, habitat recovery plans would have been "non-regulatory," meaning unenforceable in courts of law (Doremus 2005: 9; Farquhar 2005: 3). There was also a proposal to pay landowners for any lost value to their private lands as a result of regulatory action on behalf of listed species.

Supporters of the ESA were deeply troubled by the Pombo proposals. Placing the definition of "good science" in the hands of a political appointee was an anathema. Peer-reviewed civic science was endangered. Undercutting the act's enforcement powers in the implementation of recovery plans made a mockery of any federal involvement on behalf of listed species. Paying private investors for potential lost value of their lands would give them incentive to impose damage on listed species and their habitats and then demand compensation from taxpayers to stop doing so. What could be better from a private goods perspective than to find listed species habitat subject to federal regulation and, as a price of ESA compliance, be paid from the public treasury?

In the end, a Republican senator, Lincoln Chafee (Rhode Island), who chaired the Senate Sub-Committee on Fisheries, Wildlife and Water (of the Senate's Environment and Public Works Committee), kept the Pombo-sponsored House legislation away from the Senate floor through the remainder of 2005, all of 2006, and until the end of the 109th Congress (Margolis 2006: 25). So, it was a Republican president (Richard Nixon) who signed the ESA in 1973, a Republican House member (Richard Pombo) who led the most serious threat to the act, and a Republican Senate subcommittee chair (Lincoln Chafee) who saved it. Chafee, however, did not return to the Senate; in the 2006 election, where voters in many districts turned against Republicans and gave Democrats control of the U.S. Congress, Chafee was defeated. Another Republican moderate-to-liberal presence in the U.S. Senate had been extinguished (Chafee 2008).

The national political scene did not openly and directly impact any Platte River–specific negotiation on any particular day. However, it was clear to USFWS leaders in the Mountain and Prairie Region that they could not expect increased budget support to help them do their tasks more effectively; further, they could not expect senior authorities in the Department of the Interior to be interested in strengthening the agency's position vis-à-vis the states and water users. At a time when the ESA was under ferocious attack, there was general apprehension among the higher levels of civil service personnel in the USFWS that it would not be wise to upset the states. The USFWS and its environmentalist allies were aware that they were on spongy political turf that made taking strong stands on behalf of the ESA difficult. USFWS regional leaders could struggle most effectively on behalf of the ESA by demonstrating the viability of a voluntary basin-wide cooperative agreement. They constantly wrestled with the political fact that the agency's political appointees in Washington, D.C., were not enthusiastic about demonstrating that the ESA, as written, could work.

CONFLICTING VISIONS

In its biological opinions and in other program-related documents since the 1980s, the USFWS had consistently advanced a vision that centered on restoring some semblance of natural water flows to restore habitats. This "natural flow" vision, which the agency referred to as a "river processes model," has been advanced in a rich scientific literature that has been neatly synthesized (Poff et al.

1997; Poff et al. 2003; Wohl 2001). This vision stresses the importance of highly variable river flows to ecosystem health and native biodiversity.

Five critical components of any flow regime are the magnitude of discharge, frequency of pulses passing a given point, duration of high water flows, timing of the peaks, and the flashiness of peaks (how quickly flows change from one magnitude to another). Diversity in flow patterns consistent with conditions under which species evolve is seen to generate a mosaic of habitat types that promote ecosystem integrity. The path to sustaining and restoring habitats for listed species on the central Platte River, in the agency's view, was to reintroduce not only minimum stream flows but also variable flows in the form of controllable flood pulses and preservation of naturally occurring peak flows that together can do at least some significant work in scouring vegetation, creating barren ephemeral sandbars, and maintaining the wide, braided, shallow channel characteristics essential to whooping cranes, piping plovers, least terns, and possibly the pallid sturgeon downriver. Negotiations prior to 2002 had emphasized reducing shortages to USFWS target flows in the aggregate; subsequent discussions shifted to the hydrological shape of those flows—naturally occurring peak flows and program-induced pulses.

Natural Flow Vision

Given the degradation of habitats associated with over 140 years of human settlement, is river restoration through the reintroduction of some approximation of natural flows a realistic goal? Yes, within limits (Poff et al. 1997: 779–781). Just as rivers can be degraded incrementally, they can also be restored incrementally. However, USFWS analysts and negotiators explicitly recognized that given a seriously damaged riverine ecosystem, any feasible program-induced natural flow regime could not carry the burden of channel restoration by itself. It would be necessary to intervene with chainsaws, bulldozers, and other mechanical equipment to clear vegetation and level out densely vegetated sandy islands that had risen too far above typical summer flow levels and thereby become heavily vegetated. Yet the agency wanted to ensure that adaptive management—whatever that concept would come to mean in the Platte context—would be about restoring a modicum of traditional natural flows. The mantra of the USFWS and environmentalists was: clear the channel, level the high islands, and rely as much as humanly possible on peaks and pulses to sustain and restore habitat qualities. Agency negotiators would push hard for program language that had "natural flow" language and substance built into it.

Defined Contribution Vision

The states and water providers fervently resisted the USFWS view and refused to accept it at any point. They pushed for clearing the channel, leveling the high islands, and mechanically ploughing. Their concerns had always centered on protecting the yields of their own water projects on behalf of their demanding customers, who expected water to be cheap, reliable, and sufficient. The law mandated that water providers serve their customers; providers have had no legal basis for questioning the economic growth games their customers have played. For them, life is simple. They have been hired—and fired—according to their capacity to build and manage their water capture and delivery systems such that the multiple and conflicting water demands of basin civilization are met.

Providers have always been wary of any program that could make endless claims on their water and treasuries. At the very heart of the resistance to a federal presence on state rivers was the state's mission to protect its water appropriation system from federal intrusion. The federal environmental agenda was making a claim for water whose adequacy could not be known, to serve the needs of species that could not clearly be known, and to do so over an unknown span of time. Such an intrusion had to be wrestled into the least damaging configuration.

For water providers, adaptive management had to center on preserving project yields in an arid environment and to operate within agreed-upon "defined contributions" of water, land, and money. Water providers viewed themselves as stewards of water projects that have made the existing form of Platte Basin society possible. Their projects had been assembled out of a bold vision, smart engineering, generations of labor, a commitment to serve a fundamental need of society, and the willingness of generations of tax- and fee payers to provide the money needed for the projects. Installing a collaborative program on the central Platte meant their customers would pay a negligible amount more for an acre foot of water (not a problem) and a tiny fraction of a dollar more for a kilowatt hour of electricity (not much of a problem), but they would also trade away important increments of drought protection on behalf of environmental accounts that would splash water downstream for species in ways that may or may not optimally serve human agendas (possibly a bigger problem in unforeseen ways). Finally, the habitat recovery program could potentially put a crack in the states' water project gates that over time could expand to accommodate a federal intruder with designs that could potentially significantly reduce project water yields—a huge problem.

In an arid high plains environment, each water provider must capture more water than needed in average to wet years to serve demand in dry years. Water tends to come in a few short, intensely stormy precipitation spikes each year. The difference between a wet year and a dry one has usually been the presence or absence of one to three large precipitation events. Those flow spikes may have created the traditional pre–European river Platte environmentalists have admired, but they are the same spikes civilization has gathered up as slack waters behind dams. The idea of watching significant fractions of precious waters surge by in the name of improved habitats for three species of birds and one fish far down-stream was not easy for water providers to contemplate. Attempting to convince state legislators and most of their clients, who advocated continual water-fueled economic growth, to accept the environmentalists' vision would be politically impossible and would make for short, unhappy careers. Anything that reduced project yields would fuel vehement protests from economic and recreational in-terests that require water to sustain their aspirations as they have evolved around dams and slack water. Furthermore, anytime water escapes storage in a world where rivers are fully appropriated, one or more junior water right holders on a state's priority list may be shorted in all but a few of the wettest years. In such a world, there would never be enough water. Any water provider had to defend existing sources and be constantly on the prowl for more.

State representatives' fear of the federal agenda was also rooted in their judg-ment that the USFWS, relying on whatever program flows could be mustered, would have too little chance in the first thirteen-year program increment of ac-tually obtaining much of the improved channel and wetlands habitat. Water pro-viders did not want to contemplate what a disappointed USFWS would do in the future when it returned to the negotiating table for greater inputs of water, land, and money. Therefore, water users objected fiercely to any attempt to "hard-wire" any part of the natural flow model into any part of the program deal.

Water interests spent years skeptically examining the USFWS's variable flow river vision and insisted on advancing their counter-vision of a program that—in an adaptive management mode—would work within carefully defined state and federal contributions. These two visions—natural flow and defined contributions—were pitched against each other for years around the negotiat-ing table and drove the discussion of many program particulars.

Environmentalists' Vision and Quandary

The Whooping Crane Trust and the Audubon Society possessed important habitat assets on the river. These environmentalists were the most experienced of any of the parties with what state interests pushed as the "clear, level, and plough" approach to habitat restoration. They had exercised that option for years. The Whooping Crane Trust, for example, had worked two tractors full-time for three or four months a year to scrape vegetation from shorelines and sandbars. During their efforts, trust workers made alliances with local land-owners who had come to appreciate the benefits of the trust's project in many ways, not the least of which has been improved fall-winter waterfowl hunting. But they knew from their experience that "clear-level-plow" needed something more—in particular, variable flows with substantial pulses. They worked in support of the USFWS variable flow vision as a central part of any program deal, but they walked a fine line in doing so, given two considerations: their need for good relationships with local landowners and the limited nature of the ESA itself.

Environmentalists operating in many other contexts had generally gained leverage by going public with an issue, elevating it to the national stage if tactically desirable, beating the drum loudly on behalf of the "good" environmental position, and mobilizing their constituencies to write letters of advocacy and to send money to fight the battle—often in courts of law. In the context of the Platte River talks, such tactics were unworkable. The negotiations involved a rich, extended, highly nuanced discussion of multiple issues that intersected in ways that could baffle even those close to the discourse. A way to an environmentally acceptable solution could not be encapsulated in bumper stickers, letters of solicitation, or threatened litigation. Any efforts at public posturing would not only alienate the state representatives but would also become a burden to the USFWS as that beleaguered agency sought ways to move states and water users toward problem solving. In addition, it would disrupt local environmentalist-landowner alliances important to the work of river restoration.

The second constraint that gripped the maneuvers of environmental representatives had to do with the nature of the ESA itself. On the one hand, they knew well that the key to river channel and wetland restoration must be greater approximation of natural flows. They were devotees of the science that held that only such flows could restore and sustain desired habitat features in their ecological wholeness. The problem was that the ESA, as written, did not visualize entire ecosystems in the way contemporary "good" ecological science demanded. Therefore, the environmental representatives and the USFWS were compelled to negotiate within a frame that focused attention on how to manage assets for species-by-species recovery after the whoopers, terns, and plovers had already been so marginalized that they were in the "emergency room" by the time talks began. The ESA, while not overtly hostile to a more encompassing ecological approach, does not make ecosystem demands; it merely requires individual species recovery limited to particular fragments of serviceable habitat. Therefore, the environmentalists' ally in the quest for Platte River habitat restoration—the USFWS—was hobbled from the outset. The agency was trying to push an ecological system-wide river processes model within the terms of an ESA that did not require ecological holism.

The environmentalists' quandary was therefore profound. Members of the camp had to somehow assist a beleaguered USFWS in getting a solid program in place that could stand up to the inspection of environmentalist skeptics. Only a viable program could forestall lawsuits from the environmental community, which, if litigation were forthcoming, could be expected to break up hard-won local alliances with central Platte property owners. Such legal actions would drive locals out of their coalitions and compel environmentalists on the river to face even greater obstacles in their quest to advance the river restoration agenda.

THE NAS-NRC REVIEW (2002–2005)

When Congressman Tom Osborne (R-Nebraska)—nudged by his water user constituencies—pushed so hard for a National Academies of Science (NAS) review of the USFWS's recovery program science, he was operating in the context of alleged "bad federal science." This "suspicious" science had supposedly occurred in the so-called lynx hoax and the bitter Klamath River episode (see Chapter 14).

On September 18, 2002, members of the Governance Committee agreed that there would be an NAS review of the federal science, as applied in making the USFWS case. The committee would proceed simultaneously with ongoing program negotiations and with the work of the U.S. Bureau of Reclamation (USBR) Environmental Impact Assessment Team, which was struggling to put together a draft EIS that would characterize and examine any eventually proposed program. This decision, in turn, triggered a DOI request for an NAS review. At the end of January 2003, a contract for the review was signed by the USFWS and NAS. The Department of the Interior agreed to pay the cost of the review.

The NAS System

The National Academies of Science was founded as an honorary society by an act of the U.S. Congress in 1863 (national-academies.org/publicaccess; accessed April 28, 2003). In 1916 a working research arm was established, the National Research Council (NRC). This nonprofit organization has systematically mobilized scientists and engineers, who volunteer their time to advise federal policy makers and all citizens on matters of scientific import in public policy matters. Through the NRC, the NAS has always operated as a politically neutral convener of scientifically competent teams of people.

In the spring of 2003, the NAS-NRC established a multidisciplinary panel of fourteen scientists to evaluate not the proposed program per se but the science undergirding the USFWS's construction of habitat needs for the four federally listed species (www4.national-academies.org; accessed April 28, 2003). Members of the panel began their work expeditiously; in addition to getting organized and reviewing pertinent literature, they conducted two public meetings in Nebraska beginning in May 2003—one in Kearney and another in Grand Island. The panel conducted closed-door hearings to take evidence and arguments from scientists and decision makers within and beyond the federal agencies and state of Nebraska water-related organizations. These sessions included time for open testimony from a diverse array of basin voices (National Research Council of the National Academies 2005).

The states, led by the Nebraska delegation, formulated specific questions to be addressed by the NAS panel (National Research Council 2005). Did current habitat conditions jeopardize the continued existence and further recovery of each of the four listed species? Did sound science support DOI conclusions about the interrelationship of river flows, sediment deposition, vegetation, and channel morphology on the central Platte? Were the methodologies used by the USFWS scientifically valid as they pertained to describing central Platte River in-stream flow recommendations such as summer species flows, annual pulse flows, and peak flows? Were characteristics described in USFWS habitat suitability guidelines for the central Platte supported by existing science, and were they essential to the survival and recovery of listed avian species? Could other Platte River habitats provide the same survival values?

Findings

The NRC team issued a draft report on April 28, 2004 (National Research Council 2004b). In that report, the committee vindicated the USFWS's science and USBR's river modeling on all accounts. To unknown degrees, current Platte conditions were found to adversely affect the survival and recovery of whooping cranes, piping plovers, and least terns. Furthermore, no equally and consistently useful alternative habitats for the three bird species could be found. In the case of least terns and piping plovers, the committee found that off-stream sandpits and reservoir beaches were not adequate substitutes for natural riverine habitat. With regard to the pallid sturgeon, the NAS reviewers found that current habitat conditions on the Lower Platte (downstream of the Elkhorn River's mouth) did not adversely affect the likelihood of the fish's survival and recovery because that river segment was viewed as retaining the essential required characteristics, including braided channels, shifting sandbars, sandy substrate, warm turbid water, and flow characteristics similar to those of the Missouri prior to dam construction. However, severe degradation of the Missouri as pallid sturgeon habitat made the Lower Platte even more important for the survival and recovery of the species. The committee adopted the view that the Lower Platte was "pivotal" in managing the fish.

The panel judged the USFWS and USBR methodologies as validated by existing science. Furthermore, habitat characteristics described as important in USFWS guidelines were found to be supported by the best science available during the 1970s and 1980s when they were formulated. New ecological knowledge had since been produced that supported the agency's general approach. Panel members endorsed the long-standing USFWS position that researchers cannot determine the importance of various habitat types for a species by simply investigating present use patterns. Species struggle with what is available, not necessarily what is best (National Research Council 2004b: 129). The fact that terns and plovers may be observed on sandpits does not justify a conclusion that sandpit habitat is somehow equivalent to properly restored channel habitat. Furthermore, when a small population of a migratory species exists, quality habitats may remain vacant simply because there are not enough species individuals to occupy them. Habitats are used in cycles of activities, and the fraction of a given ecological patch that is actually used may depend upon what is happening in other regions.

Without using the phrases "river processes" and "natural flows," the NAS scientists directly addressed the knotty question regarding the interrelationship of river flows, sedimentation, vegetation, and desired habitat characteristics—including wide, shallow channels with braided, un-vegetated ephemeral sandbars. Can the central and Lower Platte riverine ecosystems be restored to pre-European settlement conditions? The answer is no. However, the committee asserted, it is possible to create an environment that contains conditions that favor the recovery of the targeted birds and fish. According to the committee: "This approach has the advantage of working from an observable premise: the connections among river flows, geomorphology, vegetation, and wildlife. Those connections are complex and not completely understood, but given our partial knowledge about them, restoration for species is possible. As this normative approach to restoration proceeds, corrections . . . in the flow regime of the river can provide for experimentation through adaptive management" (National Research Council 2004b: 87–88). In using the word "normative," the committee was advancing its view of what "ought" to be done on behalf of species survival and recovery. It had constructed the idea of a normative flow regime, a virtual synonym for "river processes" and "natural flow" regimes. The NAS panel was explicitly endorsing the USFWS's vision of habitat restoration through "natural flows."

Implications

For months, all parties represented on the Governance Committee had waited anxiously for the NAS report. It came in the form of a pre-publication draft on April 28, 2004 (National Research Council 2004b). The final report was released in February 2005 (National Research Council 2005).

Four things were apparent. First, federal science in general had received a substantial boost. Second, the USFWS's vision of "river processes" as an essential element in habitat restoration had been endorsed by the most prestigious scientific review panel in the land. Third, even as the states' position had been weakened overall, Nebraska at least had found important political cover in the fact that opponents of the recovery program could no longer claim that the USFWS and the USBR were getting away with shoddy science and that Nebraska negotiators were too weak regarding the matter. Fourth, as the federal position was strengthened, the USFWS could press water users harder—especially the Nebraska districts (CNPPID and NPPD)—to deal constructively with the full range of issues that had to be confronted to achieve a more desirable pattern of flow on the central Platte. Those issues in particular involved sedimentation-vegetation, peak flows, pulse flows, in-stream summer species flows, channel capacity, bypass flows, and hydro-cycling. The NAS-NRC study gave extra leverage to push both the science behind natural flows as a tool of river restoration and the political deal being hammered out at the negotiating table.

The states pointed out that just because the NAS team had made recommendations, it did not mean the Governance Committee had to follow its lead. Whatever "normative flows" meant, the states would not abandon their defined contributions approach. For them, holding on to the defined contributions principle was more important than ever. Yet they knew future program critics could use the NAS recommendations to exploit program vulnerabilities. The states defined the NAS effort as "academic big-picture stuff." Big-picture science had insinuated itself into the program deliberations and was to be minimized to the greatest possible extent. However, the three states—representatives of which had long argued for big-picture general and conceptual program commitments that were not too detailed so as not to hardwire specific habitat restoration requirements—were now pushing to reject the big-picture approach. That, in turn, meant they would have to work out the practical details of specific outstanding issues—exactly what the regulatory process would require in producing viable environmental impact statements and developing a program proposal that could win a non-jeopardy biological opinion.

Regime of the River

Colorado and Nebraska Nightmares

There was a tangle of issues connected to the "regime of the river." The term had come up initially in Federal Energy Regulatory Commission (FERC) re-licensing discourse about the environmental account (EA) that had been installed at Lake McConaughy and signed as an official FERC–Central Nebraska Public Power and Irrigation District (CNPPID)–Nebraska Public Power District (NPPD) deal effective in 1998. Regime of the river had come to mean the flow characteristics of the North Platte, South Platte, and central Platte rivers that existed as of mid-1997, when the Cooperative Agreement (CA) had been signed (Cooperative Agreement 1997: tab 1A).

Regime-of-the-river conflicts were tied to each other. Failure to work out satisfactory arrangements regarding any one conflict would cripple attempts to deal with the others. The regime of the river had been central to discussions before and after the construction of the 1997 CA (see Chapter 10 regarding Nebraska's challenge to Colorado on the South Platte and Chapter 11 regarding *Nebraska v. Wyoming* on the North Platte). But important aspects had been left to the future. By 2003–2004, that future had arrived.

No party relished involvement in the coming struggle, but no state could wiggle away because the federal regulatory process required substance to feed the analytical mills that would produce draft and final environmental impact statements (EISes) and a final biological opinion. Federal agencies planned to stay away from the states' struggle over sharing basin waters; it was the intent of the U.S. Fish and Wildlife Service (USFWS) and the U.S. Bureau of Reclamation (USBR) to simply focus on flows to critical habitat and let the chips fall where they may. By early 2003, talks had dragged into their sixth year, and either there would be a viable program or there would not. If not, states would be left without regulatory certainty and would doubtlessly be caught up in unwelcome individual Endangered Species Act (ESA) Section 7 consultations and environmentalist-inspired lawsuits. If there were to be a program, with all its advantages for water interests, states would have to face some of their darkest nightmares.

NEBRASKA'S NIGHTMARE

Nebraska was particularly concerned that its water users not be placed in a position wherein they would be trying to serve FERC licensing requirements on behalf of the listed species from a declining surface water supply from Colorado and Wyoming. FERC, in consultation with the USFWS, had placed clear stipulations on outflows from Lake McConaughy. Insofar as the traditional regime of the river stayed the same into the future vis-à-vis Wyoming and Colorado, CNPPID and NPPD could fulfill their obligations. But if Colorado or Wyoming placed new consumptive uses on either the South or the North Platte, the depletions would reduce inflows to Nebraska. Either USFWS-FERC would allow greater flexibility in the districts' operations at McConaughy (not likely) or Nebraska would "eat" the losses from upstream. Nebraska's other option in this historical negotiating moment was to ensure that the 1997 regime of the river was maintained in perpetuity. Negotiators representing Nebraska were unyielding in their push to protect what they viewed as their historical 1997 baselines.

During the arduous negotiations leading up to the 1998 FERC re-licensing settlement, federal analysts in the USFWS—using the USBR Operational Study Model of central Platte River flows—estimated how the waters in the EA account would work. As they did so, they paid little attention to issues involving the Nebraska-Colorado South Platte Compact and the *Nebraska v. Wyoming* lawsuit that was ongoing and not yet memorialized in a U.S. Supreme Court settlement in May 2000. Historical flows available to Nebraska had been built into the federal calculations that informed FERC re-licensing.

The EA section of the June 1997 CA that had framed all subsequent negotiations had indicated that "the EA contribution by the Districts . . . is based on the understanding that the flows available . . . remain representative of the Current Regime of the River except for changes . . . which are compensated, mitigated or offset" (Cooperative Agreement 1997: tab 1A, B1, p. 4). The FERC deal signed later, in May 1998, incorporated this same position. This core of Nebraska's argument had therefore been noted by all other interests at the recovery program negotiating table early in the program construction process.

What standing would a federal model of water flows at Lake McConaughy, as part of a separate negotiation with FERC, have in subsequent Nebraska negotiations and possible court proceedings with its upstream neighbors? The answer: little to none. But if flow regimes generated by the model of flows in and out of McConaughy were accepted by the states as part of the habitat recovery program, the models would become binding.

The CNPPID and the NPPD faced a big squeeze. Heavy summer irrigation demand had combined with pressure to fully employ CNPPID facilities for revenue-enhancing electrical power production. CNPPID was a latecomer on the river in the Nebraska prior appropriation scheme, thereby ensuring that the district's diversion rights were junior and highly sensitive to any loss in Platte flow volumes. Any nontrivial shrinkage of river volumes could push district diversion priorities out of the river under certain dry scenarios. Furthermore, Nebraska knew it had to serve a fixed EA commitment to downstream critical habitat as part of the FERC deal. EA water could be expected to flow on behalf of habitat without great sensitivity to Lake McConaughy's ever lower storage volumes in the current or any future drought.

Another aspect of Nebraska's nightmare was the possibility that inflows from Colorado's South Platte and Wyoming's North Platte would be diminished by some unexamined flaw in those states' plans to offset their future depletions (post-1997). In all but well-above-average years, any deficit would have to be compensated by increased flows from Lake McConaughy. Unless Nebraska could draw Colorado into an agreement not to deplete its South Platte waters to the full extent permitted by the South Platte Compact and could prevent additional unmitigated depletions in Wyoming, Nebraska would be in danger of "eating" losses. If such losses were to occur, Nebraska must not be left alone to absorb them. The price of getting Nebraska to sign on to the habitat recovery program would be to secure Nebraska's conception of the regime of the river.

The two Nebraska districts' nightmare was rich in irony. They feared upstream well depletions not fully offset by their upstream neighbors. Yet while Nebraska negotiators were concerned about ways and means of getting well pumping under control in two upstream states, they were also under ferocious attack by Nebraska groundwater interests mobilized in Natural Resource Districts (NRDs) that were energetically resisting anything the state of Nebraska might do to exercise control over depletions Nebraskans were placing on the main stem of the same river in their own state.

COLORADO'S NIGHTMARE

The entire reason for Colorado to construct its Tamarack Plan Project supplementing South Platte River flows to replace historical depletions (pre–July 1, 1997) and offset new ones (post–June 30, 1997) on behalf of the listed species was to get on with the business of creating possible additional Colorado South Platte consumptive uses, as needed because of economic growth within the terms of the 1923 Nebraska-Colorado South Platte Compact. Colorado would abide by the terms of that interstate treaty but felt no obligation to help Nebraska with its potential FERC squeeze. When it came to fundamentals, life was simple: Nebraska must not be allowed to use the negotiations to rewrite the compact. Waters in excess of USFWS target flow requirements and compact stipulations must be available for Colorado purposes.

The fact that Nebraska and the two districts made assumptions about water flows from Colorado and Wyoming during the FERC negotiations and wove them into their re-licensing deal was very interesting. However, the upstream states were not bound by those assumptions. Insofar as Nebraska was calling for a reduction of Colorado's consumptive uses on the South Platte, Nebraska was undertaking an unacceptable negotiating gambit, for at least two reasons: (1) it was nothing less than an ill-disguised attack on the 1923 Nebraska-Colorado South Platte Compact, and (2) it questioned the integrity of Colorado's Tamarack Plan and its capacity to truly offset Colorado depletions.

In 1997–1998, at the time of the birth of the Cooperative Agreement and the FERC arrangement, there was little concern in any of the states that the re-licensing stipulations would be troublesome. A much simpler vision of where the negotiations would go existed at that time—the direction would be toward reducing shortages to target flows, providing suitable land for habitat, and constructing an integrated monitoring and research plan (IMRP). In this context, Colorado had agreed to admit language into its plan to offset future depletions (post-1997): "New water related activities in Colorado will not adversely affect the 'Current Regime of the River'" (Cooperative Agreement 1997: tab 3B, 1). Colorado meant what it said. But at that earlier moment, Colorado did not fully anticipate the ways Nebraska would use those words. As the years passed, negotiations were confronting previously unimagined complexities that accompanied the USFWS's insertion of peak and pulse flow requirements.

Just when the talks were bogging down in the face of the new complexity, Colorado and Wyoming began to fear that Nebraska was using its FERC arrangements—in which Colorado and Wyoming were only tangential participants—to isolate the CNPPID and the NPPD from the new program demands on the basin. FERC, an independent-minded organization that paid virtually no attention to Platte Basin issues, had checked the regulatory re-licensing boxes and granted forty-year licenses to the Nebraska districts. The upstream neighbors feared that the receipt of those licenses had reduced incentives for Nebraska authorities to shoulder the state's burdens regarding the habitat recovery program. The districts appeared to be using the FERC deal to isolate themselves from the new demands and to press Colorado and Wyoming on the regime of the river. Colorado and Wyoming had their nightmare: Nebraska would use the FERC deal to "put a fence" around Nebraska's Platte waters. Neither upstream state could possibly guarantee that no future project would ever have a negative impact on the river;

if and when that were to happen, Nebraska would have to accept some erosion of its position in the overall flow regime.

THE PREMISE OF COLORADO'S TAMARACK PLAN

The major idea Tamarack Plan Phases I and III shared (Tamarack II was not mandated to reduce shortages to target flows) was to divert Colorado waters at times of excess to target flows and receive USFWS credit in reducing target flow shortages for the fraction that returned to the river at times of species habitat needs. Colorado had always operated with the understanding that Colorado users could exploit flows upstream of the Nebraska border in excess of target flow commitments as long as they were covered by Tamarack Plan Phase II accretions. If net accretions were to occur, it would be Colorado's prerogative to make use of them. This was the notion Nebraska set about to challenge.

NEBRASKA'S NIGHTMARE
INTENSIFIES COLORADO'S NIGHTMARE

Nebraska representatives had long had concerns about Colorado's Tamarack Plan. What would Tamarack I do to Nebraska flows for the Nebraska districts, which were caught in their commitments to FERC and the USFWS? Similarly, what would Tamarack III do? Nebraska had generally accepted Phases I and II as part of the mid-1997 CA, but state representatives had never had a chance to review Tamarack III. Behind all this, however, was a deeper, more threatening question never fully explored by either party—the division of "excesses" to target flows produced by Colorado's re-timing projects. Colorado had always fervently resisted any discussion of this issue.

For Colorado, the compelling fact was that the South Platte Compact had divided the waters of the two states in 1923, which meant there was simply nothing to discuss. Nebraska felt there was little alternative but to use the CA negotiations to re-visit the interstate division of flows, compact or not. The federal and environmental communities stood aside in hopes that the question would not cause the entire proceeding to blow up and send everybody into individual ESA Section 7 consultations.

Specifically, Nebraska was concerned that when the USBR-USFWS team ran its "operational study" model, which scored the water action plan components at the top of the critical habitat, it did not take into account the way each proposed project would impact Nebraska district operations. The models operated at a general reconnaissance level of analysis and could not reveal features of project-by-project interactions across the three states. The federal model could speak to getting quantities of water to the habitat but could not display the subtleties of the regime of the river.

Calculations had established that for Tamarack I facilities to produce an annual average of 10,000 acre feet of accretions to the river at times of habitat need, a total of about 30,000 acre feet/year needed to be diverted into recharge pits (Cooperative Agreement 1997: tab 3A, p. 4). Of that total, there would be losses, such as those associated with evaporation and with re-pumping some of the same water back to the pits. Colorado had always understood that it would use about 16,000 of the 20,000-acre-foot difference. The water may not arrive in the river channel at the proper time to earn Platte River Habitat Recovery Program credit, but it was still valuable water.

Nebraska's two districts (CNPPID and NPPD) had estimated that Colorado would not use much, if any, of the 16,000 acre feet because the flows would return low in Colorado's system and be swept into Nebraska by gravity. A key incentive for Nebraska to agree to Tamarack I in 1997 was the unstated expectation that it would have access to all or a major fraction of Colorado return flows beyond the 10,000 acre feet due to species habitat recovery. The Nebraska districts, caught in their FERC commitments, argued that any reduction in access to the Tamarack inflows would hurt their operations, even if those waters were in "excess" to USFWS target flow commitments. In Nebraska's eyes, when their authorities signed off on Tamarack I, they were expecting something in the range of 16,000–20,000 acre feet/year, not just 10,000. There was water to be had, and Nebraska would fight for it.

Nebraska's decision to push hard on this demand was rooted in several factors. First, Nebraska and Colorado had never gone through a prolonged and difficult period of trying to understand each other, as had occurred between Wyoming and Nebraska during the ten years of litigation that had led to the Supreme Court settlement in 2000. As painful and expensive as that experience had been, it had created grounds of mutual understanding that augured well for Nebraska-Wyoming's adaptive management future. There was no equivalent experience between Nebraska and Colorado—no years of gaining a deep understanding of each other's operations, constraints, and latitudes for action. In Nebraska's eyes, some mutual understanding had emerged over the years of basin habitat recovery talks, but the going had been tough given Colorado's refusal to go far beyond its mantra: compact, compact, compact; Tamarack, Tamarack, Tamarack.

Second, although Nebraska had fully participated in the prolonged negotiations on the water plan matters incorporated in the 1997 CA, the state had always wanted a project-by-project discussion of impacts—a conversation that would once again open old issues regarding the fair share division of water flows (see Chapter 10). Nebraska worried that as the years went by and Colorado placed increased consumptive uses on the South Platte above the compacted firewall at the Balzac-Cooper gauge, Nebraska would be shorted.

In Colorado's view, Nebraska was issuing nothing less than a call for renegotiating the South Platte Compact; it would have none of it. Colorado delegates strongly asserted the right of state water users to use any "excess" flows to compact minimums and USFWS targets. Colorado conceded that some return flows after Colorado beneficial uses would be available for Nebraska, but Colorado could not commit to any particular quantity at any particular time. Colorado was operating in good faith with its 1997 Cooperative Agreement pledge not to adversely impact Nebraska's regime of the river because (1) it believed its Tamarack Plan efforts would work, and (2) the long-term trend on Colorado's South Platte had been toward an increasing volume of annual flows. Any damages to Nebraska would be nonexistent or trivial. The re-timing of water flows from winter to spring months would be positive for Nebraska power and agricultural production, given that those months are times of significant demand in Nebraska.

Colorado noted that since the EA at Lake McConaughy would be drawn down virtually every year, it would thereby create a "hole" in the reservoir, which Nebraska representatives loved to lament. However, opening storage capacity behind Kingsley Dam—in wet years and otherwise a full reservoir—would permit the capture of peak flows from the North Platte system. Prior to the EA, those volumes would have been spilled downstream. No one knew when wet times would reappear, but when they arrived Nebraska would not be risking as much damage to its interests as the state's representatives claimed. Furthermore, if Nebraska was concerned about multiple agricultural uses of Tamarack return flows in Colorado, it should be equally concerned about multiple uses of EA water at McConaughy. Colorado argued that Nebraska would do with EA water exactly what Colorado planned to do with a fraction of Tamarack water: it would run it through its systems on its way to critical habitat.

Nebraska was pushing for something more than Colorado could give— permission to involve itself in the management of Colorado waters. Colorado could not accept any built-in presumption of need for Colorado to mitigate Nebraska losses that would be written into any habitat recovery program document. Therefore, the way forward was to avoid the difficult problem of trying to parse out Tamarack flows, look at the big picture of a generally gaining Colorado South Platte, and focus on the use of adaptive management to incrementally serve species habitat needs.

Nebraskans responded that they remained uncomfortable about the workings of Tamarack Plan components and, further, that the historical trend of an increasing volume of annual flows in the South Platte could be reversed in the future. Nebraska signaled that it was open to Colorado's argument that the South Platte is a gaining river and may continue to be so. But Colorado needed to provide enforceable assurance Nebraskans could count on over the long run. As Colorado irrigators turn toward greater individual efficiency by adopting center-pivot irrigation systems, return flows to the river may diminish. Furthermore, as cities such as Denver and Aurora pursue urban reuse of effluent to serve parks and golf courses, additional consumptive uses are placed on scarce water supplies, which could mean less future flow downstream to the Nebraska border. In a system in which users have always been dependent on return flows from those above them, individual rationality in pursuit of so-called water savings could create a collective problem for downstream users in both Colorado and Nebraska. For Nebraska, there were reasons to be skeptical about promises of a continually gaining river. Constrained by the terms of the Nebraska-Colorado South Platte Compact, Nebraska could not reach up above the firewall at the Balzac gauge, but it could point out in the negotiations that it was frightened of what Colorado might do to increase consumptive uses above that firewall. The way to get at the problem was to examine Tamarack Plan flows closely and stake a claim to at least some of them.

Amid the struggle, one thing that could be agreed on: by April 2003, Nebraska was sufficiently anxious about Colorado's Tamarack Plan that representatives of each state saw that it would be to their mutual advantage to strip the project proposed under Phase III out of the current talks. It would be best to work on getting Tamarack I in suitable shape to work for each of the two states and for the species to be protected. Therefore, Nebraska agreed to postpone any further inspection of Tamarack III until sometime during the first program increment.

In late 2002 and early 2003, negotiations had been dragging, even compared to the low expectations established in earlier years. Talks were bogged down over almost the full range of "skunky" issues. Now the long-delayed regime of the river had to be addressed; nobody could clearly envision a mutually satisfactory solution. Negotiators were weary, discouraged, and deeply irritated by aspects of each other's positions. Each party felt it had long been too indulgent of the others. Each also believed it was losing.

A COLORADO TIME-OUT

On Tuesday, May 27, 2003, members of the Governance Committee gathered at a hotel near Denver International Airport. All principals knew this session was critical. Each community of interest had its senior negotiators at the table, most notably Colorado, which had a spotty record of incorporating its governor's political representatives over the preceding four years. The topic was the regime of the river. Nebraska would make its case. The group would take a lunch break. Colorado would then reply.

A spokesperson for the CNPPID articulated Nebraska's case. The presentation was an uncompromising statement of the problem as district authorities saw it. The spokesperson carefully described Nebraska's plumbing heading at Korty Canal on the South Platte and inflows and outflows at Lake McConaughy on the North Platte. Attendees gained a clear overview of how the district's networks of canals, reservoirs, and rivers laced the South and North Platte streams together in a tight interdependency. If Colorado increased its consumptive uses on the South Platte, then Nebraska would have to make up the difference with increased releases from Lake McConaughy. The operational implications of various combinations of wet and dry summer conditions along with higher and lower levels at Lake McConaughy were considered. Interactions between power production and irrigation water demand were reviewed. All this was brought to bear on the main point: given FERC requirements, historical North and South Platte supplies, and already negotiated water action plan proposals for species habitat, "Nebraska has been squeezed down to a point where there is no slack left. Nebraska has no choice but to protect its supply base."

The message could not have been clearer: further depletions to Colorado and Wyoming waters must be mitigated or compensated. If Nebraska was to sign on to any proposed habitat recovery program, the price would be that Colorado could not continue to hide behind the 1923 Nebraska-Colorado South Platte Compact. It would need to put Tamarack excesses to target flows on the table for discussion. For its part, Wyoming could not expect to make a stand on the terms specified by the 2000 U.S. Supreme Court settlement, which asserted that the impacts of Wyoming groundwater wells just above the Nebraska border must be mitigated. By implication, the message was that Nebraska districts had paid their dues for the proposed ESA program in their 1998 FERC settlement; they would not take additional losses. The burdens of uncertainty had to be shifted to those upstream of Nebraska's borders.

For the upstream states, this was a harsh message. Colorado and Wyoming representatives expressed skepticism about the seriousness of Nebraska's water plight. But the presentation—so clear, so stark, so uncompromising—provided little opening for Wyoming or Colorado negotiators to reach for common ground. Plus, it was time for lunch; each community of negotiators would caucus separately.

Colorado's delegation had expected to hear a general policy position that would invite a problem-solving discourse. The state's representatives now expressed deep dismay and anger. The negotiations were clearly going off the rails. What could be done to repair them? Given that Nebraska was clearly using the habitat recovery program to try to reopen compact issues, were these negotiations really the best vehicle for obtaining federal ESA sanctions for Colorado water facilities? Colorado needed federal permits, but it might now have to obtain them in a separate deal. The risks of such a venture were enormous, but they were now being seriously contemplated. What should Colorado's strategy be?

The problem of responding to Nebraska's presentation was located within the larger context of unresolved problems that had emerged over the years, only nibbled at around the edges and left to bedevil negotiators now. The entire direction of things was very different from, and more threatening than, what the states thought they were getting into in 1997. The talks had shifted from provision of land, water, research, and monitoring to natural flows, peak flows, pulse flows, solutions to river channel choke points far above critical habitat, and open-ended commitments to take a walk with the USFWS in a "habitat recovery park" using an amorphous concept of adaptive management. Colorado's future depletions plan was seriously questioned by Nebraska and was simultaneously under attack by the USFWS because the agency wanted peak flows preserved for habitat purposes. In the midst of all these problems, was it productive to return to the negotiating room and engage Nebraska in a discussion of details of an unwanted challenge to the Tamarack Plan? The conversation had to be reframed.

While dining together in a private place, separate from the others, delegation members launched into an animated discussion of the problems, tactics, and strategy. They all agreed about the nature of the problem—it was unacceptable that, for several years, negotiations had moved from the subject of protecting and enhancing species habitat to one of protecting the regime of the river for two Nebraska districts whose facilities had done much to threaten that habitat in the first place. Regrettably, the talks had drifted to protection of an FERC deal the Nebraska districts had arranged for their own purposes without meaningful participation by either Colorado or Wyoming. They could agree about the nature of the problem, but what could be done? As one member later put it, "We were at a loss as how to right the ship."

Colorado's delegates were angry about Nebraska's posture and were divided among themselves. Given the long buildup of unresolved issues over several years and the particular events of that morning, could the Colorado team return to the room and be constructive? The answer was no. They would return to the conference room to listen as their leader, agricultural commissioner Don Ament, informed the assembly that he had determined that time was required for review and reflection. He emphasized that Colorado was not withdrawing from the negotiations but would need the month of June to pull its stance together on the issues. This decision should be interpreted as a time-out, not a permanent walk-out. The team would return to Governance Committee talks in July.

DOUBLE IMPASSE

The Colorado team met in various locations across town all of the following day (May 28), reviewed issues, and began to put together a position paper. In addition to the substantial list of other "skunks," members had to deal with at least two pressing problems: (1) coming up with a way to do something constructive and justifiable under Colorado law and compact stipulations regarding Nebraska's position on the regime of the river, and (2) determining what would be acceptable to the administration of Colorado governor Bill Owens.

State leadership teams in Wyoming and Nebraska had solidified early in the negotiations, well before the 1997 Cooperative Agreement, and they had maintained a consistent presence. This had not been the case in Colorado. The membership of Colorado's delegation had shifted over the years and had to deal with two governors with very different philosophies regarding the ESA. Colorado's changing political leadership, as well as the state's problems with Nebraska, contributed to the delegation's decision to take a time-out.

The USFWS was worried about the senior political leadership in George Bush's Department of the Interior, environmentalists at the table had to contemplate dealing with others in their movement who were more radical, Wyoming had to carefully maneuver around Upper North Platte Valley irrigators, and Nebraska representatives were always mindful of groundwater users. In Colorado, since January 1999 the concern had been about obtaining sufficient support from Governor Bill Owens and the team he had assembled to administer the state's water resources.

Owens, a conservative Republican and former lobbyist for the oil and gas industry, had served for twelve years in the Colorado House of Representatives. In the November 1998 election, he defeated Democratic candidate Gail Schoettler in a very close contest. After taking office in January 1999, Owens reacted to the challenges posed by the Platte negotiations in a much cooler manner than had his predecessor, Democrat Roy Romer. Romer and his senior administrators had taken a "can-do" problem-solving approach combined with openness to the Nebraska, Wyoming, and federal perspectives. Romer had accepted the regulatory framework that had evolved to administer the ESA and simply wanted to move forward with a solution that would work for all parties.

Other states now found Colorado less open and engaging than had been the case during the Romer era; in particular, years of a much more withdrawn Colorado had not helped the Nebraska-Colorado relationship. Also, Owens did not work closely with Platte River water interests or environmental groups to formulate a clear and consistent policy that would give the negotiators a direction. Team members feared that if the signals became clear, they would have a strongly negative impact on their efforts to develop a Colorado contribution. Some water user interests concluded that at times the Owens administration seemed to be seeking a way out of the talks or might be willing to take risks with the Platte River Habitat Recovery Program in the service of its broader, anti-ESA ideological stance.

During many negotiating sessions following the installation of Owens's administration, senior Colorado administrators who could speak authoritatively for the state were not in attendance. In the months preceding the Colorado timeout, a highly competent civil servant represented the Owens administration. He served on the staff of the Colorado Water Conservation Board and had been told not to devote more than 25 percent of his time to the Platte recovery program.

He could articulate Colorado negotiating interests on a meeting-by-meeting basis but could not construct the necessary political coalition among state agencies. That would have to be done by the governor's office.

At this critical juncture (mid- to late 2003), it was essential to get the Colorado negotiation posture right, as defined by the South Platte water community. Then the team needed to convey the water users' message to the governor in a manner that would gain his support. Looking at the big picture, there were three repositories of water knowledge within the state apparatus, each linked to the governor. First, there was the Colorado Department of Natural Resources (DNR), led by Owens appointee Greg Walcher—an outspoken critic of the ESA as written; he reflected Owens's proclivity to want the kind of reform George W. Bush's administration would endorse. Second, there was the Attorney General's Office, administered by Kenneth E. Salazar, a Democrat and an adversary of the governor who had been elected to that position in 1998; he remained in the office until January 2005, when he took a seat in the U.S. Senate. Third, there was the Colorado Water Conservation Board (CWCB), directed by Rod Kuharich and mandated to assist in the implementation of Colorado water policy.

Water users had long had productive links to the CWCB, and the agency was intimately connected to the Platte talks because its representative was acting as leader of the delegation. Obtaining support for a South Platte policy was the problem. Governor Owens, Greg Walcher, and the water users had not found a way to cooperatively construct a Colorado policy and negotiation stance that promised to work within the existing ESA Cooperative Agreement framework. The water user community in general supported weakening the law, but this was not the time to be talking about how South Platte water users could be used as a battering ram in any larger, longer-term anti-ESA crusade. They needed regulatory certainty, and they wanted to construct a coherent Colorado approach—now. They needed to count on the governor's eventual support in pushing a successfully negotiated proposed program through the Colorado General Assembly.

Water users had to construct a political path along which to lead their governor. They could follow the path led by one conservative Republican or another path, more to their liking, led by a different conservative Republican. Greg Walcher, director of the DNR, was a voice of the Western slope. He was known to have little sympathy for Eastern slope water user agendas; as a past president of Club 20 (a political interest group that had organized Western slope interests against Eastern slope designs for obtaining Western slope water), he had battled for many years against some of the same South Platte interests he was now representing in his statewide office. Furthermore, the Platte Basin issues were much more complicated and the water interests there much more powerful—particularly Denver Water and the Northern Colorado Water Conservancy District—so Walcher and associates tended to back away and remain only sporadically engaged. When these Owens people checked in on the Platte proceedings from time to time, they were overwhelmed by the intricacies of the long history of the talks and the fact that the strongly Republican water constituency on the South Platte wanted a successful habitat recovery program as a means to acquire regulatory certainty. One option for Governor Owens would have been to instruct Walcher to fully engage with the Platte River Basin problem and follow it through to a solution, whatever that turned out to be. South Platte negotiators, however, were determined to minimize the likelihood that such a scenario would develop.

Another Republican political leader could clear a path to a solution for the governor. Don Ament was an Owens appointee as agricultural commissioner. He had grown up in Lower South Platte territory and had long been a resident of Sterling, Colorado, an agricultural trade center about fifty-eight miles upstream of the Nebraska border. Prior to taking his cabinet post in 1999, he served twelve years in the Colorado General Assembly: four years in the House of Representatives and eight in the Senate. He had solid relationships in the northeastern Colorado communities along the South Platte and was the only senior Colorado policy maker who had systematically pushed the South Platte water user agenda in the recovery program talks. The question was, given that he was an agricultural commissioner—not a leader of the Department of Natural Resources, not a staff member in the water-related units of the Attorney General's Office, not a director of the CWCB—did he have sufficient support from Governor Owens to work out a water deal for South Platte users?

The question of which path Governor Owens would follow had been lingering in the minds of Colorado delegates since January 1999. Now it was May 2003, and there was still a lack of clarity about what the governor would be willing to endorse. But that which had lingered unresolved now needed immediate attention. Colorado had promised to clarify its stance and return to the table by mid-July. Obviously, one option would be to arrange a meeting with Walcher, specify the stakes, make the case for the South Platte water users' preferences, and solicit his support. However, that would entail the considerable danger that the delegates would back Walcher into a corner and thereby trigger a disaster in the form of his decision to order a Colorado pullout.

For years, the essence of the Owens-Walcher argument had been that even with a habitat recovery program in place, water users would still have to enter into Section 7 consultations—the streamlined version that would accompany a successful effort—and be "nipped" somewhat on water guaranteed to Colorado by the Nebraska-Colorado Compact. This would mean that even when the compact had been fulfilled, it would be possible for a Colorado project to be denied—to them an unacceptable prospect. Furthermore, in average years only a small amount of water would be available for new Colorado uses. Coloradoans would need to put that water to beneficial use, and the USFWS should not be empowered to hold back a portion in the name of peak flows for listed species.

South Platte water interests had countered the Owens-Walcher view over the years by pointing out that the recovery program promised huge benefits that could be obtained no other way. Such a program would protect all water uses prior to July 1, 1997, and in addition protect—through the new depletions plan—new water uses that would come with future economic growth. That would constitute the erection of meaningful protection for virtually all South Platte water. The compact could not protect pre- or post-1997 depletions to the river in individual Section 7 consultations, but a viable program would.

In this context, Colorado negotiators pieced together their negotiating strategy; that, in turn, meant being careful not to trigger a Walcher directive to abandon the talks. Then, a quiet backstage campaign was mounted to send messages to Bill Owens and his inner circle to the effect that the Platte River Habitat Recovery Program was important. Many "rock-ribbed Republicans" communicated this message in one way or another: do not mess with the Colorado Tamarack Plan for the species. Water providers associated with the Platte River Project and the South Platte Lower River Group coordinated a campaign to emphasize the problems that would ensnare them if the program collapsed. They appealed to Governor Owens to push ahead with support for continued negotiations.

As the summer transformed into the fall of 2003, Governor Owens—who had never been particularly engaged in the negotiations—signaled his intent to remain detached. He now saw the risks of abandoning the cooperative agreement process, and he indicated that he would trust his agricultural commissioner to watch over the South Platte territory. Greg Walcher, who had never had strong linkages to the South Platte communities, backed away from whatever intent he may have had to interfere with the water scene in Don Ament's territory. In January 2004 Walcher announced his resignation as director of Colorado's DNR to run for election to the U.S. House of Representatives.

In mid- to late 2003, therefore, Ament consolidated support for his South Platte leadership among the state's higher echelons. But the leader of the political coalition needed legal assistance from the Attorney General's Office. Kenneth Salazar, who won the post of Colorado's attorney general in a 1998 election and began service in January 1999, was a Democrat who tangled with Governor Owens over several highly contested public issues. One of those issues was a bitter and bruising conflict over a Republican re-districting plan (a gerrymander Democrats called the "midnight map"), introduced and passed in the waning hours of the 2003 session of the General Assembly (Martinez 2004: B3). But the issue at hand was water; on that issue, party politics would be set aside in defense of the state's interest in holding on to all possible consumptive uses.

As a partial political vacuum opened up when Walcher decided not to engage in the Platte leadership, Salazar appointed a leader to the Colorado team from the Attorney General's Interstate Water Division, Steve Sims. He had worked on the Republican River settlement among Colorado, Nebraska, and Kansas and since at least early 2002 had been in a position to closely follow the Platte River proceedings. By June 2003 he was actively involved in Colorado's preparations to terminate the time-out. Working with Don Ament and other water users, Sims placed the negotiations front and center, negotiated essential understandings among Colorado team members, and pressed forward. In the summer and fall of 2003, Colorado's negotiating team had reconstituted itself around a Democrat from the Attorney General's Office and a conservative Republican who, together, would lead their governor to a solution regarding the Platte River. Owens, in turn, would signal that he wanted a tidy, defensible solution that would not cost too much. The solution would have to be all that if the governor was going to sell the habitat recovery program to the legislature.

BACK TO WORK

In Colorado's absence, there had been no June Governance Committee session. When the principals gathered on July 14–15 near Denver International Airport, Colorado and Nebraska spent the first morning in closed caucus. They were in session together "cold," without backstage mutual exploration of each other's positions—a fact that concerned everyone. Wyoming, which knew the shape of the day, did not appear until the time for everyone to gather in an afternoon general session. Federal representatives took the opportunity to convene upstairs. Environmentalists occupied the food service area in the lobby. People were thinking about the Colorado-Nebraska session going on behind closed doors and were considering their options depending on the message that would be forthcoming. Were the two adversaries driving the process ahead? Were they aborting it?

The stakes were high. At the states' request, the Department of the Interior had funded the National Academies of Science review of the federal science that had driven the rationale for the USFWS jeopardy opinions in the basin, and its findings were expected to be released no later than early 2004. If the federal science was vindicated, the regulatory process would soon produce a draft environmental impact analysis of whatever proposed program the states had to offer. Would the states want to bear the burdens that would accompany public disclosure and assessment of an obviously incomplete and possibly deeply flawed proposed habitat recovery program, or would they agree to produce adequate substance? The draft EIS would need to be released as soon as humanly possible, in any case no later than 2004. It was imperative to obtain as much resolution as possible before its release. The time for regulatory cruising had been exhausted.

Wyoming had its federal reservoir yields to protect; the Nebraska districts did not want to suffer a FERC reopener. Colorado, in the short run, needed the program to cover new depletions that would be imposed by new water projects just coming on-line. Denver Water, for example, looked forward to switching on its celebrated reuse project (re-diverting waste water to supply over 17,000 acre feet of water to industrial and outdoor irrigation uses) in early 2004 (www.denverwater.org/recycle/recycled_facts). Placing a second consumptive use by recycling South Platte River flows would impose a new depletion that would require coverage from the program. If Denver Water lost faith in the Cooperative Agreement process, it could send its agents to buy up water on the lower river and trigger an individually rational "race to water" on Colorado's Lower South Platte among many thirsty Front Range cities and industries. In such a scramble, the wealthier customers exercising their individual rationality in the quest for offset water would out-bid more poorly financed clients—especially smaller towns and farmers—and turn the Lower South Platte into a sacrifice zone. It would be a full-employment policy for lawyers and hydrologists, who would suck up untold millions of dollars while drying up communities and producing no benefit for endangered and threatened species downstream. In the longer run, Colorado knew it needed a viable interstate program to protect the waters the Nebraska-Colorado Compact had reserved for the state.

When Colorado caucused with Nebraska that July day, its list of sore subjects included the division of so-called excesses to target flows at Tamarack, peak flows, and Nebraska's attempt to protect the two districts from any non-trivial loss at Lake McConaughy—a posture Colorado labeled a "super-right." Problems were not solved that day, but the two states agreed to invite each of the other negotiating camps to submit their outstanding concerns. The expanded list soon became known as the "dirty dozen."

The water user representatives were acutely aware that 2004 was a general election year. They knew "friendly" secretaries of the interior do not stay in office forever; they come and go, especially toward the end of first presidential terms and at the beginning of new ones. For these reasons, the players had arrived at a point where they each had powerful incentives to implement a successful habitat recovery plan. A serious struggle over clashing principles was going on behind closed doors and, as one senior Nebraska negotiator later put it, there was no more time to "diddle-diddle."

INCREASED NEGOTIATING DISCIPLINE

The Colorado time-out had galvanized a determination among the negotiating teams to accelerate problem solving. This meant doing at least three things: (1) cleaning up the negotiating process by removing staff members and stripping down to core senior negotiators, (2) employing a team of professional facilitators, and (3) setting forth an aggressive schedule of priority topics, as defined by the parties at the table. Colorado's temporary departure was remembered not so much as a sign of collapse but rather as a harbinger that collapse was a distinct possibility. They needed to prevent that from happening.

There was general agreement that the size of the negotiating group needed to be reduced. When senior members discussed matters at the level of general principles and were able to stay at that level, they could come to terms with each other. Problems tended to arise when technical staff brought forward endless distracting details. Therefore, it was agreed that staff people would be kept on call but that only seniors would inhabit negotiating rooms, except for specific and compelling reasons. This approach remained in effect for the duration of the talks.

At the July session, the parties agreed to employ a team of professional facilitators to organize and conduct every negotiating session of the Governance Committee from August to December 2003. Facilitators would work with participants prior to meetings to learn their flexibilities and rigidities on issues and would attempt to formulate possible paths to solutions. They shuttled back and forth among adversaries behind the scenes to find common ground that could be endorsed in open sessions. In the meetings, they kept control of the agenda, worked to keep everyone focused on the points of discussion, extracted clarity from statements, and confirmed understandings. They worked to prevent any party from becoming cornered by any other party and reduced opportunities for people to take unnecessary potshots at each other.

Governance Committee members established an aggressive schedule of meetings and discussion topics in the late summer and fall of 2003. Negotiators set a self-imposed deadline. Knowing they would be engaging in "do-or-die" discussions over the coming months, they agreed to do everything possible to achieve the maximum possible resolution of issues by November 2003. The proposed program document, such as it would be at that time, would provide grist for the draft environmental impact statement that would emerge in early 2004. That document would not only characterize the proposed program, it would also assess it as compared to possible alternatives and would be widely distributed to interests from every camp throughout the basin and beyond.

COLORADO RESPONDS: ATTACK THE SUPER-RIGHT

Nebraska had been claiming that it would have to be compensated for any negative impacts to water volumes at Lake McConaughy and to other CNPPID and NPPD water uses that occurred as a result of Colorado and Wyoming operations on behalf of the proposed habitat recovery program. If Colorado and Wyoming let such claims stand (and if they could sell that idea to water constituencies in and around their respective executive, legislative, and judicial branches—a virtual impossibility), the upstream states would have thereby effectively granted Nebraska a "super-right" at McConaughy. Flows into that tub would become the top water priority in the basin without regard to the history of legally sanctioned arrangements among the three states. This Nebraska district stance was unacceptable to both Colorado and Wyoming.

The Colorado-Nebraska caucus on July 14 encompassed a substantial list of Colorado concerns, most dealing with aspects of the regime of the river. Colorado presented its position while Nebraska listened calmly. At the center of Colorado's negotiating strategy were three moves that had been discussed for years among Coloradoans and signaled to Nebraskans, but two of which Colorado players had previously been reluctant to advance to the negotiating table.

First, Colorado made a general point to the effect that each state would need to explore many possibilities in developing its water supply projects on behalf of the habitat recovery program. Many unknowns would need to be addressed as each state implemented its water action plans and future depletions plans during the first thirteen-year program increment. Each state must be given the opportunity to succeed or fail and make essential adjustments. This was a way of politely telling Nebraska to back away from attempts to denigrate and micro-manage Colorado's Tamarack Plan re-timed flows. The next two points were more threatening.

Colorado's second move came in the form of calling for a revision of the 1998 deal between Nebraska's two districts and FERC. Why, Colorado asserted, should the districts obtain forty years of regulatory certainty through their re-licensing arrangements while Colorado and Wyoming could look forward to only thirteen years of such grace? The districts had been granted a condition that isolated them too much from the requirements of the proposed habitat recovery program. The program should not grant more regulatory certainty to Nebraska than was made available to Wyoming and Colorado. The districts would be asked to agree to have language placed in the FERC settlement that would level the regulatory field on which the first program increment would be played out.

Colorado then played its third card, the one it had been most reluctant to put on the table. If Nebraska continued to rigidly hold to its position on the regime of the river, Colorado was prepared to withdraw non-native South Platte River flows from its contribution to the habitat recovery program. Such a move would leave only native flows to be counted upon. To potentially diminish the flows Nebraska could expect to be in the river at the state line, and to do so explicitly in a program document would be a bold and threatening move. Not only was there water loss at the Colorado border to contemplate, but any FERC licensing reopening could place all of the two districts' water portfolios at risk. In the words of one negotiator, Colorado was threatening to "drop a heavy hammer on many Nebraska tootsies."

Questioning the Terms of Regulatory Certainty

When the first thirteen-year increment was approaching its conclusion, neither Colorado nor Wyoming would want to be in a position in which the two Nebraska districts could maneuver to disassociate themselves from any newly established program requirements by simply telling the two upstream states to go away and take care of the problems with only minimum CNPPID-NPPD involvement. Colorado argued, with Wyoming's tacit support, that the districts should accept revised language in their FERC settlement that explicitly specified that the districts must meet recovery program performance standards; as a means to ensure that, the districts would accept language granting them the same time period of regulatory certainty that was available to Wyoming and Colorado: thirteen years. Environmentalists agreed with Colorado; they could see no benefit in leaving everything up to FERC on a forty-year review cycle.

When district representatives heard about this Colorado proposal, they were furious. From their point of view, no serious consideration could be given to tampering with the FERC re-licensing settlement in the way Colorado had proposed. The 1998 FERC deal was a deal. It would be unthinkable to open it up to such proposed reconsideration. So, on this issue on that July day, there was no agreement. But Colorado was soon back at the negotiating table. The two adversaries worked on the issue in the series of facilitated meetings. As time went by, Nebraska sent signals to the effect that it was more accepting of Colorado's arguments on behalf of Tamarack. Colorado began saying that its interests might be served by obtaining a better understanding of the strictures on the Nebraska districts that were laced into the FERC licenses.

Each side knew it had a rock to throw at the other as discussions proceeded. But each also knew that carelessly thrown projectiles could push one party or the other into a corner from which that party could not deliver its essential constituencies to support any proposed program. That, in turn, would cause the negotiations to blow up and would send them all individually into ESA Section 7 negotiations—a situation no one wanted to contemplate.

Non-Native Water Threat

Two kinds of water flowed across the Colorado-Nebraska border. That fact had major implications for any attempt to divide Tamarack Plan program flows; those implications had long been avoided in discussions among Colorado, Nebraska, and the USFWS because they had the potential—unless handled with extreme care—to collapse any cooperative effort. But now, in 2003, Nebraska's insistence that Tamarack Plan re-timed waters be carefully examined was compelling Colorado to bring to the surface a long-recurring nightmare.

One kind of water available in the South Platte is that identified as native flow—water captured within the boundaries of the river basin, which has historically coursed downstream where users have diverted it for beneficial uses with the sanction of Colorado courts. In general under Colorado law, such water can be given one consumptive use by a diversion right holder, thereby making unused portions of the diversion available to others through return flows. The inability of any given user to put to consumptive use all of the diverted native flows made possible, by the return to the river system, civilization on the Platte and its tributaries. Junior priorities have lived off of upstream return flows of native water from earliest irrigation times.

A second category of water has been known as "foreign water" or "trans-basin water." This water is that "which has been introduced into a stream system that would not reach that system if left to flow in its natural historic course" (Corbridge and Rice 1999: 515). Under Colorado law, once a water provider has succeeded in taking flow from one watershed to another, that user has earned a privilege not available to the diverter of native flows—namely, the right to make successive uses of that water. In the extreme, such water can be used and reused to extinction.

The South Platte has long been a gaining river. Its flows have increased because of a history of Eastern slope water providers drawing "foreign water" into the basin (Thaement and Faucett 2001: 139–147). In the 1990s, in negotiations leading to the 1997 Cooperative Agreement and thereafter, Colorado had steered around the issue of trans-mountain flows and their meaning for participation in the recovery program. The subject was a "sleeping dog" the Colorado team had preferred to let rest undisturbed. The entire premise of the Colorado Tamarack Plan had been that the South Platte's volume of flow had increased as a result of two factors: (1) the conversion of agricultural land to urban and suburban uses, which reduced water use because the growing number of rooftops had been somewhat less water-consumptive than growing corn; and (2) the importation of foreign water. Colorado's participation in the habitat recovery program had always depended on pumping surface flows at times of excess to USFWS-imposed target flows, diverting them into recharge pits designed to return the water to the river at times of shortages to target flows. In this scenario, Colorado negotiators thought it best not to distinguish between native and foreign waters because much of the gain in Colorado's South Platte regime of the river was attributable to sources beyond the basin.

For years, Colorado had been willing not to raise the issue of water composition in the swelling South Platte; it was willing to allow Nebraska to take that water as an undeclared enhancement after Colorado users had taken their "bites." But under Colorado law, there could never be an explicit agreement whereby Colorado could allow Western slope water to count as habitat recovery program flows into Nebraska. Any such attempt would invite revolt from South Platte water users who counted on that water for future uses and from others across the Continental Divide in the Upper Colorado Basin who had reluctantly parted with it. They would not abide allowing Eastern slope water interests to obtain regulatory certainty by playing fast and loose with Western slope water that was to be used to extinction in-state. This was a touchy subject within Colorado, given that Eastern slope providers were seeking additional Western slope water and Western slope water interests were attempting to mobilize their own supplies to fulfill ESA obligations under the Upper Colorado River Endangered Fish Recovery Program (Kanzer and Merritt 2001: 303–317).

In return for leaving the issue alone, Colorado thought it had an understanding with Nebraska authorities to the effect that they would stay away from details such as those behind the Tamarack Plan and, for that matter, that they would not ally with the USFWS in the agency's desire for peak flows (see Chapter 20). Under this tacit deal, Nebraska would have access to important portions of a gaining Colorado South Platte carried to the state by gravity, and Colorado would have its compact. Furthermore, Colorado—on behalf of the species— would take care of its historical and future depletions through Tamarack I, II, and III. All this made for a much larger South Platte at the state line than existed at the time of the 1923 compact. Nebraska, in Colorado's view, should back off, remain quiet, and be happy with what it had.

By threatening to insist on explicit language in the program's water plan and noting that such water was available to be used to extinction in Colorado under state law, Colorado had reframed the entire negotiation. If Nebraska insisted on meddling with Tamarack, it would confront the prospect of a much smaller Colorado South Platte water pie. That would mean more draw on Lake McConaughy storage to compensate. The explicit reservation of foreign water for Colorado uses would, in turn, drive Nebraska away from any constructive relationship with Colorado. Careless handling of this issue could produce a nightmarish chain of events that threatened to destroy any chance of getting long-sought relief from jeopardy through a viable cooperative habitat recovery program.

FINDING A SOLUTION

During the morning caucus on July 14, Colorado presented its positions on the regime of the river and other outstanding issues; Nebraska reacted quietly but rigidly. Members of both teams left the room with a sense of foreboding. There were no obvious solutions. Yet the negotiators could see that calamity would ensue if they gave up the task. A strict ESA would not go away. Somehow, each side would have to find a way to compromise on issues that had become mutually irreconcilable. Beginning in August and throughout the ensuing fall 2003 facilitated sessions, the two states struggled to find a way to live together in a habitat recovery program world.

Since early 2003, negotiators had worked to develop an agreement that would provide substance for the USBR team's draft environmental impact statement. They had given themselves a self-imposed deadline of November 1, so the draft EIS could be ready in early 2004 before politics in an election year became even more difficult than they already were. On October 30, just ten minutes before the Nebraska team had to leave for Denver International Airport, the Governance Committee arrived at a point where members could say they had some major issues in hand, especially those pertaining to the regime of the river.

How had the adversaries made peace? First, they narrowed the field of disagreement by focusing attention only on Tamarack Phase I, Colorado's plan to provide a net annual average of 10,000 acre feet of target flow shortage reduction at the Nebraska border. In particular, this left Tamarack III wide open for future negotiations early in the first thirteen-year program increment. Nebraska succeeded thereby in keeping Colorado accountable to its desires in the not-so-distant future. Colorado succeeded thereby in getting Nebraska to back away from the close inspection of Tamarack I project operations and the explicit division of excess flows for which the Nebraska districts had so vigorously pressed.

Second, diplomatically the parties stepped around a fundamental issue. In the original 1997 Cooperative Agreement (tab 1A, B1, p. 4), Nebraska had secured language that, in effect, said that its participation in the program was rooted in the premise that the regime of the river as of that year would continue or, if altered negatively, the changes would be compensated or mitigated. This was an implicit endorsement of Tamarack II, the phase that would fill in Colorado's new depletions holes in the river. The original 1997 CA language was preserved in the October 2003 agreement and would be incorporated in the final program document in 2006. However, an important addition was made to the EA language (III.A.1:7). Immediately following the Nebraska language, in the same paragraph the agreement read that "nothing in this EA document is intended to impose any additional or independent obligations, requirements, or restrictions of any sort on Colorado or Wyoming. For as long as there is a program, if Colorado and Wyoming re-time flows in accordance with their Tamarack Plan . . . and Pathfinder Modification Plan, existing and new water related activities in Colorado and Wyoming will be included in the Current Regime of the River" (III.A.1:7). Each side had its protective language. The outcome was an implicit decision to abandon a search for reconciliation on irreconcilable principles and to move ahead with trust that the parties could work things out on a case-by-case basis as part of the larger adaptive management process.

Third, Colorado gave Nebraska increased assurance that Tamarack I would be operated in a manner that would be friendly to downstream interests. Colorado pledged to shift more Tamarack Plan recharge facilities closer to the state line. Doing so would accomplish at least two things: there would be fewer opportunities for senior Colorado diversion rights to capture that water (a benefit to Colorado and its downstream partner), and there would be less loss to seepage, thereby increasing Nebraska's confidence that the scheme would work. Water rights for Tamarack Plan activities would be obtained according to Colorado water law for beneficial uses in Colorado, as long as such operations did not interfere with the basin-wide habitat recovery program or Tamarack II new depletions activities. The beneficial uses would include, but not be limited to, habitat improvement for a Colorado species of concern—a variety of native fish species not yet federally listed under the ESA but the focus of research and management by the Colorado Division of Wildlife at Tamarack (see Chapter 9). Also, there would necessarily be interception by senior right holders for agricultural use. But Tamarack I waters, while first serving a combination of Colorado beneficial uses, were pledged to deliver to the Colorado border a rolling ten-year average annual reduction in shortages to USFWS target flows of at least 10,000 acre feet.

Furthermore, it was agreed that Tamarack Plan Phase II waters (destined to replace post-1997 Colorado depletions) in excess of species program requirements could be employed for purposes other than the three-state habitat recovery program. Colorado had in mind two non-program uses: habitat improvement for Colorado native fish species and the provision of offset water on behalf of Colorado groundwater wells below the Balzac-Cooper gauge, in the Lower South Platte. Recall (Chapter 9) that the South Platte Compact calls for Colorado lower river diverters with rights junior to 1897 to shut off their diversions during the irrigation season if South Platte flows at the border fall below 120 cubic feet per second. Furthermore, under Colorado law, junior well priorities must not impose harm on senior surface diversions. For both of these reasons, it was important for water users on the lower river to secure sufficient augmentation water to cover their well depletions to the river or face shutting down their operations just when water tended to be needed most, for summer-season crops. The promise that a portion of their augmentation needs could be provided by part of the Colorado Tamarack Plan (Phase II) effort constituted an important side payment that induced lower river cooperation with Front Range water providers that needed the habitat recovery program.

Nebraska had always been concerned about the mechanics of Colorado recharge and re-regulation operations. When water disappeared into a pit, just how much went in and how much came out in a given time period? What exactly would happen to that water on its journey to the Nebraska border? To allay these fears, Colorado agreed to employ detailed monitoring of and accounting for the operation of Tamarack Plan facilities and to report specific data to the Governance Committee. Nebraska was given assurance that depletions caused by both program and non-program water activities would be accounted for and replaced by Colorado depletions plans. Administrators of the Tamarack Plan would also coordinate in specific ways with the USFWS EA manager at Lake McConaughy.

Colorado's plan anticipated the installation of up to forty recharge wells (and canal lift facilities) to get water to recharge pits at the proper distance from the river. Given an analysis of historical data showing how Tamarack recharge facilities would have worked in the 1973–1994 study period, the average annual diversion was estimated to be 29,640 acre feet per year; that volume would produce an annual average of just over 12,000 acre feet of re-timed water for ESA listed species habitat. Colorado therefore agreed to accept a total pumping cap of 30,000 acre feet per year and a river diversion flow of no more than 225 cubic feet per second at any given time for its Tamarack I facilities (*Platte River Recovery Program* 2006: attachment 5, Water Plan, section 3, A1). The re-timed return flows would be picked up at the border and delivered by Nebraska water administrators to be measured at Grand Island.

The parties agreed that Colorado would employ a stream depletion factor (SDF) method, endorsed by the U.S. Geological Survey, to calculate water returns to the river. Observation wells would be located between recharge basins and the river so that groundwater gradients and return flows could be monitored. Any Tamarack accretions intercepted by Colorado canals would be accounted for and depletions to them would not be counted toward fulfilling Colorado's target flow obligation. Times of target flow shortages would be measured against flow conditions established by the USFWS in its studies that produced the profile of target flows prior to adoption of the Cooperative Agreement that became operative on July 1, 1997. This meant, for example, that Tamarack operations would be based on the availability of excess flows at Grand Island, as documented in the 1997 CA (Cooperative Agreement 1997). The Governance Committee would monitor all procedures in a manner transparent to the parties involved.

Both sides found common ground by agreeing to shift targeted times for Tamarack re-timed waters to return to the channel. Originally, the plan had been for a major portion to hit the river during the summer season on behalf of increasing base flows through the critical habitat. As years went by, it became apparent that species habitat needs could be served by a Colorado contribution that would (1) make its greatest diversions from the river to recharge pits in the December–January period, when the greatest excesses to target flows could be expected at the critical habitat; (2) produce return flows to the river at the Colorado border from February through June, when downstream diversions by agriculture were at their lowest level; (3) produce base flows on which to build pulses with McConaughy EA water; and (4) minimize production of accretions to the river during July–August, a time of the greatest canal interceptions and channel losses as a result of low flows below diversions. Needs for in-stream summer flows during periods of high agricultural demand would be better served by

McConaughy EA flows and a combination of return flows from CNPPID canal operations.

Nebraska agreed that it would ensure that consumptive uses of groundwater wells in existence at the time of the July 1, 1997, CA not be expanded or modified in any manner that would cause an increase in shortages to target flows. Offset water to cover their historical depletions would be provided by Nebraska water action plan projects. This principle was also applied to all groundwater wells tributary to the South Platte, North Platte, and the Platte main stem put in operation after July 1, 1997. Such depletions would be replaced by Nebraska's new depletions program. Any Nebraska water designed to offset historical or new depletions must come from sources in excess of target flows and would not rely on flows occurring from the upstream states or from accretions attributable to Colorado's new water-related activities—those activities that contribute to a gaining South Platte.

If disputes arise about the quality of information regarding Nebraska wells that is made available to the Governance Committee, resolution will be reached by a panel of three experts in groundwater hydrology—one to be named by Nebraska, one named by Colorado, and one employee of the U.S. Geological Survey. Pending completion of any dispute resolution process, Colorado, in consultation with the USFWS, would be authorized to continue to operate the Tamarack Plan in ways consistent with Colorado's commitment to the program, state law, and the South Platte Compact. Such continued operation will be considered adequate for meeting habitat recovery program milestones.

Each upstream state agreed to protect its program accretions within its own river reaches and to make the river "whole" at its Nebraska border. Likewise, in Nebraska, new depletions that occur along the series of river diversions must be fully replaced. There will be a string of depletions and accretions down the North and South Platte and main stem channels all the way to Grand Island.

IMPLICATIONS

By December 2003, negotiations on the regime of the river and other issues yet to be discussed had produced a proposed program document that could serve the federal regulatory process. The principal components of a basin-wide recovery program were in place: a water plan, a land plan, and an integrated plan for monitoring and research that would hope to show whether program efforts in the first thirteen-year increment would work. The USBR EIS team had an important component of the material it needed to proceed with producing a draft environmental impact statement that would eventuate in January 2004.

Each partner had agreed to walk into the future with the other while embracing its own ironic contradiction. Colorado built its entire Tamarack Plan on the premise of the continuation of a gaining South Platte River, as calculated in terms of annual flows. But it could not explicitly abandon the idea that the river might deplete to compact minimums. Nebraska, on the other hand, knew it was the beneficiary of a larger river, but it could only obtain the greatest possible assurance of gaining access to it if it did not explicitly demand such access.

Regime of the River—Sharing Peak Flows

Colorado and the USFWS Struggle on the South Platte

The frequency and magnitude of river flow peaks are determined by many variables. In general, they vary directly with precipitation intensity, speed of snowmelt, and slope steepness. They tend to vary inversely with soil infiltration rates, vegetation density, and diversions to reservoir storage. In the Platte Basin, flow peaks produced by snowmelt have tended to arrive in May and early June. They also appear in response to intense summer storms that can, with devastating suddenness, send walls of water crashing down river channels—uprooting vegetation, carrying heavy sediment loads, configuring sandbars, and generally rearranging riparian habitats for people and other living things. They lose energy and concentrated mass with increasing distance as they disappear into bank storage, river bottoms, revived wetlands, and diversion and storage structures. Peak flows are prized as essential to river restoration and diversity in biotic webs. They are also treasured by water providers who have not yet put together the capital, technology, and organization to capture these remnants of the pre-settlement river and to divert them for thirsty customers. How could peak flows be divided among the conflicting agendas?

AN UNWELCOME CONVERSATION

The North Platte River had been collared by a series of on-channel dams. The shape of its flows would be largely determined by manipulating gates from Seminoe and Pathfinder all the way to McConaughy. However, the South Platte stream had not been dammed below Denver, which meant its tributaries with mouths north and east of Denver—Clear Creek, St. Vrain, Big Thompson, Poudre, Bijou Creek, and Lodgepole Creek, to name a few—could capture and deliver flashy flow spikes to the main South Platte channel. U.S. Fish and Wildlife Service (USFWS) analysts would hang a critical part of their biological opinion on the importance of preserving some fraction of Colorado South Platte peak flows.

In Colorado's view, the entire point of its plan to replace post-1997 depletions was to send sufficient water downstream to fill in the holes in the river imposed by South Platte water users. Now the USFWS was saying the depletions plan that had been formulated and placed into the 1997 Cooperative Agreement (CA) would not sufficiently protect post-1997 depletions. To South Platte water users, the concept was shocking. What had begun as a straightforward plan—cover historical depletions with Tamarack I and III, offset new depletions with Tamarack II, participate in program acquisition of habitat lands, support monitoring and research—had descended into a tangled mess. For water providers, the idea—the division of peak flows under a federal environmental agenda—represented an unwelcome "skunk" at the table.

The success of the overall negotiations was importantly held hostage to the outcome of the peak flow discussions. If Colorado and the USFWS could not make peace on the issue, the entire three-state negotiation could disintegrate, and all the water users would find themselves standing among the tormented in line at the door of Endangered Species Act (ESA) Section 7 consultations.

The issue was so important and potentially polarizing that for years it had been briefly and repeatedly broached and quickly abandoned. It had surfaced in discussions in 1994, just prior to the agreement that year among the governors of the three basin states to engage in a systematic effort to negotiate a program that would eventuate in the 1997 CA. But the very thought that the USFWS would stake a claim to an unknown fraction of peak flows so greatly alarmed the states, especially Colorado, that the subject was put aside in time for the governors and the Department of the Interior (DOI) to sign the CA.

At no time did the states' negotiators accept the logic advanced in the USFWS in-stream flow document (Bowman 1994), which incorporated language advocating the preservation of peak flows. Water provider rejection of the federally proposed package held fast without exception, even when the final program document was released in December 2005 and revised in 2006 prior to being signed by the governors of the three states and DOI authorities. Prior to launching the cooperative habitat recovery program on January 1, 2007, the states placed disclaimers at several points in the text of the final program document (*Platte River Recovery Program* 2006), disassociating themselves from any endorsement of USFWS in-stream flow recommendations. Most specifically, in the Platte River recovery agreement the states secured this language:

> The signing of this Recovery Agreement does not constitute any agreement
> by either party as to whether the Service's flow recommendations in the PBO

[programmatic biological opinion] are biologically or hydrologically necessary to recover the target species or meet the needs of designated critical habitat
in Nebraska. (*Platte River Recovery Program* 2006: attachment 5: Water Plan; see,
for example, Colorado Future Depletions Plan, revised October 24, 2006: 18)

But the USFWS refused to let go of its demand for an unknown fraction
of flow peaks, which presented an entirely new challenge to contemplate. The
program would need to stop Colorado South Platte water users from diverting
and thereby flattening the peaks beyond some point. What fraction would the
USFWS want to preserve for species habitat restoration and sustenance? What
fraction would be left for water users, to serve their new depletions plans? What
fraction would remain for new uses? Whatever answers eventually emerged, it
had been clear all along that no matter how strongly the states opposed agency
thinking on the matter, the USFWS, with its in-stream flow recommendations
in hand, would judge the program's sufficiency. Even though they were rejected
by the states, USFWS in-stream flow recommendations would always be in play.
The agency would not be able to get them adopted by the states, but the states
would still be unable to get them out of their water users' lives.

FEDERAL REGULATORY PRESSURE

From early 1994 to January 2005, the shadow of the long-unresolved peak flow
problem hung darkly over the negotiations. But the federal regulatory process
had to move forward. By 2003 it was time to move ahead with the best program
that could be constructed at the time and have it reviewed, at least in a preliminary manner. With each passing year of negotiations, the states were de facto
extending their regulatory certainty without sufficient commitments to species
recovery. How long could that go on? Negotiators were edging reluctantly toward the moment wherein the toughest problems would have to be addressed,
the peak flow issue among them.

Furthermore, the Department of the Interior had paid for a review of federal science that appeared in draft form in April 2004. The analysis endorsed the
USFWS's science in support of its natural flow vision (National Research Council
of the National Academies 2004a). The states now had to dismiss any hope that
the agency's position regarding its natural flow model would weaken. By mid-
2004 there was little option but for Colorado's newly reconstructed negotiating
team to lead the states to a solution for living with the USFWS's agenda for river
flow peaks as traced out on the South Platte hydrograph.

THE FEDERAL CASE

The USFWS could not seriously consider stepping away from its statutory authority to implement the ESA. In the context of the Platte, that clearly meant

it was necessary to review the impact of the states' new depletions plans on the variety of in-stream flows at the critical habitat. The Operational Study Model (see Chapters 12 and 16), applied in the 2001–2003 sedimentation-vegetation analyses by analysts in the U.S. Bureau of Reclamation (USBR) and the USFWS, found that the program provided insufficient benefits for the interior least terns and plovers. The way to fix that problem was to preserve existing flow peaks and create pulses to sustain an open channel laced with shifting sandbars.

The North Platte would have to serve habitat recovery by manipulating gates at Pathfinder and McConaughy. That left the South Platte to produce sediment that rode with some semblance of Mother Nature's peak flows. Peak flows have been viewed as absolutely critical to biotically healthy riverine ecosystems (Poff et al. 1997; Poff et al. 2003; Wohl 2001). Variable flows with peaks are what distinguish an ecologically viable river from a canal. Channels braid at high stream power produced by flow peaks—a result of discharge volume, slope, velocity, and sediment load. At other times of lower flood pulses and small summer-winter flow quantities, they will throw loops and meander, creating ecological niches supportive of biodiversity. That diversity is essential to habitat recovery on behalf of listed species.

New diversions from the river on behalf of economic growth projects threaten to strip away what remains of flow peaks; therefore, the USFWS must have a strong hand in determining (1) how proposed future depletions plans will protect the frequency and magnitude of flow peaks, and (2) a process for conducting project-by-project reviews of new water use proposals of any significant size. In the case of the Colorado South Platte, the agency could not provide carte blanche authority for Colorado water providers to divert peak flow waters and assert that any reductions in peak flow volumes were covered in the state's depletion plan.

In 1994 the USFWS released two reports that estimated in-stream flow shortages at Grand Island, Nebraska, by examining 1943–1992 historical daily flows (Bowman 1994; Bowman and Carlson 1994). Then, in an analysis never accepted by the states, agency hydrologists divided the calendar year into seven periods (for example, February 1–March 22); looked at the flow data in terms of wet, normal, and dry years; and computed an aggregate shortage value to what the agency defined as its target flows—an annual average of 417,000 acre feet. The target flow figure combined what came to be known as species flows plus pulse flows. Peak flow data were excluded from that analysis. Beginning in 2002 and continuing well into 2005, the issue of flow pulses and peaks sparked sporadic heated conversations as the agency released updated in-stream flow documents (see USFWS 2002a). As draft followed draft, some points were clarified, but the essential message remained constant. Peak flows were viewed as an essential factor in restoring, recovering, and preserving riverine ecosystems. In each new draft, the USFWS plainly stated its objective to minimize reductions in the frequency and magnitude of peak flows. Agency in-stream flow documents consistently defined flow types as follows:

1. Species flows, in a general sense, were defined as all flow recommendations taken together; in a more specific sense, they were defined as minimum channel flows for each of the seven time periods in each category of years—wet, normal, and dry. For example, the recommended species flow from February 1 to March 22 in a normal year was 1,800 cubic feet/second (cfs). In a wet year, the flow for that time period should also be 1,800 cfs, and in a dry year the value was established at 1,200 cfs (USFWS 2004–2005: 3).

2. Annual pulse flows were characterized as recommended flows in excess of species flows. They would have a duration of seven to thirty days and be expected to occur on average in about three of every four years. Rates of flow were expected to be in the range of 2,000 to 3,600 cfs. This category could be created or augmented by program efforts.

3. Peak flows referred to the highest flows maintained for five consecutive days in any given year. Peaks in excess of 12,000 cfs "will be natural occurrences beyond the control of water resources managers in the Platte river basin" (USFWS 2004–2005: 4). The program could neither create nor augment flows of such magnitude, but it would be agency policy to protect them as much as possible. Losses to diversions by water users would not have to be compensated by state depletions plans, but the USFWS would review any new (post-1997) water projects with a sharp eye to see that any threat to flow peaks would not be too damaging.

4. Target flows were a summation of annual pulse flows and species flows. These flows were to be employed to evaluate and "score" program-produced water flows in the aggregate against the 130,000–150,000 acre foot/year first increment goal of flow enhancement.

5. Within the peak flow category, a subset was identified as "short-duration high flows." These were flows with magnitudes approaching, but not exceeding, channel capacity in the habitat reach. Program water will not be employed to enhance such flows if such action would cause flows to rise above flood stage, as defined by the National Weather Service (USFWS 2004–2005: 5). As with any other peak flow waters, they were not to be included in calculating shortages to target flow requirements.

Putting a viable program in place would not mean there would be no individual new water project ESA Section 7 consultations. A winning habitat recovery program would mean that a project that fit within a given depletions program's coverage capacity would receive an expedited USFWS review. Assuming the proposed post-1997 projects were within prearranged program parameters, water providers would—on a project-by-project basis—emerge from a streamlined review process with a favorable biological opinion. If a proposed project X would place depletions on the river beyond the available state depletions program's capacity to offset, there would need to be further analysis and possibly some form of mitigation appropriate to site-specific circumstances. Project X would be evaluated according to its estimated impacts on all types of flows. Large projects entraining significant depletions to pulses and peaks would clearly be unlikely to pass USFWS muster. Much to the dismay of state negotiators, the agency articulated its intent for a strong future-shaping federal presence on the Platte in the form of project-by-project analyses of new water diversion proposals in the basin.

THE STATES' CASE

The issue affected Colorado the most, in its role as steward of a free-flowing South Platte River below Denver. Colorado delegates therefore led the charge against the federal peak flow stance. There was simply no way Colorado could leave the USFWS an opening to reserve peak flow quantities for its habitat agenda as it wished. If the message ever got out to Colorado water constituencies and state legislators that the federal environmental agenda in central Nebraska would crowd out Colorado's right to appropriate waters, as granted by the Nebraska-Colorado South Platte Compact, and that the whims of federal middle-level managers were to be part of Colorado's appropriations doctrine, the political-legal-administrative blowup would be enormous.

Years of intermittent, highly unsatisfactory peak flow discussions weighed heavily on the Colorado delegation when it took its May 2003 time-out from the regime of the river negotiations with Nebraska (see Chapter 19). The USFWS's in-stream flow document made it harder for Colorado negotiators to push their arguments on behalf of participation in a cooperative program; that paper—in all its iterations—strengthened the position of Owens administration opponents of the basin-wide cooperative effort to implement the ESA. Water provider leaders at the negotiating table feared those opponents would succeed in employing the peak flow problem and derail the whole effort. For years, the entire discussion was a political minefield.

The states pointed out that there had been no milestone in the 1997 CA to build a habitat recovery program specifying any peak flow commitment. Although the CA did include state commitments to preserve and enhance species and pulse flows, at no time did the states make any commitment—express or implied—to preserve any fraction of any peak flow. Then (in the years 2002–2005), the USFWS had identified peak flows as an "essential component of the suite of recommended flows" (USFWS 2002a: 6). The states viewed the entire peak flow discussion, as framed by the USFWS, as illegitimate.

Colorado and every other basin state had always counted on the use of flow peaks to divert—at least in part—to new consumptive uses and, most immediately, to future depletions plans to offset water. Which flows would be defined as in "excess" of program requirements so the states could plan on using them for their own future depletions plans and for meeting future economic growth demands?

> THE USFWS (February 28, 2003): We will get a much better idea of what fractions of peak flows are needed as further analysis is done and as we proceed during the first program increment within an adaptive management mode. Do not be so paranoid.

> COLORADO: We have every reason to be paranoid about any federal agency entering our state's allocation system with unknown demands. It is easy to quantify target flows, no matter how much we may disagree with them. We can also comprehend the meaning of pulse flows of specified frequency and magnitude. However, what constitutes a peak flow? We all agree that no sharp distinction can be made between pulse and peak flows under some circumstances because pulse flows will sometimes contribute to peak flows. Where, however, is the clear-cut line between the point at which a pulse flow ends and a peak flow begins? We have, at the insistence of the USFWS, entered an "Alice in Wonderland" world of fuzzy logic. This is a domain in which the USFWS wants us simply to accept that the agency will know a flow peak when it sees one. This is a world wherein middle-level agency managers—project by project, site by site—will somehow figure out what peak flows are and approve or disapprove a proposed water project according to changing visions over time. Our promise of regulatory certainty for post-1997 water projects—in exchange for which we agreed to build future depletions facilities—has been effectively discarded. The USFWS peak flow stance betrays what we originally set out to do. We need an answer to the fundamental question: what is going to be left for us?

> THE STATES: If the states put together a program that can deliver one three-day 8,000 cfs "peak flow" and fulfill summer species target flows, would that be sufficient?

> USFWS: We do not really know. We have always assumed that Colorado will take "bites" out of peak flows. We do not have enough information to know how big that Colorado bite will be or how much of a bite we will require. Colorado's concern that regulatory certainty will disappear is greatly overstated. The states will have regulatory certainty for all water uses prior to mid-1997. You will have great likelihood of success in getting a positive evaluation for projects in the post-1997 era if they fit the coverage of the depletions plan for support of species and pulse flows and do not significantly damage peak flows. That fact is important and assured. Furthermore, we "have agreed that water replacement obligations for new water projects covered by a depletion plan will be determined on the basis of [the] extent to which they create or increase shortages to species flows and annual pulse flows only, on average, relative to pre-1997 conditions. There are no replacement obligations . . . to peak flows . . . for projects covered by a depletions plan" (USFWS 2002a: 7). You will be obtaining significant regulatory

245

certainty in a world where peak flows are critical. Furthermore, a great deal of regulatory certainty rides with effective depletions plans and viable program efforts to build pulses. Future proposed water projects that leave peaks alone, or damage them only minimally, in the context of an overall effective habitat restoration program can enjoy a good deal of regulatory certainty. These benefits are not trivial.

COLORADO: You are dancing around two fundamental issues. First, the peak flow water you are discussing is properly available to Colorado diverters under the terms of the 1923 South Platte Compact. It is not within the USFWS's purview to grant rights to or withdraw that water. Second, even if we join you in a meaningful conversation about a division of peak flows, you admit that you cannot answer a central question: what will be the state's fraction for its needs? Among other things, our depletions plans require offset water that may well come from junior diversion priorities that cannot divert until high points on peak flows are reached.

USFWS: We are trying to work with you to find a cooperative and mutually satisfactory solution to this problem. Peak flows are ecologically important and cannot be dismissed. You are uncomfortable with this discussion no matter what we do. On the one hand, you fear the idea of an arbitrary and capricious federal agency making judgments on the availabilities of Colorado peak flow waters. On the other hand, all of us are even more uncomfortable about the danger of defining a decision principle that cannot adequately address situations that may arise in a complex, unknowable future. We will work with water users on a case-by-case basis. Future project proposals without large storage components and with only small depletions to peak flows—meaning those covered by a state's depletion plan—will earn agency approval in the streamlined ESA Section 7 consultation process made available by virtue of a viable cooperative program. It is the best that can be done. This approach—open to inspection by all members of the Governance Committee and the public at large—minimizes the potential for arbitrary and capricious decision making. Please work cooperatively with us.

COLORADO: We should not be involved in such a conversation. This is why the states have not accepted and will not accept the USFWS's in-stream flow document as part of the Platte River Habitat Recovery Program.

SCIENCE CLARIFIES THE PROBLEM

The highly charged peak flow discussion presented an empirically addressable question: just what impact did Colorado flow peaks, as part of the 1997 baseline, have on critical habitat? The USFWS needed to know so it could write a defensible draft environmental impact statement and, eventually, a biological opinion. Furthermore, Colorado team members knew that their best possibility for extracting themselves from the mess was to get the agency to accept depletions plan coverage up to some level of flow volume. Then it might be possible to negotiate with the USFWS about how to approach the problem of handling depletions to flows above that volume level. All of this would require credible analysis of historical data.

In November 2002 the USFWS announced that it had contracted with Hydrosphere Resource Consultants, Inc., of Boulder, Colorado, to examine the potential effects on peak flows of future Colorado water exploitation. During December 2002 and the winter-spring of 2003, all parties waited for the results. A draft report was released to the USFWS on June 4, 2003 (Hydrosphere Research Consultants 2003). The project leader then met in closed session with Colorado authorities—representatives of Denver Water, the Northern Colorado Water Conservancy District, the Colorado Water Conservation Board, and a representative from the environmental community. Meanwhile, USFWS analysts were busy incorporating the results into the federal Operational Study Model of Platte flows. On July 14 the draft report was summarized for the Governance Committee, but a full discussion did not take place until August 18.

Hydrosphere's Method

In collaboration with the USFWS and South Platte water providers, Hydrosphere analysts constructed a "reasonable worst-case scenario" (Hydrosphere 2003: 8–17). They conjectured (1) a huge 400,000-acre-foot/year storage project in the area of the defunct Two Forks Dam and Reservoir upstream of Denver, (2) an expanded version of the proposed Northern Integrated Supply Project involving a major on-stream reservoir (300,000 acre feet) and producing a new yield in the range of 90,000 acre feet/year for users on the Cache la Poudre River, (3) a major diversion and pump-back scheme on the South Platte below Greeley that would serve Denver metro-area providers, and (4) multiple reservoirs and dispersed gravel pit storage on tributaries to the South Platte. Furthermore, the scenario included reuse to extinction of "foreign," or trans-mountain, water, which would be of particular concern to water users downstream who with each increment of new upstream consumptive use would struggle harder to keep their canals served and their reservoirs full—units such as Empire, Jackson, Riverside, Prewitt, North Sterling, and Julesburg. These priority tubs would require more time to fill each spring as a result of upstream reuse, so they could be expected to increase their absorption of whatever spring-summer flows were available, including short-term flow peaks.

Where can Colorado South Platte water providers secure water for their customers' future dreams? What threat would future depletions to these sources pose for peak flows? Analysts examined the six major options Colorado water providers have available to collect water for their customers, two of which presented potential problems:

1. Trans-mountain water importation, which increases basin flows.

2. Exploitation of non-tributary groundwater. Mining such waters causes problems, but it is no threat to peak flows. Non-tributary water sources add water to the river.

3. Conversion of in-basin irrigation water rights to new uses, especially municipal and industrial (M&I) uses. In general, an increased number of houses and industry does not place more consumptive use on the river than does growing corn and dry beans. Under many conditions, moving water from agriculture to M&I uses increases river flows as a result of return flows, especially in the fall, winter, and spring months when urban forests and lawns are not being irrigated.

4. Water conservation. Interior household use, in the context of effective piping and sewage treatment systems generally, is not seriously depletive. Problems of water quality may become apparent, but—certain industrial uses aside—much of the volume that goes into a city comes out, especially in the fall, winter, and spring. In general, such water conservation has little effect on stream flows.

5. Water reuse. Those who possess a right to divert "foreign" water have, under Colorado law, a right to use their trans-basin project water to extinction. This does pose a potential threat to peak flows. However, the Northern Colorado Water Conservancy District, the largest diverter of trans-mountain water, represents an exception. It initially adopted a policy prohibiting its allottees from making more than one use of project water because the project was designed to allow return flows to serve users downstream within district boundaries (Tyler 1992: 477). The district could only build facilities to serve its upstream users and had no alternative but to rely on the main stem to deliver supplemental flows to district allottees below Greeley. Denver Water and the metropolitan-area water users it served placed no such restriction on themselves, however. Denver Water switched on its reuse plant in the spring of 2004. It was designed to capture and process 17,660 acre feet of wastewater for outdoor and industrial uses (www.denverwataer.org/recycle), but for the most part metro entities have not yet paid the costs of capturing the foreign component of their wastewaters and have put them to additional consumptive uses. Therefore, they have permitted these unused return flow fractions to travel downstream for use by people and other living things. As they increase consumptive uses of their trans-mountain flows, the river will accordingly be impacted by shrinkage of all flows, including peak flows. Therefore, analysts assumed that metropolitan Denver water providers would use all of their foreign water to extinction for purposes of constructing the worst-case scenario.

6. Diversion of South Platte native flows. Future projects could only divert such waters when all senior right holders are satisfied. In principle, under specified conditions, such diversions could be expected to reduce peak flows.

The study then identified one-day, three-day, and thirty-day peak flow events that had historically occurred during the months of February through July each year from 1947 through 1994 at three locations: (1) on the central Platte, as measured at Overton; (2) upstream in Colorado on the South Platte, at the Kersey gauge below Greeley; and (3) at the Julesburg gauge at the Nebraska border. Flow travel times were considered along with the factors that attenuate flow peaks over distance.

All scenario components were aggregated to arrive at an estimate of a worst-case set of depletions (Hydrosphere 2003: 7). The analysis then tracked the aggregate impact of the worst-case scenario on the central Platte forty-seven-year pre-1997 historical peak flow regime.

Results

Future water projects can generally only make new diversions, and therefore impose new depletions, during times when unappropriated water is available. That would be when all other, more senior water diversion rights are fully satisfied. In relatively wet years, such times occur only during April through early July (Hydrosphere 2003: 2). In drier times and in midsummer months, waters of the South Platte Basin are heavily appropriated. Water is diverted and re-diverted repeatedly by sufficiently senior rights. There are times and locations during the non-irrigation season (November 1–March 30) when unappropriated water will be available to new depleters. However, these months are not generally times of peak flows on the central Platte—namely, April through early July.

Return flows generated by first water uses tend to appear at low, steady rates and do not constitute a major portion of South Platte peak flow patterns (Hydrosphere 2003: 3). As water providers proceed to reuse their trans-mountain waters to extinction over time, there will be no direct major depletive effect on peak flows. However, an indirect effect on peak flows can be expected as a result of the diminished supply of return flows to downstream South Platte reservoirs. Reservoirs can be expected to continue to divert for longer periods than has historically been the case; such extended diversions could reduce peak flow volumes.

About one-third of the peak flow events during the period of record occurred across all three flow categories (one, three, and thirty days) during February and March. Such events were rarely depleted by water user calls on the river (Hydrosphere 2003: 25). Flow peaks are typically higher in April, May, and June; like those of the earlier months, however, they were generally little depleted by historical river calls.

Colorado South Platte flow peaks were greatly attenuated as they traveled roughly 180 miles from Julesburg, Colorado, to Overton, Nebraska. Peaks lose their mass and energy as they disappear into river bottoms, bank storage, wet

Table 20.1. Summary of Worst-Case Scenario Impacts on Peak Flows

Peak Flow Reduction (percent)	One-Day Peak	Three-Day Average Peak	Thirty-Day Average Peak
Minimum	0.0	0.0	0.0
Average	7.6	9.5	11.3
Median	0.1	1.1	4.4
Maximum	63.9	64.7	58.4
Peak Flow Reduction (cubic feet/second)			
Minimum	0.0	0.0	0.0
Average	644	785	618
Median	5	38	136
Maximum	5,473	5,919	4,210

Source: Hydrosphere 2003: 27.

meadows, and dense vegetation; this fact limited any negative impacts of the worst-case Colorado scenario on Nebraska peak flows as observed at Overton (see Table 20.1).

The largest reductions to peak flows occurred in years wherein peaks rode on relatively high base flows during "free river" conditions—that is, when there were no calls on the river for irrigated agriculture. When flow volumes were sufficiently large that all rights could be served and still leave water in the channels, the worst-case scenario took its greatest toll (see depletions maximums in Table 20.1). Therefore, in large flow years, especially when peaks were in excess of 12,000 cubic feet per second, the percentages of loss were much higher than was the case in low-flow years characterized by lower peaks.

PEACE AT THE PEAK

The Hydrosphere study had established that the worst reasonable Colorado South Platte depletions case—virtually impossible to actually be realized in the foreseeable future—would impose small to modest impacts on peak flows at Overton, Nebraska, just above the critical habitat. However, there would be diminished high wet-year peaks.

The findings opened the door to a political possibility: the construction of "soft landings" for each party. Colorado could once again be comfortable at the negotiating table after its May–June time-out and July 2003 return. It looked as though it would be possible to have a viable program while keeping Nebraska and the federal community out of Colorado's administration of the South Platte. The state's future depletions plan would have an important fraction of the flow peaks to protect. The USFWS could hold on to its natural flow model while easing away from a demand for most, if not all, access to peak flows.

Each party would have to think through the implications of the proposed plan and work out its negotiating position. That work would require the remaining months of 2003 and all of 2004; it was well into 2005 before the parties had their mutual accommodations in place. Much of the delay was occasioned by pressures to address other "skunky" issues in a highly constrained monthly negotiation format. The resolution was advanced in a meeting of the federal community of negotiators and a Colorado delegation on January 5, 2005.

The deal was then circulated among, and examined by, the other parties. As terms and conditions emerged, the arrangement became straightforward. The USFWS acknowledged, as it always had, that many river flow re-regulation projects designed to offset depletions pre- and post-1997, while benefiting the listed species habitat, would themselves negatively impact the frequency and magnitude of peak flows. There would be no replacement obligations for such depletions. The parties agreed that there would be replacement obligations for new depletions to species and pulse flows associated with post–June 30, 1997, water projects that were not part of recovery program new depletions plans. The baseline against which the amount of deficit would be determined was the pre–July 1, 1997, flow pattern. The nature of the offset obligation would be determined on a case-by-case basis according to how much the proposed project would be estimated to increase a shortage to annual species flows and pulse flows. As had always been the USFWS's position, there was to be no requirement for replacement of depletions to any peak flow, a wild phenomenon beyond program control.

It was agreed that any large Colorado South Platte main stem dam and reservoir project ever proposed downstream from Denver would not be covered by the state's future depletions plan (Colorado Future Depletions Plan 2006: 5). Any such structure would interfere with the transport of sediment to the main stem of the Platte. The USFWS could clearly foresee the damage to wide sandbarbraided river channel qualities additional deliveries of clear water returns would inflict. This aspect of the peak flow deal was not controversial because there was no meaningful prospect that any such facility would be built under any recognizable future conditions.

Colorado and USFWS negotiators, in a series of backstage sessions, then found a way to draw a line through peak flows in a manner each could abide. The USFWS had acknowledged, by virtue of its own internal analyses, that decrements to peak flows identified by Hydrosphere were no threat to the habitat qualities of the three listed bird species. But the Hydrosphere (2003) analysis had shown that under some conditions, losses to peak flows imposed by the worst-case scenario could cause as much as a one-inch reduction in flow stage on the Lower Platte, the habitat of the pallid sturgeon. Flow surges, the biologists believed, provide spawning cues. Therefore, it was important to preserve something of the pre-1997 South Platte peak flow regime on behalf of the species. The USFWS still had much to learn about the habitat requirements of this fish; it was therefore important for the agency to keep open the possibility of enhancing spring flow peaks on that segment of the Lower Platte. That meant holding on to some fraction of South Platte peak flows. The USFWS saw itself as retaining the option of making South Platte and main stem Platte peak flow claims. Water users saw the agency as simply holding on to a weak straw—ignorance about sturgeon needs way downstream—to keep its peak flow arguments alive for possible future use.

In the end, after much difficult discussion, Colorado accepted an average annual depletions cap on flow peaks of 98,010 acre feet per year. This number placed a limit on how much South Platte flows can be further diminished and still be covered by the state's depletions plan (Colorado Future Depletions Plan 2006: 5). This number would define how far water providers could go while staying within the boundaries of streamlined ESA Section 7 consultations. What was its meaning?

The 98,010-acre-foot cap represented the additional quantity of native flows and reusable return flows Colorado could divert to beneficial uses during the period February 1–July 31 of the average hydrological year relative to the July 1, 1997, flow baseline and still be covered by the habitat recovery program. The baseline average was generated by the federal Operations Study Model from the mix of wet, dry, and normal years in a database extending from 1947 to 1994. As time passes, the period of record will be adjusted, with the concurrence of the Governance Committee. The cap value was not a limit on consumptive use or a diversion limit. Much of the water diverted from a river at a given time and place is not used consumptively; rather, it works its way back to the stream. Colorado and USFWS analysts estimated that about 36 percent of the new water supplied for M&I users would be consumptively used. The cap number was also not a reduction in peak flow volume. Deliveries of new water will occur mostly when there are no flow peaks in the river to shave off.

Whenever a newly proposed water activity would cause annual cumulative depletions to the supply of native water and reusable return flows to exceed the 98,010-acre-foot limit during the February–July period, Colorado's plan for future depletions will not be available for purposes of ESA compliance. Furthermore, it was agreed that the Colorado plan will not cover any hydropower diversion and return projects that would divert water and sediment from the main stem of the South Platte downstream of Denver, thereby returning clear water to the channels and contributing to unwanted channel incision.

The cap was defined by an awkward number: 98,010 acre feet. How was it computed?

The USFWS and Colorado negotiators accepted figures from the Colorado future depletions plan (Colorado Future Depletions Plan 2006; Cooperative Agreement 1997: tab 3B). Over the course of the first program increment, defined as the years 2007–2020, it was estimated that the population in the Colorado

South Platte River Basin would grow by approximately 1.1 million people. This, the parties calculated, would represent an added annual demand for about 297,000 acre feet of water by 2020. That increased demand would be served by a mix of the six available water sources delineated earlier in this chapter, two of which represented a threat to peak flows: storage of native waters and reuse. Then the question was posed: what portion of the gross additional water demand, in an average hydrological year, will be supplied by the storage of native waters and reusable return flows? The calculated answer was 121,000 acre feet (about 41 percent). The remaining water to be supplied (about 59 percent) would come from the four other sources, three of which tend to sustain and enhance river flows.

Peak flows are not a phenomenon equally distributed across the calendar year. They tend to concentrate in the period starting in February through the summer. The USFWS originally favored using the 121,000-acre-foot cap for the entire year. Colorado worried that such an approach would unduly constrain its appetite for swelling river flows in the fall and winter. For Colorado, it was important to have a free hand to divert South Platte waters from August through January within the limits of its law, the Nebraska-Colorado South Platte Compact, and arrangements specified by the cooperative habitat recovery program. Therefore, the two parties agreed that Colorado would accept a lower cap in return for confining new gross water deliveries against a cap that will be operative during the months of February through July. The number "98,010 acre feet per year" was calculated by the USFWS. The agency estimated that this value would provide about the same peak flow protection as would an annual 121,000-acre-foot cap operated over a full twelve-month period.

By 2005, then, the deal was struck. If Colorado delivers its full complement of water—27,000 acre feet/year of water from Tamarack I and Tamarack III (or its equivalent), plus roughly 1,800 acre feet/year for every additional 100,000 people in the South Platte Basin—Colorado water providers can get access to an additional nip of flow peaks up to 98,010 acre feet/year from August through January. They can do this while benefiting from a streamlined approval process made available by the USFWS as long as a viable habitat recovery program is in place. Supplies available to Colorado, particularly after the summer irrigation season closes at the end of October, will be an essential source for re-regulating river water on behalf of the listed species. Then there will also be something left for water providers to exploit on behalf of their customers in ways now largely unforeseen.

The parties had found a way to make peace over South Platte River flows at the peaks of the South Platte hydrograph. Yet neither the state water users nor the federal negotiators ever found a way to embrace the other's perspective. Sometimes it is possible to honor the dreams of one's adversary while staying true to one's own.

Regime of the River

Wyoming and Nebraska Address New Depletions

Historically, Nebraska has had an interest in seeing that Wyoming reservoirs maintain their yields because Nebraskans have lived primarily on Wyoming direct and return flows. About 80 percent of the water captured behind Wyoming's North Platte reservoirs is typically destined for Nebraska water providers. Furthermore, in the early years of the basin-wide discussions in the 1980s and 1990s, Nebraskans had feared that they would be left solely responsible for creating a reasonable and prudent alternative in the form of river habitat restoration. Nebraska felt a need to ensure that Wyoming and Colorado were brought into the negotiations in such a manner that water users in those two states would share the regulatory burden.

Unlike Nebraska's relationship with Colorado, which is defined by an interstate compact, Nebraska's relationship with Wyoming had been defined by a 1945 U.S. Supreme Court decree and subsequently by a 2000 modified decree—the product of long negotiations that occurred inconveniently during the Platte recovery program negotiations (1985–2000; see Chapter 11). Anything Wyoming wanted to do on the North Platte drainage could be called into question by its downstream neighbor.

For fifteen years, the push and pull of *Nebraska v. Wyoming* cast a great pall of uncertainty over the Platte River talks. On the positive side of the ledger, preparation for the court case allowed the two adversaries to learn about each others' water opportunities and constraints in a manner that was useful in the three-state habitat recovery talks. Yet on the negative side, for all the mutual exploration and deal making that went into the settlement and the modified decree, the outcome had not clarified certain important aspects of the two states' water relationship. In Nebraska's thinking, a regime of the river "skunk" needed to be flushed out and made fit for the work of developing the proposed cooperative habitat recovery program.

CONTEXT

For all practical purposes, the terms of the 2000 settlement stipulation that resulted in the modified Wyoming-Nebraska U.S. Supreme Court decree (Olpin 2001) capped Wyoming North Platte irrigation consumptive uses at existing levels. Guernsey Reservoir releases its impoundment of North Platte water approximately forty-two miles above the Nebraska state line. Wyoming was enjoined from permitting the diversion of water from the North Platte River and its tributaries—including water from hydrologically connected groundwater wells upstream of Guernsey—for intentional irrigation of more than 226,000 acres during any one irrigation season, exclusive of the Kendrick Project (Olpin 2001: 28–29). No more than 35,000 acres of land in the first unit of the Kendrick Project served by Seminoe Reservoir may be irrigated. No more than approximately 24,000 acres may be irrigated in the Casper-Alcova District.

The two states then agreed to the imposition of consumptive use limits on two stretches of the river—above Pathfinder Dam and Reservoir and between Pathfinder and Guernsey. Many technical details are not mentioned here, but Wyoming agreed to observe a ten-consecutive-year consumptive use cap of 1.28 million acre feet upstream of Pathfinder. Below Pathfinder, the ten-year consumptive uses must cumulate to no more than 890,000 acre feet. After the first ten years of administration under the modified decree, the methodology and the ten-year limit will be reviewed and, if mutually agreed, procedural improvements can be made (Olpin 2001: 28–30).

Essential parameters of the Wyoming plan to offset new depletions were fixed by the outcome of the fifteen-year *Nebraska v. Wyoming* struggle. No significant new additional consumptive uses or net increases in irrigated acreage are possible on the Wyoming North Platte. Wyoming therefore simply asked the habitat recovery program negotiators to accept the patterns of water use as of 1997—and as adjusted and capped under the 2000 U.S. Supreme Court stipulation and modified decree—to serve as the baseline for its post-1997 future depletions plan.

WYOMING DEPLETIONS PLAN

On November 2, 2006, the Cooperative Agreement Governance Committee approved Wyoming's plan for offsetting future depletions and thereby maintaining the pre-1997 regime of the North Platte River (*Platte River Recovery Program* 2006: attachment 5, section 7). Details fill twenty-nine pages of single-spaced text. The essence of the plan is centered on (1) establishing historical baselines (computed from river flow and use data gathered during the period 1992–1996 because Wyoming was preparing for the trial with Nebraska during those years), (2) comparing annual water use data after mid-1997 to the baselines, and (3) holding state authorities responsible for providing offset water at the Nebraska state line to keep the river whole if, over the course of a water year, Wyoming users have created an acreage or consumptive use overrun.

Annual net baseline depletion overruns by Wyoming water users with priorities prior to July 1, 1997, will have to be compensated. Offset water sources consist of the Wyoming account made possible by the Pathfinder Modification Project (20,000 acre feet; see Chapter 11), Wyoming's allocation of Glendo Dam and Reservoir storage water, non-hydrologically connected groundwater, and, possibly, water imported into the basin. In addition, future new water project proponents can exploit abandoned water rights, retired water uses, and conversion of agricultural land to less water-consumptive uses.

State authorities will employ two baselines that reflect the 1997 regime of the river against which net underruns and net overruns of water use will be calculated for the irrigation season (May 1–September 30) and the non-irrigation season (October 1–April 30). Overruns on one baseline cannot be offset by underruns on another. However, within each baseline domain there are multiple sub-basins. Within these units, it is possible to apply excesses of water in one to cover deficits in another.

Baseline one was applied to all irrigation water use on the North Platte drainage above Guernsey Reservoir. That area was divided into two sub-basins—one from the Colorado state line to Pathfinder and the other from Pathfinder to Guernsey. Baseline two applied to the river and its tributaries in the North Platte drainage below Guernsey Dam and Reservoir, where four sub-basins were identified. This second baseline was applied to all irrigation, municipal, industrial, and other uses not covered under baseline one. Within each sub-basin, authorities will calculate the historical range of water use, with special attention paid to maximum historical consumptive uses. Within the respective baseline areas and water-use categories, permissible flexibility is allowed within the overall caps. This was essential to retain flexibility so permit users could use more water in wet years while decreasing uses in dry times.

IMPLICATIONS

Although many of the terms of the Supreme Court settlement were not what Wyoming had hoped to secure, the outcome clarified the rules for living with its downstream neighbor. Lifting the cloud of uncertainty about what the future would hold for the Wyoming-Nebraska water relationship alleviated anxiety. In particular, Wyoming benefited from securing Nebraska's endorsement of the Pathfinder Modification Project, from which Wyoming municipalities could be served. In the aftermath of the settlement and of incorporating its provisions in the modified decree, several points stood out in clear relief.

First, given that there will be little or no new net North Platte Basin water use, post-1997 new water depleters will have to find sources of offset water, primarily by arranging transfers from existing pre-1997 beneficial uses to new ones. The only other alternatives are for them to find ways to tap into non-tributary groundwater to pay their river debts or obtain state sanction to tap into either Wyoming's new water account provided by the Pathfinder Modification Project or an older account at Glendo Reservoir. Such water is obviously limited and can be expected to go primarily to thirsty cities.

Second, any proponent of a new water use within a federal nexus will have to apply to Wyoming state authorities and then to the relevant federal action agency and fulfill U.S. Fish and Wildlife Service (USFWS) requirements when the agency is engaged in the consultation. In Colorado and Nebraska, future depletions plans placed water users under the protective cover of the habitat recovery program as long as it was found to be viable. New depleters in those two states will secure coverage unless their proposed depletions fail to qualify. However, in Wyoming the opposite is the case. A new depleter would typically be "out" of coverage until declared "in" by state authorities. This can be expected to occur in circumstances where state authorities know of water available under the acreage and consumptive use caps, which will come from the abandonment of a water right or new flow additions to the Platte River system. The fundamental reality, however, is that responsibility for mitigation of future depletions will rest squarely on new water project proponents.

Third, any new proposed water use by a party outside a federal nexus will not be subject to the strictures of the Endangered Species Act (ESA). However, Wyoming state authorities must review such proposals to ensure that no injury will be imposed on existing water users. These proposals will be held up for examination against essentially the same criteria as those the USFWS would likely employ. An application for a new water use will trigger a review by the Office of the Wyoming State Engineer. In general, consultations will be about how the proponent will replace each acre foot of new depletion. Or, in certain circumstances, a variation may be appropriate wherein the proponent may choose to undertake a project-specific analysis using models and tools developed by the state engineer, the USFWS, or both. The intent would be to allow the proponent to demonstrate that either the depletion's impact on the river will be less than the standard formulas suggest or the depleter will arrive at a means to pay the debt to the river in more creative, yet defensible, ways. The costs of such analysis will be borne by the project proponent.

Fourth, given the fact that Nebraska's Lake McConaughy served as a buffer between the Wyoming-Nebraska state line and the critical habitat far downstream, Wyoming authorities knew they were insulated from the difficult conversation Colorado was having with the USFWS about building river pulses and preserving flow peaks. There simply could not be a plausible negative impact on peak and pulse flows below McConaughy created by Wyoming. The state was free to build its future depletions plan to preserve its river flow baselines without becoming entangled in such complexities.

PROBLEMS

During the years of preparation for the Supreme Court litigation (1985–2000), it was difficult for the two states to openly discuss any plans, especially their options for offsetting future depletions. Discussions were severely constrained by attorneys on both sides, who wanted to reveal as little as possible to the adversary. However, after the 2000 settlement, open discussion could be sustained. Two looming problems had been sidestepped during the years of preparation for the trial. But in the context of the post-settlement basin-wide habitat recovery talks, between 2002 and 2006 three "skunks" were awakened as Wyoming's depletions plan took shape.

Baseline One: Water Quantity Problems

For Nebraskans, the entire point of Wyoming's (and Colorado's) future depletions plan was to provide offset water to preserve the pre-1997 pattern of flows in quantity and time. (Note: The USFWS was also very interested in preserving water inflows to McConaughy because any loss to base inflows would erode the environmental account, which is filled by assigning it a percentage of inflow.)

Wyoming pointed out that in wet years, when the Platte system was sufficiently full that USFWS target flows were fulfilled, its water users should have no obligation to send additional water to offset depletions across the Nebraska state line. Wyoming's depletive overruns, to whatever extent they had occurred, had not caused a problem. Therefore, no redress was required. Nebraska took exception to this view; it wanted Wyoming's depletions covered no matter the nature of gauge readings at the top of critical habitat.

Another aspect of water quantity needed to be addressed. The 2000 U.S. Supreme Court settlement did not specify exactly what could happen with non–irrigation season (October 1–April 30) flows from Guernsey Reservoir to the state line. What if, Nebraska asked, Wyoming were to place new winter uses on the stream and thereby diminish flows to Nebraska during this period? Wyoming replied to the effect that its water users had the latitude to do so. Nebraska responded no, they do not.

Nebraska made the point that Wyoming must not place new non–irrigation season consumptive uses on the North Platte River and its tributaries between Guernsey and the Nebraska state line unless Nebraska's Lake McConaughy and reservoirs upstream were full. Given its Federal Regulatory Energy Commission (FERC) mandate and constraints, Nebraska must not fall prey to new consumptive uses upstream of the state line.

Wyoming (like Colorado regarding the South Platte) noted that the Nebraska districts had made assumptions about future North Platte flows at the Wyoming state line during the FERC negotiations. Wyoming was in no way bound by them. The Wyoming-Nebraska water relationship in this basin was controlled by the 2000 settlement stipulation and the modified decree, which clearly left open the possibility of new consumptive uses between Guernsey Reservoir and the state line during non-irrigation months. Wyoming's obligation was to get the necessary offset water—as calculated against the logic of the two baselines—to the state line, from which point Nebraska authorities could conduct it to Lake McConaughy. If ten acre feet of offset water appeared at the state line, Wyoming should receive program credit for ten acre feet. If Nebraska irrigators and electrical power producers together diminished the Wyoming delivery by three acre feet, Nebraska authorities must see to it that those three acre feet were fully replaced in the environmental account on behalf of the listed species. Wyoming, under the U.S. Supreme Court stipulation and modified 1945 decree, had no further obligation.

Nebraska acknowledged that the settlement terms did not address the issue of non–irrigation season consumptive use. Yet the terms of the settlement were one thing and the terms of any new agreement on behalf of the listed species quite another. Nebraska authorities were adamant that they had no alternative but to defend the regime of the river as it had emerged across history prior to mid-1997. Colorado's Tamarack Plan promised offset water to Nebraska for all its new depletions year-round on the South Platte. The price of Nebraska's participation in the three-state habitat recovery program would be a deal that ensured that Wyoming would also cover its post-1997 non–irrigation season depletions below Guernsey.

Baseline Two: A Timing Problem

Wyoming contended that since Lake McConaughy served as a buffer between times of Wyoming offset water delivery and habitat needs, aggregate shortages to target flows could be addressed by Wyoming supplying augmentation water to the environmental account anytime in any season.

Nebraska would not accept Wyoming's position. Insofar as Wyoming's offset water contributions would flow primarily to McConaughy in non-irrigation months, they were less valuable to Nebraska. If habitat recovery program offset water flowed down the North Platte when there was no irrigation demand, Nebraska panhandle agricultural water users would not have an opportunity to divert any fraction of it along the way. Traditionally, those Nebraska water users had an opportunity to "take a bite" from all Wyoming return flows, deplete them a little, and then send the remainder on to McConaughy. Wyoming's plan transferred welfare away from western Nebraska irrigators in favor of listed species. That should not be permitted because Nebraska water users had already made sufficient sacrifices at the altar of the 1998 FERC deal.

Wyoming replied that it had only two obligations: (1) to fulfill the terms of the U.S. Supreme Court settlement and modified decree by paying attention to the baselines logic, and (2) to deliver on its commitments to the basin-wide habitat recovery program. It had no legal commitment to maximize western Nebraska panhandle irrigators' capacity to divert water. Wyoming believed Nebraska representatives should withdraw their objections. Nebraska replied in straightforward language. If a voluntary cooperative habitat recovery program was going to be developed that would produce regulatory certainty for all, Wyoming must take on a third responsibility: it must commit to delivering its new depletions program offset water in a manner that protects the interests of western Nebraska panhandle water users.

MITIGATING FRICTION

After 2001, the two states conducted their conversation intermittently across the years. As pressure mounted from the federal community to move ahead with the draft environmental impact statement (EIS) in January 2004, the pace of the talks quickened. Yet resolution did not emerge until early 2006, as the final EIS was about to come out in April and the final biological opinion was in the late stages of preparation.

The first part of the two-state peace plan was a reassertion of two incompatible principles. Nebraska included language in the environmental account description (*Platte River Recovery Program* 2006: EA Account: 3) to the effect that contributions to the EA account at Lake McConaughy "are based on an understanding that flows available at Lewellen [the point at which inflows are measured into McConaughy] . . . remain representative of the current regime-of-the-river except for changes that are compensated, mitigated, or offset." In the same document (pages 7–8) Wyoming (along with Colorado) asserted its countervailing principle: "Nothing in this . . . document is intended to impose any additional . . . obligations, requirements or restrictions of any sort on . . . Wyoming. For as long as there is a program . . . existing and new water related activities . . . in Wyoming will be included in the current regime-of-the-river." Each adversary was thereby staking out its position and giving up nothing in case the conversation was ever reopened.

With regard to Wyoming's obligation in water-abundant years, it was agreed that in seasons when sufficient water was flowing in the North Platte system to cause reservoirs behind Guernsey and Kingsley dams to spill, Wyoming would be given an option to present evidence to the Platte River program Governance Committee that any excess consumptive water use by Wyoming in that season did not adversely affect habitat recovery program purposes. In such an instance, Wyoming could—at the discretion of the Governance Committee—be relieved of any necessity to provide offset water.

In the matter of the potential for additional wintertime groundwater extraction and consumptive use, Wyoming agreed that new (post–June 30, 1997) non–irrigation season groundwater depleters must either secure offset water from the newly established Wyoming Water Bank (discussed later in the chapter) or make other arrangements to provide sufficient offset water to cover their river depletions (*Platte River Recovery Program* 2006: attachment 5, section 7, Wyoming Depletions Plan: 24).

The timing problem had arisen because by the time administrative authorities in the Office of the Wyoming State Engineer were able to analyze the summer-season data, compare uses to baselines, and draw conclusions, compensating offset water could not likely be delivered to the state line during that same summer or winter season. The solution was straightforward. Language was inserted into the Wyoming depletions plan document (*Platte River Recovery Program* 2006: Wyoming Depletions Plan: 21) to the effect that any depletion overruns in Wyoming water uses in a given season of a given year will be replaced in that same season the *following year*. Western Nebraska irrigators, after waiting one year for the rotation of offset flows to start, would have their annual opportunity to divert and re-divert return flows from Wyoming project operations in addition to the delivery of replacement water.

ALLEVIATING SCARCITY ON THE LARAMIE RIVER AND HORSE CREEK

A physical problem also needed to be confronted. During most years, the main stem of the Platte River in the stretch below Guernsey Reservoir to the Nebraska state line has had sufficiently available surface and groundwater supplies so that diversion priorities could be served without placing the stream under strict regulation by the Office of the Wyoming State Engineer. There has therefore been an opportunity to secure the necessary water resources with which to keep river appropriators whole within the scope of the two baselines. However, water users diverting surface and groundwater on tributaries to the North Platte below Guernsey (primarily on the Laramie River and Horse Creek) have historically been less fortunate. They have generally confronted scarcity such that there is little prospect that some users in these reaches could find sources of offset water to cover any new depletions during most years.

Wyoming decided on a cross-sub-basin approach to resolve the problem. This would mean establishing a state-administered water bank to broker available water supplies generated by water right abandonments, reducing consumptive uses, producing non-tributary groundwater, maintaining available surface storage water, and possibly—in the future—importing water. Users caught up a tributary without the prospect of finding or delivering offset water could, through the Wyoming Water Bank, gain access to accretion credits (measured in acre feet) and use them to cover their new depletions. This type of exchange is permissible within and among the sub-basins. The bank will begin with a small water portfolio, and only time will tell the extent to which it can be enlarged over the coming decades. But within the Wyoming Water Bank's constraints, Wyoming senior appropriators will be protected from the depredations of new junior priorities in accordance with Wyoming appropriation law, as well as from Nebraska's water agenda, and still serve the needs of the habitat recovery program.

Wyoming would be able to expand its new consumptive uses upstream of the border in the non-irrigation season as long as users remained within the U.S. Supreme Court–imposed restrictions and as long as the new depleters found ways to deliver water appropriately to offset their new post-1997 depletions. Wyoming offset water volumes, insofar as they are depleted during their Nebraska travels to Lake McConaughy, must be made whole by Nebraska depleters—meaning the diverter must return the water destined for the environmental account to the river and replace any consumptive losses to the river as adjusted by the Nebraska state engineer's estimates of what would have been lost in the river channel if the diversion had never been made.

During the years of wrangling, it became apparent that most new Wyoming depletions would not likely come from a post-1997 granting of new diversion priorities. Such would be life under the terms of the 2000 U.S. Supreme Court settlement caps. The real threat to water administrators and users in both states would come from a more fulsome exploitation of pre-1997 priorities, some of which had rarely been fully employed to their legal limits—certainly not in the recent years of extended drought. As wetter times return and demands for Wyoming water increase, depletions may rise above the historically established benchmarks and still be within established Wyoming priorities. At that challenging moment, the Wyoming state engineer will be responsible for fulfilling the state's settlement and modified decree obligations to Nebraska.

Water providers in both states gained an advantage by finding ways to keep the large North Platte reservoirs protected against even greater attacks on their yields. That was the big tradeoff—give up something for the listed species, gain regulatory certainty, and avoid having to give more to the habitat later under possibly more stringent terms during individual ESA Section 7 consultations. But to hold on to the deal, all three states would have to make the program work—authentically work—on behalf of the listed species, as tested by open, publicly informed civic science not controlled by any sitting power-that-be. Now, as a critical part of making the proposed habitat recovery program work, Nebraskans—while having put Wyoming and Colorado through a critical examination—would have to confront themselves and their own history of water use.

Regime of the River

Nebraska Confronts Its History

The regime of the river Nebraska was in the process of defending vis-à-vis Colorado and Wyoming was falling apart within its own borders. In mid-1997, when Nebraska authorities signed the Cooperative Agreement (CA) and thereby promised to prevent or offset post-1997 depletions, they had no legal basis to prevent new groundwater exploitation or expansion of irrigated acreage. In many places the groundwater commons was unsustainably exploited, and solutions could not be found in a continued self-seeking pursuit of satisfaction of individual preferences in marketplaces. There would have to be large-scale collective action. The historical abundance of the groundwater resource, combined with the overwhelming political dominance of groundwater well users and the industries that constituted their supply chain, meant there were deficiencies in Nebraska law and water administration in matters involving surface-groundwater interdependence. The arrival of the endangered species agenda on the socio-political horizon in the late 1980s and 1990s would force two difficult conversations, one internal to the state's water administration and the other about external relationships with the federal government and two upstream states.

With each passing month, new groundwater wells were being installed. They would entrain years of new depletions and, along with older wells, contribute to the escalating water debt owed to the river. Even if all wells were shut off forever on a given day, the depletions imposed would hit the river with varying lag times for years to come. Those debts to the Nebraska Platte system were considerable and would require rapidly increasing amounts of scarce offset water to repay the bill. The question was, to whom was the bill owed? First and foremost, to increasingly restive surface water users who historically had been first on the river and whose canals were being deprived. Second, to the needs of habitat restoration, as defined by the federal regulatory process in the service of the Endangered Species Act (ESA). During the years 2001–2006, hard-pressed Nebraska water leaders at all levels tried to confront not only Wyoming and Colorado at their borders but also their own history, cursed by a great groundwater abundance that had induced them to neglect internal regime-of-the-river problems.

Fixing things required time, of which there was too little. Nebraska water authorities were heavily invested in their lawsuit against Wyoming (1986–2001; see Chapter 11), which was all about the regime of the river at that border. Securing the Supreme Court settlement with Wyoming would release energy that could be applied to Nebraska's internal and external agendas, but there would be only a few years to install a revised Nebraska order of things to resolve highly charged issues that had been dodged for decades.

GROUNDWATER BOOM

By the end of 2005, the state of Nebraska had registered more than 91,000 large-capacity groundwater wells (Table 22.1). On average, that amounted to over 1 well per square mile. Over decades of open access to the groundwater commons, Nebraska irrigators were conducting a massive and uncontrolled experiment regarding the impacts of removing water at alternative points of diversion (not through traditional surface canal headgates) and placing that water in expanded consumptive uses (see Table 22.1).

In general, the increasing numbers of groundwater wells reflected dollar savings that came with shifting from more labor-intensive irrigation practices to

Table 22.1. Nebraska's Registered Irrigation Wells, 1966–2005

Year	Wells	Decadal Net Increase	Year	Wells	Annual Net Increase
1966	27,102	—	1997	78,373	1,072
1976	49,478	22,376	1998	79,395	1,022
1986	71,338	21,860	1999	81,483	2,088
1996	77,301	5,963	2000	82,478	995
			2001	83,571	1,093
			2002	84,681	1,110
			2003	86,223	1,542
			2004	88,301	2,078
			2005	91,328	3,027

Source: http://www.neo.state.ne.us/statshtml/73a.btml. Accessed November 15, 2006.

Table 22.2. Net Increases in New Wells and Groundwater Irrigated Acres in Natural Resource Districts (NRDs) Hydraulically Connected to the North, South, and Central Platte, 1997–2005

NRD	Total Irrigated Acreage	Net Increase in Acreage	Net Increase in Wells
North Platte	3,307,000	15,300	323
South Platte	1,661,000	16,700	118
Twin Platte	2,736,300	53,500	477
Tri-Basin	971,700	33,200	616
Central Platte	2,136,500	74,500	1,032
Column Totals	10,812,500	193,200	2,566

Source: Luckey, Woodward, and Carney 2006: 11.

center-pivot sprinkler systems (served by high-capacity turbine pumps) that could significantly reduce the need for expensive farm labor. As the drought deepened, especially after the extremely dry year in 2002, the pace of well drilling quickened. Furthermore, in many parts of the state after 1997, farmers knew that serious discussion was under way about limiting future well installations. Therein lay a source of inspiration to drill while unhindered access to the groundwater commons was still available. In addition, there was the spur of drought. Table 22.1 reveals that after the record low water year of 2002, the annual number of new well installations jumped markedly.

It is important to narrow the focus to the area tributary to the Platte River system from the Wyoming and Colorado borders through the central segment. Richard Luckey, Duane Woodward, and Clint Carney (2006), using Cooperative Hydrological Study (COHYST) simulation models to examine and project stream depletions, have reported the growth of groundwater well installation and the expansion of irrigated acreage in the domain tributary to the Platte from 1997 through 2005. Table 22.2 shows their findings.

Nebraska groundwater users had worked carefully for decades to ensure that their water extraction would not be controlled by the Office of the Nebraska State Engineer but rather would be subject to the policies of the NRDs, which they dominated. They had enjoyed virtually free access to the groundwater commons, subject only to the loose constraints of the correlative rights doctrine (share and share alike), and they would fight to keep it that way. Yet they had, through their individually rational self-interested decisions, created a collective situation that could no longer be sustained.

MOBILIZING TO REGULATE THE GROUNDWATER COMMONS

On July 29, 2002, forty-nine members of the newly constituted Nebraska Water Policy Task Force assembled for the first time. Earlier that year, the unicameral legislature had enacted Legislative Bill (LB) 1003, which created the task force. According to the legislature's directive, Governor Mike Johanns appointed its members. They represented a variety of Nebraska water interests—irrigation districts, NRDs, canal irrigators, the Central Nebraska Public Power and Irrigation District (CNPPID), the Nebraska Public Power District (NPPD), recreational entities, environmental organizations, and the public at large. Their central mandate was to examine the surface-groundwater relationship with an eye to finding ways to better induce the state and its twenty-three NRDs to proactively anticipate and resolve conflicts between purveyors of the two kinds of water supply. Additionally, they were charged to examine issues surrounding the ways and means of facilitating water transfers from location to location and use to use.

Forty-nine members constituted too large a group to be effective, so fourteen people were selected to serve on an Executive Committee that would set agendas, allocate responsibilities, and push discussion. In the end, the committee met eighteen times and, in December 2003, submitted a set of recommendations that in 2004 were incorporated into a new law that significantly changed the shape of Nebraska water policy and its organizational landscape.

The task force confronted topics so toxic that they had been avoided for decades. Fulsome public discussion risked further inflaming tense relationships between representatives of surface and groundwater interests, already made difficult by those who marched militantly under the banner of Nebraskans First (see Chapter 15). The task force operated by consensus; any one participant could block a decision. There were many points of major disagreement, and task force members relied greatly on mediators.

How could the two divergent surface and groundwater systems be reconciled? The question pressed hard because water leaders confronted at least two dynamics:

1. Growing threats from the surface water community to the effect that the state of Nebraska had not sufficiently protected their waters from the depredations of groundwater well users. If litigation on behalf of an injured surface water user proved successful and established that the injury was a direct outcome of negligent state water administration, the liabilities placed on the state treasury could be enormous. A formula for computing historical damage to a given surface water user could conceivably be applied to similar cases of injury across the state. Water leaders were already spending millions of dollars in a struggle with Kansas over Nebraska's failure to control its groundwater exploitation in its portion of the Republican River Basin. Might it be better to pay the relatively modest costs associated with a meaningful groundwater policy change rather than risk facing potentially much larger bills on the Platte later? Failure to get Nebraska's water house in order could produce a financial, legal, and administrative nightmare no one wanted to contemplate.

2. The looming need to get back to the 1997 baseline of water use that was written into the ESA habitat recovery CA. In the CA, Nebraska authorities had pledged to prevent or offset any depletions to the river post–July 1, 1997. That meant limiting and regulating the number of wells.

It was for these reasons that the Nebraska Water Policy Task Force was constituted by law, gathered immediately, and pressed to work things out as soon as possible. But in a state in which these issues had been avoided for so long, why create the task force at that time? In a state where there was little organized support for the ESA agenda, it would be the internal Nebraska surface-groundwater struggle—long submerged by powerful groundwater interests—that would call for a task force to engage in the largely unwanted surface-groundwater conversation.

Spear T Ranch

Pumpkin Creek begins near the Wyoming border in the western Nebraska panhandle country and flows for about eighty-five miles in a wiggly fashion, skirting south of the Wildcat Hills, then heading east and north to its mouth on the North Platte near the community of Bridgeport. For decades until the mid-1960s, even including the drought-stricken 1930s, Pumpkin Creek's central tendency was to contribute 20,000 to 30,000 acre feet of surface water to the North Platte annually (*Platte River Odyssey* 2006: 28; Sievers and Golden 2005: 16). However, two factors severely diminished Pumpkin Creek flows: (1) soil conservation techniques, such as building terraces, kept rainwater on fields rather than returning swiftly to the creek; and (2) rapid growth of groundwater wells interrupted and reduced what had been the steady movement of water in the aquifer toward the stream bottom. By 1980 farmers and ranchers in the valley had drilled 412 large-capacity irrigation wells in the Pumpkin Creek water commons; by 2000 that number had grown to 642. By the 1990s there was little to no surface flow along extended stretches. For years, as surface water users watched their water resource decline, groundwater irrigators fiercely resisted any NRD attempt to limit their access to what for them was a wide-open common pool. Finally, after years of travail, the North Platte NRD acted; it banned more wells in the watershed, a small fraction of the NRD's territory.

Spear T Ranch straddled Pumpkin Creek and had historically diverted surface water from the stream under the terms of two priorities, one dated November 1954 and the other granted in December 1956. In an integrated system of priorities, these water diversion rights would have had clear seniority over most of the wells pumping Pumpkin Creek water at their alternative points of diversion. However, no Nebraska law compelled groundwater users to defer to surface priorities. Nevertheless, in 2002 the owner of Spear T filed a lawsuit in the State District Court for Morrill County against upstream groundwater irrigators (*Spear T Ranch v. Knaub*), claiming that their groundwater pumping had dried up the ranch's surface water appropriations. The court dismissed the lawsuit on the grounds that there was no Nebraska law to guide the judge in making a decision. The dismissal was appealed; the case was then heard by the Nebraska Supreme Court.

The legal maneuvering, substantive arguments, and related court actions have been detailed elsewhere (Aiken 2006). In essence, Spear T Ranch advocates (other surface water users intervened in the appeals process) contended that Pumpkin Creek water flows were a product of tributary groundwater and that conflicts between surface- and groundwater users should be settled under the terms of surface water law administered by the Office of the Nebraska State Engineer; priorities would be defined by the principle of first in time, first in right. The defendants replied that existing law precluded the courts from re-solving disputes between surface- and groundwater users. The issue, the defen-dants held, had been resolved by the unicameral legislature when it passed the legislation that originally established the NRDs. Furthermore, they contended that applying surface water law to the Spear T case would undermine extant state groundwater management statutes and place Nebraska's Republican River settlement with Kansas at greater risk.

On January 21, 2005, the Nebraska Supreme Court handed down its deci-sion in what has been cited as one of the most important rulings in a generation (Aiken 2006). The central finding was that Spear T Ranch could bring its lawsuit against the groundwater users but that the issues would be settled according to the terms of the correlative rights doctrine. The court found, not surpris-ingly, that Nebraska's surface water law of prior appropriation did not apply to groundwater. It did recommend that the Nebraska legislature pass legislation to address the issue raised by Spear T Ranch. Finally, the court ruled that ground-water appropriators should not be held responsible for injury to surface water users unless the well pumping had a direct and substantial effect on those users and caused them unreasonable harm. Spear T parties took their case back to the district court and proceeded with a trial in Morrill County, wondering—along with many onlookers—exactly how much injury could be imposed on a given surface water user before a judge and jury would find "direct and substantial effect." Yet one critical point had been clarified—the ruling established the prin-ciple that under some circumstances, still to be clearly defined, groundwater pumpers could be held accountable for injury to surface water users. That was a new and startling development.

Years before the 2005 supreme court decision in *Spear T Ranch v. Knaub* was forthcoming, Nebraska authorities contemplated the unhappy state of affairs that could emerge from such a trial in the district courts. How would a judge and jury calculate the harm? What kind of formula would be concocted to redress injury to surface users? How many years would a district court look back in attempting to address injury that had been imposed for decades? What would the implications be for all other Nebraskan surface water users who had reason to claim injury from well owners? When all this was eventually appealed to the Nebraska Supreme Court, what would happen? Water leaders had to head off the potential financial and administrative calamity. In 2002 and 2003 *Spear T Ranch v. Knaub* was a spur to action.

The Central Nebraska Public Power and Irrigation District

A second, simultaneous sequence of events called into question the historical division of water law and administration in Nebraska's "big house" of irrigation. The Central Nebraska Public Power and Irrigation District was seeking to obtain redress for water lost to undisciplined groundwater extraction above Lake McConaughy.

When Kingsley Dam was originally sited, a key consideration was to capture return flows from upstream irrigation projects on the Wyoming North Platte. The planners in the 1930s did not foresee the subsequent massive growth of groundwater well installations above Lake McConaughy that would later intercept those return flows in the wide alluvial underground conveyor belt that is the North Platte Valley—so much at the expense of stream flows to the McConaughy tub.

Hydrologists had long ago learned that groundwater depletions were shrinking North Platte flows, but it was the onset of serious drought in 1999 and 2000 that focused CNPPID attention on the problem. As reservoir levels fell along Wyoming's North Platte, the U.S. Bureau of Reclamation (USBR) reduced allocations to Wyoming and the Nebraska districts. This, in turn, meant reduced return flows to the river just at the time hard-pressed irrigators were pumping their wells harder and longer. Furthermore, farmers added new wells under the Nebraska open access regime, further exacerbating matters. News spread about possible moratoriums to be placed on new well drilling in the name of protecting surface diverters and an impending possible ESA listed species habitat recovery program. These visions provided further incentive to drill quickly.

Over the five-year period 2001–2006, the CNPPID calculated that as the result of a combination of drought and increased groundwater exploitation, the annual average inflow to Lake McConaughy equaled 496,781 acre feet—a little more than half of the thirty-year average of 989,665 acre feet and just under half of the historical average of 1,017,841 acre feet (*Communicator: Newsletter of CNPPID* 2006: 1, 4). What part of the loss was caused by drought, and what portion resulted from increases in groundwater pumping? The answer was murky, but the proliferation of Nebraskan wells above McConaughy was clearly having a significant impact. The CNPPID estimated that up to 100,000 acre feet per year was being depleted by well pumping from the North Platte and its tributaries, water that district authorities thought should be going into the reservoir (CNPPID 2005a: 1).

Lake McConaughy water levels plunged during and after the record drought year of 2002, and, as they did so, CNPPID reduced its water volume allotments to its irrigators downstream of Kingsley Dam. By 2005 Lake McConaughy contained only about 21 percent of its capacity. Whereas in some years 18 inches of water per acre had been delivered per twelve-week season, by 2005 deliveries had been reduced to 6.7 inches/acre in an eight-week season (CNPPID 2005a: 1). In CNPPID's view, uncompensated injury had occurred across the district's landscape, a significant amount as a result of upstream Nebraska groundwater pumping. The district was determined not to let the matter rest.

The Republican River Basin Struggle

The Nebraska segment of the Republican River is fed by three prairie streams, none of which is served by a mountain watershed. The streams arise from the capture of sparse seasonal natural eastern Colorado precipitation and are supplemented by shallow water bearing geologic strata that produce springs. The North Fork of the Republican heads out southwest of Wray, Colorado, and moves directly to Nebraska, where it receives tributary flows from the Arikaree, a stream that also arises in Colorado. The South Fork emerges east of Limon, Colorado, and flows northeast across the northwest corner of Kansas to a point where it joins the North Fork at Benkelman, Nebraska. The Republican main stem then proceeds in a shallow arc to the north and east just above the Kansas border before it bends south and enters central Kansas.

In May 1998 the state of Kansas filed a complaint with the U.S. Supreme Court claiming that Nebraska and Colorado groundwater irrigators were depleting waters of the Republican River Basin to an extent that was violating the interstate Republican River Compact (Nebraska Department of Natural Resources 2003b). Moves and countermoves were made as the legal story unfolded (ibid.). Kansas argued that the compact restricted all groundwater use; Nebraska and Colorado took somewhat different positions, but neither agreed with Kansas's interpretation. In mid-November 1999 the Court referred the dispute to a special master to investigate; his first report found in favor of Kansas to the extent that under the 1943 Republican River Compact, consumption of groundwater was covered to the extent that Nebraska consumptive uses of groundwater reduced river flows to Kansas. A number of remaining issues needed to be sorted out, which would take additional time. On December 16, 2002, the three states announced that they had reached an out-of-court settlement, and the U.S. Supreme Court gave its formal approval in May 2003.

The terms of the settlement did not change the original 1943 compact, which had allocated flows according to what was then Republican Basin irrigated acreage in each of the three states—49 percent to Nebraska, 40 percent to Kansas, and 11 percent to Colorado. Furthermore, each state would continue to have its original allocation. The problem arose, however, because (1) the special master had found that groundwater depletions in tributary aquifers counted against Nebraska and Colorado allocations, and (2) basin irrigators had greatly expanded their tributary groundwater extraction in subsequent years. Their wells had been found to place depletions on the stream in an amount undreamed of in the early 1940s. Meaningful fractions of those greater depletions had, in turn, been found to have diminished flows to Kansas and thereby imposed injury. The entire situation was deeply problematic before the onset of a drought in 1999–2000, and a sustained lack of precipitation combined with intensifying groundwater withdrawals during a time of water scarcity only made the situation worse. Farmers had bills to pay; that meant pumping more.

What would it cost to fix the situation in the Nebraska Republican Basin? Who knew? A huge unpaid mortgage had built up on the Republican system. It consisted of the expense of covering not only post–1997–1998 depletions but also the depletions produced over a long string of earlier years, the effects of which lagged by varying durations and were currently hitting the river. Irrigation farmers on the Republican, just like their counterparts on the Platte, had drawn against their groundwater supplies during wetter times without thinking they would have to pay the system back. They now had to confront the unhappy fact that just like many credit card holders, their line of credit was exhausted, and they owed a great deal for their earlier streams of benefit. While watching this situation unfold between 1998 and 2003, Nebraska authorities knew they must do everything possible to minimize damages being risked on the Platte. The state treasury could not withstand a repeat of the Republican disaster, at least as long as politicians wanted to keep taxes low in the interest of attracting new business enterprise to the state and its fully appropriated and over-appropriated river basins.

In sum, by 2002–2003, in the midst of a deep drought, conflict between surface- and groundwater users was openly erupting in the matter of *Spear T Ranch v. Knaub*; it was also rumbling near the surface in the CNPPID's insistence that the North Platte NRD take effective action to protect inflows to Lake McConaughy. In addition, water users on the Republican River were confronted with a compact settlement, the terms of which portended substantial sacrifice. State authorities needed to address the rapidly escalating challenges, but how? The answer was to create the Nebraska Water Policy Task Force and charge it with finding a solution. For these reasons, the initial task force gathering on July 29, 2002, and its subsequent work over the next eighteen months were of critical importance.

PARSE THE PROBLEM, STRUCTURE THE CHOICES

To many Nebraskans involved in the groundwater sector, the question for years had been: do you like the ESA habitat recovery agenda on the Platte River? Answers tended to vary between "no" and "hell no." It was imperative to push the discourse further and into authentic problem solving. Leaders within the Nebraska Department of Natural Resources (DNR) proposed a way to do so. They believed it was essential to separate the state's surface-groundwater issue from the federal three-state cooperative program on behalf of ESA listed species.

The way forward was to establish the Nebraska Water Policy Task Force and provide it with a compelling mandate: construct a proposed law that would reconcile groundwater use with the surface water prior appropriation system. Invited members and their constituencies could choose to assist in this endeavor in this manner, or they could refuse and face even worse problems within the context of Nebraska law in the not-so-distant-future. That was the lesson of *Spear T Ranch v. Knaub*, CNPPID's quest to restore lost flows, and the mess in the Republican Basin. By stripping out the state's surface-groundwater problem (where the greatest costs were found), Nebraska citizens and policy makers could set aside the challenges of the Platte River Habitat Recovery Program and focus on immediate internal threats.

A significant number of groundwater users could see the prospect of at least two kinds of payoffs in exchange for supporting the task force agenda. First, many knew that decades of investment in irrigated agriculture were hanging in the balance. Failure to move ahead with some kind of solution would do damage to all parties, and that damage would eventually have to be repaired at even greater cost and risk. Uncontrolled groundwater exploitation was, in some instances, hurting other groundwater users as well as surface diverters. For these people, it was time to protect their past investment by much more carefully shaping any new investment in selected areas. Support for the Nebraska Water Policy Task Force agenda was equivalent to support for long-term security of irrigation investment.

Second, for groundwater users upstream of Lake McConaughy, authentic progress on the matter of integrating groundwater with surface flows would likely induce the CNPPID to "stand down," at least temporarily, in its quest for redress. In the Republican Basin it would not be realistic to expect that Kansas would be satisfied with the task force's proposals, but getting legislation in place in Nebraska that would solve the problems would be a critical step in developing Republican Basin solutions. Support for the task force agenda was therefore important in developing a better relationship with Kansas, at least in the minds of some.

The DNR, especially its director, then made a game-changing tactical move. The only way Nebraska state authorities could even approach the NRDs with the thought of integrating the administration of groundwater resources with surface supplies, let alone receive a decent hearing, was to make a promise. The state of Nebraska would pay for producing offset water that would address both problems that vexed the districts—the internal problem of groundwater pumping depredations and finding offset water for the federal ESA program.

This was an audacious gamble. No manager of any state department or division could commit the state legislature or the governor to any state expenditure. Yet what other option was there? In the years following the signing of the 1997 Cooperative Agreement, Nebraska authorities could not tell new depleters in any meaningful way what their obligation would be. Therefore, given the lack of essential laws to empower state intervention in groundwater administration, coupled with the lack of a complete set of COHYST groundwater models essential to inform decision making, state authorities could not simply say: we cannot stop your expansion of well drilling and irrigated lands, but we will tell you later about the nature and extent of your obligation. Furthermore, the immediate effect of the promise was to greatly reduce the NRDs' opposition to the two agendas. This, in turn, isolated the more radical opponents of change—well drillers and members of Nebraskans First.

There were sound arguments for the state of Nebraska to pay at least an important fraction of the total costs of the regime change. The state had an interest in sustainable and viable communities, made possible by irrigated agriculture in western and central Nebraska. A pecuniary interest was to preserve the tax base to fill state coffers. Also, it was the state that had allowed groundwater irrigators to get into an unsustainable position in the first place. The unfortunate circumstances of a dual irrigation administration had been created by pressure from self-seeking groundwater users, who had used their years of dominance in Nebraska water politics to seal themselves away from any responsibility to the larger water community. Still, the state had enabled them to do so; it was therefore argued that the state should shoulder some of the blame and the burden.

The politics of water had suddenly changed. How could majorities of groundwater users adamantly resist coming to grips with the internal surface-groundwater issue if the state was going to cover the costs? Furthermore, public tax dollars spent on the long-neglected state agenda would do double duty; payoffs for addressing the surface-groundwater problem could be expected to contribute importantly to the federal ESA program. NRD members, who historically had evidenced no willingness to even contemplate the words "fully appropriated" or "over-appropriated," would abide a conversation on the subjects if the state pledged to cover the costs of rectifying matters. Most were prepared to acknowledge that a federal endangered species program was advancing, and most understood that the deal offered them was preferable to anything they could expect without new Nebraska water laws and participation in the three-state–federal cooperative habitat recovery program. The real downside would be experienced by state and NRD taxpayers who would pick up the tab.

A NEW LAW: LB 962

At the conclusion of eighteen months of challenging discussions, the Nebraska Water Policy Task Force presented its report to the governor on December 18, 2003. The group's recommendations were immediately encoded into proposed new legislation that would be taken up for consideration by the unicameral legislature when it convened in January 2004 (Nebraska Department of Natural Resources 2004).

Teams of DNR staff had been active in presenting the case for water law integration during the task force deliberations, and they continued to travel around the state during early 2004 as the legislature deliberated. In the early going, the DNR teams met with deep skepticism from audiences. Many voices openly suggested that the task force and DNR attempts to push reform would go nowhere. But representatives of the state government, the eastern Wyoming and western panhandle irrigation districts, the CNPPID, the NPPD, and mutual irrigation companies ("ditch companies") pushed on with their case on behalf of the task force's work. Increasing numbers of people began to pay close attention as the months passed, especially after the task force issued its recommendations and its members returned to their communities and argued strongly for the proposed legislative package. As the stakes, options, and incentives became increasingly clear, resistance diminished. The more radical opponents split away from the majorities who were prepared to adapt to new demands.

Legislative Bill 962 was introduced without a name; it was simply identified as an "Act relating to water management" to amend sections of a long list of Nebraska water laws and laws pertaining to water laws. The text consumed 147 pages. The task force informed legislators that the proposed legislation had emerged following tortuous negotiations and strongly recommended that the assembly not confuse the water reform process by attempting to change any component of the deal; doing so would threaten to unravel the entire enterprise. The bill was read for the first time in the Natural Resources Committee on January 9, 2004; legislators refrained from making substantive alterations and enacted the bill by a large majority on April 13. Governor Johanns signed it into law on April 15. LB 962 became operative on July 16, 2004 (Nebraska Department of Natural Resources 2004).

In practical terms, LB 962 did at least two significant things. First, it gave the Nebraska Department of Natural Resources the authority to participate meaningfully in the governance of groundwater extraction. This was new. LB 962 left the separate realms of surface (prior appropriation) and groundwater (correlative rights) law intact. However, the new legislation required NRDs to undertake appropriate management action when state authorities declared that a given river basin (or sub-basin) was fully appropriated or over-appropriated. A fully appropriated unit is defined as one wherein—taking into account the lag in the impacts of depletions over time—if further depletions were to occur, the balance between water use and water supplies could not be sustained (Nebraska Department of Natural Resources 2004). An over-appropriated basin or sub-basin is one in which the extent of existing permitted water use is not sustainable over the long term.

The law also authorized the DNR to annually review the balance between water consumptive uses and water recharge; the department was then charged to declare any given river basin (or sub-basin) where no excess supply was found as either fully or over-appropriated. Discretion on this critical decision was not left to the NRDs. The law designated all or portions of nine NRDs in western and central Nebraska on the Platte and Republican river drainages as fully appropriated as of July 16, 2004. The law further empowered the director of the DNR to identify any over-appropriated basin by no later than September 15, 2004. Accordingly, the DNR moved to so declare the Platte Basin above Elm Creek (sixteen miles upstream from Kearney and just downstream of Overton) at the diversion point of the Kearney Canal, which holds a very senior water right. It also happens to be at the upper end of critical habitat for the listed species. In basins declared by the state to be fully or over-appropriated, the state DNR must work with the relevant NRD to place immediate stays on the authorization of any new wells or surface diversions. Then the DNR and the NRD will be required to jointly develop a basin-wide plan to guide appropriate groundwater decision making. Plans must incrementally reduce gaps between actual and acceptable water withdrawals, as determined by the DNR. Acceptable withdrawals on a basin-wide basis are determined by doing what is necessary to restore a balance between recharge through precipitation and canal seepage on the one hand and extraction on the other.

Although no specific mention could be made in a Nebraska statute of any state agreement with the two other states and the federal Department of the Interior that would impose a water-use baseline, state participation in NRD groundwater administration would be the key to either reducing or offsetting post-1997 new depletions, as called for by the terms of the habitat recovery CA.

NEBRASKA'S NEW DEPLETIONS PLAN

As the Nebraska Water Policy Task Force worked away during 2002 and 2003 and LB 962 was born in mid-2004, Platte River habitat recovery negotiations were hanging by a thread. Keeping all of the regime of the river discourse together was no small challenge for each and every party, state and federal.

Nebraska faced special challenges. The state had little option but to promise to pick up the costs of providing offset water from July 1, 1997, onward. But for what period of time? Originally, the answer was, up to the end of 2000, when a viable habitat recovery program was supposed to be ready. But when that moment arrived, Nebraska had no COHYST tool to inform decision making and no legal basis to shut down wells or deny new ones. Furthermore, no habitat recovery program had yet been initiated. There was nothing to do but retreat. The deadline was backed up to December 2003, then to a year later. Finally, in the wake of the passage of LB 962 in 2004, Nebraska had advanced to a place in its internal politics from which it could impose a workable deadline of December 31, 2005. After that date, new Nebraska depleters would have to assume the full costs of keeping the river whole.

Meanwhile, Colorado and Wyoming fretted that Nebraska was not going to be able to control and reduce its groundwater extraction. Insofar as that proved to be true, it meant that Colorado and Wyoming water contributions would be sucked up by Nebraska pumps and the proposed cooperative habitat recovery program would die of thirst. Members of the environmental and federal communities at the negotiating table were deeply concerned that Nebraska was falling behind with its new depletions planning; skepticism grew with each passing year when Nebraska could not provide the data essential to the USBR Environmental Impact Assessment Team and to USFWS personnel who were working on a biological opinion. A general conceptual plan might work for a draft environmental impact statement and biological opinion, but representatives of the two upstream states, the federal government, and environmentalists wanted to see numbers justified by a detailed and defensible analytical system. For years, such numbers were simply not to be had. In August 2004 the USFWS called for detailed depletions plans from all parties by February 1, 2005. Nebraska was not ready. Nebraska finally submitted its best effort in a document dated December 7, 2005 (*Platte River Recovery Program* 2006: attachment 5, section 8).

BACKING UP THE DEPLETIONS TRAIN

LB 962 established the new policy. COHYST would provide an essential tool for implementing that policy. The policy objective would be to replace water depletions in the amount, time, and location needed to prevent harm to Nebraska water users and the federal habitat recovery program agenda. Three tasks needed to be addressed simultaneously.

First, the new law and the COHYST tool would be employed to protect essential river flows for state water users, especially surface appropriators. State laws therefore needed to require sufficient flows for surface water diverters, Nebraska in-stream flow requirements, and recharge of aquifers. State-protected flows were identified in specific reaches of the North and South Platte, the Platte's main stem, and their tributaries above Chapman, Nebraska, that would be required to satisfy Nebraska diverters—agricultural, municipal, and industrial.

Second, there was a need to develop a plan to get back to the 1997 regime of the river to serve Nebraska commitments to the state-federal cooperative habitat recovery program. Here the emphasis was on reestablishing base flow conditions on the North Platte, South Platte, and Platte rivers above the city of Chapman, located at the downstream end of the critical habitat.

Third, Nebraska needed to produce water to augment the rivers to the extent that post–June 30, 1997, hydrologically connected groundwater depletions up to December 31, 2005, had shriveled the streams. Any new party that proposed imposing a new depletion on or after January 1, 2006, would bear the costs of delivering the needed offset water to the river at the appropriate place and time. The state pledged that by January 1, 2007, state authorities would report new and expanded water uses in COHYST-modeled areas that occurred after June 30, 1997, and up to December 31, 2005, upstream of Chapman, Nebraska. Furthermore, by December 31, 2008, in collaboration with the relevant NRDs or other applicable entities, the authorities would present specific measures to offset existing depletions imposed during the 1997–2005 period (*Platte River Recovery Program* 2006: attachment 5, section 8, p. 5).

How much water did tributary groundwater depleters owe the river? The eventual answer would vary depending on many factors, among them distance from a river and the hydro-geology of the well site. At the core of the matter, however, groundwater well debts—individual or collective—depend on the extent to which cumulative depletions over a given time period diminish stream flows of interest. In the Nebraska instance, these are state-protected flows and USFWS target flows. Over time, much of the consumptive use of a given well or set of wells will diminish river flows. It may be a matter of weeks, years, or decades for the full depletion to impact a hydrologically connected stream. Therefore, it was practical to discuss depletions in terms of the amount of consumptive use that appears as a depletion to stream flow within a specified time period—for example, forty years.

The next question became, what amount of consumptive use within a given time period will be permitted before a political-legal-organizational obligation is stipulated? Decades ago, the U.S. Geological Survey established that quantity as 28 percent. The number had no particular hydrological significance but was selected by agency analysts because it set a particular parameter in the equation as equal to one, a handy computational device (Warner, Altenhofen, and Odor 1994). Although technically arbitrary, the 28 percent figure took on political-legal significance when it became part of the 2002 Nebraska-Wyoming Supreme Court settlement and the modified North Platte decree.

Given all this, in the world of Colorado, Wyoming, and Nebraska water, it had become commonplace to define a hydrologically connected groundwater well of some minimum size (generally fifty gallons per minute or more) as one so located and constructed that if water were withdrawn continuously for forty years, the cumulative stream depletion would be equal to or greater than 28 percent of the total water withdrawn. Groundwater wells imposing impacts of less than 28 percent are then viewed as not sufficiently hydrologically connected to be of concern. A given well's stream depletion factor (SDF) then becomes the amount of time (calculated in the number of twenty-four-hour days) it takes for its depletion at the well site to impact the river in the amount of 28 percent of the total groundwater withdrawn. Therefore, wells that deplete that percentage or more within a given time period are defined as having an obligation to replace depletions. Each of the three states, in their own separate histories, adopted this SDF logic in demarcating tributary groundwater.

Using the SDF logic, Nebraska would use its COHYST groundwater models to draw a map defining which of the state's groundwater wells were within the tributary zone as defined by the forty-year, 28 percent line. Well users were expected, through collective action organized by NRDs, to secure the water necessary to fill in the "holes" in the river at the places and times necessary to protect other Nebraska water users and the needs of ESA listed species.

COHYST models, along with other analytical tools, stood at the core of Nebraska's future depletions plan. They were essential to determine the amount, timing, and location of depletions to state-protected flows and USFWS target flows. They were viewed as critical to ensuring that newly developed water offset projects would be operated in a manner that actually works while not causing additional shortages to either kind of state or federal program flow. Yet Nebraska modelers were having trouble obtaining the quantity and quality of data essential to build models that would reasonably reflect complicated real-world hydrological conditions. Their study area included 23,900 square miles distributed across forty-three counties, in whole or in part (Water Management Committee 2004). To provide the information necessary for decision making regarding specific wells and to draw a defensible 28 percent/forty-year line, the analysts constructed three separate models that would aggregate data in half-mile–by–half-mile squares (nodes). They built in assumptions about the consumptive uses of each kind of crop—corn and others. This kind of resolution would permit the calculation of depletions to stream flows reach by reach, month by month on the North, South, and main stem Platte rivers and parse out the net depletive effects of groundwater pumping on state-protected and federal listed species program river flows.

Federal analysts needed solid data to justify the writing of draft and final environmental impact statements and biological opinions. Environmentalists despaired over continuing delays as river channels degraded under the effects of drought, increased pumping, and thickening vegetation. Colorado and Wyoming worried about Nebraska's capacity to live up to its promise to deliver their water to the critical habitat. All parties saw the situation as very serious. The federal community and environmentalists overtly communicated their anxiety. Colorado and Wyoming fretted more quietly. Nebraska sought time to get a grip on a problem that, if not satisfactorily resolved, could sink the entire program.

Nebraska replied to the other parties' concerns in two ways. First, have patience; we are operating in good faith and are doing the best we can within the limits of our resources. Second, for all its importance, COHYST simply generates numbers node by node. Those numbers constitute nothing more than statements of impact at particular sites. More significant is the nature of Nebraska's overall future depletions plan, which will use the COHYST numbers. The larger concepts are more important. Focus on the larger picture, and employ the general concepts in your work on the evolving environmental impact statement and biological opinion. If progress is slower than had been hoped, Nebraska can always employ a partial set of COHYST models and insert more assumptions than may be desirable, but there will be sufficient substance for moving ahead.

Colorado and Wyoming representatives had always seen the advantages of relying on general conceptual plans for the habitat recovery program in their federal relationships, but in this matter they remained deeply concerned about Nebraska's capacity to fully and quantitatively justify its future depletions proposals. The efforts of the two upstream states would be rewarded according to the USFWS scoring of water volumes arriving at proper times at the top of the critical habitat. Nebraska deficiencies in controlling groundwater pumping could severely compromise those scores.

Where would Nebraska authorities obtain the required offset water? State authorities were pledged to cover depletions to federal target flows and all depletions imposed by well drilling from mid-1997 through December 2005. Beginning January 1, 2006, responsibility for offsetting new depletions was to be shared between the state and the appropriate NRD accountable for permitting a new depleter. Furthermore, Nebraska well owners had long been employing their equivalent of a credit card by initiating pumping, the depletions of which would not hit the streams for years. Those lagging impacts of earlier pumping in the 1960s through the 1990s would be depriving the river as the future depletions plan attempted to restore flows. The old bills incurred without any serious intent to ever repay them could no longer be hidden by an open-access groundwater resource organizational system that required little to no accountability. The old debts must be exposed, measured, and paid during a drought and a time of immense pressure on the state and NRD public treasuries. Most of all, those old water debts must be paid within a context in which all seven NRDs with territory upstream of Elm Creek have been declared "over-appropriated." The NRDs must work to get back to a condition of being only "fully appropriated" under the terms of LB 962.

Starting in 2010 and every five years thereafter, the state pledged to conduct a new land-use inventory to assess the sufficiency of NRD and state water offset activities. If more offset water has been produced than is needed to cover new state and cooperative habitat program depletion requirements, the excess will be available to mitigate the effects of new depletions. Within two years after the completion of each assessment, the state and its NRD partners will put in place any required additional offset projects. All offset projects will be constructed so that none increases additional shortages to USFWS target flows or state-protected volumes.

What will be the cost of providing the offset water? Nebraska, like Colorado and Wyoming, has confronted real water supply limits within its hydrological-organizational system. Clearly, post–January 1, 2006, new depletions have been severely constrained by the costs of building offset water projects. A huge central Nebraska groundwater mound has been built up by seepage from CNPPID's canal system, but there are real limits as to what can be done with it without damaging supplies needed for state-protected flows and federal-state cooperative habitat recovery efforts. There is a large pot of high-quality groundwater in the Sandhill country. Potentially, such water could be brought into the central Platte, but at what cost? What water use could justify the expense? Nobody seems to know.

CONCLUSION

For years, many groundwater irrigators within the Nebraska Platte River system intensely disliked the thought of an Endangered Species Act agenda being implemented in their valleys. That included people associated with the CNPPID and the NPPD. But in the context of events along Pumpkin Creek and a growing problem with Kansas on the Republican River, the requirements of the ESA habitat recovery agenda triggered events that would lead to a discourse long sought by the two districts.

The two districts, unenthusiastic partners with the state Department of Natural Resources as that agency struggled to cope with the implications of the ESA, wanted to do as little as possible on behalf of the listed species beyond what they had been compelled to pledge to secure their 1998 Federal Energy Regulatory Commission (FERC) re-licensing. But it was the specter of a probable federally inspired habitat recovery program that sparked the creation of the Nebraska Water Policy Task Force in combination with a serious discussion of the state's internal issue that eventuated in LB 962. If the CNPPID and the NPPD were going to fulfill their obligations to FERC and ultimately to the encompassing state-federal cooperative program for habitat restoration, they needed to sustain historical inflows at Lake McConaughy. Those flows were threatened by Nebraska groundwater irrigators. The two districts, no friends of the ESA, became among the first beneficiaries of the unwelcome discussion of that federal environmental agenda.

Regime of the River—Building a Federal Depletions Plan

States Confront the U.S. Forest Service

Other regime-of-the-river fights had pitted state against state and Colorado, at least, against the U.S. Fish and Wildlife Service (USFWS) over peak flow issues on the South Platte. But another river regime "skunk" needed to be wrestled. In this instance, the states would unite against the U.S. Forest Service (USFS). The states believed the USFS's timber management policies posed a threat to the river's twentieth-century flow regime. Forests catch, hold, transpire, and release surface water downstream. The USFS's management practices were, at least in the view of the states' representatives, deeply entangled in regime-of-the-river considerations and, in the states' perspective, were depriving states of their proper water supplies.

Federal agencies have been the source of river depletions, just as state water providers have. For example, the U.S. Bureau of Reclamation's environmental restoration activities may interrupt return flows to basin streams, the U.S. Army Corps of Engineers may engage in water supply or flood control activities that impose depletions, the U.S. Bureau of Land Management may be involved in the construction of small reservoirs and stock ponds, the U.S. Department of Energy may engage in commissioning or decommissioning power production facilities that affect stream depletions, the U.S. Natural Resources Conservation Service (formerly the Soil Conservation Service) might—in the name of improving farm irrigation water application efficiencies—advance programs that could reduce return flows, or the USFS could impose depletions by virtue of fulfilling its recreational and landscape management missions.

Some kind of federal depletions replacement plan was needed. It was in the context of putting the plan together that debate erupted about the USFS's management of vegetation in Platte Basin watersheds. This mobilized water users to call for the USFS to develop a portfolio of water with which to repay Platte Basin streams (Bucholz 1999; Leaf 1999a, 1999b) and to contribute significantly to replacing the agency's historical depredations to water flows. Later, especially during the years 2004–2006, in the context of piecing together the federal post-1997 future depletions plan, the debates again intensified.

The states were willing to work with federal agents in hammering out proposals for replacing federal agencies' many small depletions—for example, those associated with campgrounds, stock tanks, wetland rehabilitation, and fish hatcheries. But for them, there was an elephant in the room that the federal community wanted to ignore—historical and future depletions to water yields produced by Platte Basin watersheds administered by the USFS, a fraction of which was attributable to agency management practices.

State representatives, pushed hard by their constituents, asserted that the U.S. Forest Service was imposing depletions on Platte River waters by virtue of conscious policy decisions to permit the thickening of forest vegetation, thereby causing diminished water flows downstream. They wanted the USFS to join the negotiations, take responsibility for their evolving balance of accretions and depletions over time, and do what the states were being asked to do: be accountable for replacing net depletions. Most of all, the states sought a way to ensure that future agency management practices would not impose new depletions that would undercut state efforts to meet their target flow requirements. The agency, in turn, consistently resisted involving itself in any such discussion. Further, it did not want to join the states in constructing a water plan to serve listed species in central Nebraska. The states cried foul.

BACKGROUND

During the years preceding organized negotiations subsequent to the 1994 governors' agreement, water users in the states had declared that if the Department of the Interior wanted more water for listed species in Nebraska, the solution should be found by looking within the federal community. State water users wanted to push the U.S. Forest Service to engage in forest-thinning practices that would produce more runoff into basin rivers. Later, when the states were casting about trying to find ways to come up with water to offset pre-1997 depletions to the Platte system, negotiators were frequently reminded by their constituents that the increasing density of forest vegetation was also a source of significant depletions to Platte River flows. They called for the USFS to step up, take responsibility, and commit itself to practices that would increase the water yields of Platte Basin forests (Bucholz 1999; Leaf 1999a, 1999b). Why, water users asked, should they be held exclusively accountable for depletions to the river system when thickening vegetation in basin national forest watersheds was clearly contributing to the problem?

The federal community wanted the issue to go away. Environmentalists were open to a discussion on the matter but were on guard not to allow the states to cut back on their water delivery commitments by substituting possible increased forest water yield. State negotiators knew that if they were to obtain the support of their water user constituents and get the proposed program through their respective legislatures, a meaningful resolution would have to be found. Failure in this matter could scuttle the habitat recovery program.

HISTORY—IRRIGATORS AND FORESTS

In the late nineteenth century, farmers on irrigated lands were witness to the ravages of undisciplined individual self-seeking rationality let loose on open-access forestlands. They saw abused forest soils becoming compacted and shedding water like a tin roof. They struggled to undo the repeated effects of spring floods loaded with heavy headgate-clogging sediment. They suffered dry riverbeds by July, just when their crops needed moisture the most. Irrigators learned a major truth: healthy forests hold water and release it slowly; therefore, they concluded that timber should not be over-cut and thereby promote devastating flash floods that eroded their soils, filled their canals with sediment, and rushed past their diversions. They also saw the wisdom of not undercutting timber either, lest forests thicken and send moisture to the sky through evapo-transpiration. That might be acceptable for rain-fed agriculture in the Midwest, but it diminished precious surface supplies in the Platte Basin. Irrigators knew, therefore, that they must mobilize to prevent the deforestation of watersheds by railroad tie cutters, other timber harvesters, and livestock grazers (Dana 1956; Steen 1976, 1991; White 1991: 408–409). They did not want soil erosion and landslides. They did want mountainsides covered with grasses, timber, and other vegetation to curb floods and slow the release of water to streams for more supply in the mid- to late irrigation season.

So it had come to pass that, pushed hard by irrigators and others after decades of debate, the U.S. Congress passed the Organic Administrative Act in 1897 (Steen 1991: 1; White 1991: 407) and thereby established the U.S. Forest Service. In doing so, language in the act specified that "[n]o national forest shall be established except to improve and protect the forest within the boundaries, or for the purpose of securing favorable conditions of water flows" (Corbridge and Rice 1999: 446).

This forest management legislation, signed by President William McKinley, gave the federal government the power to regulate the use of forest reserves and provide means to regulate grazing and commercial lumbering so as to provide continuous supplies of water, timber, and hydroelectric power generation (White 1991: 407). Securing water by conserving forests was at the heart of the legislation.

FORESTS AND WATER

Studies have shown a substantial increase in forest vegetation density relative to the pre-settlement (pre-1850) and European settlement (1850–1900) periods (MacDonald 2002: 6–8; MacDonald, Stednick, and Troendle 2003; Stednick 1996; Troendle and King 1987; Troendle and Nankervis 2000; Troendle, Nankervis, and Porth 2003). In general, the greatest increase in vegetation density tends to occur in lower- to mid-elevation ponderosa pine and mixed conifer forests—those most susceptible to wildfires. In his summary of the literature, Lee MacDonald (2002: 6) noted that logging (without respect to cut patterns, such as clear-cuts of large patches and clumps or removal of single trees scattered across a stand) tends to increase water yields in proportion to the percentage of the forested canopy removed. This relationship holds as long as the cut areas are not exposed to wind scour that produces high rates of evaporation. Therefore, as forest density increases, forest water yields downstream tend to diminish. The potential for increased yields is generally greatest on north-facing slopes, as they exhibit the greatest density and highest rates of snow retention.

The States' Case

> [U.S.] Forest Service staff seem to think that since they have not opened a headgate to divert water, there is no depletion.
> —VIEW OF WATER USER, AUGUST 21, 2001

For water users and their state representatives at the negotiating table, the problem was straightforward. If the USFS, on a given set of Platte Basin watersheds in the years before 1997, harvested "X" board feet of timber per year and if, in the post-1997 era, the agency dropped the cut (and if the loss to fire and disease was constant or also in decline), there would be a net depletion to the river. The equitable thing to do, given the habitat recovery program's demands for water, was for the USFS to estimate that depletion and provide offset water. That would protect the stream flow baselines from which states and their water providers would obtain their habitat recovery program water.

All the parties knew well that there was no way to protect and usher any increased stream flow increments from forest boundaries all the way to the critical listed species habitats in central Nebraska. Tactically, within Wyoming, given its large North Platte on-stream reservoirs, and within Colorado, given the many off-stream reservoirs and irrigation canals that divert stream flows, any increased forest water yield would be buffered out in regular river and reservoir management operations. However, the states were concerned to preserve and enhance their base flows, from which they would pull water to fulfill habitat recovery program requirements.

If the USFWS contended that there had been a shortage to target flows amounting to an annual average of 417,000 acre feet at the critical habitat, a fraction of that shortage has resulted from U.S. Forest Service management practices that prevented Mother Nature from doing what she has always done: thinning vegetation through fire and disease and thereby opening up forest canopies to produce historical water runoff patterns. As a result of USFS suppression of fires in the twentieth century, forest vegetation has increased in density, and water yields have been diminishing. The states believed the USFS should bring its forest management plans to the Platte River Habitat Recovery Program negotiations, subject its work to inspection by all parties, and produce a viable plan to address pre- and post-1997 depletions—just as the states were required to do.

To press the states' case, in the early 1980s some citizens (mostly ranchers and farmers) representing water user interests in the three states formed a nonprofit advocacy organization, the Coalition for Sustainable Resources (Bucholz 1999). The coalition was based in Walden, Colorado. Its members were convinced that their representatives at the negotiating table were overly occupied with finding ways to satisfy USFWS regulatory requirements so they could obtain their needed permits and regulatory certainty (Bucholz 1999). They therefore feared their representatives were too willing to overlook the potential for increased flows from Platte Basin national forest watersheds. Therefore, in the summer of 1998 the coalition filed suit against the USFS in the U.S. District Court in Cheyenne, Wyoming (*Coalition for Sustainable Resources v. U.S. Forest Service*, 48 F. Supp. 2d 1303 [D. Wyo. 1999]) (Coalition for Sustainable Resources 1999).

The purpose of the lawsuit was to compel the USFS to improve water yields in Platte Basin watersheds, especially those in the Medicine Bow National Forest, for the benefit of Endangered Species Act (ESA) listed species in Nebraska. Specifically, the lawsuit held that the U.S. Forest Service was knowingly causing an increasing depletion of basin rivers and thereby was unjustly requiring state water users to offset depletions imposed by federal forest management. The U.S. District Court dismissed the lawsuit on the grounds that it was not "ripe." The USFS would presumably work out an accommodation with the actors participating in the habitat recovery program that had not yet been completed. Therefore, it was not appropriate for the court to intervene. The coalition then filed an appeal in the U.S. Tenth Circuit Court of Appeals on August 7, 2001 (Coalition for Sustainable Resources 2001; details at http://colo.washburnlaw.edu/cases/2001/08/99-8060.htm), which affirmed the Wyoming district court's earlier ruling and dismissed the case for lack of ripeness.

Deeply frustrated and having just lived through a severe drought year (2002), members of the coalition used their strong links to the Wyoming State Legislature to formulate and pass a joint resolution on the matter. In the words of one coalition member, the legislature "blasted the U.S. Forest Service" for its

287

position (Joint Resolution 2003). In endorsing the resolution, the two legislative houses noted that over the years the federal government had ignored repeated appeals from Wyoming water users for relief from diminished water flows imposed by USFS policies that led directly to what they viewed as "national forest overgrowth." That "overgrowth" served no legitimate federal or state purpose and was, the resolution asserted, depriving the state of Wyoming of its legal entitlement to waters as promised by the 1897 Organic Administrative Act. The resolution gave the federal government 180 days from the date of its passage to respond appropriately, after which the legislature would direct the governor to ask the Wyoming attorney general to consider preparing, filing, and pursuing a lawsuit on behalf of the state to—among other things—compel the U.S. Department of Agriculture and the USFS to take actions appropriate to the outcome of the possible lawsuit.

There was no serious intent in the wake of two court dismissals to undertake the threatened lawsuit at that time, but the joint resolution still sent a message. Wyoming water users were unhappy with U.S. Forest Service management, and some were not particularly happy with their own state delegation's participation in the negotiations regarding the development of a federal–three-state cooperative habitat recovery program that, they feared, would be too soft on the USFWS.

These discussions contained some irony. It had only been in the late 1980s and early 1990s that the U.S. Forest Service, in consultation with the USFWS, had pressured Colorado water users to provide "bypass" flows on the Upper Poudre River in the name of ecological responsibility and thereby sent shockwaves across the entire West (see Chapter 4). Now, in the late 1990s and the early twenty-first century, some state water users were pushing back with claims that the agency should step up and do what it had asked of them—take responsibility to produce increased river accretions in the name of listed species habitat in central Nebraska.

The U.S. Forest Service Case

In the view of USFS decision makers, the Platte River negotiations had veered into dangerous territory when the players at the table pushed questions pertaining to forest water yields and their relationship to variability in vegetation patterns. The potential for augmenting water supply through vegetative manipulation raised serious issues not yet carefully thought through. The nation was undertaking other large landscape ecological restoration projects, such as those on the Upper Colorado, in the San Francisco Bay Delta region, the Chesapeake Bay, and the Florida Everglades (Doyle and Drew 2008). But none of those efforts had broached the knotty problem of national forest water obligations to ecological restoration efforts beyond forest boundaries.

The very idea that the U.S. Forest Service could be viewed as a river depleter was an anathema. Forest depletions could not be put in the same category as depletions by a corn farmer. The agency could not abide the view that under primarily natural conditions, timber growth would impose a river flow depletion or that cutting trees should be evaluated as to potential accretions downstream of forest boundaries. If national forest depletions came under the ESA for review in this dimension and if the U.S. Forest Service were held accountable for depletions against some kind of baseline, that would be precedent setting for the nation.

But the states were pushing for answers now. The regulatory process was moving the negotiations forward. The USFS had to move with extreme caution not to yield to the pressure of the immediate situation on the Platte and thereby trap itself in untenable positions in other hot spots—particularly the Pacific Northwest and California on many issues, especially the needs of habitat recovery for highly politicized salmon. Points needed to be clarified in ways that would permit the development of sound policy for the nation as well as the basin.

First came the easy part. The agency would pledge to continue to do what it had already been doing. It would consult with the USFWS under the terms of ESA Section 7 regarding future depletions associated with its periodic forest management plans on matters involving actual water diversions from forest streams—for example, those associated with campground water pumps, housing and offices, fire fighting, and internal forest habitat improvements on behalf of fish and wildlife. These small depletions would be addressed in the federal depletions plan.

A second contentious, possibly precedent-setting, issue also needed to be tackled. What should be done about pre- and post-1997 stream flow depletions attributable to increased vegetation density? On August 21, 2001, during a Governance Committee negotiating session, two representatives of the states—one each from Wyoming and Nebraska—put the question directly to the forest supervisor of the Arapaho-Roosevelt National Forest in north-central Colorado: does the USFS see itself as being covered under the Platte River recovery program for its Platte Basin depletions prior to July 1, 1997?

A "yes" would mean the agency saw itself as part of the responsible basin community and would join the negotiations. A "no" would indicate that the U.S. Forest Service saw itself apart. The forest supervisor simply noted that, in the agency's view, vegetation management activities were not in themselves water depletions. As for the relationship between vegetation density and forest water yields, the forest supervisor gave no specific answer. On March 4, 2002, in response to the same line of questioning, the supervisor stated in the context of a discussion of the effects of vegetative clearing on water yields at forest boundaries: "We in the Forest Service disagree with many in this room who believe that

Forest Service vegetative management has been, or is, negative with respect to water supply. We disagree that the Forest Service should participate in the federal depletions plan."

The USFS's reluctance to confront the issue had long eroded federal credibility among state representatives. By the fall of 2001 and winter-spring of 2002, the USFS stance had become an open festering wound in the state-federal relationship. The situation was not made any easier by the attempts of water users in the three basin states to push ahead with their lawsuits and, later, the passage of the joint resolution by the Wyoming legislature. During a time when negotiations were deeply troubled over the range of other regime-of-the-river issues, the regional director of the U.S. Fish and Wildlife Service made a series of appeals to the regional forester who, with reluctance, directed staff members on his watershed team to address the issue. The agency would review studies critical of USFS timber management practices as they pertained to water yield (Leaf 1999a, 1999b). The USFS would then respond. Much to the relief of the USFWS, this development showed a hint of movement by the USFS.

The USFS representatives—like state water users on other topics—did not want to get into specifics. Nor did they want to provide any opening for water users to push a policy that would take forest conditions back toward what had existed in the late nineteenth and early twentieth centuries—an era witness to massive over-cutting, eroded slopes, and ravaged streams. The age and density of Platte headwater forests in the late nineteenth century represented historical lows. Forest age and density had generally increased during the twentieth century as a result of natural forest growth and human-induced fire suppression, especially in ponderosa pine stands at lower elevations. As forests recovered from the ravages imposed by European immigrant settlers, their consumptive uses undoubtedly increased, and more water evaporated from their thickened canopies. But that, in the USFS view, was as it should be.

In this heated context, in mid-March 2002 the Intermountain Region Office of the Forest Service released a policy statement on the matter (USDA Forest Service 2002). The statement provided a region-wide response to water users in the several states in language that was as specific as the agency wanted it to be.

First, the USFS team pointed out that the primary influences on water yields are precipitation, elevation, snowmelt patterns, and size of drainage areas. Of these, the most important is quantity of precipitation. In the short run, precipitation is highly variable, but it has tended to be constant over the long run. Therefore, any solution for the states must be found primarily in precipitation patterns and other factors well beyond the control of the U.S. Forest Service.

Second, it is true that in the context of smaller watersheds more amenable to study, clearing out forest cover does, in fact, increase water yield. Yields increase with little regard for any particular silvicultural design. However, it takes a large percentage (25% or more) of vegetation removal all at once to achieve barely measurable on-site water yield increases. Perhaps lesser percentages would produce measurable net water gain if the watershed under treatment is large enough. In general, it is neither feasible nor defensible to undertake large vegetation removals because of considerations regarding a variety of matters, such as law (multiple use mandates), practical budget limits, and biologically driven needs to maintain and restore aquatic ecosystems.

Within a year, the USFS advanced another argument, a logical-legal one. The USFWS, the agency contended, is mandated to review proposed actions. But an agency taking "no action"—even if that non-action permitted national forest vegetation to thicken and thereby increased depletions to river flows—was not subject to ESA Section 7 consultations. Simply put, non-actions cannot require a USFWS Section 7 review. This rule has been applied to state actors whose non-actions have been allowed to cumulatively "trash rivers." What causes an entity to have to undergo an ESA Section 7 review is a proposed action—seeking to do something that will involve the promoter in a relationship with the ESA. According to the U.S. Forest Service, the agency does not trash rivers, but what applies to state actors applies to the USFS as well. Changes to the water yield of federally managed forested landscapes resulting from natural variability of forest conditions are consequences of non-actions. Any depletions associated with this natural variability are not proper subjects for USFWS review. (Note: water user and state representatives viewed this argument with deep skepticism; they noted that the U.S. Tenth Circuit Court of Appeals, in its dismissal of the Wyoming Coalition for Sustainable Resources case because of its lack of ripeness, also acknowledged that "administrative inaction" may—under specific circumstances—be grounds for court review [Coalition for Sustainable Resources 2001: 6]).

The talks stalemated. They continued in sporadic and backstage venues but were not revived in a sustained manner until 2005 and 2006. They were again undertaken less because there were newly apparent solutions acceptable to the contending parties than because the regulatory process was pushing talks toward a make-or-break deal. The players needed to find a passable solution, at least for the first years of any habitat recovery program. A succession of draft federal future depletions plans was offered for review, but they all dodged the outstanding issues. Mishandling these plans could arouse fierce opposition to any proposed basin-wide habitat recovery program among water users, environmentalists, or both.

WALKING A HIGH WIRE

The politics of the situation were troubling. While the states were pushing, on behalf of their water user constituents, for U.S. Forest Service commitments to produce more stream flow, environmentalists were vociferous in their stand against logging national forests for water (Kassen 2000). The USFWS could not impose policy change on the U.S. Forest Service; that agency, in turn, could not be responsive to the USFWS, the states, or environmentalists. First, was it wise or even defensible to develop a national forest water policy on the Platte? Second, during the Clinton administration, in the late 1990s, policy emphasized shutting down forest roads while managing for scenic and recreational values—hardly the recipe for thinning forest vegetation. Later, after the turn of the twenty-first century, the Bush administration—in the wake of extraordinary large and intense fires across the West—touted its "healthy forest" initiative. The initiative was generally endorsed by water users, but many environmentalists viewed it as little more than political cover for opening forest assets to the pillaging of commercial loggers. On one hand, the parties were deeply "dug in" in defense of their respective positions, even well into 2005–2006. On the other hand, each party could see danger in clinging rigidly to its stance. Each had to negotiate a high-wire act.

States on the High Wire

Representatives of the states could not let the issue die. To do so would mean losing credibility with their water provider constituents, the three basin state governors, and the state legislative assemblies. Politically and technically, state water constituency proposals for thinning timber and other vegetation (Bucholz 1999; Leaf 1999a, 1999b) had to be kept on the table for at least two reasons: they kept pressure on the federal community at the negotiating table, and their presence mollified activist water user critics. There was simply no way the states could allow the U.S. Forest Service to hold itself above the entire Platte River Habitat Recovery Program negotiating process while it was perceived to be slowly eroding basin base flows.

On the other hand, there was great danger to the states' water agendas if their representatives pushed too hard. The states did not have the political power to compel the U.S. Forest Service to change its vegetation management policies in the direction they would have preferred. But if the agency became greatly pressured on the issue, it would have two options to increase forest water yields. First, it could actually find merit in the states' proposals and proceed to do what the states would define as the appropriate thinning—an unlikely prospect. A second, much more probable and frightening possibility was that the USFS would simply agree to measure its depletions at forest boundaries, as requested, and then obtain the water it needed to cover its future depletions by "extorting" it from the water providers when they came—hats in hand—seeking permit renewals for their facilities on national forest lands. The price of a renewed permit would then become increased bypass flows through water user facilities and the consequent loss of water project yields. In such a scenario, water users would become party to "shooting themselves in their own feet."

The USFWS on the High Wire

The USFWS, a creature of the Department of the Interior, was not eager to engage in any more fights with any entities. Its limited resources were stretched by tending to the negotiations as they were. Least of all, it did not want to push a struggle with the U.S. Forest Service, a unit of the Department of Agriculture. Some state participants in the Platte River negotiations expected the USFWS to compel the Forest Service to participate in the habitat recovery program, but the law contained no grounds to support such a move. But in the USFWS's perspective, a terrible scenario loomed as a nontrivial probability. The states would push hard in the political arena to advance their claim that the agency should participate in the program and come up with offset water by making changes in its vegetative management. The USFS's reply would be no. If the issue escalated and began to involve members of the U.S. Congress, senior political decision makers in the Department of the Interior could find themselves under pressure to call for the USFS to join the recovery program negotiations. The Forest Service could again be expected to say no. The issue would then escalate to the U.S. Department of Justice. An extremely sensitive, politically charged, critical issue would be addressed by policy makers in the bureaucracy's political echelon, far removed from the specifics of future habitat restoration programs. Did the USFWS feel comfortable with that possibility? Again, the answer was no.

What could the USFWS actually do to sanction the USFS for noncompliance with the ESA, if it ever came to that? The USFWS would assert some version of an ESA national forest water depletions review criterion. What would that criterion look like? Would it be constructed around holding national forest depletions constant compared to a baseline? What would the national implications be? What would all this imply for forest policy and recovery of salmon in the Pacific Northwest? What would it imply for state and private forests? Such questions were overwhelming. The key to moving ahead with the Platte Basin negotiations was to avoid escalating the tangle of scary issues.

USFWS leaders exerted themselves to encourage informal discussions with forest supervisors and the regional forester. The trick would be to include the states' timber management perspective (Bucholz 1999; Leaf 1999a, 1999b) while not driving away environmentalists who were deeply disturbed by that perspective and to secure the USFS's attention—not as participants in but as observers of the process. If the agency's attention could be sustained, meaningful backchannel discussion could possibly take place. Therefore, in mid-2000 the appropriate USFS authorities were invited to attend all Water Committee and Governance Committee sessions. Forest Service personnel did begin to attend the sessions, especially the water program manager in the regional supervisor's office. The USFS's intent was to keep the problems from escalating beyond basin boundaries.

Therefore, on the one hand, the USFWS was doing what it could to defuse the potentially explosive situation by trying to involve the USFS in the Platte

Basin talks. This required a gentle touch regarding inter-departmental and inter-agency relationships. On the other hand, the USFWS was in a logically difficult position. If the agency were to temporize with the USFS by not adequately looking at the 1997 flow situation, if not pre-1997 historical depletions; if USFS management produced increased consumptive uses in watersheds; and if the states' water contributions were held constant over time, Platte Basin stream flows would slowly erode. To permit this to continue would be tantamount to admitting that target flow commitments could be eroded. Deficiencies to target flows were what had justified the agency's series of jeopardy biological opinions. To ignore erosion of the baseline would be to admit that the analyses in the Platte River biological opinions were not so sacred after all. The USFWS would not want to send such a signal.

Environmentalists on the High Wire

Environmentalists were clearly in favor of proper vegetation management practices and believed appropriately designed selective cutting would produce increased forest water yields. Such base flow enhancements would be welcome in the basin's streams, even if they could not be easily measured or disentangled from the various state uses. On the other hand, environmentalists were strongly opposed to state water providers' attempts to count any such accretions as reducing their commitment to produce a net increase of shortage reduction in the range of 130,000 to 150,000 acre feet per year.

Yet this was exactly what the states were proposing to do. The states wanted "reformed" USFS vegetation practices to generate forest water yields as a substitute for an unknown fraction of water provider contribution. That was what the 1999 Coalition for Sustainable Resources lawsuit, filed in the U.S. District Court in Cheyenne, Wyoming, was all about. That was what the representatives of state water providers were promoting with gusto.

At a time when no one could predict the outcome of the Wyoming lawsuit or foresee how the U.S. Tenth Circuit Court of Appeals would rule, the states were pushing hard to get the U.S. Forest Service into the business of what many environmentalists called "logging for water"—an environmentalist-coined term of derision (Kassen 2000). The term carried heavy connotations of carelessly designed, crudely implemented clear-cutting. Environmentalists who had taken the risk of participating in the basin-wide negotiations (Environmental Defense, the Audubon Society, the Whooping Crane Trust) were already under critical fire from more radical voices in the movement who contended that the participants had "sold out" to a fundamentally flawed negotiating process (Echeverria 2001). If somehow the national forest watershed lands along the Rocky Mountain Eastern slope were "logged for water" to reduce the burden on water providers that needed federal permits and if moderate environmentalists at the negotiating table signed off on such a deal, it would be a disaster for them. Their constituencies would be seriously alienated. If state negotiators gave their constituencies what they wanted—enhanced national forest water yields produced by timber thinning, with the promise written up front in the program agreement—moderate environmentalists would have little recourse but to abandon the talks and mobilize their constituencies against such proposals. Years of promising work on Platte habitat recovery would be reduced to shambles.

For several years following the formulation of the 1997 Cooperative Agreement, the states and water users tended to be decidedly unsympathetic to the environmentalists' plight. A common refrain of several water user spokespersons was something along the lines of this: environmentalists are now experiencing what the states have experienced all along; their constituents do not like what the program is—or should be—proposing. They must do what the states have been compelled to do—namely, educate their publics about national forest management history and potential. We cannot let the environmentalists off the hook just because some so-called environmental priorities have created a big stream depletion problem that is hurting everybody, including the ESA listed species in Nebraska.

Discussions of the matter were episodic and unproductive. As time went by, the states could see wisdom in not pushing too hard on the issue. By mid-2000 it was clear that they had failed to get a highly resistant USFS to commit to contributing to their water action plan; by 2002 it was clear that the Wyoming lawsuit centering on Medicine Bow was going nowhere, at least in the short term. Furthermore, there was the disturbing prospect of disaffected moderate environmentalists walking out of the negotiations and preparing to take their case to court. That would likely be costly and time-consuming—not a happy prospect for water providers that needed the relief from jeopardy a successful habitat recovery program could provide.

In this context, the states and environmentalists came to see prospects for finding common ground. It was agreed that there were sometimes compelling political reasons for taking a proposal off the table, such as the proposal to put enhanced forest accretions directly into the water supply plans. Colorado could not abide the thought of putting water from Beebe Draw into a water action plan (see Chapter 9). Likewise, Nebraska could not accept Colorado money for producing program water on Colorado's behalf at any site close to critical habitat. Now that environmentalists were sweating about "logging for water" as a program activity, the states could accept the idea of becoming more flexible with environmentalists. Although that thought was advanced in the spirit of fair play, the states' willingness to back off a little was not entirely altruistic. Water users had come to appreciate the problematic implications of pushing for enhanced water yields from national forest watersheds. The USFS had the potential to

295

squeeze its needed depletions offset water directly out of water providers at times of permit review.

THE LITTLE LEVER OF SMALL DEPLETIONS

With the signing of the 1997 Cooperative Agreement, it was understood that federal agencies would have their historical pre–July 1, 1997, depletions grandfathered in along with state users. Federal agencies had diversion rights for virtually no water, and therefore—with the possible exception of revised national forest vegetation management on behalf of increased yields—they possessed none to contribute to a reduction of shortages to USFWS target flows. But the U.S. government had secured its place at the depletions offset table by having agreed to fund 50 percent of the recovery program's cost.

The basic concept was simple. A federal agency imposing a depletion would have a choice: it could replace the new depletion by retiring an equivalent federal one, or it could pay the appropriate state provisioner of offset water to produce the needed quantity at the appropriate time and place. Two central principles would guide such efforts: (1) any arrangement must avoid diminishing program water supplies, and (2) state depletions plan projects must be protected. As each federal project is planned, a National Environmental Policy Act (NEPA) review will occur in the form of an environmental impact statement or assessment. Therefore, all parties can be assured that there will be open and detailed discussion of each new federal activity as the years go by.

In late 2001, the USFWS contacted all federal entities that could conceivably impose depletions to Platte Basin stream flows and held a workshop with their representatives. Each organization provided a description of possible post–June 30, 1997 depletions. The USFS attended the session and asserted its view that vegetation management was not a depletions issue but agreed to consider potential depletions under its forest-planning processes and to consult with the USFWS on a case-by-case basis.

The key question became, how much future stream flow depletion would the federal government want to cover? How high would the cap on federal agency depletions be set? Based on the information gathered at the federal depletions workshop, by 2004–2005, USFWS analysts had settled on a number. The cap would be established at 1,050 acre feet per year. The cooperative habitat recovery program—with assistance from state authorities to find appropriate suppliers—would be expected to offset post–June 30, 1997, federal depletions up to that amount. Divided equally among the three states, federal depletions would be offset in each state up to 350 acre feet per annum. Any future federal project that would impose a depletion greater than the amount available under the appropriate state cap would have to seek offset water from sources other than the habitat recovery program.

By April and May 2005, the long standoff between the states and the U.S. Forest Service had reached a critical point. It was past the time to get on with production of the final environmental impact statement (FEIS)—to be followed by a final biological opinion (FBO)—but the entire process was being held hostage to several regime-of-the-river issues, including this one. The federal agenda, led by the USFWS, was to get all depletions plans (particularly the federal plan) into a final form that could be endorsed by all parties. Then it would be possible to move ahead with the required analysis in support of the FEIS and the FBO.

The states' agenda, led by the Colorado team, was to use the opportunity presented by the federal need for small depletions offset water to push for resolution of the USFS's vegetation management. The states linked the two issues and employed the 350-acre-foot/year depletions coverage to compel the USFWS and the Forest Service to discuss national forest depletions to water yield.

THE STATES' REFRAIN: We cannot just do recharge downstream for a federal habitat recovery program while the U.S. Forest Service depletes watersheds upstream.

USFWS REPLY: It is not feasible to force a major legal battle on a major national policy issue by manipulating language in a proposed program document. Furthermore, it is not appropriate to try to address an issue of national policy by attempting to pressure the offices of a forest supervisor or a regional forester.

STATES' REPLY: We disagree with the USFWS's inclination to allow the U.S. Forest Service to address vegetation management depletions independent of the recovery program. Colorado is now working with the USFS at the Region 2 Level (Denver). Resolution of the issue must occur before Colorado will accept the federal depletions plan.

USFWS REPLY: It is too late in the negotiations to once again bring up this issue and attempt to resolve it. The federal request for 350 acre feet of offset water from each state must be divorced from the inter-agency issue.

HIGH-WIRE DANCING TOGETHER

Bring on Science

All parties at the table recognized their common need for an analytically defensible database from which to better inform their discussions. After years of hearing the pleas of state water users, the USFWS and the regional forester—also headquartered in Lakewood, Colorado—agreed to undertake a study in 2006, the last year of talks (Cables 2005). The U.S. Forest Service had used earlier studies to make its case that potential gains from any type of responsible timber management would be neutral to modestly positive (USDA Forest Service 2004: 1–5). But the studies (Troendle and Nankervis 2000; Troendle, Nankervis, and

Porth 2003) on which the Forest Service had staked its claims were limited to the North Platte Basin. No comparable systematic studies had been conducted on the South Platte.

Therefore, during the course of 2006, with the active support of the USFS and the USFWS, a study was undertaken designed to replicate the methodology of the earlier North Platte Basin research (Troendle, Nankervis, and Peavy 2007). Historical forest timber-stand conditions from 1860 through the present and projections to 2060 were modeled, along with their attendant water yield simulations. Vegetation stands were then analytically moved in and out of various age categories over time in the same manner that had been accomplished in the North Platte Basin studies. Various combinations of human intervention and natural disturbance conditions (fire and insects) were examined. The objective was to determine "potential changes in water yield that may have, or might occur as a result of past or proposed activities that alter vegetation composition or density" (Troendle, Nankervis, and Peavy 2007: 3).

Water yields in the national forest watersheds of the South Platte were found to have been the greatest around 1920 and to have declined in proportion to increases in vegetation density. The states found vindication in this fact. Yet the net reduction in water yield from the three forests of the South Platte Basin watersheds from 1920 to 1997 was only about 1.8 area inches—about 260,000 acre feet from 1.7 million acres of national forest land. As current timber stands mature, water yield from national forest lands can be expected to decline another 0.5 area inch (about 72,000 acre feet) by 2060 if current vegetation density is not interrupted by active management or by a natural catastrophe, such as increased fire or major insect infestations. However, in both the North and South Platte Basins, the process of producing water is cyclical. As stands mature, water yields decline; as stands lose density to harvesting, insects, disease, or fire, water yields are enhanced. Fundamentally, any enhancement of water yields from forest-thinning practices would likely be modest (Stednick 2008: 3–7; Troendle, Nankervis, and Peavy 2007: 3).

A major insect infestation under way at the time—that of the pine bark beetle—had been thinning stands across Colorado, nearby states, and Canada for roughly a decade. The potential effects—especially in lodgepole pine stands—may be far more extensive and significant in their impact on water yield than even those of fire: "Mortality from the current mountain pine beetle infestation may recapture much of the decline in water yield caused by growth or re-growth of forest stands over the past 80–90 years" (Troendle, Nankervis, and Peavy 2007: 3). In the decade and a half since 1996, the pine beetle infestation has significantly killed timber on about 1.5 million acres of Colorado and Wyoming forested land and by 2006 was moving to Eastern slope lands of the Rocky Mountain Front Range in those two states (Pankratz 2008: 1A, 10A). Thanks to a bug and its capacity to reproduce and spread in mature, even-aged forest stands weakened by extended drought and a series of warm winters, the threat to the 1997 forest water yield baseline might be greatly reduced.

Fires Cool the Conflict

There was also the consideration that larger, hotter, and more frequent fires thin forests. Stephen Pyne (2001) has chronicled the intensely active 1910 fire season. The devastation that summer fundamentally shaped USFS fire policy throughout the twentieth century, which centered on an all-out effort to fight virtually all fires within the agency's domain. However, in suppressing wildfires, the USFS was simultaneously throttling one of Mother Nature's greatest janitors (Hessel and Lemaster 2007: 24–26; Matthews 2001: 1, 11).

In the wake of twentieth-century fire suppression, in the post–World War II era a steady flow of people and their homes penetrated forested landscapes adjacent to national forests. Accumulating fuel loads could then, under the right climate conditions (heat and drought), produce hot mega-fires that jumped from thick "dog-hair" sapling stands to the tops of the oldest and tallest timber, moved speedily though forest crowns, and reached the temperatures of a Bessemer furnace—sufficient to melt glass bottles and steel culverts. The fires could also scald and seal topsoils. In general, the more extreme the forest floor fuels overload, the less extreme the climate has to be to trigger super-hot mega-fires. In the human political economy–national forest interface, fire managers lost their capacity to simply allow wildfires to do their natural forest density janitorial cleanup work.

The fire problem at its core is a land-use management problem. Humans—with too little knowledge of how to live in a natural wildfire environment—have built entire local economies around people living, doing business, and recreating in highly fire-prone environments. Individual self-seeking rationality, abetted by county commissioners seeking enhanced tax bases, has caused housing and commerce to be located in dangerous areas. Thousands of individually rational acts have thereby combined to produce a major collective problem. Therefore, controlled burns and other fuel management practices have become deeply problematic in many places. The mismanagement of fire, forests, and land use and the causes and effects of mega-fires constitute a story much too complex to be captured in these pages. That story has been addressed elsewhere (Elliot et al. 2004; Goudie 1986: 26–36; Hessel and Lemaster 2007; MacDonald, Stednick, and Troendle 2003; Running 2006; Veblen et al. 2003; Westerling et al. 2006).

Fire management policy was never the direct and sustained focus of the Platte Basin habitat recovery negotiations, but the implications of the increased frequency of hot mega-fires were significant. The simple reduction of forest biomass (as proposed by the Bush administration's Healthy Forest Initiative) would probably be insufficient for reducing the risk of large-scale hot fires (Westerling et al. 2006). Furthermore, the USFS cannot be expected to control global warming dynamics that may be part of the problem. Environmentalists, water providers, and the USFS could find common ground, however, with which to address the issue of thickening forest vegetation. Given the hot fires and pine bark beetle devastation, everyone could see merit in thinning the national forest vegetation.

THE DEAL

There had been little room to negotiate. U.S. Forest Service representatives did not agree with premises advanced by the states; the states could not accept those advanced by the USFS. Yet the regulatory process needed to grind habitat recovery program grist. The results had to be reported in a final environmental impact statement and biological opinion. For this to occur, there had to be a final program proposal document. For that document to be complete, there had to be a federal depletions plan. For there to be such a plan, a deal had to be reached.

A team of Colorado representatives had taken the lead in a series of conversations (during 2005 through autumn 2006) with the U.S. Forest Service, especially at the level of the regional forester in Denver. Until late 2006, members from both sides viewed the talks as unproductive.

Somehow, the states and the U.S. Forest Service would have to find a way to agree to disagree and to do so in a manner that would permit the adversaries to move ahead without having their heads handed to them by their respective constituencies. If the discussion were able to proceed with reduced rancor, then there was a small amount of common ground on which to construct at least a limited agreement.

The adversaries agreed to disagree about the proper obligations of the U.S. Forest Service in the matter of vegetation management and water yields. Given political space by credible scientific analysis, which suggested that the stakes were not as large as some had thought and that fire and insects would be thinning timber on a scale not previously contemplated, the adversaries agreed to undertake further inquiry and conduct focused discussion during the first program increment. When the USFWS again raises the issue of water requirements for habitat recovery for the second increment (slated to begin in 2020), all parties agreed that they needed to make that future conversation solidly based on data.

Resolution of the conflict came in three parts. First, a disclaimer was inserted at the beginning of the federal depletions plan (*Platte River Recovery Program* 2006: attachment 5, section 10, pp. 2–3): "This plan does not address 'the impacts . . . of past and future management' by the U.S. Forest Service (USFS) in the Platte River Basin. Such impacts will [be] the subject of further research and analysis during the First Increment of the Program." Then, in footnote one on the same two pages: "It is the position of the Forest Service that changes to water yield from forested landscapes resulting from the natural variability of the forest conditions are not federal actions and do not constitute depletions that require consultation under Section 7(a)(2) or any other provisions of the Endangered Species Act. Several entities represented on the Governance Committee do not agree with this position taken by the Forest Service."

Second, all parties understood that under the existing provisions of the ESA, new forest management plans are subject to ESA Section 7 consultations. It can be reasonably expected that the USFWS will examine any newly proposed plan with an eye toward assessing its impacts on basin stream depletions and thereby on shortages to target flows, as well as possible harm to pulse flows. Nobody could know with certainty where the next ten to thirteen years would take them on their voyage of habitat restoration discovery, but they could count on one thing: as long as the ESA remained intact, the USFWS would have its sequence of Platte Basin biological opinions to defend. If those opinions retained their integrity, the agency would have to be alert to stop any significant diminishment of the 1997 flow baseline from any source—even the USFS.

Third, the regional forester had made explicit commitments to the recovery program in a letter that had been the subject of much discussion and been re-peatedly re-drafted during the months prior to its release (Cables 2005). The let-ter, dated December 2, 2005, reflected the then-current status of the USFS-state negotiations. In it, the regional forester reiterated a long-standing agency point: the long-term sustainable solution to the stalemate in the negotiations was to be found in aggressively managing federal forestlands in ways that promoted healthy forest conditions consistent with the National Forest Management Act. Healthy forests capture and release water over time in ways that best serve soci-ety. The Forest Service Regional Administration would:

1. Actively participate in implementation of the Federal Depletions Plan, and consult separately on any depletions which are not covered by the Federal Depletions Plan.

2. Track Forest Service vegetation management activities (timber harvest and fuels treatment) in the Platte River Basin on an annual basis. Analyze changes to water yield from these activities on a five-year basis, or more frequently if needed to evaluate effectiveness of the first increment of the Recovery Program.

3. Conduct an analysis for the South Platte Basin parallel to the May 2003 report "Impact of Forest Service Activities on the Streamflow Regime in the Platte River" (Troendle, Nankervis, and Porth). [Author's note: This study was, in fact, completed by early 2007; see Troendle, Nankervis, and Peavy 2007. This study, in draft form, informed negotiations in the fall of 2006, as discussed earlier.]

4. Conduct a renewed basin-wide analysis of water yield . . . using the most currently available vegetation data, at least once in twenty years or one year prior [to] the end of the first increment, whichever occurs first, or as may be

agreed to in writing. . . . In addition, this analysis will include a comparison with the 1997 water yields modeled in the May 2003 report by Troendle, Nankervis, and Porth, and in the report from item 3 (above), and a projection into the future for at least one program increment.

5. Analyze the predicted changes in water yield from the 2003 North Platte Study and the planned 2006 South Platte Study to determine when the simulated effects of the forest regrowth, if actualized, would be reflected in stream gage [sic] data, using the references gages [sic] identified in Troendle et al. 2003.

6. Ensure that the reference stream flow and precipitation monitoring sites identified in Troendle et al. (2003) remain in operation.

7. Provide support to the National Academies of Science study titled "The Hydrologic Impacts of Forest Management," which has been contracted by the Department of [the] Interior. [Author's note: Frustrated by the stalemated talks, the states, led by Colorado, pushed hard to reframe the negotiations by calling for research on the relationship between forest vegetation management and water yields to be conducted by a disinterested party—specifically, the National Academies of Science/National Research Council. The assembled investigating committee met and received its charge on March 22, 2006, at the Mirage Hotel in Las Vegas, Nevada. For details, see www8.nationalacademies.org/cp/project viewaspx?Key=1935.]

8. Work on an ongoing basis with the [program] Water Management Committee to determine what additional studies may be needed to inform these issues, and develop appropriate timeframes for funding, contracting, and completing any needed studies. (Cables 2005)

So by late 2005 a deal had been struck that permitted each party to hold on tightly to its essential position. The U.S. Forest Service had avoided joining the program and overtly taking responsibility for any net forest depletions that could be traced back to its landscape management practices. The agency thereby ducked challenging regional and national policy problems that could not be properly resolved at the Platte River Basin level. The states kept the issue alive and securely riveted to the habitat recovery program agenda. Most of all, they had created grounds for future data-based discourse such that if the USFWS came seeking additional state water contributions as a result of declines in the 1997 regime of the river, the federal community would have to take a hard look at any depletions imposed by U.S. Forest Service vegetation management. That future conversation will be informed by studies opened to independent peer review. States and their water providers had thereby girded themselves with a defense against what they viewed as unjust federal extraction of their waters. Environmentalists were saved from having to associate themselves with a habitat recovery program that would engage in "logging for water." A legal-political problem with potentially major implications for the future of the basin, the nation, and the habitat recovery program had been converted into a research and information-sharing problem.

POSTSCRIPT: REGIME OF THE RIVER AND DEPLETIONS PLANS

In the early days of the negotiations, some had thought that the states could collaborate, put their depletions plans together, and then approach the negotiations with the federal community with at least a measure of solidarity. However, the states' respective political economies of water were so different that they could do little more than refrain from openly saying "no evil" about another's depletions plan. Even that was not possible when Nebraska wanted to closely critique Wyoming's and Colorado's plans.

Each state's plan was importantly unique. Colorado's plan was designed to protect all water providers within the South Platte Basin, including new users who can be accommodated within limits. In Colorado, users are "in" unless declared "out." Wyoming, given constraints imposed by the *Nebraska v. Wyoming* settlement, covers only North Platte existing water users as of June 30, 1997. After that, new users are "out" unless declared "in." Nebraska's depletions offset programs cover western and central Platte water providers above the mouth of the Elkhorn. Below that point, new users have to enter into other negotiations and undertake appropriately designed programs to provide the necessary replacement water to the river system.

The state depletions plans did reflect some common principles. All depletions plans are implemented within the state where depletions have occurred and will occur. Water yields of future (after mid-1997) depletions plans will not count toward the recovery program's first increment historical (prior to mid-1997) reductions in shortages to target flows, as those yields must mitigate only new water uses. This is a roundabout way of saying that water replacements cannot be counted twice. Responsibility for tracking and protecting program offset waters rests with each state's water administration. No state can track a given acre foot of water through sequences of diversions, uses, and return flows over hundreds of miles. They can, however, calculate consumptive uses and reductions in return flows and provide sufficient offset flows at the respective state lines or, in Nebraska's case, just above the critical habitat.

The federal depletions plan provides ESA coverage for a maximum of 1,050 acre feet per year of new federal depletions between July 1, 1997, and the end of the first program increment. Reductions in flows will be quantified by state administrations at the appropriate points. Each state has agreed to assist the USFWS and cooperating federal agencies in securing up to 350 acre feet per year to offset federal depletions in the state in which the depletion occurred. Each federal agency will fund the costs of supplying the necessary offset water.

Federal agencies must always take their depletions plan waters from sources of state-produced offset water for new depletions. Such water must not come from sources designed to reduce shortages to USFWS target flows.

Regime of the River

Inserting Pulse Flows

Impounded water made it possible to build a civilization that required the capture of spring flood peaks and other pulses so they could be distributed across time and space for intensified agricultural production and to fulfill urban demand. But prior to dam building, unconstrained rushing floodwaters had determined the geomorphology of the basin and the diversity of its wildlife habitats. Although the states did not agree, to the U.S. Fish and Wildlife Service (USFWS) riverine habitat restoration meant at least a modest insertion of pulse flows with the objective of scouring vegetation and redistributing sediment to help maintain a shallow, wide, braided river as habitat.

The USFWS doggedly pursued a goal of preserving some remnants of peak flows on the South Platte below the dams upstream of Denver and of reintroducing program-managed pulse flows on the central Platte segment of the river designated as critical habitat. The agency had conducted technical workshops in March and May 1994 (Bowman 1994; Bowman and Carlson 1994) that identified peak and pulse flows as top priorities for habitat restoration. The states had reacted negatively. The entire set of concepts was found to be unacceptable; the states seriously threatened to abandon the talks rather than endorse any part of the agency's vision on the matter. This fight took place within the context of the bitter struggle over target flows and land for habitat. The agency then determined to pull back its in-stream flow analyses and recommendations (Bowman 1994; Bowman and Carlson 1994); by so doing, it temporarily defused some of the conflict.

The USFWS then proceeded to center the troubled conversation on its target flow logic and eventually worked out an arrangement for reducing shortages to target flows from 417,000 to 130,000–150,000 acre feet per year. The first increment habitat land commitment was also reduced, from 29,000 acres to 10,000. By making these two compromises and taking pulse flow issues off the table, the agency had saved the negotiations. The 1997 Cooperative Agreement could then be completed.

In 2002 the issue of in-stream, peak, and pulse flows resurfaced (U.S. Fish and Wildlife Service 2002a), much to the consternation of the states and their water providers. During the worst drought year, irrigation water took up all of the channel's carrying capacity at a stretch near the city of North Platte, and the USFWS could not find room for its environmental account (EA) flows. It was one thing for the states to agree to deliver 130,000–150,000 acre feet of aggregate shortage reductions to target flows over the course of a year and receive program compliance credit, but it was quite another to send water downstream in pulses at particular times in specific river conditions. Building a pulse with EA water and little help from Mother Nature could be quite a job. Furthermore, the states knew that whereas reduction in shortages to target flows was an empirically measurable phenomenon, adequacy of pulse flows had no similar independently verifiable measurement of goal achievement. Furthermore, no one knew what the birds really needed. That which one management team found acceptable at a given time could be altered by another. The states—never enamored of the USFWS natural flow (river processes) vision and holding tight to their defined contribution perspective—looked at agency plans with deep, undisguised skepticism.

The states refused to endorse the USFWS's natural flow concepts. In the final program document, produced in 2006, the states inserted language noting that "[t]he states have not agreed that peak flow 'pulses' or other FWS identified flows are biologically or hydrologically necessary to benefit or recover the listed species" (*Platte River Recovery Program* 2006: 11). Given the clash of river visions (see Chapter 18), any pulse flow conversation was going to be difficult. There were also other problems.

In the early years of negotiations under Central Nebraska Public Power and Irrigation District (CNPPID) and Nebraska Public Power District (NPPD) Federal Energy Regulatory Commission (FERC) re-licensing auspices, the USFWS faced an enormous problem. How could it grasp the complexities of a large-scale basin-wide recovery program for three birds and a fish within the context of a three-state complex of rivers, canals, reservoirs, and power plants? The situation was mind-numbing. Yet the USFWS would have to lead the way to a proposed FERC re-licensing about which the agency would have to write a defensible biological opinion (BO). Then there would be another BO about the more encompassing three-state Platte River Habitat Recovery Program that was on the horizon. But in the late 1980s and early 1990s, no one could pretend to be sufficiently all-knowing that it would be possible to write a specific action program for each of the listed species that would minimally reflect the opportunities and constraints of the three states' water systems. That would also be true for the immediately impinging FERC discussions.

Players on all sides cast about for ways to develop an approach to building a habitat recovery program under the FERC umbrella that would be both meaningful and sensible. Finally, a significant organizing concept was advanced by the Nebraska Department of Natural Resources, under the administration of Governor Ben Nelson: install an EA at Lake McConaughy and send water to the critical habitat. It would be labeled the Nebraska Plan—a bold stroke that cut through the morass of complexity that had negotiations tied in knots.

There were two problems, however. After installing the EA at Lake McConaughy in the wake of the FERC deal, it would be up to negotiators to figure out how to actually use the EA water on behalf of the listed bird species. That reality, in turn, entrained another problem. As soon as the CNPPID and the NPPD secured their renewed licenses (1998), other negotiators at the Platte River table—especially the USFWS and environmentalists—would lose significant leverage in extracting additional concessions from the two Nebraska districts, which would have every incentive to defend their FERC arrangement and to move beyond it as little as possible. The FERC deal set a template for the two Nebraska districts that would be hard to break and re-design because any FERC re-licensing reopener would be costly in time and money. The Nebraska Plan was bold in concept, but it had to be implemented using the plumbing of two districts that had not agreed to any implementation specifics and, further, whose capacities to impose their terms on the Platte River negotiators would be markedly enhanced as soon as their 1998 FERC deal was finalized.

In endorsing the FERC re-licensing deal, the USFWS had traded away any opportunity to do river restoration above Lexington, Nebraska, back up toward Lake McConaughy or downstream below Chapman. It had placed its habitat restoration hopes on one seventy-mile-long river channel basket. The USFWS therefore had determined to place heavy emphasis on making its variable flow river processes vision work there. For their part, the states and their water providers did not want to be dragged into any discourse that would further diminish states' control over their water agendas. They had never accepted the USFWS's target flow logic, and they certainly did not want to venture into territory beyond the compromise they had already reluctantly accepted: reduction of target flow shortages and the 10,000-acre commitment for habitat. They did not want to get involved in any negotiation of program commitments affecting the Platte between Kingsley Dam and the critical habitat.

THE ENVIRONMENTAL ACCOUNT

The NPPD and the CNPPID received their FERC licenses on July 29, 1998. By the end of September of that year, as stipulated by the FERC deal, the CNPPID had entered into an agreement to install an EA at Lake McConaughy. The contract specified conditions for storage and release of that EA water (*Platte River Recovery Program* 2006: attachment 5, section 5, pp. 1–14).

At its core, the agreement provided that at the end of each month from October through April, the EA will be credited with 10 percent of the storable natural inflows to Lake McConaughy up to an annual limit of 100,000 acre feet. The total quantity in the EA may never exceed 200,000 acre feet. Water flows will be measured by the Nebraska Department of Natural Resources. Regardless of the source, the water entering the EA loses any separate identity. Water may be carried over from one year to another, subject to certain constraints. Contributions to the EA will be protected from either the appropriate state line or, within Nebraska, from the source to Lake McConaughy. Nebraska water user contributions to the account were made contingent on flows upstream remaining representative of the 1997 regime of the river.

The FERC re-licensing agreement provided for an EA manager. This person, an employee of the USFWS, was granted authority to request releases from the EA from the CNPPID and to manage the environmental water asset on behalf of the four target species. Central's role is to deliver the EA water within the rules, just as the provider would serve any other customer. The manager is expected to develop an annual operating plan in conjunction with a committee populated by representatives of the recovery program players—the states, the U.S. Bureau of Reclamation (USBR), the two Nebraska districts (CNPPID and NPPD), and environmentalists. The committee is expected to meet at least twice a year, more frequently if needed. In addition, a Reservoir Coordination Committee was established to advise the EA manager in matters having to do with movement of water in and out of basin storage facilities. The EA manager and the two districts retained their authority to construct their own individual operational plans.

All EA water, or any other program-designated water that passes through Lake McConaughy (or any other program-approved storage facility), can be diverted into project facilities by the districts at their discretion. The districts, in turn, are required to return the environmental water to the river, with replacement of any losses of water in excess of that which the Nebraska Department of Water Resources has determined would otherwise occur if that diverted water had been transported by way of the Platte River system.

EA water is therefore available to be put to as many Nebraska-defined beneficial uses as possible as it moves from an open gate at Kingsley Dam toward the critical habitat. The obvious bad news from an environmental perspective was that program water was to be diverted from river channel in-stream flows; the better news was that Nebraska would replace any losses. In effect, the FERC arrangement traded away minimum in-stream flows and pulse flows in the river stretch below Lake McConaughy and above the critical habitat to obtain the

EA. The USFWS then wanted to concentrate waters as much as possible into in-stream and pulse-making flows that would course through the designated habitat.

THE USFWS'S PULSE VISIONS

Calculating pulse flow requirements for habitat restoration was no simple task. The entire central Platte stream will not respond uniformly to a given quantity of water. Many variables are at play. Most are beyond the control of program management. To name a few, there are matters of the channel cross-section profile, canal diversion and return flow patterns, river gradients, frequency of bridge occurrence (they narrow channels), effects of human bank stabilization projects, variation in riverbed substrate and riverbank soils, type and density of channel vegetation, constraints on availability of EA water, precipitation patterns and associated natural flows on which pulses may ride, and the timing and frequency of large uncontrollable flood peaks. The actual impact of a given program-produced flood pulse will therefore vary significantly from one river segment or time period to another.

The USFWS's goal was to install a habitat recovery program capacity to flexibly mount appropriate pulse surges given prevailing conditions. Pulse flow management would be conducted within a participatory framework established by adaptive management methodologies. The plan meant the creation of short-duration flows with the banks nearly full through the big bend critical habitat stretch. They would be sufficient to reshape and shift most existing sandbars while scouring out annual vegetation growth. The flows were expected to promote the formation of sandbars high enough to maintain and expand roosting habitat free of vegetation, maintain sloughs and backwaters, and support adjacent wetlands and wet meadows. Pulses were to be timed for late winter, prior to the crane migration season, or during late spring to set the table for plover and tern nesting. The USFWS was anxious that sandbars be sufficiently elevated so that plover and least tern nests and fledglings would experience less probability of being washed away by summer rises produced by thunderstorms.

Agency river modelers concluded that desirable things happened when pulses reached a volume of about 8,000 cubic feet per second (cfs) in the habitat reach. If one could employ about 3,000 cfs of non-program water flowing in the channel(s), a program-supplied supplement from the EA of 5,000 cfs for one to three days at the top of the habitat would meaningfully enhance habitat sustenance and restoration (U.S. Department of the Interior, Bureau of Reclamation, and U.S. Fish and Wildlife Service 2006: 3:39–40). Pulse flows would be constructed during times of low irrigation demand (October 1–April 30). In real-world conditions, the target range was estimated to be between 6,000 and 9,000 cfs where full bank capacity was roughly 10,000 cfs (U.S. Department of the

Interior, Bureau of Reclamation, and U.S. Fish and Wildlife Service 2006: 3:39–40). In addition, the USFWS's in-stream flow plan called for a minimum of 800 cfs of continuous flow during summer irrigation season (May 1–September 30) (U.S. Fish and Wildlife Service 2002a). The summer minimum flow was designed to maintain the biotic web on behalf of the least terns and piping plovers.

How would the water move from Lake McConaughy to the top of the critical habitat? There were three primary water sources and two general routes. Water could come from the McConaughy EA on the North Platte River (plus the 34,000-acre-foot EA in Wyoming's Pathfinder Reservoir), from the NPPD Sutherland power plant loop fed by the Korty Canal on the Nebraska South Platte plus the Keystone diversion on the North Platte, and from non-program (CNPPID irrigation and general precipitation) flows and return flows. The EA flows could move as much as possible on top of natural North and South Platte flows supplemented by Colorado Tamarack Plan waters to the top of the critical habitat through either the river channel or CNPPID's canal system. Water re-timed through the canal network would be returned to the river through direct canal releases (Jeffrey, Johnson no. 1, and Johnson no. 2 power plant returns) or in the form of irrigation system seepage and deep percolation returns. It was generally understood that the bulk of the return flows get back to the river by the time flows reach the Kearney area, well above the critical habitat.

There were admittedly huge unknowns in all of this, but the USFWS representatives noted that the faster the proposed habitat recovery program could be put together, the more quickly alternative hypotheses about pulses and their impacts could be tested in adaptive management modes. That would be better for everybody. State water representatives—especially those representing the two Nebraska districts—steadfastly refused to endorse the vision, but the federal regulatory process tugged them along.

CHANNEL CAPACITY

What good was the EA account, and many other recovery program components, if the USFWS could not reliably get that water downstream to the designated habitat? By fall of 2002 the river "choke-point" issue took the Governance Committee negotiations to another in a long series of low points.

The National Weather Service (NWS) announced on September 9, 2002, that it was lowering the definition of flood stage of the North Platte River near the Nebraska city with the same name. Up to that time, the NWS had defined flood stage at 6.0 feet of water flow depth (corresponding to a flow of about 3,800 cfs); the announcement reported a decision to lower the flood stage to 5.7 feet, a level that accommodated about 1,980 cfs (Sato and Associates 2005: 1). In July and August 2001, flows of roughly 3,000 cfs had caused "nuisance flooding" of properties located a short distance upstream of a Nebraska Highway 83 river crossing. There had been another episode in July 2002. At the request of local property owners, NWS personnel visited the site and reported their assessment, which resulted in the lowering of the marker (Sato and Associates 2005: 1–2).

The NWS determination followed an administrative eruption of the channel capacity problem a few months earlier. The summer of 2002 brought the severest drought conditions since European settlement in the basin. Farmers called for their irrigation water sooner, longer, and in greater quantities than during more normal times. Given the limits of channel capacity in the North Platte choke-point stretch, irrigation water took up the full delivery capacity of the river channel. Serving cornfields meant that bird habitat downstream had to do without the benefits of EA water just when it needed that water most. After years of "kicking this can down the road," two developments compelled negotiations over North Platte channel capacity to restart immediately—the NWS flood stage announcement and the fact that EA water was held back in deference to irrigation flows.

There was no joy among the states' representatives in contemplating any of this. In their view, it was bad enough to be compelled to be a party to the construction of program pulses for critical habitat. Now that unwelcome enterprise was engendering a confrontation with problems upstream of that habitat, which, in turn, raised the specter of greater federal intrusion on the river. The states' representatives were contemplating difficulties in selling the habitat recovery program to many of their constituents (especially state legislatures) even under the best of the probable circumstances. To permit federal agencies to dictate river conditions upstream of the critical habitat would add greatly to the political burden. In fact, it could be a showstopper.

In the negotiations leading up to the 1998 FERC-NPPD-CNPPID re-licensing deal, the USFWS secured a major fraction of what would amount to about one complete Kingsley Dam gate flow, approximately 5,700 cfs. Not far downstream, NPPD's Sutherland Canal headgate could be generally expected to divert about 1,800 cfs, leaving around 3,900 cfs of EA water for the main North Platte channel. That water was destined for critical habitat restoration purposes, along with return flows out of NPPID's and CNPPID's systems downstream. But given the National Weather Service's lowering of the North Platte flood stage, what was the point of having up to 3,900 cfs available in the recovery program EA if the manager could not send it downstream in a pulse-building manner?

The lowered flood stage also constrained CNPPID's capacity to send its irrigation water to customers. In the pre-1998 period, when the FERC re-licensing talks were ongoing, no one had imagined such a capacity problem. That meant the USFWS had secured no provision in the arrangement for proportional reductions of flows between CNPPID irrigation water and EA outflows in cases where the river channel filled. EA water would then be held back in deference to irrigation. In addition, the FERC agreement provided that there would be no EA releases that would cause flooding (CNPPID and NPPD 1998). Furthermore, if the state of Nebraska knowingly sanctioned water releases to the river in excess of channel-carrying capacity, it would bear liability.

Two large questions surfaced: (1) what could the CNPPID do to alleviate matters in the immediate future before the habitat program was launched, and (2) what would the habitat recovery program do to fix current problems? The continuation of severe drought eased pressure on the CNPPID to take immediate action. The heavy draw-down of Lake McConaughy in 2002 and subsequent years compelled the district to cut back its irrigation deliveries, thereby leaving space in the choke-point river segment. In addition, the drought-deprived riverbed became so dry at many points that the EA manager stopped attempting to run account water to the critical habitat in futile efforts to maintain minimum stream flows. Pressure to do something immediately on behalf of EA water eased. But how could a longer-term program solution be devised?

Causes

In the fall of 2002, the CNPPID engaged Parsons Engineering Science of Denver to undertake a preliminary assessment of the channel capacity problem in the river reach immediately upstream of North Platte, Nebraska (Lewis and Roerish 2003). The report, made available to the Governance Committee on January 14, 2003, concluded that the capacity of the main channel per se had not significantly diminished since 1991 and therefore did not account for recent flooding problems. In the twelve years preceding the investigation, there had been a recent rapid growth of *Phragmites australis* and purple loosestrife, which did resist and elevate flows. Furthermore, over-bank flow chutes had been blocked by vegetation, and rock crossings installed by people had elevated river flow levels, as had beaver dams. Some drainage chutes downstream had been intentionally blocked by property owners. An artificial drain installed by the state sometime around 1970 had ceased to function because of a lack of maintenance. Finally, large transient sandbars had formed in the main channel and entered new locations, thereby contributing to rising water levels.

The implications were clear and to the states' advantage. If degradation of channel capacity as such could not explain the flooding, the two Nebraska districts—and the three states in general—were not responsible for improving matters. The findings and their implications were not what the USFWS or environmentalists wanted to hear.

Also on January 14, a USBR river modeler reported on another analysis to the Governance Committee negotiators. It was rooted in a then-recent study of the sediment-vegetation problem, as addressed in Chapter 16 (Murphy and Randle 2001). That day's report (Randle 2003) endorsed the points the Parsons engineers had made. However, the USBR analysis took a broader perspective and found that channel capacity began declining in 1952 but that flood flows in 1971 restored some capacity temporarily, as did another flooding episode in 1983. Overall, the picture was one of North Platte River channels cycling up and down over time, but the long-term capacity trend was downward. By the 1990s, near the city of North Platte, the river capacity was in the 1,700–1,900 cfs range.

The report made another point: the North Platte River gauge elevation for flows within a range of plus or minus 20 percent of 2,000 cfs had risen in a linear fashion since 1940, when Kingsley Dam was being completed. Rising riverbed elevations caused constant or even reduced flow volumes to flood. In the years following the closing of the gates at Kingsley, there had been an insufficient volume of flow to carry sediment through the choke-point area (about twelve river miles). Sediments that clear water dam releases had scoured and lifted upstream were dropping out of smaller, slower flows and thereby aggrading the streambed. As the channel bed continues to rise, the river will form new channels through the floodplain. This would pose a long-term threat to the use of the EA, and, in addition, CNPPID could face the necessity of reducing water deliveries to its irrigators in high-demand times.

When the facts of local flooding were placed in this perspective, the USFWS and environmentalists could better compel a conversation about big-picture river processes. Representatives of the three states—especially those of the two Nebraska districts—saw their long-standing fears materialize. This angle of vision placed them directly in the crosshairs of the USFWS's river restoration agenda above the critical habitat.

The States' Case

THE STATES: the National Weather Service waltzes in with a lowered flood stage, and the sky falls. The choke point has been there all along. The USFWS simply did not raise it as an issue during years of negotiations. Now the USFWS is forcing a conversation about a so-called jeopardy issue that emerged during a summer drought like no other. The agency is trying to hold the states hostage to a rare event to push a river recovery program as distinguished from a species recovery program. We do not want a critical habitat recovery effort for the species to mushroom into a river recovery program for an eighty-mile stretch above the critical habitat. That is not what the states signed on to when we committed ourselves to the 1997 Cooperative Agreement.

The proposed program simply cannot do what the USFWS wants it to do— that is, build a "nirvana" for listed birds with pulse flows produced far upstream at Kingsley Dam. There are other, more feasible ways to restore critical habitat. There are many possibilities, and none of us now knows what combination will work best. The agency should take the assets already provided by the negotiated proposed program and go to work. Perhaps the program could use the money available to build a re-regulation reservoir just above the critical habitat (enthusiasm for this idea was centered especially in Wyoming and Colorado). Pulses released from a nearby source would use scarce water much more effectively in creating desired habitat characteristics. Furthermore, there are likely to be opportunities to gather water resources from Nebraska's program of water leasing on lands along the central Platte River close to the habitat; then, no additional channel capacity will be needed at the North Platte stem choke point. Other Nebraska action plan projects will be designed to reduce shortages to target flows that will be located much closer to critical habitat. Their releases to the river will not be constrained by any known choke points. Furthermore, if all this is insufficient to deliver water levels adequate to drive the nesting birds high enough onto sandbars, it would be possible to install variable height check structures in the channel to elevate summer species flows to the desired level. Strategically placed gates, shunting excess flows into side channels, could also possibly protect nesting birds from summer thunderstorm–induced rising waters. The USFWS needs to soften its commitment to its natural flow model and work more creatively with other options.

The federal community has forced this issue in an unwanted replay of the 2000–2001 sediment-vegetation negotiations (see Chapter 16). Those talks were difficult because the USFWS attempted to push the states into taking responsibility for the eighty-mile stretch between Kingsley Dam and the top of the critical habitat. The federal demand, in that context, that the states micro-manage a river segment in private ownership was then unacceptable. Now, in the context of this pulse and species flow conversation, the repetition of the old demand must again be rejected. The states are willing to work with the federal community and environmentalists to make possible productive use of the EA at Lake McConaughy, but any deal must preserve state control over the river.

It is dangerous to allow a discussion of the 8,000 cfs pulse flow figure to occur because it could turn out that flows in the 12,000–17,000 cfs range may be required to build the USFWS required sandbars. Negotiations around the proposed pulse flow figure will start the entire adaptive management process down the wrong road, down the "river processes" path. The agency will always want additional pulse water to create a river that simply cannot be what the USFWS wants it to be.

The USFWS must not ask the states to formally sign on to any natural flow model. The states must not position themselves to have to perform preordained tasks on a long stretch of river upstream of the critical habitat over which the Nebraska state water administration has, at best, very limited control. It does not control, among other things, local land uses. If county commissioners endorse bad land-use planning practices and permit people to encroach on floodplains in ways that are destructive to channel capacity and themselves, agents of the federal community may talk to county and city authorities. There is no way the states or the proposed program can guarantee that the river channels will always serve the USFWS agenda as the agency defines it. Also, if one choke point goes away, another will usually emerge somewhere. Who knows what the implications will be? States do have some responsibility for floodplain management, but they are not responsible for specific characteristics of a given channel at a particular point. Furthermore, Colorado and Wyoming representatives are not eager to sign on to a program in which they would be expected to pay for solutions to problems caused by a combination of Nebraska's dam impacts and deficient local land-use permitting.

In their resistance to the federal agenda, the states did not want to destroy the negotiations. They simply wanted the USFWS to be clear that the states were not going to go where the agency wanted them to go on this issue—namely, to hardwire specifics of a natural flow model into the program document, the final environmental impact statement (EIS), and the BO. In the states' view, the federal EIS writing team must not be allowed to build into the proposed habitat recovery program the solution the agency had always preferred but the states had never accepted.

The USFWS's Case

THE USFWS: we are all presented with an opportunity to construct a solution that is a "win-win-win." It will help the CNPPID deliver its water to its customers, reduce flooding jeopardy for citizens near the city of North Platte, and provide benefits for the listed species. Certainly, all the players on the Governance Committee should be able to meaningfully address the issue.

The program EIS and the BO must do two things: show clear-cut benefits for target species and present defensible methods by which to produce those benefits. The states worry about eventual Endangered Species Act (ESA) compliance issues, that in the future a federal authority will point to a given statement in a program document and declare the states to be not in compliance. The states should be less concerned about that possibility within a well-constructed habitat recovery program guided by collaborative adaptive management principles. They should be more concerned with an ESA compliance issue that is immediate and compelling: there must be clear, specific language in the proposed program describing concrete actions that the writers of the EIS and the BO can analyze. Only then can a defensible judgment be made as to the proposed program's sufficiency.

It is not possible to put the entire issue off in loosely constructed language that permits undisciplined drift in the future adaptive management process. That process must be tied to a vision of practical means and ends. The program and the pertinent regulatory documents must clearly show how the EA water will get to the critical habitat in ways that will enhance habitat recovery. Do the states really want to see an EIS without a defensible proposed program? That would only lead to a jeopardy biological opinion.

There is a place for bulldozers and chainsaws in river restoration, but there can be no substitute for restoring some semblance of natural flows and their associated river processes to create and sustain essential habitat characteristics. It is not possible to separate river restoration from production of species benefits. The agency will work with states to build options to deliver that water through adaptive management processes. States should join the USFWS in developing options for moving pulse water from Kingsley Dam to the critical habitat. There must be sufficient detail so federal analysts can inspect the data and draw conclusions justifiable to critical outside audiences and peer reviewers.

ON THE SAME HOOK

The USFWS and the water providers shared a common interest: neither wanted to contemplate individual ESA Section 7 consultations. The ESA placed all parties on the same hook. The adversaries were clearly accountable to produce tangible benefits for listed species in ways critics on all sides could appreciate.

The environmentalists were becoming restless. With the continued deep drought and lagging negotiations, the central Platte riparian habitats were degrading as a result of rapidly thickening vegetation on re-colonized dried-out channel bottoms. The delay was imposing high costs on the habitats. Would it be necessary to reopen FERC licenses for the CNPPID and the NPPD? Would such a move reenergize the effort to find viable solutions? Along with all the water providers, the two Nebraska districts were directly in environmentalists' crosshairs.

On February 19, 2003, the senior Governance Committee negotiating team gathered in a hotel conference room near Denver International Airport. For months the federal community had repeatedly invited the state representatives to write a problem-solving plan to address the choke-point problem. The state representatives had no enthusiasm for the task and had hung back. The February 19 session was designed to stop the cycle of hostile charges and countercharges. That morning, after months of carping and fully cognizant of the possibility that FERC re-licensing would be reopened, the states would work with senior leaders from the federal and environmental communities. They peered at a computer-driven projection of their unfolding language. They parsed their statement word by word, sentence by sentence, paragraph by paragraph. They had vented their emotions for months and had worked out their own positions within each allied group. Each side could anticipate and articulate the other's stance point by point. After lunch, more revisions were made. Tired of wrangling, their voices were civil; the tone was one of mutual problem solving. When everything was done for that day, the negotiators had addressed the issue at two levels:

1. They would collaborate in forging a general adaptive management philosophy. There was a general agreement that the USFWS BO analysts and the USBR-EIS team would assess a suite of options. The text of the agreement would contain escape language that would leave room for the states to stay disconnected from any particular USFWS plan.

2. They would agree to specific reconnaissance-level components that the states would accept as possibilities. These options could be elements from which federal analysts could construct a reasonable and prudent alternative. There would then be substance for the regulatory documents. Meaningful numbers (for example, 5,000 cfs of EA pulse water delivery to the top of the critical habitat to add to other flows in the off-season; 800 cfs of EA summer flows) could be advanced without tying the states to those numbers. It was explicitly acknowledged that the possible options were examples that could possibly work in restoring species habitat, but they were examples only, not fixed standards. The states agreed to work with the USFWS to identify options that could deliver a range of water quantities. Among them, the agency's preferred quantities were inserted. For its part, the USFWS agreed to accept general reconnaissance-level analysis for the purpose of writing its regulatory documents.

The parties did not agree about the need for pulse or other in-stream flows. However, it was acknowledged, for example, that the USFWS believed the program should have the physical capacity to deliver 5,000 cfs of program water to the upper end of the critical habitat for three days during the non-irrigation season when conditions permitted. They could agree that the program currently lacked such capacity and, therefore, that it was not possible to test the hypothesis in an adaptive management mode that held that 5,000 cfs was the "right" amount to secure benefits for the listed species. Therefore, the program would explore and implement options that would incrementally enhance the capability to deliver program water. Following the precedent established in the sediment-vegetation agreement (Chapter 16) and in combination with those stair-step manipulations, the merits of alternative flow-sediment shifting scenarios for providing improved habitats would be examined. The language produced that day was later additionally vetted—in particular on March 7, 2003—but the substance was preserved.

CONCLUSION: FURTHER STUDY

On July 5, 2005, the Governance Committee awarded a contract to a consulting firm, Sato and Associates, which would review the literature on the issue and conduct its own field investigation (Sato and Associates 2005). By the end of August, a set of preliminary findings was in hand, and the final report was available by December 1. The findings would be available for inclusion in the final EIS (April 2006) and BO (June 2006).

The analysis confirmed the earlier findings, as presented by the Parsons and USBR analysts (Lewis and Roerish 2003; Murphy and Randle 2001; Randle 2003). The report offered seven alternatives that could be added to the base set of actions in various combinations (Sato and Associates 2005: 2–13).

The consultant's report provided substance for the regulatory documents. However, all parties at the table knew that this preliminary report would have to be supplemented by a systematic study of specific behavior of the plumbing system on the North, South, and main Platte stem that could inform detailed preparations for running an actual pulse flow early in the program's first increment. To this end, in conversations between mid-June and mid-October 2004, the Governance Committee agreed to initiate a more extensive study of pulse-building options at the program's inception and to complete it by no later than the conclusion of program year 2. Specifically, the study would identify how to muster 5,000 cfs of program water for three days of a pulse flow during the non-irrigation season. Furthermore, the study would evaluate specific ways to produce sufficient program water so that 800 cfs would be available at the top of the critical habitat during the irrigation season. If proper deliveries prove to be infeasible, the negotiators agreed to identify new water supply and conservation projects, or other means, to ensure the program's ability to deliver the necessary water during the first program increment. If feasible, it was hoped that the USFWS-specified pulse flows would be operational by program year 5.

Boyle Engineering of Lakewood, Colorado, won the contract and launched its study in the late summer of 2007; it produced a draft report in early 2008 (Boyle Engineering Corporation 2008). The Final Environmental Impact Analysis, released in April 2006, would incorporate thirteen alternatives for achieving the desired flows as defined by the USFWS (U.S. Department of the Interior, Bureau of Reclamation, and U.S. Fish and Wildlife Service 2006). State support for the two studies meant that the states and their water providers were following up on their words from 2003 with a willingness to carefully address optional solutions. The states had seriously reengaged the negotiations.

Locked into an Awful Dance

Bypass Flows and Hydro-cycling

The U.S. Fish and Wildlife Service (USFWS) pushed for a commitment from the Central Platte Public Power and Irrigation District (CNPPID) and the Nebraska Public Power District (NPPD) to provide, under some pulse-building circumstances, bypass flows of Lake McConaughy environmental account (EA) water. These flows would be created if the CNPPID and the NPPD would temporarily waive their right to divert such water into their networks of canals, small reservoirs, and power plants. Bypass flows were those left in the river; they would bypass NPPD's Keystone headgate and CNPPID's Tri-County diversion to be routed down the Platte River channel.

In average to wet years, there would likely be no need for pulse-building bypasses. But under dry conditions, federal river modelers had learned that the best habitat restoration outcomes, with minimum losses to the EA, occurred when EA water could be added directly to CNPPID's irrigation water in the main channel. But if the two districts' diversions swept away most or all of the channel waters, downstream return flows from irrigation would provide insufficient base flow on which to send EA water. The prospect of EA water disappearing into the river bottom upstream of the critical habitat gave serious pause to U.S. Bureau of Reclamation (USBR) formulators of the environmental impact statement (EIS) and USFWS evaluators of proposed program sufficiency in their biological opinion.

There was another problem—one primarily involving the USFWS, CNPPID, NPPD, and the Federal Energy Regulatory Commission (FERC). During dry times, under specific circumstances, Johnson Lake power plant no. 2 (J-2) operations produced small flow pulses that could potentially harm whooping cranes settled on the river at night, as well as tern and plover nesting. These two battles, one about bypass flows and the other concerned with power plant hydro-cycling, came up late in the negotiations and threatened to destroy any chance of assembling a winning program in 2005 and 2006.

BYPASS PROBLEM

Water from Colorado on the South Platte and from Wyoming and Nebraska on the North Platte became most valuable to habitat restoration when it was able to ride with CNPPID's agricultural flows. The bypass issue centered on USFWS negotiations with the CNPPID and the NPPD in venues beyond the Platte River Habitat Recovery Program talks. Whereas the USFWS would have preferred to have the negotiations over bypass flows conducted in general Governance Committee sessions, the Nebraska districts did not want to air particulars in the presence of the other two states and environmentalists. Among other considerations, the other actors at the table would potentially pressure the districts' delegations to arrive at a quicker, possibly less advantageous resolution. Wyoming and Colorado refrained from meddling, but they followed the matter with interest.

There had been no discussion of bypasses during the FERC negotiations. The wet 1990s had kept the issue from emerging. But in 2001 and 2002, USFWS hydrologists, whose computer models were simulating severe drought-induced conditions in and above the critical habitat, became deeply concerned that their precious EA water be given every possible advantage. Some fraction would be accommodated within CNPPID's canal system, but an insufficient quantity would be released at the low end of the district's system to build the desired pulse. Therefore, additional water had to be delivered down the river channel—some natural and agricultural flows supplemented with bypassed EA water. The USFWS would therefore want to cooperate with the CNPPID. Bypass flows would be an important part of any solution. The CNPPID, however, would resist that solution.

In this context, the USFWS proposed a significant idea. If sufficient flows (including EA water) could be sent through the CNPPID canal system and then be quickly released to the river out of Johnson Lake (J-2 return) above the critical habitat, they could ride downstream "on top" of base flows. Together, such assets could constitute flows in a range of quantities from 5,000 to 9,000 cubic feet per second (cfs), depending on river conditions and management decisions. This option would employ EA water most effectively to generate pulse flows.

The proposed USFWS solution was a problem for the CNPPID in at least two ways. First, at the visceral level, the district did not relish the prospect of a federal agency meddling in its daily operations. It owned the plumbing, it was operating within the terms established by the 1998 FERC settlement, and it did not want the USFWS to establish claims that could impact operations throughout the district's system. The CNPPID was willing to discuss general possibilities that might be worked out over a period of years, but it was not willing to commit to specifics in an open-ended restoration process when no one knew what was most feasible or effective. It certainly did not want to see particular "possibilities" printed in public regulatory documents, the environmental impact statement (EIS) and the biological opinion (BO). As constituencies became aware of those possibilities, there was a risk that they would take on a life of their own beyond the control of district management.

At another level, the CNPPID pointed out that if it were to waive its right to divert in the name of occasional pulse-building opportunities, there would be lost power production at its three electrical generating plants on its canal system—Jeffrey, Johnson Lake no. 1 (J-1), and Johnson Lake no. 2 (J-2). It was also conceivable that there could be revenue losses at Kingsley Dam if water destined for a pulse was spilled at a time of insufficient electrical supply. At the very least, Central would demand compensation for lost electrical power revenue. The FERC agreement explicitly provided for compensation for revenue losses as a result of future re-timing of water though the systems of the two districts (U.S. Federal Regulatory Commission 1998).

The CNPPID's Case

The district had made an agreement during the re-licensing process on behalf of improving habitat for the listed species. That arrangement was made final in July 1998 and was signed by the CNPPID, the NPPD, the U.S. Department of the Interior (DOI), the states of Colorado and Wyoming, and, among others, the National Audubon Society, the Whooping Crane Trust, the Sierra Club, American Rivers, and the Nebraska Wildlife Federation (U.S. Federal Energy Regulatory Commission 1998). In addition to providing the program EA at Lake McConaughy, the CNPPID and the NPPD agreed to provide 2,650 acres of program habitat land located on both sides of the river downstream of the J-2 return. That land parcel, known locally as the Cottonwood Ranch property, included two miles of river channel and was adjacent to land owned and managed by the Whooping Crane Trust and the Nature Conservancy. The districts had furthermore agreed to cooperate in the program's water conservation and supply activities. The districts had concluded that this was sufficient payment for regulatory certainty.

The FERC deal specifically provided that all program water yield that could be placed in the Lake McConaughy EA could be used for hydropower production. Furthermore, it had been agreed that the two districts would not be required to exercise their system capacities to store EA releases. There was one exception: if the EA manager determined that EA water flows became unsteady and thereby posed a problem for the river and the irrigation system, it was understood that the districts' canal storage and reservoirs could be used to dampen fluctuations. This provision was intended to cope with emergencies, however, and was not an offer of storage to the habitat recovery program.

In their view, the districts had made a deal and honored it. The USFWS could not unilaterally assert demands to alter the 1998 arrangement. Mutually satisfactory solutions might be found, but the present talks were proceeding in a time of too many uncertainties. The USFWS had accepted the FERC stipulations in 1998 and should do so now as well. Specifically, there was no warrant to discuss the possibilities of employing J-2 as a program water re-regulation tool.

The USFWS's Case

During the negotiations that led to the 1998 FERC stipulations, federal analysts did not fully understand the implications of severe drought as experienced in 2001, especially in 2002, and during the following years. The USFWS was now the beneficiary of new information; that new knowledge must be incorporated in any proposed habitat recovery program.

State and USFWS representatives had long discussed what might be done to build pulse flows. But the states and the two Nebraska districts had refused to help anyone in the federal community actually figure out how to build the necessary pulses. Now a winning biological opinion was required. The USFWS needed a clear understanding of how things can work; that understanding could only be gained if the districts—particularly the CNPPID—worked with the federal community of analysts. Building a habitat recovery program must be a cooperative effort. Cooperation means, if necessary, undertaking new commitments beyond those of 1998. That means everyone needed to join together in a discussion about how to get at least 2,000 cfs through the CNPPID canal and reservoir system while, in coordinated fashion, getting at least 3,000 cfs through the choke point in order to assemble a 5,000 cfs pulse. All sides had to collaborate to build realistic pulse-building scenarios for disclosure in the EIS and evaluation in the BO.

It is undoubtedly true that any workable arrangement on behalf of pulse flows will impose additional financial costs on the districts. The USFWS has fully appreciated that during dry times, there may be—in limited circumstances—lost electrical power production revenue. However, the districts must also recognize the benefits that come with such costs. Beyond avoiding the enormously expensive challenges of reopening the FERC deal in the wake of a failed recovery program, the proposed habitat recovery enterprise will deliver increased water supplies from Wyoming's restoration of long-lost capacity at Pathfinder

Dam. This means additional return flows will be captured at Lake McConaughy. Furthermore, each of the three states will add water supplies from its water action plan projects, in addition to the original three (Tamarack I, Pathfinder EA, EA at McConaughy). Furthermore, the program will address the choke-point issue, to the districts' advantage. That effort will help the CNPPID deliver its irrigation water, which also produces electricity for sale to the NPPD. Districts may see costs rise because some water will be bypassed for a few days each year, but significant gains will be produced by a viable program. Drop your defensiveness and work with us.

THE NEBRASKA DISTRICTS' RESPONSE

CNPPID and NPPD authorities faced a devil's choice. They knew, ultimately, that if they bolted from the negotiations, they would bring the recovery program down on their own heads and face a reopening of the FERC re-licensing process. If that happened, they would undoubtedly be required to do many of the same things they were now resisting, such as addressing the North Platte channel choke-point problem and building a sufficient pulse. They would be doing all that and more without a coordinated Wyoming, Colorado, and DOI collaboration that would provide major cost sharing. If they were not going to abandon the basin-wide collaborative program, they had to choose one of two unwanted options.

First, they could decide to work out an arrangement such as the one proposed by the USFWS, compromise bits and pieces of their 1998 FERC deal, and try to get as much financial compensation for electrical power interference as possible. Or, as a second possibility, they could do something Colorado had advocated for years: build a downstream reservoir somewhere just upstream of the critical habitat, divert and store pulse water there, and release it at times of need, as determined by the EA manager at Lake McConaughy.

A downstream water re-regulating reservoir would reduce the impact of the USFWS agenda on CNPPID's daily operations—a happy thought. However, such a proposal could be socially and politically disastrous. Many Nebraskans held the view that Nebraska was paying too high a price for participation in the collaborative riparian habitat recovery program. They had long resented the fact that the two districts, caught in the federal licensing nexus, had dragged the state into unwanted negotiations in their quest for regulatory certainty. When CNNPID and NPPD managers contemplated their options, they saw danger in proposing a re-regulation reservoir on other people's land, adding the concept to two public documents that would be read closely by opinion leaders across the landscape, and doing all this when political tumult existed regarding Nebraska's need to impose limitations on groundwater well drilling.

323

Compensation

Without abandoning their stand that the 1998 FERC terms should remain sacrosanct, the CNPPID and the NPPD chose to treat the problem as a compensation issue, thereby permitting negotiations with the federal community to proceed. However, they were rigid in asserting an argument that can be synthesized as follows: we have a deal with the federal government, we paid the agreed price for obtaining our forty-year licenses, and we do not want to expand on that settlement. Given our situation, we must always consider the possibility of going all the way to an FERC reopener rather than yielding.

The CNPPID did not want to waive its FERC-granted right to divert EA water at will during low-flow conditions unless it could be assured of financial compensation. Nearly 80 percent of CNPPID's total annual revenues came from electrical power generation and sales (*Platte River Odyssey* 2006). To keep Central whole, the district proposed compensation for foregone power revenues at rates consistent with its power sales agreements with its sole customer, the NPPD. Furthermore, the CNPPID was being asked to insert new operating rules in a system never designed to implement those rules, especially moving substantial quantities of water around to create flood pulses.

The CNPPID also pleaded poverty. Years of drought-induced low inflows into Lake McConaughy had produced a budget squeeze. As lake water levels dropped, irrigation deliveries were reduced, and power generation revenues fell while routine operating expenses increased—especially as a result of rapidly rising costs (see Table 25.1).

Most Central irrigators had paid $24.49 per acre for contracts that historically had generally delivered eighteen acre inches per year. However, as a result of the drought, the district was compelled to drop its allotments in 2005 and 2006 to 6.7 and 8.4 acre inches, respectively. It was difficult for the districts' board of directors to ask farmers to pay more for allotments that had shriveled. Over time, the CNPPID hoped rising electricity prices would provide increased revenue and relax the budgetary squeeze.

Over the first thirteen-year program increment, Central estimated that the net effect of a three-day EA bypass would mean a loss of power generation revenue of about $2,145,000 as a result of lost sales (CNPPID 2005a: 3). In addition, the NPPD—the purchaser of Central's power—would be obliged to buy replacement energy on the spot market at an estimated net additional cost of about $936,000 during the first thirteen years.

Furthermore, Central noted that it had made a $10 million capital investment for the purchase and rehabilitation of the Cottonwood Ranch property. Other significant expenditures on behalf of riverine habitat restoration were required as part of the FERC deal. In this context, representatives of CNPPID fought for financial compensation for any waters the habitat recovery program would ask to be bypassed around district powerhouses.

Table 25.1. CNPPID Irrigation Deliveries, Expenses, and Power Generation Revenues, 2001–2005

Year	Irrigation Deliveries (thousands of acre feet)	Operating Revenues (millions of $)	Total Electricity Sold (millions of kilowatt hours)	Operating Expenses (millions of $)
2001	92.23	12.16	276.31	13.34
2002	115.18	10.75	210.90	12.54
2003	111.00	9.22	146.31	13.53
2004	98.42	9.32	128.17	14.29
2005	49.89	9.52	125.01	14.31

Source: CNPPID 2005a.

Consternation

The federal community, environmentalists, and the three states knew they had little leverage given the terms of the FERC settlement. At a time when the USFWS was pressing the states hard to get a viable recovery program in place (2003–2005) so a viable EIS and final BO could be produced by no later than 2006, was it prepared to reopen negotiations with the CNPPID and the NPPD through FERC—a large, deliberate, slow-moving regulatory agency? The process could take years. Meanwhile, environmentalists were reminding everyone that critical habitat conditions were rapidly deteriorating, given the effects of the drought and in the absence of a viable program effort to reverse the situation.

In the view of others at the table, the two Nebraska districts had not paid an extraordinarily high price for their license renewal. If the CNPPID was facing difficult budgetary situations, the proper remedy would be to raise its irrigation water and electricity prices sufficiently to cover its costs. Was it not the case that markets were supposed to send price signals to consumers about something approaching the real costs of production? The beneficiaries of irrigation water and electricity should pay the costs directly. Costs should not be socialized to the federal treasury and the program contributions of the other states. It was important to Colorado and Wyoming that if any compensation were made to the Nebraska districts, it would not come from the pool of monetary or water contributions they had agreed to provide.

Furthermore, senior USBR authorities, responsible for Wyoming's Pathfinder and Kendrick projects (not to mention other facilities across the West), were perplexed at the prospect that the bureau might be put in a position to be paying compensation to two non-federal projects for implementing the ESA. Not only could the costs on the Platte prove to be substantial, but what kind of precedent would be established for other ESA-mandated habitat restoration programs involving the USBR? Costs of the 1998 FERC settlement had been borne by the regulated projects; no federal compensation was provided. Was that principle to be abandoned? Was it possible that the federal government would agree

325

to shoulder a cost burden on behalf of two districts that had caused the problems that led directly to jeopardy for the listed species? (Districts' response: federal authorities should not change signed FERC agreements that did not call for pulse flows and that promised compensation for any additional costs imposed by implementation of the FERC arrangement.) The implications were significant. For its part, the USFWS initially refused to even consider paying the two districts for use of the agency's own EA water. Whatever costs were imposed on the districts would have to be absorbed by them. However, that position had to confront the realities of the FERC settlement, which contained contrary provisions.

HYDRO-CYCLING

During the protracted and bitter bypass negotiations (2002–2006), a simultaneous sideshow was unfolding. When USFWS field analysts were assembling a viable BO, they became aware that under certain conditions, CNPPID's turbines that drove electrical generators at Jeffrey, J-1, and J-2 started, stopped, and operated at speed ranges in ways that could send unwanted surges into the river channel. In a world where the USFWS contended that at least one large annual pulse flow in the range of 5,000 cfs and above was highly desirable, little pulses in particular circumstances were not.

The CNPPID's Problem

From 2001 to 2006, the CNPPID faced increasing difficulty moving irrigation water down its canal delivery systems; as flows diminished, seepage losses mounted in both river channels and canals as a proportion of total flows. This meant less water for hydroelectric plants. When flows were too low to be efficient producers of electrical power, management shut down the water supply to turbines at Jeffrey, J-1, and J-2 to then build up storage all along the main canal system and in reservoirs such as Johnson Lake until a point was reached where sufficient water was available to operate the power plants efficiently and without harm to the equipment. Hydro-cycling, therefore, involves stopping water flows through the plants, storing them, and then releasing flows though the turbines. After flows pass through turbine blades, they splash into the river channel. The necessity for hydro-cycling was built into the design of the irrigation and power production system in the 1930s.

Johnson Lake was constructed on the main supply canal about sixty-five miles downstream of the Tri-County Canal diversion near North Platte. It has served as the largest and best available water level–regulating reservoir in the CNPPID system; it accepts variable upstream river and canal flows, provides modest short-term storage, and permits management to manipulate lake levels within a narrow range of elevations (usually about one foot) so as to release a steady stream in the proper quantities to the turbines of the J-1 and J-2 facilities (Drain 2006). After doing their electrical production work, power plant outflows are either directed downstream to irrigators or back to the river at a point near Lexington, Nebraska.

Under normal water supply conditions, the CNPPID releases enough water from Lake McConaughy during the non-irrigation season to divert about 1,200 cfs at its Tri-County diversion dam to Central's main supply canal. Historically, the district has had considerable flexibility in selecting among its hydro-cycling options during low-flow times. Management has responded to a wide range of conditions when making decisions, including precipitation events, best turbine operating speed ranges, Johnson Lake levels, canal levels, icing conditions, farmer demand for irrigation water, equipment conditions, and transitions in and out of irrigation water deliveries (Drain 2006).

One critical consideration was cavitation. Under certain conditions, a swiftly moving solid object (such as a turbine blade) can create many partial vacuums (bubbles) in a liquid (for example, water). When these bubbles burst under pressure, over time they can pit and wear away a solid surface by forming cavities. Cavitation is a threat to the long life of expensive metal and concrete structures, such as those at the heart of CNPPID's power plants. Therefore, a key rule for CNPPID was to operate turbines at the Jeffrey, J-1, and J-2 powerhouses at speeds that avoided cavitation. There was a direct implication: turbines were typically operated with substantial flow levels or were shut off entirely.

There have been two cavitation-free water flow windows for the turbine at J-2; one ranged from 250 to 475 cfs, and another appeared from 1,050 to 2,100 cfs. Generally, the CNPPID has wanted to operate J-2 at a maximum efficiency level of about 1,750 cfs. When flows decline to an amount below 1,400 cfs, Central managers typically resort to hydro-cycling tactics rather than permit their turbines to drop into damaging speed ranges. Depending on river and irrigation conditions, the starting and stopping of flows frequently in the range of 1,400 to 1,900 cfs can have a significant impact on the river channel and other life forms, including roosting birds.

The USFWS's Problem

In the drought years 2001–2006, the CNPPID managed main canal flows frequently in the range of no more than 800–900 cfs for extended periods. If the district were to maximize its power production and revenue, there was little option but to hydro-cycle. Central therefore resorted to switching the turbines and generators on and off twice a day. During this same period, USFWS analysts were doing their best to work with all the parties to piece together a proposed program that could justify a non-jeopardy biological opinion. They became alarmed about the implications of CNPPID's hydro-cycling practices.

In the lead-up to the 1998 FERC agreement, USFWS analysts did not see the surges produced by hydro-cycling when they examined the historical record because they were looking at data aggregated into monthly, not daily or hourly, units. Therefore, the FERC re-licensing deal did not address the problem. Even if hydro-cycling issues were not addressed in the agency's BO on the FERC re-licensing, it is reasonable and necessary to raise the issue and resolve it in the context of the Platte River Habitat Recovery Program. The CNPPID and the NPPD cannot choose to stand on the 1998 arrangement and employ its stipulations to refuse to address the needs of listed species. When the CNPPID and the NPPD entered the basin-wide habitat recovery program negotiations, they did so to address species needs, not just to defend the 1998 FERC deal.

The USFWS was concerned that EA water, dedicated to serve the listed birds, would be hydro-cycled to their detriment. That situation could not be permitted. Sharp fluctuations in the range of a few inches to a foot or more could be a problem. On the positive side, to a limited extent, the little surges might move some sediment and reduce vegetation encroachment, thereby delivering habitat benefits (U.S. Fish and Wildlife Service 2006a, 2006b). Yet in general, the magnitude of flow variations would be too small to significantly improve channel characteristics while being large enough to destroy plover and tern nesting sites, eggs, and chicks during late spring and summer (U.S. Fish and Wildlife Service 2006a, 2006b). The variations could also possibly harm night-roosting whooping cranes on the river channel.

When suitable dry, barren sandbars are available, terns and plovers will nest on the central Platte River. Sandbars need to be high enough to provide expanses of dry sand and avoid nest inundation during rain events, but they must be low enough to be part of the active channel and thereby not succumb to vegetation encroachment. Hydro-cycling in general raises water levels quickly and inundates sandbar areas that otherwise would provide prime habitat. Danger to piping plovers and least terns can be expected, for example, at cool, wet times during irrigation seasons. At such times, farmers will reject their canal water, which must be shunted to the river through the J-2 return. If low canal flows then prompt spasms of hydro-cycling at J-2, combined with a rising river as a result of precipitation, there is a high probability that otherwise safe areas will become inundated, to the detriment of tern and plover nests, eggs, and chicks.

As for whooping cranes, given the potential magnitudes, frequency, and rapidity of changes in river flows during different stages, there is a meaningful chance that during their spring and fall stopovers, roosting birds could be flushed from the protection of shallow river bottoms in ways that could expose them to injury or death. Like most birds, whooping cranes do not normally fly at night. When flushed from their roosts in the dark by quickly rising flows, they become vulnerable to in-flight collisions with each other, as well as with sandhill cranes, tree branches, fences, wires, and power lines. Furthermore, when the cranes have located themselves in a given roost with an appropriate water flow level, sudden drops in river stage caused by closing the gate at J-2 may expose whoopers to harm from predators by reducing the capacity of the river to provide secure habitat free from disturbance. Abrupt transitions to lower flows reduce the channel's attractiveness as a place of secure habitat for birds at roost and those in the air making decisions about where to roost. Hydro-cycling impairs the normal behavior of both sandhill cranes and whooping cranes. Given the already tiny population of whooping cranes, the dangers induced by hydro-cycling pose a substantial threat to the species.

If hydrological conditions remain similar to those documented in the late 1940s through the late 1990s and assuming that no EA water is released during whooping crane migration season, the average frequency of hydro-cycling occurrence has been estimated to be about 58 percent of the time during spring migration (March 23–May 10) and about 46 percent of the time during fall migration season (October 1–November 15) (U.S. Fish and Wildlife Service 2006a, 2006b). These numbers are averages and do not predict events for any given year, but they portray a real threat that must not be overlooked in evaluating the sufficiency of the proposed program. The most pronounced impacts on whooping cranes have occurred between the J-2 return and the city of Kearney, where amplitude of the ascending and descending flow cycles is greatest. The Cottonwood Ranch property is situated a short distance downstream of the J-2 return. This and adjacent properties dedicated to habitat restoration represent a critically important habitat complex, and their importance will increase as restoration efforts make the Cottonwood-Kearney segment even more attractive to the birds (U.S. Fish and Wildlife Service 2006a, 2006b). The USFWS duly noted, however, that as the channel is restored, it will widen. Greater width will lower the amplitude of surges. Careful tracking will be needed to better determine the impacts of hydro-cycling over time.

Without ever addressing hydro-cycling per se in the 1998 FERC agreement, analysts could see the danger of such inundation as a result of farmer water rejection combined with precipitation-driven rising river flows. Therefore, the parties agreed in Article 412 of Central's newly granted Project 1417 license that the CNPPID must use its "best efforts" to attenuate increased flows in the Platte River that may result from farmer rejection of irrigation water during the June 1 to August 15 nesting season (U.S. Federal Energy Regulatory Commission 1998). Therefore, Central should build on this commitment and work constructively with the USFWS to create a solution to the problem posed by more recent understanding of the effects of hydro-cycling on the three listed bird species.

Stalemate

Discussions between Central and USFWS representatives began in June 2002. During sporadic and unproductive exchanges, the USFWS probed for discussion of CNPPID operations relevant to the problem but was largely rebuffed. CNPPID management saw danger in any discussion that could introduce significant open-ended uncertainties into a revised FERC deal. Even if a reopened FERC negotiation was avoided, meaningful discussions of hydro-cycling could lead to changes in the design of powerhouse turbines that would be costly and immensely disruptive to operations. All this would come at a time when CNPPID revenues were falling and operational expenses were rising.

For its part, the USFWS had limited options. It could take a confrontational approach and use Section 9 of the ESA to make a case that hydro-cycling amounted to at least harassment of the listed birds and, in specific instances, would impose injury and even death. That meant "species takes" and constituted grounds for reopening ESA Section 7 consultations with FERC. Moving ahead with direct confrontation could be justified on the grounds that the agency had new information not available during the proceedings leading to the 1998 FERC grant of licenses. However, Section 9 violations could be difficult to prove; extended inconclusive haggling would be destructive to the negotiations as well as the habitat.

A move by the USFWS to pursue an ESA Section 9 "incidental take" approach would be seen by all the state representatives as truly sinister. Such a ploy would strengthen the hand of recovery program rejectionists everywhere, including that of Colorado governor Bill Owens's administration. It would push the CNPPID and the NPPD into a position from which they might abandon the negotiations. The USFWS generally opted to hold back Section 9 incidental take matters while simultaneously advancing the possibility of reopening ESA Section 7 negotiations.

As the hydro-cycling situation was being reported to the Platte River Governance Committee negotiators on July 12, 2005, this exchange occurred:

FEDERAL VOICE: Do the districts take the position that nothing in the FERC deal can be changed over the forty-year license period?

CNPPID VOICE: There are processes for reopeners. [Note: Nothing in the habitat recovery negotiations had risen to the level of threatening a FERC reopener except in the case of failure to produce a viable reasonable and prudent alternative to the status quo.]

FEDERAL VOICE: Does the recovery plan's need for bypass flows and mitigation of hydro-cycling constitute a need to reopen the FERC deal?

CNPPID VOICE: Silence.

FEDERAL VOICE: If the districts opt for a Section 7 FERC reopener, they will foot a big bill on their own.

In late May 2006, the manager of the CNPPID let it be known to the Platte River senior negotiating team that the CNPPID board of directors had indicated its willingness to abandon negotiations if a solution acceptable to the district on bypass and hydro-cycling matters could not be found.

There were additional risks to the USFWS taking the directly confrontational approach. Would FERC, in reopening Section 7 proceedings, perform the way USFWS analysts hoped? FERC was viewed by many as a large, lumbering, deliberate bureaucracy attentive to thousands of projects across the nation. The Platte River program was a small item on the larger FERC horizon. Who could be sure what would happen? One thing was certain: a reopening of the licensing situation would bring back all the intervening parties that were signatory to the deal. What new directions would be introduced? In the words of one USFWS participant, it would be a "crapshoot." Also, the 2004 national elections had sustained the George W. Bush administration and its allies in Congress; they were no friends of the USFWS or the ESA.

Breaking the Impasse

There was another option, an opportunity to modify the FERC agreement without reopening FERC re-licensing processes. Some statements in the 1998 FERC re-licensing documents regarding water levels at Lake McConaughy and other smaller reservoirs in the CNPPID system had been found to be in error. To redress the situation, FERC authorities appointed the CNPPID to be FERC's agent in making the necessary corrections (Drain 2006). On June 9, 2004, Central filed an application with FERC to amend its license to raise the "normal maximum surface elevations" of specified reservoirs. A year later, on June 10, 2005, FERC designated Central as its non-federal representative to conduct informal consultations with the USFWS on the potential impacts of the proposed changes (Drain 2006). Central then engaged in consultations under Section 7 of the ESA regarding the potential impacts of the higher lake levels, particularly those of Jeffrey and Johnson lakes.

This situation offered an opportunity to work out a deal on hydro-cycling and to make it a supplement within the FERC licensing framework. Given the dangers of pursuing a direct confrontation with the CNPPID over the matter of "incidental takes" and thereby driving the district into a corner, the USFWS pulled back its threat. In return, CNPPID signaled a willingness to work out a deal within the FERC framework. If CNPPID did not use this opportunity to make an amendment, it would risk a great deal. First, it would find itself undergoing extensive review under a FERC licensing reopener, with all the signatory parties—environmentalists, Colorado, Wyoming, the federal community—at the table capable of raising virtually any issue and questioning any stipulation. Second, in the wake of collapsed negotiations, the districts would be facing individual ESA

Section 7 consultations amid the wreckage of their relationships with Colorado, Wyoming, and the federal community. Also, by 2005–2006, the cooperative habitat recovery program was tantalizingly close to realization. The parties therefore backed away from their most confrontational options.

A Deal Is Made

In July 2006 an agreement emerged to modify CNPPID's hydro-cycling practices (Drain 2006). The arrangement would appear in an amendment to the 1998 FERC re-licensing language. The deal was critical to keeping the proposed program viable, but it would not be part of the Platte River Habitat Recovery Program.

The CNPPID committed to employ its "best efforts" to operate J-2 in a manner that could be expected to minimize the chances of harm to the listed bird species. Part of this would entail timely notification of the USFWS's EA manager regarding current and anticipated hydro-cycling operations during specific periods when the birds were vulnerable. CNPPID would keep careful records of its hydro-cycling activities, and that information would be available to the EA manager.

The USFWS and the CNPPID agreed to cooperate in collecting baseline data essential to monitoring and evaluating habitat conditions as they are affected by hydro-cycling. In addition, limits were placed on hydro-cycling operations (U.S. Fish and Wildlife Service 2006a). A detailed analysis occupied the core of the USFWS's biological opinion (U.S. Fish and Wildlife Service 2006a). No summary here can do the arrangement justice. The parties agreed that from March 18 to April 30 and from October 17 to November 10 each year (and on any additional days when whooping cranes are known to be present), the CNPPID will hydro-cycle J-2 in a series of stepped-up releases during certain hours of the day such that the amplitude of overnight flow-stage increases will be reduced downstream.

On behalf of terns and plovers, during the first seven days of May each year, J-2 will not be restricted in its hydro-cycling. The working hypothesis was that higher surges during this time period will drive the birds' nesting activities higher on the sandbars, thereby protecting them from precipitation spikes during the following summer days. In the course of any hydro-cycling later in May, the CNPPID agreed to use its best efforts to operate the J-2 facility so that any peak surge flows will be "similar to or less than" a benchmark flow at the Overton gauge, the river flow measuring location just above the critical habitat (U.S. Fish and Wildlife Service 2006a: 6). That benchmark flow value is to be established "annually at a level equal to the highest flow during May, or at another flow rate set by the Service [USFWS] based upon data regarding nesting locations or desired nesting locations and flows that are believed not to inundate known nests, and with cognizance of CNPPID's limited storage capacity at Johnson Lake" (U.S. Fish and Wildlife Service 2006a: 6). This arrangement will apply to the full tern and plover nesting season: May 1–August 15. Adjustments to the benchmark value can be made or suspended by mutual consent. The magnitude of river-stage changes produced by hydro-cycling was predicted to diminish because the actions of the habitat recovery program were expected to produce wider, shallower channels. The USFWS therefore had reason to expect that hydro-cycling would present a diminished threat over time.

The USFWS issued its BO on the hydro-cycling arrangement on July 28, 2006 (U.S. Fish and Wildlife Service 2006a). Within less than three days, the CNPPID included it in a packet of materials that constituted the proposed amendment to the 1998 FERC grant of a license. Postmarked July 31, the package was sent on the last day permitted under the regulatory amendment window. A major stumbling block had been overcome. Would the birds be adequately served? Who knew? All parties did know that as long as a strong, uncompromised ESA is in place, the USFWS can pursue new options within the terms of future adaptive management during program implementation. If those activities fail to remove any identified jeopardy, a viable USFWS will once again address the problem.

BACK TO BYPASS

The USFWS could not give the proposed program a passing grade in any BO without a capacity to deliver 5,000 cfs to the top of the critical habitat. In the face of that pressure, the two districts opted to take their case to senior DOI authorities in the George W. Bush administration.

On November 17, 2005, representatives of the two districts, the USFWS, and the USBR met in Washington, D.C., to make their respective cases. The CNPPID and the NPPD contended that the 1998 FERC license conditions should not be changed. Furthermore, if the districts chose to cooperate with the habitat recovery program by permitting EA flows to be bypassed in some measure, they should receive full financial compensation for any resultant revenue losses. The DOI authorities did not find their rationale persuasive. In the words of one district participant, "We did not feel listened to." The Nebraskans did hear two messages they had rejected for years: (1) there would be revenue losses, but program benefits outweighed those costs; and (2) work out a viable deal with the USFWS in the context of the Platte recovery program negotiations. Get going on a deal. Do not escalate the Platte Basin matter to the very highest authorities in the DOI. The USBR wants its Colorado, Wyoming, and western Nebraska panhandle facilities covered by a viable basin-wide habitat recovery program.

The CNPPID and NPPD representatives were unhappy. Informal messages were conveyed that the districts were seriously considering withdrawing from the negotiations and taking their chances with a FERC licensing reopener. That meant recommending that Nebraska governor David Heineman not sign any proposed program document. That meant blowing up the program for all parties at this very late moment. If something could be worked out that would be acceptable to the districts and to every other party, however, the districts would become much-needed champions of the proposed program.

ANOTHER DEAL IS MADE

How could the problem be addressed? Given that resolution had been achieved on the matter of hydro-cycling by the end of July 2006 and that more productive conversations had been ongoing from May through July of that year, final program language on the matter of bypass flows was inserted into the program document dated August 8, 2006 (*Platte River Recovery Program* 2006: attachment 5, section 1).

The bypass solution was framed at several levels. First, it was agreed that the EA manager at Lake McConaughy could request that the CNPPID or the NPPD regulate EA flows in the interest of building short-duration pulses. The manager would request such bypasses only when needed, when it was determined that the necessary pulses could not be otherwise constructed. The EA manager would also take into consideration what peak flow events had occurred during the past year. If a peak flow of high magnitude (about 8,000 cfs or greater) had occurred and if it had accomplished effective channel scouring and sediment shifting, the EA manager would be expected to consider making another pulse during the subsequent twelve months a low-priority use for EA water. Use of EA water as bypass flows to build pulses for purposes of studying the effectiveness of alternative flow routing would be appropriate. Under these conditions, it was agreed that the districts would not unreasonably decline requested re-timing of EA waters and flow bypasses.

To assist in creating short-duration pulse flows below the J-2 return, the CNPPID agreed to regulate up to 12,000 acre feet of water (of CNPPID's power use appropriation) diverted at Keystone and re-time the return of that water to coincide with Lake McConaughy EA releases. Provision of this water will be subject to certain constraints—especially avoidance of damage to CNPPID facilities, downstream flooding, and FERC-imposed operational rules. To further assist in building pulse flows, the NPPD agreed to coordinate the operations of its Gerald Gentleman Power Plant Project and feeder canal loop with the EA manager and the CNPPID. This would permit re-timing of NPPD flows in ways useful to the proposed program.

Then came the money provision. It was agreed that the EA manager would not call for re-regulation of water, with or without bypassing flows, that would result in total program payments exceeding $3,081,000 for the first thirteen-year program increment unless additional sums were approved by the Governance

Committee. Payments could be made to compensate the CNPPID for lost power production revenue and the NPPD for the higher net costs of purchasing replacement electricity on the spot market. Rates were to be consistent with applicable power sales agreements. Other associated costs could be compensated—for example, bank sloughing in canals and reservoirs subjected to rising and falling water levels occasioned by program-required manipulations and damages to third parties, such as fisheries, private river facilities, and equipment. The program, using other funds, would purchase liability insurance to cover at least $1 million worth of documented claims that could be attributed to habitat recovery program manipulations of water.

As the major money channel for the federal portion of the habitat recovery program, it would be a troublesome precedent for the USBR to pay compensation directly to the districts. But given the fact that the districts' participation was essential to the recovery program, that they were needed as the leading Nebraska champions of the program, and that the 1998 FERC licensing conditions promised compensation for such losses, there was no other option than to find a way to provide some compensation. It would therefore be necessary for the habitat recovery program taken as a whole to pay compensation. Just as program dollars could be invested in relaxing the constraints of the North Platte choke point or in addressing the sediment-vegetation issue, program dollars could be used to assemble a pulse flow package. The costs of power production foregone by EA bypasses were thereby shifted from the districts' books and placed under the habitat recovery program's tent. Where did the $3,081,000 commitment come from? From the USBR budget. Year by year, those USBR dollars would be shifted into program accounts and thereby take on a recovery program identity. The practice was distasteful, but the USBR and the other parties could live with it. After all, the agency's Wyoming dams and reservoirs had been important contributors to the decline of listed species habitat in central Nebraska. Most of all, the USBR needed regulatory certainty for all its facilities in the three states.

The maneuver saved the habitat recovery program negotiations at a late moment after thirty years of negotiations. Until then, in the words of one federal participant in the drama, "We had been locked into this awful dance." The price of halting that mutual agitation was to socialize the districts' bypass flow losses to the federal treasury. Within three months, the governors of the three basin states would begin signing off on the completed recovery program document.

The Pallid Sturgeon Habitat Gamble

Available evidence suggested that the pallid sturgeon was in extreme danger of becoming extinct (U.S. Fish and Wildlife Service 2000a: 7). In the view of the U.S. Fish and Wildlife Service (USFWS), the pallid sturgeon's plight could not be ignored. If the habitat recovery program focused exclusively on the needs of the three listed bird species far upstream, the agency and the states would be vulnerable to being compelled by environmentalist-inspired lawsuits to enter individual ESA Section 7 consultations regarding the pallid sturgeon's needs. In principle, a separate habitat recovery program could have been developed, but no one wanted to contemplate the complexities of mobilizing virtually all the same parties, along with new ones, in separate negotiations.

CONTEXT: THE LOWER PLATTE RIVER AS HABITAT

Within the larger picture of the Mississippi River and its Missouri tributary, the relative importance of the Lower Platte River to the pallid sturgeon is unknown (Lutey 2002: vii). In general, the stretch from the mouth of Nebraska's Elkhorn River to the Missouri is thought to be important, especially given the destruction of habitat by human-engineered works on the Missouri River. Upstream of its confluence with the Platte, there is evidence that the pallid also uses the lower portion of the Elkhorn.

The Lower Platte River segment represents only a tiny fraction of the Lower Missouri River drainage. Yet the Lower Platte is the only tributary where the pallid has been captured with some regularity (National Research Council of the

the National Academies 2005: 193). This reach of the Platte appears to possess the essential combination of discharge, substrate, and channel morphology essential for sustaining the fish's three major life stages—larval, juvenile, and adult (Lutey 2002: vi; National Research Council of the National Academies 2005: 193). It seems to provide the turbid flows and shifting sand substrate thought to typify much of the Missouri River prior to the federal dam and reservoir–building campaign. Of the twenty-nine confirmed occurrences of pallid sturgeon reported in the Lower Missouri Basin (that is, below Gavins Point Dam) between 1980 and 2000, twelve were from the Platte River near its confluence with the Missouri (U.S. Fish and Wildlife Service 2000b: 28).

Habitat recovery program flows are only a small fraction of the upper main stem waters. There is clearly some connection between the organization of upper main stem flows on behalf of the three target bird species and pallid sturgeon habitat, but it is likely a modest one. Beginning with the Loup just downstream of Columbus, Nebraska, the Lower Platte River becomes much larger. As measured at the Loup confluence, the upper main stem of the Platte contributes only about 25 percent of the total flow of the lower river. During the span 1950 to 1980, the Loup River contributed about 40 percent of the total flow, the Elkhorn about 21 percent, and other, smaller streams about 14 percent (U.S. Department of the Interior, Bureau of Reclamation, and U.S. Fish and Wildlife Service 2006: 1:4–116–117). In average to wet years, the program contribution, in all probability, will be undetectable. However, especially in dry years, the USFWS contends that program-enhanced flows could make a positive difference.

BUREAUCRATIC SUPERSTAR

The Missouri River is highly regulated by one of the most powerful agencies in the U.S. government—the U.S. Army Corps of Engineers (USACE) (Clark and McCool 1996; McCool 1987; Schneiders 1999). The USACE delivers a broad stream of utilitarian benefits across a wide spectrum of congressional districts. Historically, the USACE has been especially effective in providing a rich array of means by which political entrepreneurs have been able to deliver "pork" to their constituencies. Interest group beneficiaries, served well by USACE projects, in turn support the politicians who take credit for those projects and work to ensure expanding federal budgets for the agency that delivers the goods. Triangular alliances incorporating local interests, congressional committees, and federal bureaucracies that deliver desirable facilities in many sectors of public life are a well-known phenomenon (Clark and McCool 1996; McCool 1978). But of all these political triangles, the one the USACE has patiently constructed over the last 180 years is rivaled only by the Pentagon. Its capacity to deliver expensive projects, highly irreversible given their crystallization in concrete and steel and thereby ensuring long-term economic and political benefit streams, has made the corps a "bureaucratic superstar" (Clark and McCool 1996).

In addition to its robust political base, in the Missouri Basin the USACE works under a complex array of obligations to its rich variety of constituencies—defined by a host of legislation including the Endangered Species Act (ESA)—and complex sets of regulations spelled out in master manuals, annual operating plans, and a litany of court orders. The agency strives to balance a diverse set of often conflicting river interests while keeping an eye on its constituents' needs in a world of irrigation, barge traffic, flat-water recreation, electrical power production, and flood control. Upstream communities—especially in Montana and the Dakotas—want more water held high, barge operators and irrigators downstream want more water releases, lake recreational interests want more water retained in reservoirs for longer periods, and environmentalists want increased and more variable water releases in the name of better native species habitats, along with the elimination of some dams. There are constituencies for and against each possible change in river management.

Environmental constituencies allied with the USFWS have never enjoyed the political dominance of federal and state politics that has been associated with the large public works sustaining the commercial agendas that underlie local, regional, and national economic growth. Environmental considerations, by their very nature, raise issues about the unpaid mortgages—un-priced in any market—historically taken out against people and other living things within the biotic web in the quest to grow the economy as cheaply as possible. It has never been especially politically popular to push for even partial repayment of old mortgages that project promoters never intended to repay. Such has been the fate of the USFWS. When the agency began to raise the issue of how to pay back a small amount of the mortgage historically taken out against the traditional Missouri River—and to do so by issuing biological opinions that found jeopardy for ESA listed species—it found the politically formidable bureaucratic superstar difficult to budge.

USFWS VS. USACE

In 1990 the USFWS issued a biological opinion that found that USACE operations on the Missouri River jeopardized the existence of the least tern and piping plover (U.S. Fish and Wildlife Service 2000a: 2). The pallid sturgeon was listed under the ESA as endangered that same year, but not in time for its habitat issues to be addressed. These actions precipitated an extended and difficult discourse about how to alter corps operations on the Missouri on behalf of the three targeted species. The conversation between the USFWS—attempting to administer an unyielding law—and a much more powerful USACE—the steward of unyielding commercial constituencies—cannot be adequately captured in these pages. When the story is told, it will be one of confrontation, delay, and bloodletting, with the USFWS doing most of the bleeding.

Among other things, throughout the 1990s and the early twenty-first century, the USACE was updating its Missouri River Master Manual, the document that describes how the USACE intended to operate Missouri basin dams and reservoirs. Issues surrounding the needs of the least tern, piping plover, and pallid sturgeon were just part of the larger effort. Revisions of its plans for the river, however, meant entering the ESA federal regulatory process. That, in turn, meant formulating an environmental impact statement and undergoing review of a USFWS biological opinion. In the course of all this, the USFWS pressed the USACE to accept its recommendations so as to produce a reasonable and prudent alternative on behalf of the three listed species. That acceptance was not forthcoming. By 2002–2003, as Platte negotiations were addressing the "skunks" that bedeviled them, no viable process for addressing issues on the Missouri River had yet emerged—at least in the view of the USFWS.

After ten years of struggle, in April 2000 the USFWS issued another biological opinion on the USACE's Missouri River operations; this one incorporated pallid sturgeon habitat considerations. The USFWS found that all too little had been accomplished during the past decade and that all three species were placed in jeopardy by the USACE's operations (U.S. Fish and Wildlife Service 2000c). At its core, the USFWS called for seasonal fluctuations in river flows to be produced at Gavins Point Dam—the lowest in the string of river barriers. There, the recommendation to the corps entailed producing a spring rise of 17,500 cfs, to a total of 49,500 cfs, in one of every three years and an annual summer low flow of 21,000 cfs (U.S. Fish and Wildlife Service 2000a). Rising waters would wash nutrients into the stream and send spawning cues. Low flows would signal nesting time to the terns and plovers and provide more shallow-water habitat for fish. Cyclic manipulations of lake levels on the upper river at Fort Peck, Lake Sakakawea, and Oahe were also recommended in the interest of providing alternating higher and lower shorelines for listed bird nesting habitat improvement and fish spawning habitat. Given conducive runoff conditions, one lake would be held a little bit low, another would be maintained at an average level, and the third reservoir would be filled higher than average on a three-year rotation (U.S. Fish and Wildlife Service 2000a, 2000c). There was also a call for the establishment of additional shallow-water habitat at priority places along the length of the river. Much of it would be produced by placing notches in riverbank armor, thereby allowing water to flow into chutes to prepared shallow basins.

The corps was not enamored of the USFWS recommendations. After additional debate, in October 2002 the USACE announced that it had decided to postpone any changes in its Missouri River management for reasons induced by the extended drought (Zaffos 2002: 5). For years environmentalists of various stripes, including upstream fishing and recreational interests, had fought hard to introduce changes in the master manual that would insert variable flows into Missouri River operations (*Environment News Service* 2004). But downstream interests in irrigation, hydropower, and barge traffic saw economic disaster in such proposals. In the overall balance of things, the corps wanted a river with steady, deeper flows for power production, irrigation, and shipping. This meant it was at a stalemate with regard to the USFWS environmental agenda; that, in turn, meant floodplain commerce and barge traffic would continue to dominate river management objectives.

The full story—including all the legal maneuvering—must escape these pages, but it can be safely asserted that the bureaucratic standoff could not continue for long. The superstar was simply not responsive to the ESA agenda. The intent of the ESA needed to be administered. What could be done? Bush administration political appointees in the Department of the Interior (DOI) intervened to amend the 2000 biological opinion. On December 16, 2003, the USFWS issued an amended agency opinion on Missouri River operations. Craig Manson, DOI's assistant secretary of fish, wildlife, and parks, issued a press release to announce the revised product (U.S. Fish and Wildlife Service 2003a, 2003b). There had been no new peer-reviewed scientific studies to warrant an amendment to the 2000 document. Furthermore, the National Research Council of the National Academies of Science had independently confirmed the findings of the 2000 biological opinion (National Research Council of the National Academies 2002a). However, during their consultations with the U.S. Army Corps of Engineers, USFWS scientific staff members who had been working on Missouri River biological opinion matters for years were removed and reassigned to other tasks (*Environment News Service* 2004; Union of Concerned Scientists 2004).

A memorandum, written by the leader of the specially selected team charged with formulating the amended biological opinion, acknowledged receiving the assignment on November 3, 2003, and noted that the amended opinion was due by December 15 that year. The team assembled in Minneapolis, Minnesota, for two November sessions and reconvened in Albuquerque, New Mexico, during the first twelve days of December (U.S. Fish and Wildlife Service 2003b: enclosure). The team reviewed the situation and evaluated proposals formulated by the USACE in an effort to construct a reasonable and prudent alternative acceptable to the corps. The team decided that current operations of the Missouri imposed no jeopardy for the interior least tern and the piping plover (Union of Concerned Scientists 2004). Members found that USACE's proposals would also prevent jeopardy for the pallid sturgeon (U.S. Fish and Wildlife Service 2003b: enclosure).

In a period of no more than five weeks, the meaning of the original biological opinion on Missouri River operations, issued in 2000, had been substantially altered in ways favored by the USACE. This was accomplished without any public hearings or scientific peer review. After learning that a new team had been

assembled and charged with amending the original document, Allyn Sapa, a retired USFWS biologist who had supervised the USFWS team that had written
the original 2000 biological opinion, noted in November 2003: "It's hard not to
think that because our findings don't match up with what they want to hear, they
are putting a new team on the job who will give them what they want" (Union
of Concerned Scientists 2004: 3).

Environmentalist critics close to the episode were outraged by the process
and the fact that the amended biological opinion, in their view, fell far short of
meeting the real needs of any of the three targeted species (American Rivers
2004; *Environment News Service* 2004). Yet the revised USACE master manual for
Missouri River operations had been validated on the corps's terms.

Given the highly constrained capacity of either the USFWS or the USACE
to significantly improve habitat for the tern, the plover, and particularly the pallid sturgeon during the 1990s and the first years of the twenty-first century, the
USFWS came to view the tidbit of Lower Platte pallid habitat as precious. That
would mean obtaining a commitment from the three states at the Platte River
negotiating table to do something to protect that habitat.

THE USFWS'S CASE

The National Research Council (NRC) had been asked, at the behest of the three
states, to review the federal science that had justified the series of Platte Basin
jeopardy opinions produced by the USFWS (National Research Council of the
National Academies 2005). A draft report was available soon after the amended
Missouri River biological opinion was released in December 2003 (National
Research Council of the National Academies 2004b). The NRC report endorsed
the USFWS's science and thereby bolstered all the parties as they struggled to
move the negotiations forward (see Chapter 18).

The NRC team found that current conditions on the Lower Platte River did
not adversely affect the likelihood of survival or recovery of the pallid sturgeon.
But the analysts concluded that, given the wider context of habitat destruction,
loss of Lower Platte River habitat would likely result in a catastrophic reduction
of the pallid sturgeon population. Furthermore, the team noted that any habitat recovery program would have to include the Lower Platte River (National
Research Council of the National Academies 2005). The USFWS was correct in
thinking that the stretch of stream was important to the pallid.

USFWS analysts became concerned that the recovery program upstream on
behalf of the three bird species might mean further loss of Lower Platte springtime flow when water users in the three states made diversions to fuel their
depletions replacement plans. Diminished flows in general—especially reduced
peak and pulse flows—might negatively impact lower river sandbar formation,
reduce the connectivity of wetland slough backwater features, and weaken

spawning cues (U.S. Fish and Wildlife Service 2006b: 210–211, 280–282). What do high spring flows in the April–June period do for spawning? They change flow depth and velocity and thereby inundate sandbars and riverbanks—all of which recycles nutrients, increases turbidity, and triggers faster temperature changes. These developments, in turn, produce spawning cues. The USFWS wanted to focus on preserving and—to the extent possible—enhancing variable natural flows of historical habitat.

The USFWS had worked hard to refine its flow tracking and accounting model for the central and Lower Platte to the point where historical evaporation and seepage losses associated with the river reaches below Grand Island could be defensibly estimated. In mid-May 2002 the agency released its preliminary findings (U.S. Fish and Wildlife Service 2002b). Employing stream flow gauge data for water years 1975 through 1994 plus—for one reach—calendar years 1997–2000, the USFWS estimated that in the Septembers of the worst years, less than 60 percent of the program-augmented flow at Grand Island reached the Louisville gauge (sixteen river miles upstream of the mouth of the Platte). That number rose to 90 percent in December–January and March–May of the best years.

Major uncertainties surrounded the estimates. During winter months, icing posed measurement problems, and during summer months there were large unknowns regarding possible negative impacts of continued groundwater pumping to stream flows. USFWS analysts concluded that, given such potential losses, program-augmented flows as measured at Grand Island will seldom exceed the range of 6,000–30,000 acre feet per month. Given measurement error, the substantial background variability of river flows, and the modest program water increments to be added, it is unlikely that they would be distinguishable at the Louisville gauge unless there were exceptionally large program water releases or exceptionally low non–program water flows (U.S. Fish and Wildlife Service 2002c: 7). Could 100 or 200 cubic feet per second of added program water have much impact? Probably not in wet, high-flow years, but they could be meaningful to habitat in dry ones. The general conclusion the USFWS drew from all this was that there was a modest connection between augmentation of river waters by program efforts for the three birds upstream and channel-shaping spawning-signal volumes.

The USFWS therefore requested the cooperation of the states in constructing a recovery program to promote a dynamic, sandy, free-flowing braided river with a preserved and at least partially restored natural hydrologic regime. It would be necessary to monitor pallid sturgeon habitat as the first program increment unfolded; it would be important to take appropriate actions on behalf of the sturgeon within an adaptive management framework as lessons are learned; and it would be important to develop baseline information on the abundance, distribution, and population structure of the fish. Then it would be important to develop population recovery objectives that include defining the minimum viable population size. Over time, people will learn more about the importance of the Platte River to pallid sturgeon recovery and about how the cooperative program's actions on the Upper Platte contribute (or not) to improved sturgeon habitat.

THE STATES' CASE

The states' representatives agreed years ago (Cooperative Agreement 1997) to participate in a process to test the assumption that the Platte River Habitat Recovery Program will have a positive impact on pallid sturgeon habitat. Now the National Research Council (2005) has determined that the Lower Platte segment does not adversely impact the chances of survival of this beleaguered species. Therefore, the USFWS should back away from writing any pallid sturgeon habitat demands into the program as it now stands. Furthermore, all parties agree that most of the traditional pallid habitat is on the Missouri and other tributaries (particularly Montana's Yellowstone and Upper Missouri rivers). The fate of this fish hinges on the Army Corps of Engineers' management of the Missouri; whatever actions are eventually determined to be helpful on the Lower Platte will constitute a sideshow.

This entire topic is fraught with danger. Given uncertain habitat requirements, when water providers eventually go into what they believe is a program-covered, streamlined ESA Section 7 consultation on a proposed project that would affect the Lower Platte, the USFWS will make one of three types of judgment: (1) the proposed water user action will be found to be covered by the program, (2) it will be determined to be partially covered, or (3) the USFWS will judge it not to be covered. These decisions will be informed by considerations now unknown. If the decision is either of the last two options, the water provider will be "kicked over" on a flow chart into a full-fledged ESA Section 7 negotiation process. Why go through all the expense of putting a Platte River Habitat Recovery Program in place if some unknown future middle-level manager arbitrarily puts the supplicant into a regulatory armlock over data and interpretations that cannot be foreseen? The entire concept of regulatory certainty is under attack.

> USFWS: It is true that no one can now see where research and monitoring will lead us. It is possible that such investigations will consume virtually all of the first thirteen-year program increment. But if research and monitoring—guided by adaptive management principles—clearly show the need for action by an earlier year, the partners in the habitat recovery program must cooperate in addressing the problem. The fixes may be cheap; they may be expensive. There can be no substitute for renegotiations when the facts come in.
>
> The states are in this position because historically your water activities have depleted flows on the Platte and have had an impact on the lower river.

Also, your future depletions plans can be expected to further diminish spring pulse flows as they draw from pulse waters to be re-timed upstream. The USFWS has never contended that water extractions associated with the states' future depletions plans would damage the three listed target bird species, but it does worry about possible negative impacts—however minor—on flows to pallid habitat.

STATES: Under the proposed program terms, we are only allowed to divert for our future depletions plans at times of excesses to target flows at the Grand Island gauge. Those times include the spring months, when the river rises. We accommodated the USFWS in this regard in our quest for regulatory certainty. Now you are implying that we will be asked to install depletions plans to offset the impacts of our depletions plans. Where does this end? We are entering an absurd Alice in Wonderland world.

USFWS: We have said nothing about depletions plans for depletions plans. Nobody wants to go down the rabbit hole with Alice. We are asking you to join in addressing the needs of the pallid sturgeon. We have much to learn, but it is clear that volume of flow is important to maintain the habitat characteristics we do know about.

STATES: By covering our historical depletions prior to 1997 and by offsetting our post-1997 future depletions, we are adding program water to the river at critical times for three bird species. If, as you say, sturgeon habitat is positively affected by greater volumes of water and if our pulse flow efforts for the birds add to springtime pulses and summer river flows, it is only logical to expect that the program flows must be good for the pallid; they cannot be bad.

USFWS: The sturgeon is in serious trouble. We cannot—as stewards of the ESA—overlook even small reductions in flows to the extent that they degrade habitat, especially spring flows that trigger spawning in the February to July time period. Program-required depletions do reduce spring peak flows. This is a problem. The law stipulates that there will be no habitat degradation.

STATES: The USFWS is using the fish to expand its control over the river. The pallid sturgeon has become a convenient tool for the agency to maneuver itself into a stronger negotiating position on peak and pulse flows during the first program increment. The fish are far downstream, and the birds are many miles above; the pallid thereby provides an opportunity for a federal agency to stick its nose into the affairs of diverters all along the length of all three major Platte segments—South, North, and main stem down to the confluence with the Missouri.

The USFWS wanted help in mounting a research and monitoring program. That activity would probably impose only modest costs in the near term and would pave the way to regulatory certainty. It would be a gamble, but future studies might demonstrate that the addition of program waters to the lower river has a trivial to nonexistent impact; if that turns out to be the case, it follows that a little depletion by water providers here or there will not hurt the fish.

Yet did the states really want to fund an aggressive research and habitat monitoring program on sturgeon requirements? In ways not then foreseeable, doing so could link them to a future program on the Missouri over which they would have virtually no control. Furthermore, it could bring about an unwanted discussion of flow volumes and sediment delivery to the Lower Platte. Two intertwined questions needed to be pursued: (1) the biological question as to how the fish will respond to changes in lower river habitat characteristics, and (2) the hydrologic question regarding what flow and sediment requirements are needed to create desired habitat characteristics. The answer to the second question could possibly mean more water flow would be needed on the Lower Platte. That, in turn, meant danger on the horizon for water provider agendas.

If the states proceeded, there could be problems not now foreseen. But if the states did not proceed, the negotiations would collapse. If the states went ahead with support for USFWS objectives on the Lower Platte, they generally agreed that they must do everything possible to encourage the USFWS to focus on rectifying the Missouri River situation, do whatever they could to keep Lower Platte efforts de-linked from the politics of the Missouri, emphasize that the Lower Platte is only a minor piece in the larger Missouri puzzle, focus research and monitoring on the biology of the fish as much as possible, and stay away from a focus on river hydrology and sediment to the extent possible. The path would be fraught with risk, but it would be the best way for the states to maneuver.

A DEAL IS REACHED

The states rejected the agency's analysis of peak, pulse, and in-stream flows at any point on the Platte outright, but both adversaries still needed a viable program. It was important to help the USFWS do what it had to do regarding the fish so the agency could deal with strong pallid sturgeon supporters within the agency and in the environmental community. It was critical to build a program on behalf of the sturgeon, or the fish would become a "loose cannon" on the program deck as soon as negotiations were completed. That would mean an immediate reopening of the pallid problem in a context of much greater ill will. The habitat recovery program must be sold to a diverse array of constituencies, and the pallid sturgeon was a necessary part of the river basin picture.

The deal was reached largely in two spasms of discourse. First, on October 31, 2002, the Governance Committee negotiators reaffirmed (the 1997 Memorandum of Agreement was the original affirmation) that the pallid sturgeon would be included as a target species during the first program increment. Furthermore, they agreed that $3,928,000 would be committed to the program's monitoring and research efforts to investigate the sturgeon's situation during the first thirteen years. That amount was later increased to $6,934,600 (*Platte River Recovery*

Program 2006: 66–68). Second, during 2003 and early 2004, within the context of the larger, more encompassing conversation on peak and pulse flows, additional elements of the bargain emerged.

The National Research Council (2004b) released its draft report on April 28; the team found that the Lower Platte was critical to pallid habitat recovery and must not be further degraded. Then, in the wake of that finding, a pivotal Governance Committee meeting on June 14–15, 2004, produced more specific and elaborated terms. That language eventually constituted the bulk of the wording in the final program document that appeared in the fall of 2006 (*Platte River Recovery Program* 2006: 12–13, and attachment 3, section V, pp. 45–46, 66–68).

The states noted that they did not agree with the NAS or the USFWS conclusions, but they did agree on the following:

1. During the first program increment, impacts to the sturgeon caused by habitat recovery program activities upstream or new water related activities would be assessed.

2. Assessment will be conducted by the integrated monitoring and research plan supplemented by the efforts of other independent researchers in the Missouri basin and its tributaries.

3. There will be a Lower Platte River stage change study to be completed by the conclusion of the third year of the first program increment.

4. If impacts of the proposed program are deemed adverse to the pallid sturgeon, the Governance Committee will construct and implement appropriate conservation measures that negate them. Those measures will be funded by the habitat recovery program.

5. The USFWS recognized, for its part, that in order to achieve the recovery program's water objectives, operation of offset water projects for pre- and post-1997 water user depletions will at times cause unavoidable adverse impacts on one or more agency recommended flows on the central Platte and [the] lower river. The Service agreed that such impacts are acceptable as long as their operation is in accordance with program approved water supply plans and future depletions plans.

6. Research specific to the targeted pallid will a) summarize existing information about the species, b) examine selection and use of habitat by juvenile and adult sturgeon relative to river conditions, [and] c) identify [the] physical effects of different rates of flow and river stages on the construction, connection, maintenance, and evolution of pallid habitat components. In addition, there will be systematic study of selected water quality indicators. There will be particular investigation of the relationship [among] flow regime, sediment transport, and the creation and maintenance of habitat. (Platte River Recovery Program 2006: attachment 3, section V, pp. 66–68)

Of the items on this list, the most urgent in the view of the USFWS was to get a study under way that would address a central question: what impact will the shaving of off-peak flows and pulse flows by diverters have on sturgeon habitat quality? Agency biologists knew they could not go before a judge in a court of law and argue convincingly that any given small decrement in the volume of flow and river stage is biologically acceptable relative to pallid sturgeon needs. The ESA is clear on this point: no harm is to be inflicted upon listed species habitat. If a 1 percent decrement were to come at the time of year most damaging to habitat—during the spawning period—the burden of impact uncertainty could not be placed on the species. It would have to be absorbed by the water depleter. But there was too little knowledge to draw defensible connections between river stages, especially during peak flow times, and implications for pallid habitat.

Over time, an intensely civic science incorporating contributions from the various interests will have to address contentious facts. As the analytical process unfolds, a USFWS and environmental community will be focused on the implications of attempts to enhance variable flows. Equally interested water providers will be holding tight to their wallets while uttering their mantra: defined contributions, defined contributions.

Reaching Sufficiency

Structuring Decision Making

Wielding the Regulatory Hammer

Seven-eighths of anything cannot be seen.

—GENERALIZED ICEBERG THEOREM

The problem in general was that environmental impact statement (EIS) and biological opinion (BO) analytical teams had been attempting to formulate publicly defensible documents in the service of a more natural variable flow vision, but the states and water providers had accepted virtually none of their ideas. How could the U.S. Fish and Wildlife Service (USFWS) go into the public arena with a draft EIS that examined a program proposal the states would not associate themselves with in major respects? Did the USFWS and the U.S. Bureau of Reclamation (USBR) really want to release descriptions and examinations of a proposed program that would quickly be disavowed by the states and their water providers? Doing so would be disastrous. Such a move would play directly into the hands of those who would welcome the collapse of the entire enterprise—especially those who opposed the intent of the 1973 Endangered Species Act (ESA)—and who would gain the advantage in the ongoing environmental policy debates if handed an important example of failure on the Platte River.

Yet by 2004, how could the USFWS not push ahead with the best possible analyses in the regulatory documents? The states had run the regulatory clock on the federal community ever since Wyoming's Grayrocks Reservoir had come up for discussion in the wake of the passage of the ESA almost three decades earlier. It had been a full decade since the three basin states and the Department of the Interior (DOI) had agreed to develop a cooperative basin-wide program.

It had been seven years since the signing of the outline of the deal in mid-1997. If the program could be initiated in 2004—which it clearly could not—the states would have then constructed a twenty-year first increment for themselves.

There was pressure from every community at the table to move ahead with something that promised to work. In particular, authorities in the Department of the Interior were feeling pressure. It was one thing to allow the beleaguered USFWS to twist in the political and administrative winds, but the USBR had billions of dollars' worth of project facilities in Colorado, Wyoming, and the Nebraska panhandle. Those facilities needed ESA coverage under the law of the land. Friends of the idea of a basin-wide cooperative habitat recovery program wanted to demonstrate that the concept could work. Among them were environmentalists in despair over a rapidly degrading river and riparian corridor under assault by both drought and the negative side effects of undisciplined individual rationality in pursuit of private goods on and near prime habitat lands. Furthermore, money was running low for program-building activities under the 1997 Cooperative Agreement. No player at the table was eager to return to state legislatures or the federal government to request additional funds for additional years of negotiation of a habitat recovery program that was incredibly complex, poorly understood by outsiders, and only partially constructed. Very few legislators or members of attentive publics could grasp the problem, the program, the issues, or the consequences of failure.

For all parties, the issues came down to defining and mutually accepting cooperative habitat recovery program starting points. What would each player agree to do to get the habitat recovery program under way? Administration of the federal regulatory process provided essential hammers and anvils for forging common program starting points, the substance of which was reported in earlier chapters. But how did the federal regulatory process assist in moving players from positions that did not, in the view of the USFWS, constitute elements of a winning habitat program to postures that could be approved?

THE REGULATORY PROCESS

At its simplest, the regulatory process consists of at least five elements: (1) construction of a proposed program to be assessed; (2) analyses that constitute a draft environmental impact statement, incorporation of public comments, and production of a final EIS; (3) the assessment provided by a USFWS BO that finds or does not find continued jeopardy; (4) a record of decision (ROD); and (5) permit granting (or not, depending on the verdict). The EIS process is responsive to the mandate incorporated in the National Environmental Policy Act (NEPA) of 1969; the environmental impact statement provides the foundational analysis of the proposed program. Upon this NEPA-mandated platform, the biological opinion analytical team produces its assessment, as charged by the ESA. The fi-

Table 27.1. Decision Documents in Federal Regulatory Process, with Dates

Draft environmental impact statement	January 2004
Draft biological opinion	August 2004
Final environmental impact statement	April 2006
Final biological opinion	June 2006
Record of decision	September 2006
Platte River Habitat Recovery Program	October 2006

Source: Record of Decision, Platte River Recovery Program, September 27, 2006. Available at http://www.platteriver.org.

nal BO reports an agency decision the USFWS is prepared to defend in future negotiations and courts of law. A ROD is then formulated. Among other things, it summarizes essential program features, describes the rationale for the DOI's decision, discusses the alternatives, directs relevant authorities to work together to implement program agreements, and calls for authorization of necessary federal funds. Given success in all this, the federal action agencies, in consultation with the USFWS and permit applicants, can proceed to approve those activities that are within the boundaries of federal regulatory compliance. Table 27.1 reports the dates of passage for each regulatory hurdle in the Platte River Habitat Recovery Program.

It is much too simple to claim that the regulatory process began with the construction of a proposed program. The regulatory process itself, and the manner in which it was wielded, had everything to do with producing the Platte River Habitat Recovery Program. Regulated actors, knowing what hurdles they were going to face, formulated their courses of action accordingly. Intense and sustained interaction among the regulators and regulated in the context of a legally mandated regulatory process does produce proposed programs.

Given the initiation of program construction in 1994, the designated federal action agency—in this instance the USBR, steward of federal water facilities in Colorado, Wyoming, and the panhandle of Nebraska—was obliged to assemble a team to analyze the environmental implications of the proposed program as compared with potential reasonable alternative courses of action. A draft EIS was released to the public much later. Public meetings were organized throughout the basin to explain the process, share findings, and solicit public comment.

Concurrently, USFWS staff—especially those in the Grand Island, Nebraska, field office—worked away at producing the groundwork for an eventual biological opinion. These staff members were occasional observers of the negotiations in earlier years but did not participate in them. There was no regulatory necessity for producing a draft biological opinion (DBO). However, in the case of the Platte River Habitat Recovery Program negotiations, water providers—knowing the complexity and sensitivity of the issues involved—requested that a DBO be

353

produced for their review. They wanted a preliminary peek at a proposed program scorecard to see how well they were doing. They would have an opportunity to address failings prior to public issuance of a final opinion. Biological opinions, especially negative ones, had the potential to produce firestorms of protest that, in turn, could unravel carefully constructed political coalitions. Therefore, as a courtesy to the water providers, the USFWS agreed to present and discuss a DBO.

Progress toward program objectives that deliver ESA compliance and regulatory certainty is measured through the achievement of milestones (see Appendix D). The habitat recovery program will serve ESA compliance requirements as long as specified milestones are fulfilled (*Platte River Recovery Program* 2006: attachment 2). In the end, ten major milestones (each with a list of specific parts) were constructed for the first thirteen-year program increment. For example, Wyoming pledged to make its "Pathfinder Modification Project physically and legally capable of providing water to the program by no later than the end of Year 4 of the First Increment" (*Platte River Recovery Program* 2006: attachment 2, pp. 1–2). Colorado was committed to complete construction of its Tamarack I Plan also by the end of year 4. Milestones were put in place to make Nebraska's promises real and enforceable, as well as to specify land plan implementation and each state's and the federal government's post-1997 water depletions plans.

WIELDING THE HAMMER

The Draft EIS: Structuring Choices

The USBR-USFWS's EIS team and the USFWS's BO team were challenged to write their respective draft documents during the series of intertwined, simultaneous, multiple skunk-wrestling matches. In the midst of all this, the agency needed to formulate those environmental impact statements and biological opinions in a manner that would foster and steer a process of problem solving.

To do this, the USBR-USFWS EIS team pulled together the disparate parts of the emerging habitat recovery program such as they were in the spring and summer of 2003. The next task was to track the impacts of those components. After years of contemplating matters and in an effort to enable eventual USFWS evaluation of proposed recovery program options, USBR staff, collaborating with the USFWS, constructed two general alternative program scenarios and projected the effects of each (U.S. Department of the Interior, Bureau of Reclamation, and U.S. Fish and Wildlife Service 2003: 3, 38–48). Those effects were then compared to 1997 baseline conditions in the light of known requirements of the listed target species. The way forward was to take extant program components and label that suite of proposed actions Governance Committee Option 1 (GC-1). The team then systematically specified an enhanced set of possible program actions—specifically, GC-2.

An EIS—draft or final—analyzes the impacts of a proposed action. It does not assert conclusions regarding ESA compliance. The EIS simply stated the facts about the probable impacts associated with alternative courses of action. Yet by organizing the data, information, and analyses around these two options, the analysts and writers signaled at least two things: (1) the configuration of program elements then in place after years of negotiations (GC-1), and (2) a possible enriched configuration that would be expected to accomplish more habitat recovery on a larger scale (GC-2). It was not the USBR EIS team's task to define program "sufficiency," but everyone understood that GC-2 would, in all probability, represent a much better approximation of what the USFWS wanted to see in any Platte River Habitat Recovery Program.

In addition to GC-1 and GC-2, each of which resembled what had been negotiated, the DBO analyzed another four options, for a total of six (U.S. Department of the Interior, Bureau of Reclamation, and U.S. Fish and Wildlife Service 2003). The additional four included a no-action option that listed federal programs from which water users drew benefits and thereby placed them in a federal nexus, a water leasing option that enhanced river flows, a wet meadow option, and a water emphasis option that shrunk habitat lands to 6,500 acres but then called for a considerably greater reduction of shortages to USFWS target flows (180,000 acre feet per year). No sustained attention was paid to these additional four options in negotiating sessions. Negotiators and their attentive publics were focused on how the proposed program was portrayed in GC-1 and what it might become under the terms of GC-2.

GC-1 represented what the states and water users had already committed to by that point in 2004. It focused on habitat land downstream, mostly below Kearney, Nebraska, where most of the best habitat for the three bird species remained. The proposal would entail less demand for a habitat restoration effort because that portion of the basin already possessed the most desirable habitat characteristics. GC-1 would therefore offer little habitat restoration in more degraded areas upstream. The choke-point problem near North Platte, Nebraska (see Chapter 24), would not be addressed; channel capacity for conducting irrigation and program water would remain constricted at about 1,980 cubic feet per second (cfs). No program measures would be taken to create short-duration near-bank-full pulse flows in the critical habitat area.

GC-2 represented a "juiced-up" GC-1; it incorporated a considerably larger package of proposed habitat recovery program actions. The emphasis was placed on more degraded habitat lands in the segment of the targeted habitat area upstream of Kearney. Because most of that land did not exhibit the characteristics most required by the three bird species, this scenario called for more restoration work than did GC-1. The choke-point constraint on water deliveries near North Platte, Nebraska, would be relaxed, and there would be program construction of near-bank-full pulse flows.

The two scenarios represented a range of possibilities. Many combinations of actions could be formulated from the basic factors at play that included locations and amounts of targeted habitat lands, extent of habitat restoration, and the program's ability to deliver water to the habitat, along with the variable shapes of those deliveries (timing, duration, and size of flow pulses). The draft EIS did not attempt to analyze possible program mixes other than the two that constituted the most basic pair.

The major issues had thereby been starkly framed for subsequent work by BO analysts. If the USFWS could have been expected to give a passing grade to GC-1, the discussion would simply have focused on how to pay for implementing it. Life would be simple at the negotiating table while the outstanding issues would be back-loaded onto adaptive management processes. However, after reviewing GC-2, states and their water providers saw new demands being placed on them. After hearing for ten years what the states thought they could live with in a habitat recovery program, the federal community had used the draft EIS to set up a regulatory review to extract more water and other assets than the states had heretofore agreed to provide. All parties could see that discussions of how to incorporate features of GC-2 would necessarily move water providers into negotiation postures they did not wish to adopt.

The States' Case

The draft environmental impact statement (DEIS), released in January 2004, was not followed by a DBO until August of that year. During the intervening months, water interests reviewed the DEIS, shared their dismay over the GC-2 alternative, submitted their views during the public comment period as part of the larger stream of public input, and pressed hard against GC-2 at the negotiating table. In general, the states contended that GC-1 represented a much stronger and better approach to habitat restoration than it was made out to be in the DEIS, and they cried foul that the USFWS had chosen to insert the GC-2 option into a public document with which state negotiators had never agreed.

The state representatives were extremely sensitive to any language in the DEIS—or any other regulatory document—that members of the public might view as characterizing the proposed program. People not involved in the negotiations might understandably see a DEIS as the public document that informs them—at least in a preliminary way—about "the deal." The DEIS has been a critical document to which the public, including state legislators, responds. When other DEIS documents have hit the streets, proponents and opponents have typically immediately interpreted the program as described to their respective constituencies. In such situations, publics on the different sides of the issues have tended to coalesce around positions that best seem to serve their interests. The danger has been that leaders at the negotiating table can quickly lose flexibility of action as they and their political superiors are compelled to respond to constituencies with fixed positions. In the case of the Platte DEIS, state authorities and water users were careful to (1) distinguish both GC-1 and GC-2 from any actual program that would be forthcoming; (2) be quietly neutral in draft EIS public review sessions, neither attacking nor supporting either of the two options; and (3) point out that much more negotiation was yet to come.

Public information is good for reasoned civic debate, but it may not always help with the politics of local coalition building, especially in the case of water providers attempting to keep their attentive publics on board during the worst drought in possibly 300 years. Any program—even GC-1—would place significant new demands on the North, South, and main stem Platte River systems, and it would have been a challenge for leaders in the three states to bring their concerned constituencies along under the best of circumstances. In the middle of all this, the federal community chose to advance GC-2 as one option, even though no state representatives had endorsed it or wanted to endorse it.

GC-2 raised the bar for reaching program compliance. It represented the incorporation of USFWS objectives regarding the restoration of natural flows or river processes. The agency was creating a new program vision not accepted by the states; that vision would no longer simply be the USFWS's view of issues on which the parties could disagree, but the variable flow vision would have achieved the status of a program objective. It would do all this without having launched an adaptive management process or field-tested a hypothesis. Rather, it had hardwired into a public document elements of particular means to reach a solution for the listed species. That vision of what a solution should look like may or may not be effective in the long run, but, in the states' view, it should not receive privileged status over other possible approaches to solutions.

For example, the aggressive GC-2 call for substantial island leveling above Kearney would arbitrarily require efforts to generate sediment and open whooping crane vision lines on a large scale yet to be tested and approved by all parties. The states had agreed to a stair-stepped adaptive management approach beginning with data gathering, further investigation of options, and a commitment to begin on a small scale and to test impacts at successively larger scales as lessons are learned (see Chapter 16). GC-2 went well beyond this.

While the DEIS noted that a range of permissible land and water management strategies existed to elicit desirable habitat responses, in the states' view there was insufficient acknowledgment that the "range" of potential actions emanated from, and was limited by, defined resource contributions. The range of possible actions on behalf of the listed species should explicitly include forest vegetation management alternatives that would increase water yields from national forest lands in basin watersheds. There needed to be a revision of the draft document that would make the program, as negotiated, a vehicle for working through future uncertainties and reacting to new knowledge within a framework of defined contributions and adaptive management.

Although nothing in the DEIS explicitly stated that GC-2 represented a better approximation of a winning approach than did GC-1, it seemed clear that any USFWS biological opinion would use GC-2 to "take another bite out of the Platte Basin apple" in a way no state representative had consented to. It would be critical to negotiate a solution before a final BO set everything in stone. State representatives felt betrayed that a DEIS had been unleashed on the public that was seriously at variance with what they had agreed to.

The Federal Case

The DEIS was not the vehicle for describing an actual program to be implemented. Rather, an EIS represented a way to create an envelope of possibilities from which selected components could eventually be creatively assembled into an effective program that might work in a highly uncertain world. GC-1 represented components already agreed to by the parties in negotiations, whereas GC-2 advanced possibilities that would more intensively impact river restoration and habitat maintenance on a larger scale. The DEIS simply traced the logical implications of each scenario. Nothing in the DEIS was viewed by the USFWS as imposing anything particularly new on the states. The DEIS was not a decision document; rather, it constituted a public disclosure statement.

Neither scenario, GC-1 or GC-2, exactly reflected the outcome of ten years of negotiations. The other four alternatives examined (no-action, leasing, wet meadow, and water emphasis) certainly did not reflect agreements made at the negotiating table. They were used to make possible comparisons of the uses and limits of different approaches, as required by NEPA. The analytical team had the luxury of making up different combinations of assets (e.g., water, land) to cast a net over a broad range of possibilities.

Later, when the USFWS team issued its final biological opinion (FBO), it would analyze the "bounded envelope" of possibilities encompassed in a final program proposal. The jeopardy/non-jeopardy call would then be made based on the substance of possibilities in that envelope of potential actions. The DEIS is a best attempt to describe to all citizens the overall envelope of environmental consequences traceable to each option.

If the state representatives and their publics look at GC-1 and GC-2 in this perspective, they will see that the states are not being compelled to accept any particular proposal. There is an important unresolved problem, however. Now that the DEIS has been released, given the pressures on everyone to develop a winning habitat recovery program, all parties must come together and take authentic ownership of a proposed program that can pass muster.

The Environmentalists' Case

To anyone who values meaningful habitat restoration, the proposed program as roughly characterized by GC-1 in January 2004 could not be seriously advanced as adequate. There was too little substance, too much back-loading of real issues onto an amorphous adaptive management process, and too much promised regulatory certainty for water providers. Virtually all of the skunky issues being wrestled were then unresolved. The need for restoration was great and was becoming greater by the day because of human- and drought-induced impacts. It was important to press hard for the best possible program. Anything less had to be resisted. What was really needed was GC-2 plus.

NAS-NRC Draft Report

In the midst of the pulling and hauling over GC-1 and GC-2, in late April 2004 the National Research Council (NRC) of the National Academies of Science (NAS) released its draft review of the science the USFWS had used to undergird its series of jeopardy biological opinions that had brought a number of Platte Basin water projects to a halt. The NRC's vindication of the USFWS's use of science and its endorsement of normative flows provided a critical boost for the agency just as the Platte Basin negotiators were contemplating the implications of GC-1 and GC-2 for an eventual USFWS BO. The states knew the USFWS would use the NRC's endorsement of the idea of normative flows as a tool for habitat restoration. They would do what they could to minimize the impact of this concept on what had been negotiated and reflected in GC-1. Yet no one could deny that the NRC report had buttressed the USFWS's case for introducing natural flow considerations to the main stem of the Platte.

Whereas for years the states had been prepared to accept that two different visions existed regarding Platte River habitat restoration—their defined contributions stance and the USFWS's natural flow perspective—they had worked hard to keep any river processes vision out of the program language. But now, in the wake of a DEIS that included an explicit statement of GC-2 and an NRC report that supported the importance of variable flows in riverine habitat restoration and maintenance, it was clear that the USFWS's commitment to a natural flow model of habitat restoration would be part of any winning recovery program.

After hearing a preview of what the USFWS was contemplating for the DBO during negotiating sessions on May 17–18, 2004, the USFWS and state representatives developed carefully parsed language that pulled together the NRC's idea of normative flows in a way the states could abide. That language would be incorporated in the eventual recovery program document and read as follows:

> During program formulation, FWS also identified additional flows such as
> short-term channel management "pulses" that are lower than peak flows but

are in excess of target flows and are deemed by the FWS to be important to creation and/or maintenance of habitat in the central Platte associated habitats. . . . The states have not agreed that the peak flows, "pulses" or such other FWS identified flows are biologically or hydrologically necessary to benefit or recover target species. . . .

The states agree that FWS may use Program water that is subject to release at its direction to reduce shortages to FWS's recommended peak, pulse, or other flows in the central Platte River as part of an attempt to achieve a more normalized flow regime (one closer to the former structure of the hydrograph) given system constraints. (*Platte River Recovery Program* 2006: 11, 12)

The new language reflected a marked shift in the negotiations toward a program that would more closely resemble GC-2. The states' appropriations doctrine was untouched. But a voluntary cooperative effort had—for the first time—accepted the USFWS natural flow notion as something with which the states would cooperate and make work within their traditions of water law. Did the states accept this with enthusiasm? No. But while maintaining their traditional appropriations systems, they would, within their constraints, cooperate to implement something resembling a natural flow model on behalf of the listed species.

This turn of events was profound. It not only opened up a path to the construction of a much more viable habitat recovery program, but any environmentalist tempted to attack the emerging cooperative program agreement would have additional reasons to think very carefully. If the program crumbled, it would take down with it the states' agreement to allow the core idea of river restoration and habitat maintenance to be introduced into the program. The states and water providers could see their future unfolding before them; that future would include living with an unwanted natural flow vision.

Draft Biological Opinion

As a matter of principle, the USFWS does not negotiate final biological opinions. It is not typical, if anything is typical in such large landscape–scale habitat recovery program efforts, for the USFWS to openly share a DBO and welcome a discussion of it. But at that moment, no clearly defined preferred alternative was on the table to be evaluated. Rather, there was a range of possible actions as denoted by GC-1 and GC-2. It was critical to employ the DEIS and the DBO to complete the formulation of a viable program. Doing so meant more negotiations. The side agreement made between the USFWS and water users in 1997, to the effect that a DBO would be provided, now proved very useful to all the parties, especially the USFWS.

A focused discussion of the draft and a quick withdrawal of the document violated no procedural requirement. In fact, there was no ESA requirement even to produce a DBO. Public distribution of the draft would not help any party at the table, and it could inflame constituencies. The original idea had been that a fully fleshed-out habitat recovery program would be ready to be evaluated, but that had not come to pass. The draft would be employed as a lever to move the states toward accepting something more than GC-1. But this was not a nefarious federal scheme to "step on the throats" of state representatives and water providers; it was done at the request of state negotiators who needed insight into the USFWS's thinking so they could find solutions in advance of being publicly hit with problems that could create tumult in their constituent relationships.

On August 10, 2004, representatives of the various interests met in a conference room at a motel near Denver International Airport. Some selected staff members of the USBR-USFWS EIS team and the USFWS's BO group were present as observers. They would be working in support of developing the eventual final environmental impact statement and biological opinion. The state representatives and water providers were about to learn how their proposed program, such as it was, had been graded and why.

Several federal representatives took their turns explaining aspects of the document and its overall meaning. The objective was to evaluate whether the effects of a federal action (the permitting of basin facilities) would likely jeopardize the continued existence of the listed species or adversely modify their critical habitat. Now was the time to get things right.

A program that resembled GC-1 was found to exacerbate the deterioration of aspects of ecosystems that depended on variable flows and natural river processes, which provide essential supply and movement of sediment, enhance preservation and channel width, prevent channel incision, control vegetation encroachment, and produce spawning cues for sturgeon and habitat improvement for all targeted species. GC-1 would, with high probability, jeopardize the continued existence of the three listed bird species but would not likely impose jeopardy on the pallid sturgeon. In general, GC-1 would not provide compliance with the ESA.

A program with the attributes of GC-2, with "some fixing," could potentially earn a non-jeopardy opinion. With further work, this configuration of program elements could be "reasonably expected" to provide ESA compliance for the first program increment. Several problems would have to be addressed, however. Among them, the North Platte choke point presented a constraint on the delivery of program water that needed to be relaxed. Results for GC-2 were based on achieving a minimum channel capacity of 3,000 cfs. Overall, management of system processes through some restoration of variable flows had to be integrated into the program plans. There needed to be a more explicit commitment to address the negative impacts of hydro-cycling through an arrangement approved by the Federal Energy Regulatory Commission. On behalf of pallid sturgeon habitat, better tracking of program water through sturgeon habitat on the Lower Platte was needed, and the program had to make explicit commitments to undertake other actions that would support better pallid habitat. GC-2, like GC-1, would be implicated in the reduction of peak flows, resulting in weaker spawning cues; that also meant possible negative impacts on habitat formation and reductions in floodplain biotic connections. Parties to the program must be willing to act on valid peer-reviewed findings of pallid sturgeon research. The program, in either its GC-1 or GC-2 manifestation, did not provide clearly defined benefits to the pallid, while existing water-use patterns were found to impose small adverse impacts. Implementation of any viable program would require a better-developed adaptive management process.

The Aftermath

The states and their water providers registered a generally strong negative reaction. The final biological opinion, in their view, should simply define modest "starting points" for getting a program under way and not make detailed demands about how to cope with "unknowables." They saw the DBO as a wholesale attack on their more loosely constructed, more flexible view of adaptive management. They saw too much hardwiring of solutions that, in their view, would unduly guide adaptive management toward the USFWS natural flow model of river restoration. The states—prior to issuance of the DEIS and the DBO—had thought they were headed toward a program that would return issues involving choke points, pulse flows, bypass flows, hydro-cycling, and everything else involving sediment-vegetation to a loosely defined adaptive management process to be thrashed out during the first program increment. Now, in GC-2, the federal community had put all these issues up front as prerequisites for getting the program under way.

> STATE VOICES: We have agreed to provide the program with 10,000 acres of improved habitat land and with 130,000–150,000 acre feet of average annual reduction in shortages to target flows. Also, we have committed to replace future depletions with waters the USFWS would not likely get its hands on under individual ESA Section 7 consultations. Furthermore, we have agreed to add millions of dollars in support of program administration and systematic monitoring and research. Yet the USFWS has now told us we are still on the hook for a jeopardy opinion. How can that be?

> USFWS VOICE: The agency must be assured that any proposed program can be implemented component by component in ways that can be demonstrated to tangibly benefit targeted species. A viable BO must be sufficiently specific that it can (1) meaningfully guide a principled adaptive management process to deliver sufficient benefits to the targeted species, and (2) stand up to reasoned third-party inspection by people on all sides of the issues.

Forks in the Road

The combination of the DEIS and the DBO had pushed the states into a corner. The USFWS was saying it knew what had to be done and wanted to lock in as much of its natural flow vision as possible up-front. The states needed to push back and induce the federal community to incorporate critical state concerns. A strategic state concern had infused the talks for years. What would prevent regulatory certainty from being withdrawn for reasons states and water users might see as arbitrary and capricious? What was to protect them from seeing their deal unravel because some biologists determined that a presently unimaginable program variant was insufficient according to some logic not even being contemplated?

"Forks in the road" became a label used to convey the message that the states did not absolutely have to have a deal. The USFWS obtained its leverage in the regulatory process because the states and water providers had learned to fear the "no-program" option. They had abetted this definition of the situation as, in the past, they themselves had demonized the idea of abandoning the talks. They had done this for at least two reasons: (1) by any reasoned calculation, a no-action option would lead them into a prolonged, costly regulatory nightmare, and (2) it had justified to their constituencies their decision to sit through years of frustrating negotiations.

Now, given a peek at their future under the proposed program as delineated in the DBO, it was time to seriously advance the thought that if they were to be pushed too far in the direction of GC-2 plus, the states would authentically consider walking away from the negotiating table. Their vision of a defined contribution program was under direct assault by the federal natural and variable flow model. The only way to get the federal community to incorporate their concerns would be to seriously restore the no-program option.

The states and water users knew the federal and environmental communities also feared the no-program path. Their representatives dreaded the thought of more than 100 individual ESA Section 7 consultations in the basin; collapse of the negotiations would mean handing a victory to anti-ESA elements in the U.S. Congress, to the advantage of the water providers. In addition, a program was by far the best way to have Nebraska groundwater exploitation issues addressed while also obtaining compliance for USBR facilities. Furthermore, the river was continuing to degrade.

The two Nebraska districts were alarmed at the implications of the USFWS positions on choke points, peak and pulse flows, bypass flows, and hydro-cycling. They viewed the implications of the DBO as advancing a federal "taking" of their facilities in the name of habitat recovery. They sent signals that they were seriously prepared to march into the nightmare of individual consultations. Colorado was not particularly sympathetic to the Nebraska districts' positions, but it saw reasons to maintain solidarity with the Nebraska delegation, given that the latter had exhibited a tendency to find solace after setbacks by looking upstream for ways to move more Colorado South Platte water into Nebraska pockets. Wyoming could live with something approximating GC-2 if it had to. Its delegation worked to hold things together among the states and wanted to find solutions because it hosted major ESA compliance–needy USBR projects.

The states could agree that the way out of the impasse would be to find ways to diminish the impact of the USFWS's hardwired content in adaptive management by obtaining firm USFWS recognition that a much wider range of options was available than merely those of the agency's natural flow model. If one is to minimize hardwiring solutions, one finds refuge in adaptive management possibilities. If one is to follow the fork in the road that leads to building a viable habitat recovery program, the means might be to construct an adaptive management approach that can abide the states' defined contributions position while incorporating the federal natural flow approach. Much would rest on what adaptive management would come to mean in its actual application along the river.

CONCLUSION

The federal regulatory process had moved the states well beyond where they had originally intended to be. What had begun on their part as an attempt to provide habitat land, an average annual amount of water, replacement for future depletions, and support for a research and monitoring program had been transformed into a program that would attempt to relax channel-carrying capacity constraints far upstream of critical habitat, produce variable flows by regulating and bypassing water with the intent to restore habitat, and require continual open-ended conversations guided by an adaptive management process. All this meant that as they continued their struggle, the states could expect to see new evaluation criteria and new demands on behalf of the species. This would continue during the second and subsequent program increments. As long as a viable ESA was in place, their future would be a succession of GC-2, GC-3, GC-4, GC-5, ad infinitum. All parties knew that, although final biological opinions were not in themselves negotiable documents, at any given time the USFWS's floor of expectations could quickly become the water users' ceiling of response. They also knew the key to a workable plan would be ascertaining how to define and manage an adaptive management process. How could adaptive management be organized to serve two conflicting visions of habitat restoration—defined contributions and natural flow river processes?

CHAPTER 28

Adaptive Management

Lashing Together Conflicting Visions with a Chinese Wall

At its core, the struggle over the draft biological opinion (DBO) was a fight about how adaptive management would be conducted on the Platte River. That fight, in turn, was about how the interests would govern themselves under uncertain conditions. Whatever adaptive management was going to mean, it had to offer a way to manage intensified conflicts regarding (1) regulatory requirements for specific front-loaded program substance—how could state commitments be tied to the delivery of measurable benefits to species while also acknowledging the states' defined contribution stance and their refusal to share in any natural flow vision; (2) politics—how to arrange for two conflicting program visions at the very center of the program to coexist; and (3) science—whose hypotheses were to be tested in the service of which river vision? A viable adaptive management plan would have to accomplish all this. The problems tormented negotiators for years, especially from 2003 to 2005.

DEFINING PROGRAM SUFFICIENCY

The Endangered Species Act (ESA) has rested on the premise that there will always be a clear-cut problem in the form of demonstrated jeopardy for a given species (Rohlf 2001). Furthermore, there will be identifiable ways to fix the problem that could constitute a "reasonable and prudent alternative" (RPA). RPAs, in turn, can be scientifically evaluated by biologists and other technical people. The legislation did not address issues posed by the huge uncertainties that accompany large landscape–scale, multiple-phase habitat recovery efforts

(National Research Council of the National Academies 1995; Rohlf 2001). How can anyone determine at a given point in time what will be "sufficient" in a first program increment when all known program impacts will be modest at best and will take decades before they provide substantial habitat recovery? Habitat restoration programs must necessarily conduct only partially controlled quasi-experiments in field settings open to various interpretations (Poff et al. 1997). At best, there can be only a tentative and incomplete understanding of interactions among the many critical variables. Practitioners cannot pretend to forecast with any certainty specific outcomes over many years in complex ecosystems.

Given all this, what could be done? It is clear that under the ESA (Endangered Species Act 1973: section 7.a.2) each federal agency has an obligation to ensure that its actions are "not likely to jeopardize the continued existence" of federally listed species or "result in the destruction or adverse modification" of their designated critical habitat. The ESA is therefore simultaneously weak and strong. It is weak in the sense that the law only requires that agency actions not hurt listed species. It is strong in the sense that it makes not doing damage to species absolute. There can be no tradeoffs between small hurts to a listed species and substantial gains in other dimensions—for example, economic gains or political coalition-building needs. Therefore, given the history of injury to habitats on the Platte, to pass muster, any proposed habitat recovery program had to demonstrate that the historical trend of habitat degradation would be reversed in a manner that would do no harm in any knowing way and provide something measurably beneficial to each of the four listed target species, as determined by the best available science. That general mandate left open a rich variety of possibilities.

Except in general terms, biology cannot specify exactly what a river ought to look like. Furthermore, even if all parties could agree on the relative worth of various restoration outcomes, there would be optional ways to pursue them. A commitment to examine clearly stated hypotheses using peer-reviewed, open civic science was necessary, but in itself it was insufficient for recovery program building. Can adaptive management alone, as a systematic investigation and technical interpretation of empirically testable hypotheses in ecosystems of theory-defying complexity, lead the way to viable river and wet meadow habitat restoration? The answer is no. The program governance process that must guide adaptive management will obtain essential information from many other sources—such as refereed literature, best guesses, understanding provided by river experience, and common sense. Adaptive management must be governed by people engaged in sustained, open civic discourse wherein generalized principles of scientific understanding are embedded with local site-specific knowledge.

THE BIRTH OF NEW PLATTE BASIN GOVERNANCE

The Platte Basin water governance community was slowly being reconstituted around new rules. Community has never meant that people need to agree with each other, but it has always meant there would be an understanding of how to conduct problem-solving discourse. The actors needed to figure out how to govern themselves under conditions in which (1) the withdrawal of any given player could wreck the common project, (2) wreckage of the project would impose high costs on everyone, (3) program actions would always be a calculated gamble, and (4) one actor—the U.S. Fish and Wildlife Service (USFWS)—had the legally endowed capacity to score the adequacy (or lack thereof) of program outcomes.

The USFWS held the ultimate trump card: it could define sufficiency and therefore program compliance. But the states could only sign on to a program that would provide maximum possible constraint on federal intrusion. An adaptive management plan had to do far more than test hypotheses and draw reasoned conclusions; it had to incorporate a way of living together by defining mutually acceptable ways to disagree within an uncomfortable, deeply divided Platte Basin community whose members were all caught in the same political-legal trap. Adaptive management issues were not so much about any particular concept, principle, or procedure. The central issue was, how will adaptive management work in a regulatory environment where the states and federal communities had incompatible policy positions and program compliance was at stake?

REACHING A DEAL

The DBO (U.S. Fish and Wildlife Service 2004a) concluded that the adaptive management portion of the proposed program was underdeveloped; it needed specific substance in the form of empirically testable hypotheses that would explicitly reflect the agency's vision of natural variable flows for river restoration. Up to that time, the differences in the parties' river visions had been papered over by keeping them out of program document language. However, the USFWS's assessment of GC-1 and GC-2 called for explicit recognition of the natural flow model in program plans. That call was directly connected to the question of program sufficiency and was bolstered by the National Research Council's (NRC) endorsement of normative flows as important to habitat restoration. The paper fig leaves had thereby fallen away; the issue of what to do with naked contrasting river restoration visions was out in the open for everyone to confront.

Forks in the Road: The States' View

The states' representatives and their water user colleagues saw the reinforcement of the natural flow vision in the DBO for what it was—a non-jeopardy decision requirement, a direct attack on their defined contribution position. An open-ended natural flow view placed in the heart of program implementation through the use of adaptive management threatened the states' defined contribution stance. The states sought to defend their embattled position by advancing their "forks-in-the-road" view of the matter. They asserted that they did not have to have a recovery program deal at the cost of acknowledging the USFWS's natural flow position in a program document. Walking away from years of efforts to negotiate a basin-wide cooperative agreement was a possible option. The stakes were high. Thoroughly professional, thoughtful, and highly skilled people on every side struggled to keep their emotions in check. The states contended that the DBO represented a betrayal of earlier understandings.

The states had been prepared to allow the USFWS to conduct adaptive management under their scrutiny and in keeping with state laws and regulations. But the DBO had clearly signaled that the agency, in their view, wanted to take the program in the direction of too much hardwired natural flow content, to the exclusion of other ways of serving species habitats. The USFWS wanted to use peak and pulse flows to move sediment to build sandbars; if that did not work, the agency would then demand more peak and pulse flows to move sediment and build sandbars. This could go on and on. Good water and money would be repeatedly thrown into an unworkable program pit. The states wanted to see science work on behalf of methods other than those required by the natural flow model. They wanted to incorporate much more in the way of mechanical manipulations on the river and more reliance on sandpit habitat for terns and plovers. Adaptive management should not be loaded with natural flow prejudice; there must not be pre-judgment as to what will best work for the species.

Since the beginning of the negotiations, the states had feared that future moment when the USFWS would want to pursue adaptive management in a manner unacceptable to them. The Governance Committee would, in all likelihood, be deadlocked over changing directions. If the situation were not resolved in favor of the USFWS, the recovery program would be declared to be out of compliance. Therefore, the states were determined never to abandon their clear-cut black-and-white defined contribution approach. As long as the states fulfilled their obligations by delivering defined contributions of land, water, and money, water users would know they had a defensible claim to regulatory certainty. However, if the states were to jump into the USFWS natural flow arena, they saw themselves as never being certain about where they stood. In that world, program compliance would come and go according to shifting and capricious considerations advanced by federal analysts who themselves could not be expected to agree on what program sufficiency should mean.

The DBO pushed the states into a corner. If the negotiations could not find a solution to governing together in a way that fully acknowledged their defined contribution stance prior to the release of the final BO, forks in the road lay ahead. Program abandonment was a distinct possibility.

Forks in the Road: The USFWS and States' Views

FEDERAL VIEW: There did not have to be only one vision of the river. There was room for multiple perspectives. But the array of visions must include a viable variable water flow regime that could serve the targeted species as determined by the USFWS. Adaptive management required a specific direction; it could not consist of little more than trial and error strung out over a long time period while the players haggled over every little decision. An adaptive management plan, unhinged from a vision of how to improve and maintain river habitat, was not defensible. The states' stance on this matter made a mockery of the entire federal regulatory process. Environmental impact statement (EIS), BO, and program documents would be vacuous. The USFWS could not administer such a plan, the courts would not defend it, and Congress would not pay for it.

The states are sovereign river managers, but their policy makers and water users must authentically buy into the program goals. The USFWS has not been comforted by the states' insistence on repeatedly asserting program document language to the effect that they do not agree that peak flows and pulses are biologically or hydrologically necessary to benefit target species. The states have resisted hardwiring specifics into program agreements, but federal law requires that the USFWS develop a BO that can stand up to public inspection, including that of juried science. A combination of federal law and a lack of cooperation from the states accounted for the so-called hardwiring. The agency had no alternative. The USFWS position was endorsed by the National Research Council of the National Academies of Science.

STATES' VIEW: We agree that the NRC report is one of many sources of material for eventual use in adaptive management. At a future time, when it is appropriate to do a peer review of management action "X," the report will be relevant. There is no reason to put any findings from the report in the adaptive management plan.

USFWS: The federal government spent a lot of money to have the NRC review done; it would be wrong to ignore it when putting program plans together. In the final analysis, there has been a pattern of significant channel degradation on the central Platte. The USFWS cannot place itself in a position where if peak and pulse flows do not work quickly and adequately, the states would have grounds to abandon the entire policy of using variable flows to help reverse channel degradation.

STATES' VIEW: We know that over the longer run the USFWS wears two hats: (1) as a partner with the states in program implementation and (2) as a judge empowered to grant or withdraw program compliance. As judge, the agency brings to our river an unclear vision of what will be necessary to attain habitat

369

restoration. In the foreseeable future, federal negotiators at this table will be replaced with new decision makers who will not have walked with us through the issues. As representatives of sovereign states, we have an obligation to protect our citizens from arbitrary and capricious reasoning future federal representatives may bring to the table. Put simply: we do not trust the USFWS to keep its failures and frustrations with its river processes model separate from overall program compliance by the states.

USFWS: We fully understand that we are all working in an uncertain world. Specific actions undertaken in the course of good-faith adaptive management may well fail. We have made it clear for years that the program can suffer failures without causing the denial of regulatory certainty. We have always supported language in the program document that provides flexibility for change in strategies, tactics, hypotheses, and objectives. We expect that our understanding of what works will expand over time. The agency has established a record of being reasonable.

STATES' VIEW: That is what you say now, but what will some future agency team say?

Forks in the Road: Environmentalists' View

Environmentalists viewed the entire scene as a dismal display of states and their water users once again refusing to do much of anything different from what they had been doing for over 100 years. They were confident that the natural flow perspective would work to advance habitat restoration—with sufficient time, assets, and a good-faith effort. But they also knew that the program, under the best of circumstances, would have only modest resources to invest in an extensively disturbed network of ecosystems. Advancing restoration would be difficult and time-consuming. The states' forks-in-the-road talk provided no comfort. Environmentalists saw in the states' posture a desire to take every avenue that promised quick abandonment of any program action that smacked of natural flow approaches. They fretted that if a given action X did not work in a short period of time, states and water users would want to abandon X in favor of the cheapest and crudest mechanical interventions. In the wake of the August 2004 DBO and the states' negative reaction that had them talking about abandoning the program, how could water providers be counted upon to enthusiastically join in the creation of the best possible circumstances for program success?

Environmentalists worried that the USFWS was being too soft on the states on the "skunky" issues, particularly with regard to the role of natural flows in an adaptive management plan. But they also sympathized with the plight of the agency in general—particularly the Lakewood, Colorado–based Mountain and Prairie Region, which was on the political hot seat. In the November 2004 elections, George W. Bush and Richard Cheney were reelected, and Republican majorities widened in both the U.S. House of Representatives and the U.S. Senate. Environmentalists watched anxiously as the regional service crew struggled to move ahead with a meaningful adaptive management plan in an openly hostile national political context while facing fierce resistance from three states on the Platte. USFWS demands that were too strong could trigger the states to bolt for intervention by DOI secretary Gail Norton. USFWS demands that were too weak would force environmentalists to resort to the courts. Either way, the costs would be high. Ammunition could too easily be placed in the hands of those who would reap political gain from a failed Platte River cooperative program.

Chinese Wall

Something constructive had to be done. The states were actively pushing a forks-in-the-road message while also mumbling about possibly escalating the entire program issue to the level of the friendly Gale Norton. The USFWS was bearing down more intensely in 2003–2005 as it moved toward a final EIS and BO that would eventuate in April and June 2006, respectively. Each side calculated that the other would yield to avoid seeing the entire program collapse. The states were gambling that the USFWS had too much at stake in the gains it had made over the years to allow them to abandon the negotiations. The USFWS, in turn, doubted that the states would bolt given the costs they would bring upon themselves. Yet meeting by meeting they were edging toward a situation neither party could afford.

How could calamity be averted? During the course of meetings and an extended conference telephone call during November–December 2004 and January 2005, negotiators agreed to build a wall. In words negotiators used repeatedly in 2004–2006, that wall would be "tall and thick and extend to the horizon as far as the eye could see." They would recognize their conflicting river visions, place considerations of program sufficiency on one side of the wall, and put their common adaptive management work on the other side.

The basic concept had been batted around for months as the parties tussled over program starting points, flexibility language, and forks in the road. There was no exact moment at which the Chinese Wall concept was born, but the critical event arguably occurred on December 13, 2004, when the Governance Committee convened for negotiations at a Denver hotel near what was once Stapleton International Airport. The negotiators worked for two days (December 13–14) in the ambiance of a large, profusely lit Christmas tree. They worked on a crowded agenda that addressed a wide range of problems, but adaptive management was front and center. Just days before (December 2–3), they had been through their first adaptive management workshop, led by five practitioners. It was clear that meaningful adaptive management regarding Platte River recovery would go nowhere unless a treaty could be signed by adherents of the two conflicting river visions. On December 13 they worked to construct a compromise text, the operative centerpiece of which stated:

> Adaptive management, in the technical sense, is a series of scientifically driven actions that use monitoring and research results to test assumptions, hypotheses, or management objectives and uses. . . . [T]he information [is used] to improve . . . them. . . . The use of any assumptions, hypotheses, or management objectives is part of the adaptive management process [and] is fundamental to concepts of uncertainty, learning, and mid-course adjustment, and is not relevant for purposes of determining ESA compliance during the first increment.

There it was, the long-sought solution. It had been found by making a critical distinction—separating the outcomes of any given set of adaptive management actions on the river from the business of fulfilling program milestones that would determine program sufficiency. The negotiators disassociated the program adaptive management plan from the fulfillment of milestones by building a Chinese Wall between the two. The adaptive management plan could incorporate federal visions of river processes, along with contrary state hypotheses, while program sufficiency would not depend on attaining any particular program objective in any particular way. The idea was to build a wall between ESA compliance as measured by milestone fulfillment on one side and the particulars of program adaptive management on the other. The bigger and longer the wall, the more the states could tolerate USFWS experimentation on the river.

The language formulated that December day would survive and be placed in the final program document, in the preface to the adaptive management plan (*Platte River Recovery Program* 2006: attachment 3, pp. 1–2). On one side of the Chinese Wall, the USFWS would evaluate program merits by comparing events to program milestones and would draw conclusions about program sufficiency. On the other side of the wall would be systematic adaptive management, any particular results of which on a given river segment during a specific time period would not be used to determine program compliance. Operating in its own niche, conceptually separate from any milestone, adaptive management would proceed within the constraints of state-defined program contributions centered on 10,000 acres of land habitat in the first program increment, 130,000–150,000 acre feet of annual average reductions of shortages to target flows, and the promised money. Construction of the wall would free the energy needed to move ahead with an adaptive management plan.

Adaptive Management Help

The draft biological opinion had demanded a strengthened adaptive management plan prior to the agreement to devise the Chinese Wall. Therefore, during the fall of 2004, members of the Governance Committee had put together a list of recommended adaptive management practitioners and voted on their preferences. On December 2 the five chosen consultants met with the Governance Committee for the first time to begin systematically working through adaptive management issues. They had never worked together, but each consultant had experience with the application of adaptive management concepts (see Appendix E). Their first task was to help the Governance Committee learn much more about adaptive management; later efforts were focused on the specifics of producing a Platte River adaptive management plan.

These practitioner-consultants also assisted with developing recommendations regarding the organization of a socially and politically safe space to examine and reflect on adaptive management results. This involved finding ways to segregate policy decisions suitable for the Governance Committee to address from tactical decisions that would be made by a recovery program director and staff, assisted by two advisory committees (ISAC and AMWG).

An Independent Science Advisory Committee (ISAC) would review the design of adaptive management interventions and provide all parties with a second opinion on what integrated research and monitoring evidence was telling decision makers about habitat changes and species response. ISAC was established to ensure the scientific integrity of data and interpretation that would be an important part of the information flowing to the Governance Committee. ISAC was made up of five independent scientists knowledgeable in the critical technical areas. The long-standing Water, Land, and Technical advisory committees—established in the 1999 Cooperative Agreement—provided an opportunity for the various stakeholders to participate in the synthesis of information and the formulation of recommendations to ISAC and the Governance Committee (*Platte River Recovery Program* 2006: attachment 3, p. 7).

Two adaptive management workshops were conducted in January and February 2005. The Chinese Wall arrangement then made it possible to assemble a technical working group representing the respective communities of interest at the negotiating table. This Adaptive Management Working Group (AMWG) held its first meeting in May 2005, then reconvened workshops each month from June through October of that year. Together with various combinations of the five adaptive management consultants, members of AMWG developed conceptual ecological models from which empirically testable hypotheses could be drawn. They eventually incorporated the contrary hypotheses advanced by the states. The workshops were contentious at times, but participants learned that each party could articulate his or her favorite hypotheses in a context in which friendly views were mixed with antagonistic ones. Nobody had to give up a favorite hypothesis—at least not until eventual data-based analysis tilted thinking one way or another. Forged amid these discourses, adversaries could better appreciate the implications of ideas they liked as well as ones they opposed.

Participants came to appreciate the potential for forging effective working relationships across interest group divisions.

THE SHOWDOWN

What had been born on December 13, 2004, had yet to be fully accepted. A smaller Governance Committee program group had been delegated to follow up by revising the Chinese Wall language, taking into account implications for future flexibility and program starting points. The group worked for three days on less than two pages of single-spaced text in preparation for an extended discussion of the work in a Governance Committee session on January 18–19, 2005. Sentence-by-sentence inspection had brought to light all the long-standing issues—the "skunks"—that were bedeviling the negotiators.

In that January Governance Committee session, Nebraska took the lead in expressing discomfort. Colorado had accepted the thrust of the Chinese Wall language but was openly worried about its longer-term implications. Central Nebraska Public Power and Irrigation District (CNPPID) and Nebraska Public Power District (NPPD) representatives were adamant that they could not take the USFWS's stated river management "objectives" to their constituencies—even if they were on the other side of the wall. They stated emphatically, "We see unresolvable issues here."

Over the years, as the program language had evolved, the word "objective" had come to mean provision of specific deliverables to the program in return for regulatory certainty. Now, in the Chinese Wall deal—the language that opened up "flexibility" for the parties—the word "objective" was being used much more loosely. "Objective" now included restoration of river habitats using USFWS variable flows lurking on the other side of the wall. This was driving the Nebraska district negotiators into a corner, with Colorado representatives fretting nearby. Adaptive management should be nothing more than a set of possible tools, the use of which must be subject to Governance Committee control during the course of the program. The USFWS agenda for river habitat restoration should not be connected to any particular tools—such as variable flows—anywhere, even on the other side of the wall. Nothing should be stated in the program language that would go deeper into the matter. There must be no more stuffing natural flow content into any adaptive management plan.

The NPPD in particular had important constituencies organized into Natural Resource Districts, mutual irrigation companies to which it supplied water, and municipalities—leaders of which were struggling to come to terms with the shock of Nebraska's new law, LB 962, which promised to integrate the management of groundwater and surface waters. The governor had signed the law only months earlier, in April 2004. In addition, the NPPD had customers for its electricity in the form of power cooperatives that had come to depend importantly on revenues from a history of growth in the use of electric motors to power groundwater wells. Co-op members did not tend to be enthusiastic about either LB 962 or Platte River habitat recovery. They openly criticized NPPD authorities for engaging in talks that might someday shut down well growth.

The districts claimed that all this adaptive management discussion was too much. Problems were crowding organizational agendas much too quickly. District linkages with constituents were overloaded with issues. Constituents were facing a whirlwind of suddenly accelerated change that had been held back for many years. For many Nebraska water users, LB 962—the legislation that would impose a measure of accountability for groundwater depletions to the river—topped the list of concerns, but the federal habitat restoration program was repeatedly described as always unreasonably demanding more and more. Where would it all end? Many constituents deeply resented the fact that the two districts had sat at the table negotiating away what they viewed as Nebraska water prerogatives during years of extreme drought in an effort to obtain regulatory certainty. Now the districts were being asked to present their disgruntled stakeholders with a deal to fix things by incorporating USFWS visions for the river in the program document. Their historical water interests might be protected by a conceptual distinction that negotiators had labeled a Chinese Wall. Yet the CNPPID and the NPPD feared too little goodwill was left in district-constituency relationships to hold things together if constituents found USFWS visions hardwired into the river restoration program plan.

There was also a deeper problem. The two Nebraska districts had obtained a deal regarding their Platte River obligations during the Federal Energy Regulatory Commission (FERC) re-licensing proceedings. Those terms and conditions stretched them as far as they wanted to go. For years there had been little incentive to push themselves beyond the FERC arrangements to accommodate additional USFWS agendas advanced since 1998. The fact that the CNPPID and the NPPD had their forty-year licenses in hand and the fact that the other parties at the table—including the USFWS—had signed on to that deal had empowered the districts to hold back from making new commitments. This had been the obvious flaw in the three-state negotiations for years. The FERC re-licensing situation had constituted the districts' trump card. Now that card was being openly placed face-up on the table. Either the USFWS would back away from including its natural flow language in program documents, or the districts were threatening to walk away from the negotiations.

In January 2005 the Chinese Wall breakthrough of the previous month was therefore near collapse. Talks had again suddenly stalemated. The newly born adaptive management compromise baby was in serious danger of being strangled in its crib. With their objections, the Nebraska districts had pushed the USFWS and U.S. Bureau of Reclamation (USBR) teams to their limits. If the

Chinese Wall construction was unacceptable to the Nebraska districts, nothing more could be offered.

That day—January 19, 2005—the choices were stark. In one last-gasp effort to hold the talks together, the Governance Committee negotiators—including those from the Nebraska districts—agreed to empower the executive director of the Governance Committee to unilaterally write a revised adaptive management plan that would specifically address the "flexibility" issue, meaning the nature of the flexibility each party would have on each side of the wall. The executive director was the most neutral person available and had followed details of the issues for years. Negotiators further agreed that the plan would be accepted or rejected by the Governance Committee without renegotiating it in any significant way. The plan would either fly or fail.

The executive director was given a mandate to present the revised package to the Governance Committee at an adaptive management workshop slated for February 23. Following that session, if the stalemate continued, the status of the entire program would be elevated to the highest levels of the Department of the Interior for review and judgment. That would undoubtedly mean either significant intervention by Washington, D.C., authorities with little sensitivity to the needs of the parties or abandonment of the cooperative program negotiations.

The February 23–24 meetings did not result in a stalemate, but they were inconclusive. When negotiators convened again on March 9–10, the tension was palpable. All three states were being drawn into a relationship with the USFWS that would somehow place USFWS natural flow concepts in the program document. The Nebraska districts were being dragged to a decision point from which they would either bolt away or step beyond their FERC arrangements into a program with an explicit federal natural river processes component.

> WYOMING VOICE: The USFWS wants a commitment from us [the three states], and we want to give it to them. The only question is, how can we do it?

> COLORADO VOICE: Colorado can abide the USFWS's need to specify hypotheses relating to the "clear, level, pulse" [see Chapter 15] as long as the adaptive management process is open to study the "clear, level, and plough." This assumes that a strong wall exists between adaptive management outcomes and program compliance.

> NEBRASKA DISTRICT VOICE: This entire process is leaving our constituents behind; this thing is a railroad job. It is unreasonable to request the states to address the adaptive management plan today without time for sufficient study.

Environmentalists and USFWS representatives looked on with incredulity. The conversation had been protracted. The states had long since inserted a disclaimer to the effect that participation in the voluntary program did not imply an agreement that peak pulse or other USFWS recommended flows were biologically or hydrologically necessary for the recovery of target species. Furthermore, the Governance Committee had earlier agreed to place a second disclaimer in the program document, namely: "Adoption of the AMP [Adaptive Management Plan] does not constitute an admission by the states or water users of support or acceptance that any hypothesis or ecological model is valid, is based on the best science available, or should be used as a measure of appropriate or reasonable accomplishments or success" (*Platte River Recovery Program* 2006: attachment 3, p. 1). How could today's need for a decision be considered a railroad job?

EXECUTIVE DIRECTOR: The Governance Committee has established a schedule. That means work on the final EIS and BO must be pushed hard quickly. If there is to be any chance of a non-jeopardy BO, the USFWS must have a completed adaptive management plan that has earned the support of each state. Its substance must include, among other things, a commitment to permit the program to experiment with alternative ways to produce a wide, braided channel. States can offer their own hypotheses, but the USFWS must also be allowed to pursue its hypotheses. Let us see if it is possible to finalize language that the states—especially the Nebraska districts—can live with.

NEBRASKA DISTRICT VOICE: Yes, let us try it and see if we can get something to take back to our constituencies.

FEDERAL VOICE: Let us set a meeting date to have a workshop on formulating alternative hypotheses and thereby open up a path for state constituencies to buy into the program.

NEBRASKA-LINCOLN TO NEBRASKA DISTRICTS: We must not get bogged down in another word-by-word debate on the adaptive management plan or the entire process will collapse. We must back off and look at the bigger picture.

FEDERAL VOICE: To reach a winning biological opinion, there must be conceptual ecological models with real substance to them and a commitment to sensible program starting points. An important rule can be: one party will not edit or otherwise argue with another party's hypothesis. A party that disagrees with hypothesis X will simply advance hypothesis non-X or anti-X.

During the afternoon of March 9, the various parties addressed issues of wording projected onto a screen. They concluded the session with an agreement that the executive director would revise the adaptive management language that evening in time for a review the next morning. The revision, responsive to points made on March 9, became the priority focus on the 10th. It was understood that the revision placed before them that second day would constitute an unfinished working document sufficient to meet the needs of the USBR Environmental Impact Assessment Team and the USFWS biological opinion workers.

On the morning of March 10, the executive director asked the districts: do you feel these revisions are a sufficient improvement?

NEBRASKA DISTRICT VOICE: We will study them and comment later.

EXECUTIVE DIRECTOR: We need to know now. If you hate the document, we have a problem and cannot move forward. If you can accept the general ideas, with an understanding that we will be open to clarification to enhance understanding, then we can move forward.

Silence.

USFWS, USBR, environmental, Wyoming, Colorado, and Nebraska-Lincoln attendees looked on as the isolated district representatives sat motionless, glumly staring ahead. Would they bolt from the room?

EXECUTIVE DIRECTOR, after a considerable pause: Do you agree that the language as revised provides a basis to go forward?

DISTRICT VOICE: Can we add new hypotheses later?

EXECUTIVE DIRECTOR: Yes.

Silence.

Many attendees stared intently at the computer-projected revised text on a screen in a corner of the room.

ENVIRONMENTALIST LEADER: I move that the revised language be memorialized by putting it in the minutes of this meeting.

The motion was seconded.

A unanimous vote in support of the first substantive motion brought to the floor of the Governance Committee negotiating sessions in years would keep the program alive. If district representatives voted no and left the session, the dead body of a failed program would be laid at CNPPID's and NPPD's doorsteps. That reality would haunt their relationships with Wyoming, Colorado, Nebraska-Lincoln, and the Department of the Interior for the rest of their lives. It would also mean their FERC re-licensing agreement would be reopened.

Discussion in soft voices slowly broke out among the other negotiators regarding small editorial points. Soon, the districts' representatives offered a few of their suggestions, which were gladly accepted as "friendly" amendments. Tension eased; the social atmosphere warmed.

MEETING CHAIR (leader of the Colorado delegation): Is there any objection to the language proposed for the minutes?

The room was quiet.

CHAIR: Are we ready to vote?

Silence.

CHAIR: All in favor say "aye."

The motion passed unanimously. Language about program flexibility, starting points, and the Chinese Wall had been blessed by all parties and placed in the official meeting minutes. In less than a day, the program had gone from the brink of an abyss to endorsement. The Governance Committee could now move on to other matters. The parties made the journey to program completion because they had lashed themselves together with a Chinese Wall.

Conclusions

Making a Mesh of Things

CHAPTER 29

Search for Approval

If there was ever a celebration of the completion of twelve years of negotiations, the nearest approximation followed a morning of discussion of the political challenges in obtaining authorizations and appropriations from the federal government. It was Monday, December 11, 2006. The setting was a hotel conference room near Denver International Airport. Members of the Governance Committee and some staff members took a break to eat cake and enjoy a cup of coffee. Some shared memories of more difficult times. This session constituted the last gathering of the people who, as negotiators, had constructed the terms of the Platte River Habitat Recovery Program. The first meeting of the program's Governance Committee—consisting of some of the same personalities—would convene on February 7 at the same location (see Appendix C) and carry on with implementation of the deal that officially began on January 1, 2007.

Negotiators had crafted an intricate program. The deal would deliver the big prize—regulatory certainty through a streamlined Endangered Species Act (ESA) Section 7 process. There would be template applications and biological opinions for new water-related activities in the Platte Basin that fell into a federal nexus. A water user soliciting federal approval of a proposed action would apply to the appropriate federal action agency. That agency, under the terms of the ESA, would determine if the project would likely negatively impact one or more listed species and, if so, would initiate a consultation with the U.S. Fish and Wildlife Service (USFWS). The agency would then determine if the proposed water user effort would fall within the scope of the Platte River Habitat

Recovery Program. If so, the USFWS would find that any negative impacts had already been analyzed in a Platte River programmatic environmental impact statement and biological opinion. Consultations under the ESA could then be handled directly and inexpensively in a matter of months. The collective action of Platte habitat restoration and maintenance will have served as the ESA compliance measure. All of this will also work for any proposed federal project that would impose a depletion on the basin's water flow system.

The three basin states and the federal Department of the Interior (DOI) had produced a collective product that promised to save all parties untold millions of dollars and years of effort while simultaneously undertaking to stop and reverse habitat degradation on the central Platte. Yet no party was deeply enamored of the final product. None had been able to strong-arm the others to impose its will beyond constrained limits. They had checked and counterchecked each other in ways that left each party with significant reservations.

If program leaders were going to obtain federal support, there would have to be unified advocacy among the three states on behalf of the program. However, each state had constituencies waiting for openings to attack the program arrangements. Unity would be difficult to forge. Furthermore, no politician in the interior West has historically been able to acquire much political capital by openly—and to public fanfare—dashing forward to advance ESA agendas that are easily made politically toxic in a bumper-sticker civitas. It takes political courage to step up as a champion of the ESA; that courage was best mustered when the politics of organizing support was conducted quietly backstage. The state representatives worked hard to hold their political coalitions together in late 2005 and 2006—the latter an election year.

Electioneering meant office seekers would open up another political silly-season—a time when jockeying for position on party-designated issues would trump serious policy thought, a time when it was more important to inflict body blows on opponents than to think creatively and constructively on behalf of a complicated ESA program. In each state, program champions were able to keep Platte River issues below electioneering notice. Yet even so, in the context of the Platte River Basin, it would be a messy business to run political traplines to arrange essential endorsements in state legislatures from governors, the U.S. Congress, and the George W. Bush administration. All this has the makings of a worthy tale, but most of it remains beyond the scope of these pages.

COLORADO

Using the social organizational capital built into the South Platte Lower River Group (SPLRG) and the Platte River Project (PRP) (see Chapter 9), water leaders set about to construct and incorporate an operational nonprofit organization to fund and implement the Colorado portion of the larger Platte Basin plan. They eventually incorporated the organization as the South Platte Water Related Activities Program (SPWRAP).

SPWRAP

The objective of South Platte water users was to develop an organization that would continually examine the balance of accretions and depletions at the Colorado-Nebraska state line, as measured at the Julesburg gauge. The entity would daily implement the Tamarack Plan on behalf of the three-state program by ensuring the proper re-timing of water flows from times of excess, as measured near Grand Island, Nebraska, to times of shortages to USFWS target flows. During the first program increment, that effort would entail installing the capacity to produce an average annual 10,000-acre-foot reduction in USFWS defined shortages to the Nebraska border to offset historical pre-1997 depletions. In addition, it would mean developing capacity to produce water offsets to cover post–June 30, 1997, "new" depletions according to a population-driven formula (see Chapter 9). Colorado agreed that Tamarack Plan depletion offset waters would amount to an annual average of 5,000 acre feet by no later than two years post–program initiation, and the quantity would increase to the full 10,000 acre feet four years after the start of the program. Furthermore, SPWRAP would provide steady representation of Colorado's water interests to the recovery program's Governance Committee.

The costs of the operation were placed squarely on South Platte River depleters in a federal nexus—specifically, those who would need a federal permit, license, or funding or whose work would need to be reviewed by a federal agency. That group includes cities, industries, and some agricultural enterprises. Many Colorado South Platte agricultural water providers (such as mutual irrigation companies and irrigation districts) have not historically been in a federal nexus; unless they expect to undertake an action (such as compromising a wetland) in the future that would place them in such a relationship, they may not see the need to join SPWRAP's collective insurance scheme.

SPWRAP, with funds provided by member annual assessments, represented the lead organization responsible for constructing Colorado's water contribution to the three-state habitat recovery program. The organization's assessments will be supplemented by financial contributions from private-sector entities (for example, Ducks Unlimited, an organization committed to the provision of wetlands). To the extent possible, SPWRAP members hope to fund Colorado's first increment $24 million cash contribution to the recovery program with dollars from the Colorado Species Conservation Trust Fund. (For the program budget, see Appendix F; for the trust fund, see http://cwcb.state.co.us/NR/rdonly/B3565C5E-5696-4B59-9B70-9B4AA0D2EA53/0/06.pdf.) That cash, along with money provided by Wyoming and the federal DOI through the U.S. Bureau of Reclamation (USBR), will fund the three-state program's cash needs.

Colorado's choice to create SPWRAP as an implementing organization had the advantage of permitting water providers to fund the bulk of Colorado's water component while avoiding an annual pilgrimage to the state legislature to request funding amid incessant political battles. SPWRAP's direct internal funding of the Tamarack Plan's water re-timing was removed from state legislative money appropriation politics; however, SPWRAP will annually trek to the Colorado General Assembly to ask for money for general habitat recovery program costs ($24 million), to be paid in installments over the first thirteen-year increment. Insofar as the General Assembly makes these funds available, that burden will be lifted from SPWRAP. However, if state of Colorado funds are not available to pay the annual installments, SPWRAP will have to juggle its assessments accordingly to fill any funding gaps.

Organizational Structure

Bylaws were adopted on May 12, 2005, as the first order of business at the inaugural board of directors meeting, held in Berthoud, Colorado (SPWRAP 2005a). At the heart of SPWRAP's structure are five classes of membership (SPWRAP 2005b). Members in good standing are issued a Certificate of Membership in one of the five categories—agricultural, industrial, municipal, other water organizational (mutual companies, irrigation districts, conservancy districts), and miscellaneous. That certification constitutes evidence of depletions coverage, recognized as such by the USFWS in the streamlined ESA Section 7 consultation process. The board of directors has the discretion to deny membership to any person or entity if that membership would require depletions offset water in amounts likely to jeopardize SPWRAP's ability to fulfill its obligations.

The concept of a SPWRAP unit is at the heart of the organization. The unit unites Platte River Habitat Recovery Program collective benefit produced (regulatory certainty) with the amount and type of member water use, amount of annual assessment to be paid, and number of votes to be cast by any given member in conducting organizational governance. Each of the five membership classes has been assigned "units" per member in ways deemed most appropriate to that class of activity.

Each unit confers one vote in the conduct of organization business. Miscellaneous class members are empowered to vote on all matters except the election of directors. Each of the four other classes of members is entitled to elect one director, except that the municipal class elects six because the distribution of units across membership classes ensures that the bulk of assessment revenue will come from the municipal category. The general estimate is that more than 90 percent of Colorado's cost of participating in the Platte River Habitat Recovery Program will be borne by cities and towns.

Assessments are expressed in dollars per unit. For example, the board of directors roughly projected a need for an amount in the range of $3 million per year for the first thirteen-year program increment, calibrated in 2005 dollars. To mobilize the necessary annual revenue, the board established a 2007 assessment rate of 30 cents per unit and continued it in 2008 (SPWRAP 2007). If a mutual irrigation company commanded 30,000 acres of irrigated land, the entity needed 3,000 units. At a rate of 30 cents/unit, that ditch system provided its share of the central Platte recovery program at a cost of only $900 per year—no small bargain when one considers the quantities of water diverted from the river to agricultural purposes. On the municipal front, there are many single-family equivalent water taps along Colorado's highly populated Front Range. Rough calculations of municipal units to be assessed in the area extending from the Denver metropolitan area and Boulder north to Longmont, Loveland, Greeley, Fort Collins, and many towns in between—given six units per single-family equivalent water tap—established the municipal assessment at $1.80 per year per six-unit tap. That amount paid the vast majority of SPWRAP's obligations. It translated to an average of 15 cents per month added to a family's municipal water bill—a pittance.

Any applicant for membership in any category must pay all earlier-year assessments that would have been imposed back to 2007, the first year of SPWRAP operations when the Platte River Habitat Recovery Program was launched. This provision ensures that latecomers cannot enjoy a free ride on past program investments. There is therefore no incentive to delay in joining SPWRAP and in shouldering responsibility for central Platte River habitat restoration and maintenance.

Knowing that SPWRAP was in place and with a push from Colorado South Platte water providers, Governor Bill Owens signed the Platte River Recovery Program document on October 26, 2006. He forwarded the four original copies (one each for the three states and one for the U.S. Department of the Interior) to Nebraska governor Dave Heineman, who affixed his signature five days later.

SPWRAP Policy Implications

SPWRAP became the exclusive means by which Colorado South Platte water diverters could obtain access to a streamlined ESA Section 7 consultation process and the regulatory certainty that comes with a successful basin-wide habitat recovery program. Thirsty water providers—especially rapidly growing cities, towns, and rural water supply districts—now had an option to protect their supply sources by joining an organization that could effectively deliver regulatory certainty at much less cost through collective action than they could accomplish by individual effort.

Not only does SPWRAP promise to cover depletions on behalf of ESA listed species at less cost than any alternative, it also has the potential to prevent a disorganized self-seeking rush to the Lower South Platte River by water-seeking Front Range communities in a careless "buy-up/dry-up" quest for water supplies to cover their individual expansion of diversions upstream. Rather than be witness to "buy-up/dry-up" activities that would deplete Colorado's Lower South Platte River agricultural and trade center business, local well owners who fulfill essential criteria can be financially rewarded for having participated in the production of Tamarack Plan recharge credits that come from re-timing water from times of excess to periods of shortage. This activity enhances, rather than shrivels, economic activity on behalf of an environmental cause. Cities and other upstream users, who need to make the river whole at the Nebraska border, have an attractive option in SPWRAP and need not therefore participate in creating an economic and social sacrifice zone among Lower South Platte communities.

NEBRASKA

In 2005 and 2006, Nebraska Platte River program supporters faced an almost perfect political storm as they struggled to garner support for state and federal approvals. In the midst of ongoing drought, Nebraskans were confronting new designations of fully appropriated and over-appropriated groundwater areas upstream of Elm Creek (whose mouth is at the top of critical habitat). The LB 962 legislative process had been rife with disputes between groundwater user majorities and surface appropriators. Natural Resource Districts (NRDs)—dominated by leaders of well users—were deeply opposed to both the internal state LB 962 water integration agenda and the requirements of the Platte River program. Yet they were the entities that would be counted on to secure offset water with which to implement the two programs, to fulfill the requirements of state law and federal ESA needs.

In addition, NRDs in the Republican River Basin were beset with demands from Kansas that Nebraska irrigators address the costly fact that their pumping race to groundwater had over-appropriated waters in violation of the Nebraska-Kansas interstate compact. Addressing Republican River liability would require a major investment of public revenues from one source or another. At a time of limited state treasury funds, a dollar spent on the Republican was one not available to the Platte. Where were the Platte program (the costs of providing offset flows for pre- and post-1997 depletions) and Republican River Compact compliance dollars going to come from in a state that wanted to lower its tax rates to attract businesses, which were always seeking the lowest possible tax environment? In addition, for many western and central Platte Nebraskans in the water sector, the simple truth was that the proposed Platte River Habitat

Recovery Program was not a top priority. Republican River Compact issues and LB 962 policy implementation were higher on the list.

Searching for a Champion

Meanwhile, the Central Nebraska Public Power and Irrigation District (CNPPID) and the Nebraska Public Power District (NPPD) were fighting to the last moments of the negotiations. It was impossible for them to go to political leaders in Lincoln and render support for a Platte River program they were threatening to abandon if they did not get their way with the USFWS. In the midst of all this, water leaders in Lincoln—especially in the Department of Natural Resources—and in the western panhandle were confronting bleak prospects for securing essential funding from the state's unicameral legislature. The majority of that assembly's members were elected by citizens in the much more heavily populated eastern districts; many looked at the state water scene with skepticism, baffled as to why the state treasury should be tapped to resolve problems created by western and central Nebraska water users.

What Nebraska desperately needed but did not have until the proverbial last minute was a well-organized Platte River Habitat Recovery Program champion, a coalition of water providers that could go to Governor Heineman and key legislative leaders and say something to the effect that "this is a critically important program that produces essential payoffs. This is what the program does. We have the support of our constituents on this. Look at the disaster that will befall us all if we drift into the no-program option. We want your support." But such a coalition did not form until the two districts cut their deal with the USFWS over hydro-cycling and bypass flows. Only then, in October 2006, could they turn their attention to securing support—just weeks before Governor Heineman was presented with a program signature sheet to sign.

Nebraska water leaders who supported the Platte River program were careful to distinguish between it and Nebraska's internal need to make well users accountable for their depletions to surface water under the new Nebraska law, LB 962. That distinction was critical because there would be no Nebraska cash contribution to the first increment of the Platte River program (see Appendix F). The major portion of the financial drain on the state and NRD treasuries would be imposed by the need to address the long-avoided internal problem of well user harm placed on surface rights and to come up with water to offset depletions placed on the central Platte post-1997 by the rush to construct groundwater wells during the state's period of forgiveness, which lasted until December 31, 2005 (see Chapter 22).

Habitat recovery program supporters pointed out the high cost of living with no recovery program in place. Water providers would have to independently self-finance the expensive business of getting back to the 1997 baseline of depletions, and they would be fiercely competitive in a highly constrained water supply environment. That prospect did not necessarily elicit love for target species habitat needs, but it could attract reluctant support from Nebraska water users. In the absence of a cooperative program, water users would be dealing directly with the USFWS without the support of the two other states in the program's Governance Committee; furthermore, the negotiated program was far superior to anything the DOI-USFWS would likely put together in individual ESA Section 7 consultations. There was no acceptable "walk-away" option. Finally, given the challenges of finding funds to address issues on the Republican River and to implement LB 962, Nebraska negotiators had arranged for the state to obtain regulatory certainty without making a cash payment out of pocket.

Building Support

Yet given the whirlwind of change pressing on central Nebraska groundwater users who dominated the relevant Natural Resource Districts, it was not clear that the proponents' arguments would prevail. On October 17, 2006, the twenty-three-member citizens' Platte River Advisory Committee, appointed by the governor, assembled in Kearney. These representatives of the several water interests had been given a mandate to carefully examine the uses and limits of the proposed Platte River Habitat Recovery Program and to recommend whether Governor Heineman should commit Nebraskans to it. The central item on the agenda was to be a vote on a motion that recommended support for the program (Potter 2006a). The atmosphere at the meeting was characterized as serious; groundwater interests let it be known that the entire process had been distasteful. Most onlookers expected a close vote, and no one would publicly predict the outcome. The vote, however, came in with eighteen in support of the motion and three opposed.

Potentially ugly scenes had been avoided. Platte River issues had been kept out of the election debates. The task force's strong positive endorsement did much to clear the political path for the governor to proceed. Heineman had not wanted to step out in support of the habitat recovery program until a series of public hearings had been completed or to do so in a way that would pre-judge the decisions of the two western Nebraska districts. The districts, in turn, would not recommend a "yes" vote until they had an arrangement acceptable to them on the issues of bypass and hydro-cycling, which happened in late July. In the wake of the hearings conducted around the state and the citizens' Platte River Advisory Committee vote, the governor announced on October 27, 2006, that he was prepared to sign the Platte River program agreement. He did so on October 31 (http://www.gov.state.ne.us/archive/news/index.html), just days before the November election. Dave Heineman won reelection handily.

WYOMING

Wyoming had well-organized Platte River program champions. They were centered in the state's Water Development Commission and among farmer-controlled irrigation districts that served as local sponsors of USBR North Platte Basin water impoundment projects. Water insiders could see that the Platte co-operative program was critical to the state's effort to protect the water yields of its large federal reservoirs. But within the state's political scene, by 2005–2006 federal implementation of the Endangered Species Act had long been a politically touchy subject that had roiled constituencies for and against ESA requirements in several contexts. There were many political minefields to avoid in the buildup to the 2006 elections. Among them was a history of rancorous debates over ESA's intent regarding grizzly bears and gray wolves (Glick 2008: 16–20; U.S. Fish and Wildlife Service 2004b, 2007; Williams 2007).

No politician in the state came out in public support of the USFWS's position on grizzly or wolf management in the years leading up to the 2006 midterm elections. Taken together, issues surrounding the grizzly bear and the status of wolves made for a political context within which it would have been difficult for any politician in any major political party to openly bless another ESA child—including the Platte River Habitat Recovery Program. Furthermore, there was unfinished business with program opponents on the Upper North Platte.

Upper North Platte Irrigators

Following the release of the draft environmental impact statement in January 2004, Upper North Platte River irrigators intensified their efforts to protect themselves from what they viewed as possible harm if the state of Wyoming—to serve municipal and industrial agendas and those of the Platte River Habitat Recovery Program—restored capacity long lost to sedimentation at Pathfinder Reservoir. Their case centered on the possibility—however remote—that if 54,000 acre feet of additional water were to someday fill the restored capacity at Pathfinder Reservoir, water rights junior to the 1904 Pathfinder right could be deprived by virtue of the increased capacity to store flows (see Chapter 11).

For years the struggle had hinged on whether, to fill Pathfinder Reservoir during the summer irrigation season, the state engineer would ever accept a request to administer water rights in a manner that would be to the disadvantage of Upper North Platte diverters. If that came to pass, irrigators with water priorities junior to Pathfinder's 1904 right would have to shut their headgates in deference to the new junior Pathfinder priority. It galled them to think they would have to suffer even the smallest loss.

Upper North Platte water users had an opportunity to attack the concept of Pathfinder modification by virtue of the fact that putting the restored water supply to work on behalf of both urban demand and the Platte River recovery program would require changes in water use. Such a change would have to win state legislative approval and would require an act of the U.S. Congress, which had originally dedicated Pathfinder's yields exclusively to agriculture. Changes of water use entailed a public process with points of political leverage for mobilized Upper North Platte citizens.

Those water users did all they could to pressure the Water Development Commission, their elected state and federal officials, and Democratic governor Dave Freudenthal to accept their critique of the Pathfinder Modification Project. In response, in 2004 the governor asked Wyoming's attorney general to examine the situation.

The attorney general addressed one central question: should the Wyoming state engineer honor a USBR call (water diversion request) on the North Platte during the irrigation season (May 1–September 30) to fill Pathfinder Reservoir under its 1904 storage right (Wyoming Attorney General 2004)? In short, the legal opinion was no. However, the matter was nuanced. Wyoming law allows flexible administration in allocating stream flows between storage and stream flow rights. The state engineer is authorized to consider a variety of factors in regulating the filling of reservoirs and balancing that demand against immediate needs of surface irrigators. A problem always rides with a downstream reservoir that comes into priority during the irrigation season and thereby imposes a call that places a demand on the entire river while making no allowance for the positive impact of return flows moving downslope from upstream diversions under junior priorities. Compelling the closure of all junior headgates in the name of filling senior reservoirs can, in this context, impose an undue burden on the juniors and thereby cause unnecessary economic loss. Therefore, the state engineer has been authorized to balance conflicting demands with an eye to minimize interference between storage rights and direct flow appropriations.

Therein lay the rub. The attorney general's opinion was clear that the state engineer should not honor a request for priority regulation of Pathfinder during the regular irrigation season, but an opportunity was left available to the state engineer to someday fill a Pathfinder hole at the Upper North Platte's expense: "Neither the U.S. Supreme Court cases nor Wyoming law requires strict conformity to the priority system between storage and direct flow rights" (Wyoming Attorney General 2004).

The Upper North Platte Valley Water Users Association, in collaboration with the Upper North Platte Valley Water Conservation Association and other groups, moved aggressively to amend the terms of the Pathfinder Modification Project and sought to insert language into the federal authorization legislation that protected their interests (Associated Press 2004; Ridenour 2008). There were many moves and countermoves. It will suffice here to note that the USBR and the state of Wyoming did not want any amendments that would restrict a water right administered under state law. That would establish a terrible precedent, with implications for all USBR projects throughout the West. Furthermore, Wyoming's Water Development Commission saw danger in any amendment to federal authorizing legislation that could potentially, and in the extreme, put the entire reservoir, not just the 53,000 acre feet of restored capacity, off limits to a federal USBR call (Straub 2007).

Wyoming water leaders and USBR authorities did their utmost to keep two issues separate. The question of a USBR call on the river during irrigation season was one thing; the question of obtaining support in the state legislature and mobilizing support for the Platte River Habitat Recovery Program authorizing legislation in the U.S. Congress was quite another. Upper North Platte water interests wanted to make support for Platte program approval conditional on a revised policy in the Wyoming-USBR relationship. The conflict dragged on (Ridenour 2008).

Wyoming Governor's Endorsement

In 2004–2006, as Platte River program leaders were attempting to build a supportive political coalition, Dave Freudenthal was a Democratic governor in a premier ESA-wary state. All three members of the state's congressional delegation were Republicans, and there was little constituency support for implementation of the ESA. Furthermore, the GOP held lopsided majorities in both chambers of the state legislature. Freudenthal won the 2002 election by only a 2 percent margin (www.cqpolitics.com/2006/01freudenthal). Any Democrat who has won a state or federal elective office in Wyoming has found it essential to reach out to independents and Republicans. In general, Wyoming water leaders worked hard to share the outlines of the Platte River Habitat Recovery Program and make clear its importance to the state's future. The two U.S. senators (Craig Thomas and Mike Enzi) and the one at-large Wyoming member of the U.S. House of Representatives (Barbara Cubin) signaled that they would not openly oppose the Platte program, but they did not want to be asked to support it either—especially prior to the November 2006 election. Governor Freudenthal knew the stakes. He tilted toward support for the Platte recovery program but moved cautiously to minimize hostility to both the program and his candidacy. He had consistently earned high job approval ratings, and he did win a second term—handily, in fact (www.cqpolitics.com/2006/01freudenthal).

The ESA never became a campaign issue in Wyoming because nobody running for office supported the federal management plans for the grizzly bear or wolves. No one wanted to arouse the hostility of irrigators on the Upper North Platte regarding Pathfinder modification. Yet it was also true that in an election year, Wyoming had no Platte River Habitat Recovery Program champions among elected officeholders at the state or federal level. The ESA was sufficiently toxic that no Wyoming politician wanted to openly bless any program that would advance an environmental cause in an election year. The Wyoming Platte River negotiating team, bolstered by the USBR, had been particularly steadfast in holding the talks together during their most troublesome moments over the years. In addition, Wyoming had much to lose if the Platte program failed and for years had worked effectively with Wyoming North Platte irrigators below Pathfinder Reservoir and secured solid support for the three states' position on the habitat recovery program among those constituencies.

After waiting a few weeks after the election earlier that month, Governor Freudenthal signed the three-state Platte River agreement on November 27, 2006. In doing so, he stated: "I have signed this agreement reluctantly. . . . There are no good choices in this area . . . but it seems to me that the only hope rests in the Platte River [Habitat] Recovery Program" (Potter 2006b). He was the last of the three governors to sign. The program still needed to secure support for an act of Congress to authorize federal funding and to endorse the Pathfinder Modification Project.

FEDERAL AUTHORIZATION

During early 2006, Platte program water leaders had two interrelated problems with respect to obtaining federal authorizing legislation. First, at that time only Colorado was in a position to openly endorse the program, but a three-state Platte River Habitat Recovery Program sponsored solely by Colorado politicians would obtain no support in Congress. Platte leaders desperately needed to find a way to get Nebraska and Wyoming into a position where they could, in a united way, push the program at the federal level. Second, Platte leaders had to proceed cautiously, given the touchiness of the ESA. Any sharp controversy could mobilize program opponents even more than was already the case. An open fight could sink any hopes for congressional authorization and appropriation of funds.

During the first year of the Platte River Habitat Recovery Program, beginning January 1, 2007, there was no federal authorization. The program launched with existing funds available from the USBR and with cash contributions from Colorado and Wyoming. On March 2, 2007—well after the November 2006 election—Nebraska senators Ben Nelson (D) and Chuck Hegel (R) introduced bipartisan legislation in the U.S. Senate to authorize the secretary of the interior to participate in the implementation of the Platte River Habitat Recovery Program and to modify the plan for Pathfinder Dam and Reservoir (Pore 2007). The bill authorized an expenditure of $157,140,000 for the first thirteen-year program increment and empowered the secretary of the interior to act through the commissioner of reclamation to implement the Platte effort in partnership with the states, other federal agencies, and non-federal entities. The sum would be adjusted annually for inflation. Colorado senators Ken Salazar (D) and Wayne Allard (R) collaborated as co-sponsors.

On the U.S. House side, Colorado representative Mark Udall (D) introduced virtually identical legislation as H.R. 1462 on March 9; by March 23 seven co-sponsors had signed on representing Nebraska, Wyoming, and Colorado. However, Marilyn Musgrave, representing Colorado's Fourth Congressional District—which included the major South Platte communities—refused to support the bill (www.congress.gov/cgi-bin/bquery).

Subsequent to internal Wyoming negotiations, the 2008 Platte River Recovery Program and Pathfinder Modification Act included in Title II, Section 203, "conditions precedent" that had not been in the original language. The section addressed concerns of Wyoming's Upper North Platte water users:

> The actions and water uses authorized . . . [regarding Pathfinder Dam modification] shall not occur . . . until final approval in a change of water use proceeding under the laws (including regulations) of the State of Wyoming for all new uses planned for Project water . . . (has been completed). Final approval, as used in this paragraph, includes exhaustion of any available review under state law of any administrative action authorizing the change of the Pathfinder Reservoir water right. (www.thomas.loc. gov/cqi-bin/query/D?c110:9.:/temp/~c110fjQMDy::)

Upper North Platte water users were greatly empowered by that language, and federal funding for the Platte recovery program could be much delayed if the act passed—not a desirable situation for program proponents. Upper valley users would advance their case at administrative hearings conducted by the Wyoming Board of Control, after which the board would issue its decision along with a supportive rationale. North Platte objectors would then examine the rationale and decide on their future course of action. If they determined that there were sufficient and compelling flaws in the state's rationale, they could seek redress in Wyoming courts. That process could pose a serious time-consuming problem. Furthermore, given that the changes in the use of Pathfinder storage water (from agricultural to municipal and environmental) were an essential component of the basin-wide habitat recovery program, the long-standing division between Upper North Platte water users on the one side and state authorities and downstream irrigators on the other would have to be directly addressed. The question became, what could the state of Wyoming do to properly address any potential economic loss to those water users? By late 2007 and early 2008, something had to be done to resolve matters. There was state senatorial support for the Upper North Platte position, widespread hostility to the ESA in general, and a need to quickly secure federal authorization of funds and changes in water use.

The full story of how a solution was reached cannot be captured in these pages. In essence, on January 3, 2008, the USBR filed a petition to be placed on the docket of the Wyoming Board of Control requesting the required changes of water use at Pathfinder. In a March hearing before the board, Upper Platte irrigators opposed the USBR request. Meanwhile, negotiations among the contesting parties had resulted in a possible solution acceptable to everyone. This backstage work made it possible to secure the essential political coalition needed to move ahead with the necessary federal legislation.

The Platte River Recovery Program U.S. House and Senate bills were integrated and packaged under Title V, Section 515—along with fifty-six other natural resource bills—of the Consolidated Natural Resources Act of 2008. The act was passed by the House of Representatives on April 29, 2008; the Senate had voted to pass it a few days earlier (www.resourcecommittee.house.gov/index. php?option =com_content&task=viewid:373). President George W. Bush signed it into law on May 8 (www.whitehouse.gov/news/releases/2008/05/200058. html).

On the Wyoming front, having gathered support for the federal legislation, necessary depositions were taken by the Wyoming Board of Control in September 2008, and formal hearings were conducted the following month. This session marked the birth of a settlement in substance when representatives of the Upper Platte irrigators signed the deal on October 16. The Board of Control met in Cheyenne to approve the arrangement on November 4. To what had the contending parties agreed? Details are found in the October 16 Stipulation and Settlement Agreement (Wyoming Board of Control 2008). The essence of the settlement is found in the second item of the agreement section (p. 3):

> Reclamation agrees that the operation and use of the 54K [thousand] AF [acre feet] portion shall not be the basis for nor be the direct or indirect cause of any request for water rights administration on the North Platte River, and its tributaries in the North Platte Basin above Pathfinder Reservoir. The foregoing limitation is for the protection of all upstream water rights junior or senior to the 54KAF portion (excepting the water right associated with Reclamation's Seminoe Reservoir) and extends to protect such rights from direct administration for the benefit of the 54KAF portion, as well as any indirect administration from the operation and use of the 54KAF that might result from administration of Reclamation's Seminoe Reservoir water right, that would not have occurred but for the existence of the 54KAF portion.

There it was at last. A solution had been reached under intense pressure almost two years after the program had been endorsed by all three state governors in the late fall of 2006. Upper North Platte water users got the protection they wanted (Adams 2008: 1, 4). The state of Wyoming belatedly secured what it required—clearance to move ahead with Pathfinder modification and the changes in water uses so essential to economic growth plans in the Casper area and downstream, as well as to the basin-wide cooperative habitat recovery program.

Policy Implications

In the West, when you touch water, you touch everything.
—WAYNE N. ASPINALL
Inscribed on Town Park Memorial, Palisade, Colorado

The Platte River system once provided paths for the great Platte River Road—the convergence of the Oregon, Mormon, California, and Overland trails through the high plains east of the Rocky Mountains (Mattes 1969). From the mid-1840s through the early 1860s, over 350,000 people of European descent traveled west on that road—one of the greatest human migrations in world history. For them, it was mostly a path to someplace else by following a river that would water them and their livestock. There was little thought of paying allegiance to that river or its encompassing prairie. Over the past 100–160 years, at least some citizens have learned to pay closer attention to a river system around which people have since settled and staked their futures (see Appendix G). Now the peoples of the basin have set about to modify the Platte River Road by launching a modest river preservation and restoration program. Their representatives have inserted new rules and tools into their relationships with each other and with the river. They have broken a new piece of trail that holds new possibilities, new allegiances, and new self-governance of their water commonwealth.

DESIGNER RIVER

The story of water management has always been one of mobilizing individually self-interested people into organized collective action so they could be empowered to do things together not possible through individual effort. To reconfigure the rivers of the Platte Basin, people had to organizationally reconfigure themselves. It has been an uncomfortable trial for those who underwent the ordeal. Each ditch, each river segment, each shared aquifer, each trans-mountain water import project has its tale of organizational, legal, and technical struggles as people sought to transcend their individual self-interests to reshape their water commons, on which their welfare ultimately depended. Asking people to set aside some measure of immediate advantage on the promise of an as yet unknown, organizationally coordinated and proportionate effort for the commonweal has never been easy or quick.

Now water leaders, as river re-designers on the Platte, have been at it again (see Appendix H). This time they have inserted an ecosystem agenda—modest to be sure—into the pattern of things. In a preliminary way, this new design element promises to implement a habitat recovery program for target species listed under the Endangered Species Act (ESA). This effort is to be accomplished on a basin-wide collaborative basis rather than permit by permit, enterprise by enterprise, water use by use. It will proceed not in cordoned-off parks, forests, or national monuments but rather across landscapes on which people conduct their regular rural and urban commerce, their personal and civic lives amid complex and rapidly evolving biotic webs. In the middle of the utilitarian quest to satisfy human preferences, an explicit but undetermined value has been placed on the worth of non-human species, a value not reflected in marketplace exchange, a value sufficiently important under the law that human agendas will reconfigure in the pursuit of it.

VALUE OF THE RECOVERY PROGRAM

By whatever measure, will the Platte River Habitat Recovery Program be any good? One may as well ask, what is the worth of a newborn baby? The worth of babies and newly born habitat recovery programs is found in their unfolding potentials. Those become apparent only as they are nurtured by the assets of enveloping communities. What is clear, however, is that the Platte River Habitat Recovery Program has constructed a new Platte River Road for water providers to move forward with their fundamental objective—to serve their mandate as enablers of economic growth. The meaning and ultimate value of the recovery program will depend largely on how the peoples of the basin transcend immediate self-seeking rationality to guide the uses of water the program has made available.

ECONOMIC GROWTH DEBATE

The Platte River Habitat Recovery Program has been designed to permit future human uses of basin waters while simultaneously restoring and sustaining habitats for target species. The economic growth agenda has never been far from the surface of the talks. Each state and its respective water providers fought hard to preserve water project yields for purposes of enhancing economic growth. Most negotiations were so heavily occupied with preserving basin water for human utilitarian agendas that for years environmentalists were frustrated that there was too little talk about species requirements. The program has been, in a most central way, about how water providers can remove species jeopardy to obtain regulatory certainty and get on with their mandate to supply water to growing economies without the uncertainties of litigation, extended delays, and monstrous expenses.

Sustained growth in gross national product and average per capita income has become a modern worldwide secular religion. Much ink has been spilled in the past forty years in arguments between growth pushers and anti-growth gloom merchants (Daly and Cobb 1994; Freeman 1992: 108–110; Kahn 1976; Meadows, Randers, and Meadows 2004). The debate quickly became sterile, however, because the real issue is not growth versus no growth but rather the composition and distribution of the products of growth. Some types of economic growth are more compatible than others with long-term social, economic, and environmental sustainability. Smart growth means providing high-density housing located close to jobs, schools, and essential services (Freilich and White 2008; Smart Growth America n.d.; Squires 2002). It includes—in locally appropriate ways—transportation options other than complete reliance on the private automobile, shrinking individual lawns in favor of public neighborhood parks. Such a growth pattern has altogether different ramifications than does sprawling, low-density housing—characterized by large individual lawnscapes—served by 4,000-pound automobiles each carrying a 160-pound person several miles to purchase a 16-ounce loaf of bread. It is not defensible to be anti-growth in some simpleminded manner; it is defensible to seek patterns of growth that can be accommodated sustainably within the finite limits of affordable water and hydrocarbon energy supplies (Burchell et al. 2002). The critical question is not should economic growth be spurred or stopped? It is, rather, how will the composition of economic growth be shaped and managed?

WATER: THE ENABLER OF GROWTH VISIONS

In an arid environment, available water constrains and enables economic growth. Historically, civic leaders across the arid West have disagreed about countless issues, but from the earliest settlement days onward they have promulgated one powerful dominating vision that united them across highly varied ideologies and landscapes: they wanted to promote economic and population growth. There was land to be had, communities to be built, income to be generated, wealth to be accumulated. Much was to be captured in the logic of private goods exchange in marketplaces. It has been a utilitarian vision that everyone could understand, and coalitions of civic-political-business leaders have been good at promoting it.

In arid and semiarid environments, one critical constraint that has limited economic growth—in a bundle of constraints, including access to transportation—has been the actual or feared lack of water supply. Civic leaders have therefore demanded that their water supply organizations continually find more water to lubricate the ongoing growth of population and the economy. To this end, they have created common property organizations (mutual ditch companies, irrigation districts, conservancy districts, municipalities, public power and irrigation districts) to empower themselves to do things together that they could not accomplish through private market transactions—build and operate dams, ditches, reservoirs, and water treatment plants and produce electricity to power up growing economies, whose sales defray significant fractions of water supply expenses. As they organized around their particular oases, these groups forged common identities rooted in the need to protect "our" water and defend it from "them." They could be an internally fractious bunch, but they found they could build politically powerful, winning coalitions around the acquisition and defense of their water projects. One longtime water broker and planner summed up the situation: "[W]ater has provided our clearest public policy consensus: we need more than we have and we will use all we can get. We do not want outsiders to think lack of water might stop our growth, and we don't want to debate future water resources too openly for fear of being overheard" (Gammage 2003: xiii).

Transcending the Prisoners' Dilemma

All competitors for the same scarce water supplies are vulnerable to being caught in a prisoners' dilemma (see Chapter 1). This is especially the case along the Colorado Front Range and the Nebraska Platte and Republican River systems. Insofar as there is a lack of effective organization that empowers people to do joint planning and enforces shared constraint, individual rationality will be dominant at the expense of any vulnerable resource commons. In insufficiently organized common pool resource situations, if actor X denies him- or herself access to the next waterhole in the name of ecological integrity or anything else, another will seek to command it. Those who accept limits are thereby punished; those who succeed in securing a new supply are, in the short term, economically and politically rewarded. Therefore, under such conditions, few civic leaders of sufficiently prosperous communities can long deny a technically feasible and economically affordable proposed water growth project.

As high-quality freshwater has become increasingly scarce, each interdependent water provider in prisoners' dilemma situations tends to grab available water immediately while postponing the more politically and organizationally challenging business of constructing defensible forms of water management and making cooperative alternative supply arrangements. In addition, any given water provider, acting independently, will be very reluctant to share any so-called excess water supply because of (1) short-run uncertainties that come with high variability in annual precipitation (what looks like an excess in a period of average to wet years may disappear in dry times), and (2) long-run uncertainties—what will global climate change do to local supply; how will the local economy grow its water demand? In the perspective of an individual actor, it is perfectly rational to race to water pell-mell, but in the longer run, undisciplined water contests may lead to collectively irrational outcomes for all players. The cure, of course, is to organize individually rational self-seeking water hunters in a manner that empowers them to transcend the prisoners' dilemma trap in at least two ways: (1) to cooperatively secure and allocate available supplies, and (2) to collectively impose rules within which markets can allocate scarce resources in the quest for more sustainable forms of economic growth.

The concept of organizing collectively to enable smarter economic growth is an old one, well ensconced in water traditions of the West. Examples abound in the ways people organized to control water in irrigation ditches and along rivers all across the West. Mutual irrigation companies and irrigation districts—organized as nonprofit farmer-owned entities—empowered people to allocate water productively and fairly, maintain their local common property ditch delivery systems, and manage conflicts (Maass and Anderson 1978). This meant repeatedly transcending prisoners' dilemma traps at the ditch level in the name of organizing sustainable irrigation communities. Today, thousands of these organizations still stand at the core of water supply and management in the western United States (Freeman 2000).

A prime interstate example of organizing to keep individual rationality from getting out of hand and leading to collective disaster was the construction of the 1922 Colorado River Compact (Hundley 1986; Tyler 2003). The alternative to the Colorado River Compact was a careless race to divert water first before other competitors could do so in the seven basin states under the doctrine of prior appropriation. Delph Carpenter, a Colorado leader and strong adherent of the prior appropriation doctrine within state boundaries, could see—along with others—that to empower water providers in each basin state to more carefully divert waters at their own rates according to their own needs, a treaty was needed among the states—a basin-wide Colorado River Compact. Failing that, there would be an individually self-seeking scramble among users in the face of a rapidly growing and politically potent California (Tyler 2003). The point of the compact was to secure the freedom to be more collectively rational on behalf of all the players by providing "security of access" under known rules of the water acquisition game. Without the compact, the doctrine of prior appropriation would have made Colorado River Basin decisions in court battles and the U.S. Congress dependent on what people did first in Los Angeles and the Imperial Valley—not on the needs of Colorado, Wyoming, New Mexico, Utah, Arizona, or Nevada. On the South Platte River, the Nebraska-Colorado South Platte Compact (1923) accomplished the same purpose; it established a regime of rules for allocating consumptive uses so that private investors could operate within a zone of political-legal-organizational security.

From the earliest European settlement days, therefore, organizing to transcend individual rationality in the world of western water has been an essential part of western arid lands community building. Now, given the birth of the Platte River Habitat Recovery Program, with a mission to produce a collective good in the name of enhancing habitat on the central Platte River and of permitting continued economic growth, the question must be asked: what will be the quality of that growth? What larger encompassing vision will the newborn habitat recovery program be enabling?

Water: Growth Horizons on the Platte

Platte Basin negotiations have been difficult primarily because water providers have long been hitting the limits of supply. The available water envelope has already been pushed hard. The evidence is found in the chapter-by-chapter tale of the fight over the disposition of water project yields in all three states.

Nebraska has struggled to secure water supplies to offset historical and future depletions. New uses in Wyoming's North Platte Basin will primarily have to come from existing uses. The exceptions will be limited to exploitation of non-tributary groundwater and, possibly, new trans-basin imports. Statewide, Colorado municipal and industrial water demands have been projected to rise substantially by 2030; about 80 percent of that increase can possibly be fulfilled by the successful completion of water supply projects under way by 2004 (Colorado Water Conservation Board 2004). That analysis has identified a 20 percent supply gap to be filled by water providers who have indicated that they foresee significant constraints on their capacity to address it (Colorado Water Conservation Board 2004: 13).

WATER AND LAND-USE PLANNING: THE COSTS OF DISCONNECTION

In this context of scarcity, water demand has been driven by considerations disconnected from supply. Water and land-use issues have been kept separate, to the detriment of the long-term sustainability of our society on the western landscapes (Babbitt 2005; Gammage 2003; Jenkins 2006: 9–13; Livingston, Riddlington, and Baker 2003). The nature of our land uses is what establishes the core of water demand. But land use has long been dominated by local economic growth interests that have not wanted to have the politics of local land-use decisions opened up to, or constrained by, statewide or river basin–level discussions of issues of either land or water supply (Jenkins 2006: 9–13). Traditionally, the pattern has been for proponents of new housing and commercial projects to acquire substantial parcels of land on the periphery of metropolitan areas to meet consumer demand for housing. Then, when a sufficient number of rooftops has been attained, big-box stores and shopping malls locate in the area, along with providers of the many services a reasonably affluent population will support. If water supplies are insufficient for long-term sustainability, the assumption has been that growing tax bases will provide the wherewithal to pull the necessary water into expanding suburban or ex-urban growth complexes over time. Promoters will have captured their gains in market exchange (typically bankers, insurance and title brokers, realtors, construction firms and their laborers) and trundled off to new projects as the risks are shifted to members of the communities who hold the properties and jobs and who must find ways and means of securing additional water sufficient to keep their communities together. A combination of market and regulatory failures, combined with problematic tax policies, has produced unnecessarily high water and energy demand landscapes (Ulfarsson and Carruthers 2006: 767–788).

Then, to make matters even more challenging, in many places supply problems—particularly during droughts—become more pronounced as older water rights holders increasingly employ their full allotments, making junior priorities harder to serve. As growth continues, highly desirable senior priorities become committed to its support, leaving latecomer housing and commercial projects beyond historical city supply areas with the dimming prospects that accompany a reliance on increasingly junior priorities.

It is commonplace for growth project promoters to buy land, have it platted, secure essential permits and authorizations, and then take years to build it out. The promoters may have provided water and sewer pipes and the like and recouped their investment through real estate sales. Yet water providers—who have had no part in land-use decisions—are then expected to provide supply. As years go by and available supplies become more constrained, the costs of providing water service to sustain the build-out tend to rise substantially.

When the water demand table is set by land uses shaped independently of water supply considerations, parties behaving in a manner that is perfectly individually rational in their quest for satisfying preferences in private marketplace exchange can produce a collective disaster. This is not to argue against market allocation of resources in the private goods sector. It is to argue for individual rationality in marketplace exchange operating within the context of a well-governed society wherein markets serve the interests of—among other things—long-term social, political, ecological, and economic sustainability. The concept of "commonwealth," as distinguished from the interest of any particular subset of society, has a long tradition in the philosophy and practice of Western Civilization. In our time, among other things, a more defensible relationship is needed between land-use decision making and our common water pool.

LEARNING TO BETTER GOVERN OURSELVES

The enduring challenge for American environmental policy, in short, is to build and maintain public support for effective governance of the environment: for managing the environment by managing ourselves.
—RICHARD ANDREWS (1999: 372)

Communities of water interests have installed a new Platte Basin governance regime designed to produce a pure collective good in the form of enhanced and preserved habitats for four species listed under the Endangered Species Act. The Platte River Habitat Recovery Program is a social organizational and political experiment. It is an effort to hold together a coalition of interests such that politics, open peer-reviewed civic science, and a regulatory process can nourish an enduring discourse about how people can build community with each other and other living things at the river basin level.

The new governance arrangement is a framework for forever managing conflict over scarce resources. People enjoying their civic freedom, spurred by the ESA, have associated themselves around what Grady Gammage (2003: 21) has called the "liquid glue" that is our water commons. In doing this, they have done what their forebears had to do—transcend self-interest to organize their local commonwealths. As the river heals at least in part, it will be because civic life across three states has been enriched. By accepting a small amount of constraint on their actions and adopting a new governance regime that ensures that water will move across the landscape in modified ways, they have freed themselves to pass on to future generations an assembly of restored riverine habitats and a system of self-governance that no amount of individual marketplace exchange of store-bought private goods could ever provide. The gift is that future generations have a better chance to witness a five-foot-tall white bird millions of years in the making, the flash of a piping plover speeding on a sandbar, the high dive of a least tern, the presence of a rare fish, and all the other life forms that share their biotic webs.

Peoples of the basin now confront an even larger challenge—additional governance organization building in the domain of land use and water planning so as to defensibly employ the waters made available by the habitat recovery program for economic growth. One new environmental enterprise sets the stage for another. Will the program become little more than a highly compromised habitat museum piece while its existence grants license for short-term individually rational local growth machines to produce unsustainable self-defeating visions of ourselves that are incapable of handing our children and grandchildren an ecologically viable and water sustainable society? What is the worth of the new Platte River Habitat Recovery Program baby? The newborn will be raised not only by people directly governing the program but also by citizens and their leaders who will determine the quality of encompassing basin land use and water self-governance. There are more Platte River Roads to be traveled, new possibilities to be seized, new allegiances to be forged, new self-governance to be adopted.

CHAPTER 31

Theory Implications

The time of spilled blood is short and the time of spilled ink goes on forever.
—LOUISE BARNETT (2006: 331)

In all societies, collective goods have been seen as essential to the production and enjoyment of private goods. Public roads and streets are necessary for the use of private automobiles. The Federal Communications Commission regulates the airwaves so that individuals and organizations can use market exchange to build, distribute, and enjoy radios, televisions, and telephones. We have recently been reminded of the importance of the Security and Exchange Commission and the Federal Reserve banking system and their roles in keeping regulatory practices up to standard so the stock markets and the banking system can function properly to allocate investment capital. National defense has always been a top-priority collective good—perfectly non-rival and non-excludable—to keep the enemy from the gates while those within enjoy their private goods and common property. Viable societies have always depended on the provision of high-quality collective goods.

We have only begun, however, to learn about how to provide large-scale environmental collective goods when ecosystems are not in public ownership and confined to designated boundaries of public parks and forests. The Endangered Species Act (ESA), at its core, held forth a policy promise that we must, at least in a limited way, constrain our willingness to take out un-priced mortgages against Mother Nature and future generations across all landscapes. What the language of the Endangered Species Act did not do, however, was specify a blueprint for its implementation.

This has been a tale of how powerful rival self-seeking water providers—historically defensive of their settled regimes—were mobilized to transcend prisoners' dilemma dynamics on issue after issue to forge a new state-federal system of water commons governance that has promised to slow and eventually reverse habitat degradation and thereby overcome the tragedy of the commons on a segment of the central Platte River. How did this happen? What was the implementation blueprint in analytical terms?

HOW CHANGE OCCURRED: CONCEPTS AND VARIABLES

What of a generalizable nature can be abstracted from all the site-specific Platte River Basin detail? What empirically researchable propositions can be formulated and advanced as hypotheses to explain mobilization for the construction of a large landscape–scale environmental collective good?

Conditions Precedent to Launching Negotiations

No attempt will be undertaken here to list the many things that may impinge on launching negotiations, but it is essential to fulfill five conditions. First, if negotiations are going to work, the geographic and social unit for talks must be determined in a manner conducive to problem solving. If the U.S. Fish and Wildlife Service (USFWS) had selected only Nebraska for the recovery program talks on the grounds that it incorporated the critical habitat, the land, and ample water, there would arguably have been a serious problem. Nebraska authorities would have ferociously resisted the imposition of habitat recovery burdens without the contributions of its upstream neighbors. The interstate struggles traced in this study are testimony to this point. An exclusive USFWS focus on Nebraska would have triggered rounds of lawsuits that would have tied up the proceedings in the courts for years. Furthermore, the USFWS needed Colorado, Wyoming, and Nebraska to pressure each other so issues could be forced into the open. For example, it took intense pressure from the two upstream states to compel Nebraska to initiate its depletions plans and institute groundwater well birth control because Wyoming and Colorado needed to assure their constituencies that upstream water contributions would reach the critical habitat. The USFWS, acting bilaterally with Nebraska, could not have mustered such pressure. Choosing the basin as the unit of analysis was an essential precondition of eventual success.

Second, essential stakeholders must be identified and made aware of the rationale for their presence at the negotiating table. Stakeholders are organizations and their policy leaders who have something to lose if negotiations fail. Third, the organizational representatives who participate in negotiations must have legitimate authority to speak on behalf of each stake-holding constituency. They

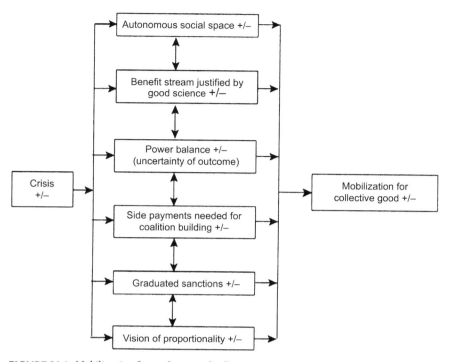

FIGURE 31.1. *Mobilization for production of collective good.*

must be accepted by others in important constituent networks and be central to those networks. Fourth, there must be sufficient information and data to allow those at the table to grasp essential aspects of the problem being negotiated. For that which is unknown, there must be the prospect that time and money will be available to find out how real-world problems operate in critical dimensions. Fifth, there must be at least some agreement on essential premises—for example, that over its history the South Platte River has been a gaining stream as measured over annual seasonal flow cycles, the pallid sturgeon population has plummeted on the Missouri River, and well pumping in a hydraulically connected aquifer will deplete river flows in ways that can be calculated according to commonly accepted methodologies.

Given the fulfillment of these conditions, Figure 31.1 displays seven variables advanced as critical to mobilize individually rational actors to construct large landscape–scale collective goods. Small changes in the values of these variables are posited to have major consequences for collective goods production. For additional theoretical and methodological comments, see Appendix B. Consideration of the variables advanced in Figure 31.1 provides a framework for reflection on the Platte River habitat recovery story.

Crisis

Crisis has always meant the presence of serious trouble that requires mobilization for new kinds of action, the reconfiguration of existing ways. Crisis is what the ESA imposes on the routine agendas of organizations that fall within its grasp. Representatives who came to the table to negotiate the proposed recovery program were all part-timers, people who had many other things to do in taking care of their regular organizational missions. Only after the ESA-induced crisis credibly threatened to block the achievement of organizational objectives did leaders reluctantly attend to matters. They sat at the table because the ESA had created a crisis for their operations that would not go away until a collective solution could be negotiated.

It is obvious but still worth noting that if the ESA-induced crisis had been relaxed or removed, resource user representatives would have immediately and understandably left the negotiations. What individually rational actor wants to spend time, money, and energy chasing after environmental restoration objectives, the payoffs of which come at a cost to organizational missions as historically defined and the benefits of which will not be any greater than those available to non-contributors? Under an open access situation, what actor wants to pay the costs of transcending the prisoners' dilemma dynamic if he or she does not have to and if another increment of asset can be grabbed for individual organizational agendas?

The ESA has often been referred to as the "great convener," which it is. But the legislation's capacity to convene is driven by the imposition of crisis. The ESA must be strong and unyielding so that resource appropriators who serve us all get the message. As one federal negotiator, reflecting on what it took to keep the states and water users at the table, put it: "negotiate in good faith or die."

Arguably, many things can be done to improve the ESA, but any change that significantly reduces its crisis-making potential must be resisted unless one wants to argue that a good society needs little or nothing in the way of environmental collective goods. There can be legitimate debate as to what constitutes social, political, and economic progress (Freeman 1992), but no serious thinker has ever contended that such progress is to be found in a society that only values that which can be priced and exchanged in marketplaces or in a view of society only as a giant, environmentally unconstrained consumer and producer goods vending machine, indifferent to the fate of the ecosystems to which it is intimately tethered.

The ESA's crisis-making demands produce political cover for political leaders who want to make use of them. They can authentically carry on a struggle on behalf of their resource appropriators, earn political capital by so doing, and then reluctantly succumb to the necessity of supporting a proposed program as the lesser of evils. The new collective good may then produce a benefit stream that becomes the fountainhead for new opportunities to produce and exchange items in the sectors of private goods and common property resources—for example, tourism around birds in Nebraska and well regulations that will protect surface water rights or, in the case of Colorado's lower South Platte, offset water to keep junior wells in play under Colorado law and the Nebraska-Colorado Compact. Such things, in turn, generate new constituencies of beneficiaries supportive of the collective good that made the private and common property benefits available. Clusters of beneficiaries are then available for coalition building by shrewd political leaders. Once collective goods are in place and private goods constituencies have learned to thrive around them, that which was once damned as useless extravagance may be defended as important to the good life.

When a disaster—in the form of a hurricane, earthquake, flood, tornado, or other natural event—hits communities, people quickly set aside their private agendas, mobilize into cooperative units to seek needed assistance, start the chainsaws and portable generators, and directly confront the problems that beset them. They quickly unite, address problems, and then, in the aftermath, return to their private agendas. However, in the case of crisis induced by the ESA, people and their organizations do the opposite. At first, constituents retreat into separate defensive camps, and only slowly and under duress do they come together to address matters.

After initial tendencies to deny the existence of the problem, the Platte River recovery negotiators found themselves seeking ways to use the regulatory process to delay meaningful action; then—when confronted with undeniable pressure to engage in good-faith problem solving—they tended to stretch the regulatory process, to embark on "regulatory cruising." Cruising was essential insofar as it enabled requisite coalition building among resource appropriators. But the prospect of endlessly avoiding problem solving provided no incentive to mobilize the coalition partners. What brought an end to the cruising? Answer: the stark certainty that no action would bring about greater calamity than would the trouble of building a viable reasonable and prudent alternative. Further, there were limits on the time and money available to build that alternative. Therefore, it was essential that multiple stakeholders mobilize to share the burdens in a predictable, organized, and proportionate manner. Episode by episode, issue by issue, the actors confronted—and eventually transcended—the prisoners' dilemma dynamic. They thereby produced a habitat recovery program designed to reverse the environmental tragedy that had been mounting on a seventy-mile segment of the central Platte River water commons.

Propositions. First, crises induced by the ESA and its regulatory process are managed crises constructed by the U.S. Department of the Interior (DOI) in interaction with state and local resource appropriators. Second, effectively managed crises are those that permit sufficient slack for coalition building in the context of an ever-present threat of a highly undesirable no-action option. Third, all players must confront limited resources of time and money with which to construct a program solution.

In the case of the Platte, the two Nebraska water and power districts—the Central Nebraska Public Power and Irrigation District (CNPPID) and the Nebraska Public Power District (NPPD)—had little interest in doing anything that was not part of their 1998 Federal Energy Regulatory Commission (FERC) re-licensing deal; this posture posed a threat to successful negotiations. Yet even their considerable power was no match for that of the USBR, a federal agency that absolutely needed a defensible recovery program to cover its facilities in Wyoming, Colorado, and the Nebraska panhandle. Eventually, the USBR's needs trumped those defined by the two Nebraska districts. To the extent that any one or a few critical players have significantly more time and money than the others to engage in regulatory cruising, to the extent that the burdens of no action would be significantly fewer than the burdens on the other parties, and to the degree that such a party is essential to the construction of the collective good, success in negotiations will be jeopardized.

Autonomous Social Organizational Space

Given the multiplicity of interests, the complexity of issues, and the necessity of coalition building, the challenge of surmounting the prisoners' dilemma dynamic is necessarily best met in a safe, autonomous social organizational space provided by entities operating above the level of individuals and below the level of central state bureaucracies.

Some have advocated that the ESA be implemented in a strong federal agency command and control operational mode that would brook little compromise and compel compliance from those who have created jeopardy (Echeverria 2001). The objectives are to speed things up, hold to higher environmental standards, and avoid compromising the intent of the law—whatever that might mean. The problem with all this, of course, is that it fails to recognize the limits of the law in general and of the ESA in particular. Tough legal stances cannot produce creative action on the rivers. Law schools and biology departments produce virtually no knowledge of how water is actually organized in particular rivers. Even if they did produce the essential competencies, federal agencies control very little water across the landscape. The kind of creative technical and organizational action that produces viable reasonable and prudent alternatives must necessarily come from people who are organized around the river, people with substantial local knowledge of opportunities and constraints. These are the people who created jeopardy in the first instance, but there is no choice but to incorporate their knowledge, energy, resources, and sustained participation into any proposed program.

The law insists that a remedy be found, but the creative construction of reasonable and prudent alternatives must emerge out of protected autonomous organizational spaces not penetrated by federal authorities or rival constituencies from within or beyond state lines. In the Platte Basin, the social, political, legal, and technical discourse was sustained by the South Platte Lower River Group (SPLRG) and the Platte River Project (PRP) in Colorado; the CNPPID, the NPPD, and panhandle irrigation organizations in Nebraska; and the North Platte and Kendrick projects (among other irrigation districts) in Wyoming. It was also found in the individual and coordinated action of the National Audubon Society, the National Wildlife Federation, the Whooping Crane Trust, and—early on—Environmental Defense.

Such organizations, as diverse as they are, share several common attributes (Freeman 1989, 2000; Ostrom 1990: 58–102). They occupy social-political-legal space in a middle domain between federal and state bureaucracies, on the one hand, and individual citizens/entrepreneurs on the other. They each have a stake in some important aspect of the resource commons. Their social organizational space is inclusive of both scientific-technical generalizable knowledge and local site-specific particulars in ways neither individuals nor public state-level bureaucracies can equal. They are potentially capable of undertaking adaptive action within the limits of encompassing laws and regulations in ways not possible by either individuals or central bureaucracies, state or federal. These middle-level organizations are crucibles of problem solving and mobilization of constituent support.

Virtually all of the creative portions of option building during program negotiations were conducted not before the Governance Committee but in safe spaces within the respective states where state, local, and sometimes federal authorities could devise solutions. Then and only then did such options surface in program advisory committees. Negotiations then become an interplay of state and federal agendas, with ideas and positions moving up and down a chain of organizations distributed across the basin landscape—in Colorado, places such as Loveland, Berthoud, Denver, Brush, Fort Morgan, and Sterling; in Nebraska, locations such as Holdrege, North Platte, Kearney, and Grand Island; and Wyoming cities and towns such as Cheyenne, Casper, Saratoga, and Torrington. Governance Committee meetings dealt with the products of extended discussions that had gestated elsewhere within middle-level organizations for months if not years.

However, two things can go awry within organizational webs. Senior federal, state, and local leaders tend to be heavily occupied with crowded agendas, most of which have nothing to do with the program negotiations. They are continually on the verge of being overwhelmed by the complexities of the many tasks before them. Urgent matters tend to drive off the important ones. The classic solution, of course, is to rely on staff. Staff members, in turn, make their way by paying close attention to details in ways that protect their leaders. Careers are not made by placing one's boss in untenable positions. Staffers, with some

413

important exceptions, tend to dwell on problems more than on opportunities, to parse issues finely while refraining from bold actions that would cut though thickets of deeply nuanced considerations.

In mid-2002, after years of frustration over obfuscation and delay, a senior Platte River negotiator blurted, "we are being paralyzed by nuance." The outburst was triggered by an attempt to read an early draft of a section that would eventually be incorporated in the program document. The negotiators' staffs had so carefully parsed the language that no drafting committee could clearly articulate the section in comprehensible program language for a wider public audience. Drafters had settled on their meanings, which, in all probability, would be lost to others. The program document drafting committee was finding it difficult to make progress in virtually any critical area.

The only solution was the sustained engagement of responsible and supportive senior leaders who had an organizational vision of the objectives to be served by successful negotiations; they then articulated that vision repeatedly so their staffs could push ahead secure in the knowledge of those understandings. What comes out of autonomous organizational space at any level depends heavily on the quality and quantity of leadership that goes in. The essentials of effective leadership, as repeatedly evidenced in the Platte negotiations, required at least two capacities. First, leaders needed the capacity to directly confront problems, assign priorities to them, establish general policy directions for problem solving, and mobilize staff to work within those boundaries. As leaders' attention drifted, processes slowed as staffers sliced and diced issues in ways that were protective of their bosses but that did little to stimulate creative problem solving. Second, leaders needed the capacity to build and nurture stakeholder coalitions that would implement program components. Organizations have missions that serve stakeholders; constituencies were therefore generally easy to define. The challenge was to work with stakeholders of long standing in such a manner that new ones, along with additional mission components, would be accepted into organizational life. Effective leaders transcended traditional organizational arrangements in coalition building.

Leadership and effective staff work were repeatedly abetted by the systematic use of workshops that enriched people's perspectives regarding problems and options. Workshops brought teams together in seminar formats and advanced common analytical frameworks within which to contemplate challenging topics, such as sediment and vegetation, future depletions plans, organizational options for habitat management, potential landholding entities, and state protocols for water tracking. Presentations and discussion allowed parties to advance their perspectives, define meanings, and better explore the implications of their own arguments and those of their adversaries. At the end of the day, participants returned to their camps and maintained their loyalties. But as they did so they were better informed, more appreciative of other positions, and better able to imagine solutions. All this took time, patience, and a willingness to appreciate multiple aspects of generally accepted truths. Problem-solving activities in autonomous organizational spaces were enhanced by infusions of reasoned thought from others in the negotiating circle, outside consultants, and the Office of the Cooperative Program Executive Director.

Proposition. Top-down central bureaucratic command and control modes of ESA implementation cannot work effectively because essential coalition-building efforts must occur in semiautonomous and autonomous middle-level organizational layers operating in the social and political space between federal and state bureaucracies, on the one hand, and individual citizens, on the other.

Benefit Stream

If the players were going to surmount the prisoners' dilemma dynamic and not defect into a no-action stance, some promise of benefits had to be taken to constituents. On the Platte, federal authorities needed to demonstrate that the ESA could be implemented defensibly, states and water users needed regulatory certainty, and environmentalists required a deal that promised meaningful habitat recovery. There are many issues to address in the analysis of benefit streams. Who wins? Who loses? In what respects? Who or what bears the burdens of uncertainty? Two fundamental questions will be noted here. First, is the benefit stream authentic and justified by sound scientific rationale? Second, how can the program and its expected stream of benefits be packaged and "sold" to audiences beyond the negotiating rooms and beyond the middle-level organizational leaderships that have been party to constructing the proposed solutions?

A Defensible Rationale. An assumption provided the foundation for the entire negotiating process—namely, that prevailing habitat conditions were significantly limiting the USFWS's efforts to recover listed species. If this assumption were seriously questioned, all rationale for negotiating and implementing a program would evaporate.

In the early years, the assumption was questioned in the informal and inadequate sense that the sessions witnessed much venting of anger. But as the talks continued, water users could see the futility of "throwing spit-wads" at USFWS target flow calculations, and they began to engage in serious discussion of possible solutions. Moderate and pragmatic voices set aside issues of "bad" science, accepted the USFWS's offers of reduced target flow figures and a division of land habitat acreage requirements (only 10,000 acres in the first program increment), and moved ahead with building a program that could deliver regulatory certainty. However, old irreconcilable interests—especially among Nebraska groundwater users—saw the negotiations slowly advance, much to their dismay. They were able to again force the issue back to the table by employing the distorted story of a purported lynx hoax and the calamitous confrontation on the Klamath River Basin. In each case, opponents of the Platte program contended that the DOI was using bad science to unjustifiably hurt people.

Proposition. If people are going to be mobilized to produce and sustain a collective good, the underlying factual rationale must be defensible as defined by the best scientific methodological procedures. Sacrificing people's private and common property resource agendas can be justified only if there is compelling evidence that a proposed collective good is required and will produce the intended benefits.

A significant idea has been placed at the center of the recovery program: program modifications will be driven in important part by independent peer-reviewed empirical research and monitoring. The logics will be open to public inspection. This places all parties in at least two continual binds. First, parties must in general accept common methodological procedures for producing facts. Different procedures predicated on different assumptions will generate different conceptions of fact. On the Platte, state water users and federal analysts never reached agreement on the USFWS's calculation that the central Platte was shorted an annual average of 417,000 acre feet. Yet technical people in all communities of interest did find common ground in USBR-USFWS models of river flow.

Proposition. The greater the degree of mutual acceptance of analytical methods, the *greater* the prospects for successful negotiations.

Insofar as issue settlements are data-based, a second negotiating bind arises. On the one hand, each party is extremely cost conscious because each faces constituent resistance to increasing allocations of dollars. Yet on the other hand, if the states, for example, do not want to fall uncritically into the USFWS's perspectives, they will have little choice but to fund quality science and monitoring that will provide justification (or not) for undertaking alternative X. The establishment of an Adaptive Management Working Group (AMWG) and an Independent Science Advisory Committee indicates a willingness to pay the costs of doing solid peer-reviewed science. In the interplay of successive studies and the interaction of differing interpretations, a healthy civic science is expected to emerge. It will be essential to the ongoing discourse.

Public Outreach Constraints. Amid the swirl of politics necessarily associated with installing a new governance regime, mounting public outreach programs can be expected to be a challenge. Nontrivial problems are inherent in involving the public, sharing information broadly, and galvanizing public support for the collective goods program and its benefits. It is one thing to have completed the necessary science to justify program construction; it is quite another to package that science and its payoff rationales in a manner that can publicly build constituent support.

In the Platte River Habitat Recovery Program, each major negotiating community of interest was responsible for developing efforts at public outreach. This was deemed necessary because each of the partners had different audiences with unique circumstances; that fact demanded politically different approaches. For example, while DOI concentrated on rolling out a draft environmental impact statement in a manner that would minimize potential lawsuits from environmentalist critics, the states had to work out messages that appealed primarily to their water user communities, which meant emphasizing the promise of regulatory certainty. Furthermore, what was said to one user community in Nebraska had to be squared with what was shared with users in Wyoming and Colorado. It was too easy to potentially trip each other up. What appealed to the environmental community might easily become ammunition for groundwater users in their campaign against the program. The reverse was also true; attempts by Nebraska authorities to develop a perfectly honest message that would assuage the fears of their irrigators could offend environmentalists. What constituted a "solution" for any given entity could quickly mushroom into "problems" for others. Opponents of the program could be counted on to exploit any carelessly constructed argument from one context to another if doing so promised to damage prospects for program success. All of this severely constrained the program proponents' ability to get their messages out.

In Nebraska, where public outreach efforts to sell program benefits were arguably needed most, Governors Mike Johanns and Dave Heineman could not declare that they were supporters. Only in late 2006—in the wake of a positive recommendation from the citizens' Platte River Advisory Committee, late resolution of the bypass and hydro-cycling issues, and endorsement of the program by the CNPPID and the NPPD—could Heineman openly declare in favor of the habitat recovery program. In this context, how could program proponents on the Nebraska negotiating team conduct an energetic and sustained public outreach effort on behalf of the program to Nebraska citizens? The answer: they could not. To do anything more than assert a litany of program merits and pitfalls, when asked, risked preempting the governor's decision.

Propositions. The greater the polarization of significant constituencies, the greater the reluctance of political leaders to endorse negotiated proposals for constructing a collective good. The greater the reluctance of political leaders to endorse projects to construct a collective good, the less opportunity negotiators have to be a public resource for careful, civil program advocacy. The greater the polarization, the less agreement there will be about either fact or value. The less agreement there is about facts and values, the less capacity there will be to conduct problem-solving public outreach efforts.

417

Power Balance

Negotiations were sustained by virtue of the fact that neither the states nor the Department of the Interior/USFWS could compel the other to do their bidding. Federal positions on issues such as target flows, riverine versus alternative habitats, and sedimentation-vegetation each in its own way drove at least some within the states to seriously consider seeking redress through pleas to friendly DOI allies in high places—even to pursue court action in compact and ESA matters—and abandoning the negotiations. Yet in each instance, voices calling for such strategies were eventually quieted by those who pointed out the uncertainties of possible outcomes and the high costs of a defeat in both time and money. In each instance, prudence dictated that the parties stay at the table.

For their part, USFWS decision makers were well aware of movements in the U.S. Congress—especially in the House Natural Resources Committee—to "reform" the Endangered Species Act in ways that would weaken the agency's capacity to implement the ESA in any currently recognizable manner. Collaborative negotiations—reasoned, flexible, patient, and backed by the prospect of individual accountability for the construction of reasonable and prudent alternatives, as required by Section 7—pointed the way to solutions and denied ammunition to those who sought to attack federal environmental agendas. Most important, the USFWS controlled no water. If water were to be re-timed for habitat restoration, the agency had little alternative but to work with organizations in the federal government (the USBR) and within the states that do control it. The USFWS had a powerful legal mandate, but under the constitution it was the states that had the water, and the USBR had to defer to state allocation doctrines and regulations.

If the balance of power shifted sharply to one side or another, it is reasonable to speculate that the organizational webs that provide essential autonomous space for creative action would not be called upon to devise new environmental collective goods. If the federal agencies were going to win the tug-of-war, they—pushed by environmentalist constituencies—could be expected to ignore or drive away the multiple tiers of water user organizations that had essential river knowledge and water control.

Environmentalist organizations had relatively little in the way of bargaining chips to cash in at the table. For the most part, their representatives sat frustrated with the slow pace of developments. However, through their steady and thoughtful presence they were able to witness the USFWS's tactical decisions. That witness served as a constant reminder that the agency had to carefully justify its decisions or possibly face litigation. The environmentalists' presence also personified the threat of the ESA's "big hammer"—fearsome individual Section 7 consultations that would be conducted within a frame of an average annual 417,000-acre-foot shortage to target flows and replacement of depletions at the state line on an acre-foot-for-acre-foot basis—which could fall on water users if they failed to produce a viable habitat recovery program.

If the states were to decisively prevail in the power struggle, it seems clear that they would have largely abandoned the quest for new environmental collective goods and thereby let traditional water uses and practices stand at the expense of habitat recovery. The extant balance of power was instrumental in making things work. Given the limits of their respective positions, each side needed the other.

Proposition. If the day arrives when one side becomes sufficiently dominant that it does not need the other, creative problem solving in the production of environmental collective goods will falter.

Side Payments

The Platte Basin negotiations clearly demonstrated the importance of making arrangements among coalition partners to compensate needed allies for their cooperation and assistance. The promise of regulatory certainty was not enough to induce the participation of essential allies because they were not all in a federal relationship. Even if the ally was in a federal nexus but needed more inducement, side payments by some coalition partners to others strengthened bonds of cooperation and smoothed collaboration.

In Colorado, water users along the Front Range, from Denver to Fort Collins, were clearly in the federal nexus and needed to comply with ESA mandates. Yet the logic of Colorado's situation made it imperative that Front Range users work out their basin recovery program contribution far downstream, close to the Nebraska border. Lower river users were not in an immediately compelling federal nexus, however, and had no incentive to cooperate. To induce lower river cooperation, Front Range users assisted their downstream partners-to-be with their well augmentation needs. Lower river groundwater users were required to expand their well augmentation for reasons stipulated by both Colorado law and the South Platte Compact. Junior well owners below the Balzac gauge had to either protect Colorado senior surface right holders and Nebraska's compact entitlement at the border or shut off wells at times of high demand, just when they were needed most. Assistance with additional well augmentation was a welcome side payment that ensured the cooperation of lower river allies.

In Wyoming, side payments were an important part of the state's alliance with its irrigation districts that draw water from the North Platte. The districts were in the federal nexus and in any circumstance would have had to undertake the long quest for regulatory certainty. The state found it advantageous to quiet opposition and smooth relationships by working out ways to address district

419

issues regarding toxic selenium concentrations in selected places, as well as dam safety issues. The promise of these side payments has kept Wyoming's internal discourse much more constructive and positive than may have otherwise been the case. However, Wyoming state water authorities failed to find a side payment satisfactory to Upper North Platte irrigators. The opposition of those water users plagued Wyoming state authorities from the beginning and was only resolved at the end of the negotiations by acquiescing to the irrigators' perspectives.

Nebraska state authorities had the highly conditional support of the state's two large districts (CNPPID and NPPD), which needed federal permits for their operations at Kingsley Dam and Lake McConaughy. Nebraska's biggest political problem was to defuse strident opposition from groundwater users, especially those beyond the boundaries of the CNPPID. Those well owners, numerically in the majority by a handsome margin and powerful within the unicameral legislature, had been mobilized for years to ensure that Nebraska state authorities did not require them to do what Colorado had required that state's well owners to do in 1969 by integrating their junior wells into prior appropriation doctrine. They fought ferociously to avoid having to subordinate their right to withdraw groundwater to senior surface water priorities. Nebraska authorities therefore offered the groundwater users a side payment—a program of state-funded offset water for all wells installed and registered after June 30, 1997, up through December 31, 2005. In return, groundwater users were asked to drop their opposition to Nebraska's participation in the basin-wide habitat recovery program.

The structuring of side payments was critical to the political coalition building that sustained the movement toward developing the habitat recovery program. Alternatively, the successful formulation of side payments importantly empowered transcendence of the prisoners' dilemma dynamic and the eventual production of the environmental collective good program. The business of negotiating a successful program in safe, autonomous organizational spaces was very much about how to secure support by building local site-specific side payments. No top-down command and control approach to ESA implementation could hope to construct the elaborate system of exchange that went into a habitat recovery–sustaining coalition.

Propositions. To the extent that the allies required to construct a large landscape collective good do not confront a crisis, side payments must be arranged to secure their cooperation. To the extent that required allies are in crisis and lack sufficient organizational assets to operate most effectively as allies, side payments are needed to strengthen these alliance partners. The primary locus of side payment discourse must be within local organizations.

Graduated Sanctions

A common complaint has been that the negotiations dragged on too long. Pushed by the USBR, Wyoming's interest was to develop a viable habitat recovery program with as much dispatch as possible, given the constraint of not breaking with its Nebraska and Colorado allies. But stalling was more than just a temptation for the other two states. Transcending the prisoners' dilemma dynamic was challenging work for all parties. Yet Colorado and Nebraska, at various times and for different reasons, found it useful to stall while contemplating internal political problems. When is regulatory cruising needed and justifiable for compelling reasons? It takes time to learn about the problem to be addressed, the available options, and each party's opportunities and constraints. Yet when is regulatory cruising little more than ducking responsible commitment? Clearly, significant incentive must exist for participants in a cooperative program construction process to devise workable and sufficient program elements.

There is, of course, the huge sanction for water users' failure to perform— USFWS withdrawal of regulatory certainty. An argument can be made that the prospect of losing regulatory certainty was sufficient to push the various interests to the table and that the years of negotiations were largely about the terms and conditions under which water providers would act in cooperative partnership to fulfill recovery program milestones. Those milestones, in turn, were effective graduated sanctions as written incrementally. In this perspective, the topic is addressed very simply: the "big hammer"—the necessity of securing regulatory certainty—holds representatives of basin water interests in the federal grip, and everything else is simply a matter of defining the terms and conditions of milestone fulfillment.

However, more nuanced points need to be advanced. No party relished the thought of actually using the big hammer. There were at least two problems with threatening to do so. First, it would be devastating to stop negotiations and thereby enter into individual Section 7 consultations; the USFWS contemplated this extreme action only as a last resort. Second, everybody knew individual Section 7 consultations were as much a nightmare for the enforcing agency as for the users; it would require a level of effort by the USFWS—in terms of personnel, budget, and procedural innovation—that was simply not available. The organizational confrontations that would be involved would be nightmarish—dozens of Klamaths—and would have constituents scurrying to call and e-mail their federal elected officials and thereby threaten the integrity of the ESA in the U.S. Congress. Meanwhile, the species would languish while futile efforts were made to get people to do individually what cannot be accomplished with anything less than a coordinated collective effort. Enforcers, who would seriously harm themselves when swinging the big hammer, became reluctant to use it.

Therefore, the big hammer, while essential to construct crises that can compel people to the negotiating table, may be supplemented by a set of graduated sanctions tailored to the program-building process. Elinor Ostrom (1990: 94–100) postulated that graduated sanctions—rewards and punishments that fit the severity and context of failed performance—constitute an essential component of long-enduring common pool natural resource organizations. Here it is suggested that they may also be important to mobilize actors to construct new governance regimes for the resource commons. Sanctions, graduated to judiciously fit the circumstances of an actor's non-performance, provide incentives to get things done with reasoned and prudent dispatch. They must spur discussion about how to best construct a habitat recovery program with milestones to be fulfilled without threatening to sink the entire discourse over repairable transgressions.

In the world of private property goods, buyers and sellers routinely put performance clauses into their contracts. Failure to deliver commodities or services on time is financially penalized. Failure to meet quality standards is sanctioned by having the provider redo the work at the supplier's cost. There is a direct connection between the scale of the problem and the size of the penalty. Ten-dollar problems are not threatened with million-dollar penalties. Yet small failures to perform appropriately can cumulate into serious problems if not meaningfully and judiciously addressed.

No cleverly formulated set of graduated sanctions could solve the periodic problems of the lack of political will encountered in Nebraska and Colorado. If such problems had become sufficiently severe, the actors would simply have withdrawn from the cooperative effort and taken their chances with individual ESA Section 7 consultations. Is it reasonable to expect that the rigid application of a configuration of smaller sanctions could have moved Nebraska ahead when authorities were having trouble assembling a state Water Policy Advisory Committee and advancing its agenda in the face of deep antagonism from organized groundwater users mobilized under the banner of Nebraskans First? The answer is no. If anything, it could be expected that oppositions would see lesser sanctioning threats as just another example of unwanted federal intrusion and use them to stir up further agitation. At such moments, the quiet potential of the ESA big hammer, situationally defined by local authorities deftly tuned in to local political realities, can be expected to be more efficacious than any formulaic offer of a carrot or threat to employ a lesser stick.

However, in contexts where fundamental political problems have been surmounted, it might be the case that a future depletions plan due from a given state or the federal agencies would be more promptly forthcoming if the actors were on notice that a delay in moving forward would cost additional money, to be contributed to the National Wildlife Foundation in the case of a state delinquency or in the form of a cash grant to reduce the initial costs the states had incurred if they were unduly victimized by a federal delay. What procedures would have to be developed for the Governance Committee to administer and adjudicate a sanctioning process?

There are real dilemmas here. The productive use of carrots and sticks is a tricky business. For example, suppose that a graduated sanctioning regime could be installed and accepted as legitimate (say, DOI could offer an increasing schedule of replacement water quantity and quality over time, combined with added quality land habitat contributions that would be required if water user efforts were not timely). Such incentives, however, may become perverse if a subset of permit-hungry users rushed to complete the task at the expense of internal state water community alliance building. Problem-solving state and local water leaders could find themselves caught between badly managed federal threats and gathering local opposition insisting on withdrawing from the talks. Such circumstances could drive problem solvers from the table while simultaneously feeding political ammunition to those opposed to the entire collective goods project. Delayed milestone completion may, in some circumstances, result in healthy negotiating processes essential to surmount special challenges.

On the other hand, if no meaningful graduated sanctions are in place, if there is the temporary relief from jeopardy that accompanies participation in a cooperative agreement, and if busy leaders are preoccupied with other agendas, there may be insufficient incentive to push ahead with deliberate speed. A basic principle is at stake: delay is costly to deteriorating habitats and must therefore exact a price. Looming additional obligations built into initial cooperative agreements to build programs do provide cover for decision makers to move ahead and request timely sacrifice from constituencies. A process that included negotiation of a reasonable set of graduated sanctions for the cooperative agreement program development phase and tied them closely to the fulfillment of specific milestones could be expected to provide incentives to move with greater speed than one that only provides a stark choice between swinging the big hammer and nothing.

Elements within the basic regulatory process as now constructed provide a framework within which additional, yet-unimagined graduated sanctions can develop. The USFWS has held steadfast to its contention that the central Platte has been shorted an average of 417,000 acre feet per year by historical water project installations in the basin, thereby causing jeopardy for the listed species. If the program fell into deep trouble, the USFWS could—through ESA Section 7 consultations and ESA Section 10 species "takings"—threaten to increase program water depletion replacement requirements. Water users, contemplating a sizable increase in their water contributions, would be boggled by such a prospect. The agency could then back off by lowering the replacement requirement in a compromising manner. Water providers could remove themselves from the cooperative program and fall into individual consultations. But the price for such a choice would be to figure out individually how to replace their particular project depletions by something more than one acre foot for one acre foot of depletion at each state boundary, in the case of Wyoming and

Colorado, or at the top of the critical habitat, in the case of Nebraska water providers.

Propositions. The Cooperative Agreement specifying the collective good must be calibrated to offer a better deal than any deal potentially available from a source other than what the negotiations are expected to produce. In the case of the Platte, the alternative to successful negotiations for any given contributing party is individual ESA Section 7 consultations. Powerful incentives to stay in the program and get things done are needed, assuming a strong ESA and a USFWS that will have the political support necessary to operate with full regulatory integrity. Graduated sanctions are not likely to be efficacious in contexts where serious political problems loom and leaders must attend to critical coalition building. To the extent that graduated sanctions can be devised that earn the support of all parties at a given time and can be attached to specific milestones, they can be efficacious in situations where non-performance is a result of organizational inattention.

Vision of Proportionality

Players can be expected to resist joining arrangements thought to be "unfair." Fairness, or the lack thereof, quickly turns on the question of whether the burdens shouldered or costs paid are roughly proportionate compared with others also asked to cooperatively sacrifice. In private market exchange, fairness is easily determined by whether willing buyers and sellers can agree on a price. Buyers who find the asking price too high will seek alternative sellers. In the domain of common property resources, such as an irrigation ditch, a "proportionate" contribution has traditionally been determined by making the costs paid equal to the proportion of benefit stream received. Irrigators who take 15 percent of the water are assessed 15 percent of the cost of operating the ditch collection and delivery system.

However, in the world of collective goods, the situation is more challenging. Costs to be shouldered can be calculated in somewhat meaningful ways, but since the benefit streams are non-rival and non-excludable, investors cannot easily calculate the value of their individual contributions to the sum of the program outcomes. What are the true benefits of improved critical habitat to Nebraska over a given span of time—a year, a decade, a century? Nobody knows. Benefits are clearly to be had from the two districts obtaining regulatory certainty, some surface water users receiving additional protection from the depredations of junior well owners, sustained tourism dropping dollars into local towns that would otherwise be bypassed, and enhanced land values resulting from a close association with desirable open space. But how do these benefits compare with those captured by Wyoming and Colorado, which also receive regulatory certainty? There is no commensurable unit with which to capture the multiple streams of benefits, to compare who gains more or less, and to permit calculation of fair share contributions.

Fair share is therefore a deeply troubled concept when applied to collective goods program negotiations. Early on, Colorado and Wyoming thought they were well served by a conception of fair share limited largely to sending money to Nebraska. Water for program purposes was viewed as potentially available in central Nebraska. Therefore, Nebraska's upstream neighbors thought it was a good idea to simply provide money to acquire the cheapest available water supplies. Fair share would then mean each state would pay one-third of the costs of re-timing the least expensive water available (Nebraska water). Not surprisingly, that vision of fair share was unacceptable to Nebraskans. Money was not viewed as an appropriate substitute for real water available for Nebraskans in perpetuity—the essential and limiting ingredient for producing income and accumulating wealth. Some in Nebraska wanted fair share to be constructed in a manner approximating an equal division into thirds of the 130,000–150,000 average annual target flow figure. That would mean water contributions in the neighborhood of 43,000–50,000 acre feet a year from each of its two neighbors. To Wyoming and Colorado, that reasoning was beyond absurd. Colorado pointed out that fair share had been determined in 1923 and was encoded in an interstate compact. Wyoming battled for its position within the framework of a U.S. Supreme Court decree in a lawsuit that took over fifteen years to decide. After settling with Wyoming and accepting that state's contribution to the program, Nebraska then discussed with Colorado the idea of protecting the "regime of the South Platte River" as a price for Nebraska's participation in any program. Colorado's regulatory certainty would have to be purchased at the price of accommodating, at least to some extent, Nebraska's vision of proportionality. That, of course, was unacceptable to Colorado.

By the fall of 1996, the discourse had advanced to the point that the Department of the Interior had agreed to provide 50 percent of the cost of the first increment of the program on the condition that the three states match the federal contribution. That concept was incorporated in the 1997 Cooperative Agreement. The states' representatives then agreed to contribute money and in-kind assets for their half share of program costs, based on a rough estimate of basin water use in each state (Strickland 2000). Negotiators incorporated into the 1997 Cooperative Agreement a provision rooted in U.S. Geological Survey estimates of water use in each state's portion of the Platte Basin as of 1990. The relative portions were computed and rounded off in a manner that established relative state shares as follows: Wyoming, 20 percent; Colorado, 40 percent; and Nebraska, 40 percent. The final recovery program budget is given in Appendix F.

Students of collective goods mobilization would do well to study carefully the manner in which alternative fair share concepts become socially constructed and with what consequences. Their impacts on the prospects for success in overcoming the prisoners' dilemma are crucial. No actor can hope to secure the support of constituencies if there are obvious flaws in the construction of their fair share that work to the disadvantage of those same constituencies. The critical questions will always be: what visions of proportionality are in play? Who supports or opposes them? Why? No issue is more critical to successful negotiations than the allocation of burdens in a manner consonant with a mutually acceptable principle of proportionality.

Propositions. The more contending parties can link their proportion of contribution to the proportion of historical negative impact on the targeted collective good, the greater the propensity to accept a common vision of fair share. Failure to construct a mutually agreeable conception of fair share in apportioning costs will result in failed negotiations.

CONCLUSION

Five conditions precedent and seven variables have been advanced as strategic to the successful mobilization of organizational actors to produce collective goods in the domain of water and the environment. Does fulfillment of these factors sufficiently explain the difference between success and failure? Probably not. Yet there are grounds for contending that they represent strategic considerations in any attempt to understand how people can be mobilized to produce and sustain collective property.

Analysts are in the position of the auto mechanic, asked if the car under scrutiny will complete tomorrow's 500-mile trip. Essential components can be checked; apparent problems can be fixed. But after the machine has passed all the tests, there is still no guarantee that the trip will be completed successfully. Factors beyond the analysis, such as being rear-ended at the first stoplight beyond the shop's parking lot, can account for failure. The best analysis can therefore never pretend to provide a blueprint for success, but analysis can highlight factors whose fulfillment can be postulated as necessary—if not sufficient—for success in a complex, theory-defying world.

What can be concluded from all this? No matter how much money and time are spent, no matter how clever and creative the individuals involved, there is no chance of implementing the collaborative initiatives needed for constructing large-scale environmental collective goods under the ESA if conditions precedent cannot be fulfilled and if

1. That legislation cannot create a meaningful crisis for the operations of organizations whose activities have created jeopardy.

2. There is a lack of autonomous social organizational space to which resource users can retreat to work out proposals, plan side payments, and build coalitions.

3. The benefit stream to be produced by collective action is thought to be unneeded according to the best available science, and justification for a new order of things is thereby lost.

4. The balance of power shifts preponderantly to either the regulators or the regulated such that local knowledge within the resource user communities

    a. is driven away by regulators, who are too little constrained and feel no compulsion to incorporate the best ideas of those communities, or

    b. is not tapped because regulation is too weak to compel serious and sustained mobilization to transcend old ways and create a revised regime.

5. Side payments cannot be devised to build essential partnerships.

6. There is a lack of effective sanctions to spur continued meaningful effort to escape the prisoners' dilemma traps that accompany each challenging issue.

7. Conflicting visions of proportionate fair shares in allocating burdens cannot be reconciled.

Under these conditions, it is postulated that attempts to mobilize stakeholder resource organizations to produce collaborative habitat recovery programs will flounder. Failure to fulfill any one of the considerations delineated here can be expected to seriously harm, if not destroy, chances of success.

The effort to assemble a Platte River Habitat Recovery Program reflects a fundamental shift in this nation's water history. One way or another, there must be as never before a continual multi-state, multilevel, interdisciplinary, citizen-technical-specialist, basin-wide discourse about how to integrate the needs of other living things into the human water agenda. Almost four decades ago, our elected representatives said on our behalf that this should be so. The Platte Basin negotiations have been about learning how to do this in the context of feuding water users and environmentalists, three bickering states, and at least three federal agencies (the USFWS, USBR, and USFS) infamous for their inability to coordinate with each other or with the states. Given all this, a new river basin arena of public policy discourse and self-governance has slowly, haltingly, and grudgingly been birthed.

As program implementation proceeds, people of the basin will always have the same two choices that were available to the negotiators who put the habitat recovery program in place. One choice will be, in the name of traditional arrangements and individual actor–level rationality, to reject the voluntary collaborative program for species habitat recovery. People would thereby choose to conduct their discourse through fragmented individual water project consultations and uncoordinated attempts to offset the damage their facilities have caused or will inflict. Beyond the technical challenges that will ride with the individual action option, observers know it will likely also be associated with high-cost intrastate, interstate, and federal-state litigation as permit-hungry organizations vie for immediate advantage at each other's expense amid a scarcity of time, money, land, water, and analytically defensible monitoring and research.

The other choice will be to continue to forge the viable voluntary partnership that is now under way. That option will continue the habitat recovery task in a less expensive, more systematic manner. Either way, there will be basin-wide discourse about how to overcome the historical unfolding of the tragedy of the commons. As long as a viable ESA is in place, along with a regulatory process that has integrity, the issue is not, should water communities be accountable for listed species habitat? The issue is, rather, how and at what cost will people conduct the essential policy talk and implement solutions to problems? How fragmented will their efforts be, and with what effectiveness will their attempts proceed?

For now, it remains to be seen whether the political will, financial resources, and organizational capacity can continue to be mobilized to sustain and invigorate habitat restoration in the Platte Basin. Whenever water and electricity consumers want another bite of basin water flows, their representatives on the production side must adjust their activities, amid the cacophony of basin voices, to the habitat requirements—to the extent they can be known—of at least three species of birds and one species of fish. There is something new under the Platte River Basin sun. It is habitat restoration produced by a richer civic life and better self-governance of an important water commons.

Appreciation

This study has been made possible by the cooperation, goodwill, and assistance of many people representing the various negotiating constituencies. To those listed and to many others not recognized here, who have been helpful in numerous ways, I extend my warmest appreciation. Any errors of fact or interpretation are solely my own.

In the federal community, I acknowledge the special efforts of Margo Zallen, Ralph Morgenweck, Mark Butler, Curt Brown, Donald Anderson, Steve Anschutz, Sharon Whitmore, Jeff Runge, John Lawson, and Polly Hayes. In the environmental community, valuable assistance was rendered by Paul Currier, Daniel Luecke, Duane Hovorka, Chad Smith, Carolyn Greene, Felipe Chavez-Ramirez, and Paul Tebbel.

In the community of states and water providers, I express thanks to David Little, Kevin Urie, Eric Wilkinson, Alan Berryman, Jon Altenhofen, Brad Wind, Allyn Wind, Deborah Freeman, Kent Holsinger, Rick Brown, Grady McNeill, Wendy Weiss, Steve Sims, Ted Kowalski, Joe Frank, Jack Odor, Bob Schott, Steve Treadway, Louis Rinaldo, Bart Woodward, Bill Condon, Mike Purcell, Norman DeMott, Kurt Bucholz, Robert Stieben, Bill Fischer, Dick Stenzel, Jim Hall, Dennis Strauch, Ann Bleed, Dayle Williamson, James Cook, Roger Patterson, Donald Kraus, Mary Jane Graham, Mike Drain, Kent Miller, Brian Barels, Richard Holloway, and Ron Bishop.

Much help was forthcoming from people not affiliated with any particular constituency. In this category I recognize the excellent assistance provided by Dale Strickland and Clayton Derby, who administered the Cooperative Agreement during the negotiating years. Dr. John Wiener of the University of Colorado and Drs. Robert Ward and Jacob Hautaluoma of Colorado State University read drafts of the manuscript and provided valuable comments. Annie Epperson, a former master's degree student in sociology at Colorado State University, and Dr. Troy Lepper, then a graduate student and now a colleague, rendered valuable assistance on an early draft of the work in 2002–2003. In addition, Troy has provided much valuable help with graphics. Cheryl Carnahan, copyeditor, and Laura Furney, managing editor at the University Press of Colorado, have done much to advance the quality of the presentation. To them I extend high praise.

Theory and Methods

> One does not apply theory to history; rather one uses history to develop theory.
>
> —ARTHUR STINCHCOMBE (1978: 1)

A major theoretical question has framed this study from the beginning: how do individually rational actors transcend the prisoners' dilemma dynamic to solve a problem requiring joint collaborative construction of a collective good to address a tragedy of the commons? An opportunity to launch such a study emerged in my own regional neighborhood within the context of the Platte River Habitat Recovery Program negotiations. After undertaking studies of irrigation organizations internationally in the 1970s and 1980s (Freeman 1989), I had turned to a more careful examination of water management organizations in the western United States—mutual irrigation companies, irrigation districts, and conservancy districts, along with forms of river administration—in the 1980s and 1990s (Freeman 2000). When I became aware of the mid-1997 signing of the Cooperative Agreement, I launched an effort to comprehend how the actors would be mobilized to undertake a basin-wide habitat recovery program. The original thought was that the negotiations would consume no more than three or four years.

This study was made feasible by my sixteen years of experience building relationships with water provider organizations in Colorado and elsewhere in the interior West. Those years gave me perspective, the language of local water culture, familiarity with project facilities, and conceptual tools with which to begin to build working relationships with water leaders involved in the three-state Platte River negotiations. If I had not been involved in the universe of local water organizations for a number of years prior to 1997, I would have had little chance to gain entrance to the organizational realm of the Platte negotiations, for at least two reasons: (1) I would not have possessed the requisite local knowledge to comprehend the explanations provided by people of goodwill, and (2) busy informants would have quickly lost patience with anyone not conversant with their social, legal, technical, social, and political world. It is obvious that in the world of research on urban gangs, for example, no researcher would parachute into a specific neighborhood and expect to accomplish anything meaningful quickly without a long prior process of establishing credibility with those representing the targeted study groups. This is at least as true in the case of attempting to enter the arena of highly defensive water communities, characterized internally by long histories of rivalry and never-to-be-forgotten scorecards composed of victories and defeats in past water battles. A researcher, even one with the highest level of technical research skills, simply cannot expect to enter a particular water management and policy domain without carefully building relationships of trust and mutual understanding over extended periods.

To pursue the study of basin-wide negotiations on the Platte, I began by conducting individual interviews with key informants representing the major constituencies. This was essential to gain knowledge about issues, positions, and actors (individual and organizational). It was also important to win acceptance of my presence among water providers at public and private meetings. In-depth interviews not only provided me with necessary understandings, they also gave me, as a researcher, the opportunity to define myself, the project, and my objectives. Informants needed to know that I was a neutral agent, someone trying to get the facts about positions and rationales while not advancing any particular political agenda. Over time, it was possible to earn at least minimal trust by demonstrating that I wanted to comprehend the issues and positions as each community of interest saw them. Three things were critical to build the essential relationships within which key informants could comfortably share their insights amid challenging bargaining. First, I attended as many meetings as possible, especially those of the Governance Committee and the Water Committee. The simple acts of consistently showing up, taking careful notes, and engaging in follow-up discussions in hallways, during lunchtimes, before meetings started, after sessions concluded, and in more private settings earned negotiators' confidence that I was serious and that I was authentically attempting to accurately represent the issues, positions, and unfolding dynamics among the various interests.

Informants were further comforted by the fact that I returned as necessary to clarify facts and perspectives. As the years went by, a number of representatives from each community of interest had systematic opportunities to read and comment on partial draft manuscripts. The first of these came when I prepared a draft manuscript to be presented at the Colloquium on Comparative Study of Ecosystem Restoration Projects, Center for Ecosystem Science and Policy, University of Miami School of Law, Coral Gables, Florida (Freeman 2003a; Doyle and Drew 2008: 58–88). Representatives of each community of interest read and reacted to that early manuscript in late 2002 and 2003. Their comments and critiques were not only valuable in improving the draft, but players were also able to see the scope and depth of the research project. They also came to know that I was making a good-faith effort to correct errors of fact and interpretation. Most important, they could see that the study was not a melodrama. There would be no story of heroes and villains and their accomplices. Rather, the study was guided by a theoretical perspective about which the representatives tended to be neutral; it was of no particular significance for their work. Nevertheless, some expressed an interest in a sociological view of their work that investigated the ways individual rationality did or did not accept the discipline of collective organization.

Later, in the fall of 2003, a heavily revised, corrected, and expanded version of the Platte story and analysis appeared in the form of a Colorado State University Special Report (Freeman 2003b). Representatives of the negotiating communities again had an opportunity to see that their earlier comments were well received and that corrections of fact and interpretations had been incorporated. Furthermore, they were invited to offer another round of fulsome critique. Was this a corruption of the research process? Absolutely not. If a research study was eventually going to be published, if it reflected a good-faith effort to seek out the understandings of those at the negotiating table, and if the work was not a hatchet job on behalf of any particular interest, all informants had an incentive to help me get the story straight. Although everyone knew I would make interpretations with which many informants might eventually disagree, in researcher-informant exchanges the issue was never whether a particular party agreed or disagreed with me. The issue was always: did I present the problems, issues, and respective positions with accuracy? Was I successful in reconstructing the Platte River negotiations as they knew them? Informants could see that my judgment regarding the negotiating process would be grounded in a theoretical perspective of my own construction, independent of any particular negotiating interest. Therefore, their interest was best served by ensuring that I correctly grasped their positions and rationales. In the fall of 2008, after a draft of the completed story and analysis had been composed, selected representatives of the same communities of interest provided their final comprehensive manuscript review.

The negotiators were stakeholders with something important to lose. As a non-stakeholding researcher, I could never be a participant observer in the fullest sense, but my presence at the various negotiating venues was accepted even after the July 2003 decision to impose additional discipline by, among other things, stripping delegations to their core by removing staff members from the sessions.

433

My demonstrated good faith in error correction was central to sustaining both effective relationships and representatives' willingness to speak freely in my presence, even during the most sensitive moments. In following the negotiations as an inside observer, I was asked to leave a negotiating room for a brief period only on two occasions. In each such case, negotiators wanted to converse with an important water policy person who had not agreed to speak candidly in my presence. Informants explained to me, after the fact, the general nature of the discussion from which I had withdrawn in deference to their need to accomplish backstage work.

All informants were assured of confidentiality. All informants were interviewed repeatedly across the years in a variety of settings. Tools for recording information were nothing more than a pen and notebook. I never used a recording device in any manner or circumstance. To have recorded evidence in any way other than writing notes on paper would have driven informants into defensive postures. In a situation of pen and paper only, informants could retain deniability; note takers are capable of error, and what I wrote was clearly my responsibility. If I had placed an operating recording device on a desk, another kind of evidence would have been made available, and shared information would have been placed in a potentially threatening format—it would have become independent evidence that could fall into the possession of an unknown third party. Key informant deniability would have been threatened. Virtually all key informant interviews were conducted with a mutual understanding that the discussion was deep background. Only with this condition in place could informants speak fulsomely and with candor. Each informant has to continue to serve his or her constituencies without having been pinned to particular views in a published monograph.

In the end, meeting and interview notes filled twenty-one large spiral notebooks. Over a ten-year period, notes from negotiating sessions, other meetings, documents, newspapers, newsletters, interviews, and refereed journals were then converted into more than 20,000 3×5-inch note cards—each with one idea, data set, or reference to a data set. Note cards were reviewed, sorted, culled, and organized into themes and topics around which chapters were written.

This Platte River Basin case study has produced a thick and rich description of local site-specific events and episodes that fleshes out a story of how local water providers, state and federal authorities, and environmentalists were mobilized on behalf of an ESA agenda. This knowledge of details has value in itself as history. But an effort to comprehend the story must serve another purpose for sociologists, other analysts in related disciplines, policy makers, and citizens. Knowledge of local and site-specific events must inform the construction of generalizable propositions that can be abstracted from the details of complex histories (Freeman 1992: 18–23; Smith 1991: 156–184).

The research enterprise was initiated because I could see that the Platte case study could address an important abstract theoretical question. Those abstractions were advanced in Chapter 1 and applied in Chapter 31. Several points are in order regarding the nature of those propositions.

First, no set of abstracted concepts and variables can pretend to capture the entirety of complex systems—natural, technical, or social (Freeman 1992: 18–23). For example, unless confronted with a trauma victim who is clearly and immediately threatened by an obviously life-ending condition, a physician would be foolhardy to forecast the exact fate of any given patient based on one analysis of any one model of the human body's respiratory system, gastrointestinal tract, and the like. Physicians operate without a comprehensive theory of the human body. They are cautious because they are fully aware that, when looking at a reasonably healthy person, one must consider many factors beyond any one abstracted model of a process and structure. Likewise, any given generalizable nomothetic proposition, abstracted from the richness of organizations and sets of organizations interacting with technical tools on dynamic ecological webs, captures at best a thin slice of the greater whole without comprehending that whole. Can inference from any particular set of abstracted propositions regarding slices of wholes explain or predict outcomes of the whole? The answer is no. Too many other variables and relationships among variables are at work. To pretend otherwise would be absurd and pretentious. Such explanation and prediction must always escape us. However, it is realistic and fruitful to abstract important slices of wholes, examine them, and evaluate them as to whether they represent something strategic in the outcomes produced by the wholes (Freeman 1992: 18–23). If so, the abstracted dimensions gain merit as worthy of attention by analysts, policy makers, and citizens as part of the assembly of other analytical tools available to advance our understandings—each in its own way casting a particular pattern of light and shadow upon the study domain.

Second, it is obvious but worth stating explicitly that no causality is to be imputed to the relationships among any variables in Figure 31.1. It would be absurd to suggest that crisis causes a change in value on any other dimension of analysis—namely, that crisis would "cause" side payments, fair share rationales, or a rough equality in the players' capacity to check the others at the negotiating table. Each variable in Figure 31.1 has been abstracted from the complexity of the story and has been advanced for consideration because it is thought to specify a condition necessary to successful mobilization for the production of a collective good. But each stands alone as a marker of an important component of success; each possesses its own causal chain, left unspecified and hidden from theoretical view by a set of simplifying conceptual benchmarks against which real-world events can be compared. Any thoughts should be set aside that would posit change in a unit of one variable to be defensibly causal of a specifiable fraction of change in another.

Third, fulfillment of a given dimension or set of dimensions can be posited to be necessary to the production of successful outcomes identified by a given abstracted dependent variable, even if those specified dimensions do not constitute sufficient explanations or predictions of outcomes in the larger complex systems of things. Just as a physician cannot predict next month's outcome for a patient with measured high blood pressure, the same doctor does well to track that parameter and—guided by an understanding of its significance—advocate for lowering blood pressure values to a specific range. The physician knows better than to predict when a given patient will die—the patient's death may be attributed to events far beyond a given conceptual model—but the healer knows well the importance of getting blood pressure values under appropriate control in the name of prolonging quality lives.

There is likewise utility in formulating abstracted generalizable (nomothetic) propositions gained from the study of myriad details of historical episodes. One acknowledges the impossibility of a theory of rich and complex wholes in favor of abstracting slices of those wholes. The slices, representing parameters posited to be necessary even if not sufficient, make better policy assessment possible. We can identify better from worse courses of action in their partial and incomplete light. As we stumble ahead in our quest for improving policy, students of the subject can add improved understanding of existing variables and their relationships, as well as advancing entire new orders of abstracted measuring sticks. It was in the service of this kind of theoretical and policy assessment vision that the study of the Platte River Habitat Recovery Program negotiations was undertaken.

Governance Committee

From 1997 to the end of 2006, the Governance Committee (GC) was the central locus of negotiations to implement the 1997 Cooperative Agreement, the objective of which was to produce a viable habitat recovery program. The GC was served by four standing advisory committees—a Water Committee, Land Committee, Technical Committee (habitat and species monitoring and peer-review processes), and Finance Committee.

GC membership included one voting representative from each of the three states; one voting representative from the U.S. Fish and Wildlife Service (USFWS); one voting representative from the U.S. Bureau of Reclamation (USBR); environmental representatives in the three states, who have two votes; North Platte water users in Wyoming and Nebraska above Lake McConaughy party to storage contracts in federal reservoirs (one voting representative); Colorado South Platte water users above Nebraska's Western Canal headgate (immediately downstream of the state line); and North Platte users (one voting representative); and water users downstream of Kingsley Dam and below the Western Canal headgate and those above Lake McConaughy without federal storage contracts (one voting representative). Votes were rarely conducted.

The governors of each state selected their respective representatives and alternates. The secretary of the interior selected representatives and alternates for the USFWS and USBR. Representatives of each of the other constituencies were selected according to protocols devised by those constituencies (see Cooperative Agreement 1997: appendix C).

For purposes of voting on any issue, a quorum consisted of member representatives (or alternates) appointed by each governor, representatives appointed by the secretary of the interior, and two other representatives. Nine of the GC members, including those appointed by each governor plus the representative of the USFWS, had to vote in the affirmative for the GC to establish a position on policy issues. Seven of ten votes were needed to establish a position on non-policy issues. Policy issues were those that affected "the term, scope, allocation of funding, or continuing viability of the Program" (Cooperative Agreement 1997: appendix C).

The structure of the Program Governance Committee, initiated January 1, 2007, has remained essentially the same. There have been modifications in vote sharing, especially among Nebraska downstream water users, but the structure of voting has held constant, as has the nine-positive-votes-out-of-ten rule on policy matters. The non-policy voting provision was dropped. An Independent Science Advisory Committee was added to the list of standing committees (*Platte River Recovery Program* 2006: attachment 6).

Program Milestones

Progress toward meeting the objectives for Endangered Species Act (ESA) compliance will be measured in terms of the achievement of ten milestones during the first thirteen-year program increment. The Governance Committee is empowered to change these first-increment milestones (*Platte River Recovery Program* 2006: attachment 2). In summary form, they are:

1. The Pathfinder Modification Project will be operational and physically and legally capable of providing water to the program by no later than the end of year 4 of the first increment.

2. Colorado will complete construction of Tamarack 1 and commence full operations by the end of year 4 of the first increment.

3. The CNPPID and the NPPD will implement an environmental account for storage reservoirs in the Platte system in Nebraska, as provided in FERC licenses 1417 and 1835.

4. The Reconnaissance-Level Water Action Plan, as may be amended by the Governance Committee, will be implemented and capable of providing at least an average of 50,000 acre feet per year of shortage reduction to target flows, or for other program purposes, by no later than the end of the first increment. (Note: this is in addition to the 80,000 af/year negotiated by 1997.)

5. The Land Plan, as may be amended by the Governance Committee, will be implemented to protect and, where, appropriate, restore 10,000 acres of habitat by no later than the end of the first increment.

6. The integrated monitoring and research plan, as may be amended by the Governance Committee, will be implemented beginning in year 1 of the program.

7. The Wyoming Depletions Plan, as may be amended with the approval of the Governance Committee, will be operated during the first increment of the program.

8. The Colorado Depletions Plan, as may be amended with the approval of the Governance Committee, will be operated during the first increment of the program.

9. The Nebraska Depletions Plan, as may be amended with the approval of the Governance Committee, will be operated during the first increment of the program.

10. The Federal Depletions Plan, as may be amended with the approval of the Governance Committee, will be operated during the first increment of the program.

Interim steps and time frames for each milestone are specified (see *Platte River Recovery Program* 2006: attachment 2).

APPENDIX E

Adaptive Management Advisory Consulting Team

AUMENT, NICK. Member of the Florida Everglades Program Team for Adaptive Research and Management, with expertise in stream/river processes and limnology

HANNA, EDWARD. President of DSS Management Consultants, Inc., of Pickering, Ontario, with expertise in forest management and the natural resources water sector

KUBLY, DENNIS. Chief of the Adaptive Management Group in the Environmental Resources Division, Bureau of Reclamation, Salt Lake City, Utah

MARMOREK, DAVID. Aquatic ecologist with expertise in research design for adaptive management; employed by ESSA Technologies Ltd., Vancouver, British Columbia

McBAIN, SCOTT. A private consultant with McBain and Trush, Inc., Arcata, California, with expertise in geomorphology and fisheries biology and experience with the Trinity River (northern California) adaptive management program

Program Budget

For the first thirteen-year increment of the Platte River Habitat Recovery Program, cash and cash-equivalent contributions will be provided by the U.S. Department of the Interior (DOI) and the three states, as summarized in the table. Dollars are valued in millions as of 2005. They will be adjusted annually for inflation.

Contributions	Total	DOI	States	Description
Cash	187.14	157.14	30.00	Colorado–24 Wyoming–6
Cash equivalents: Land	10.00		10.00	
Cash equivalents: Water	120.19		120.19	From three initial projects
Total	317.33	157.14	160.19	

Source: *Platte River Recovery Program* 2006: attachment 1.

Photo Gallery

Top left: *Whooping crane (© Al Mueller / Shutterstock).* Top right: *Interior least tern (courtesy, Executive Director's Office—Platte River Recovery Implementation Program [PRRIP]).* Bottom left: *Piping plover (courtesy, Executive Director's Office—Platte River Recovery Implementation Program [PRRIP]).* Bottom right: *Pallid sturgeon (photo from U.S. Fish and Wildlife Service).*

Top left: *Gurnsey Dam and Reservoir (photograph from the U.S. Bureau of Reclamation).* Top right: *Kingsley Dam at Lake McConaughy (public domain photo).* Bottom left: *Infrared photograph of a densely vegetated segment of the Platte River (courtesy, Executive Director's Office—Platte River Recovery Implementation Program [PRRIP]).* Bottom right: *Platte segment after clearing (courtesy, Executive Director's Office—Platte River Recovery Implementation Program [PRRIP]).*

Top left: *Pathfinder Dam (photo from U.S. Bureau of Reclamation).* Top right: *Seminoe Dam (photo from U.S. Bureau of Reclamation).* Bottom left: *Glendo Reservoir (photo from U.S. Bureau of Reclamation).*

Top left: *Clayton Derby (left), deputy administrator; Dale Strickland, executive director, Governance Committee support.* Top right: *Felipe Chavez-Ramirez (left), executive director, Whooping Crane Maintenance Trust; Dan Luecke, Environmental Defense and National Wildlife Federation.* Bottom left: *Kevin Urie (left), environmental planner; David Little, director of planning, Denver Water.* Bottom right: *John Altenhofen, NCWCD engineer who represented NCWCD in assembling Colorado's Tamarack Plan. (Photographs by author.)*

Top left: *Ann Bleed, deputy director and director, Nebraska Department of Natural Resources.* Top right: *Nebraska's core negotiating team (left to right): Brian Barels, NPPD; James Cook, legal counsel to the NDNR; Donald Kraus, manager CNPPID; Dennis Strauch, manager Pathfinder Irrigation District.* Bottom left: *Ronald Bishop, manager Central NRD.* Bottom right: *Kent Miller, Twin Platte NRD. (Photographs by author.)*

Top left: *Ralph Morgenweck, USFWS, regional director, Mountain and Prairie Region.* Top right: *John Lawson, USBR, area manager, Great Plains Region.* Bottom left: *Margot Zallen (left), U.S. Department of the Interior; Mark Butler, USFWS, designated Platte recovery program team leader.* Source: *Photographs by author.*

449

Top left: *Richard Holloway, assistant manager Tri-Basin NRD.* Top right: *A cathedral of the high plains: grain storage for global economy, Holdrege, Nebraska.* Bottom left: *Wyoming core negotiating team: Mike Besson (left), Wyoming Water Development Commission; Mike Purcell, consultant and former director of same commission.* Bottom right: *Colorado core negotiating team (left to right): Steve Sims, formerly Colorado Attorney General's Office, later a private contractor; Ted Kowalski, legal counsel, CWCB; Alan Berryman, NCWCD; Donald Ament, agricultural commissioner. (Photographs by author.)*

Left: *Steve Anschutz, USFWS, supervisor, Grand Island Field Office.* Right: *Sharon Whitmore, USFWS EA account manager at Lake McConaughy, in Grand Island Field Office. (Photographs by author.)*

450

Chronology

Extracted from Echeverria (2001: 593–604); U.S. Fish and Wildlife Service, In-
stream Flow Recommendations: Proposed Definitions and Usage for the Platte
River Recovery Program, 2002a; History of ESA Consultations on Platte River
Target Species, in Final Environmental Impact Statement, vol. 2, Platte River
Recovery Program, April 2006; Record of Decision, Platte River Recovery
Program, September 2006; and other program-related documents.

March 11, 1967	The whooping crane was listed as an endangered species under the Endangered Species Preservation Act.
December 1969	Passage of the National Environmental Policy Act (NEPA).
1970	Six electric utilities formed a consortium to construct a coal-fired power plant and the associated Grayrocks Dam and Reservoir on a tributary of the North Platte River in Wyoming.
December 28, 1973	The Endangered Species Act (ESA) signed into law.
March 1977	The National Wildlife Federation and other groups intervened in *Nebraska v. Rural Electrification Administration*, a suit challenging the Rural Electrification Administration's (REA) issuance of loan guarantees for the Grayrocks Project, objecting that the REA had not adequately considered the project's impact on downstream habitat. The suit also challenged the U.S. Army Corps of Engineer's (USACE's) analysis of the project.

March 1978	The USACE issued a Section 404 permit for the Grayrocks Project, over the U.S. Fish and Wildlife Service's (USFWS) objection that additional studies were required to evaluate impacts on downstream habitat.
May 15, 1978	The USFWS designated fifty-one miles of the Platte River in the big bend reach as "critical habitat" for the whooping crane.
October 2, 1978	The Federal District Court concluded that the REA and the USACE violated NEPA and the ESA and invalidated the loan guarantees and the Section 404 permit.
December 8, 1978	The USFWS issued a jeopardy biological opinion to the USACE and the REA for impacts on habitat associated with the Wyoming Grayrocks Project on the Laramie River. It called for establishment of a $7.5 million trust fund for protecting whooping crane habitat. The USFWS formally requested that the Federal Energy Regulatory Commission (FERC) consult under the ESA on the application of the Central Nebraska Public Power and Irrigation District (CNPPID).
December 4, 1979	FERC requested a formal consultation with the USFWS under the ESA.
1980	Parties to the Grayrocks litigation reached a settlement, leading to the creation of what would become known as the Platte River Whooping Crane Habitat Maintenance Trust.
January 20, 1983	The USFWS issued a biological opinion concluding that the U.S. Bureau of Reclamation's (USBR's) proposed Narrows Unit on the South Platte River in Colorado would jeopardize threatened and endangered species under the ESA.
March 25, 1983	In the aftermath of the decision on the Narrows Project, the USFWS and the USBR agreed to establish the Platte River Management Joint Study.
June 28, 1984	CNPPID and the Nebraska Public Power District (NPPD) (the districts) submitted their initial re-license applications to FERC.
November 1984	Water interests in Colorado, Nebraska, and Wyoming successfully petitioned the secretary of the interior to establish a joint State/Federal Platte River Coordinating Committee to oversee the Platte River Management Joint Study.
December 7, 1984	FERC informed the districts that their applications were deficient and that they had ninety days to amend them. Deficiencies included inadequate analysis of the long-term impacts of the projects' operations on vegetation and wildlife, a lack of study of the feasibility of operating alternatives, and a lack of proposed mitigation measures.
May 28, 1985	Interior least tern is listed as an endangered species.
December 11, 1985	Piping plover was listed as a threatened species.

January 20, 1987	The U.S. Supreme Court reopened *Nebraska v. Wyoming* by allowing Nebraska to file a petition to enforce the decree and to seek injunctive relief.
April 20, 1987	The U.S. Supreme Court, in *Nebraska v. Wyoming*, issued an order granting Wyoming leave to file a counterclaim alleging that Nebraska had violated the decree in various respects.
May 28, 1987	The USFWS asked FERC to formally consult under the ESA prior to issuing annual licenses for CNPPID and NPPD projects.
June 30 and July 29, 1987	Original licenses for CNPPID's and NPPD's licenses expired. FERC issued the first of many annual licenses for the projects.
July 20, 1987	The USFWS issued a non-jeopardy biological opinion to the USACE on the Wyoming Deer Creek Project. To preclude future jeopardy judgment, the USFWS agreed to accept Wyoming's offer to fund a whooping crane habitat area in Nebraska's central Platte region. The Deer Creek Project was not built.
August 17, 1990	The pallid sturgeon was listed as an endangered species.
May 17, 1993	The Platte River Management Joint Study Team released its report, envisioning elements of a possible Platte River Habitat Conservation Program.
May 23, 1994	In-stream flow recommendations for the central Platte River were prepared by David Bowman, USFWS, in a report presenting results of a workshop held March 8–10, 1994, at the National Ecological Research Center of the National Biological Survey, Fort Collins, Colorado.
June 2, 1994	The secretary of the interior and the governors of Colorado, Nebraska, and Wyoming entered into a Memorandum of Agreement (MOA) initiating the construction of a basin-wide program for endangered species protection in the Platte River Basin. The USFWS estimated an average of 417,000 acre feet/year of historical in-stream flow shortages relative to the agency's in-stream flow recommendations.
June 2 and July 1, 1994	The USFWS issued biological opinions for six reservoirs undergoing re-permitting on Arapaho-Roosevelt National Forest lands in northern Colorado. The opinions concluded that unless the impacts of these projects were successfully mitigated, their operations would cause jeopardy to downstream critical habitat in central Nebraska.
March 15, 1995	The U.S. Department of the Interior (DOI), on behalf of all parties, issued a fifteen-page memorandum that briefly outlined program elements to be negotiated and basic principles for the conduct of negotiations. It came to be known informally as the "sideboards" agreement.
February 14, 1996	FERC released its biological assessment on the re-licensing applications under the ESA and requested initiation of formal consultations with the USFWS under Section 7 of the ESA.

December 4, 1996	The DOI issued its draft biological opinion on the proposed re-licensing of the CNPPID and NPPD projects for FERC.
July 1, 1997	The secretary of the interior and the governors of Colorado, Nebraska, and Wyoming entered into a Cooperative Agreement for Platte River Research and Other Efforts Relating to Endangered Species Habitats along the Central Platte River, Nebraska (CA). The CA established a Cooperative Agreement Governance Committee consisting of representatives from the Department of the Interior (USFWS and USBR), each of the three states, water providers, and nongovernmental environmental organizations. The Governance Committee functioned as an entity responsible to develop a Platte River Habitat Recovery Program that could win a non-jeopardy USFWS biological opinion and thereby serve as a reasonable and prudent alternative, as required by the ESA.
July 25, 1997	The USFWS issued its final biological opinion based on the CA and the proposed environmental water account in Lake McConaughy.
January 15, 1998	The CNPPID, NPPD, and the other major parties to the re-licensing proceedings filed an agreement on "all issues" with FERC.
July 24, 1998	FERC issued a final environmental impact statement (EIS) on the re-licensing applications based on the terms of the CA.
July 29, 1998	FERC issued an order approving new forty-year licenses for the CNPPID and NPPD projects.
February 24, 2000	The Governance Committee extended the original three-year CA for six months, July 1–December 31, 2000.
May 10, 2000	On the eve of the trial in *Nebraska v. Wyoming*, the parties arrived at an agreement in principle to settle the entire litigation without specifically addressing habitat conservation issues. The Governance Committee agreed to extend the CA to June 30, 2003, with an option to extend it for an additional six months. This decision was driven primarily by a preliminary analysis of the sedimentation-vegetation problem.
August 3, 2000	The USFWS informed the Governance Committee that the proposed recovery program as then configured could not serve as a reasonable and prudent alternative. Sedimentation-vegetation and other issues would have to be addressed.
September 14, 2000	Boyle Engineering Corporation delivered its report, Reconnaissance-Level Water Action Plan, to the Governance Committee. The report defined possible water re-timing projects in the three basin states that could potentially produce an annual average of 130,000–140,000 acre feet for recovery program purposes.

October 1, 2000	The USBR (Murphy and Randle) released a draft report (Platte River Channel: History and Restoration) that described anticipated continued erosion of medium-sized sand and channel narrowing downstream from Grand Island, Nebraska, over the next several decades unless changes were made in the management of the river. The report also recommended short-duration vegetation scouring flows as one component of a strategy to restore a portion of the historical Platte River channel.
March 2001	Nebraska and Wyoming agreed to an out-of-court settlement in *Nebraska v. Wyoming* (1986). In November, the U.S. Supreme Court approved the settlement and the accompanying modified decree of 1945.
July 2002	The USFWS provided a draft memorandum to the Water Committee summarizing all agency in-stream flow recommendations and defining species flows, pulse flows, and peak flows. This was followed by a revised draft dated December 23, 2002.
July 17, 2002	The USFWS announced that the USBR-EIS team had found that the revised program that incorporated sedimentation and vegetation manipulations could serve as a reasonable and prudent alternative. Other issues remained to be resolved.
September 11, 2002	Designation of critical habitat along Nebraska's central Platte for the threatened piping plover.
January 31, 2003	Contract signed between DOI and the National Academies of Science (NAS) for an NAS review of selected aspects of the science undergirding the proposed habitat recovery program.
December 9, 2003	Governance Committee approved extension of the CA from January 1, 2004, to June 30, 2005, with a possible extension until December 31, 2005, if needed.
December 18, 2003	The Nebraska Water Policy Task Force presented its report to Governor Johanns. The report recommended means to integrate critical aspects of groundwater and surface water administration. Contents of the report were encoded in legislation known as LB 962.
January 26, 2004	Draft EIS on the proposed Platte River Habitat Recovery Program was released to the public. Public comment period began.
April 13, 2004	Nebraska unicameral legislature enacted LB 962, hailed as one of the most significant water laws in recent decades. LB 962 took effect July 16, 2004.
April 28, 2004	The National Research Council of the NAS released its draft report, Endangered and Threatened Species of the Platte River (2004b), endorsing the bulk of the USFWS's use of science that justified the need for the Platte River Habitat Recovery Program.
August 2004	Draft biological opinion on the proposed Platte River Habitat Recovery Program was released for Governance Committee review and quickly withdrawn.

455

January 1, 2005	The National Research Council of the NAS published its final report, *Endangered and Threatened Species of the Platte River*.
May 17, 2005	The Governance Committee approved extending the CA to December 31, 2005.
October 27, 2005	The Governance Committee approved extending the CA to October 1, 2006.
January 2006	Platte River Habitat Recovery Program document was released with placeholders in some sections as substitutes for final language yet to be adopted. This program plan provided the basis for review by the USBR-EIS team and the USFWS biological opinion team.
April 2006	Final EIS released.
June 16, 2006	Final USFWS non-jeopardy biological opinion released.
July 28, 2006	Draft non-jeopardy biological opinion released on the matter of amending hydro-cycling operations on CNPPID's Johnson no. 2 power plant in the Kingsley Dam Project.
September 14, 2006	Governance Committee approved extending the CA from October 1, 2006, to December 31, 2006.
September 27, 2006	Record of Decision released. DOI officially announced its endorsement of the Platte River Habitat Recovery Program.
October 24, 2006	Platte River Habitat Recovery Implementation Program document published. Produced by the Platte River Cooperative Agreement Governance Committee, it was more than 500 pages long.
October 26, 2006	Bill Owens, governor of Colorado, signed the Platte River Recovery Program Agreement.
October 31, 2006	Dave Heineman, governor of Nebraska, signed the Platte River Recovery Program Agreement.
November 27, 2006	Dave Freudenthal, governor of Wyoming, signed the Platte River Recovery Program Agreement.
December 7, 2006	Dirk Kempthorne, Secretary of Interior, signed the Platte River Program Agreement
January 1, 2007	Platte River Habitat Recovery Implementation Program began. The Program Governance Committee, as distinguished from the Cooperative Agreement Governance Committee, assumed responsibility for implementing the Platte River Recovery Program.
May 8, 2008	President George W. Bush signed the Consolidated Natural Resources Act of 2008, incorporating the Platte River Recovery Program and Pathfinder Modification Act under Title V, Section 515, along with fifty-six other natural resource bills.

References

Abbott, Carl. 1976. *Colorado: A History of the Centennial State*. Boulder: Colorado Associated University Press.

Abell, Robin A., David M. Olson, Eric Dinerstein, Patrick T. Hurley, James T. Diggs, William Eichbaum, Steven Walters, Wesley Wettengel, Tom Allnutt, Colby J. Loucks, and Prashant Hedao. 2000. *Freshwater Ecoregions of North America: A Conservation Assessment*. Washington, D.C.: Island.

Adams, Tori. 2006. "Upper Platte Water Users Want Certainty." *Rawlins* (Wyoming) *Daily Times*. November 29.

———. 2008. "Settlement Reached with Water Rights, Pathfinder Modification." *Rawlins* (Wyoming) *Daily Times*. November 14.

Aiken, J. David. 1980. "Nebraska Ground Water Law and Administration." *Nebraska Law Review* 59: 917–1000.

———. 1999. "Balancing Endangered Species Protection and Irrigation Water Rights: The Platte River Agreement." *Great Plains Natural Resources Journal* 3, 2 (Spring): 119–158.

———. 2006. "The Spear T Decision." *Nebraska Law Review* 84: 962–996.

Allen, Robert P. 1952. *The Whooping Crane*. Research Report 3. New York: National Audubon Society.

———. 1969. "The Whooping Crane's World," in *Our Natural World,* ed. Hal Borland. Philadelphia: J. B. Lippincott, 605–610.

American Rivers. 2004. "Losing Missouri River Fish and Wildlife." Available at www.amrivers.org. Accessed July 24, 2004.

Anderson, Stanley. 1998. "The Evolution of the Endangered Species Act," in *Private Property and the Endangered Species Act*, ed. J. Shogren. Austin: University of Texas Press, 8–24.

REFERENCES

Andrews, Richard. 1999. *Managing the Environment, Managing Ourselves: A History of American Environmental Policy*. New Haven: Yale University Press.

Ashworth, William. 2006. *Ogallala Blue: Water and Life on the Great Plains*. New York: W. W. Norton.

Associated Press. 2004. "Platte River Users Get Lawyered Up." *Casper* (Wyoming) *Star-Tribune*. February 9.

Austin, Jane E., and Amy L. Richert. 2001. *A Comprehensive Review of Observational and Site Evaluation Data of Migrant Whooping Cranes in the United States, 1943–1999*. U.S. Geological Survey, Northern Prairie Wildlife Research Center, Jamestown, N.D. Available at http://www.npwrc.usgs.gov/resource/2003/wcdata.

Babbitt, Bruce. 2005. *Cities in the Wilderness: A New Vision of Land Use in America*. Washington, D.C.: Island.

Baden, John, and Douglas Noonan (eds.). 1998. *Managing the Commons*. Bloomington: University of Indiana Press.

Barnett, Louise. 2006. *Touched by Fire: The Life, Death, and Mythic Afterlife of George Armstrong Custer*. Lincoln: University of Nebraska Press.

Barry, Hamlet "Chips." 1997. "Water Management: The Equitable Sharing of a Scarce Resource." *Colorado Water* 14, 5 (October): 19–24.

Bean, Michael. 1999. "Endangered Species, Endangered Act?" *Environment* 41: 12–18, 34–38.

Becker, Jo, and Barton Gellman. 2007. "Leaving No Tracks." *The Washington Post*. June 27.

Bethell, Thomas N. 1986. *The Native Home of Hope: People and the Northern Rockies*. Salt Lake City: Home Brothers.

Blake, Tupper A., Madeleine G. Blake, and William Kittredge. 2000. *Balancing Water: Restoring the Klamath Basin*. Berkeley: University of California Press.

Bleed, Ann S. 1993. "Climate and Hydrology," in *Flat Water: A History of Nebraska and Its Water*, ed. C. A. Flowerday. Lincoln: University of Nebraska–Lincoln, 45–49, 54, 56, 60–62.

Blumm, Michael C. 1994. "The Rhetoric of Water Reform Resistance: A Response to Hobbs' Critique of Long's Peak." *Environmental Law* 24: 171–188.

Bowman, David. 1994. "Instream Flow Recommendations for the Central Platte River, Nebraska." National Ecology Research Center, Fort Collins, Colo., May 23.

Bowman, David, and David Carlson. 1994. "Pulse Flow Requirements for the Central Platte River." U.S. Fish and Wildlife Service, Lakewood, Colo., August 3.

Boyle Engineering Corporation. 2000. "Reconnaissance-Level Water Action Plan." Report to Platte River Recovery Program Governance Committee, Lakewood, Colo.

———. 2008. "Water Management Study, Phase I (Draft)." Technical Report to Governance Committee, Platte River Recovery Program, Denver, January 29.

Bromley, Daniel. 1992. *Making the Commons Work: Theory, Practice, and Policy*. San Francisco: Institute of Contemporary Studies Press.

Brower, Ann, Chaual Roedy, and Jennifer Yelin-Kefers. 2001. "Consensus vs. Conservation in the Upper Colorado River Basin Recovery Implementation Program." *Conservation Biology* 15: 1001–1007.

Bucholz, Kurt. 1999. Letter to Committee on Resources, U.S. House of Representatives. Written on behalf of the Coalition for Sustainable Resources, Inc., Walden, Colo., July 24. Letter on file with author.

Bunch, Joey. 2003. "Mallach Resigns from the Water Board." *The Denver Post*. August 8.

Burchell, R.W. 2002. *Costs of Sprawl—2000*. Washington, D.C.: National Academy Press.

Burger, Joanna, Elinor Ostrom, Richard B. Norgaard, Daniel Policansky, and Bernard D. Goldstein (eds.). 2001. *Protecting the Commons: A Framework for Resource Management in the Americas*. Washington, D.C.: Island.

Cables, Rick D. 2005. Letter to Dale Strickland from Rick D. Cables, Regional Forester. U.S. Forest Service, Region II, Lakewood, Colo., December 2. File Code 2500/2670. Topic: Relationship between Forest Condition and Water Yield. Available as Attachment B, Federal Depletions Plan, *Platte River Recovery Program*, October 24, 2006.

Chafee, Lincoln. 2008. *Against the Tide: How a Compliant Congress Empowered a Reckless President*. New York: St. Martin's.

Clark, Jeanne Nienaber, and Daniel C. McCool. 1996. *Staking Out the Terrain: Power and Performance among National Resource Agencies*. Albany: State University of New York Press.

Clarren, Rebecca. 2001. "No Refuge in the Klamath Basin." *High Country News* (Paonia, Colo.). May 7.

———. 2008. "No Refuge in the Klamath." *High Country News* (Paonia, Colo.). July 16.

CNPPID. 1999. "Annual Report." Central Nebraska Public Power and Irrigation District, Holdrege, Neb.

———. 2005a. "Annual Report." Central Nebraska Public Power and Irrigation District, Holdrege, Neb.

———. 2005b. "Responses to Questions in M. Butler's Email of October 17, 2005." Unpublished memorandum. Central Nebraska Public Power and Irrigation District, Holdrege, Neb., December 6.

CNPPID and NPPD. 1998. "Offer of Settlement in the Re-licensing Proceedings for the Kingsley Dam Project no. 1417 and North Platte/Keystone Project no. 1835 on the Platte River in Nebraska." Holdrege and Kearney, Neb., May 15.

Coalition for Sustainable Resources. 1999. *Coalition for Sustainable Resources v. United States Forest Service, Department of Agriculture*. 48 F. Supp. 2d 1303 (D. Wyoming) D.C. no. 98-CV-174-B.

———. 2001. *Coalition for Sustainable Resources v. United States Forest Service, Department of Agriculture*. Case number 99-8060. Appealed from U.S. District Court, District of Wyoming, D.C. no. 98-CV-174-B, to U.S. Court of Appeals, Tenth Circuit. Filed August 7.

Collier, M. P., R. H. Webb, and E. D. Andrews. 1997. "Experimental Flooding in Grand Canyon." *Scientific American* 276, 1 (January): 82–89.

Colorado Future Depletions Plan. 2006. Attachment 5, Water Plan, *Platte River Recovery Program*. Governance Committee, October 24.

Colorado Water Conservation Board. 2004. *Statewide Water Supply Initiative (SWSI)*. Report, Executive Summary. Denver: Colorado Department of Natural Resources, November.

Communicator: Newsletter of CNPPID. 2006. Vol. 21, 5 (November–December).

Cooperative Agreement. 1997. "Cooperative Agreement for Platte River Research and Other Efforts Relating to Endangered Species Habitats along the Central Platte River, Nebraska." States of Colorado, Nebraska, Wyoming, and the U.S. Department of the Interior. Unpublished document, July.

Corbridge, James N., Jr., and Teresa A. Rice. 1999. *Vranesh's Colorado Water Law*. Niwot: University Press of Colorado.

Cottam, Clarence. 1996. "The Whooping Crane." Appendix A in *The Whooping Crane: North America's Symbol of Conservation* by Jerome J. Pratt. Prescott, Ariz.: Castle Rock Publishers, 122–129.

Cox, James L. 1967. *Metropolitan Water Supply: The Denver Experience*. Boulder: Bureau of Governmental Research and Science.

Currier, Paul J., and Craig A. Davis. 2000. "The Platte as a Prairie River: A Response to Johnson and Boettcher." *Great Plains Research* 10: 69–84.

Currier, Paul J., Gary R. Lingle, and John G. Van Der Walker. 1985. *Migratory Bird Habitat on the Platte and North Platte Rivers in Nebraska*. Grand Island, Neb.: Platte River Whooping Crane Critical Habitat Maintenance Trust.

Daly, Herman E., and John B. Cobb Jr. 1994. *For the Common Good: Redirecting the Economy toward Community, the Environment, and a Sustainable Future*. Boston: Beacon.

Dana, S. T. 1956. *Forest and Range Policy*. New York: McGraw-Hill.

Denver Water Board. n.d. *Denver Water Resources: Features of the Denver Water System*. Denver Water Board, Denver.

Diffendal, R. F., Jr. 1993. "Understanding Groundwater Starts with Rocks: Geological Framework, Groundwater Occurrence and Irrigation Development in Nebraska," in *Flat Water: A History of Nebraska and Its Water*, ed. C. A. Flowerday. Lincoln: University of Nebraska–Lincoln, 50–54.

Dolsak, Nives, and Elinor Ostrom (eds.). 2003. *The Commons in the New Millennium: Challenges and Adaptation*. Cambridge: MIT Press.

Doremus, Holly. 2005. "Endangered Species Act Gets Listed." *Christian Science Monitor*. September 29.

Dornbusch, A. J., Jr., B. M. Vining, and J. L. Kearney. 1995. "Total Resource Management Plan for Addressing Groundwater Concerns," in *Conservation of Great Plains Ecosystems: Current Science, Future Options*, ed. S. R. Johnson and A. Boujaher. Dordrecht: Kluwer Academic Publishers, 231–252.

Doyle, Mary, and Cynthia Drew (eds.). 2008. *Large Scale Ecosystem Restoration: Five Case Studies from the United States*. Washington, D.C.: Island.

Drain, Michael A. 2006. "The Central Nebraska Public Power and Irrigation District, Project Number 1417, Application for Amendment of License—Consultations with the U.S. Fish and Wildlife Service and the Nebraska Game and Parks Commission." Letter to Magalie Roman Salas, secretary, Federal Energy Regulatory Commission, Holdrege, Neb., July 31. Attachments.

Dreeszen, Vincent H. 1993. "Water Availability and Use," in *Flat Water: A History of Nebraska and Its Water*, ed. C. A. Flowerday. Lincoln: University of Nebraska–Lincoln, 82–86.

Dunbar, Robert. 1983. *Forging New Rights in Western Waters*. Lincoln: University of Nebraska Press.

Echeverria, John. 2001. "No Success Like Failure: The Platte River Collaborative Watershed Planning Process." *William and Mary Environmental Law and Policy Review* 25: 559–604.

Eisel, L., and J. D. Aiken. 1997. "Platte River Basin Study: Report to the Western Water Policy Review Advisory Commission." U.S. Department of Commerce, Springfield, Va.

Elliot, J. G., M. E. Smith, M. J. Friedil, M. R. Stevens, C. R. Bossong, D. W. Litke, R. S. Parker, C. Costello, J. Wagner, S. J. Char, M. K. Bauer, and S. R. Wilds. 2004. "Analysis and Mapping of Post-Fire Hydrologic Hazards for the 2002 Hayman Coal Seam and Missionary Ridge Wildfires, Colorado." USGS Colorado Water Science Center, USGS Scientific Investigative Report 2004-5300. Available at http://pubs.usgs.gov/sit/2004/5300. Accessed January 6, 2008.

Endangered Species Act. 1973. 16 U.S.C. 1531–1534, 87 Stat. 884. Public Law 93-205. Approved December 28.

Environment News Service. 2004. "Appeal Seeks to Restore Missouri River's Natural Flow." Available at www.ens-newswire.com/ens/jul2004/2004-07-13-11.asp. Accessed March 12, 2008.

Eschner, T., R. Hadley, and K. Cromley. 1981. "Hydrologic and Morphologic Changes in Channels of the Platte River Basin: A Historical Perspective." U.S. Geological Survey, Denver.

Farquhar, Bradie. 2005. "Pombo Takes on the Endangered Species Act." *High Country News* (Paonia, Colo.) 37, 19 (October 17).

Ferrell, John. 1993. *Big Dam Era: A Legislative and Institutional History of the Pick-Sloan Plan.* Omaha: Missouri River Division, U.S. Army Corps of Engineers.

Forbush, Edward Home, and John Richard May. 1955. *A Natural History of American Birds of Eastern and Central North America.* New York: Bramhall House.

Freedman, Warren. 1987. *Federal Statistics on Environmental Protection: Regulation in the Public Interest.* New York: Quorum Books.

Freeman, David. 1989. *Local Organizations for Social Development: Concepts and Cases of Irrigation Organizations.* Boulder: Westview.

———. 1992. *Choice against Choice: Constructing a Policy-Assessing Sociology for Social Development.* Niwot: University Press of Colorado.

———. 2000. "Wicked Water Problems: Sociology and Local Water Organizations in Addressing Water Resources Policy." *Journal of the American Water Resources Association* 36: 483–491.

———. 2003a. "Organizing for Endangered and Threatened Species Habitat in the Platte River Basin." Paper presented to the Colloquium on Comparative Study of Ecosystem Restoration Projects, Center for Ecosystem Science and Policy, University of Miami School of Law, Coral Gables, Fla., January 22–24.

———. 2003b. "Organizing for Endangered and Threatened Species Habitat in the Platte River Basin." Special Report 12. Fort Collins: Colorado Water Resources Research Institute, Colorado State University.

———. 2008. "Negotiating for Endangered and Threatened Species Habitat in the Platte River Basin," in *Large-Scale Ecosystem Restoration: Five Case Studies from the United States,* ed. Mary Doyle and Cynthia Drew. Washington, D.C.: Island, 59–88.

Freilich, Robert, and S. Mark White. 2008. *21st Century Land Development Code.* Chicago: American Planning Association.

Gammage, Grady, Jr. 2003. *Phoenix in Perspective: Reflections on Developing in the Desert.* Tempe: Herberger Center for Design Excellence, Arizona State University.

Gaul, Steve. 1993. "Politics and Policy," in *Flat Water: A History of Nebraska and Its Water,* ed. C. A. Flowerday. Lincoln: University of Nebraska–Lincoln, 203–207, 209–230.

Gellman, Barton. 2008. *Angler: The Cheney Vice Presidency.* New York: Penguin.

Gerber, Leah R., Douglas P. DeMaster, and Simona P. Roberts. 2000. "Measuring Success in Conservation." *American Scientist* 88: 316–324.

Gillilan, David M., and Thomas C. Brown. 1997. *Instream Flow Protection: Seeking a Balance in Western Water Use*. Washington, D.C.: Island.

Glick, Daniel. 2008. "Still Howling Wolf." *High Country News* (Paonia, Colo.) 40, 20 (November 10).

Gordon, Nancy. 1995. "Summary of Technical Testimony in the Colorado Water Division 1 Trial." Rocky Mountain Forest and Range Experiment Station, Fort Collins, Colo.

Gottlieb, Robert, and Peter Wiley. 1982. *Empires in the Sun: The Rise of the New American West*. New York: Putnam.

Goudie, Andrew. 1986. *The Human Impact on the Natural Environment*. Cambridge: MIT Press.

Grooms, Steve. 1991. *The Cry of the Sandhill Crane*. Minnetonka, Minn.: North Word.

Halbert, C. L. 1993. "How Adaptive Is Adaptive Management? Implementing Adaptive Management in Washington State and British Columbia." *Reviews in Fisheries Science* 1: 261–283.

Hanna, Susan S., Carl Folke, and Karl-Goran Maler (eds.). 1996. *Rights to Nature: Ecological, Economic, Cultural, and Political Principles of Institutions for the Environment*. Washington, D.C.: Island.

Hardin, Garrett. 1968. "The Tragedy of the Commons." *Science* 162: 1243–1248.

Hendee, David. 2006. "Reservoirs Thirsty for Snowmelt." *Omaha World Herald*. October 17.

Herbert, Bob. 1995. "Health and Safety Wars." *The New York Times*. July 10.

Hessel, Dave, and Dennis Lemaster. 2007. "Protecting Front Range Forest Watersheds from High-Severity Wildfires." *Colorado Water* (August–September): 24–26.

Holling, C. S. 1978. *Adaptive Environmental Assessment and Management*. New York: John Wiley.

Hundley, Norris, Jr. 1986. "The West against Itself: The Colorado River—An Institutional History," in *New Course for the Colorado River: Major Issues for the Next Century*, ed. Gary D. Weatherford and F. Lee Brown. Albuquerque: University of New Mexico Press, 9–51.

Hydrosphere Resource Consultants. 1999. "Metropolitan Water Supply Investigation." Report prepared for the Colorado Water Conservation Board, Boulder.

———. 2003. "Potential Effects of Colorado's Future Water Development on Central Platte River Peak Flows." Report prepared for the USFWS, Mountain and Prairie Region, Lakewood, Colo. Draft, June.

Inspector General, Office of. Department of the Interior. 2007. "Investigative Report: On Allegations against Julie MacDonald, Deputy Assistant Secretary, Fish, Wildlife and Parks." U.S. Department of the Interior, Washington, D.C. Available at www.docoig.gov/upload/Macdonald.pdf. Accessed July 30, 2007.

Interagency Ecosystem Management Task Force. 1996. "The Ecosystem Approach: Healthy Ecosystems and Sustainable Economies." National Technical Information Services, Washington, D.C.

Jenkins, Matt. 2006. "The Perpetual Growth Machine." *High Country News* (Paonia, Colo.) 38, 11 (June 12).

———. 2008. "Peace on the Klamath." *High Country News* (Paonia, Colo.) 40, 12 (June 23).

Jerke, Bill. 2006. Chair, South Platte Basin Roundtable. "Memorandum Regarding Water Needs Assessment Refinement" to Eric Hecox, Manager, Office of Interbasin Compact Negotiations, Colorado Department of Natural Resources, Denver, September 29.

Johnson, W. Carter. 1994. "Woodland Expansion in the Platte River, Nebraska: Patterns and Causes." *Ecological Monographs* 64: 45–84.

Johnson, W. Carter, and Susan E. Boettcher. 2000. "The Pre-Settlement Platte: Wooded or Prairie River?" *Great Plains Research* 10: 39–68.

Joint Resolution. 2003. Fifty-Seventh Legislature of the State of Wyoming, General Session. File no. 0003. March 1. Available at http://legisweb.state.wy.us/2003/enroll/sj0003.pdf. Accessed November 15, 2007.

Kahn, Herman. 1976. *The Next 200 Years: A Scenario for America and the World.* New York: William Morrow.

Kanzer, David A., and David H. Merritt. 2001. "Mitigation of Trans-Mountain Diversions? Re-operation!" in *Transbasin Water Transfers: Proceedings of the 2001 USCID Water Management Conference,* ed. Jerry Schoock. Denver: U.S. Committee on Irrigation and Drainage, 303–317. June 27–30.

Kappas, Uli. 1997. "Wise Water Stewardship through Partnerships." *Colorado Water* 14, 5 (October): 16–19.

Kassen, Melinda. 2000. "Report on Water Yield from Forest Management in the North Platte." Letter on Trout Unlimited letterhead to Dan Luecke, Environmental Defense, Boulder, Colo., July 3.

Kearney Hub. 2007. "Johnson Lake Level Drops to Maintain Big Mac." July 17.

Keohane, Robert O., and Elinor Ostrom (eds.). 1995. *Local Commons and Global Interdependence.* London: Sage.

Keyes, John. 2002. Commissioner, Bureau of Reclamation, U.S. Department of the Interior. "Statement on Endangered Species Act: The Platte River Cooperative Agreement and Critical Habitats." Committee on Resources, U.S. House of Representatives. Field Hearing in Grand Island, Neb., February 16.

Kittredge, William. 1996. *Who Owns the West?* San Francisco: Mercury House.

Knight, Samuel H. 1990. *Illustrated Geologic History of the Medicine Bow Mountains and Adjacent Areas, Wyoming.* Laramie: Geological Survey of Wyoming.

Kraft, Michael E. 2006. "Environmental Policy in Congress," in *Environmental Policy: New Directions for the Twenty-First Century,* ed. Norman J. Vig and Michael E. Kraft. Washington, D.C.: Congressional Quarterly Press, 124–147.

Krech, Shepard, III. 1999. *The Ecological Indian: Myth and History.* New York: W. W. Norton.

Larson, T. A. 1965. *History of Wyoming.* Lincoln: University of Nebraska Press.

Leaf, Charles F. 1999a. "Forest Hydrology Issues for the Twenty-First Century: A Consultant's Viewpoint by Robert H. Swanson." *Journal of the American Water Resources Association* 35, 1 (February): 193–194.

———. 1999b. "Past, Present, and Future Effects of Forest Service Management Policies on North Platte River Water Yields." Research Paper PRHRC-6. Platte River Hydrologic Research Center, Merino, Colo., September.

Lee, K. N. 1993. *Compass and Gyroscope: Integrating Science and Politics for the Environment.* Washington, D.C.: Island.

Lee, K. N., and J. Lawrence. 1986. "Adaptive Management: Learning for the Columbia River Basin Fish and Wildlife Program." *Environmental Law* 16: 431–460.

Levy, Sharon. 2003. "Turbulence in the Klamath River Basin." *BioScience* 53, 4 (April): 315–320.

Lewis, Gary L., and Eric Roerish. 2003. "Preliminary Evaluation of Channel Capacity in the North Platte River at North Platte, Nebraska." Report prepared for the Central Nebraska Public Power and Irrigation District. Parsons Engineering, Denver, January.

Lewis, Harry. 2005. "Have We Painted Ourselves into a Corner?" *The Denver Post.* May 1.

Lipsher, Steve. 2007. "Aiming to Tip the Scales Back." *The Denver Post.* August 2.

Livingston, Ann, Elizabeth Riddlington, and Matt Baker. 2003. "The Costs of Sprawl: Fiscal, Environmental, and Quality of Life Impacts of Low-Density Development in the Denver Region." Report. Environment Colorado Research and Policy Center, Denver, March.

Lochhead, James. 2000. "Chronic and Emerging Water Issues in the South Platte/Front Range Corridor," in *Water and Growth in the West: Proceedings of the Twenty-First Summer Conference.* Denver: Natural Resources Law Center, University of Colorado School of Law, June 7–9.

Longo, Peter J., and Robert D. Miewald. 1989. "Institutions in Water Policy: The Case of Nebraska." *Natural Resources Journal* 29: 751–762.

Luckey, Richard R., Duane A. Woodward, and Clint P. Carney. 2006. "Estimated Stream Depletion in the Nebraska Platte Basin Due to New Irrigated Land Developed after July 1, 1997." Report: A COHYST Cooperative Hydrology Study. Nebraska Department of Natural Resources, Lincoln, October 3.

Luecke, Daniel F. 2000. "An Environmental Perspective in Large Ecosystem Restoration Processes and the Role of the Market, Litigation, and Regulation." *Arizona Law Review* 42: 395–410.

Lutey, James M. 2002. "Species Recovery Objectives for Four Target Species in the Central and Lower Platte River." Greiner Woodward Clyde, consultants. Report Prepared for the USFWS, Mountain and Prairie Region, Lakewood, Colo., June 26.

Maass, Arthur, and Raymond L. Anderson. 1978. *. . . and the Desert Shall Rejoice: Conflict, Growth, and Justice in Arid Environments.* Cambridge: MIT Press.

MacDonald, Lee. 2002 . "Effects of Changes in Colorado's Forests on Water Yields and Water Quality." *Colorado Water* 18 (October): 6–8.

MacDonald, Lee, John Stednick, and Charles Troendle. 2003. "Forests and Water: A State-of-the-Art Review for Colorado." Report 196. Colorado Water Resources Research Institute, Colorado State University, Fort Collins.

MacDonnell, Lawrence J. 1985. "The Endangered Species Act and Water Development within the South Platte Basin." Completion Report 137. Colorado Water Resources Research Institute, Colorado State University, Fort Collins.

———. 1988. "Colorado Law of Underground Water: A Look at the South Platte Basin and Beyond." *University of Colorado Law Review* 59: 579–625.

———. 1999. *From Reclamation to Sustainability.* Niwot: University Press of Colorado.

Mapstone, B. D., R. A. Campbell, and A.D.M. Smith. 1996. "Design of Experimental Investigations of the Effects of Line and Spear Fishing on the Great Barrier Reef."

C.R.C. Reef Research Centre, James Cook University, Townsville, Queensland, Australia.

Margolis, Jon. 2006. "The Green Republican: Back from the Dead?" *High Country News* (Paonia, Colo.) 38, 16 (September 4).

Marmarek, D. R., and C. Peters. 2001. "Finding a PATH towards Scientific Collaboration: Insights from the Columbia River Basin." *Conservation Ecology* 5, 2: 2–8.

Martinez, Julia. 2004. "Map Ready for 04 Election." *The Denver Post.* January 25.

Mattes, Merrell J. 1969. *The Great Platte River Road.* Lincoln: University of Nebraska Press.

Matthews, Mark. 2001. "The West Goes to Work Cleaning up Its Forests." *High Country News* (Paonia, Colo.) 33, 9 (May 7).

Matthiessen, Peter. 2001. *The Birds of Heaven: Travels with Cranes.* New York: North Point.

McCay, Bonnie, and James Acheson (eds.). 1987. *The Question of the Commons: The Culture and Ecology of Communal Resources.* Tucson: University of Arizona Press.

McCool, Daniel C. 1987. *Command of the Waters: Iron Triangles, Federal Water Development, and Indian Water.* Tucson: University of Arizona Press.

McDonald, Peter M., and John G. Sidle. 1992. "Habitat Changes above and below Water Projects on the North Platte and South Platte Rivers in Nebraska." *Prairie Naturalist* 24, 3 (September): 149–158.

McKee, Thomas B., Nolan J. Doesken, John Kleist, and Catherine J. Shrier. 2000. *A History of Drought in Colorado.* Report 9. Fort Collins: Colorado State University, Water Resources Research Institute, February.

Meadows, Donnella H., Jorgen Randers, and Dennis Meadows. 2004. *The Limits to Growth: The 30-Year Update.* Junction, Vt.: Chelsea Green.

Melious, Jean, and Robert Thornton. 1999. "Contractual Ecosystem Management under the Endangered Species Act: Can Federal Agencies Make Enforceable Commitments?" *Ecology Law Quarterly* 26: 499–542.

Morgenweck, Ralph. 2001. "Untying the Gordian Knot: How to Recover Endangered Species in Nebraska and at the Same Time Allow Water Users to Recover Their Water." *Colorado Water: Newsletter of the Water Center of Colorado State University* 18: 20–24.

Murphy, Peter J., and Timothy J. Randle. 2001. "Platte River Channel: History and Restoration." Technical Service Center, Sedimentation and River Hydraulics Group, U.S. Bureau of Reclamation, Denver.

National Research Council of the National Academies. 1995. *Science and the Endangered Species Act.* Washington, D.C.: Committee on Scientific Issues in the Endangered Species Act, National Academies of Science.

———. 2002a. *The Mississippi River Ecosystem: Exploring the Prospects for Recovery.* Washington, D.C.: National Academies of Science. Available at www4.nationalacademies.org/news.nsf/isbn0309083141?OpenDocument. Accessed March 12, 2008.

———. 2002b. *Scientific Evaluation of Biological Opinions on Endangered and Threatened Fishes in the Klamath River Basin: Interim Report.* Washington, D.C.: National Academies of Science.

———. 2004a. *Endangered and Threatened Fishes in the Klamath River Basin.* Washington, D.C.: National Academies Press.

————. 2004b. *Endangered and Threatened Species of the Platte River.* Washington, D.C.: National Academies Press. Draft. April 28.

————. 2005. *Endangered and Threatened Species of the Platte River.* Washington, D.C.: National Academies Press.

Nebraska Department of Natural Resources. 2003a. *Reports to the Cooperative Agreement Basin-Wide Recovery Program Governance Committee. July 1, 2000–June 30, 2001 and July 1, 2001–June 30, 2002.* Lincoln: Nebraska Department of Natural Resources, October 4, 2001, and February 13, 2003.

————. 2003b. *Republican River Basin: Report of Preliminary Findings.* Lincoln. May 20. Available at www.dnr.ne.gov/Republican/Report05-20-03pdf. Accessed August 24, 2007.

————. 2004. "LB962 Enacted into Law." Brochure. Lincoln: Nebraska Department of Natural Resources, April.

Nestor, William. 1997. *The War for America's Natural Resources.* New York: St. Martin's.

Neuman, Janet C., and Michael C. Blumm. 1999. "Water for National Forests: The Bypass Flow Report and the Great Divide in Western Water Law." *Stanford Environmental Law Journal* 18: 3–30.

Official Nebraska Government Website. 2006. "Registered Irrigation Wells in Nebraska, 1966–2005." Available at http://www.neo.state.ne.us/statshtml/73a.html.

Ogden, J. C., and S. M. Davis. 1994. *Everglades: The Ecosystem and Its Restoration.* Del Ray, Fla.: St. Lucie.

Olpin, Owen (special master). 2001. "Final Report of the Special Master in the Supreme Court of the United States." *State of Nebraska (Plaintiff) v. State of Wyoming et al. (Defendant),* Washington, D.C.

Omaha World Herald. 2007. "Irrigation Empire: Part 3: Pivot Irrigators Prospered in Groundwater Basin." April 1.

Opie, John. 1993. *Ogallala: Water for a Dry Land.* Lincoln: University of Nebraska Press.

Ostresh, Lawrence M., Richard A. Marston Jr., and Walter M. Hudson (eds.). 1990. *Wyoming Water Atlas.* Cheyenne: Wyoming Water Development Commission and University of Wyoming.

Ostrom, Elinor. 1990. *Governing the Commons: The Evolution of Institutions for Collective Action.* New York: Cambridge University Press.

————. 1998. "A Behavioral Approach to the Rational Choice Theory of Collective Action." *American Political Science Review* 92, 1 (March): 1–22.

Ostrom, Elinor, and Vincent Ostrom. 2004. "The Quest for Meaning in Public Choice." *Journal of Economics and Sociology* 63, 1 (January): 105–147.

Ostrom, Elinor, Larry Schroeder, and Susan Wynne. 1993. *Institutional Incentives and Sustainable Development: Infrastructure Policies in Perspective.* Boulder: Westview.

Outwater, Alice. 1996. *Water: A Natural History.* New York: Basic Books.

Pankratz, Howard. 2008. "Catastrophic: The Beetle Infestation That Is Expected to Kill All of Colorado's Mature Lodgepole Forests within Five Years Is Moving into Wyoming and the Front Range." *The Denver Post.* January 15.

PEER (Public Employees for Environmental Responsibility). 2007. "New Bush Plan to Gut Endangered Species Act." Released in collaboration with the Center for Biological Diversity. March 27. Available at www.peer.org/news/news_id.php?/. Accessed April 4, 2007.

Peirce, Neal. 1972. *The Mountain States of America: People, Politics, and Power in the Rocky Mountain States*. New York: W. W. Norton.

Pisani, Donald. 1989. "The Irrigation District and the Federal Relationship: Neglected Aspects of Water History in the Twentieth Century," in *The Twentieth Century West: Historical Interpretations*, ed. Gerald D. Nash and Richard W. Etulain. Albuquerque: University of New Mexico Press, 257–292.

———. 2002. *Water and the American Government: The Reclamation Bureau, National Water Policy and the West, 1902–1935*. Berkeley: University of California Press.

Pitzer, Gary. 2005. "Turning Water into Electricity: Hydropower Projects under Review." *Western Water* (September–October): 4–5.

———. 2006. "Unlocking the Mysteries of Selenium." *Western Water* (March–April): 4–13.

Platte River EIS Team. 2000. "Central Platte River 1998 Land Cover/Use Mapping Project, Nebraska." U.S. Department of the Interior, Bureau of Reclamation, and U.S. Fish and Wildlife Service, Denver.

Platte River Management Joint Study. 1993. "Platte River Habitat Conservation Program." U.S. Bureau of Reclamation, Mills, Wyo.

Platte River Odyssey. 2006. Report. Lincoln: College of Journalism and Mass Communications, University of Nebraska, in association with the *Lincoln Journal Star*.

Platte River Recovery Program. 2006. Governance Committee Cooperative Agreement. Looseleaf document in three-ring binder, October 26.

Poff, N. LeRoy, J. David Allan, Mark B. Bain, James R. Kerr, Karen L. Prestegaard, Brian D. Richter, Richard E. Sparks, and Julie C. Stromberg. 1997. "The Natural Flow Regime: A Paradigm for River Conservation and Restoration." *Bioscience* 47, 11 (December): 769–784.

Poff, N. LeRoy, J. David Allan, Margaret A. Palmer, David D. Hart, Brian D. Richter, Angela H. Arthington, Kevin H. Rogers, Judy L. Meyer, and Jack A. Stanford. 2003. "River Flows and Water Wars: Emerging Science for Environmental Decision Making." *Frontiers in Ecology and Environment* 1, 6: 298–306.

Pore, Robert. 2007. "Nelson, Hegel Unveil Bill to Protect Wildlife of the Platte River." *Grand Island* (Nebraska) *Independent*. March 3.

Potter, Lori. 2006a. "Platte Program Gets Majority, but Not without Much Hesitation." *Kearney Hub*. October 18.

———. 2006b. "Wyoming Governor 'Reluctantly' Signs Platte Plan." *Kearney Hub*. November 27.

Poundstone, William. 1992. *Prisoner's Dilemma*. New York: Doubleday.

Pratt, Jerome J. 1996. *The Whooping Crane: North America's Symbol of Conservation*. Prescott, Ariz.: Castle Rock.

Pyne, Stephen J. *Year of the Fires: The Story of the Great Fires of 1910*. New York: Viking.

Randle, Tim. 2003. "Flood Stage on the North Platte River Near North Platte." U.S. Bureau of Reclamation, Denver. Undated report delivered to the Governance Committee, January 14.

Record of Decision. 2006. *Platte River Habitat Recovery Implementation Program*. U.S. Department of the Interior, Final Environmental Impact Statement, September.

Reisner, Marc. 1986. *Cadillac Desert: The American West and Its Disappearing Water*. New York: Viking.

Ridenour, Shelley. 2008. "Water Users Fight Pathfinder Plan." *Casper* (Wyoming) *Star-Tribune*. May 26.

Ridgeway, Marian E. 1955. *The Missouri Basin's Pick-Sloan Plan: A Case Study in Congressional Policy Determination*. Urbana: University of Illinois Press.

Riebsame, William, and James J. Robb. 1997. *Atlas of the New West: Portrait of a Changing Region*. New York: W. W. Norton.

Ring, Ray. 1999. "Saving the Platte." *High Country News* (Paonia, Colo.) 31, 2 (February 1).

Rogers, Peter. 1996. *America's Water: Federal Roles and Responsibilities*. Cambridge: MIT Press.

Rohlf, Daniel J. 2001. "Jeopardy under the Endangered Species Act: Playing a Game Protected Species Can't Win." *Washburn Law Journal* 41: 114–163.

Ruckelshaus, William D. 1997. "Stopping the Pendulum," in *Law and the Environment: A Multidisciplinary Reader*, ed. Robert V. Percival and Dorothy C. Alevizatos. Philadelphia: Temple University Press, 397–401.

Rundquist, Brad. 1993. "North Platte Decree Began in Argument Arising out of 1934 Drought," in *Flat Water: A History of Nebraska and Its Water*, ed. C. A. Flowerday. Lincoln: University of Nebraska, 210–211.

Running, Steven W. 2006. "Is Global Warming Causing More, Larger Wildfires?" *Science* 313, 5789 (August 18): 927–928.

Ryman, Russ. 2008. "Reuniting a River." *National Geographic* 214, 6 (December): 134–155.

Sato, J. F., and Associates. 2005. "North Platte Channel Capacity Study." Final Report to the Water Management Committee, North Platte Cooperative Agreement, Littleton, Colo., December 1. Report available in *Platte River Recovery Program*, 2006.

Schneiders, Robert Kelley. 1999. *Unruly River: Two Centuries of Change along the Missouri*. Lawrence: University Press of Kansas.

Shabecoff, Philip. 2000. *Earth Rising: Audubon Environmentalism in the 21st Century*. Washington, D.C.: Island.

Sievers, LeRoy W., and Jocelyn Walsh Golden. 2005. "Nebraska Water Law Changing." *The Water Report* 21 (November 15): 16–21.

Simons and Associates Inc. 2000. "Physical History of the Platte River in Nebraska: Focusing upon Flow, Sediment Transport, Geomorphology, and Vegetation." U.S. Department of the Interior, Bureau of Reclamation, and U.S. Fish and Wildlife Service, Platte River EIS Office, Lakewood, Colo.

Smart Growth America. n.d. "What Is Smart Growth?" Available at www.smartgrowth america.com. Accessed February 11, 2008.

Smith, Dennis. 1991. *The Rise of Historical Sociology*. Philadelphia: Temple University Press.

Smith, Zachary. 1989. *Groundwater in the West*. San Diego: Academic Press.

———. 2000. *The Environmental Policy Paradox*. Upper Saddle River, N.J.: Prentice-Hall.

South Platte River Compact. 1923. "Signatories: Colorado and Nebraska," April 27. See Colorado Division of Water Resources. 2000. "A Summary of Compacts and Litigation Governing Colorado's Use of Interstate Streams." Available at http://water.state.co.us/pubs/compact_00.pdf. Accessed April 11, 2002.

SPWRAP (South Platte Water Related Activities Program). 2005a. Bylaws. Adopted by the original directors at the organizational meeting, May 12. Available at the principal office, Northern Colorado Water Conservancy District, Berthoud.

———. 2005b. Articles of Incorporation. Robert V. Trout, Registered Agent, 1112 Lincoln Street, Suite 1600, Denver.

———. 2007. Meeting Minutes of Board of Directors. Northern Colorado Water Conservancy District, Denver Water, September.

Squires, G. (ed.). 2002. *Urban Sprawl: Causes, Consequences and Policy Response.* Washington, D.C.: Urban Institute.

Stednick, John D. 1996. "Monitoring the Effects of Timber Harvest on Annual Water Yield." *Journal of Hydrology* 176: 79–95.

———. 2008. "Effects of Pine Beetle Infestations on Water Yield and Water Quality at the Watershed Scale in Northern Colorado." *Colorado Water* 25, 3 (May–June): 3–7.

Steen, Harold. K. 1976. *The U.S. Forest Service: A History.* Seattle: University of Washington Press.

———. 1991. *The Beginning of the National Forest System.* FS-488. Washington, D.C.: USDA Forest Service, May.

Stephenson, Kurt. 1994. "Governing the Commons: History and Evaluation of Local Democratic Groundwater Management in the Nebraska Upper Republican Natural Resource District." PhD diss., Department of Economics, University of Nebraska, Lincoln.

Stinchcombe, Arthur L. 1978. *Theoretical Methods in Social History.* New York: Academic Press.

Straub, Noelle. 2007. "Platte River Recovery Plan Debated." *Casper* (Wyoming) *Star-Tribune.* April 26.

Strickland, Dale. 2000. "Program Budget Analysis." Memorandum distributed to Finance Committee, March 13.

Thaement, David K., and Andrea H. Faucett. 2001. "Evolution of Transmountain Water Diversions in Colorado," in *Transbasin Water Transfers: Proceedings of the 2001 USCID Water Management Conference,* ed. Jerry Schaack. Denver: USCID Water Management Conference, U.S. Committee on Irrigation and Drainage, June 27–30, 139–147.

Troendle, Charles A., and R. M. King. 1987. "The Effect of Partial and Clearcutting on Streamflow at Deadhorse Creek, Colorado." *Journal of Hydrology* 90: 145–157.

Troendle, Charles A., and James M. Nankervis. 2000. "Estimating Additional Water Yield from Changes in Management of National Forests in the North Platte Basin." Final Report. Prepared for the Platte River EIS Office, U.S. Department of the Interior, Denver, Colo., May 12.

Troendle, Charles A., James Nankervis, and A. Peavy. 2007. "Historical and Future Impacts of Vegetation Management and Natural Disturbance on Water Yield from Forest Service Lands in the South Platte River Basin." Report. Submitted to Polly Hays, water program manager, Rocky Mountain Region, U.S. Forest Service, Lakewood, Colo. Technical Services Contract 53-3187-5-6008.

Troendle, Charles A., James M. Nankervis, and Louise S. Porth. 2003. "The Impact of Forest Service Activities on the Streamflow Regime in the Platte River." Final Report. Submitted to the Office of the Hydrologist, Rocky Mountain Region, U.S. Forest Service, Lakewood, Colo., May 22.

Tyler, Daniel. 1992. *The Last Waterhole in the West: The Colorado–Big Thompson Project and the Northern Colorado Water Conservancy District.* Niwot: University Press of Colorado.

———. 2003. *Silver Fox of the Rockies: Delphus E. Carpenter and Western Water Compacts*. Norman: University of Oklahoma Press.

Ugland, R. C., B. J. Cochran, M. M. Hiner, and R. D. Steger. 1993. "Water Resources Data. Colorado Water Year 1993. Volumes I and II. USGS Water Data Reports CO-93-1 CO-93-2." U.S. Geological Survey, Denver.

Ulfarsson, Gudmunder, and John I. Carruthers. 2006. "The Cycle of Fragmentation and Sprawl: A Conceptual Framework and Empirical Model." *Environment and Planning B: Planning and Design* 33, 5 (September): 767–788.

Union of Concerned Scientists. 2004. *Scientific Integrity in Policy Making*. Online report. Excerpt pertaining to USFWS Missouri River Amended Biological Opinion. Available at www.ucsusa.org/scientific-integrity/interference/the-endangered-species-act.html. Accessed March 12, 2008.

U.S. Bureau of Reclamation. 1987. "North Platte Basin Reference Map." Mills: Wyoming Area Office, Great Plains, Region, March 31. No. 20-703-5199.

U.S. Department of Agriculture. 2002. "National Agricultural Statistics Service, 2002 Census of Agriculture, State Data." Available at http://www.nass.usda.gov/census/census02/volume1/us/st99, table 10. Accessed December 8, 2006.

U.S. Department of the Interior. 2006. "Record of Decision: Platte River Recovery Program." Signed by Secretary of the Interior Dirk Kempthorne, September.

U.S. Department of the Interior, Bureau of Reclamation, and U.S. Fish and Wildlife Service. 2003. *Platte River Recovery Program: Draft Environmental Impact Statement*. One vol., December.

———. 2006. *Platte River Recovery Program: Final Environmental Impact Statement*. Summary, three vols., April.

U.S. Federal Energy Regulatory Commission. 1998. "Order Issuing New License. FERC Project 1417, CNPPID; FERC Project 1835, NPPD." Issued July 29. Also: "Agreement on All Issues." 1995. Washington, D.C. Issued January 15.

U.S. Fish and Wildlife Service. 1995. "Unpublished Internal Memorandum: Platte River Recovery Program." Known informally as the "Sideboards Document." U.S. Fish and Wildlife Service, Denver.

———. 1997a. "Biological Opinion on the Federal Energy Regulatory Commission's Preferred Alternative for the Kingsley Dam Project (Project no. 1417) and the North Platte Keystone Dam Project (Project no. 1835)." Department of the Interior, Grand Island, Neb.

———. 1997b. "Biological Opinion on the Federal Energy Regulatory Commission's Preferred Alternative for the Kingsley Dam Project (Project no. 1417) and North Platte Keystone Dam Project (Project no. 1835)." U.S. Fish and Wildlife Service, Grand Island, Neb.

———. 1997c. "Cooperative Agreement for Platte River Research and Other Efforts Relating to Endangered Species Habitats along the Central Platte River, Nebraska." U.S. Fish and Wildlife Service, Lakewood, Colo.

———. 2000a. "Missouri River News and Information: Questions and Answers Regarding the Biological Opinion on Missouri River Operations." Available at www.fws.gov/mountain-prairie/MissouriRiver/archive/qanda_92000.htm. Accessed March 12, 2008.

———. 2000b. "Biological Opinion: Impacts to Federally Listed Threatened and Endangered Species in Nebraska from the Proposed Western Sarpy and Clear Creek, Nebraska Flood Control Project Located in Sarpy and Saunders Counties." Proposed project of the U.S. Army Corps of Engineers. U.S. Fish and Wildlife Service, Ecological Services Branch, Nebraska Field Office, Grand Island, Neb., December 18.

———. 2000c. "Biological Opinion on the Missouri River Main Stem Reservoir System, the Bank Stabilization and Navigation Project, and the Kansas River Reservoir System." U.S. Fish and Wildlife Service, Grand Island, Neb., and Lakewood, Colo., April.

———. 2002a. "USFWS Instream Flow Recommendations: Proposed Definitions and Usage for the Platte River Recovery Program." U.S. Fish and Wildlife Service, Mountain and Prairie Region, Region 6, Lakewood, Colo. Draft, December 23. Subsequent drafts: November 18, 2003; September 1, 2004; April 13, 2005.

———. 2002b. "Estimated Historic Losses by Stream Reach in the Platte River below Grand Island, Nebraska, and Implications for Program-Augmented Flows." Unpublished report. U.S. Fish and Wildlife Service, Mountain and Prairie Region, Region 6, Lakewood, Colo. Draft, May 15.

———. 2002c. "Summary Report on the Potential of Changes in Central Platte Flow Conditions to Affect Flows in the Lower Platte." Unpublished document. U.S. Fish and Wildlife Service, Mountain and Prairie Region, Region 6, Lakewood, Colo. Draft, December 6.

———. 2003a. "Amendment to the 2000 Biological Opinion on the Operation of the Missouri River Mainstem Reservoir System, the Bank Stabilization and Navigation Project, and the Kansas River Reservoir System." December 16. Available at www.fws.gov/feature/pdfs/FinalBO.pdf. Accessed February 17, 2007.

———. 2003b. "News Release." Craig Manson, assistant secretary, Fish and Wildlife and Parks, Department of the Interior. Enclosure: "Memorandum from Regional Director, Great Lakes–Big Rivers Region. Subject: Missouri River Biological Opinion Assignment. To: DOI Assistant Secretary, Fish and Wildlife and Parks," December 17. Available at www.fws.gov/mountain-prairie/PRESSREL/03-87.htm. Accessed March 12, 2008.

———. 2004a. "Platte River Recovery Program: Draft Biological Opinion." U.S. Fish and Wildlife Service, Lakewood, Colo., August.

———. 2004b. "Questions and Answers: Wolf 10j Final Rule." Available at www.fws.gov/mountainprairie/species/mammals/wolf. Accessed December 23, 2004.

———. 2004–2005. "Upper Colorado River Endangered Fish Recovery Program and San Juan River Basin Recovery Implementation Program. Program Highlights 2004–05." Available at www.mountain-prairie.fws.gov/infopackets. Accessed February 17, 2007.

———. 2006a. "Draft Biological Opinion and Incidental Take Statement Regarding an Agreement on Hydrocycling Operations at the Central Nebraska Public Power and Irrigation District Johnson no. 2 Powerplant in the Kingsley Dam Project (FERC no. 1417)." U.S. Fish and Wildlife Service, Lakewood, Colo., July 28.

———. 2006b. "Biological Opinion on the Platte River Recovery Program." U.S. Fish and Wildlife Service, Ecological Services Field Office, Grand Island, Neb., June 16.

————. 2007. "Wolf Recovery in North America: Fact Sheet." www.mountain-prairie. fws.gov/species/mammals/graywolf. Accessed February 2, 2007.

U.S. Geological Survey. 1990. *Water Fact Sheet: Largest Rivers in the United States*. Reston, Va.: U.S. Geological Survey.

USBR/Northern Colorado Water Conservancy District. 1938. "Contract between the United States and the NCWCD Providing for the Construction of the Colorado Big Thompson Project, Colorado." U.S. Department of the Interior, Bureau of Reclamation, and the Northern Colorado Water Conservancy District, Greeley, Colo.

USDA Forest Service. 2002. "Drought Conditions and Conservation Measures." Memorandum to forest supervisors. File code 2500. USDA Forest Service, Intermountain Region, Ogden, Utah, March 14.

————. 2004. "USDA Forest Service Vegetation Management Plan." Unpublished report. USDA Forest Service, Rocky Mountain Region, Lakewood, Colo., January 8.

Veblen, Thomas T., William L. Baker, Gloria Montenegro, and Thomas W. Sanborn (eds.). 2003. *Fire and Climate Change in Temperate Ecosystems of Western America*. Ecological Studies vol. 160. New York: Springer.

Walkinshaw, Lawrence. 1973. *Cranes of the World*. New York: Winchester.

Walters, C. J. 1986. *Adaptive Management of Renewable Resources*. New York: Macmillan.

Walters, C. J., L. Gunderson, and C. S. Holling. 1992. "Experimental Policies for Water Management in the Everglades." *Ecological Applications* 2: 189–202.

Walters, Carl. 1997. "Challenges in Adaptive Management of Riparian Coastal Ecosystems." *Conservation Ecology* 1, 1 (no pages).

Warner, James W., Jon Altenhofen, and Jack Odor. 1994. "Recharge as Augmentation in the South Platte River Basin: Groundwater Program Technical Report #21." Department of Civil Engineering, Colorado State University, Fort Collins.

Water and Power Resources Service. 1981. *Project Data*. Denver: U.S. Government Printing Office.

Water Management Committee. 2004. "Advisory Committee to Governance Committee, Minutes." Water Management Committee, May 14.

Weiss, Wendy, and James R. Montgomery. 1999. "*Nebraska v. Wyoming*: The End of Collaboration?" in *Natural Resources Law Center 20th Annual Summer Conference*. Boulder: University of Colorado School of Law, no pages.

Westerling, A. W., H. G. Hildalgo, D. R. Cayan, and T. W. Swetnam. 2006. "Warming and Earlier Spring Increase of Western U.S. Forest Wildfire Activity." *Science* 313, 5789 (August 18): 940–943.

Western Water Policy Review Advisory Commission. 1997. "Water in the West: The Challenge for the Next Century." Western Water Policy Review Advisory Commission, Denver.

White, Richard. 1991. *It's Your Misfortune and None of My Own: A History of the American West*. Norman: University of Oklahoma Press.

Whitman, Walt. 1982. *Complete Poetry and Collected Prose*. New York: Viking.

Whooping Crane Conservation Association. 2006. http://www.whoopingcrane.com. Accessed December 19, 2006.

Williams, Ted. 2002. "Lynx, Lies, and Media Hype." *Audubon* 104, 3 (May–June): 24–33.

————. 2007. "Incite: Back Off!" *Audubon* 109, 3 (May–June): 50–53, 84–87.

Wohl, Ellen E. 2001. *Virtual Rivers: Lessons from the Mountain Rivers of the Colorado Front Range*. New Haven: Yale University Press.

Wohl, Ellen E., Robert McConnell, Jay Skinner, and Richard Stenzel. 1998. "Inheriting Our Past: River Sediment Sources and Sediment Hazards in Colorado." Technical Report. Colorado Water Resources Research Institute, Colorado State University, Fort Collins.

Wood, Mary Christine. 1998. "Reclaiming the Natural Rivers: The Endangered Species Act as Applied to Endangered River Ecosystems." *Arizona Law Review* 40: 197–286.

Woodward, Clyde. 1981. "Interim Report: South Platte River Basin Assessment, Colorado." Colorado Water Conservation Board, Denver.

Wyoming Attorney General. 2004. Office of the Attorney General, Patrick J. Crank, Attorney General. To Honorable Dave Freudenthal, Governor, State of Wyoming. Re: "Request for Opinion Evaluating the Legal Basis for Administering a Call for Regulation to Fill Pathfinder during the Irrigation Season." Formal Opinion no. 2004-01. Cheyenne, August 31.

Wyoming Board of Control. 2008. "In the Matter of the United States Petition to Change the Use . . . for a Portion of the United States of America, Appropriation Permit no. 609 Res, Pathfinder Reservoir, Storing Water from the North Platte River with a Priority of December 6, 1904." Stipulation and Settlement Agreement. Wyoming Board of Control Docket no. I-2008-1-7.

Young, Oran. 1982. *Resource Regimes: Natural Resources and Social Institutions*. Berkeley: University of California Press.

——— (ed.). 1997. *Global Governance: Drawing Insights from the Environmental Experience*. Cambridge: MIT Press.

——— (ed.). 1999. *The Effectiveness of International Environmental Regimes*. Cambridge: MIT Press.

Zaffos, Joshua. 2002. "Corps Stands behind the Status Quo." *High Country News* (Paonia, Colo). November 11.

Zallen, Margot. 1997. "Integrating New Values with Old Uses in the Relicensing of Kingsley Dam and Related Facilities." Natural Resources Law Center, University of Colorado School of Law, Boulder.

Index